MASTER PHOTOSHOP 5.5

VISUALLY™

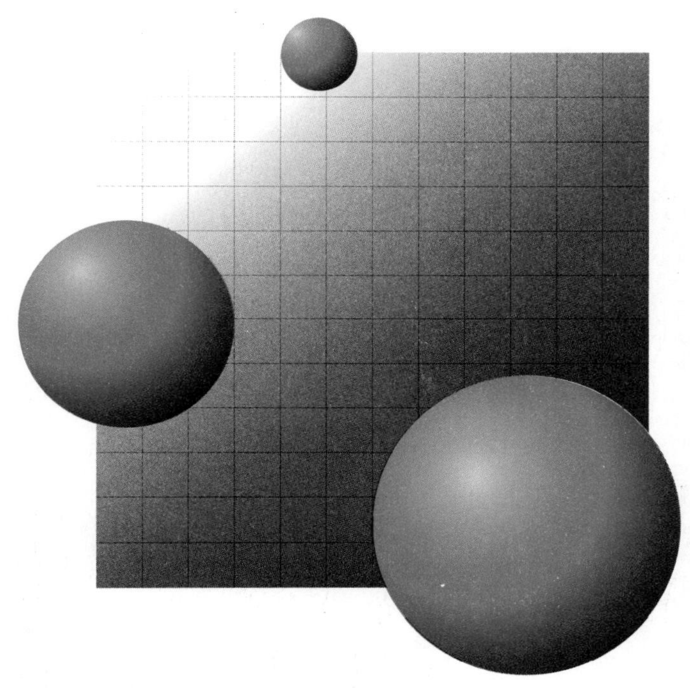

IDG's 3-D Visual Series

Ken Milburn

IDG Books Worldwide, Inc.
An International Data Group Company
Foster City, CA • Indianapolis, IN • Chicago, IL • New York, NY

Published by
IDG Books Worldwide, Inc.
An International Data Group Company
919 E. Hillsdale Blvd., Suite 400
Foster City, CA 94404
www.idgbooks.com (IDG Books Worldwide Web site)

Library of Congress Catalog Card No.: 99-10950

ISBN: 0-7645-6045-X

Printed in the United States of America

10 9 8 7 6 5 4 3 2 1

1P/QV/QR/QQ/FC

Distributed in the United States by IDG Books Worldwide, Inc.

Distributed by CDG Books Canada Inc. for Canada; by Transworld Publishers Limited in the United Kingdom; by IDG Norge Books for Norway; by IDG Sweden Books for Sweden; by IDG Books Australia Publishing Corporation Pty. Ltd. for Australia and New Zealand; by TransQuest Publishers Pte Ltd. for Singapore, Malaysia, Thailand, Indonesia, and Hong Kong; by Gotop Information Inc. for Taiwan; by ICG Muse, Inc. for Japan; by Intersoft for South Africa; by Eyrolles for France; by International Thomson Publishing for Germany, Austria and Switzerland; by Distribuidora Cuspide for Argentina; by LR International for Brazil; by Galileo Libros for Chile; by Ediciones ZETA S.C.R. Ltda. for Peru; by WS Computer Publishing Corporation, Inc., for the Philippines; by Contemporanea de Ediciones for Venezuela; by Express Computer Distributors for the Caribbean and West Indies; by Micronesia Media Distributor, Inc. for Micronesia; by Chips Computadoras S.A. de C.V. for Mexico; by Editorial Norma de Panama S.A. for Panama; by American Bookshops for Finland.

For general information on IDG Books Worldwide's books in the U.S., please call our Consumer Customer Service department at 800-762-2974. For reseller information, including discounts and premium sales, please call our Reseller Customer Service department at 800-434-3422.

For information on where to purchase IDG Books Worldwide's books outside the U.S., please contact our International Sales department at 317-596-5530 or fax 317-596-5692.

For consumer information on foreign language translations, please contact our Customer Service department at 800-434-3422, fax 317-596-5692, or e-mail rights@idgbooks.com.

For information on licensing foreign or domestic rights, please phone +1-650-655-3109.

For sales inquiries and special prices for bulk quantities, please contact our Sales department at 650-655-3200 or write to the address above.

For information on using IDG Books Worldwide's books in the classroom or for ordering examination copies, please contact our Educational Sales department at 800-434-2086 or fax 317-596-5499.

For press review copies, author interviews, or other publicity information, please contact our Public Relations department at 650-655-3000 or fax 650-655-3299.

ABOUT IDG BOOKS WORLDWIDE

Welcome to the world of IDG Books Worldwide.

IDG Books Worldwide, Inc., is a subsidiary of International Data Group, the world's largest publisher of computer-related information and the leading global provider of information services on information technology. IDG was founded more than 30 years ago by Patrick J. McGovern and now employs more than 9,000 people worldwide. IDG publishes more than 290 computer publications in over 75 countries. More than 90 million people read one or more IDG publications each month.

Launched in 1990, IDG Books Worldwide is today the #1 publisher of best-selling computer books in the United States. We are proud to have received eight awards from the Computer Press Association in recognition of editorial excellence and three from Computer Currents' First Annual Readers' Choice Awards. Our best-selling *...For Dummies®* series has more than 50 million copies in print with translations in 31 languages. IDG Books Worldwide, through a joint venture with IDG's Hi-Tech Beijing, became the first U.S. publisher to publish a computer book in the People's Republic of China. In record time, IDG Books Worldwide has become the first choice for millions of readers around the world who want to learn how to better manage their businesses.

Our mission is simple: Every one of our books is designed to bring extra value and skill-building instructions to the reader. Our books are written by experts who understand and care about our readers. The knowledge base of our editorial staff comes from years of experience in publishing, education, and journalism — experience we use to produce books to carry us into the new millennium. In short, we care about books, so we attract the best people. We devote special attention to details such as audience, interior design, use of icons, and illustrations. And because we use an efficient process of authoring, editing, and desktop publishing our books electronically, we can spend more time ensuring superior content and less time on the technicalities of making books.

You can count on our commitment to deliver high-quality books at competitive prices on topics you want to read about. At IDG Books Worldwide, we continue in the IDG tradition of delivering quality for more than 30 years. You'll find no better book on a subject than one from IDG Books Worldwide.

John Kilcullen
Chairman and CEO
IDG Books Worldwide, Inc.

Steven Berkowitz
President and Publisher
IDG Books Worldwide, Inc.

Eighth Annual Computer Press Awards 1992

Ninth Annual Computer Press Awards 1993

Tenth Annual Computer Press Awards 1994

Eleventh Annual Computer Press Awards 1995

IDG is the world's leading IT media, research and exposition company. Founded in 1964, IDG had 1997 revenues of $2.05 billion and has more than 9,000 employees worldwide. IDG offers the widest range of media options that reach IT buyers in 75 countries representing 95% of worldwide IT spending. IDG's diverse product and services portfolio spans six key areas including print publishing, online publishing, expositions and conferences, market research, education and training, and global marketing services. More than 90 million people read one or more of IDG's 290 magazines and newspapers, including IDG's leading global brands — Computerworld, PC World, Network World, Macworld and the Channel World family of publications. IDG Books Worldwide is one of the fastest-growing computer book publishers in the world, with more than 700 titles in 36 languages. The "...For Dummies®" series alone has more than 50 million copies in print. IDG offers online users the largest network of technology-specific Web sites around the world through IDG.net (http://www.idg.net), which comprises more than 225 targeted Web sites in 55 countries worldwide. International Data Corporation (IDC) is the world's largest provider of information technology data, analysis and consulting, with research centers in over 41 countries and more than 400 research analysts worldwide. IDG World Expo is a leading producer of more than 168 globally branded conferences and expositions in 35 countries including E3 (Electronic Entertainment Expo), Macworld Expo, ComNet, Windows World Expo, ICE (Internet Commerce Expo), Agenda, DEMO, and Spotlight. IDG's training subsidiary, ExecuTrain, is the world's largest computer training company, with more than 230 locations worldwide and 785 training courses. IDG Marketing Services helps industry-leading IT companies build international brand recognition by developing global integrated marketing programs via IDG's print, online and exposition products worldwide. Further information about the company can be found at www.idg.com.

1/24/99

CREDITS

Acquisitions Editor
Michael Roney

Development Editor
Katharine Dvorak

Technical Editor
Steve Kimball

Copy Editor
Ami Knox

CD-ROM
Media Development

Project Coordinator
Linda Marousek

Production
Booklayers.com

Quality Control Specialist
Chris Weisbart

Book Designer
maran Graphics

Proofreading and Indexing
York Production Services

ABOUT THE AUTHOR

Ken Milburn is a photo-digital illustrator and author. More than 250 of his articles and reviews on computer graphics and multimedia have appeared in *InfoWorld*, *PC World, MacWeek*, *Mac User, Popular Computing, PC Computing, Computer Graphics World, Publish,* and *Windows* magazines. Ken has also worked as a user-interface design consultant for Mannequin, an application developed by the HumanCAD division of Biomechanics Corporation of America and the predecessor to Fractal Design's Poser. Milburn began his career as a fashion and travel photographer in Beverly Hills and now specializes in photo-digital illustration.

ACKNOWLEDGMENTS

First, I have to thank the IDG Books Worldwide editorial folks who have made a significant contribution to this book. Mike Roney, my acquisitions editor, Katharine Dvorak, my development editor, and Ami Knox, my copy editor, are exceptionally intelligent, conscientious, patient, and fair. These are people any author should leap at the chance to work with.

Kudos to Janine Warner for her constant help, support, friendship, and humor during the writing of this book. Also, thanks to Sonita Malan for giving me a reason to want to finish sooner, rather than later.

A special thanks to Steve Kimball, my technical editor. I wish I'd had more time to communicate with him in person. I think he probably doesn't even know that I think he's the best technical editor with whom I've ever had the pleasure of working. Steve understands the practical application of Photoshop features to an even greater extent than most professionals.

I'd also like to acknowledge two digital camera manufacturers for making it possible to create almost every illustration used in this book: Olympus Camera and Agfa-Gavaert.

The camera I used from the beginning to the end of this project is the Olympus D-500L digital camera. This is the least expensive and lowest-resolution single-lens reflex digital camera on the market today. As any professional photographer will tell you, a single-lens reflex camera is a requirement for serious hand-held picture-taking because you always see the exact composition, perspective, and depth-of-focus as dictated by the image pickup device. All three cameras from Olympus (the D-500L, D-600L, and D-620L) have the same built-in, all-glass, aspherical F2.8 autofocus 3x zoom lens. Many reviewers have called this the highest-quality lens available on a sub-thousand-dollar digital camera. My experience leads me to concur.

The other camera I used was the Agfa ePhoto 1280. The 1280 is a breast-pocket-size megapixel digital camera with a 3:1 zoom lens that rotates 280-degrees. The flash head is mounted in the same swiveling housing as the lens, so no matter where you rotate the lens, the flash is also aimed at the subject. After working with this camera during the writing of this book, I confess that I love this camera. It is small enough to be with me always; it captured shots that I would not otherwise have made. Its controls are flexible and easy to access. Finally, the swivel lens enables the user to hold the camera at virtually any height or angle, making it easier to take photos from eye-catching perspectives.

Both the Agfa and Olympus cameras use an ultra-thin memory card called SmartMedia. I like this memory device because it is low in cost per megabyte of storage and because they are small enough to make it practical to carry dozens on a trip without feeling even slightly burdened. You can slip them into a floppy disk adapter or a Lexar SmartMedia Reader and quickly download the images into any computer that can read standard high density floppies — all without draining your camera batteries. Lexar Media was kind enough to provide me their 8MB card; I used it in both cameras and never ever had an error.

ATI provided high-resolution video cards suitable for use with 19- to 21-inch monitors for both Windows and Macintosh. All the calibration tests were performed using these cards. For Windows, the card was the Xpert@Work. For the Mac, the card was the Nexus GA. Both cards had 8MB RAM installed, run from a PCI bus, and accelerate both 2D and 3D graphics processing.

Mactell Corporation also supplied a Powerjolt 250 MHz G3 accelerator card with a 512K cache. This proved to be the most affordable way to bring my Power Computing PowerCenter 132 into the realm of the G3.

PHOTOSHOP 5.5

I GETTING STARTED

1. Photoshop Basics
2. Photoshop File Management

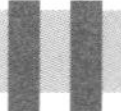

MAKING IMAGE ADJUSTMENTS

3. Changing the Size of an Image
4. Adjusting Image Quality
5. Retouching Images

ISOLATING PARTS OF THE IMAGE

6. Making Selections
7. Working with Paths
8. Working with Masks
9. Working with Layers
10. Channel Operations
11. Text and Text Effects

PHOTOSHOP FOR ART'S SAKE

12. Using Photoshop's Brushes
13. Applying Darkroom Effects
14. Working with Textures
15. Using the Artistic Filters
16. Using the Distort Filters
17. Using the Noise, Pixelate, and Stylize Filters

ADVANCED TECHNIQUES

18. Using Layers to Combine Effects
19. Automating Photoshop with Actions
20. Preparing Images for a Composite

PREPARING IMAGES FOR THE WEB

21. Preparing and Previewing Web Images
22. Designing Interactive Graphics
23. Making Animations from Photos

Appendix A: Color Management

Appendix B: What's on the CD-ROM

Index

End User License Agreement

CD-ROM Installation Instructions

TABLE OF CONTENTS

GETTING STARTED

1 PHOTOSHOP BASICS

Getting to Know the New Photoshop 4
Set Up Windows to Compliment Photoshop 12
Set Up Your Mac to Compliment Photoshop 14
Set General Preferences 15
Set Preferences for Saving Files 16
Set Preferences for Display and Cursors 17
Set Preferences for Transparency and Gamut 18
Set Preferences for Units and Rulers 19
Set Preferences for Guides and Grid 20
Set Preferences for Plug-ins and Scratch Disks 21
Set Preferences for Memory and Image Cache 22
Recover from Mistakes 23
Use Quick Edit Mode to Overcome Limited RAM 28

2 CHAPTER 2: PHOTOSHOP FILE MANAGEMENT

Get Organized 30
Organize Projects by Folder 31
Make Contact Sheets 32
Open a New File 33
Open Existing Files 34
Save the Current File 36
Save a Copy of the Current File 38
Get Information About the Current File 40
Create Contact Proof Sheets Automatically 42
Place a Conditional Mode Change into an Action 44
Make a Picture Package or Job Print 46
Make a Scrapbook Page 48

Import Images from a TWAIN Device 50
Import Images from a Digital Camera 52
Import Images from a Flatbed Scanner 54
Import Images from a Slide Scanner 56

II MAKING IMAGE ADJUSTMENTS

CHAPTER 3: CHANGING THE SIZE OF AN IMAGE

Image Size Basics 60
Change the Image Size 62
Change the Canvas Size 64
Crop the Image 66
Crop the Image to a Specific Proportion 68
Crop the Image to a Specific Size 69
Crop the Image to a Fixed Size and Resolution 70
Crop the Image to a Specific Proportion or Dimension 71

CHAPTER 4: ADJUSTING IMAGE QUALITY

Control Overall Image Quality 72
Correct Overall Color Balance 84
Use Color Correction Aids 86
Adjust Brightness and Contrast 87
Alter Color with Hue/Saturation 88
Lose All Color with Desaturate 90
Create a Tonal Effect with Invert 91
Swap One Color for Another 92
Mix Color Channels 94
Make an Adjustment with Variations 96
Create a Tonal Effect with Equalize 98

TABLE OF CONTENTS

Switch Color Palettes 100
Correct Tonal Values with the Levels Command 102
Correct Tonal Values with the Curves Command 104
Correct Some Color Values with the Curves Command ..106
Create Special Effects Color Changes with Curves 108

CHAPTER 5: RETOUCHING IMAGES

Correcting Mistakes 110
Use the Eyedropper to Pick Up Color 116
Use Offset Cloning 117
Use Aligned Cloning 118
Automatic Spotting with the Dust & Scratches Filter 119
Automatic Spotting with the Gaussian Blur Filter 120
Correct Blending Defects 121
Hand-Spotting with the Brushes 122

III ISOLATING PARTS OF THE IMAGE

CHAPTER 6: MAKING SELECTIONS

The Art of Making Selections 128
Make Polygon Selections 130
Automate Selection with the Magic Wand 131
Automate Selection with the Magnetic Lasso 132
Magnetic Lasso Options and Keyboard Shortcuts 134
Use the Color Range Command 135
Use Quick Mask Mode 136
Make Compound Selections 138
Edit Selections 140
Modify Selections 142

Modify Selections with Grow and Similar 144
Make Wholesale Selection Changes 146
Blend Selections 148
Magical Erasing with the Magic Eraser 150
Erase Backgrounds 152

CHAPTER 7: WORKING WITH PATHS

Making and Using Paths 154
Draw a Path 158
Draw Complex Paths 160
Draw Freehand Paths 162
Convert Selections to a Path 163
Automate Path Tracing with the Magnetic Pen 164
Edit and Reshape a Path 166
Make and Use a Clipping Path 168
Export and Save Paths 169
Paint a Path 170

CHAPTER 8: WORKING WITH MASKS

Making and Using Masks 172
Save and Load Selections 180
Edit Masks 182
Edit Masks with Brushes 184
Edit Masks with Fills 186
Edit Masks with Quick Mask Mode 188
Make Texture Masks 190
Use Texture Masks 192
Make a Mask from a Color Channel 194
Make a Threshold Mask 196
Make a Layer Mask 198

TABLE OF CONTENTS

CHAPTER 9: WORKING WITH LAYERS

Using Layers 200
Create a New Layer 210
Stack and Reorder Layers 212
Show and Hide Layers 213
Merge Layers 214
Use Transparency with Layers 216
Delete Layers 217
Change the Size of Layers 218
Use Layer Blend Modes 220
Effects of the Layer Blend Modes 221
Stretch Layers, Selections, and Paths 222
Make Multiple Freehand Transformations 224
Make Numerically Precise Transformations 226
Link Layers 228
Make and Use a Clipping Group 229
Make and Use Adjustment Layers 230
Make a Layer Mask 232
Make and Use Layer Effects 234
Make and Use Layer Effects continued 236

CHAPTER 10: CHANNEL OPERATIONS

Using Channel Operations 238
Split Out the Channels 244
Make a Separate Channel for Spot Colors 245
Merge Channels to Create Special Effects 246
Merge Channels from Different Files 248
Use the Apply Image Command 250
Use the Calculations Command 252

CHAPTER 11: TEXT AND TEXT EFFECTS

Using Text 254
Using the Type Tools 258
Edit a Type Layer 260
Use the Type Selection Tool 262
Use Transparency and Blend for Type Effects 264
Enter Vertical Type 266

IV PHOTOSHOP FOR ART'S SAKE

CHAPTER 12: USING PHOTOSHOP'S BRUSHES

The Photoshop Brushes 272
Choose the Right Brush 278
Set Airbrush Options 280
Set Paintbrush Options 281
Set Pencil Options 282
Set Eraser Options 283
Save and Load Brush Palettes 284
Create Custom Brush Shapes 286
Create a Brush from Type 288
Create a Brush from a Postscript Image 289
Paint from a Snapshot 290
Get Even More Painterly with the Art History Brush 292

CHAPTER 13: APPLYING DARKROOM EFFECTS

Correcting Details 294
Create Simple Tonal Effects 298
Suck Up Color with the Sponge Tool 302
Match Color with the Paintbrush Tool 303

Add Color Tone to the Image 304
Hand-color a Monotone Image 308
Control Focus: Blurring and Sharpening 310
Eliminate Artifacts from Compressed Images 322
Eliminate More Artifacts 324

CHAPTER 14: WORKING WITH TEXTURES

Creating Textures with Photoshop 326
Apply Texture Filters 331
Apply Craquelure Texture 332
Apply Grain Texture 333
Create Mosaic Tiles 334
Create a Patchwork 335
Create Stained Glass 336
Apply Texturizer Textures 337
Create New Textures from Photos 338
Create Seamless Pattern and Texture Tiles 340

CHAPTER 15: USING THE ARTISTIC FILTERS

Painterly Filter Effects 342
Create a Painting by Filtering Specific Areas 362
Texturize an Image with a Sketch Filter 364
Apply the Colored Pencil Filter 366
Apply the Cutout Filter 367
Apply the Dry Brush Filter 368
Apply the Film Grain Filter 369
Apply the Fresco Filter 370
Apply the Neon Glow Filter 371
Apply the Paint Daubs Filter 372
Apply the Palette Knife Filter 373
Apply the Plastic Wrap Filter 374
Apply the Poster Edges Filter 375
Apply the Rough Pastels Filter 376

Apply the Smudge Stick Filter 377
Apply the Sponge Filter 378
Apply the Underpainting Filter 379
Apply the Watercolor Filter 380
Apply the Accented Edges Filter 381
Apply the Angled Strokes Filter 382
Apply the Crosshatch Filter 383
Apply the Dark Strokes Filter 384
Apply the Ink Outlines Filter 385
Apply the Spatter Filter 386
Apply the Sumi-e Filter 387
Apply the Bas Relief Filter 388
Apply the Chalk & Charcoal Filter 389
Apply the Charcoal Filter 390
Apply the Chrome Filter 391
Apply the Conté Crayon Filter 392
Apply the Graphic Pen Filter 393
Apply the Halftone Pattern Filter 394
Apply the Note Paper Filter 395
Apply the Photocopy Filter 396
Apply the Plaster Filter 397
Apply the Reticulation Filter 398
Apply the Stamp Filter 399
Apply the Torn Edges Filter 400
Apply the Water Paper Filter 401

CHAPTER 16: USING THE DISTORT FILTERS

Warping and Morphing 402
Distort with the Diffuse Glow Filter 410
Distort with the Displace Filter 411
Distort with the Glass Filter 412
Distort with the Ocean Ripple Filter 413
Distort with the Pinch Filter 414

TABLE OF CONTENTS

Distort with the Polar Coordinates Filter 415
Distort with the Ripple Filter 416
Distort with the Shear Filter 417
Distort with the Spherize Filter 418
Distort with the Twirl Filter 419
Distort with the Wave Filter 420
Distort with the ZigZag Filter 421
Apply a Third-Party 3D Surface Filter 422

CHAPTER 17: USING THE NOISE, PIXELATE, AND STYLIZE FILTERS

Breaking Up Is Easy to Do 424
Apply the Add Noise Filter 433
Apply the Despeckle Filter 434
Apply the Dust & Scratches Filter 435
Apply the Median Filter 436
Apply the Color Halftone Filter 437
Apply the Crystallize Filter 438
Apply the Facet Filter 439
Apply the Fragment Filter 440
Apply the Mezzotint Filter 441
Create a Texture with the Mezzotint Filter 442
Apply the Pointillize Filter 444
Apply the Diffuse Filter 445
Apply the Emboss Filter 446
Apply the Extrude Filter 447
Apply the Find Edges Filter 448
Apply the Glowing Edges Filter 449
Apply the Solarize Filter 450
Apply the Tiles Filter 451
Apply the Trace Contour Filter 452
Apply the Wind Filter 453
Create Your Own Filter Effects: The Custom Filter 454

Save and Load Custom Filters 456
Sharpen with the Custom Filter 457
Create Directional Blurs with the Custom Filter 458
Emboss with the Custom Filter 459

V ADVANCED TECHNIQUES

CHAPTER 18: USING LAYERS TO COMBINE EFFECTS

Using Other Features Expressively 462
Combine Filter Effects Using Layers 464
Define and Save Patterns 466
Paint with Fills 468
Make Nonlinear Gradient Fills 470
Make and Edit Gradient Styles 472
Choose Colors 474
Make Custom Swatch Palettes 476

CHAPTER 19: AUTOMATING PHOTOSHOP WITH ACTIONS

Simplify Life with Actions 478
Create a New Action 482
Save and Load a Set of Actions 484
Edit an Action 486
Play Actions 488
Play Actions in Batches 490
Insert the Unrecordable 492

CHAPTER 20: PREPARING IMAGES FOR A COMPOSITE

Organization Is the Key to Success 494
Collect and Prep Images 496
Integrate Images in a Collage 498

TABLE OF CONTENTS

Clean Up the Edges 500
Rearrange Items on a Layer 502
Cast Shadows 504

VI PREPARING IMAGES FOR THE WEB

CHAPTER 21: PREPARING AND PREVIEWING WEB IMAGES

Getting to Know ImageReady 508
Optimize PNG-8 in ImageReady 513
Optimize GIF Files in Photoshop 5.5 514
Optimize JPEG Files in ImageReady 516

CHAPTER 22: DESIGNING INTERACTIVE GRAPHICS

Image Slicing 518
Slice It Up 522
Modify Slices 524
Specify Slices 528
Assign Rollovers to Slices 530
Animate a Rollover State 532

CHAPTER 23: MAKING ANIMATIONS FROM PHOTOGRAPHS

Create Motion Tweens 534
Tween a Cross Fade 536
Animate a Series of Photos 538
Create a Slide Show 540

Appendix A: Color Management 542

Appendix B: What's on the CD-ROM.............................554

Index...559

IDG Books Worldwide, Inc.
End-User License Agreement 580

CD-ROM Installation Instructions 590

SECTION I

I PHOTOSHOP BASICS

Getting to Know the New Photoshop 4
Set Up Windows to Compliment Photoshop 12
Set Up Your Mac to Compliment Photoshop 14
Set General Preferences 15
Set Preferences for Saving Files 16
Set Preferences for Display and Cursors 17
Set Preferences for Transparency and Gamut 18
Set Preferences for Units and Rulers 19
Set Preferences for Guides and Grid 20
Set Preferences for Plug-ins and Scratch Disks 21
Set Preferences for Memory and Image Cache 22
Recover from Mistakes 23
Use Quick Edit Mode to Overcome Limited RAM 28

GETTING STARTED

2 PHOTOSHOP FILE MANAGEMENT

Get Organized 30
Organize Projects by Folder 31
Make Contact Sheets 32
Open a New File 33
Open Existing Files 34
Save the Current File 36
Save a Copy of the Current File 38
Get Information About the Current File 40
Create Contact Proof Sheets Automatically 42
Place a Conditional Mode Change into an Action 44
Make a Picture Package or Job Print 46
Make a Scrapbook Page 48
Import Images from a TWAIN Device 50
Import Images from a Digital Camera 52
Import Images from a Flatbed Scanner 54
Import Images from a Slide Scanner 56

GETTING TO KNOW THE NEW PHOTOSHOP

Photoshop 5.5 is not radically different from Photoshop 5, or from Photoshop 4, for that matter, but its changes are well worth understanding. What you have in front of you is an amazingly powerful program. But, not to fear, as with any program, once you master the basics, the rest will come easy.

In Photoshop 5 and 5.5 we see incremental improvements in the user-interface: an indispensable unlimited undo feature that doesn't hog RAM; much better implementation of scripting and automation (think Actions Palette); a couple of new, useful layers; improved calibration and color management support (color sync); several new masking features; greater support for text; and possibly the biggest change, the addition of ImageReady — Adobe Systems' program for processing Web images. There are also a host of smaller improvements, including new tools, support for spot colors, new file formats, new keyboard shortcuts, and even something called 3D transformations.

New Keyboard Shortcuts

Old	New	What It Does
None	⌘/Ctrl+PgUp or PgDn	Moves image view left or right by a full screen.
None	Shift+⌘/Ctrl+PgUp/PgDn	Moves image view left or right by a nudge.
None	⌘/Ctrl+Shift+Z	Previous history entry.
None	⌘/Ctrl+Opt/Alt+Z	Next history entry.
None	Opt/Alt+arrow key	Duplicates selected path when an arrow key is pressed. Hint: You need press only once to duplicate the path. Continuing to press the arrow key moves the path one pixel at a time.
None	Shift++	Cycles through all the Blend modes for the currently chosen tool.
None	Shift+-	Cycles through all the Blend modes for the currently chosen tool.
None	=	Chooses the Pen Add Point tool.
None	-	Chooses the Pen Delete Point tool.
A	J	Selects the Airbrush tool.
None	A	Selects the Path Select tool.
Letter	Shift+*letter*	Alternates between tool slots (for example, Shift+L alternates between the Lasso, Polygonal Lasso, and Magnetic Lasso tools).

Following is a brief description of the latest improvements in Photoshop:

Descriptive Tool Status Lines

Way back in Photoshop 4, the status line (see the top figure) didn't tell you much about how to use the chosen tool, whereas now the Photoshop status line (see the bottom figure) is almost as informative as this book.

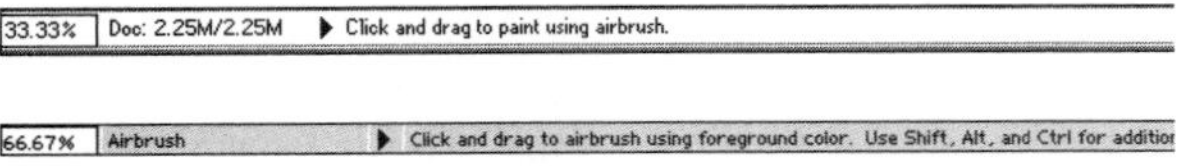

Cancel Sign

If you try to use a tool at in an "illegal" place or sequence, your cursor will turn into a cancel sign (the international symbol of a circle with a slash through it), as shown in the following figure. If you click the Cancel sign in an attempt to choose the tool, you'll get a beep. If you double-click, a message will appear telling you why you can't use the tool.

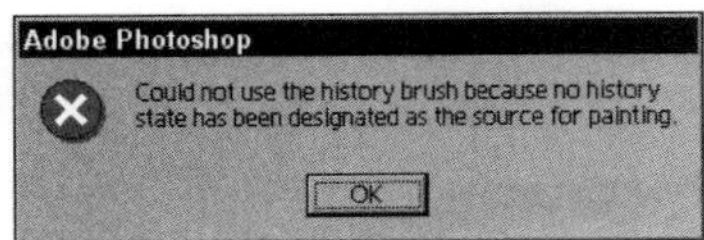

Instant +/- Zoom and Scrolling

Photoshop 5 and 5.5 enables instant zooming and scrolling for drag-based tools. You can zoom in and out of and scroll around the screen while you're dragging to complete a selection or path. Just press the spacebar without letting go of the mouse button (or lifting the pen tip) to scroll. To zoom in, press the = key and keep making the selection. To zoom out, press - without releasing the mouse button and keep making the selection.

This is very handy, but you may find that, at times, scrolling or zooming while selecting or making a brush stroke causes the selection to jump to an unpredictable place. If this happens, just finish making the selection, and then subtract from the selection to correct the mistake. Chapter 8 shows you how to subtract from a selection.

Scrolling and zooming while dragging works with the following tools: Lasso, Polygon Lasso, Magnetic Lasso, Magnetic Pen, and Freehand Pen.

Purge History and Purge All

Photoshop 5 introduced multiple undo capability in the form of the History palette. The state of the image for each stage in the History palette is kept in a memory buffer called the *History buffer*. You can now delete all the History buffers at once. Photoshop will leave the image as is and start building a new history automatically. From the Edit menu, select Purge ⇨ Histories to delete a History buffer. Select Purge ⇨ All to delete all of them at once.

Save Selection Dialog Box

The Save Selection dialog box now enables you to name a new channel at the same time you save a selection (see the following figure). You no longer have to first double-click the channel name or otherwise call up the Channel Options dialog box before you can name the channel.

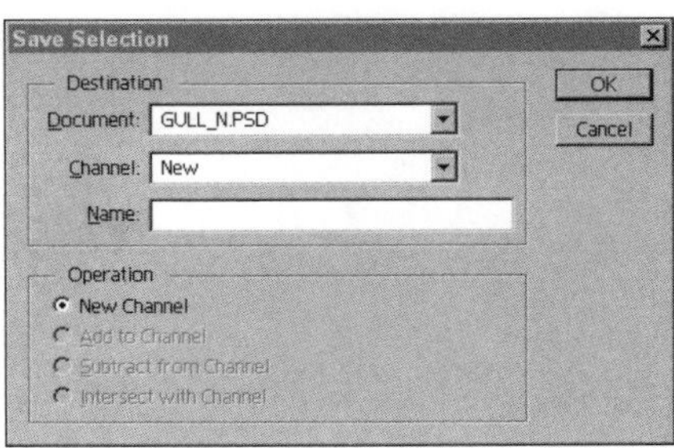

CONTINUED

GETTING TO KNOW THE NEW PHOTOSHOP CONTINUED

Clipping Path

Clipping Path controls no longer appear in the EPS Format Options dialog box. Select Path Palette ➪ Clipping Path to bring up the Clipping Paths dialog box instead.

Clone Tool

The Clone tool no longer clones from the current state of the document, but from the original state of the document.

New Tools

For those upgrading from an earlier version of Photoshop than Version 5, or who are first-time users of Photoshop, the following tools may be new. Nine new tools were introduced in Version 5. Following is a run-down of them:

- **Multipoint Color Sampler**: A new kind of Eyedropper tool, the Color Sampler, appears on the Color Pickup tool pop-out menu. Using this tool, you can click up to four different samples in an image and get a precise read-out of the color of each in the Info palette.
- **Magnetic Lasso**: At last! Photoshop decided to include one of the most popular tools featured in other paint programs: the Magnetic Lasso tool. It automatically snaps the selection marquee to the nearest contrasting pixels. In other words, you can (somewhat) loosely trace around a shape, and the Magnetic Lasso selects it for you.
- **Magnetic Pen**: The Magnetic Pen tool draws a vector path with the same method the Magnetic Lasso tool uses to draw a marquee. It automatically draws the path at the closest border between contrasting pixels.
- **Freeform Pen**: The Freeform Pen tool lets you draw freehand and then automatically converts that sketch to a vector path. The default path smoothing is surprisingly good, so you won't have to spend much time editing the path to the exact shape you had in mind.
- **Measure**: The Measure tool reports the length of a dragged line. At the end of the line, you can press Opt/Alt and drag to see an angle.
- **Vertical Type**: Use to be if you wanted to create vertical type in Photoshop, you had to do it one letter at a time, and then carefully arrange the letters one under the other. Now all you have to do is choose the Vertical Type tool from the Type fly-out menu.
- **Vertical Type Mask**: With the Vertical Type Mask tool you can also make a selection with vertical type. Using a selection for type makes it easy to fill the type with a gradient or an image, bevel the type, or create drop shadows.
- **Pattern Stamp**: The new Pattern Stamp tool replaces the From Pattern choice in the Clone Options palette. Now, you simply paint from any saved pattern.
- **History Brush**: The History Brush takes the place of the From Snapshot option in the old Clone Options dialog box. It will paint from any version of the image in the history record.

- **Art History Brush:** The Art History Brush is brand new in Photoshop 5.5. Like this History Brush, it paints from a Snapshot, but at the same time, it imposes its own "style." The brush works by sampling the color from a snapshot at the moment you press the mouse button, then smearing and changing the color of those pixels as you drag.

New Gradient Types

No longer do you have to depend on third-party filter sets for cylindrical, conical, or diamond gradients. These are all available directly from the Gradient tool fly-out menu.

History Palette

Every time you do anything, such as paint a brush stroke or run a filter effect, Photoshop automatically records the result on the image. It records as many actions as your available memory can stand. The default number is 20, but you can set the number in the History Options dialog box. The name of each operation appears in the History palette.

Layer Effects

A new Layer ➪ Effects submenu makes it possible to automatically create a drop shadow, an inner shadow, an outer glow, an inner glow, and to bevel and emboss. The Bevel and Emboss option further includes options for creating inner bevel, outer bevel, emboss, and pillow emboss effects. You can apply any combination of these effects to any layer. The effects are dynamic, so you can adjust the effect or remove it any time you change your mind. Each effect has its own dialog box, and you can switch effects from the pull-down menu at the top. More about using layer effects appears in Chapter 9.

Type Layers

Type layers aren't new, but now they're re-editable by double-clicking the layer name in the Layers palette. You can control tracking, kerning, and baseline shift in these layers. Some of the best news is that you can have multiple fonts on the same layer and different styles for the same character (as long as each is a different occurrence of that character). Finally, you are able to see live previews as you type (which works really well on dual-monitor systems) so the dialog box doesn't cover the image. Chapter 11 covers in more detail how and when to use type layers.

Adjustment Layers

There's a new kind of Adjustment layer as well as a much improved Hue/Saturation dialog box. The new Channel Mixer layer lets you remix the levels of any of the existing color channels. For instance, you could say that the blue channel now consists of 70 percent of the original content, plus 5 percent of the red channel and 15 percent of the green channel. More about how to use and when to apply these new Adjustment layers appears in Chapter 9.

Improved Actions and Automation

The Insert Menu Item command now sports a Find button, so you can type in part of the command name and Photoshop will retrieve the most likely candidate. This is a nice time-saver when typing is faster than point-and-click-and-drag. Also, measurement units are now based on the current units for the target file. Finally, numerous commands that formerly couldn't be recorded in an action are now available, including the following:

Palettes

- History
- Layers
- Paths

CONTINUED

GETTING TO KNOW THE NEW PHOTOSHOP CONTINUED

Tools

- Crop
- Gradient
- Lasso
- Line
- Magic Wand
- Marquee
- Move
- Paint Bucket
- Polygon
- Type

Menu Commands

- Apply Image
- Calculations
- File Info
- Free Transform

3D Transform

The new Filter ➪ Render ➪ 3D Transform command enables you to select a shape in an image and then wrap it around a three-dimensional shape. This is a major help in making accurate photomontages (composite photos).

Transformations

The location of the Transformations command has been changed. The old Layer ➪ Transform commands are now, more logically, Edit ➪ Transform commands.

Your ability to make transformations has been improved in several respects: You can move the center of the transformation, which changes the way the transformation stretches or rotates. A transformation can be repeated any number of times by selecting Edit ➪ Transform ➪ Repeat. A selection can be transformed without first having to convert it to a layer by selecting Selection ➪ Transform. You can even transform a path—just select a path and then select Edit ➪ Transform.

Color Management Changes

If you are used to the color management commands in previous versions of Photoshop, they will seem almost totally unfamiliar in Photoshop 5 and 5.5. All the File ➪ Color Settings dialog boxes have been changed. (See Appendix A, “Color Management,” for details.)

16-Bit Channel Support

Photoshop supports 16-bit channels. This means that Hue/Saturation, Brightness/ Contrast, Color Balance, Equalize, Invert, and Channel Mixer can now be used in 16-bit mode. Also, the Crop, Rubber Stamp (Clone), and History Brush tools can be used on images with 16-bit channels. Finally, Image Size and Rotate ➪ Arbitrary also work with 16-bit channels.

Spot Color Support

Through the new command Channels Palette ➪ New Spot Channel, you can situate spot colors in a channel by placing images or painting in them. Another new command, Channels Palette ➪ Merge Spot Channel, merges a selected spot color channel with any of the standard color channels. Also, if you convert a duotone to RGB, the individual channels in the multichannel are converted to spot color channels.

Inclusion of Adobe ImageReady

New with Photoshop 5.5 is Adobe's world-standard image-editing solution for print and the Web, ImageReady 2.0. No longer sold as a separate program, ImageReady in Photoshop 5.5 enables you to design interactive Web graphics or prepare sophisticated images for print with power and ease.

The Image Ready interface is intentionally reminiscent of Photoshop's, but you will also see some major differences that are related to ImageReady's primary task. Chief among these are the Animations, Slice, and Rollover palettes that default to appearing at the bottom of the workspace. Also, there's an Optimize palette, where you will spend most of your productive ImageReady time.

Additional File Formats

Photoshop has always been compatible with an abundance of cross-platform graphics file formats. Still, changes and developments are par for the course in the industry, and this is reflected in Photoshop 5 and 5.5 by its inclusion of a few new formats.

Photoshop now supports the Flashpix Import/Export format. Flashpix, the new multiresolution format invented by Live Picture, is quickly being incorporated into Kodak's Photodisc and into the products of many digital camera, scanner, and graphics software manufacturers.

PDF files can now be imported and rasterized in Photoshop. Portable Document Format (PDF) is the file format employed by Adobe Acrobat, which can be used to create portable on-screen displays of desktop-published documents. If you import multipage PDF documents, Photoshop has a new command (File ➪ Automate ➪ Multipage PDF to PSD) that automatically converts them to a multipage Photoshop (PSD) format. Also, now when you save to PDF, you can control the degree of JPEG and ZIP compression.

Finally, support for the DCS 2.0 format saves color separations to a single file. It also includes alpha and spot color channels. In addition, DCS 1.0 format is still available.

Additional Changes

Many additional changes have been made to Photoshop in Version 5 and 5.5. Here is a run-down:

- Previewing a CMYK image has been enhanced by the inclusion of separate preview modes for individual separation plates as well as the composite CMYK image.

CONTINUED

GETTING TO KNOW THE NEW PHOTOSHOP CONTINUED

- New Alignment commands for layers enable you to align and evenly space objects in relation to one another. (Of course, objects to be aligned must be smaller than the canvas and on an otherwise transparent layer.)
- A new command has been added to the Select menu: Select ➪ Reselect (shortcut Shift+⌘/Ctrl+D), which restores the last-used selection whether you saved it or not. This is extremely useful because of the ease with which a selection can be accidentally dropped.
- Three new Action scripts appear in the Automate menu: Contact Sheet II, Picture Package, and Web Photo Gallery. Contact Sheet II places filenames directly underneath thumbnail images; Picture Package lets you print multiples of the same image at different sizes on the same page; and Web Photo Gallery creates contact sheets that can be published to the Web.
- Conversion from millions of colors to 256 indexed colors has also been improved. First, a new Adaptive palette more accurately reflects colors in the original image. You can choose between the speed and quality of conversion with a new Best Quality option. The need to be able to convert solid colors in text and logos to the same Web-safe color has been addressed as well — now there's a Preserve Exact Colors option in the Indexed Color dialog box. Checking the option ensures that colors in the original that are the same as in the target palette will not be dithered. Finally, the Indexed Color dialog box now gives you the option to preview the image before finalizing it.
- Device N support for duotones has been added to PostScript 3 support.

- A new plug-in type, Actions plug-ins, has been added. This enables plug-ins, generally in the form of *Wizards*, to be added to Photoshop's functionality. To find installed Actions plug-ins, select the Help menu and select File ➪ Automate. Included Actions plug-ins are the Resize Image Wizard, the Export Image with Transparency Wizard, the Automate ➪ Batch command, the Automate ➪ Conditional Mode Change command, the Automate ➪ Contact Sheet command, the Automate ➪ Fit Image command, and the Automate ➪ Multipage PDF to PSD command.
- A new option is available in the File ➪ Save As dialog box that enables you to specify the addition of a lowercase file extension.
- It's faster to save large files when also saving thumbnails. In addition, you can now save Mac and Windows thumbnails independently. This means you can store both with the file so that when it's transported to another platform, you will still be able to load a thumbnail.
- It's no longer necessary to load a plug-in if you have a pressure-sensitive tablet.
- The Save Copy dialog box has some new options that make it easier to eliminate saving unwanted information so that you can save the smallest possible file size for a given image.
- In the Mac version only, the Edition Manager is no longer used. You can now make brushes as large as 32,000 pixels in diameter — although trying to paint with such a huge brush could be mighty slow, unless your machine is a dual-processor G3 hotrod with more than 256MB of RAM.

SET UP WINDOWS TO COMPLIMENT PHOTOSHOP

You don't really have to do anything special to make Windows and Photoshop work well together. Still, you can do certain things to enhance their coexistence.

First, unless your work will be strictly in black and white, you want to set your monitor to display as much of the subtle tonalities in a photo as possible. Set your monitor to either High Color (thousands of colors) or True Color (millions of colors).

Second, it's a good idea to get rid of as many of the extraneous colors surrounding a photo as possible. Don't use colored wallpapers and screen savers or any of the appearance schemes provided by Windows or invented by others. Colors outside the picture you're working on can influence your ability to accurately adjust and choose colors within the image.

Of course, if you're just occasionally using Photoshop to edit and size a Web graphic or to enhance photos for a family album, you can leave your desktop color scheme just as it was. But if you're a serious artist, graphic designer, or prepress specialist, your ability to judge colors accurately becomes much more critical.

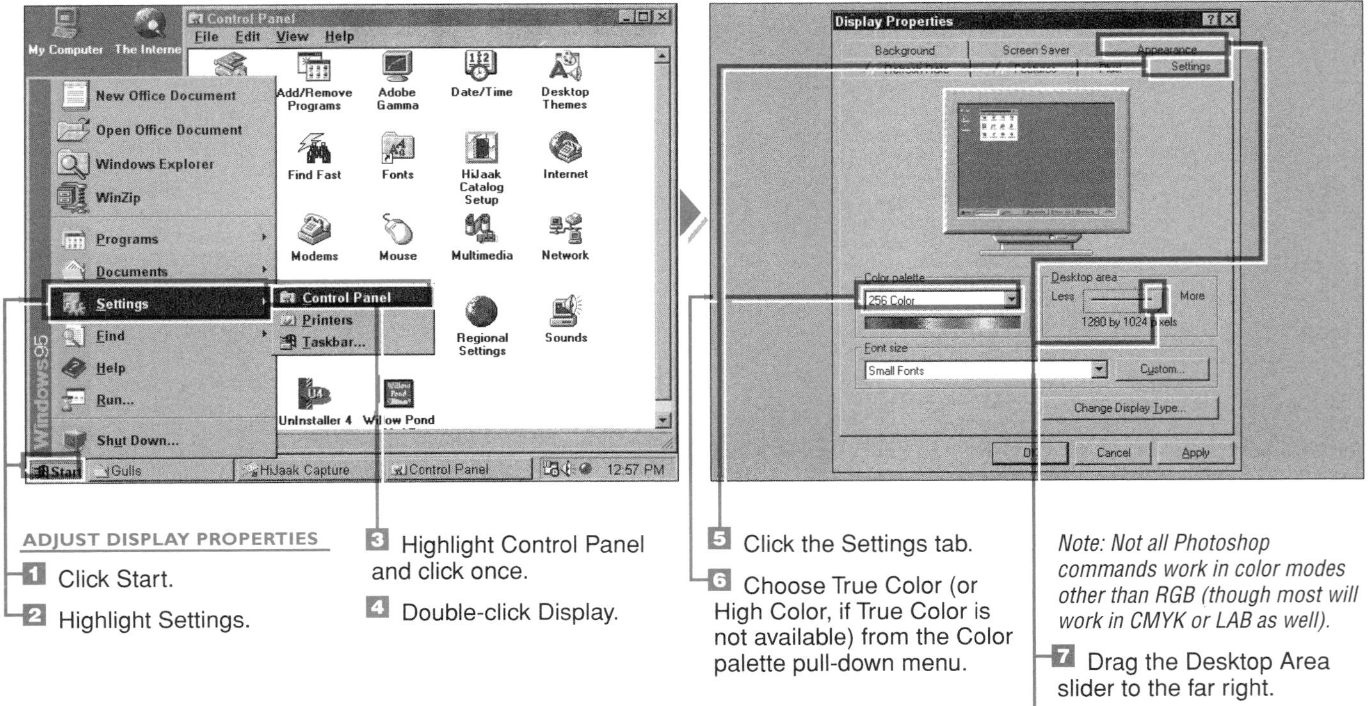

ADJUST DISPLAY PROPERTIES

1 Click Start.

2 Highlight Settings.

3 Highlight Control Panel and click once.

4 Double-click Display.

5 Click the Settings tab.

6 Choose True Color (or High Color, if True Color is not available) from the Color palette pull-down menu.

Note: Not all Photoshop commands work in color modes other than RGB (though most will work in CMYK or LAB as well).

7 Drag the Desktop Area slider to the far right.

8 Click the Appearance tab.

TIPS

Is there a way to switch settings more quickly?

Yes. Place the cursor on the desktop and right-click. Then choose Properties from the In-Context menu. Or, you could place a shortcut to the Display Properties window on the desktop. To do that, open the Control Panel. Click the Display icon to highlight it, and then right-click to bring up the Windows in-context menu. Choose Create Shortcut. Click Yes when Windows asks if you want to place the Shortcut on the desktop.

Is there a way to save my new settings and wallpaper so I don't have to repeat these steps every time I want the same look?

First make sure all your Appearance settings are okay. Then, in the Display Properties window, click the Appearance tab. Click Save As. Name the scheme and click OK.

How do I get rid of the wallpaper and patterns that were in effect before I changed the settings?

In the Display Properties window, choose None from both the Pattern and Wallpaper lists, and then click OK.

Can I use a black or gray background (wallpaper) for the desktop?

Yes. Open a new file in Photoshop and make it approximately 16 pixels square (see Chapter 3 to learn how to do this). Select Edit ⇨ Fill or the Paintbucket tool to fill the image with solid black. Save the image as a Windows bitmap (.BMP) file. Place it in the C:\Windows directory (folder). In the Display Settings window, click the Background tab. In the Wallpaper box, choose the Tile radio button and click Browse. Locate the file you saved and click OK.

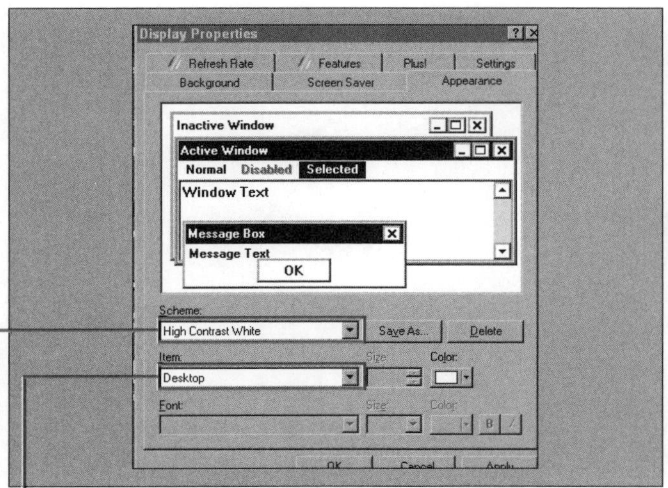

9 Choose Desktop from the Item pull-down menu.

10 Choose High Contrast White in the Scheme pull-down menu.

Note: You can choose to use smaller or larger letters. Smaller letters let you see more of the image you are editing, but larger letters in window titles and menu names are easier to see.

11 Click OK.

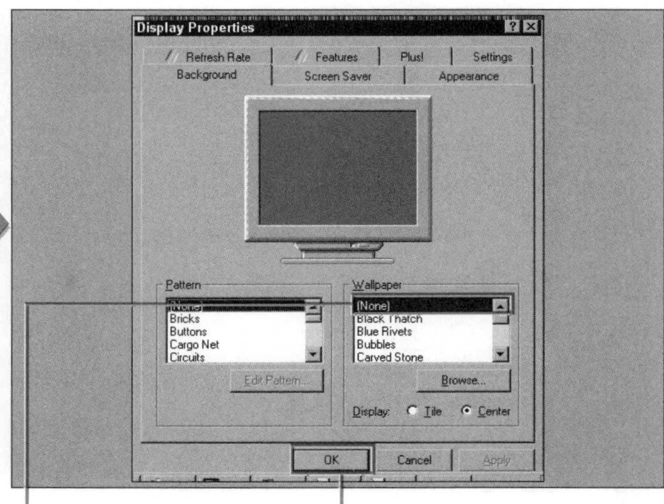

12 Choose None from the Wallpaper list

13 Click OK.

SET UP YOUR MAC TO COMPLIMENT PHOTOSHOP

Setting up the Macintosh desktop to give the most accurate preview of color images is even easier than in Windows.

First, unless your work will strictly be in black and white, you'll want to set your monitor to display as much of the subtle tonalities in a photo as possible. Set your monitor to either High Color (thousands of colors) or True Color (millions of colors).

Second, it's a good idea to get rid of as many of the extraneous colors surrounding a photo as possible. Don't use colored backgrounds, background patterns, or pictures for the desktop. The colors outside the picture you're working on can influence your ability to accurately adjust and choose colors within the image.

Choosing the appropriate resolution setting based on the size of your monitor is important for image quality. Here's a hint: If your monitor is 12 to 15 inches, set the resolution to 640 × 480; 17-inch monitors should be set to 800 × 600; and 19 - 21-inch monitors to 1024 × 768.

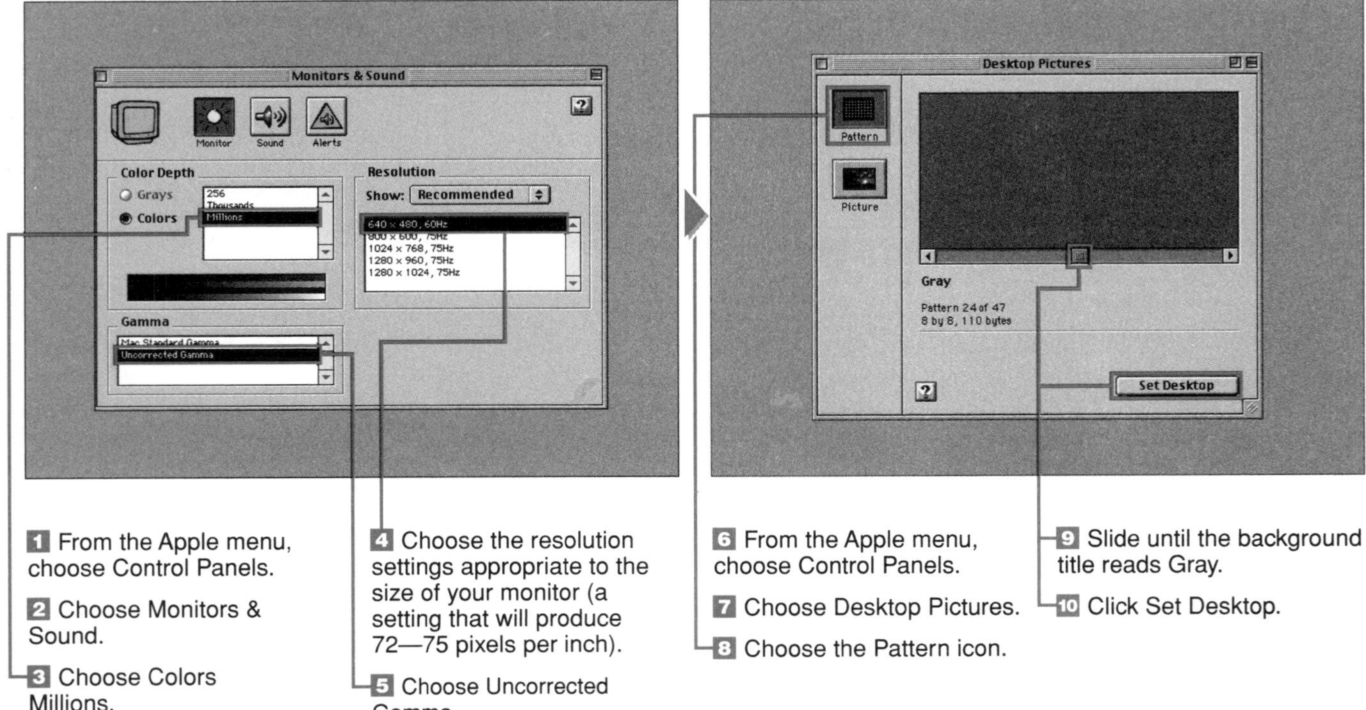

1. From the Apple menu, choose Control Panels.
2. Choose Monitors & Sound.
3. Choose Colors Millions.
4. Choose the resolution settings appropriate to the size of your monitor (a setting that will produce 72—75 pixels per inch).
5. Choose Uncorrected Gamma.
6. From the Apple menu, choose Control Panels.
7. Choose Desktop Pictures.
8. Choose the Pattern icon.
9. Slide until the background title reads Gray.
10. Click Set Desktop.

SET GENERAL PREFERENCES

Before you start working in Photoshop, you want to tidy up the darkroom, put all your supplies in the right drawers, and hang all the controls and accessories on the right pegs. The first thing you need to do is open the Preferences dialog box. From this dialog box, you will be able to change the settings for all the Preferences categories: General, Saving File, Display & Cursors, Transparency and Gamut, Units and Rulers, Guides and Grid, Plug-ins and Scratch Disk, and Memory and Image Cache.

You can choose your preferred type of Color Picker, either Photoshop's or your Mac/Windows native picker. All the exercises in this book that use the Color Picker use Photoshop's, so you should set yours that way — at least while you work through the exercises in this book. You can also choose the type of Interpolation that Photoshop will use when you enlarge an image. Unless you're using a really slow computer that's short on memory, choose Bicubic. (You can always change the interpolation method with the Image ➪ Image Size command.)

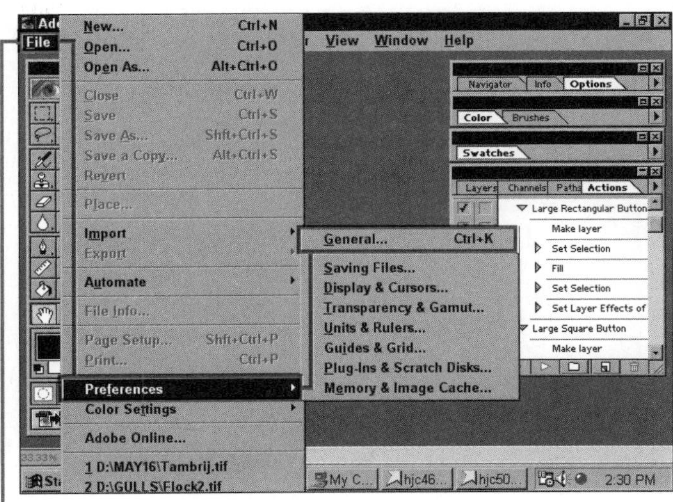

1 Choose File ➪ Preferences ➪ General.

■ The General Preferences dialog box appears.

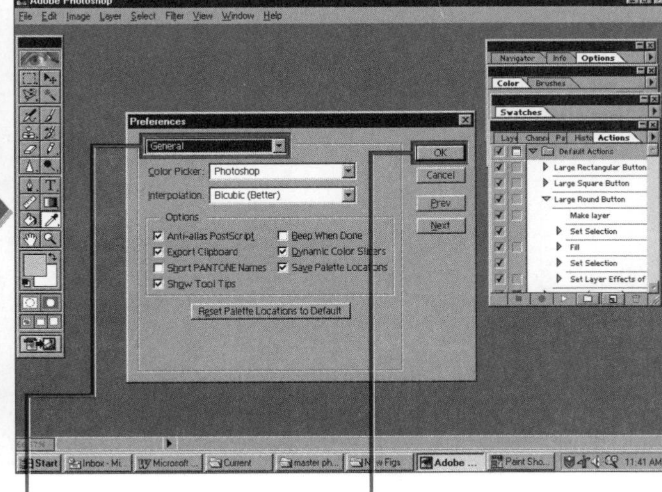

2 Choose the settings you want in the Preferences dialog box.

3 Click OK.

Note: If you want to set preferences of another specific type, choose from the pull-down menu.

SET PREFERENCES FOR SAVING FILES

Setting preferences for saving files is the simplest job in the series of setting preferences — and one of the most important. These are the options that affect how Photoshop saves your files: with or without thumbnails, preview icons, and DOS file extensions, for example.

Macintosh users get a few more options for saving files than PC users do. For example, the Mac can save picture icons to the desktop and full-size 72 dpi thumbnails for use as accurate size placeholders in publishing programs.

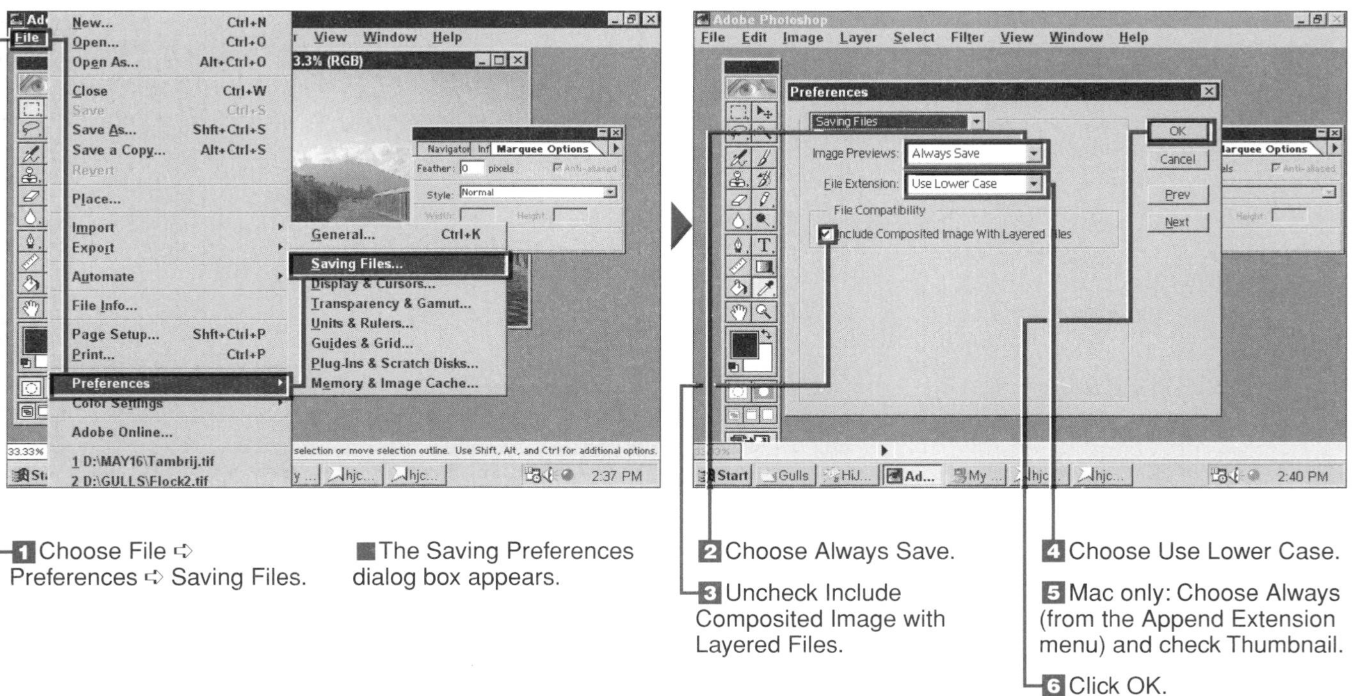

1 Choose File ➪ Preferences ➪ Saving Files.

■ The Saving Preferences dialog box appears.

2 Choose Always Save.

3 Uncheck Include Composited Image with Layered Files.

4 Choose Use Lower Case.

5 Mac only: Choose Always (from the Append Extension menu) and check Thumbnail.

6 Click OK.

SET PREFERENCES FOR DISPLAY AND CURSORS

Photoshop lets you choose the methods for displaying colors and the shapes in which the cursors will appear.

In the Display & Cursors Preferences dialog box, checking the option for Showing Color Channels in Color may provide you with a display that can help you stay oriented as to which channel you're viewing, but you may have a tougher time judging tonal values accurately. Turn off Use System Palette unless you are stuck with a 256-color display. Also turn off Use Diffusion Dither and Video LUT animation — you can set these independently if you later find you need them.

Photoshop differentiates between the cursors used by brushes (which Photoshop calls *painting cursors*) and all other cursors. Under Painting Cursors in the dialog box, if you choose Standard, you may find that the tool's icon gets in the way of your work. The Precise option helps you to make exact pixel placement of strokes (as in pixel-by-pixel retouching). Most of the time, however, you'll have trouble seeing the cursor. I find it most helpful if the cursor represents the actual size of the brush.

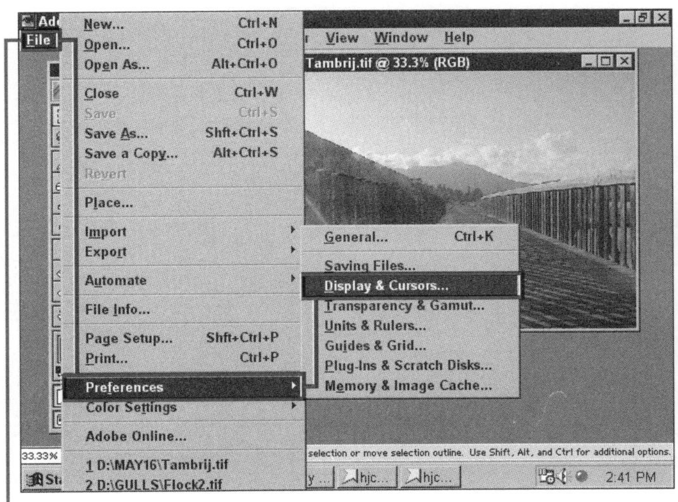

1 Choose File ⇨ Preferences ⇨ Display & Cursors.

■ The Display & Cursors Preferences dialog box appears.

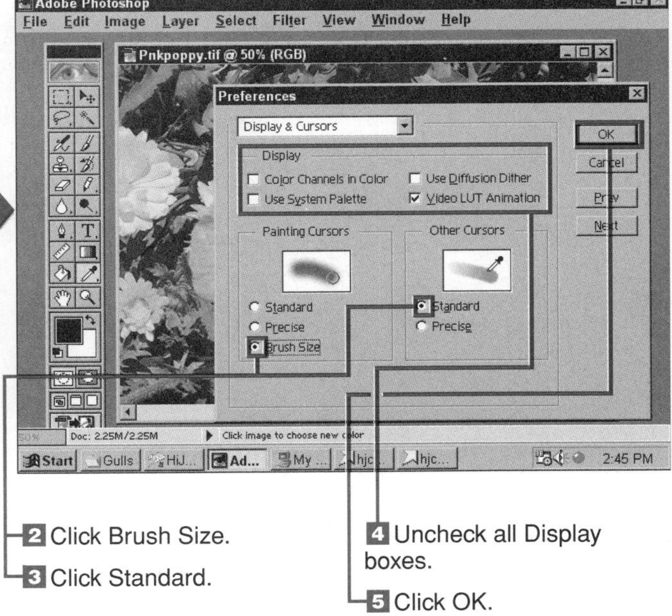

2 Click Brush Size.

3 Click Standard.

4 Uncheck all Display boxes.

5 Click OK.

SET PREFERENCES FOR TRANSPARENCY AND GAMUT

Transparency and Gamut preferences are the settings that determine how Photoshop displays a transparent background and how it alerts you when you've chosen colors for your image that are outside the range of the intended (CMYK) color printer. RGB (the default color scheme used by your monitor) colors that can't be accurately interpreted by a CMYK color printer are called *out of gamut colors*. Photoshop can show these as a garish, flat color to let you know that you'd better make image adjustments to get the proper printed output. (You learn how to make color adjustments in Chapter 4.)

To alert you when part (or all) of your image contains absolutely nothing — in other words, is transparent — Photoshop displays a checkerboard pattern. The transparency settings let you choose the color and size of that checkerboard so it will appear in obvious contrast to the rest of your image.

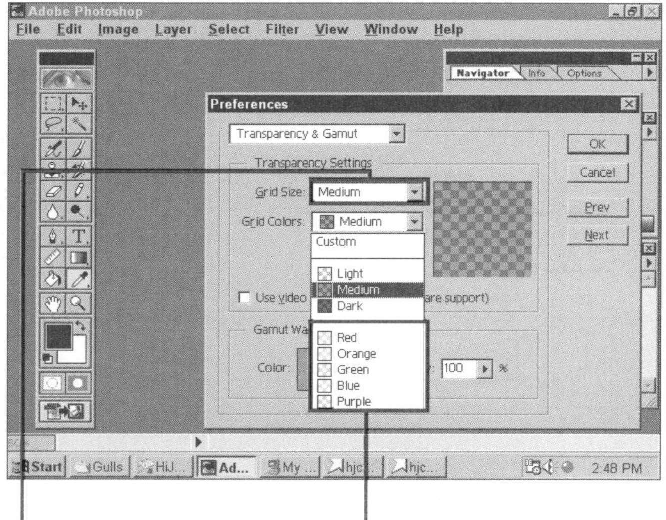

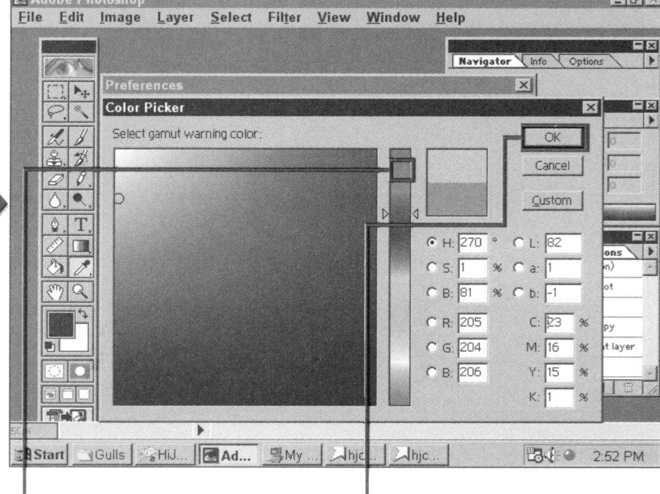

1 In the Transparency & Gamut Preferences dialog box, choose Grid Size: Small, Medium, Large, or None.

Note: Most often the Default Transparency Settings are used.

2 If you want to change color for any of the items, click the appropriate color square.

■ The Color Picker dialog box appears.

3 Click the sliding Hue bar to choose color.

4 Click the Saturation/Brightness preview box to choose color intensity.

5 Click the Next button in the Preferences dialog box to move to the next setting type or click OK.

SET PREFERENCES FOR UNITS AND RULERS

Units and Rulers preferences let you choose the system of measurement that will be used throughout your Photoshop session to measure the size of images, selections, layers, and canvas (the work area — including the image and its borders). You can also set column size and point/pica size.

It is recommended that you use pixels as your base unit of measurement, as resolution is variable. In other words, an image 1-inch wide could be any number of pixels wide. On the other hand, if most of your images will be printed in a specific publication at a particular resolution, you may want to use inches or picas.

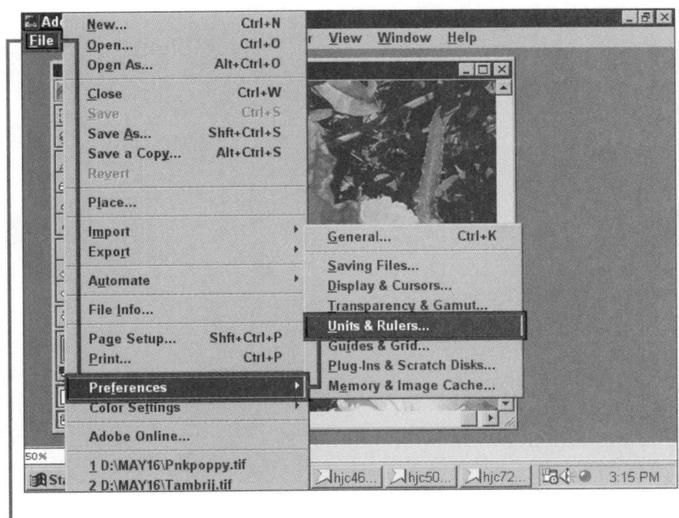

1 Choose File ⇨ Preferences ⇨ Units & Rulers.

■ The Units & Rulers dialog box appears.

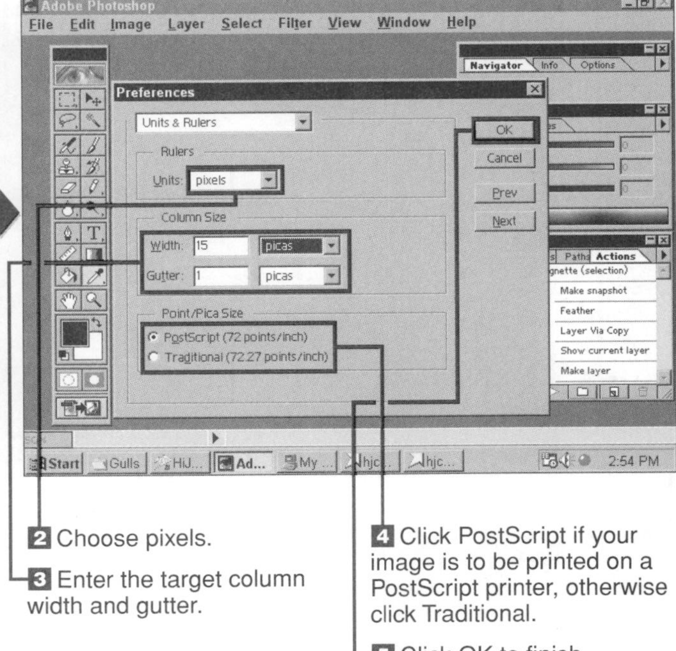

2 Choose pixels.

3 Enter the target column width and gutter.

4 Click PostScript if your image is to be printed on a PostScript printer, otherwise click Traditional.

5 Click OK to finish.

SET PREFERENCES FOR GUIDES AND GRID

Guides and grids are nonprinting visual aids used to help place elements (such as type) accurately within a composition. If you're a beginning artist, you may also find it easier to paint from scratch if you draw on grid paper or make ruler guides for the compositional "rule of thirds." Here, the computer beats the traditional methods because you can hide your "amateur" guidelines when you've finished your image.

The Guides & Grid Preferences dialog box enables you to choose a color for your grids and guides. It's a good idea to pick separate colors for these, just in case you find a reason to use the two together.

Finally, you can choose to use either solid lines or dashed lines for both grids and guides. If you have an image that uses a lot of straight lines (such as venetian blinds or mattress-ticking type fabric patterns), dashed lines can be easier to see.

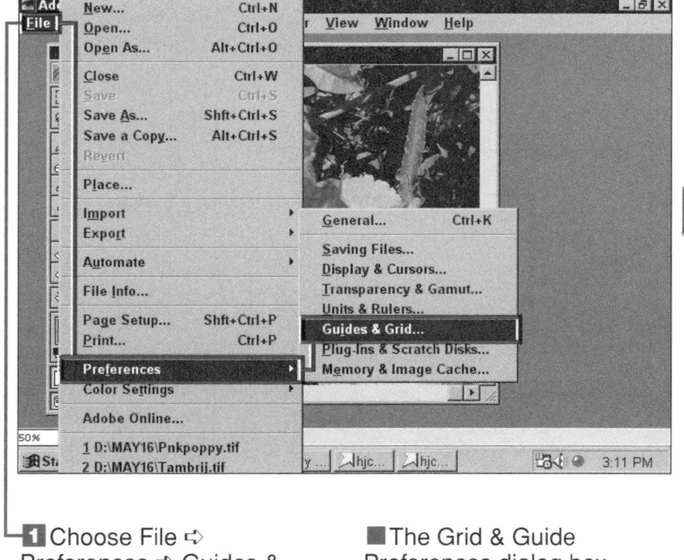

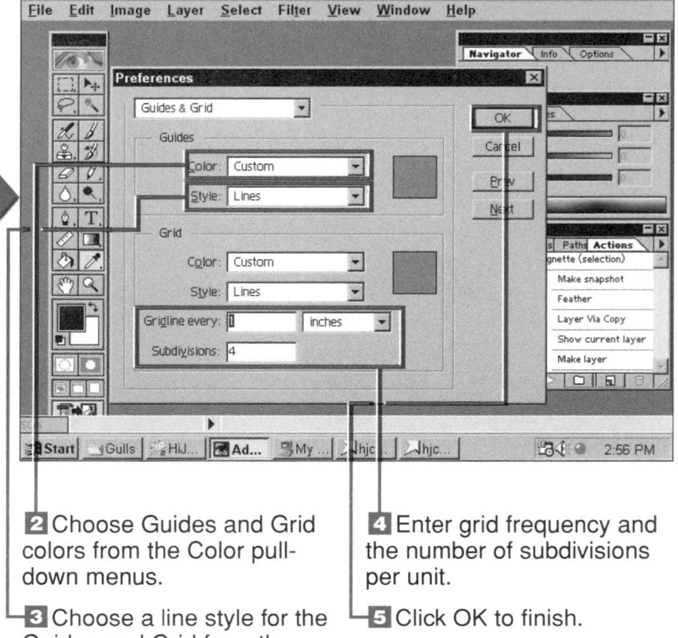

1 Choose File ➪ Preferences ➪ Guides & Grid.

■ The Grid & Guide Preferences dialog box appears.

2 Choose Guides and Grid colors from the Color pull-down menus.

3 Choose a line style for the Guides and Grid from the Style pull-down menus.

4 Enter grid frequency and the number of subdivisions per unit.

5 Click OK to finish.

SET PREFERENCES FOR PLUG-INS AND SCRATCH DISKS

Plug-ins are programs written so that they will work inside Photoshop to add greater functionality to Photoshop.

Photoshop comes with a default Plug-ins folder to store your Photoshop plug-ins, but you can put them in any folder you like. (I recommend using defaults whenever possible, because this makes it much easier to troubleshoot long after you've forgotten how you set up the program.) Note: The settings you make now won't take effect until you restart Photoshop.

Scratch disks refers to where Photoshop stores its temporary virtual memory files. Photoshop assumes you only have one hard disk, so it stores these files, called scratch files, on the same disk with your system software. If you have more than one hard disk, you can tell Photoshop to store its temporary files elsewhere.

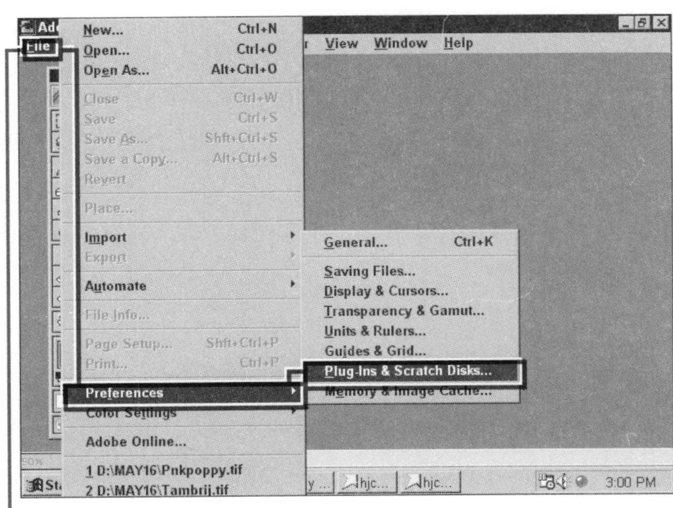

1 Choose File ⇨ Preferences ⇨ Plug-Ins & Scratch Disks.

■ The Plug-Ins & Scratch Disk Preferences dialog box appears.

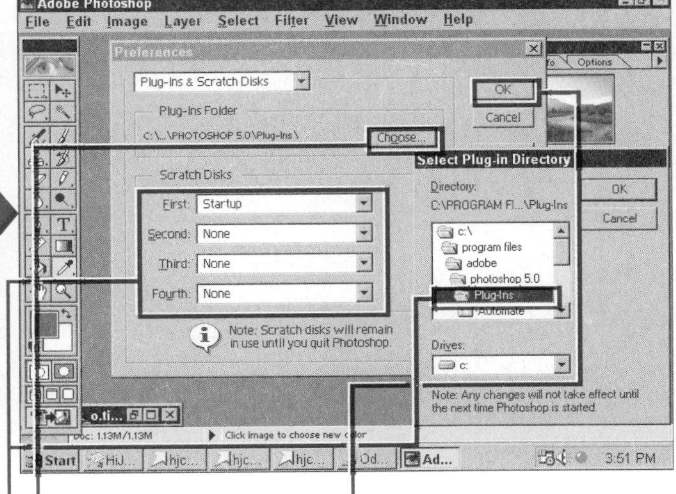

2 Click the Choose button.

■ The Select Plug-in Directory browse box appears.

3 Navigate to the folder you wish to save your plug-ins in and select it.

Note: You can also choose the third and fourth disks, if you have that many drives or partitions.

4 Click OK.

SET PREFERENCES FOR MEMORY AND IMAGE CACHE

Photoshop, in versions since 4.0, uses a memory-caching scheme to speed its operations. Photoshop stores multiple resolutions of the currently active file in a cache, for example, so the program can access the resolution closest to the zoom level you're working in.

There are two preferences to set for the image cache: the number of cache levels and whether to use the cache for drawing histograms. *Histograms* are the graphs Photoshop draws in the Image ⇨ Adjust ⇨ Levels, Image Adjust Histogram, and similar dialog boxes. If you check the box, histograms will be drawn faster, but won't be as accurate. So leave the box unchecked unless you really need the speed or until you can afford more memory.

Note: The settings you make now won't take effect until you reboot Photoshop.

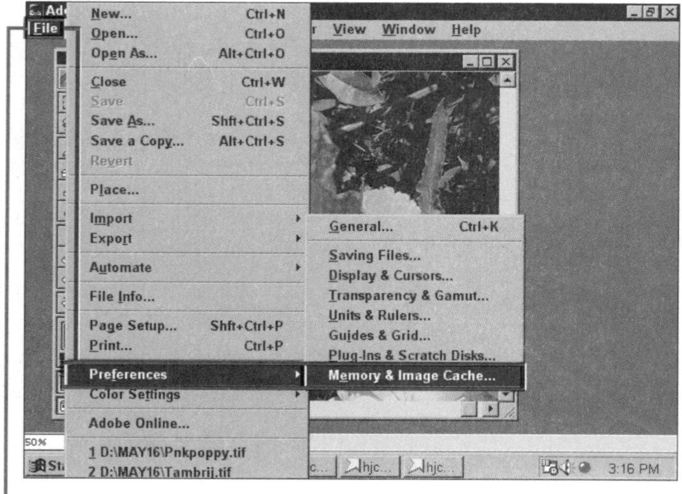

Note: The settings you make now won't take effect until you reboot Photoshop.

1 Choose File ⇨ Preferences ⇨ Memory & Image Cache.

■ The Memory & Image Cache Preferences dialog box appears.

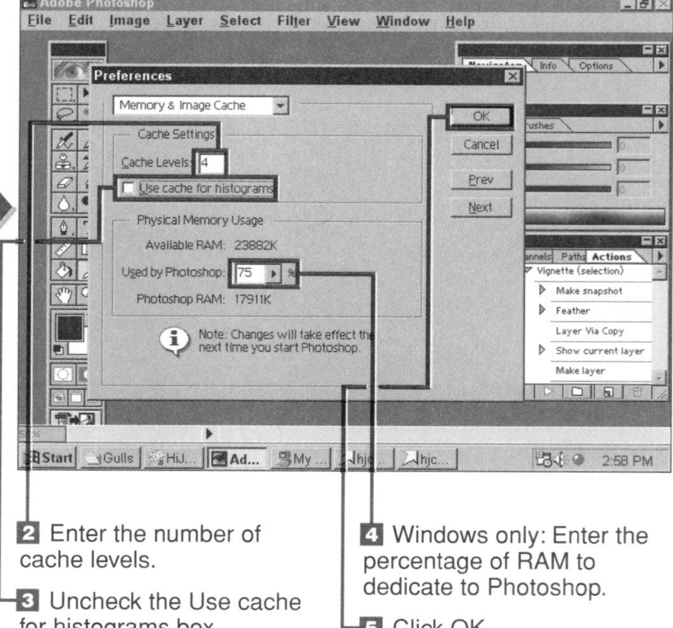

2 Enter the number of cache levels.

3 Uncheck the Use cache for histograms box.

4 Windows only: Enter the percentage of RAM to dedicate to Photoshop.

5 Click OK.

RECOVER FROM MISTAKES

One of the most fundamental things to understand about Photoshop is that it works with *raster* (sometimes called *bitmap*) images. You can't edit items in a raster image, such as an orange or a face, for example. Instead, you must edit the pixels that make up those items — and those pixels are part of a matrix that encompasses the whole layer. So, if you goof on part of the picture, you've messed up the entire layer.

Photoshop 5 gives you six ways to recover from such mistakes without having to recreate the entire image: use Undo or Revert, duplicate a layer, use the history list, take a snapshot, or take a merged snapshot. If you understand the fundamental methods of recovery, and which to use when, you will save yourself enormous amounts of time in the long run.

UNDO

Undo is the fastest way to recover from a single-step mistake, such as a misplaced brush stroke. It is useless after performing more than one action, however.

UNDO COMPLETELY

1 Choose Edit ➪ Undo.

Note: The name of the previous operation follows the Undo command. Undo also removes the last operation from the History list.

Note: If you change your mind, you can repeat this operation or press ⌘/Ctrl+Z again. The second time you repeat the operation, the command is called Redo last operation.

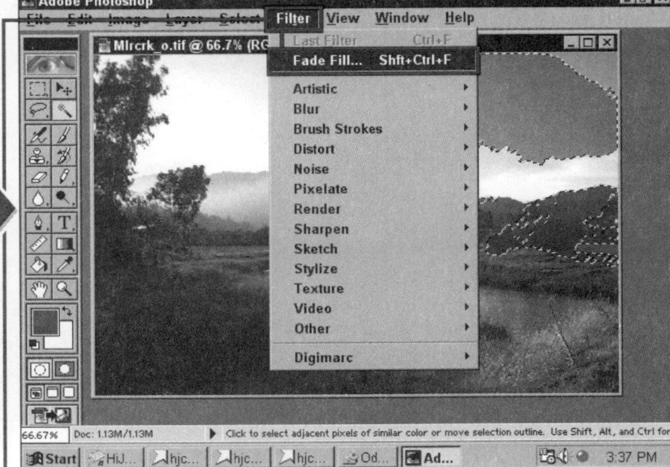

FADE THE UNDO

1 Choose Filters ➪ Fade last operation.

■ The Fade dialog box appears. Drag the slider to set opacity, then choose Mode ➪ Apply.

Note: The quickest and most important way to undo is ⌘/Ctrl+Z. It's a good idea to get in the habit of keeping your fingers near these keys.

CONTINUED

RECOVER FROM MISTAKES CONTINUED

REVERT

Choose File ➪ Revert to retrieve the last saved version of your image. Always keep your project saved to Photoshop (.PSD) format until it is complete. This way you will have access to all layers, channels, and other Photoshop features (except the History list).

Even with the addition of the History list, it's a good idea to save your file each time you complete what you consider to be a major stage of the work you're going to do on that file. Then, if you decide you want to go back to a version that precedes the number of steps available in the history file, you can do so.

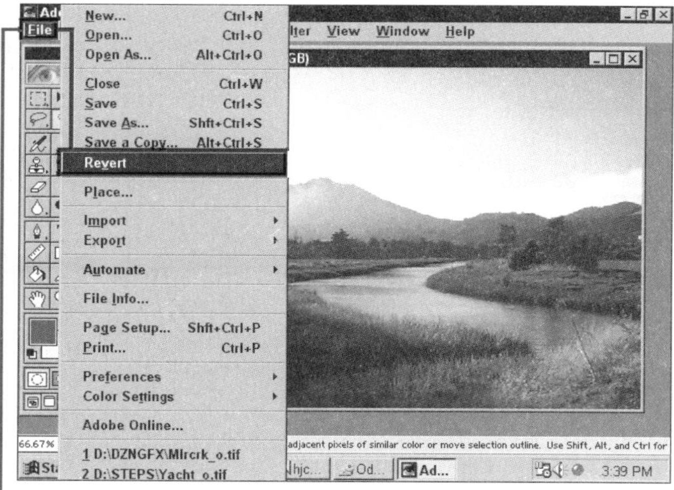

1 Choose File ➪ Revert.

■ The file is directly restored to its last saved version.

■ Any steps taken since the last save are gone. There is no way to recover.

Note: Get in the habit of saving a file each time you get to a stage where you know you're please with the overall effect. Then you can always revert, and you haven't wasted RAM with unneeded snapshots.

RECOVER FROM MISTAKES CONTINUED

DUPLICATE A LAYER

Most Photoshop commands work only on the currently selected layer. If you want to experiment with the content of a layer and then be able to recover quickly if you (or your client) hate the result, make a duplicate of the target layer. This way, if you don't like the result, you can just trash the layer. You can also turn it off and on until you decide whether you really like the result.

Another reason you might want to duplicate layers is so that you can have different versions of the same layer. You'll then be able to make quick comparisons by simply turning the layers on and off.

One problem with creating several duplicate layers is that having lots of layers requires lots of file space (and RAM, if you're a Mac user). Be sure to delete or merge layers once the need to keep them independent has passed.

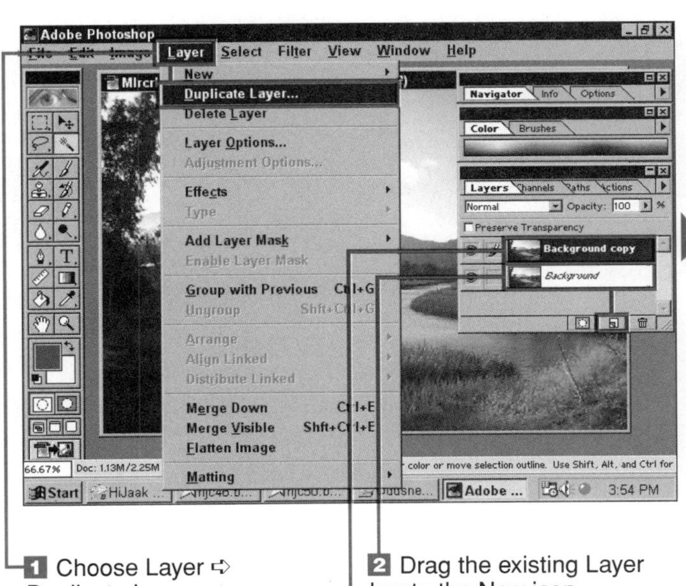

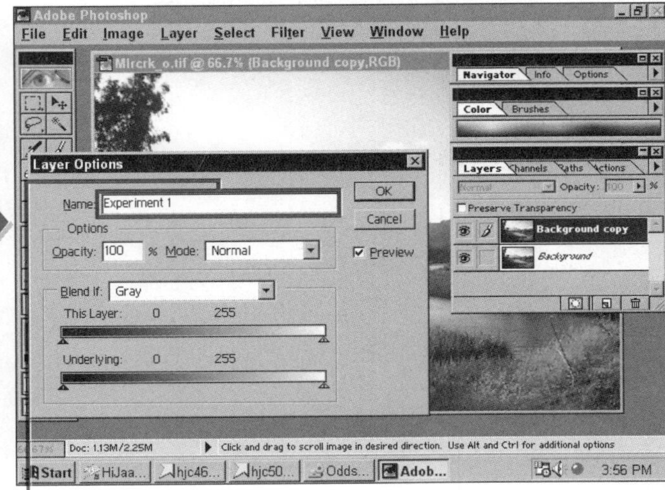

1 Choose Layer ⇨ Duplicate Layer.

2 Drag the existing Layer bar to the New icon.

3 Double-click the new layer to bring up the Layer Options dialog box so you can enter a new name.

4 Enter a descriptive name for your new layer.

Note: Be sure to delete layers you're sure you'll no longer need. Unneeded layers hog file space.

CONTINUED

RECOVER FROM MISTAKES CONTINUED

USE THE HISTORY LIST

Photoshop 5's new History list now provides a means for recording each brush stroke, command, or any other operation. Everything you do is entered onto a list by the name of the command or tool used. This list looks like any of the other Photoshop palettes, such as the Layers palette. You can return to any stage of the creation of your project by selecting (highlighting) an operation's name bar.

You can set the number of operations that the History list will record in the History Options dialog box. The default is 20. Of course, the more levels you specify, the more memory your system will require. You can also choose to automatically create the first snapshot (for more about snapshots, see the next exercise in this chapter) and whether to allow a nonlinear history. If you check Allow Non-linear History in the History Options dialog box, you can go back and insert steps anywhere in the sequence.

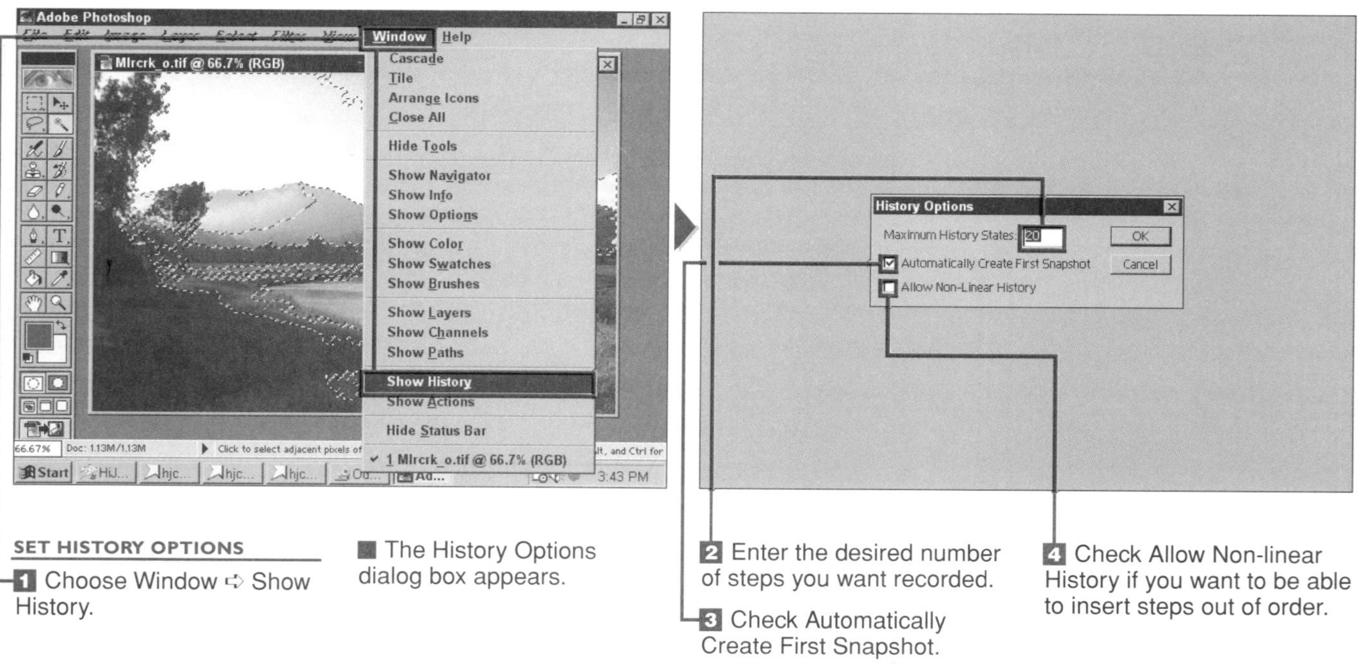

SET HISTORY OPTIONS

1 Choose Window ⇨ Show History.

■ The History Options dialog box appears.

2 Enter the desired number of steps you want recorded.

3 Check Automatically Create First Snapshot.

4 Check Allow Non-linear History if you want to be able to insert steps out of order.

RECOVER FROM MISTAKES CONTINUED

SNAPSHOTS

Whenever you want to record an image that is the result of all the steps you've performed up to that point, use the History palette menu to take a snapshot of the image. You will then be able to recreate the image as it looked at that stage simply by selecting the snapshot in the History list. You can also "erase to the snapshot" by selecting the snapshot and using the History Brush.

When you want to record all the visible layers as a single image to the History list, use the New Snapshot command. When the New Snapshot dialog box appears, choose Merged Layers from the pull-down menu. You can choose which layers are visible by clicking the Eye icon box so that the Eye icon is visible. Layers that have no Eye icon showing in the Layers palette list will not be merged.

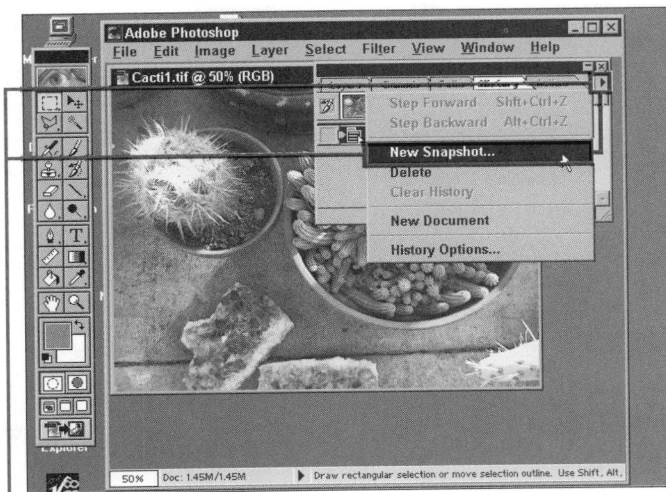

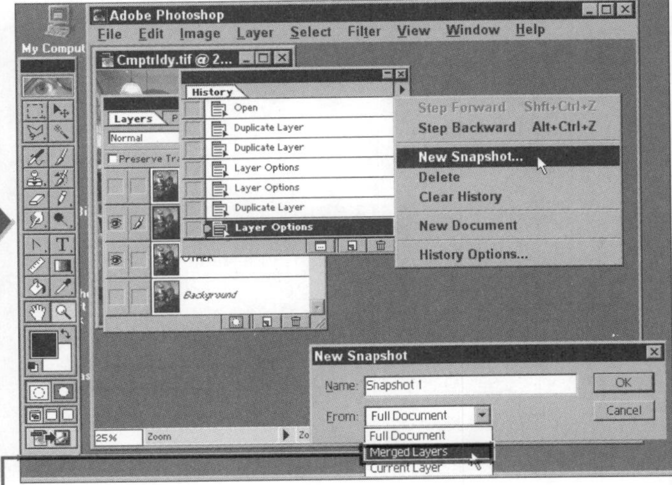

TAKE A SNAPSHOT

1 Click the History palette arrow to show the palette menu.

2 Choose New Snapshot.

■ The Snapshot icon appears at the top of the History palette list.

TAKE A MERGED SNAPSHOT

1 Choose Merged Layers from the From pull-down menu in the New Snapshot dialog box.

Note: You can also make a snapshot of all layers, visible or not, by choosing Full Document or of a single layer by choosing Current Layer. Make sure the layer you want to shoot is the one that's currently chosen.

USE QUICK EDIT MODE TO OVERCOME LIMITED RAM

If you're just getting started with Photoshop, and your machine has only the 16MB to 32MB of RAM typical of office and personal computers, you might find yourself enduring long waits while the hard-disk grinds. The reason: The file itself is probably larger than your available memory, so the computer substitutes hard-drive disk space.

Photoshop provides an often-overlooked alternative to opening entire files called *Quick Edit*. Quick Edit lets you work on any small portion of a file, using only as much memory as needed for that portion, and then integrates the altered segment seamlessly into the whole image.

Alternatively, you can automatically divide an image into same-size sections, and then work on each with the same command(s) to end up with a uniform result. To get an idea of how handy this can be, imagine changing the overall brightness and contrast of the image — one section at a time.

The beauty of Quick Edit is that you only need as much RAM as is necessary to edit that small portion of the whole image. Quick Edit is a Photoshop plug-in that can be found on your Photoshop installer CD-ROM in the Goodies/Quikedit folder.

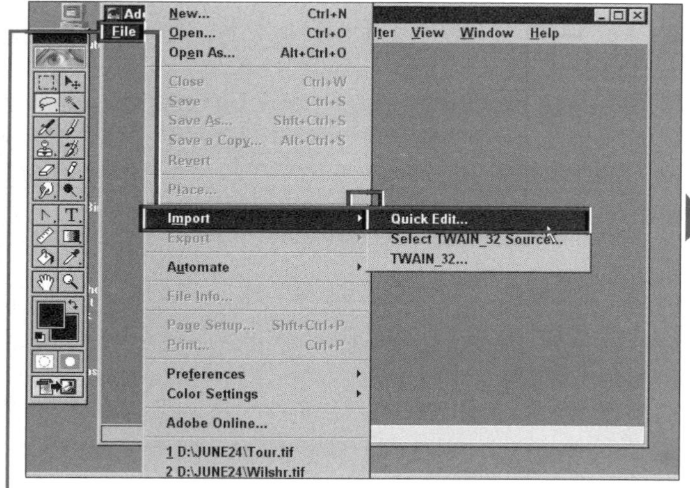

1 Click File ➪ Import ➪ Quick Edit.

■ The Open dialog appears.

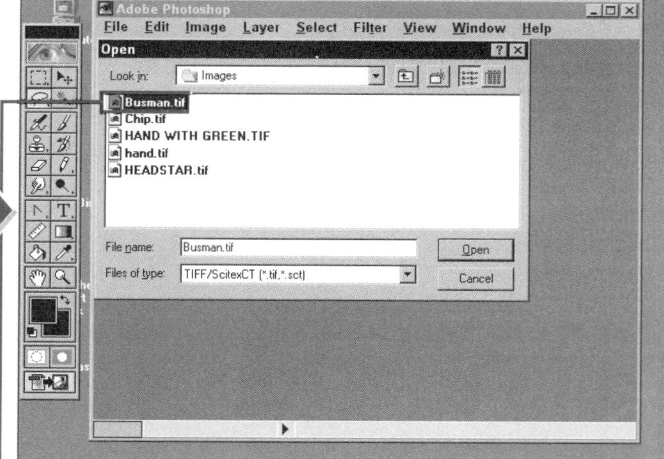

2 Double-click the filename of the file you want to edit.

Note: The hard way to do the preceding step is to choose the file. When its name appears in the File name field, click Open. The Quick Edit dialog box appears.

TIPS

Is Quick Edit really a substitute for lots of RAM?

No, but then you can never have enough RAM. If you're going to work regularly on large files, the money it takes to buy 128MB or more of RAM will be well spent. On the other hand, even those who have hundred of megabytes of fast memory and a fast computer will eventually find good use for this feature.

What if I want to do something that needs to affect the whole image at once, such as using a special-effects filter?

No problem. Follow the Quick Edit procedure until you get to the Quick Edit dialog box. Then check the Grid check box. To change the number of columns and rows, click the + and - buttons. Then click in the section you want to edit first. After editing each section, choose File ⇨ Export ⇨ Quick Edit Save. Repeat for each of the other sections.

What if I want to work on a file that's not in one of the three formats (Scitex, TIFF, or Photoshop 2) that work with Quick Edit?

Simply use File ⇨ Open to open the file in Photoshop. Next, use File ⇨ Save As and choose TIFF from the Save As pull-down menu.

Can I use Quick Edit at any stage of working on a file?

No. You can't import layers, and if you make them during a Quick Edit, they will flatten upon saving. If you want to work with layers, make several copies of the file, use Quick Edit on each file individually, and then use the Move tool to drag each copy into each file as a layer (if you have enough RAM).

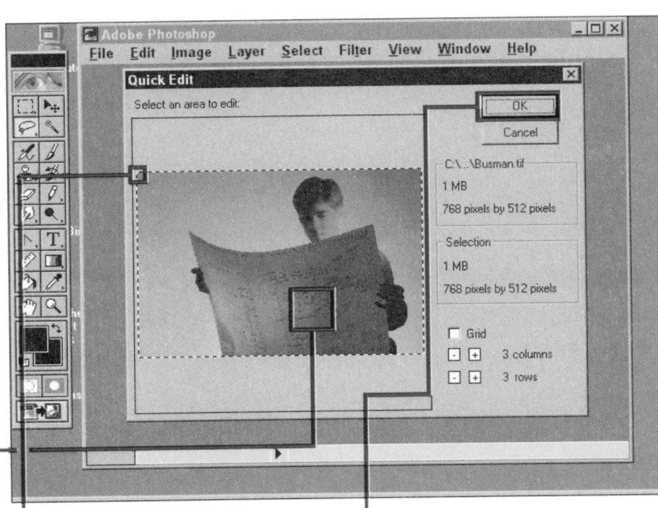

3 Position the cursor (a gray cross-hair) at one corner of the section you want to edit.

4 Drag the cursor until the dashed line rectangle encloses the area you want to edit.

5 Click OK.

■ The indicated portion of the file opens. When finished working on the section, export to Quick Edit so that the section you modified can be reunified with the whole.

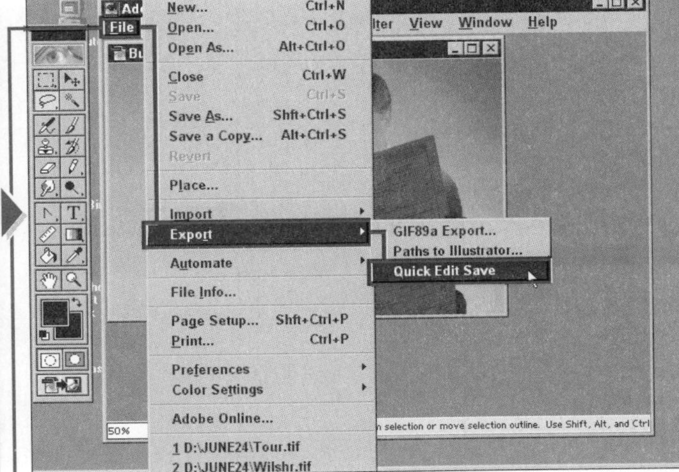

Note: It is very important you remember to save your Quick Edit as follows. Otherwise, you may accidentally overwrite the original file with the Quick Edit section.

6 Choose File ⇨ Export ⇨ Quick Edit Save.

Note: It may seem as though nothing happens next, but your edit will rejoin seamlessly the larger, original file.

GET ORGANIZED

This chapter shows you the aspects of Photoshop that have the potential to help you get organized. There are no new products to buy. In fact, some of the topics covered deal with everyday file management. You don't even have to own Photoshop to do those exercises.

The topics covered in this chapter are all concerned with how to better manage files while working on a Photoshop project:

- Organize projects by folder
- Make contact sheets
- Open a new file
- Open existing files
- Save the current file
- Save a copy of the current file
- Get information about the current file
- Import images from a digital camera
- Import images from a flatbed scanner
- Import images from a slide scanner
- Import images from a TWAIN device

Putting Your Files Away

The truth of the matter is most of us tend to complete projects in a fairly haphazard way. We try something, throw it out if it doesn't work, and then go find new images or experiment with new techniques. Every once in a while, a miracle happens, and we make art. It's fun, but it's usually not a reliable way to make money or ensure deadlines are met.

A project will move along in a more sane and efficient way if you organize your images in folders by type and purpose and your projects in folders that are subdivided into components and stages of production. This organization can be simple or complex, depending on how involved the project at hand is.

Getting Down to Business

Once you've done all your organizing, it's time to go to work. You can either open an existing image to use as the subject of your project or open a new file and start from scratch. If you have questions about using Photoshop's New File dialog box, you'll find the answers in this section.

ORGANIZE PROJECTS BY FOLDER

Once you've worked with Photoshop for a while, you'll probably find yourself accumulating hundreds or thousands of images (and their edited variations). Once this happens, trying to find the right file becomes a challenge.

The way around this is simply to get organized. Think about how your images should be categorized and how your jobs should be broken down. For example, if you were working on several projects at once, create a master file folder for each client and a subfolder for each assignment. In each subfolder, create separate folders for backgrounds, props (images that will contribute to a composite), and variations.

You also want to organize all your images. Here again, what system is best suited to the way you collect images and using them will vary. I like to organize master folders or disks by source (for example, Nikon, Digital Camera, PhotoCD). The next level of folders is usually divided by date. Finally, images are further organized by subject or location.

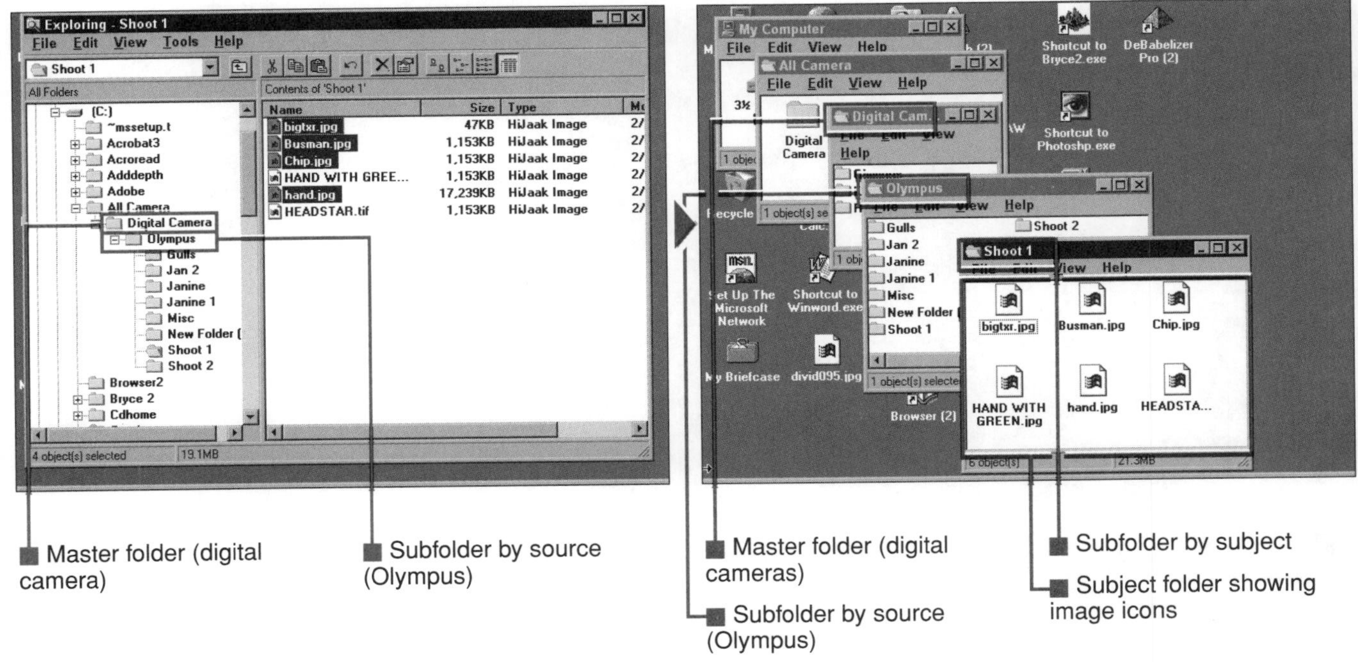

MAKE CONTACT SHEETS

You will have a much easier time finding your image resources if you use Photoshop's new Automate plug-in to make contact sheet files for each of your image directories. A *contact sheet* is a collection of thumbnail images organized by directory, enabling you to quickly view each image. You can print out these contact sheets (in full-color, if you have a color printer) or keep them in a contact sheet directory where you can refer to them online.

Another tip: If you have a CD-ROM recorder to enable you to store files on CDs, or if you have had Kodak PhotoCDs made of your images, you can also keep contact sheets of the images contained on a CD in the CD's jewel case or envelope.

Contact sheets make it easy to distinguish between multiple versions of the same image or completely different shots with similar filenames.

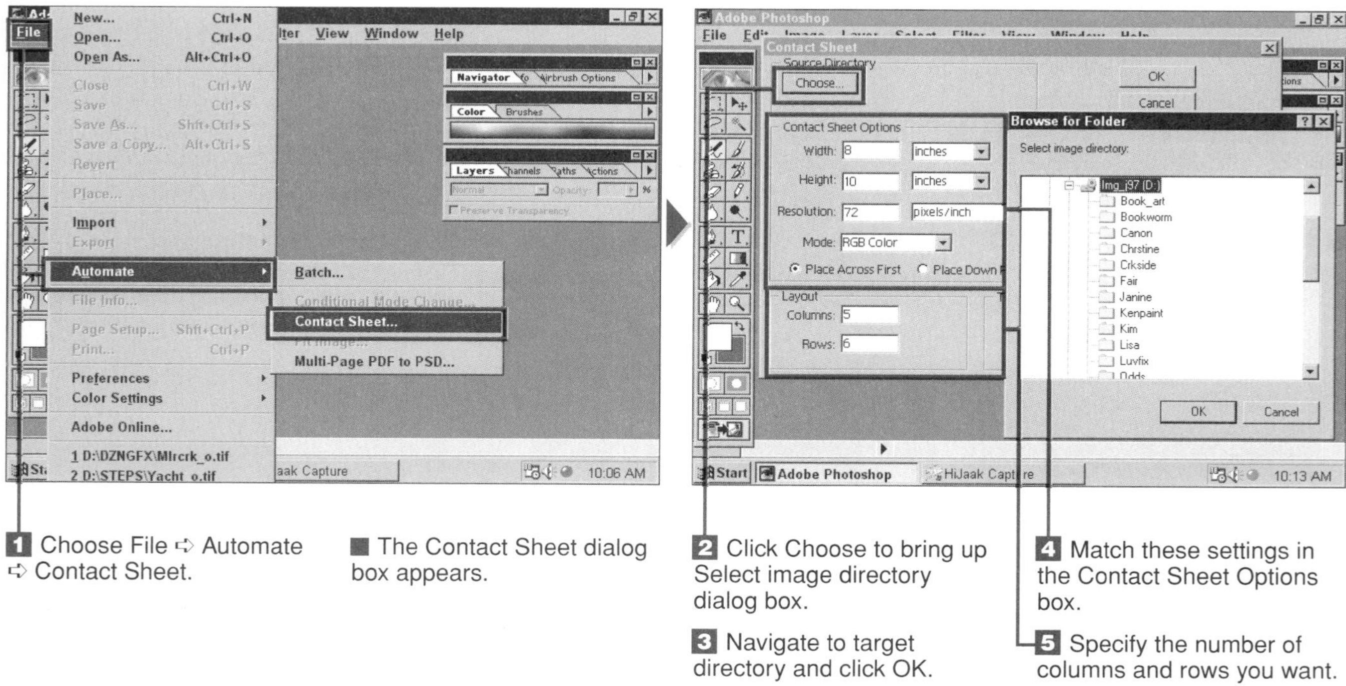

1 Choose File ➪ Automate ➪ Contact Sheet.

■ The Contact Sheet dialog box appears.

2 Click Choose to bring up Select image directory dialog box.

3 Navigate to target directory and click OK.

4 Match these settings in the Contact Sheet Options box.

5 Specify the number of columns and rows you want.

OPEN A NEW FILE

To start a new image, Photoshop needs to know several things that aren't required by other types of programs: the output resolution of the file you want to create, the units of measurement you want to use while you create your image, and the size of the canvas you want to create the image on.

It also wants to know what color you want the canvas to be, or whether you'd rather it were transparent.

If you have an image in the Clipboard (as a result of an earlier Copy or Cut command executed on another image), however, Photoshop automatically enters the dimensions and Color mode of that image. You can enter numbers for a smaller or larger canvas, but it's better to make the canvas larger with the Image ⇨ Canvas Size command and to crop it with the Crop tool.

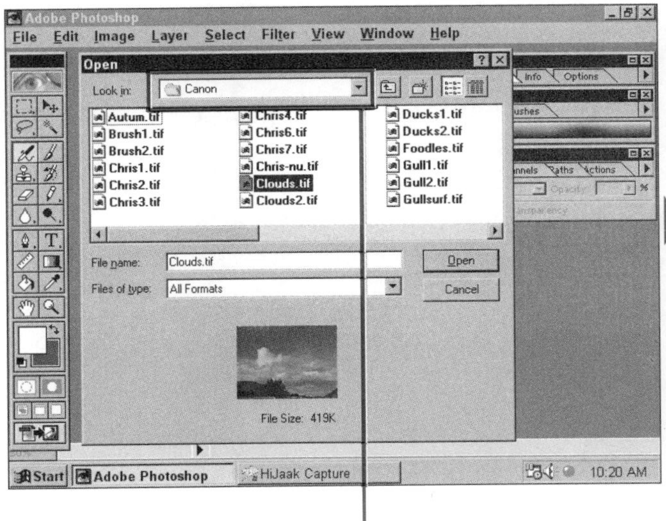

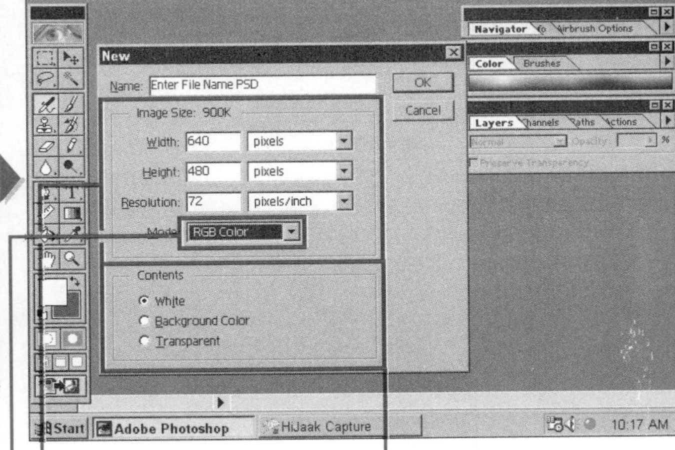

1 Choose File ⇨ New (or ⌘/Ctrl+N).

■ The New File dialog box appears.

2 Enter a filename.

3 Enter dimensions in the Image Size area of the New dialog box for canvas width, height, and resolution.

4 Choose a Color mode from the pull-down menu.

5 Choose the canvas color in the Contents area.

Note: Choose Transparent if you want to paint or paste an irregular shape that can later be comb ıed with new layers without the nʊed for further masking.

OPEN EXISTING FILES

The process of opening an existing file in Photoshop is basically the same as that for any other application running under the Mac OS or Windows. There are a few things to know and a few caveats, however.

First, although Photoshop is compatible with most bitmap and some vector (Encapsulated PostScript, Adobe Illustrator, Quark Generic EPS files) image formats, you may encounter new formats all the time. It's possible you may need to open a format that isn't on the Open dialog box's Files of Type pull-down menu. In such a case, you have several options for opening the non-Photoshop-compatible file: Check the Adobe Web site (`www.adobe.com`) for a plug-in, or open the file in the program native to that format and then save it to a Photoshop-compatible one, or use a file conversion program such as DeBabelizer from Equilibrium Software to convert the file to a format Photoshop can open.

If you want to open a file using a plug-in (such as GIF89a), choose File ⇨ Import ⇨ *format name*. If you want to open a file under a new name (in other words, a copy, to ensure preservation of the original), choose File ⇨ Open As.

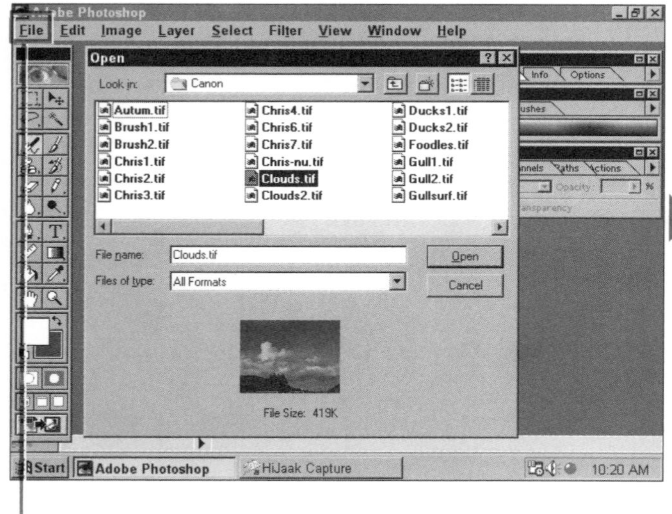

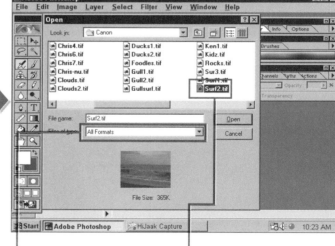

1 Choose File ⇨ Open.

■ The Open dialog box appears.

2 Choose All Formats from the Files of Type pull-down menu.

■ All types of files, whether Photoshop-compatible or not, appear.

3 Double-click the file you would like to load.

■ Any Photoshop-compatible file will open in Photoshop.

TIPS

What should I do if Photoshop won't open the file, even though it appears to be in a compatible format?

A few applications seem to store certain formats (such as GIF and JPEG) in a variant Photoshop doesn't understand. Open the file in that application and save it to another Photoshop-compatible format. Reopen the file in Photoshop and save it again in the format you want to use.

I tried the preceding and it didn't solve the problem. Any other suggestions?

If you're in Windows, you may have given the file the wrong extension when you saved it. Try using the Open As command and test some different formats until one of them works. Of course, you may have an irreparably damaged file.

What if I can't find the file I want to open?

Start out by assuming you didn't accidentally erase the file. You probably stored it under a forgotten filename or on a different drive than you remembered. Use your operating system's Find command to search all the local drives. Then use it on all your CDs and removable media.

How do I figure out which image goes with which filename in a long list of files?

If you're working on a Mac, you probably have thumbnails of your images as file icons. Regardless of the platform, just click a filename in the File Open dialog box. A thumbnail appears at the bottom of the dialog box (provided one was saved with the image).

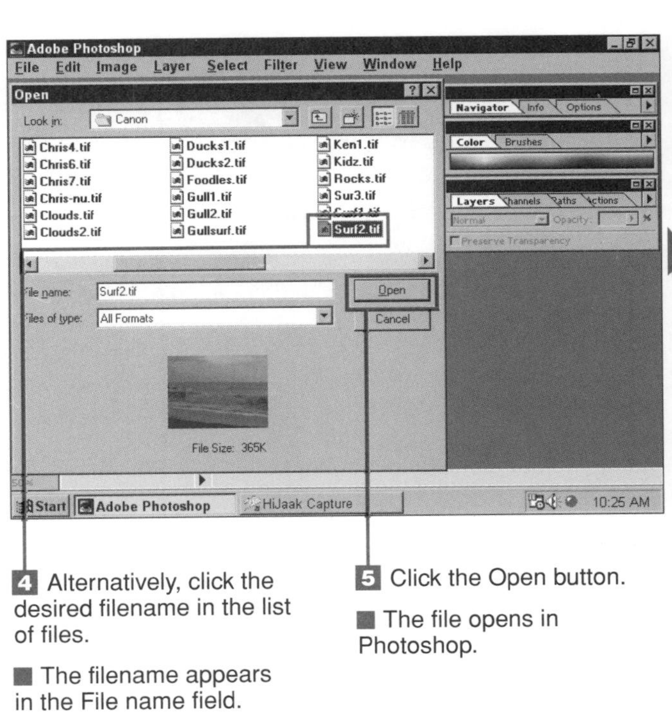

4 Alternatively, click the desired filename in the list of files.

■ The filename appears in the File name field.

5 Click the Open button.

■ The file opens in Photoshop.

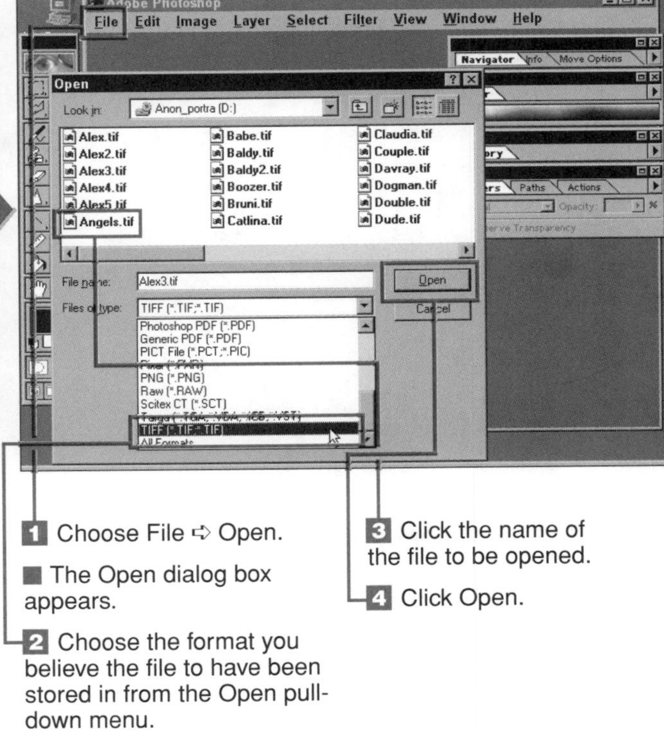

1 Choose File ⇨ Open.

■ The Open dialog box appears.

2 Choose the format you believe the file to have been stored in from the Open pull-down menu.

3 Click the name of the file to be opened.

4 Click Open.

SAVE THE CURRENT FILE

There are several ways to save the current, or open, file. You can perform a simple save by pressing ⌘/Ctrl+S or choosing File ➪ Save.

You should get in the habit of using this command to ensure you can retrieve all the successful work you've done to that point by choosing File ➪ Revert. You are also thus ensuring you can recover your work after an unexpected computer crash.

A slightly more complicated alternative to the Save command is File ➪ Save As. Save As lets you convert the file to a different file format, save it under a new name, or save it to a different disk location. This is the command to use when you want to try a risky experiment, because you can always go back to the original.

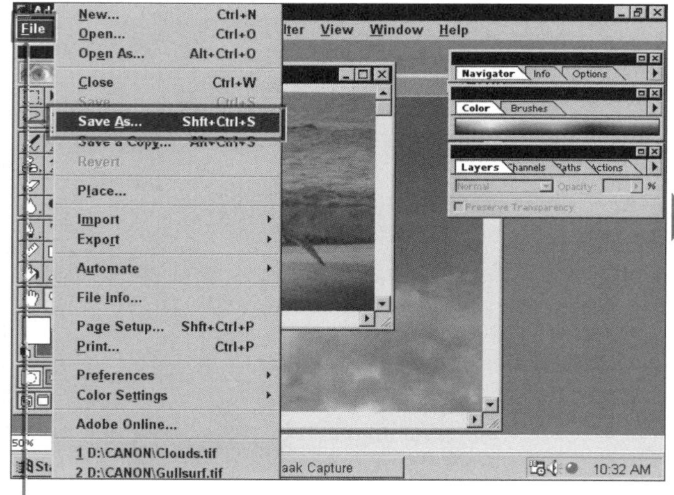

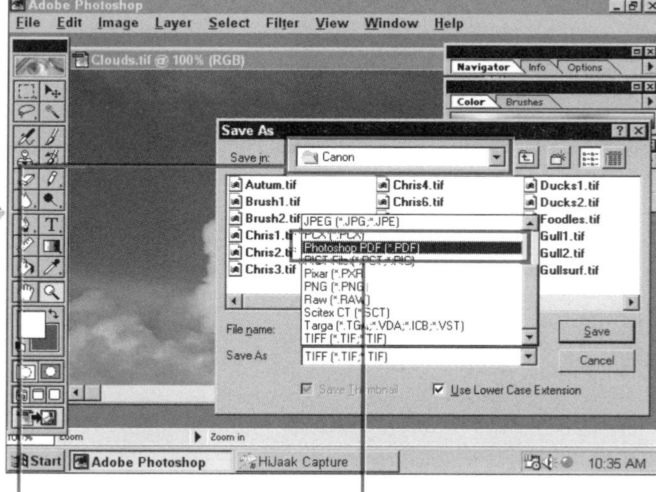

1 Choose File ➪ Save As.

■ The Save As dialog box appears.

2 Use the Save In pull-down menu to navigate to the folder where you want to save this file. Mac users can navigate to other drives or folders using the pull-down menu above the file list.

3 Choose the format you want to save to from the Save As pull-down menu.

4 Enter the filename you want to use in the File name field.

TIPS

I like your suggestion that files be saved in several formats. Is there a faster way to do this?

The best plan is to use an external file conversion application, such as Equilibrium's DeBabelizer. It can automatically convert a whole disk or directory (folder) of .PSD files.

Should I always save image previews?

Almost always. Preview thumbnails add to the file space used — an important consideration when saving files for the Web. It's also a waste of space if the file is going to be used to illustrate a publication or application and won't be reopened by an application such as Photoshop.

Is there more than one version of Photoshop file? Does it matter which version I use to save files?

There's Photoshop 2 and the current format, which has been in use since Version 3.0. However, in Windows, the Save As Photoshop 2 option has been dropped, as there is no advantage to saving to that format over saving to TIFF format. You can also specify a backward-compatible format that saves both a layered and a flattened version of the file. This format is useful if you need to edit individual layers at a later time, but uses significantly more file space.

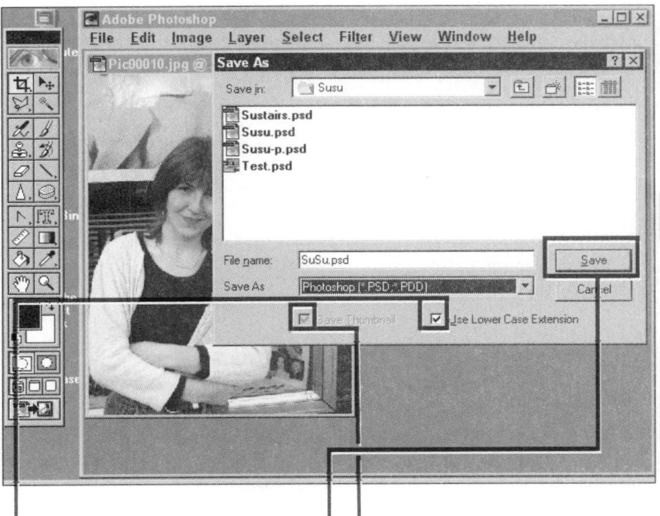

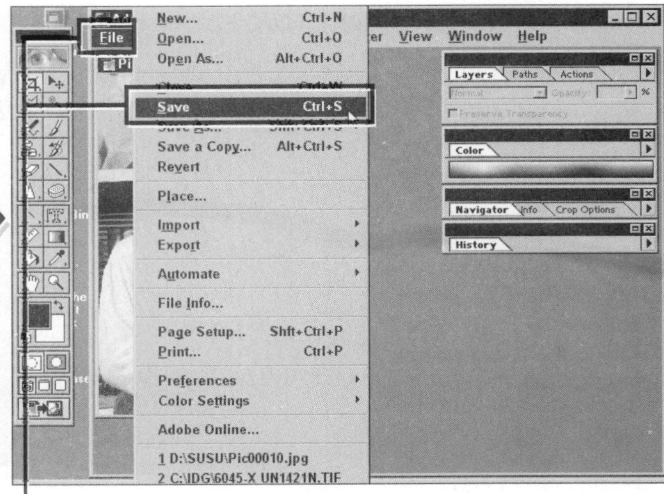

5 Click Use Lower Case Extension to make files cross-platform compatible with UNIX.

Note: Compatibility with UNIX may be especially important if UNIX is the OS used by your Web server or service provider.

6 Click Save Thumbnail if you are saving a file to be opened later.

7 Click Save.

8 Choose File ➪ Save or press ⌘/Ctrl+S.

■ The file is saved to the same drive and folder to which it was last saved.

SAVE A COPY OF THE CURRENT FILE

The File ➪ Save a Copy command does far more than its name suggests. You can use it to flatten all the layers, save to another file format, save the file under an entirely different name, exclude any data that doesn't belong to the image, and exclude all alpha channels. All these options will help you to minimize file size.

The File ➪ Save a Copy command is the most direct way to save a version of the current file for use in another program without affecting your original. This way, you can keep the layers and masks intact in the original in case you want to make changes later. At the same time, you create a file that's more portable or that works in another application (such as a desktop publishing program that requires a flattened file).

The keyboard shortcut for saving a copy is ⌘/Ctrl+Opt/Alt +S. You can also force the use of a lowercase extension — an especially good idea when sending files to a Web server or placing them on a cross-platform or hybrid CD-ROM.

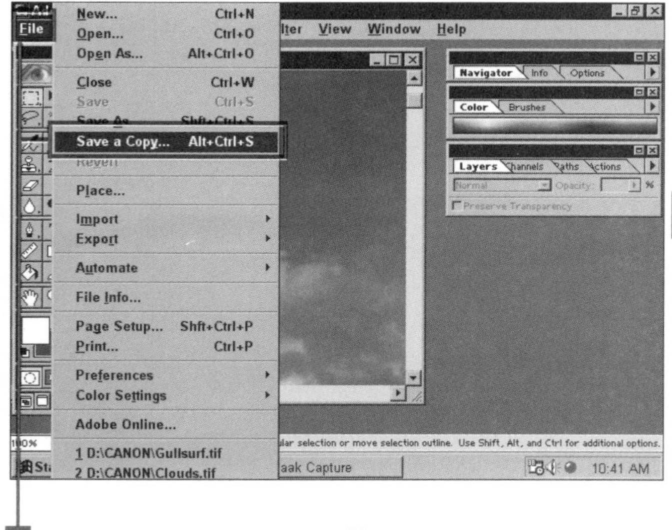

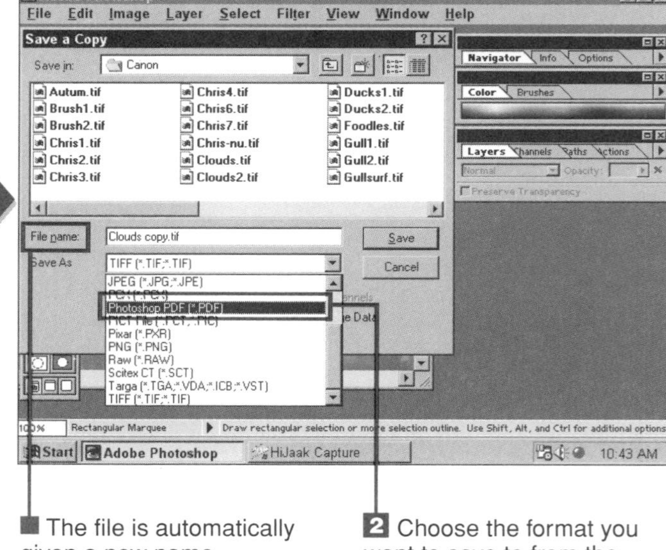

1 Choose File ➪ Save a Copy (or press Opt/Alt+⌘/Ctrl+S).

■ The Save a Copy dialog box appears.

■ The file is automatically given a new name.

2 Choose the format you want to save to from the Save As pull-down menu.

TIPS

Why use Save a Copy instead of Save As?

Saving a copy duplicates the current file and saves it as well. So whatever you've done in the original that's valuable is backed up and protected. Saving a Copy also lets you convert the file to another format, customize the minimization of file size, and rename the file — all within a single operation. However, it's important to remember that the "copy" file is now not open in Photoshop — it's only saved to your drive.

The Flatten Image check box is almost always grayed and checked. Why?

No other format supports layers, so the image is automatically flattened when you save to another format. Flattening the image is an elective only when saving to Photoshop format.

Why would I decide not to include alpha channels?

Alpha channels are masks. *Masks* are grayscale images that are the same size as the original image. They don't use as much file space as a color image, but they still use a lot. If you have multiple masks (not unusual), the masks could use considerable file space. So if you don't need the masks, unload them by checking the Exclude Alpha Channels check box.

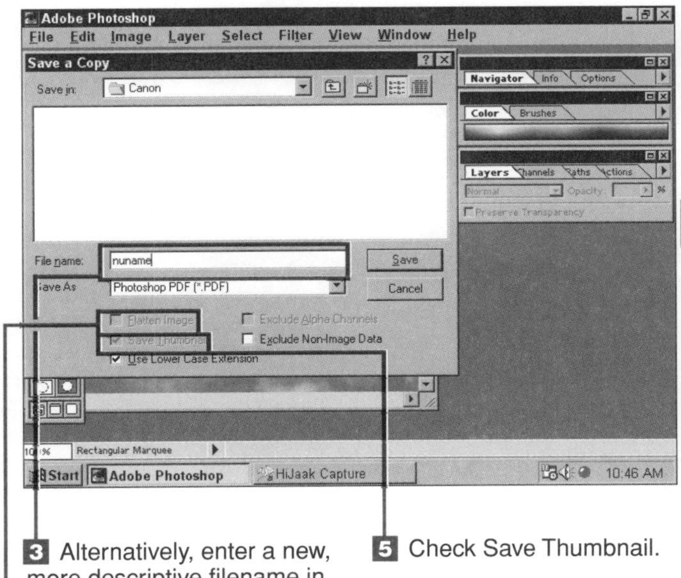

3 Alternatively, enter a new, more descriptive filename in the File name field.

4 Check Flatten Image.

Note: A check mark means the file will be flattened.

5 Check Save Thumbnail.

Note: Save Thumbnail will be grayed if you have chosen "Always Save Thumbnail" in Photoshop Preferences.

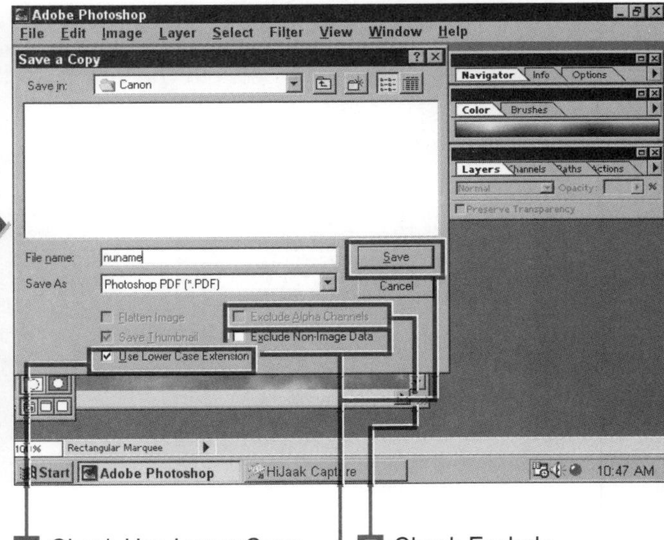

6 Check Use Lower Case Extension (Windows only).

Note: Checking Use Lower Case Extension ensures universal portability between platforms. You can set this on the Mac under File ➪ Preferences ➪ Saving Files.

7 Check Exclude Alpha Channels.

8 Check Exclude Non-Image Data.

9 Click Save.

GET INFORMATION ABOUT THE CURRENT FILE

Photoshop 5 stores and enables you to retrieve six categories of information about the current file: captions, keywords, categories, credits, origins, and copyrights and URLs. As you gain experience with Photoshop, you will discover more and more uses for this information.

Each category of information has its own fill-in form dialog box. These dialog boxes let you enter information according to standards set up by the Newspaper Association of America (NAA) and the International Press Telecommunications Council (IPTC) to help identify remotely transmitted news images.

You can save file information when you save any file in Photoshop, TIFF, and JPEG formats. If you're on the Macintosh, you can save file information in any format.

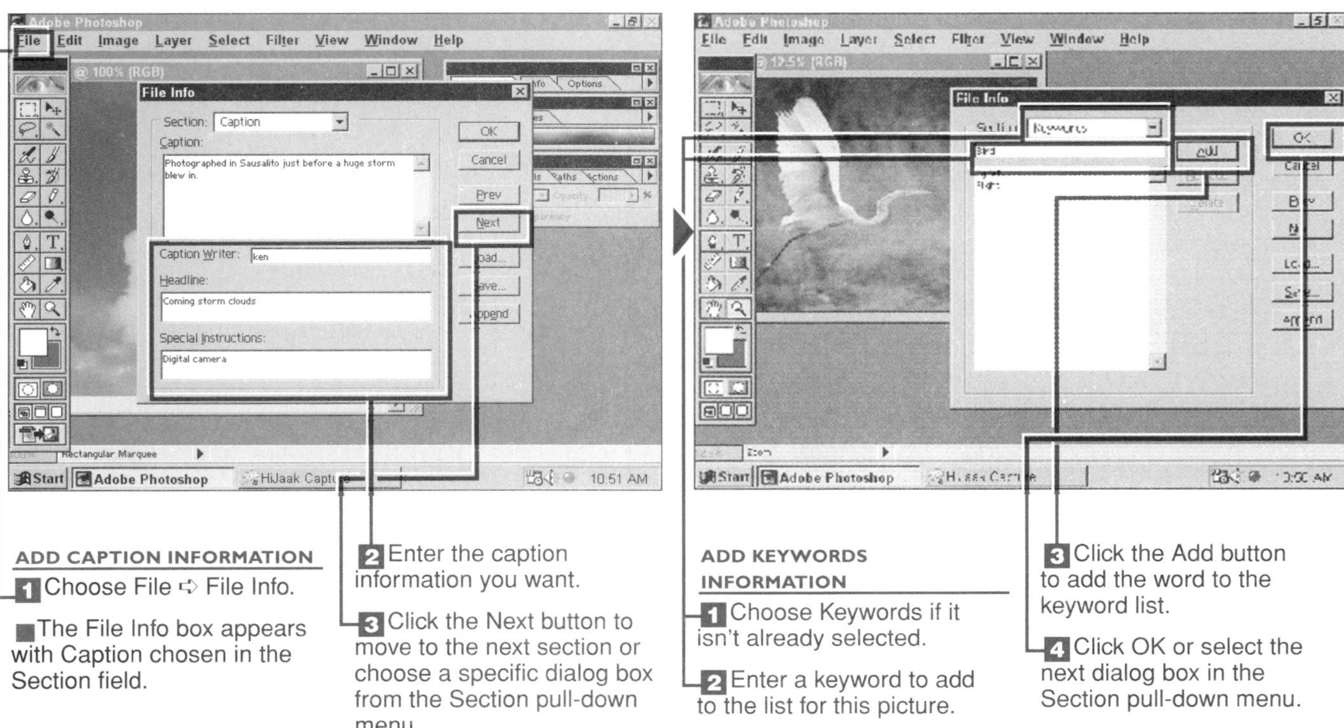

ADD CAPTION INFORMATION

1 Choose File ⇨ File Info.

■ The File Info box appears with Caption chosen in the Section field.

2 Enter the caption information you want.

3 Click the Next button to move to the next section or choose a specific dialog box from the Section pull-down menu.

ADD KEYWORDS INFORMATION

1 Choose Keywords if it isn't already selected.

2 Enter a keyword to add to the list for this picture.

3 Click the Add button to add the word to the keyword list.

4 Click OK or select the next dialog box in the Section pull-down menu.

Are there secrets to entering data in such a way that it's likely to be understood later — or by other parties?

If you want to order a group of files by their importance, sequence, or viewing priority, use the Urgency pull-down menu in the File Info Categories dialog box.

An awful lot of the information for a particular file is the same as for several other files. Can I save the information in the current file for use in another file?

Yes. Just click the Load and Save buttons that reside on the right side of all the File Info dialog boxes. If you load a "boilerplate" file, you can give it a new name when you click the Save button. To modify the record that stays with your image, just edit the contents of the newly loaded file in the normal way.

I don't belong to a news organization. Why else might I want to store this data?

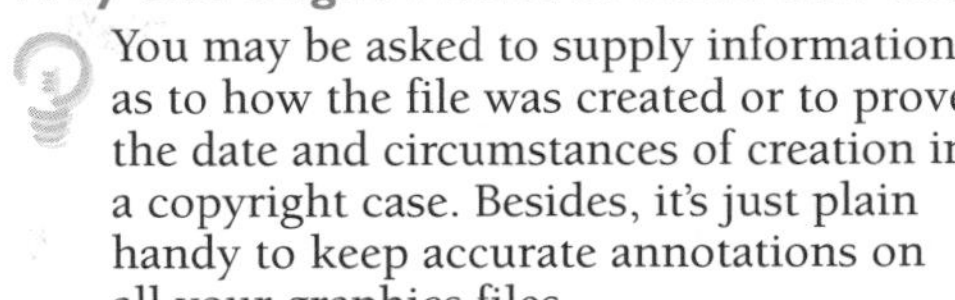

You may be asked to supply information as to how the file was created or to prove the date and circumstances of creation in a copyright case. Besides, it's just plain handy to keep accurate annotations on all your graphics files.

Are the buttons on the right side of the various dialog boxes the same for each dialog box?

Yes. Clicking OK stores the information with your file. The Prev and Next buttons move you up or down the list of dialog boxes. Load and Save let you save the information for this file to an external file. Append lets you store the file info at the end of an existing list.

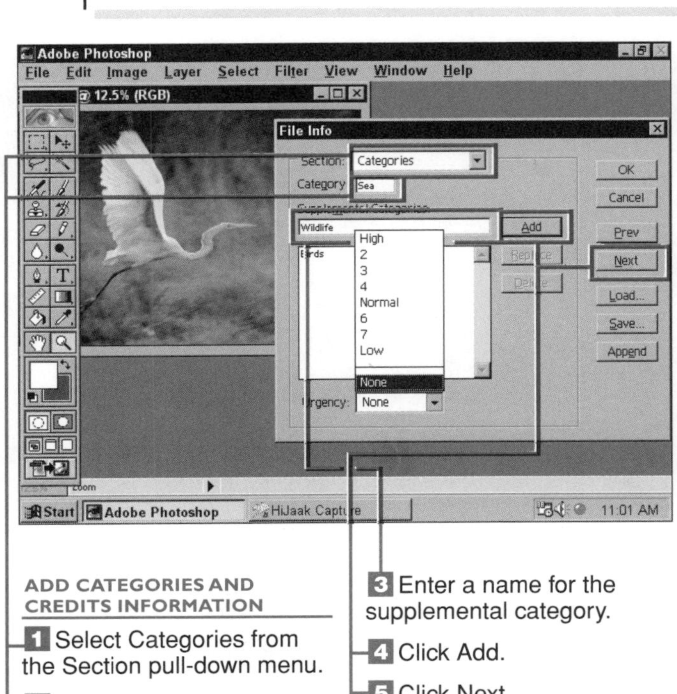

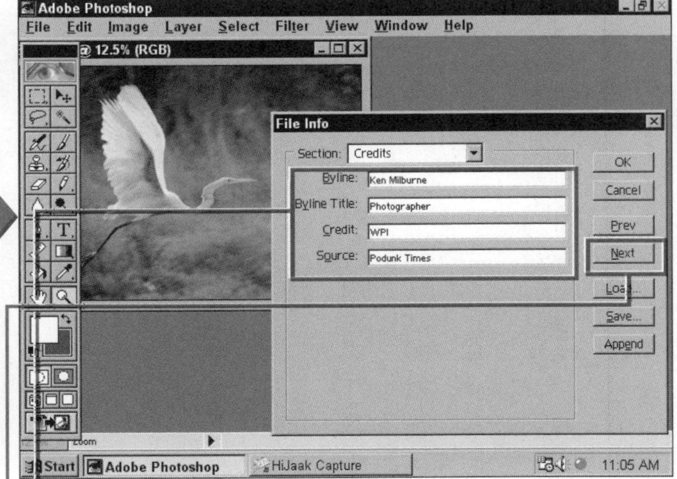

ADD CATEGORIES AND CREDITS INFORMATION

1 Select Categories from the Section pull-down menu.

2 Enter a three-character category name.

3 Enter a name for the supplemental category.

4 Click Add.

5 Click Next.

6 Enter the information you wish to include.

7 Click Next.

■ The File Info Origin dialog box appears.

Note: You are free to enter any information that will fit in most fields. However, if you want to subscribe to the NAA/NTPC standards for transmitting news photos, follow the guidelines of those organizations at www.iptc.org/iptc/catguide.html.

CREATE CONTACT PROOF SHEETS AUTOMATICALLY

Managing images can quickly become a problem for most Photoshop users because they tend to create a lot of images. Then they complicate matters by creating numerous variations of those images. Before long, you may find yourself opening several versions of the same file just to figure out which file is the file you want.

Mac users get thumbnail previews of images and Windows 98 offers a preview mode, but neither of these is an ideal solution. The Mac thumbnails are too small to see subtle differences and the Windows previews take forever to generate. The solution is to create visual proof sheets of all your images.

Photoshop 5 included a command that would automatically make a contact sheet for you, but you had to type in all the filenames by hand. Photoshop 5.5 types them in automatically for you.

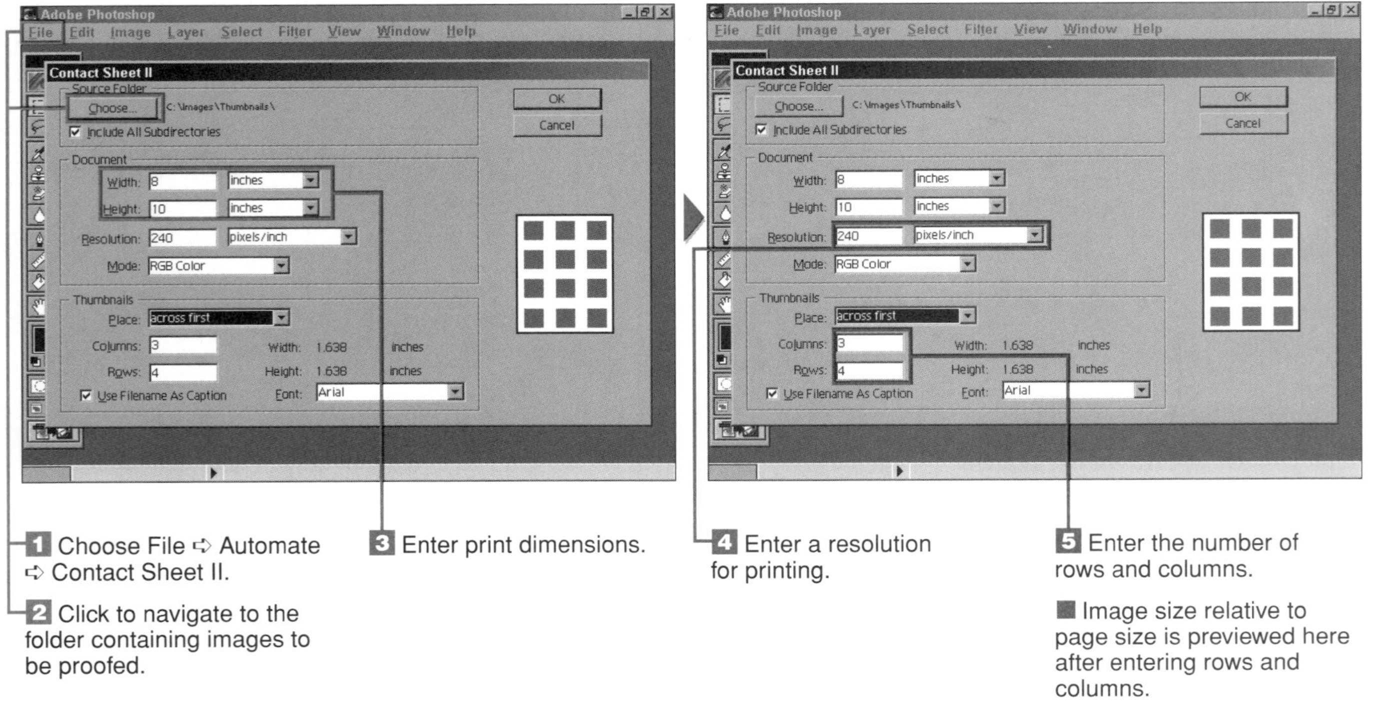

1 Choose File ⇨ Automate ⇨ Contact Sheet II.

2 Click to navigate to the folder containing images to be proofed.

3 Enter print dimensions.

4 Enter a resolution for printing.

5 Enter the number of rows and columns.

■ Image size relative to page size is previewed here after entering rows and columns.

TIPS

What resolution should I use for printing the contact sheet?

Typically, about one-third of the resolution of your color printer. This is because the resolution of your printer is the number of dots made by all three color printheads. (Black doesn't count because it is added to the image wherever needed to add contrast.)

What color mode should I use?

Read your printer manual. Most modern inkjet printers print in CMYK colors, but print from an RGB image. Therefore, most of the time you should use RGB.

How many rows and columns should I use?

You can preview to see what works best for you. I find 3 columns and 3 rows works best for easy viewing.

What if I want to use a label other than the filename?

Not a good idea. The thumbnail won't tell you what file it relates to. You can use long, descriptive names if you don't have to save these images to the Web or to a CD-ROM.

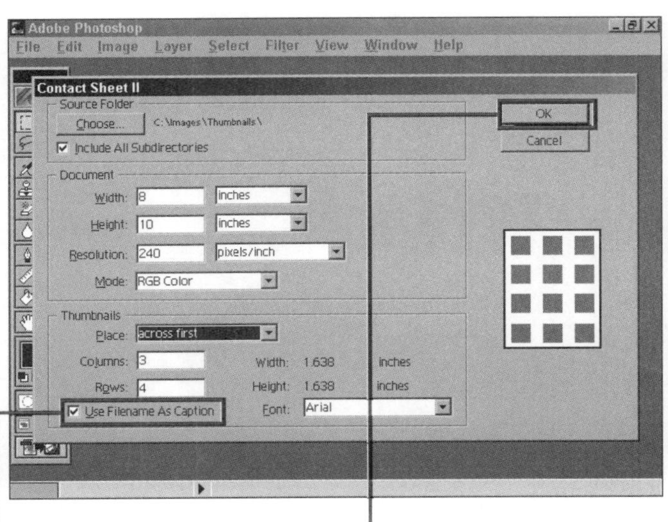

6 Check if you want to label thumbnails with the existing filename.

7 Click OK when you re ready to execute.

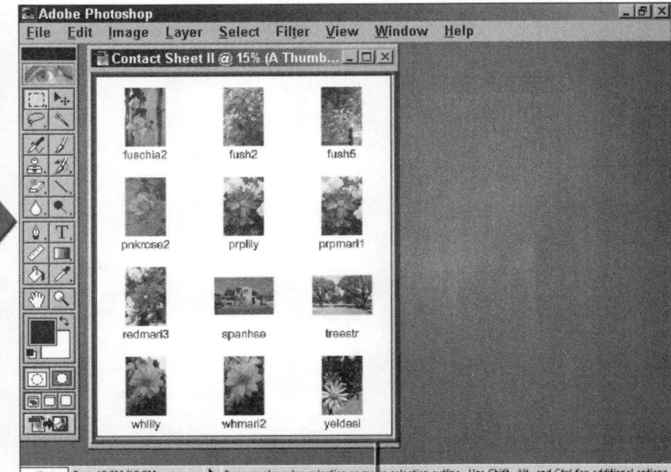

■ The contact sheet will be made automatically.

■ Here we see the finished contact sheet. Had there been more than 12 images in the folder, Photoshop would have made as many pages as necessary to fill the page.

PLACE A CONDITIONAL MODE CHANGE INTO AN ACTION

There will be times when you want to create an Action that requires your image(s) be in a particular color mode in order to work. If that is the case, there is an Automate command in Photoshop 5.5 that will help you out. It is called Conditional Mode Change.

Conditional Mode Change changes the color mode of the Action's target images on two conditions: they are already in a particular mode and the images' current mode is different than the target mode. If the conditions aren't met, the file is simply left unmodified.

This exercise assumes that you already know how to use the Actions palette.

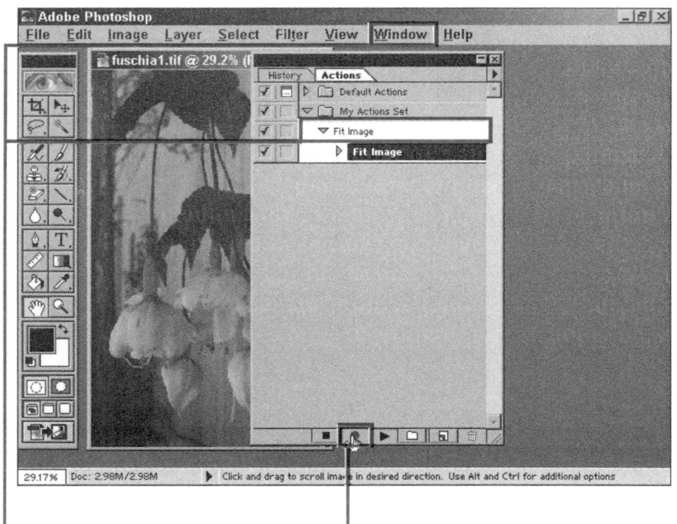

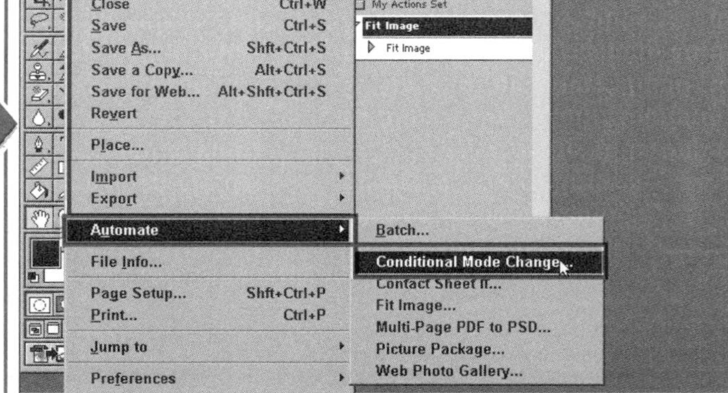

1 Choose Window ➪ Show Actions.

2 Select the command preceding the point where you want to add the conditional mode change

3 Click the Begin Recording button.

4 Choose File ➪ Automate ➪ Conditional Mode Change.

TIPS

What happens to the original file when I use a Conditional Mode Change?

This command will permanently change the file it affects. If you don't want to change the mode of the original, be sure to organize your files so that you're working on a copy.

What happens if you click the None button?

You won't make any conversions. The purpose of having the None button is to clear all previous entries so that you can start fresh.

Why can't I select more than one Target Mode?

Because there's no need. You are only changing modes here so that you can operate a command that wouldn't operate in any other mode.

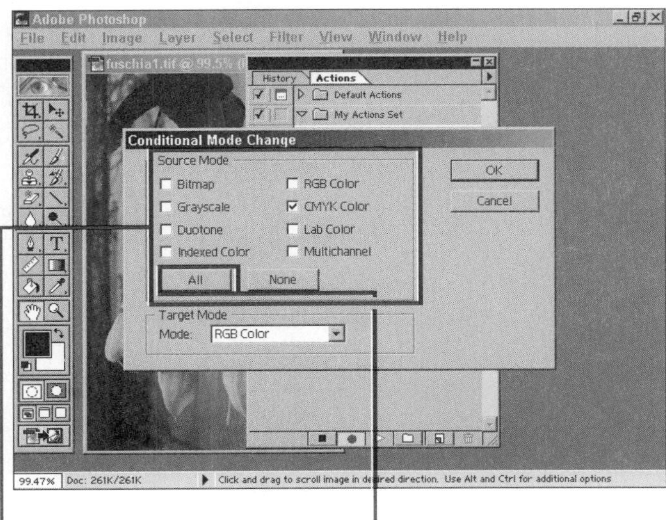

■ The Conditional Mode Change dialog box appears.

5 Check any modes that you may want to convert from.

6 If you want to select all modes, click All.

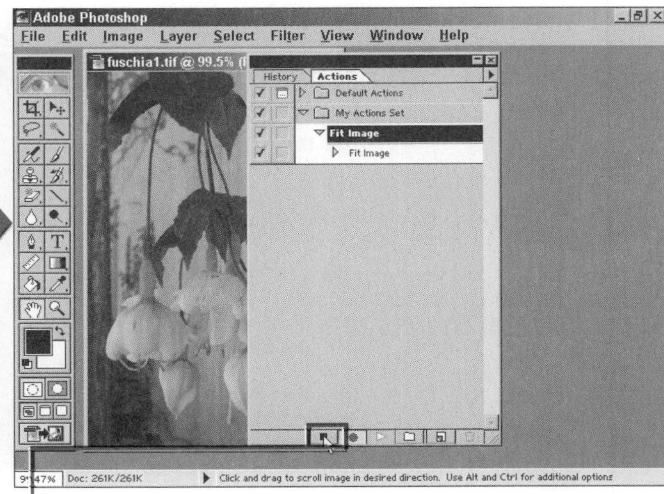

7 Unless you want to add other commands to the currently active Action, click the Stop recording button.

MAKE A PICTURE PACKAGE OR JOB PRINT

Picture packages and *job prints* are interchangeable trade terms for making multiple prints of the same subject on the same sheet of paper.

Wedding and events photographers have long used job sheets as a way to offer a package deal on multiple prints, knowing that the process also cuts costs by cutting printing time and eases the task of sorting an order by keeping like items together.

Photoshop 5.5's Picture Package command enables you to place as many as three different sizes of prints on the same page.

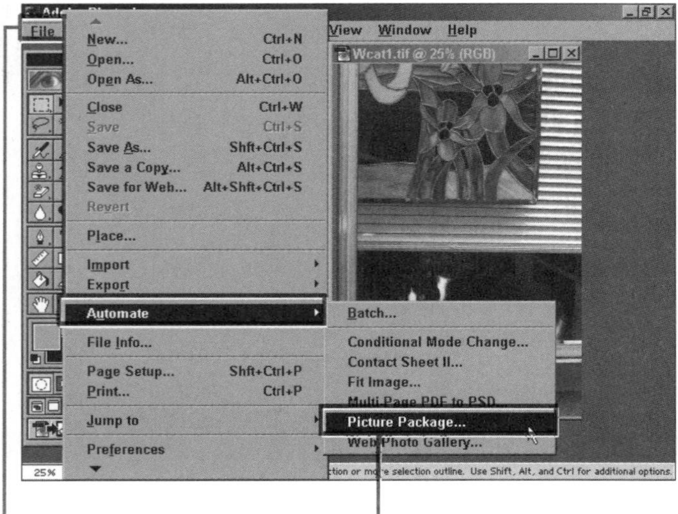

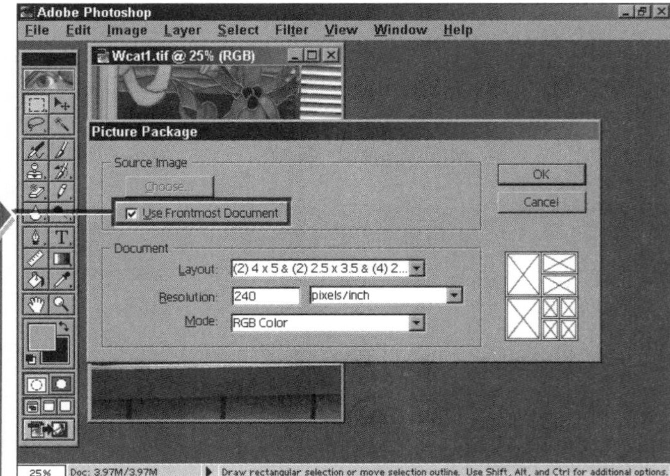

1 Open the image you want to print as a Picture Package.

2 Choose File ➪ Automate ➪ Picture Package.

■ The Picture Package dialog box appears.

3 Check Use Foremost Document.

Note: If you haven't opened the file you want to print, you can click the Choose button to browse for it. You won't be able to make image adjustments before printing, however.

What should the desired printing resolution be?

Generally, you want the printing resolution to be one-third the resolution that you set your printer for. That resolution equals the sum of the number of dots that will be printed in each of the three primary colors.

Can I use anything but the sizes shown on the menu?

Only if you put together your job print manually, using Photoshop's layers.

Why did you choose RGB color mode for your CMYK printer?

That's the way most inkjet color printers work. Be sure to double-check with your printer manual, however.

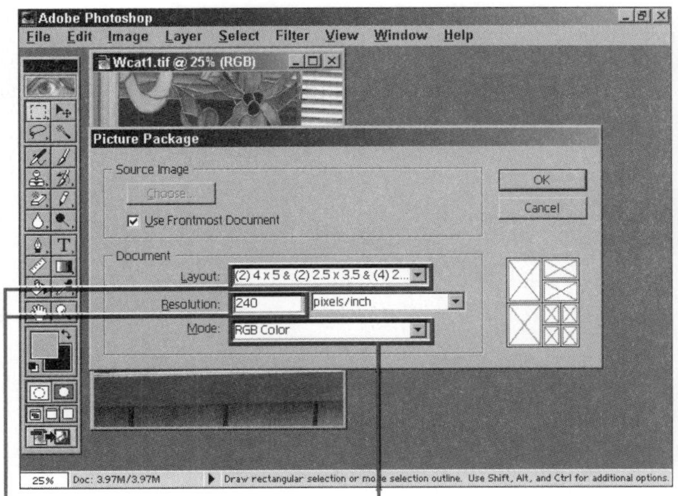

4 Choose the layout you d like to use.

5 Enter the desired printing resolution.

6 Choose the color mode for your printer.

■ You get to watch as Photoshop opens each image and drags it onto a layer in the Picture Package window, then resizes and positions it.

MAKE A SCRAPBOOK PAGE

Making job sheets is a terrific way to automatically print multiple images on a page . . . as long as the image is the same and as long as the duplicates are the size you want them to be.

However, there are also times when it may be handy to be able to print multiple different images on a single sheet of paper. This is handy for making up scrapbook pages or for doing a very rough layout for a catalog or magazine page, for example.

The procedure involves creating a new file, then opening all the files you want to put on the page at once, rotating and sizing them, and then dragging each image onto the new page. It's really an easy process, so don't be intimidated by the apparent number of steps.

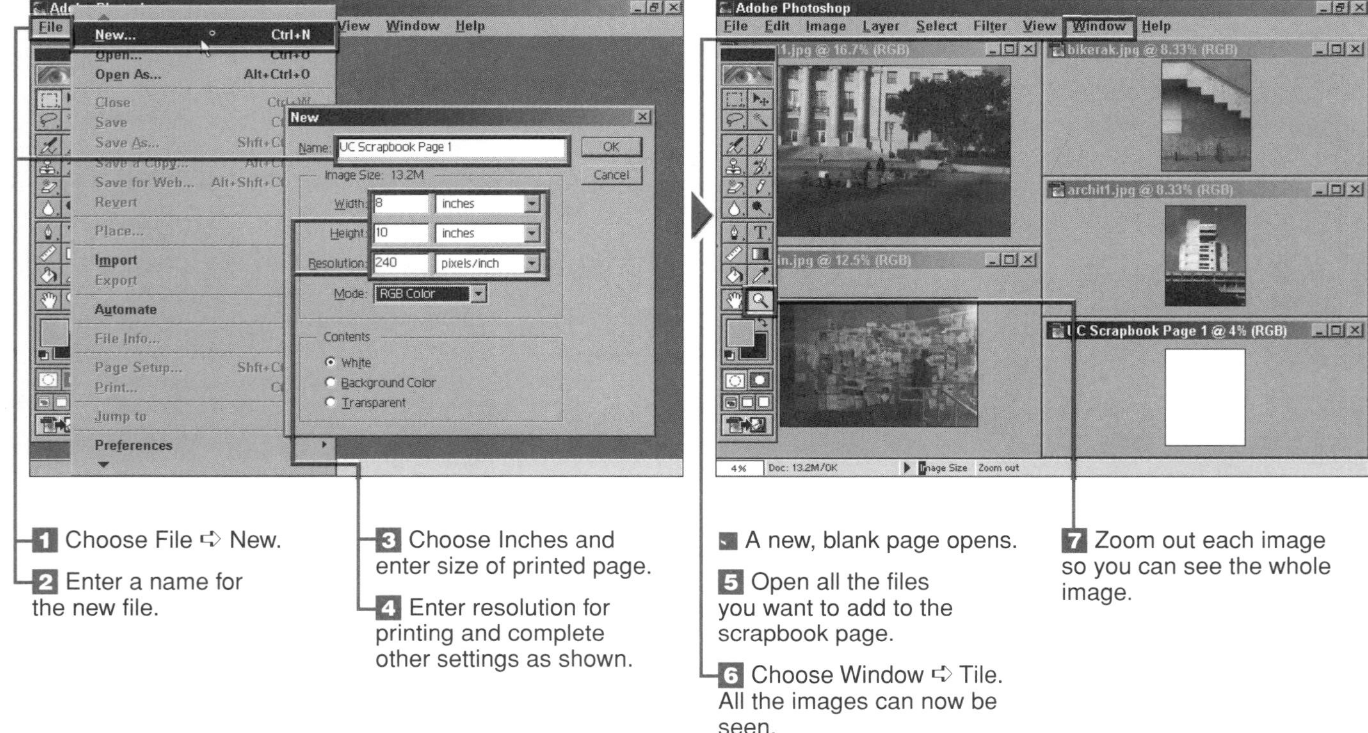

1 Choose File ➪ New.

2 Enter a name for the new file.

3 Choose Inches and enter size of printed page.

4 Enter resolution for printing and complete other settings as shown.

■ A new, blank page opens.

5 Open all the files you want to add to the scrapbook page.

6 Choose Window ➪ Tile. All the images can now be seen.

7 Zoom out each image so you can see the whole image.

TIPS

Do you really print on 8×10-inch paper?

You need to leave at least a half-inch margin. Also, if you put the contents into and 8×10-inch area, they will fit inside a standard-size picture frame. Of course, if your printer prints larger sizes of paper, you can make the whole page larger.

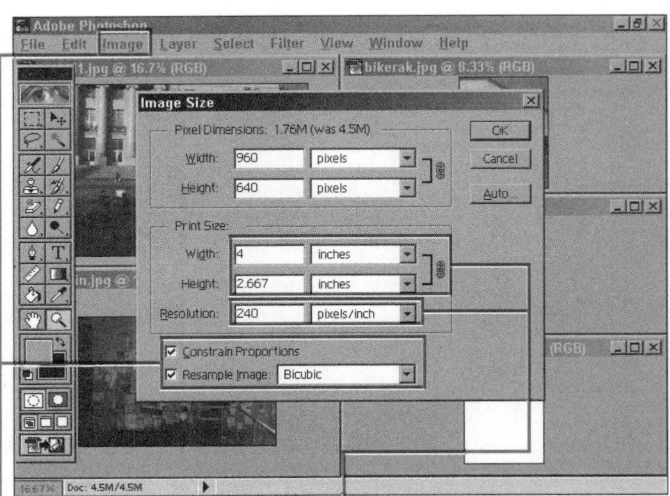

■ Repeat these steps for each of the picture images:

8 Choose Image ⇨ Image Size.

9 Make sure these are checked.

10 Enter the same resolution as you entered for individual images.

11 Enter scrapbook width and height and click OK.

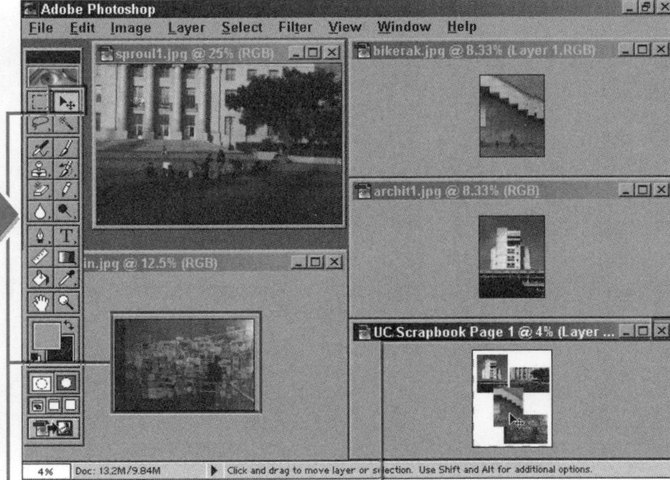

12 Choose the Move tool.

13 Drag each image onto the scrapbook page and position it.

14 Close all the image files without saving (to avoid overwriting the original with a smaller image).

IMPORT IMAGES FROM A TWAIN DEVICE

TWAIN (short for *Technology Without An Interesting Name*) is a protocol used on PCs and (more recently) Macs to communicate with all types of image acquisitions devices, including digital cameras, video cameras, scanners, and slide scanners.

The advantage of TWAIN is that the manufacturer of the device doesn't need to write a driver to each specific type of software or application. If the software (such as Photoshop) understands TWAIN, the device will automatically work with that software.

To use a TWAIN device, follow the instructions in that device's manual for installing the TWAIN drivers in your operating system. Then, when you select a TWAIN device (shown in the steps that follow), all the devices that have been installed on your system will show up in your Windows directory. Once you've selected the device, you then have to import your images from the TWAIN device. The software for whichever device you've preselected will appear on your desktop to prompt you through this process.

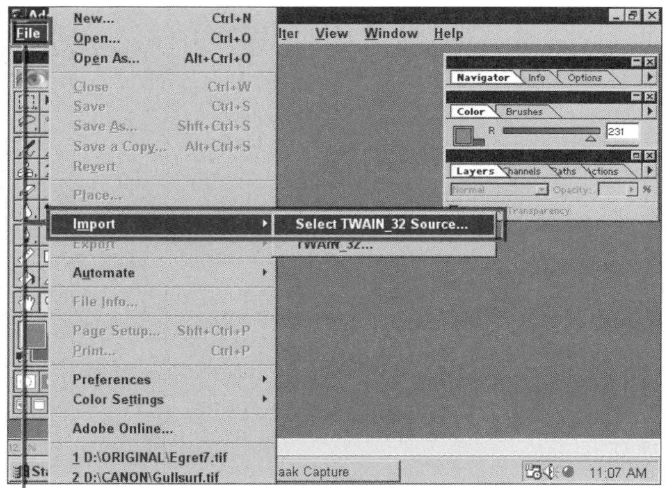

1 Choose File ⇨ Import ⇨ Select TWAIN 32 Source (or Select TWAIN Source if you have an older 16-bit operating system or device).

■ The Select Source dialog box appears.

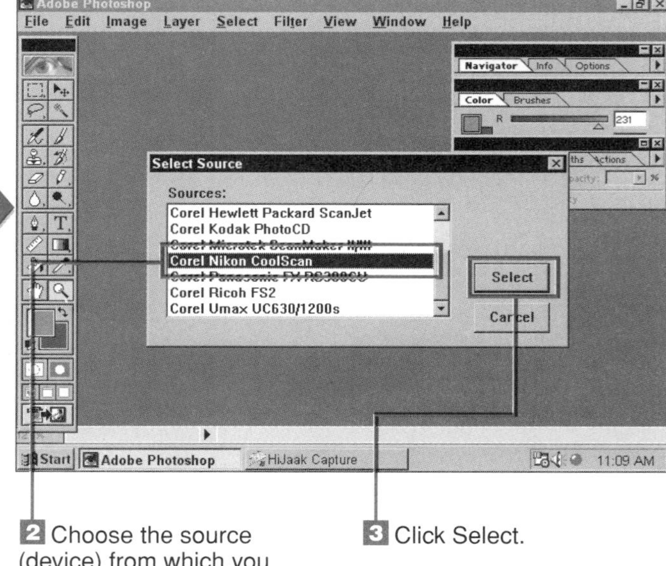

2 Choose the source (device) from which you want to import images.

3 Click Select.

TIPS

My TWAIN device has a much different-looking interface than that shown here. Where do I find out what to do next?

All TWAIN software interfaces are unique. Most are fairly obvious and work much like those for the three types of devices shown on these pages. If you have more specific questions, refer to the user manual that came with your device.

What if my device doesn't have a TWAIN driver or a Photoshop plug-in?

You will have to run stand-alone software outside of Photoshop. If you have allocated most of your system's memory to Photoshop operation, you may have to first close Photoshop, and then open the device's software.

I haven't seen many TWAIN devices for the Mac. Why?

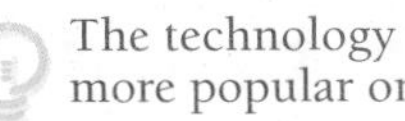

The technology is just now becoming more popular on the Mac platform.

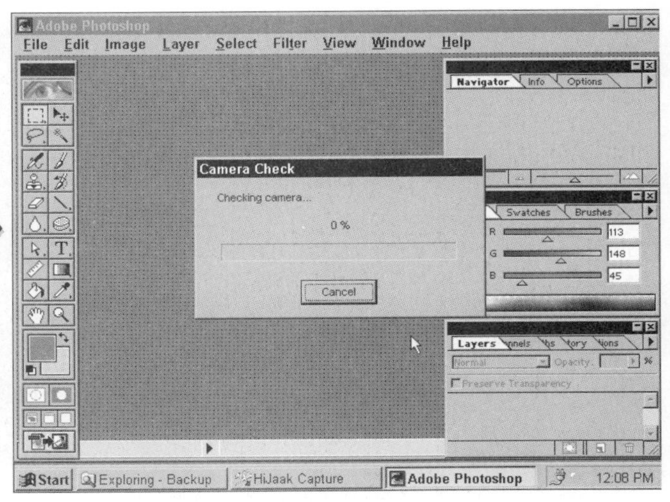

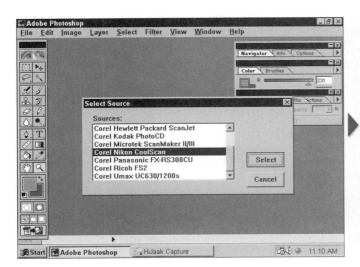

Note: What happens here depends on the software for the TWAIN device you have chosen.

■ After you click Select, a dialog box may appear to advise you that information is being transferred.

■ Or, you may jump straight to the software interface for the TWAIN device you have chosen.

Note: What happens here depends on the software for the TWAIN device you have chosen.

IMPORT IMAGES FROM A DIGITAL CAMERA

One of the easiest devices from which to import images directly into Photoshop is the digital camera. A huge variety of digital cameras are available, ranging in resolution from 300 × 220 pixels to better-than-film resolution. In price, they range between $250 and $50,000. You'll get the best compromise from a sub-$1,000 point-and-shoot camera with "megapixel" resolution and a zoom lens.

Almost all the popularly priced digital cameras come with a Photoshop import plug-in for both Macs and PCs. Others, such as the Olympus DL500 (shown in the example that follows), are TWAIN devices.

There is an alternative to using the camera's plug-in software for acquiring images. Many digital cameras store their images on *smart cards* or *flash memory cards*. These can be placed into a Personal Computer Memory Card Interface Adapter (PCMCIA) that can be read as an external disk by most of today's laptop computers. You can also buy PCMCIAs for desktop computers. Files are usually stored in JPEG format, so they can be opened with Photoshop's File ⇨ Open command.

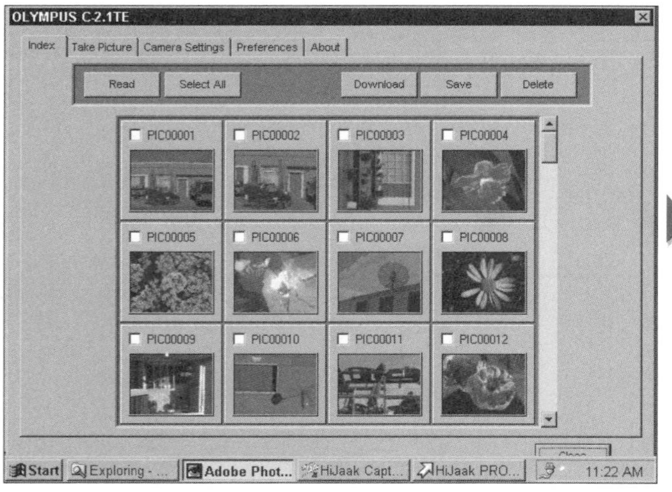

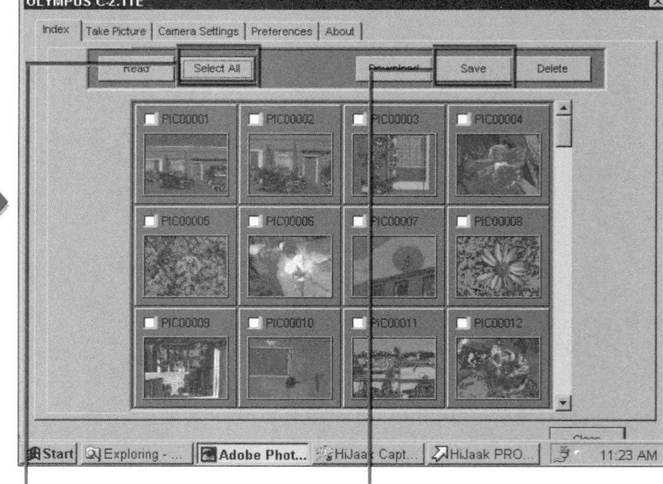

1 Choose File ⇨ Import ⇨ Select TWAIN 32 Source.

2 Choose the source (device) from which you want to import images.

3 Click Select.

■ The digital camera's software dialog box appears.

4 Click Select All.

■ The thumbnails turn gray to show they have been selected.

5 Click Save.

■ The File Save dialog box appears.

If the resolution of popularly priced digital cameras is limited to making a 5-×-7 photographic-quality print, are these cameras worth the investment?

Probably, but that really depends on your goals. For instance, I often use digital camera images as "instant sketches" for illustrations that are heavily processed by special effects filters and overpainted by hand. The original resolution is thus of little consequence. They are also practical for collecting details to be included later in larger compositions, for record-keeping purposes (such as insurance photos or employee databases). Finally, for Web publication purposes, the creative potential of these cameras is unlimited.

What effect does the number of images saved in a digital camera have on image definition?

Some manufacturers actually give you a choice of resolution. Obviously, you can save more 640 × 480 images than 1280 × 1024 images. Also, all digital cameras give you a choice of quality (compression) levels. More compression results in blotches and smears called *artifacts*, which are tolerable for record-keeping and sketchpad purposes. Artifacts become more pronounced when Image ⇨ Adjust commands are used.

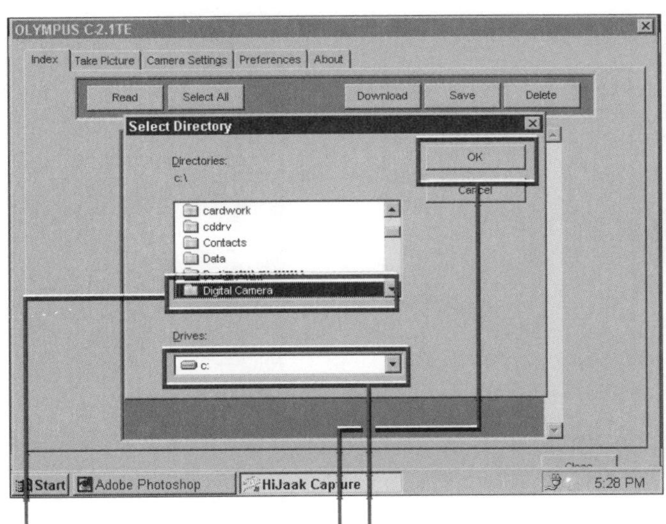

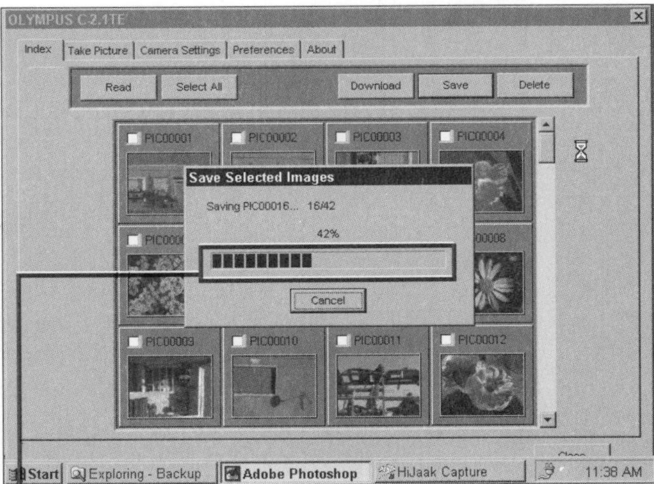

6 Navigate to the folder where you want to store these images.

Note: This folder should not contain other files that may have the same names as those in the camera. It is best to create a new folder for each download.

7 Use the Drives pull-down menu if you want to store the images on a different drive.

8 Click OK.

9 Wait until the Save Selected Images meter reaches 100 percent and the dialog box disappears.

10 Click Close.

IMPORT IMAGES FROM A FLATBED SCANNER

Although it is certainly possible to paint an original image in Photoshop, most of us use the program to enhance images acquired from another source.

The most versatile image acquisition device is a flatbed scanner. Actually, for purposes of this exercise, it could just as well be a handheld or sheetfed scanner. Flatbed scanners, however, tend to have higher optical resolution and greater color depth. Furthermore, you can scan small 3D objects and thick books on a flatbed scanner.

Before you perform the steps that follow, ensure the glass of your scanner is clean. Also check that the art you're going to scan is clean. Photoshop is good at retouching, but why make work for yourself? Finally, make sure the scanner is turned on and that the scanner's plug-in software has been installed properly.

Dozens of makes and models of scanners will work with Photoshop. The figures shown on these pages were created using a Umax PowerLook scanner. Not all scanner software is this versatile, but this should give you a general idea of what's involved.

Be sure to keep your scanner manual handy, too. Some scanners require that you scan using independent software, and then save the resulting file in a Photoshop-compatible format. If you have such a scanner, refer to its manual.

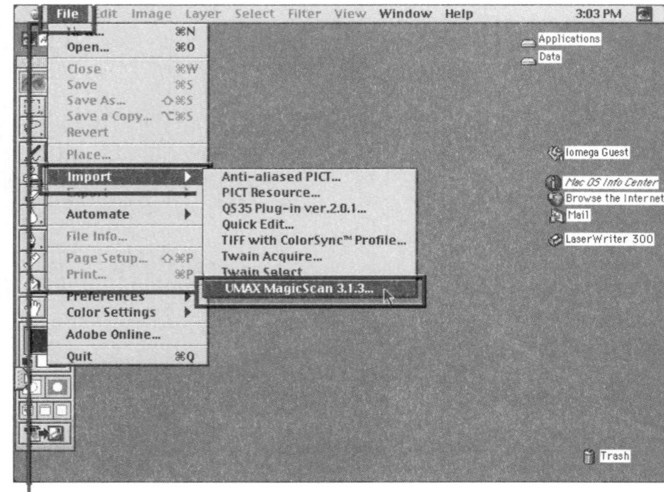

1 Choose File ➪ Import ➪ your scanner (in this case, Umax Magic Scan).

■ The scanner s software dialog box appears inside Photoshop.

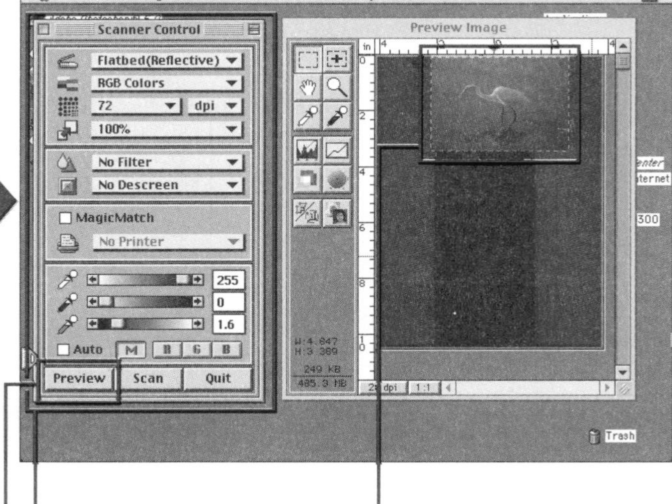

2 Use settings similar to those seen here.

3 Click Preview to see the picture in position on the scanner bed.

4 Drag the selection marquee to restrict the scan to the intended picture.

TIPS

What do the image size controls do in the scanner software?

They have nothing to do with image size control in Photoshop, except the resolution in pixels helps you to preview how large the Photoshop image will be on screen. It's a good idea to set the units for those measurements in pixels.

My scanner software doesn't offer as many adjustments as I see in this Umax screen. Do I need to buy another scanner?

Probably not. Photoshop is capable of "fixing" almost anything. Buy the best scanner you can afford, but don't avoid buying a scanner if you can't afford the best.

What should I look for in a scanner?

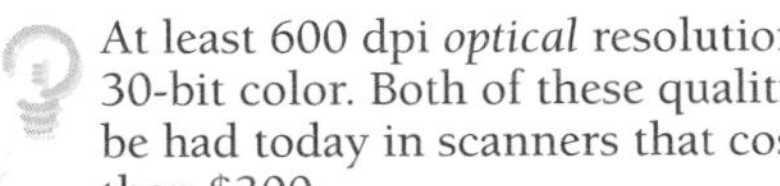

At least 600 dpi *optical* resolution and 30-bit color. Both of these qualities can be had today in scanners that cost less than $300.

What if I don't know how I'm going to end up using the scanned image? How should I make the preview look?

Scan an image that has the truest color balance and the widest possible range of tones. Then you'll have a library image that will give you the most flexibility when modifying the image later.

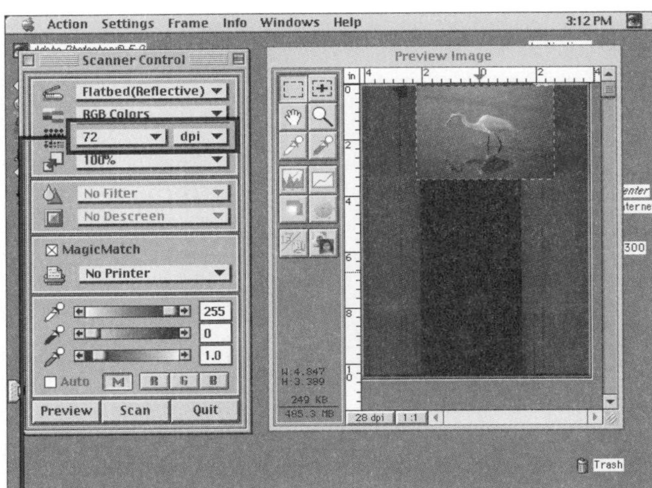

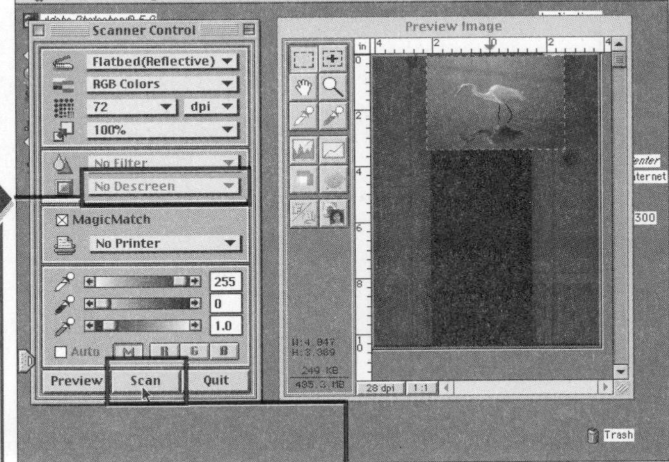

5 Choose or enter (depending on your software s interface) the resolution of the file you want to bring into Photoshop.

Note: Stick to your scanner's range of optical resolutions, per the scanner's manual. This way, you'll have an easier time enlarging the image in Photoshop.

Note: Use the scanner software to make your scanner preview look as much like you want your end product to look.

6 If scanning publications, look for and select Descreen or Despeckle.

■ Make any other adjustments that seem appropriate (options vary widely from scanner to scanner).

7 Click Scan.

IMPORT IMAGES FROM A SLIDE SCANNER

If you want the highest quality images from your original photos at the most affordable price, a slide scanner is the way to go. *Slide scanner* is a bit of a misnomer. The best desktop slide scanners capture a 35mm image at about 2,700 dpi at 30- or 36-bits-per-pixel, which greatly increases shadow range and depth. The resulting file is approximately 27MB, large enough to produce a professional-quality, full-page magazine ad.

The drawback to slide scanners is their cost and lack of versatility. You'll spend between $600 and $2,000, and you'll still need another scanner for reflective materials. The least expensive scanners will work with APS (24mm Advance Photo System) as well as 35mm film, but generally resolve only 1800 dpi. Transparency scanners are also available for larger format images, but count on paying closer to $5,000. This approaches the price of drum scanners, which provide the highest-quality image.

Make sure your film is clean and that it is inserted emulsion-side toward the imager. Some scanners require that you run an acquire filter before loading the film, so be sure to refer to your manual.

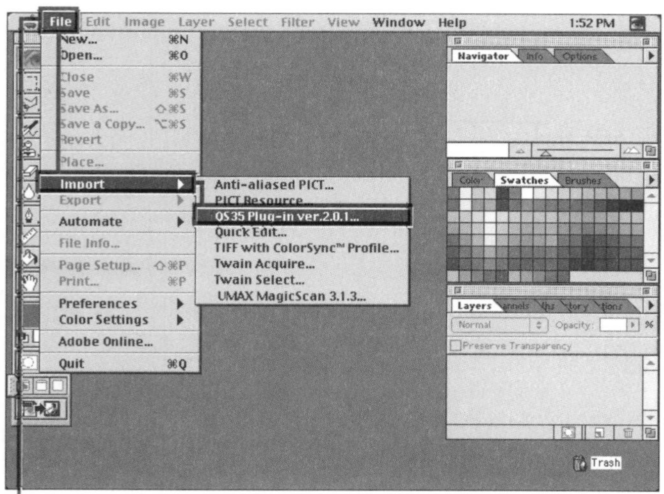

1 Choose File ⇨ Import ⇨ *your slide scanner* (in this case, Minolta QuickScan 35).

■ The slide scanner's software dialog box appears.

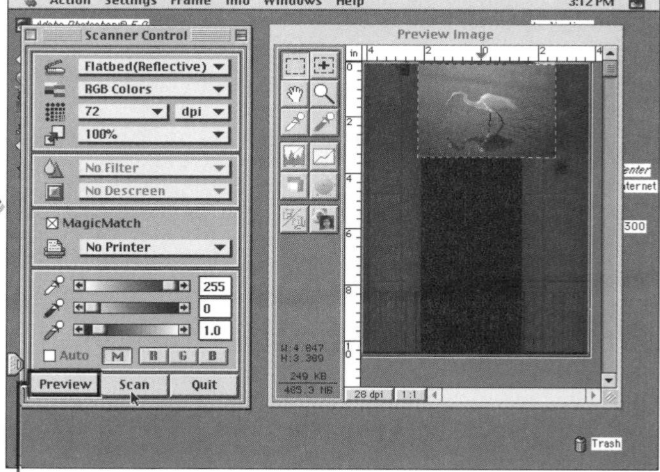

2 Insert the slide or the film holder into the slot in the scanner.

3 Click Preview or Prescan.

■ After about a minute, an image will appear in the preview box.

TIPS

Most of my photography is on color negative film. Do I have to make prints and scan them on a flatbed scanner?

No. Most popular slide scanners will scan negatives and convert them. There's no need to make a print at all.

Why not use a much less expensive transparency attachment on my flatbed scanner to scan slides?

Resolution isn't good enough to scan a 35mm frame intended for publication-quality work. If the format is 6 × 9 or larger, you will be more likely to get a large enough scan at high enough resolution. Try to use a scanner with 1200-dpi optical resolution.

Is a transparency adapter good for anything?

Yes, indeed. It's a great way to make contact sheets of 35mm negatives. You can also do a decent job of scanning Web images, because these usually have a maximum size of 640 × 480 pixels.

What do I do about film strips that are too long to fit in the film holder?

Film holders usually accommodate up to six frames. If you've already cut your film into longer strips, you'll have to cut them again. Ask your film lab to cut your film into six-frame strips.

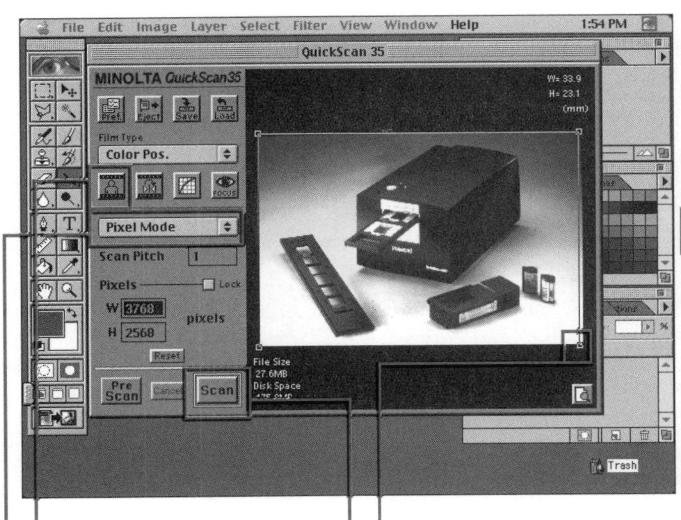

4 Click to rotate the image, if necessary.

5 Adjust color balance and contrast (slider area).

6 Drag the selection marquee to crop out any unneeded part of the image.

7 Click Scan.

■ The scanned image appears in a work window in Photoshop.

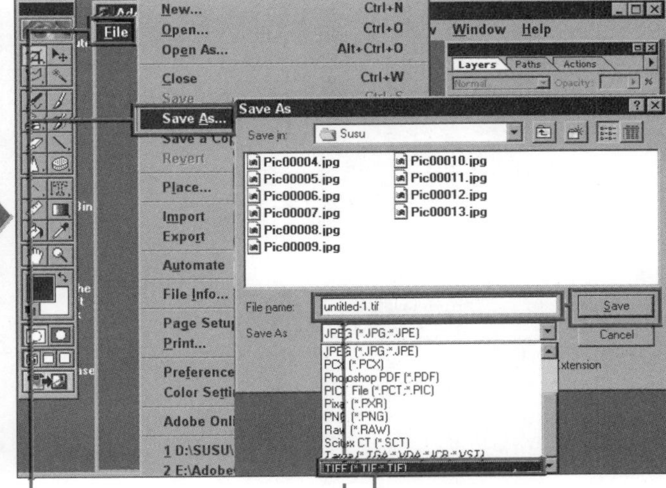

8 To save the file to a portable format, choose File ➪ Save As.

■ The Save As dialog box appears.

9 Choose TIFF (or another preferred format) from the Format pull-down menu.

10 Type the filename you want to use.

11 Click Save.

SECTION II

3 CHANGING THE SIZE OF AN IMAGE

Image Size Basics 60
Change the Image Size 62
Change the Canvas Size 64
Crop the Image 66
Crop the Image to a Specific Proportion 68
Crop the Image to a Specific Size 69
Crop the Image to a Fixed Size and Resolution 70
Crop the Image to a Specific Proportion or Dimension 71

4 ADJUSTING IMAGE QUALITY

Control Overall Image Quality 72
Correct Overall Color Balance 84
Use Color Correction Aids 86
Adjust Brightness and Contrast 87
Alter Color with Hue/Saturation 88
Lose All Color with Desaturate 90
Create a Tonal Effect with Invert 91
Swap One Color for Another 92
Mix Color Channels 94
Make an Adjustment with Variations 96
Create a Tonal Effect with Equalize 98
Switch Color Palettes 100
Correct Tonal Values with the Levels Command 102
Correct Tonal Values with the Curves Command 104

Correct Some Color Values with the Curves Command 106
Create Special Effects Color Changes with Curves 108

5 RETOUCHING IMAGES

Correcting Mistakes 110
Use the Eyedropper to Pick Up Color 116
Use Offset Cloning 117
Use Aligned Cloning 118
Automatic Spotting with the Dust & Scratches Filter 119
Automatic Spotting with the Gaussian Blur Filter 120
Correct Blending Defects 121
Hand-Spotting with the Brushes 122

IMAGE SIZE BASICS

This chapter shows you how to change the size of an image, either by changing the size of the whole image (*resizing*) or by *cropping*, which is a photographer's term for trimming an image to a smaller size than the original.

Before you consider changing the size of an image, you should understand that any Photoshop image consists of a fixed number of *pixels*, tiny square dots of image data, placed in a matrix made up of rows of pixels of a fixed number and columns of pixels of a fixed number. Each pixel is assigned a specific color.

Now, if you make the picture smaller, you have to remove pixels (remember, the size of the pixels themselves is fixed). Which pixels are thrown out is determined by a mathematical formula built into Photoshop, and the choices might not always be the ones you'd make. Nevertheless, you usually get less loss of image quality when you reduce an image than when you enlarge it.

If you make the image larger, Photoshop must duplicate some pixels. If you make it much larger, Photoshop has to duplicate *lots* of pixels. How Photoshop duplicates those pixels depends on the resampling method you choose from the Resample Image pull-down menu in the Image Size dialog box, as shown in the following figure. *Resampling* blends the colors of added pixels so that they make a smoother transition between sharply contrasting original pixels.

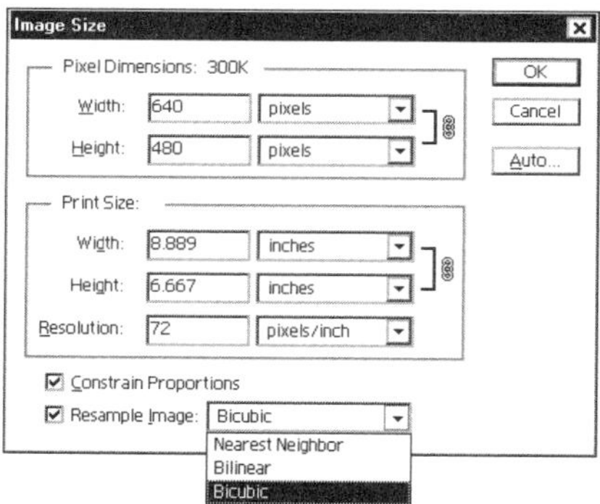

The three resampling methods are Nearest Neighbor, Bilinear, and Bicubic. Nearest Neighbor, as shown in this figure, is fastest, but most pixelated.

The next figure illustrates Bilinear resampling which is faster than Bicubic, but transitions between neighboring pixels are not as smooth. (These figures appear at 800 percent enlargement over the original image.)

CHANGE THE IMAGE SIZE

Photoshop includes two commands for changing the size of the current image: Image Size and Canvas Size. If you want to change the size or proportions of the current image, choose Image ⇨ Image Size. (To make changes to the size of the canvas, choose Image ⇨ Canvas Size, as discussed in the next exercise.)

This exercise shows you how to change the size of an image, but it can't guarantee that you'll like the result. Anytime you grow or shrink an image, Photoshop has to add or subtract pixels from the original. It's important to remember that Photoshop can't add detail; it has to guess according to various mathematical formulae which pixels to duplicate and whether to duplicate them exactly or to change their colors according to the colors of their surrounding pixels.

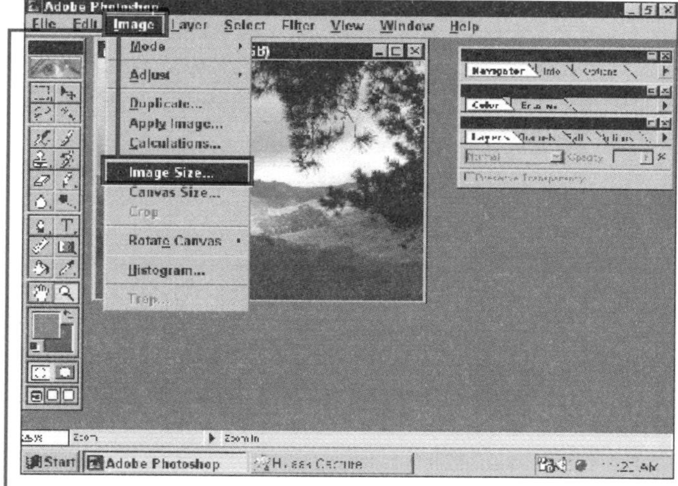

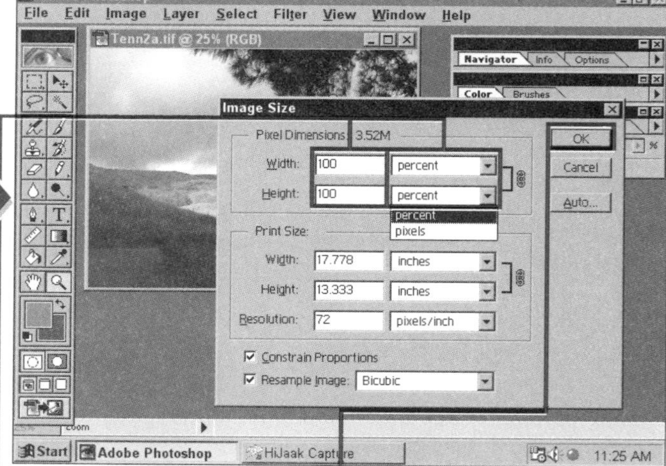

CHANGE IMAGE SIZE

1 Choose Image ⇨ Image Size.

■ The Image Size dialog box appears.

2 To change the size of the image by a percentage without changing the proportions, choose percent from the Height and Width pull-down menus.

3 Enter the percentage.

Note: If Constrain Proportions is checked, you need enter the percentage in only one field. The other is entered automatically.

4 Leave other settings at defaults (shown) and click OK.

TIPS

What does Resample accomplish?

If you turn Resample off (uncheck the box), Photoshop assigns more pixels to the representation of each original pixel by the amount specified. This results in jaggies.

How do I get rid of the out-of-focus effect that seems to occur when I change the size of an image significantly?

Use the Unsharp Mask filter or the Sharpen Edges filter. The most beneficial settings will depend on the colors and contrast of the image, so you will need to experiment. One technique is to use the default settings and then repeat the command by pressing ⌘/Ctrl+F. When sharpening has gone too far, press ⌘/Ctrl+Z to undo the last filtration.

How do I know what resolution is needed for a particular size output from a particular printer?

Divide the printer's output resolution by the number of colors used (three for RGB and LAB, four for CMYK). For instance, an Epson Stylus Color printer at 720 dpi is printing one dot of each color. So the resolution of the image doesn't need to be more than 240 dpi. A print intended for a large format printer typically needs to be only 100 dpi because those printers rarely print at more than 300 dpi. Large prints for exhibition are generally viewed at a greater distance, so the end result may look the same.

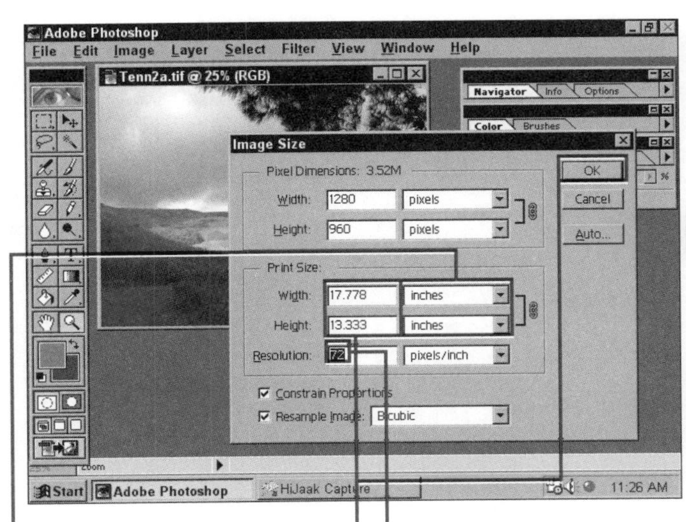

5 To resize the image by changing the Print Size dimensions, choose inches, percent, cm, points, picas, or columns from the Print Size pull-down menus.

6 Enter the resolution for the output.

7 Enter the dimensions for the final print.

8 Click OK.

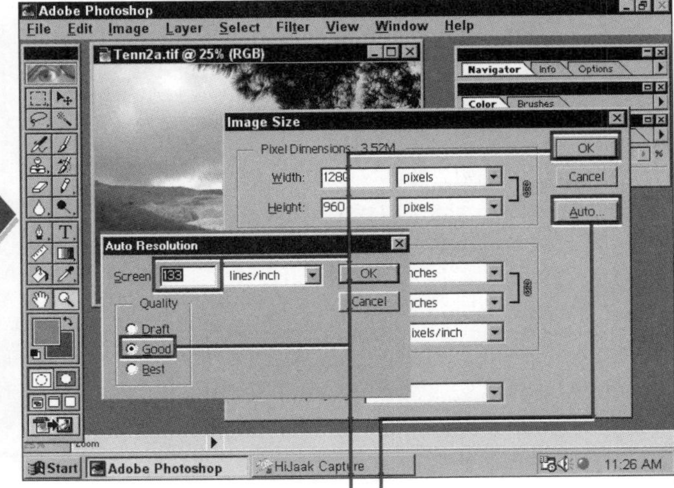

■ An easy way to specify size to match printed output in a publication is to click the Auto button.

9 Enter the dimensions for the printed image in the Print Size Width and Height fields.

10 Click the Auto Button.

11 Enter screen lines per inch/centimeter.

12 Click Quality radio button for Draft, Good, or Best.

13 Click OK.

CHANGE THE CANVAS SIZE

The Canvas Size command enables you to change the size of the workspace without changing the size of the picture. This way you can change the proportions of the image and leave room for a border, border effect, or drop shadow.

If you resize the canvas so that you can change the proportions of the image, you'll have some solid background color at the perimeter of the image. If the image background is a solid color, you can pick up color with the Eyedropper tool and fill the blank space with the Paint Bucket.

Pay attention to where you place the image on the canvas. The location of the gray square in the Canvas Size dialog box's Anchor box dictates where the outside borders will fall. If you are adding a symmetrical border (or border-effect or drop shadow), be sure you leave the image centered (the default position).

1 Choose Image ➪ Canvas Size.

■ The Canvas Size dialog box appears.

2 Enter desired canvas dimensions in the Width and Height boxes.

3 Select the desired units of measurement.

4 Click to place current image in desired location on canvas.

5 Click OK.

■ The canvas will assume the current background color.

TIPS

Why may I want a transparent background?

You may want to do this so you could put another background or a textured border around the image. The next exercise shows you how to make a transparent background.

What if I want to place the image on the canvas so that the borders are not equidistant on all sides?

Make the canvas large enough so that you can crop the image. Then use the Crop tool to define the borders on the top and sides

How can I make a drop shadow on the canvas border?

Select the image and press ⌘/Ctrl+ J to lift the image to a new layer. From the menu bar, choose Layer ➪ Effects ➪ Drop Shadow. Adjust the settings according to your preferences, and click OK.

Note: Canvas size has been increased as shown.

6 If the borders of the image contrast with the border color, choose the Magic Wand.

7 Click in the border.

8 Press ⌘/Ctrl+Shift+I to invert the selection.

9 Press ⌘/Ctrl+ J.

10 Choose Window ➪ Show Layers

11 Drag the background layer to the trash.

■ The border around the canvas is now transparent.

CROP THE IMAGE

Often, information in the edges of the image detracts from the main subject. You will also find that sometimes the image is the wrong height versus width proportion to fit your intended layout or print frame. The process of trimming the edges of the image to fit is called *cropping*.

The first lesson you learn when you study the art of photographic composition is to crop out any subject matter that detracts from the intended center of attention. So, though cropping may be simple, it is also important.

Photoshop gives you two means of cropping an image: the Crop tool and the Marquee tool. The methods for using both tools are shown in this exercise. The first three figures show the use of the Crop tool, and the fourth figure shows how to crop with the Rectangular Marquee selection tool. Both tools are found on the Marquee tools fly-out menu that appears by clicking and holding the Marquee tool in the toolbox.

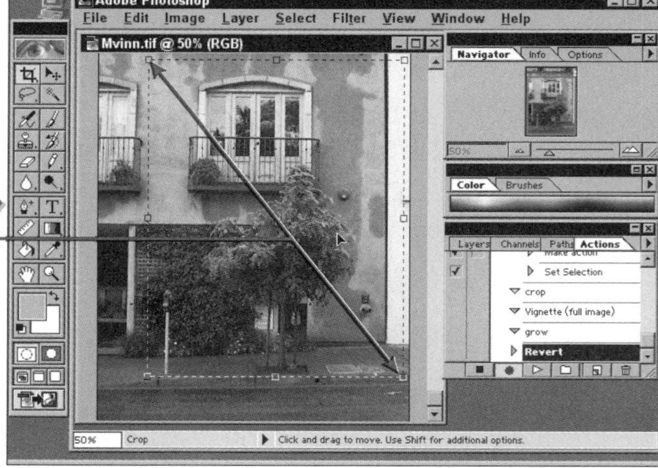

CROP WITH THE CROP TOOL

1 Click and hold the Marquee tool from the toolbox and choose the Crop tool from the fly-out menu.

■ The Crop tool appears in the upper-right corner of the toolbox.

2 Drag diagonally across the image to create a marquee approximating the area of the image to be cropped.

■ Sizing handles appear around the marquee with a target to indicate the image center.

Note: You needn't be precise in sizing the marquee. Use the sizing handles to get the exact trim.

Which is the more accurate of the two cropping methods?

There is no technical difference, but the Crop tool enables you to size and rotate after you've dragged the marquee. It is definitely the more versatile of the two tools.

Is there a way to crop the image without reducing the Canvas size?

You have to cheat. Indicate the area you want to crop to with the Marquee tool. Press ⌘/Ctrl+Shift+I to invert the selection. Choose Edit ➪ Fill ➪ Background Color. Because the color of the canvas is the background color, you will have accomplished your goal.

Is there a method for cropping the image without cropping the original?

Yes. It's almost the same process as the one just described. Indicate the area you want to crop to with the Marquee tool. Press ⌘/Ctrl+C to copy the image to the Clipboard. Press ⌘/Ctrl+N to create a new file. In the New File dialog, click OK (the file is already sized to fit the Clipboard image). When the New File window opens, press ⌘/Ctrl+V to paste the image. Now save the image under a new name.

3 To rotate the area to be cropped, place the cursor just outside any corner handle. When the cursor changes to a double-headed arrow, drag to indicate rotation.

4 To resize the trim border, drag any sizing handle. To resize proportionately, press Shift+drag.

5 To crop, double-click inside the marquee.

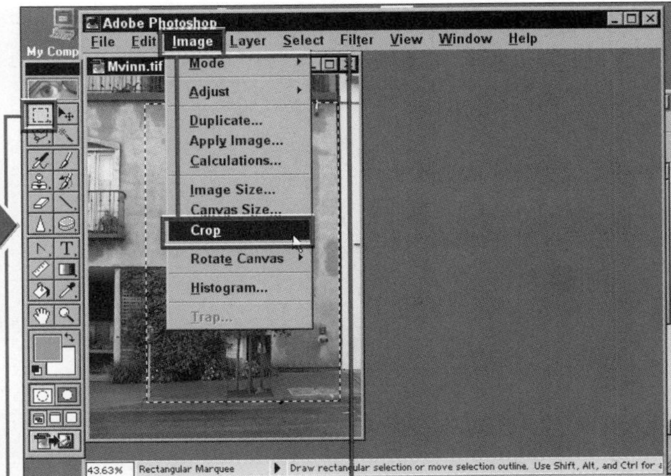

CROP WITH THE MARQUEE TOOL

1 Choose the Rectangular Marquee tool or press M until the Rectangular Marquee tool appears in the toolbox.

2 Drag to indicate the border you wish to crop to.

3 When the marquee is the right size, choose Image ➪ Crop.

CROP THE IMAGE TO A SPECIFIC PROPORTION

Often you may be required to produce an image that is a specific proportion. For instance, you might want to produce Web thumbnails or components in an ad layout that all have the same proportionate shape.

You can easily use Photoshop to perform proportionate cropping. You do not, however, use the Crop tool. Instead, you use the Rectangular Marquee together with the Image ⇨ Crop command.

Note, however, you may want to make a series of images that have been cropped to a specific proportion fit a specific size. If that is the case, you have to use the Image ⇨ Image Size command after cropping. Remember, the greater the size change, the more detail that will be lost.

1 Double-click the Marquee tool from the Marquee tools fly-out menu.

■ The Marquee Options tab appears.

2 Choose Constrained Aspect Ratio from the Style pull-down menu.

3 Drag to place the marquee. Proportions are maintained, regardless of where you drag.

Note: Drag inside the marquee to position the marquee as desired.

4 Choose Image ⇨ Crop.

■ *Everything outside the marquee is cropped.*

CROP THE IMAGE TO A SPECIFIC SIZE

The Rectangular Marquee tool also can be used to crop out an area of specific height and width from an image. This is another technique useful for making thumbnails. It is also extremely useful for cropping out sections of textures to be used as seamless tiles for texture mapping.

The only difference between the way you crop to a fixed size and the way you crop proportionately is the settings you choose in the Marquee Options dialog box.

Once you have entered a fixed size in the Width and Height fields of the Marquee Options dialog box, any place you click with the Marquee tool is where the upper-right corner of a marquee of those dimensions appears. If the marquee is bigger than the image, the entire image is selected, even if you click inside the image.

1 Double-click the Marquee tool from the Marquee tools fly-out menu.

2 Choose Fixed Size from the Style pull-down menu.

3 Enter the desired pixel measurements in the Height and Width fields.

4 Drag to place the marquee. It will always maintain proportions, regardless where you drag.

Note: Drag inside the marquee to position it as desired.

5 Choose Image ⇨ Crop.

■ Everything outside the marquee is cropped.

CROP THE IMAGE TO A FIXED SIZE AND RESOLUTION

At times you may want to trim an image to a specific pixel width and height and, at the same time, render it at a specific resolution. Photoshop lets you do that by checking the Fixed Target Size option in the Crop Options palette.

Note that the object here is to end up with a cropped image that has an exact proportion and that is of a specific resolution when cropped to that proportion. In the Crop Options palette, if you change the height or width and don't reenter resolution, the resolution will automatically change in the end result. On the other hand, if you don't change the height and width entries, but do change the pixels per inch (or centimeter) of resolution, the Image Size specification will change the height and width to make the image the correct size at the specified resolution.

If you click on the Front Image button, the current dimensions and resolution become your starting point. If you don't, simply specify height and width and resolution. The image will size itself accordingly.

1 Double-click the Crop tool.

■ The Crop Options palette appears.

2 Click to check the Fixed Target Size box.

3 Click Front Image.

■ The current image size information appears.

4 Enter the desired dimensions and resolution for the resized image.

5 Drag diagonally to create a marquee approximating the area of the image to be cropped.

■ Sizing handles appear around the marquee.

6 Drag corners to change size of the crop boundaries or drag outside to rotate boundaries.

CROP THE IMAGE TO A SPECIFIC PROPORTION OR DIMENSION

It is possible to crop images to a consistent size and resolution or to a set proportion of height and width. To do this, you have to use the Rectangular Marquee tool.

These options can save you significant time and hassles when you want to crop images to fit in uniform spaces on a print page (think of the portraits in a year book) or on a Web page (think of image thumbnails). You'll also find fixed-size crops handy for cutting out patterned portions of an image for use as tiled fill patterns.

1 To make a fixed proportion crop, double-click the Rectangular Marquee tool.

2 Choose Constrained Aspect Ratio.

3 Drag to indicate the size of the crop.

4 Choose Image ⇨ Crop.

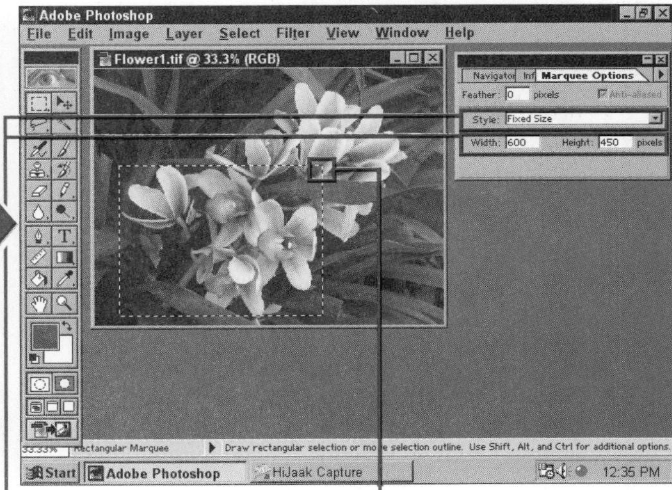

1 To make a fixed height and width crop, choose Fixed Size from the Style pull-down menu in the Marquee Options dialog box.

2 Enter the pixel dimensions you desire.

3 Click to place the upper-right corner of the marquee.

4 Choose Image ⇨ Crop.

CONTROL OVERALL IMAGE QUALITY

The visual exercises in this chapter show you how to control the characteristics of your image, in whole or in part. The image characteristics that are specifically discussed include overall tonal range (gamma), contrast (the difference between the brightest and darkest portions of the image), color balance, and overall brightness. The specific commands discussed are all found on the Image ⇨ Adjust submenu, shown in the following figure.

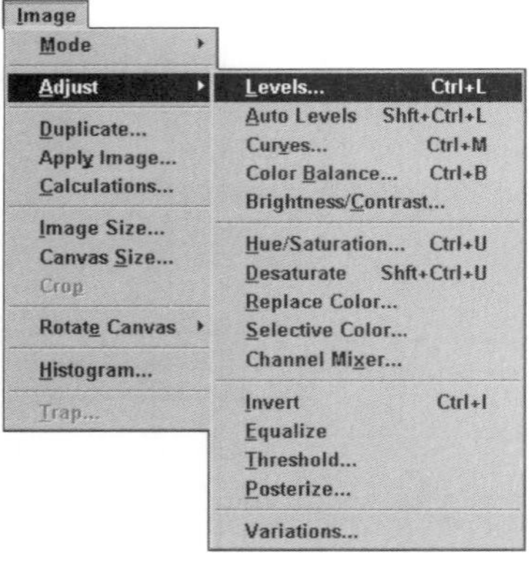

All these commands (except, as noted, a few that don't work with adjustment layers) can be applied to the following:

- An entire layer
- Any specific part of the image enclosed by a selection
- An adjustment layer, which will affect the entire image

The advantage of making image adjustments on adjustment layers are threefold:

- All the layers below the adjustment layer are equally affected (otherwise, image adjustments work on only one layer at a time).
- You can change the adjustment at any time (or delete it), because it doesn't actually change any of the pixels in the underlying layers (unless, of course, you flatten the image).
- You can specify the intensity (Adobe calls it *opacity*) or transparency of the effect.

Levels

The Levels command is used to compress or expand the image's range of brightness values by moving any of three input sliders in the Levels dialog box, one each for shadow, midtone, and highlight as illustrated in the following figure. The histogram shows the density of the pixels within a given tonal range. This is one of the easiest and most powerful color correction tools and usually the best place to start working in color correction as soon as an image has been digitized.

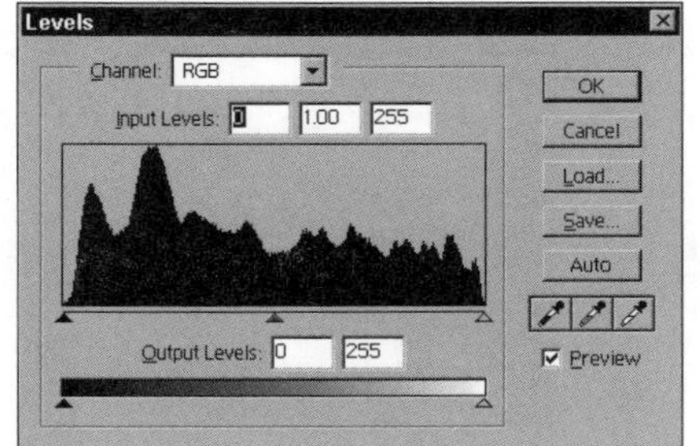

Levels Dialog Box Contents

Component	Function
Channel pull-down menu	Enables you to change the entire image or a particular color channel.
Input Levels fields	Specify the shadow, midtone, and highlight points by exact number.
Histogram	Reflects the population of pixels at a particular brightness level.
Input Levels sliders	Indicate the level of the darkest, median, and brightest pixels in the image.
Output Levels fields	Specify the darkest and lightest tones to be output by exact number.
Output Levels bar	Displays a smooth blend from black to white to help you judge where you're setting the output sliders.
Output Levels sliders	Enable you to decrease image contrast in highlights and shadows.
Load button	Loads previously stored levels setting.
Save button	Stores the current levels setting.
Auto	Executes the Auto Levels command.
Sample Eyedroppers	Each Eyedropper — Shadow, Midtone, and Highlight — enables you to select a pixel to specify the matching tone.

CONTINUED

CONTROL OVERALL IMAGE QUALITY
CONTINUED

Curves

The Curves command is another powerful image adjustment command that gives you control over every aspect of an image's brightness, contrast, and color. The Curves command enables you to move the mid- and end points of the gamma spectrum for the composite channel or any of the color channels. Through this command, you can also change the brightness value of any color of any pixel in the image to any other brightness value. You do this by specifying a brightness curve along the input/output axis. Create this curve either by dragging control points or by drawing it freehand. The Curves dialog box is shown here.

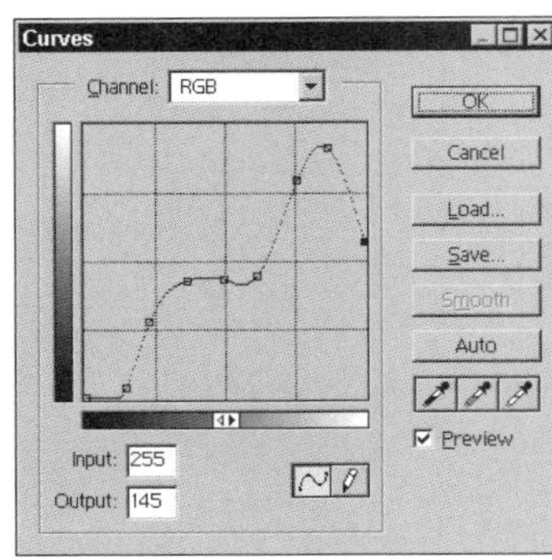

Curves Dialog Box Contents

Component	Function
Channel pull-down menu	Enables you to change the entire image or a particular color channel.
New Brightness Values bar	Indicates the direction in which new values are displayed by the graph.
Curves graph	Reflects any redistribution of the brightness range of pixels.
Input field	Displays a numerical value for the input. You can enter a value from 1 to 255.
Output field	Displays the numerical value for the output. You can enter a value from 1 to 255.
Curve Point button	Enables you to change the shape of the curve by clicking to enter a point, and then dragging the point to change its value. Always results in a smooth curve.
Load button	Loads a previously stored levels setting.
Save button	Stores the current levels setting.
Smooth button	Converts a freehand curve to one with control points.
Auto	Executes the Auto Levels command.
Sample droppers	Each dropper — Shadow, Midtone, and Highlight — enables you to select a pixel to specify the matching tone. Shadow, Midtone, and Highlight droppers select a pixel as the matching tone.

Color Balance

The Color Balance command makes generalized color corrections. Shadows, midtones, and highlights can be controlled individually through the Color Balance dialog box as shown in the following figure. To change the balance of any of the primary colors, you simply drag a slider. This is an excellent tool for beginners, as well as for those who want instant feedback on overall color balance changes.

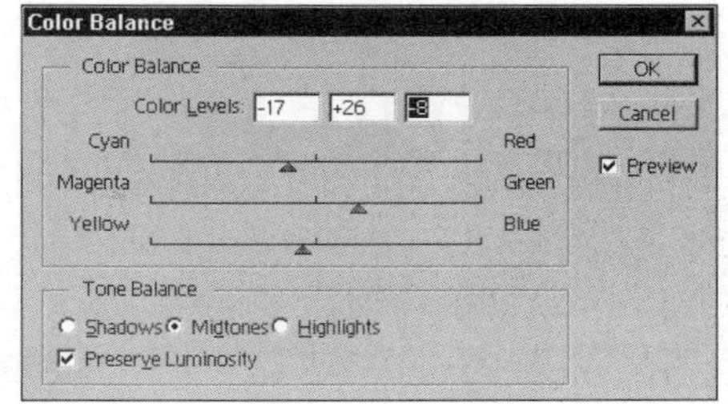

Color Balance Dialog Box Contents

Component	Function
Color Levels fields	Indicate, from left to right, the levels of cyan/red, magenta/green, and yellow/blue. Enter a positive number to move slider toward the primary color (for example, red), negative to move toward the compliment (for example, cyan).
Color Levels sliders	Enable you to interactively set the color level for each channel.
Tone Balance radio buttons	Determine which range of tones will be affected by your settings. Controls can be set at different levels for each range, one at a time.
Preserve Luminosity check box	If checked, prevents alteration of luminosity when color is changed.

CONTINUED

CONTROL OVERALL IMAGE QUALITY CONTINUED

Brightness/Contrast

Brightness/Contrast is the simple command for controlling brightness and contrast. A pair of sliders makes the whole area lighter or darker and more or less contrasting as illustrated here.

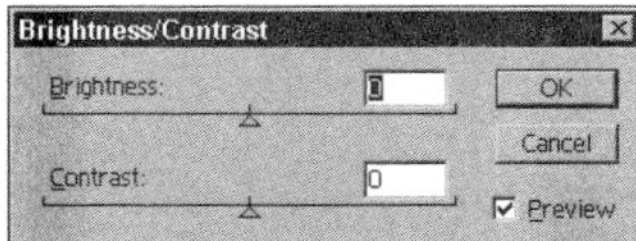

Brightness/Contrast Dialog Box Contents

Component	Function
Brightness slider	Increases or decreases overall lightness.
Contrast slider	Increases or decreases overall contrast.

Hue/Saturation

The Hue/Saturation command is especially useful for pepping up the colors in an image. This command enables color correction through independent control of Hue, Saturation, and Lightness values, as shown in the following figure. You can control all colors simultaneously or any of the primary and complimentary colors individually. You can also designate which colors are to be affected by selecting them from the Edit pull-down menu, and then targeting a particular range of pixels by clicking them with the three Eyedropper tools. The Hue/Saturation command can also color the entire image if you click the Colorize check box.

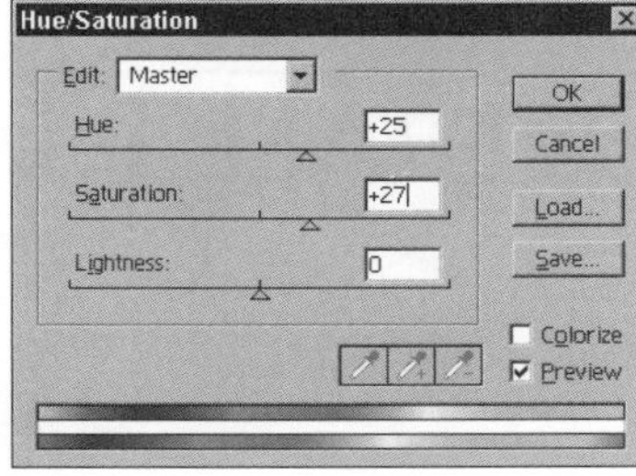

Hue/Saturation Dialog Box Contents

Component	Function
Edit pull-down menu	Enables simultaneous or individual editing of all primary and complimentary colors.
Hue slider	Infuses the image with the hue, causing a shift in color balance.
Saturation slider	Intensifies or mutes the intensity of colors.
Lightness slider	Intensifies or mutes the brightness of colors.
Input Hues bar	Represents the normal spectrum of colors.
Output Hues bar	Represents the shift of the spectrum according to the position of the hue slider.
Load button	Loads a previously stored levels setting.
Save button	Stores the current levels setting.
Colorize check box	Makes a monochrome tint of the slider settings.

CONTINUED

CONTROL OVERALL IMAGE QUALITY CONTINUED

Replace Color

The Replace Color command enables you to replace all the pixels within a given range of color with pixels from another range of color. You use the droppers to select the color(s) you want to change; indicate a range of brightness surrounding that color with the Fuzziness setting; and then use the Hue, Saturation, and Lightness sliders shown here to change the color in the Sample box to a shade that pleases you. If you want to change the color of one particular object in a scene, but the scene contains other objects of that color, be sure to mask the target object with a selection marquee first.

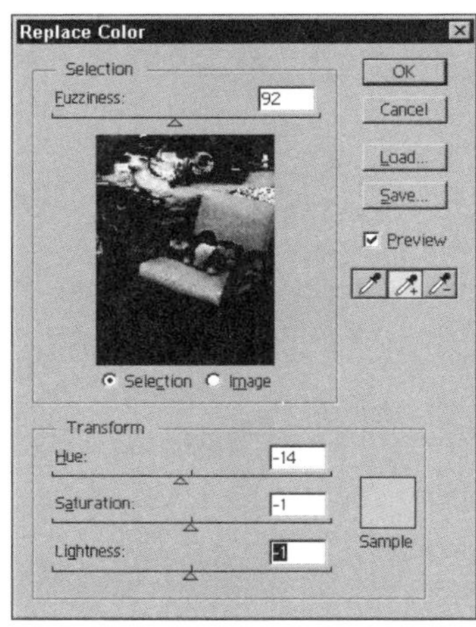

Replace Color Dialog Box Contents

Component	Function
Fuzziness field	Indicates spectrum range of color. Enter a number from 1 to 200.
Fuzziness slider	Enables you to specify spectrum range of color by dragging the slider.
Preview window	Shows selected colors as white (selection) or as adjusted (image).
Selection radio button	Indicates preview image will be shown as a selection.
Image radio button	Indicates preview image will be shown as an image.
Hue slider	Infuses the image with the hue, causing a shift in color balance.
Saturation slider	Intensifies or mutes the intensity of colors.
Lightness slider	Intensifies or mutes the brightness of colors.
Output Color Sample box	Previews the color that will be substituted for the selected pixels.
Load button	Loads a previously stored levels setting.
Save button	Stores the current levels setting.
Color droppers	Enable you to select pixel that represents the color to be substituted. Plus and Minus droppers add to or subtract from the selected range of colors.

Selective Color

The Selective Color command lets you substitute any CMYK color for any of the primary or complimentary colors as well as neutral colors, blacks, or whites. Used primarily in press applications for controlling CMYK ink levels, this command is also capable of producing unusual visual effects. The Selective Color dialog box is shown here.

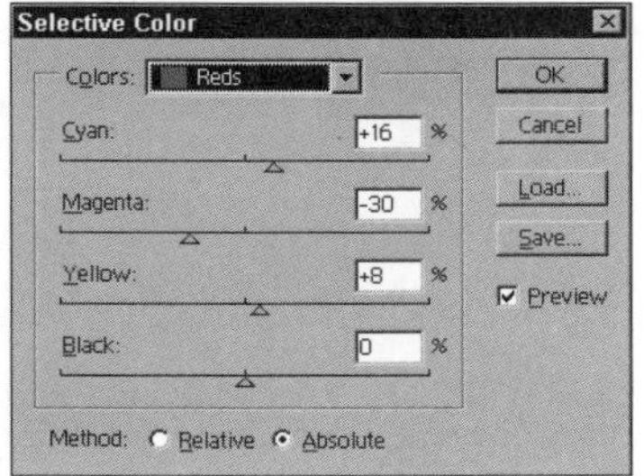

Selective Color Dialog Box Contents

Component	Function
Colors pull-down menu	Lets you choose area of color to be adjusted.
Color sliders	Control the amount of cyan, magenta, yellow, or black ink that will be applied to the chosen color range.
Method radio buttons	Determine whether indicated changes will be relative to amount of ink color or an absolute percentage of ink color.
Load button	Loads a previously stored levels setting.
Save button	Stores the current levels setting.

CONTINUED

CONTROL OVERALL IMAGE QUALITY CONTINUED

Channel Mixer

The Channel Mixer command, the dialog box for which is shown in this figure, makes it possible to mix the color from multiple channels. This command is particularly handy for rescuing images from the blahs after they've been converted to CMYK from RGB or Lab color. By checking the Monochrome box, you can also use this command to create a monochrome image from a color image while remaining in a true-color color space, thus enabling control of color values based on the information contained in one or more specific color channels. This command is disabled when in Lab Color mode.

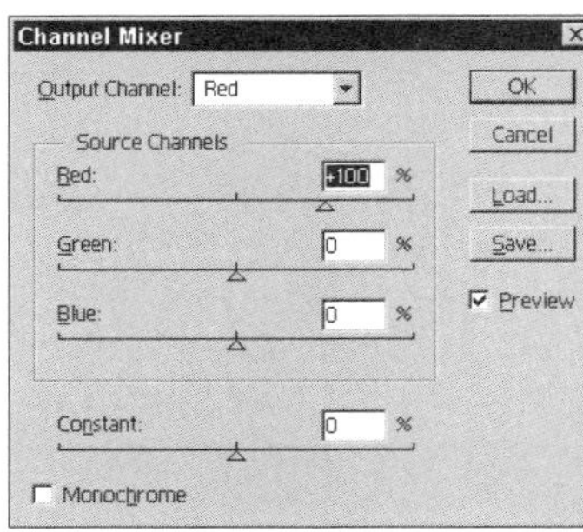

Channel Mixer Dialog Box Contents

Component	Function
Output Channel pull-down menu	Lets you choose color channel into which colors from other channels will be mixed.
Color sliders	Control the amount of color that will be infused from existing channels.
Constant slider	Adds an opacity channel to the output channel. Drag to the left to decrease opacity, to the right to increase it.
Monochrome check box	If checked, creates a monochrome image within the current color space.
Load button	Loads a previously stored levels setting.
Save button	Stores the current levels setting.

Threshold

The Threshold command creates a black-and-white image by pushing all the pixels brighter than a certain level to white and all those below a certain level to black — a capability you can take advantage of to automatically make certain types of masks. Also, for an instant line drawing, try using this command in conjunction with the Find Edges filter. The dialog box for this command is shown here.

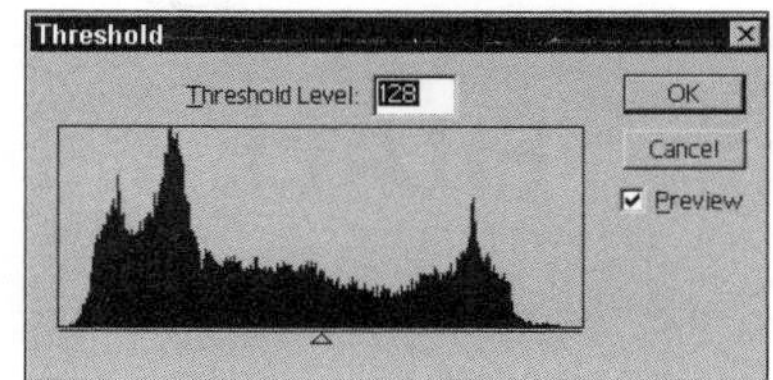

Threshold Dialog Box Contents

Component	Function
Threshold Level field	Indicates the value of the grayscale level. Enter a value from 0 to 255.
Histogram	Displays a graph of pixel density at a given level of brightness.
Threshold slider	Enables you to set the threshold. The value for the level automatically appears in the Threshold Level field.

CONTINUED

CONTROL OVERALL IMAGE QUALITY CONTINUED

Posterize

The Posterize command reduces all the colors in the image to a particular number of brightness values, as specified in the Posterize dialog box depicted here. The result looks like a high-impact color poster drawn with hard edges and flat-colors.

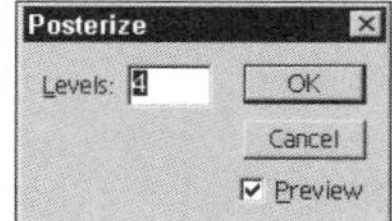

Posterize Dialog Box Contents

Component	Function
Levels field	Enter any number of brightness values from 0 to 255.

Variations

The Variations command lets you control brightness and color balance by clicking on preadjusted thumbnails. Values for shadows, midtones, and highlights can be controlled separately in the Variations dialog box shown here. This command is very easy to use and can be a good place to start experimenting with adjustments in color, saturation, and gamma. Be aware, however, that it is hard to judge the precise effect of these adjustments from the relatively small thumbnails that are your only means of previewing the image. You may want to note your settings, and then use the File ➪ Revert command or the History palette to restore your image to its previous state after examining the result at full size. You can then make corrections by using the Curves or Levels commands to make more precise adjustments to the final image.

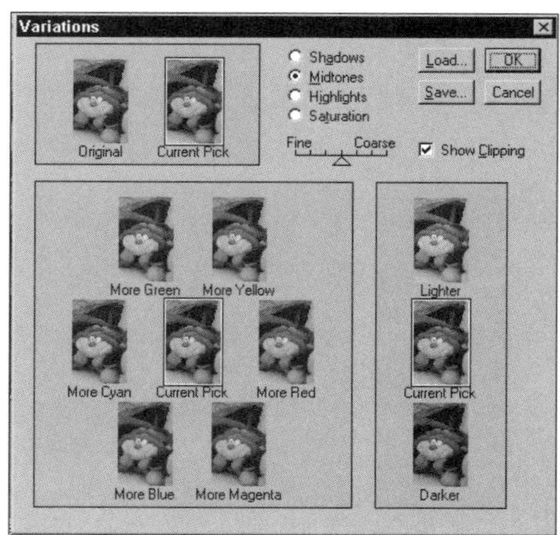

Variations Dialog Box Contents

Component	Function
Original thumbnail	Shows the image as unaffected by any variations.
Current Pick thumbnail	Shows the image as altered by any series of choices you have made.
More *Color* thumbnail	Clicking any of these thumbnails infuses an even measure of that color into the original image. You can multiply the effect by clicking more than once, and you can click on multiple color thumbnails. The effect is cumulative.
Lighter and Darker thumbnails	Make the image lighter or darker according to the position of the Fine/Coarse slider.
Tonal Range radio buttons	Enable you to restrict changes to one of the listed tonal ranges.
Saturation radio button	Enables you to restrict variation thumbnails to changing only level of color saturation.
Fine/Coarse slider	Sets the intensity of the effect that occurs when you click a thumbnail.
Load button	Loads a previously stored levels setting.
Save button	Stores the current levels setting.

Adjustment Commands Without Dialog Boxes

The following commands work automatically, with no intervention from dialog boxes. Note that none of these commands work on adjustment layers.

- **Auto Levels:** Automatically defines the lightest pixel as white and the darkest as black, and then proportionately distributes those pixels that are in between. You can use the Auto button in either the Curves or Levels commands to do exactly the same thing.
- **Desaturate:** Lets you turn an area into grayscale without leaving a true-color mode, so all commands available in RGB will still be available. You can do the same thing in the Hue/Saturation dialog box by moving the Saturation slider to the extreme left.
- **Invert:** Reverses the light and dark tones, as well as changing colors to their compliments. In other words, this command creates a color negative (but with no orange mask). You can use the Curves dialog box to create the same effect by dragging the leftmost point to the top of the Curves graph and the rightmost point to the bottom. The graph should then be a diagonal line from top left to bottom right.
- **Equalize:** Interprets the brightest pixel as white, the darkest as black, and then evenly distributes the brightness values of all the pixels in between. This command is potentially useful for maximizing the detail in highlights and shadows. You can get a similar result with the Auto button in either the Curves or Levels dialog boxes.

CORRECT OVERALL COLOR BALANCE

The Color Balance command is the easiest way to correct color casts that affect overall image quality. For example, this command enables you to correct unattractive color casts that may have resulted from poor film processing or poor lighting that existed at the time of the shooting. More often, it is used to correct a hastily made scan. To bring up the Color Balance dialog box, press ⌘/Ctrl+B or choose Image ➪ Adjust ➪ Color Balance.

All the commands for making tonal and color corrections work on adjustment layers. Otherwise, the effect is limited to the currently selected layer. Because the Color Balance command is usually most effective when applied to all layers, this example demonstrates it in that context. An exception to this rule is commonly encountered in making composite images. In that case, you want to color balance each layer so that together they look as though they belong in the same place and time.

You can also use color balance to change the mood of a photo or create a special effect. Also, you can limit the area in which color balancing occurs by making a mask or selection (see Chapter 7 for more on making selections).

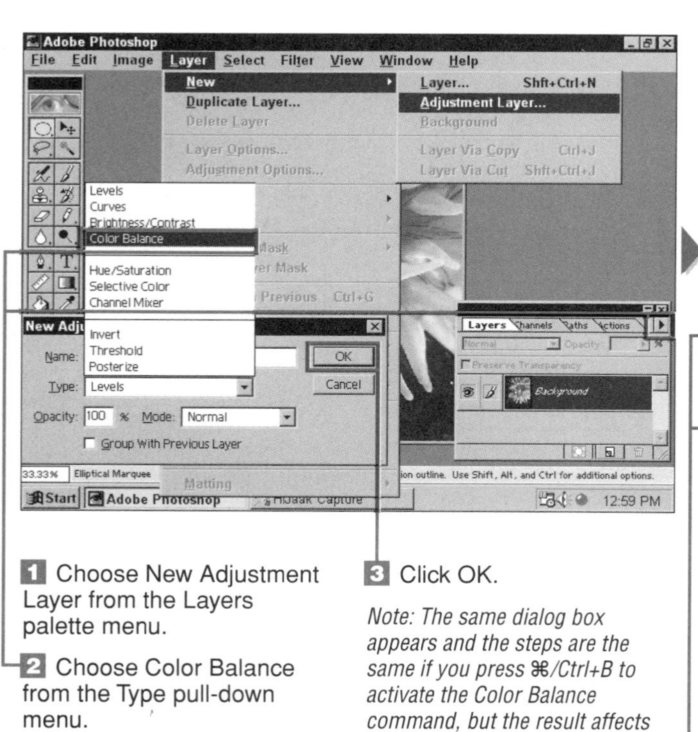

1 Choose New Adjustment Layer from the Layers palette menu.

2 Choose Color Balance from the Type pull-down menu.

3 Click OK.

Note: The same dialog box appears and the steps are the same if you press ⌘/Ctrl+B to activate the Color Balance command, but the result affects only the current layer.

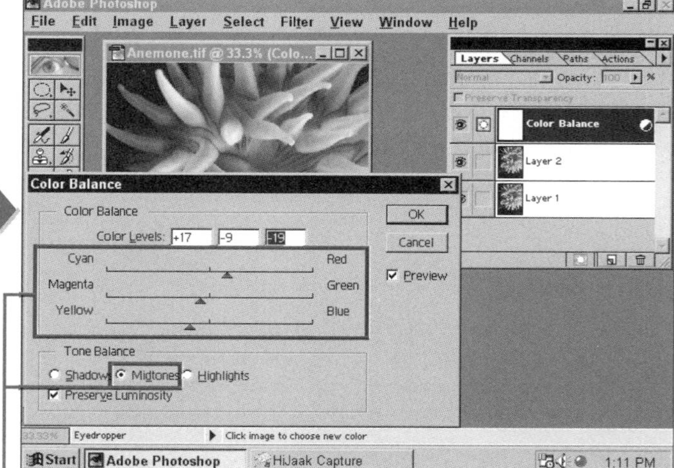

■ Preview and Preserve Luminosity boxes are on (checked) by default.

4 Click to activate midtones.

5 Drag sliders to increase color in the direction of label.

Note: Shadow, midtone, and highlight adjustments can be made before closing the dialog box, which you should do if you want one set of color balance adjustments to affect all areas of the image equally.

TIPS

Is it better to correct a poor scan with the Color Balance command or to rescan the image?

On rare occasions, you may be able to improve on the best your scanner can do, because all scanners aren't created equal. Still, you owe it to yourself to get the best you can out of your scanner. Remember, the more detail you have to work with in the first place, the better.

Is that why 30- or 36-bit scanners are more prized than 24-bit scanners?

Yes. The more bits per pixel your CCD device produces, the more information Photoshop has to work with, provided you work in the 16-bits-per-channel mode.

How do I make it easier to see my image when the Color Balance dialog box covers most of it?

Everyone has his or her favorite work habits, but most find it advantageous to see the whole image when balancing overall color. Before you open the Color Balance dialog box, drag the image window to about one-quarter of your active screen size, and then zoom out until the image is small enough to fit within that window. Drag the window to the upper-right corner of the screen. Finally, open the Color Balance dialog box.

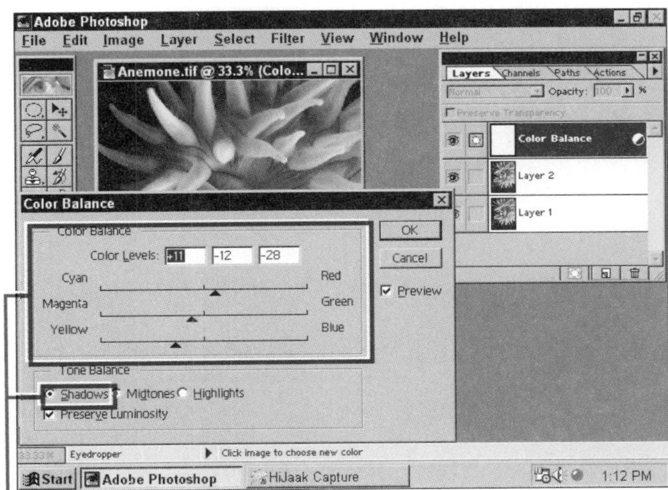

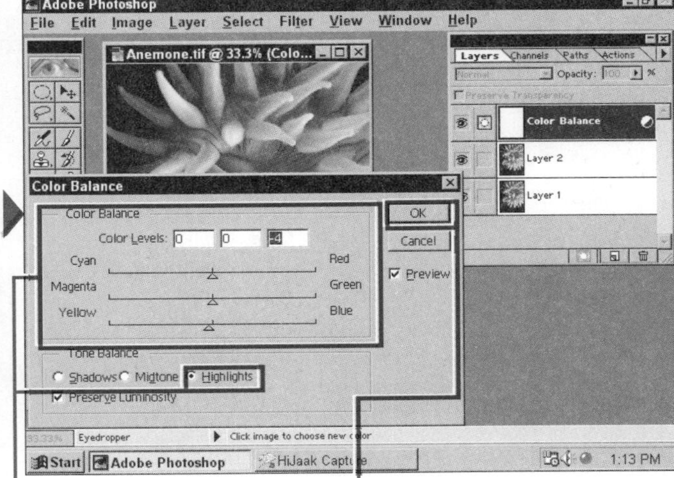

MODIFY THE BALANCE IN THE SHADOWS

6 Click to select Shadows.

7 Either drag sliders to indicate color shift or enter numbers for any or all slider bars.

Note: Enter positive numbers to move slider to the right of center, negative numbers to move slider to the left of center. Press Tab to cycle through the three number boxes.

MODIFY THE BALANCE IN THE HIGHLIGHTS

8 Click to select Highlights.

9 Either drag sliders to indicate color shift, or enter numbers for any or all slider bars.

Note: Enter positive numbers to move slider to the right of center, negative numbers to move slider to the left of center.

10 Click OK.

USE COLOR CORRECTION AIDS

Although all the commands and dialog boxes used to make the image corrections discussed in this chapter are found on the Image ➪ Adjust submenu, some helpful assistants are not found there: the Color palette and the Info palette. These can be used with the Eyedropper tool in a way that makes it quite easy to note color correction changes with absolute precision.

To do this, first open the Info Palette (Window ➪ Show Info). Use the Eyedropper tool to test up to four samples of color from the image itself. Place the pick up points in the areas that most need to be changed by your image adjustments. Next, open the Color Palette (Window ➪ Show Color).

Now, let's say you want to make a color correction using the Levels, Curves, Color Balance, Hue/Saturation, Replace Color, Selective Color, or Channel Mixer command. Place the cursor anywhere in the image, and it changes to the Eyedropper icon. Click in the color area that concerns you most. Now, any change you make with the correction command is reflected in the setting of the Color palette sliders and in the color samples in the Info palette.

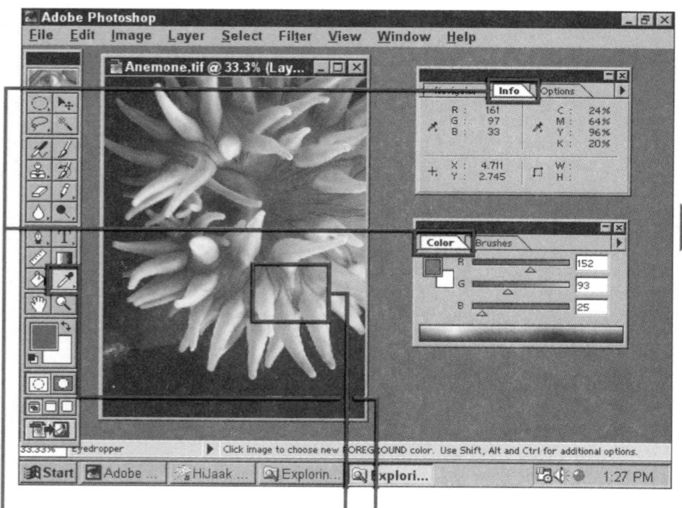

1 Choose Window ➪ Show Info to open the Info palette.

2 Choose Window ➪ Show Color to open the Color palette.

3 Choose the Color Sampler tool.

4 Click up to four sample areas.

■ Exact colors of each sampled pixel are shown (brackets #1-#4).

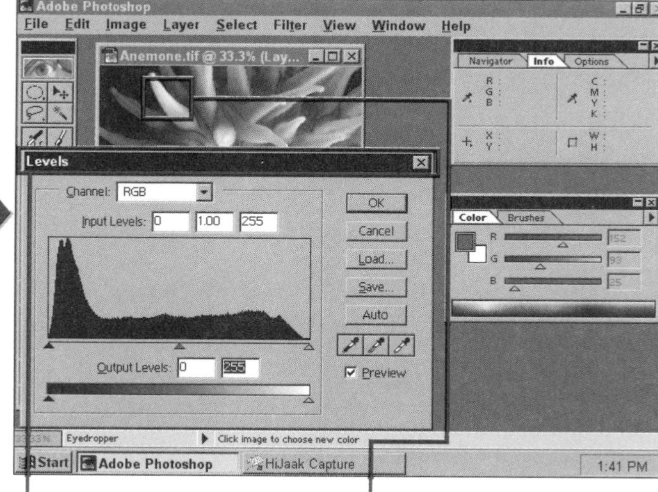

5 Choose any of the color correction commands you wish to use.

■ The command s dialog box appears.

6 Click a color in the workspace. Color settings change in response.

7 Make an adjustment in the command dialog box. Changes in the sample are shown.

ADJUST BRIGHTNESS AND CONTRAST

One of the quickest and easiest adjustments to make is to an image's brightness and contrast, because of the lack of flexibility of this type of change. You can't separately modify the intensity of highlights and shadows, for instance. There may be times, though, when you won't want to do a lot of tweaking.

You can limit the area that will be influenced by brightness and contrast either by making a selection or by selecting a layer on which the subject has a transparent background. You cannot, however, work on individual channels with this command. This means you can't use it to influence color balance in any way.

No shortcut key exists for the Brightness/Contrast command, so you may want to make an Action for it and assign it to a function key (see Chapter 19 for more information on how to automate Photoshop with Actions). If you make an adjustment you don't like, remember the trick of pressing ⌘/Ctrl to switch the Cancel button to Reset and then clicking Reset.

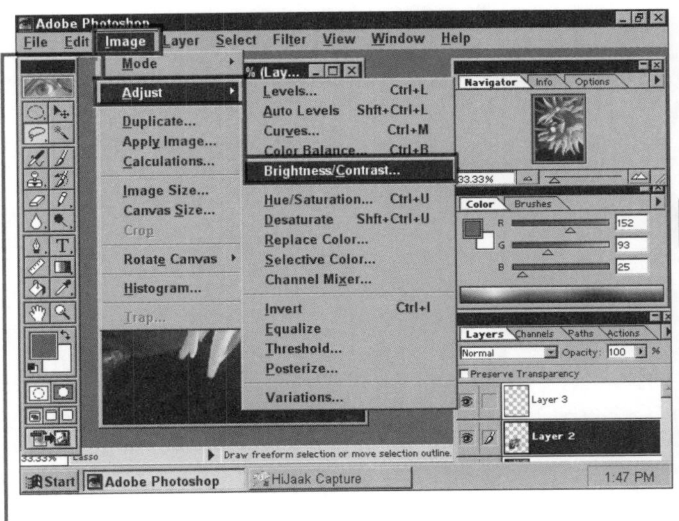

1 Choose Image ➪ Adjust ➪ Brightness/Contrast.

■ The Brightness/Contrast dialog box appears.

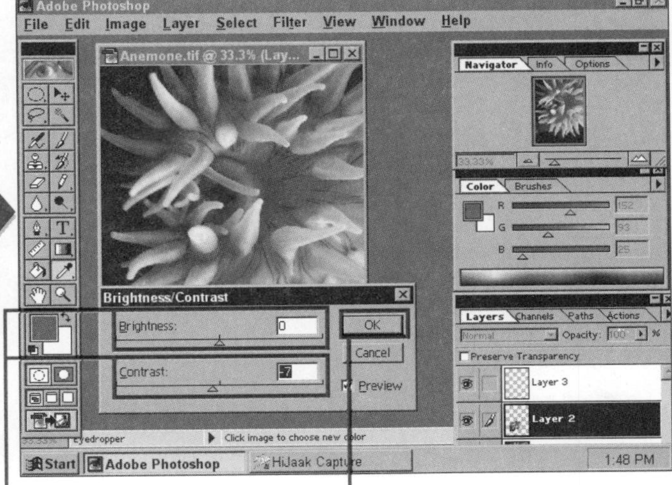

2 Drag the Brightness slider to the left of center to darken or to the right of center to lighten the image.

3 Drag the Contrast slider to the left of center to lower contrast or to the right of center to increase contrast.

4 When you re satisfied with the result, click OK.

Note: Be sure the Preview box is checked; otherwise, you may not be able to judge the results of your adjustments.

ALTER COLOR WITH HUE/SATURATION

The Hue/Saturation command (Image ➪ Adjust ➪ Hue/Saturation or ⌘/Ctrl+U) actually performs several types of jobs. You can change any combination of color balance, color saturation, or image brightness for the overall image. You can also work on individual channels of color and their complements. Finally, by checking the Colorize box, you can change the overall color of the image.

The Hue/Saturation command can be used to either affect the current layer and selection or multiple layers in an adjustment layer. The Hue/Saturation dialog box's appearance has changed slightly in Photoshop 5. Gone are the radio buttons that set the primary color range(s) to be adjusted, replaced by an Edit pull-down menu.

A new dual spectrum bar at the bottom of the dialog box serves a two purposes. If you choose Master and move the Hue slider, the lower spectrum bar moves to show the relationship between it and the old colors. If you choose a color, the area affected is shown by a bar and a pair of movable brackets, which you can drag to increase the chosen color range on either side of the primary color.

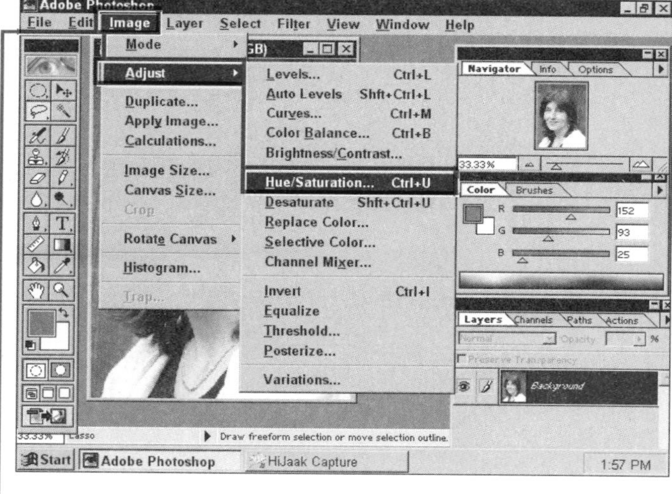

1 Choose Image ➪ Adjust ➪ Hue/Saturation.

■ The Hue/Saturation dialog box appears.

MAKE OVERALL ADJUSTMENTS TO THE LAYER

2 Choose Master from the Edit pull-down menu.

3 Drag the Hue slider to change the color tint.

4 Drag the Saturation slider to increase or decrease color intensity.

5 Drag the Lightness slider to lighten or darken the image.

TIPS

What happens when I want to make several adjustments in series?

The adjustments you make in the Hue/Saturation dialog box are cumulative, so you can make an adjustment to all colors followed by several to individual colors, and then make a selection and colorize it. All the changes will be registered when you click OK.

When I choose a color from the Edit menu, am I limited to affecting areas in the image that are in that color family?

Click any color in the image, and it, too, will be changed when you make adjustments for the color family chosen from the Edit pull-down menu.

When I choose a specific color from the Edit menu, will I be modifying only that exact color?

No. You are adjusting all tones that are in that color's family. You can also widen or narrow the range of colors to be modified by dragging the bracket on either side of the color bar that appears between the spectrum bars.

How can I select a range of colors that matches a specific area in the image?

Shift+drag the cursor over the area in the image that you want to affect.

MAKE ADJUSTMENTS WITHIN A RANGE OF COLORS

1 From the Edit pull-down menu, choose the color range you want to modify.

2 Click the color that you want to change.

Note: You can expand the range of colors surrounding the chosen color by moving the bracket sliders.

3 Drag the sliders to modify the color range.

CHANGE THE IMAGE TO AN OVERALL MONOTONE

1 Click the Colorize check box.

2 Drag the sliders to change the tint, intensity, and image brightness of the monotone.

■ These settings create a nice sepia tone, like that of an antique photograph.

LOSE ALL COLOR WITH DESATURATE

Using the Desaturate command (Image ➪ Adjust ➪ Desaturate or Shift+⌘/Ctrl+U) is a one-step no-brainer. After choosing the command, your image suddenly becomes grayscale, without your having to specify options in an intervening dialog box. If the result isn't your objective, quickly press ⌘/Ctrl+Z to undo, choose File ➪ Revert, or delete the command from the History list. (There's no Reset button because there's no dialog box.)

You may well ask why not simply change the Color mode to Grayscale. Well, if you do so, you won't have accomplished the same thing. You have to be in a Color mode (Indexed, RGB, CMYK, or Lab) when you issue the Desaturate command. Because you are still in that Color mode, you can now directly recolor the image.

To recolor a monochrome image, choose a brush and, in the Brush Options palette, choose Color from the Apply Modes pull-down menu.

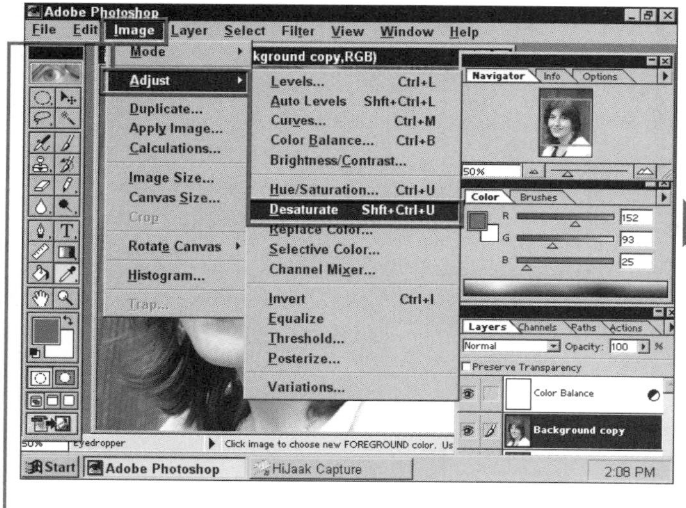

1 Choose Image ➪ Adjust ➪ Desaturate.

The image loses all color but is still in full-color mode. This means you can color the image or add additional colored layers.

Note: You can have the image fade from grayscale to full color by first making a mask that is filled with a white-to-black gradient. Load the mask as a selection, and then issue the Desaturate command.

CREATE A TONAL EFFECT WITH INVERT

Issuing the Invert command (Image ➪ Adjust ➪ Invert or ⌘/Ctrl+I) causes a reversal of all the tones in an image. In other words, Invert makes a photographic negative of a positive image. It's also useful for converting scans of black-and-white negatives into positives. Unfortunately, this won't work on color negatives because those negatives use an orange mask, which Photoshop doesn't take into account.

To use Invert, you execute the command and — bingo! — you have a negative (or a positive, if you started with a negative).

You may also find Invert useful for making a channel mask, especially if the mask is subsequently hand-retouched so that the masking is limited to very specific areas. You can make a negative mask in the Channels palette by dragging any of the color channels to the New Channel icon. Select the resulting new alpha channel, and press ⌘/Ctrl+I.

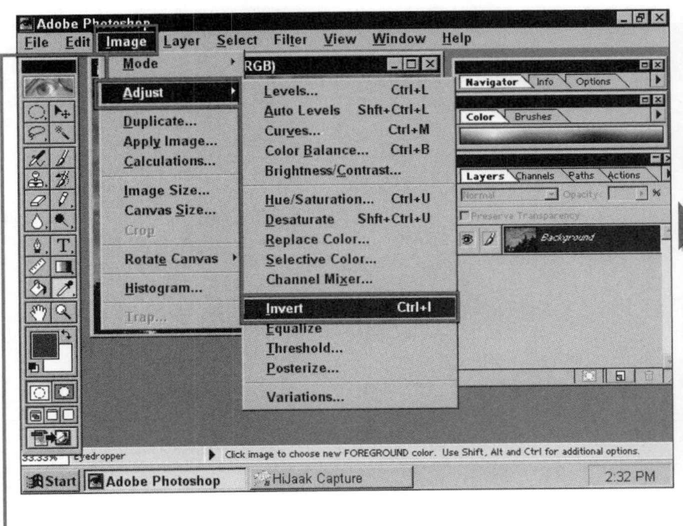

1 Choose Image ➪ Adjust ➪ Invert.

■ All tonal values are reversed in the current image.

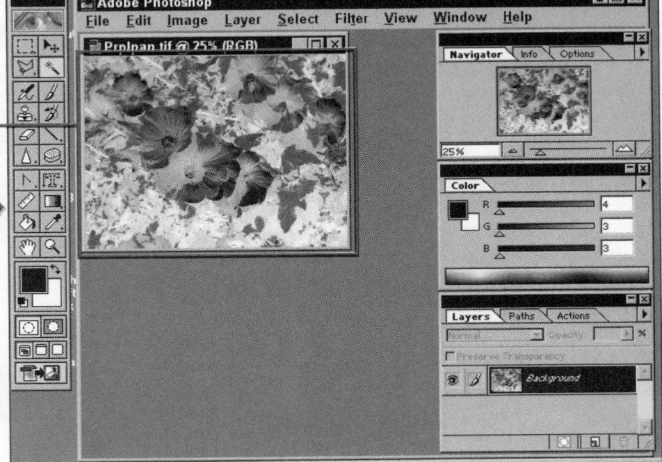

■ Notice the resulting negative image.

SWAP ONE COLOR FOR ANOTHER

The Replace Color command (Image ⇨ Adjust ⇨ Replace Color) enables you to recolor parts of an image. It does this by making a mask and then letting you adjust the hue, saturation, and color. In other words, it's the Replace Color and Brightness Hue/Saturation/ commands in one dialog box. Often, you may want to restrict the area for recoloring. In such a case, select the area or areas to be affected before issuing the Replace Color command.

Making adjustments is a matter of dragging sliders to alter the degree of change. You choose the color you want to change by simply clicking in the image. You can add and subtract colors from the selection by choosing Plus (+) and Minus (–) Eyedropper tools and continuing to click in the image. The Fuzziness slider broadens or narrows the range of color surrounding the chosen colors. It isn't just the color itself that you can change — you can also control the saturation and lightness of the color you swap.

Load and Save buttons make it possible to save the Replace Color adjustments so that they can be applied to other images. These buttons bring up standard file loading and saving dialog boxes.

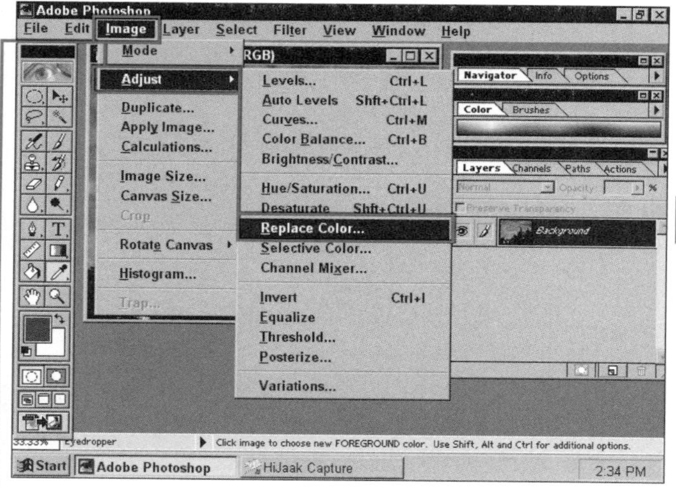

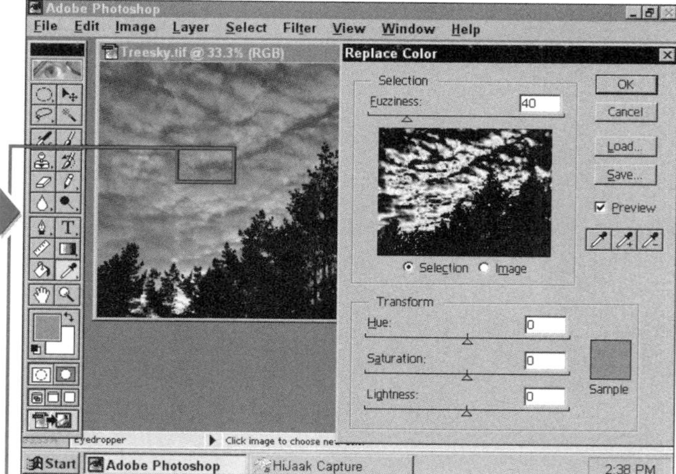

1 Choose Image ⇨ Adjust ⇨ Replace Color.

■ The Replace Color dialog box appears.

2 Click in the image to indicate the color you want to replace.

■ The area covered by your selection appears as white in the Preview box.

Note: The Sample box at lower right displays the color (including hue, saturation, and lightness) that will replace the colors you've chosen. To change this color, adjust the sliders.

TIPS

The Replace Color dialog box seems very familiar. Does another Photoshop dialog work in much the same way?

The Select ➪ Select Color range dialog box has almost identical controls. You could use it to replace color by first choosing the replacement color as the foreground color, and then using the Edit ➪ Fill command in conjunction with the Color Apply mode.

Is there an easy way to see the whole image when I am zoomed in closely on the image?

You can see the whole image in the Preview window if you click the Image radio button under the Preview window.

Do I have to click the Plus and Minus Eyedroppers to add and select colors?

No. In this dialog box (or any other that features Plus and Minus Eyedroppers), you can Shift+click in the current image to add colors or Opt/Alt+click to subtract colors. This is much faster because the cursor never needs to leave the image.

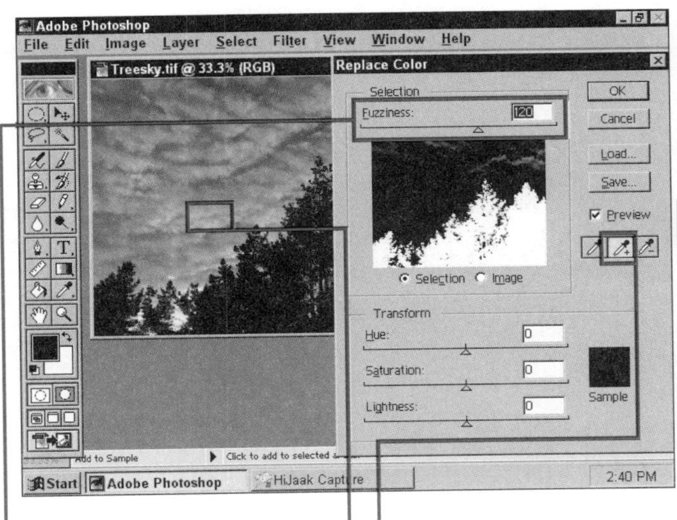

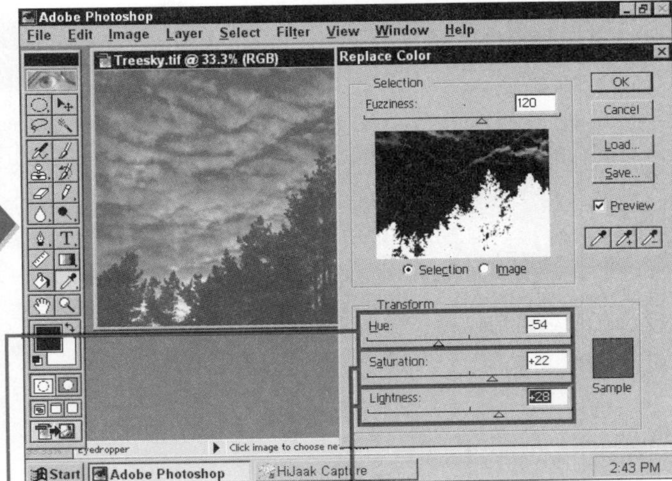

3 Drag the Fuzziness slider to increase the selected range of color.

■ The area of white in the Preview window expands and contracts as you move the slider.

4 Click the Plus Eyedropper to add other colors to the selection or the Minus Eyedropper to subtract colors.

5 Click in the image to add or subtract colors.

6 Drag the Hue slider to replace the chosen color.

Note: If the Preview box is checked, you see the color change previewed in the image.

7 Drag the Saturation slider to change the intensity of the replacement color.

8 Drag the Lightness slider to change the brightness of the replacement color.

MIX COLOR CHANNELS

You can choose Image ⇨ Adjust ⇨ Channel Mixer to change the mix of colors that contributed to a particular color channel. Although it is possible to change color balance (drastically) by this method, its real purpose is to create special effects. The most readily understandable and useful applications include custom sepia tinting of grayscale images and using channel data to create a mask. Mathematically, the Channel Mixer creates output channels that reflect your adjustments to the existing channels plus a constant brightness value. The constant value is adjustable by dragging the Constant slider at the bottom of the dialog box.

The Channel Mixer is meant to replace operations that would require channel calculations or layer blending in earlier versions of Photoshop. These effects generally fall into the areas of grayscale conversions, mixing and matching of channels for making custom masks, and bizarre special effects. Talented prepress types can also use the command for making custom-mixed separation plates.

Note: You won't be able to use the Channel Mixer unless you are viewing the Composite channel (RGB, CMYK, Lab).

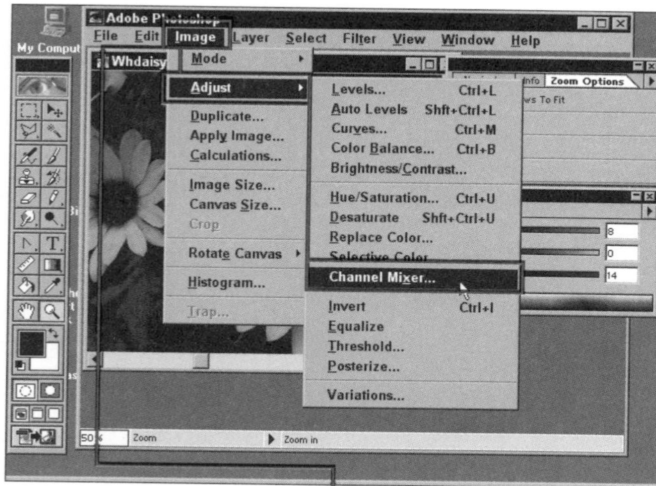

1 Choose Window ⇨ Show Channels.

2 Click the Composite channel name bar to make sure it's selected.

3 Choose Image ⇨ Adjust ⇨ Channel Mixer.

■ The Channel Mixer dialog box appears.

4 Choose the primary color channel you want to adjust from the Output Channel pull-down menu.

5 If not checked, click the Preview box.

TIPS

How do I use the Channel Mixer to create a monochrome or duotone effect, such as a sepia tone?

Try setting the source channels for the Red output channel at Red = +132, Green = 0, and Blue = 0. For the Green source channel, try Red = 0, Green = +42, and Blue = +22. For the Blue source channel, try Red = 0, Green = 0, and Blue = +32. These exact settings may not be to your liking, but you can experiment from there. Using the Channel Mixer produces a sepia effect that still has some hint of color, whereas the effect produced by the Mode ➪ Duotone command uses only the specified colors and produces a more traditional look.

How can I use the Channel Mixer to make a custom mask?

Copy the layer you want to mask. Click the Monochrome box to check it and make adjustments to the channels until you see the contrasts you are looking for in the mask. When you see something close to the mask you want, click OK. Press ⌘/Ctrl+A to Select All and then ⌘/Ctrl+C to copy the contents of the layer to the Clipboard. Switch to the Channels palette, and click the New Channel icon. Select the new channel, and press ⌘/Ctrl+V to paste in the layer contents.

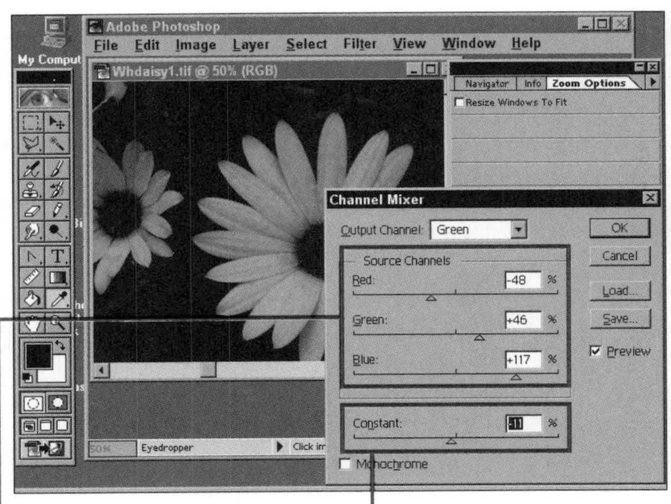

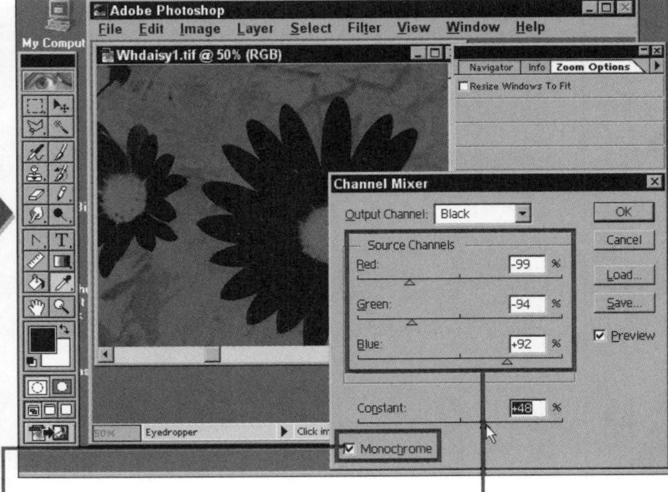

6 Drag the color sliders until you see the approximate effect you want.

■ The colors shift in the workspace window.

7 Drag the Constant slider to change the image contrast and to fine-tune the effect of the channel adjustments.

8 To make a monochrome image, layer, or mask, click to check the Monochrome check box.

■ The layer becomes monochromatic.

9 Drag any combination of sliders to achieve the desired tonal values in the monochromatic image.

Note: This mode is often used to create mask channels.

MAKE AN ADJUSTMENT WITH VARIATIONS

The Variations command (Image ➪ Adjust ➪ Variations) is the easiest way for the uninitiated and the most efficient way for the experienced to make adjustments in color balance, exposure, and contrast. It's easy because the image is shown as it will look if adjusted in several different ways. You make any combination of adjustments. When the preview image looks the way you want it to, click OK.

The Variations command is best for making corrections that apply to the entire layer (or image, if it's used on an adjustment layer). It will, of course, work on masked areas, but you can't see the effect very well. The Variations dialog box occupies almost your entire screen, so there's no workspace preview. Generally, the thumbnails prove too small to give you a good preview of even smaller masked areas.

Note: It is possible that the Variations command doesn't appear on your Image ➪ Adjust menu, because Variations is an Adobe-supplied plug-in that may not have been installed. The solution is to find the plug-in on the disks that shipped with the program. Drop the plug-in into the Adobe Photoshop 5 Plug-ins directory and restart Photoshop.

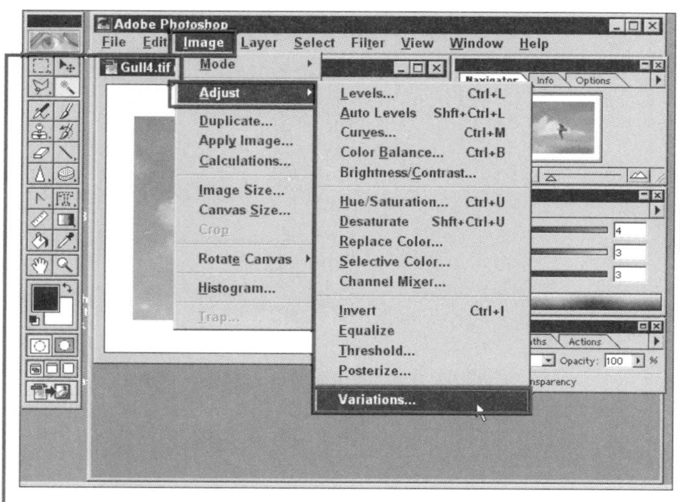

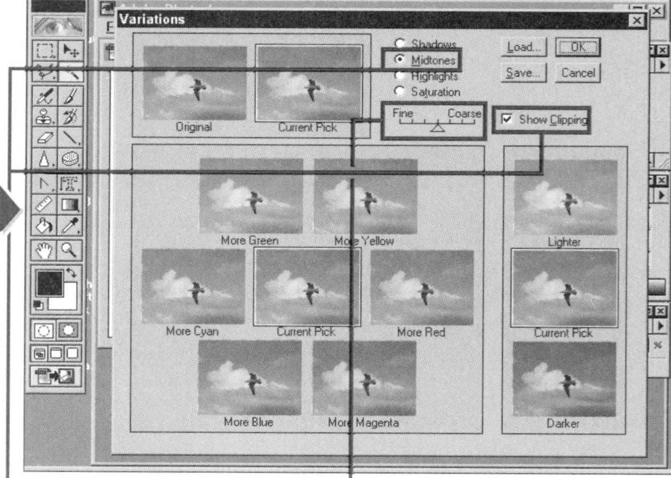

1 Choose Image ➪ Adjust ➪ Variations.

■ The Variations dialog box covers nearly the entire Photoshop workspace. This has been done to give you the largest possible thumbnails, as no workspace preview is provided.

2 Click the Show Clipping radio button.

3 Click the Midtones radio button.

4 Drag the Slider to make the differences between thumbnails more or less pronounced.

■ Each tick mark indicates a doubling of the intensity of the effect.

Is an experienced user likely to ever use the Variations command?

It can be a good way to get an image closer to the desired final result. You could then use any of the Adjust commands for fine-tuning. It's also a quick check for loss of detail due to clipping. Clipping occurs when the colors go to pure black (in the shadows) or pure white (in the highlights). Just make sure the Clipping box is checked.

If I use Variations as a prelude to tweaking with other Adjust commands, am I likely to lose data?

You could, if you make adjustments that cause clipping. You can give yourself additional headroom by working in 16-bit-per-channel mode — at least until you are ready to save the file.

Should I keep the Show Clipping box checked?

It's a good idea. If the box is checked, you'll see neon color blotches appear in areas where the detail will be lost in highlights or shadows

What if I overadjust?

There are many ways to recover. First, you can click the complementary color thumbnail opposite the one that caused the overadjustment. If you want to return to the state of the original image, press ⌘/Ctrl and Opt/Alt+click the Cancel button when it changes to Reset or click the image box titled Original. Of course, you can also press ⌘/Ctrl+Z to undo the change.

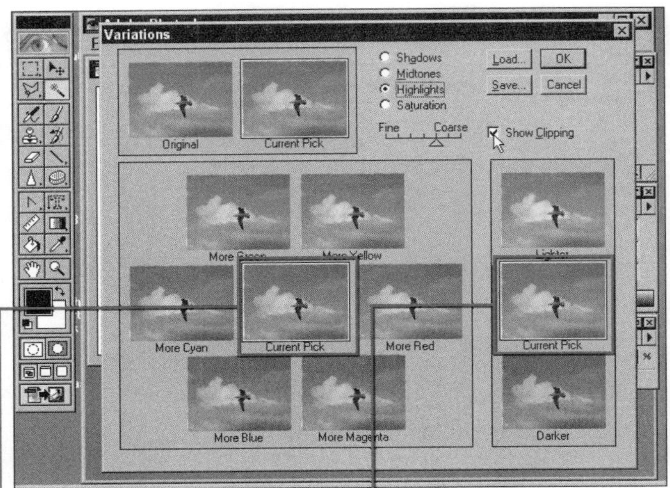

5 Click any color thumbnail to shift color in that direction.

■ The result appears in the Current Pick thumbnail.

6 Click the Lighter or Darker thumbnail to change image brightness.

■ The result appears in the Current Pick thumbnail.

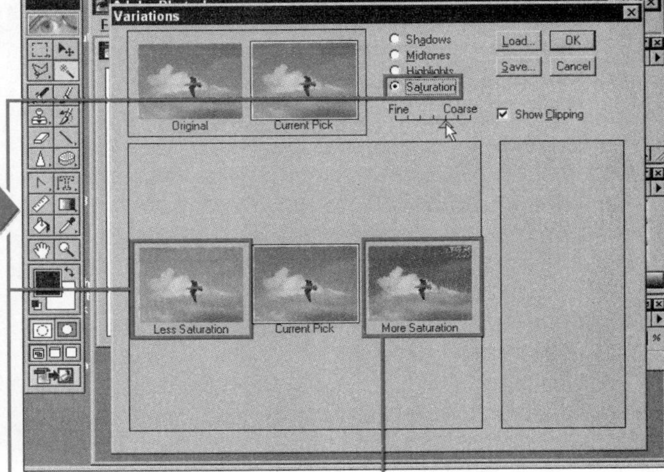

7 To change the hue intensity (color brightness) of an image, click the Saturation radio button.

8 Click Less Saturation to dull colors.

9 Click More Saturation to brighten colors.

Note: You can click the OK button any time you are satisfied with the appearance of the Current Pick thumbnail.

CREATE A TONAL EFFECT WITH EQUALIZE

Choosing Image ➪ Adjust ➪ Equalize causes all the tonal values in an image to be evenly distributed in a single step. You may be thinking why on earth would someone want to use this command? Usually, it's because an image (from a camera or scanner) has been acquired that's messed up to the extent that all its values are compressed. In other words, the picture has too much contrast or is flat as a pancake. Fortunately for us, most digital capture devices produce files that have more color depth than is apparent on screen.

Another way to use Equalize is to make a selection first. You can then choose whether to equalize only within the selected area or to equalize the entire image according to the tonal range contained within the selection.

Once you've used the Equalize command, you may very well want to use the Levels, Curves, or other Adjust commands to further refine or interpret the values in the image.

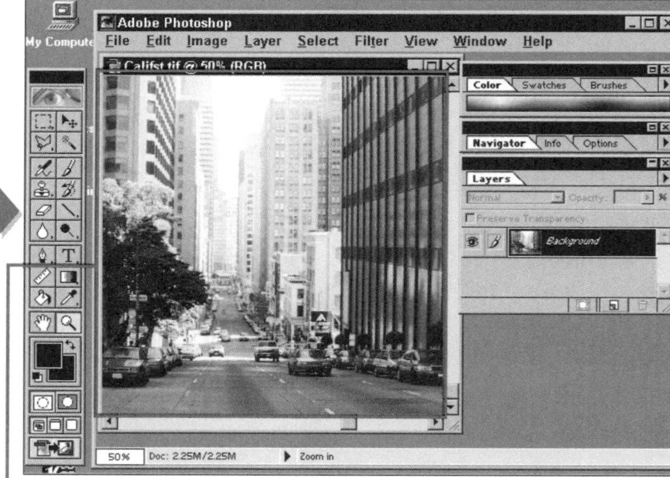

1 Choose Image ➪ Adjust ➪ Equalize.

■ Photoshop finds the absolute highlight (white point) and absolute shadow (black point) in the image's data and evenly distributes all data in between according to brightness value.

■ Notice the highlight and shadow detail that wasn't there before in this digital camera image.

TIPS

Is the "Equalize entire image based on selected area" option a good way to increase shadow detail in a specific area of the image?

It can be a good starting point. Usually, however, you'll get too much shadow detail for the image to seem realistic. Use the Levels or Curves commands after applying the Equalize command (but while the selection is still active) to darken the selection.

Can I use the "Equalize entire image based on selected area" option to highlight and separate an object from its surroundings?

You are so smart! That's one of the most useful things you can do with this command.

Are there other commands commonly used before or after the Equalize command to create special effects?

Of course. The capability to combine commands and filters in Photoshop makes it possible for you to create an endless variety of special effects. Here's one I like: Copy the image to a new layer and equalize the whole image to a shadow area. Edges will become more defined. Run a Stylize filter such as Find Edges. Now try combining the new layer with the old layer (see Chapter 10).

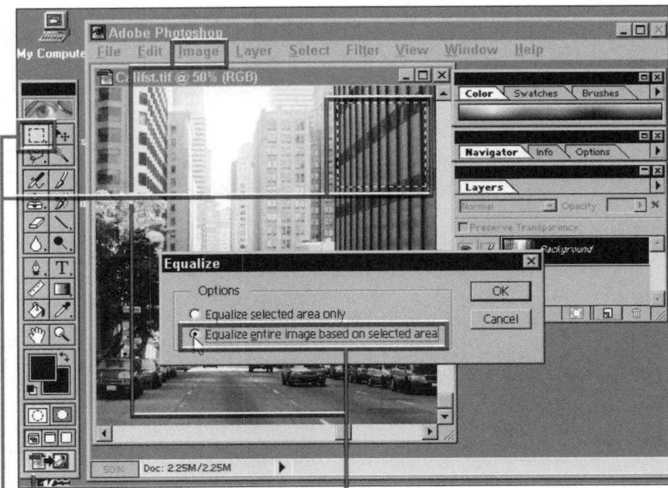

2 To equalize the entire layer according to the contents of the selection, choose any of the selection tools.

3 Make a selection.

4 Choose Image ➪ Adjust ➪ Equalize.

5 Select the option "Equalize entire image based on selected area."

6 To equalize only the area within the selection, choose Image ➪ Adjust ➪ Equalize.

7 Select the option "Equalize selected area only."

Note: Experiment with using this method when the selection has been made with the Magic Wand or Lasso tool.

SWITCH COLOR PALETTES

The use of Color palettes applies only to indexed color images. This means you won't be able to access these commands unless you first convert your image to indexed color. At that point, you will be able to influence which palette is used in two ways: 1) You can specify which palette and dithering method to use when initially. 2) You can subsequently switch to another palette through the use of the Image ➪ Mode ➪ Color Table command.

There are two main uses for the Image ➪ Mode ➪ Color Table command: 1) To view the colors assigned to each palette position (index). 2) To change the colors assigned to the current color table (often called a Color palette).

The Color Table dialog box enables you to load any saved palette file for use with the current image. This is useful for creating a new image from scratch that uses only colors assigned to a specific palette, such as the Web palette or the System palette of an operating system. It is also useful for previewing images that will be incorporated into a multimedia production that limits all images to a single palette — as is often the case with such programs as Macromedia Director.

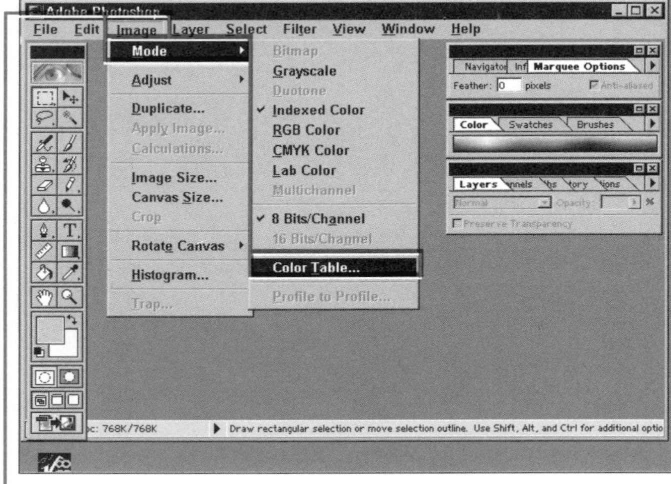

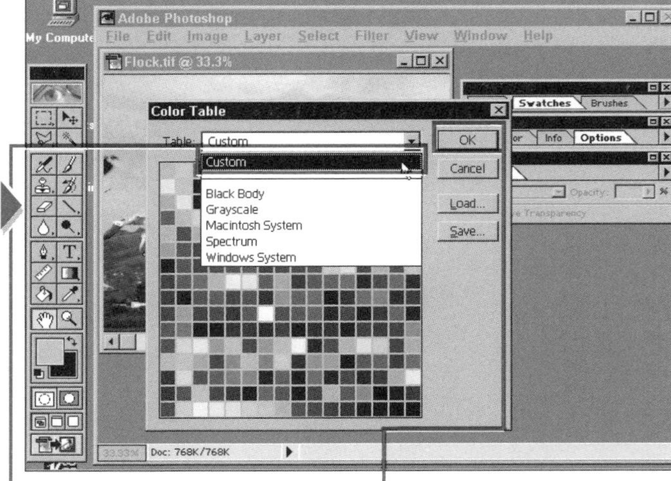

1 Choose Image ➪ Mode ➪ Color Table.

Note: This command will not be available unless you are already in Color Table mode.

■ The Color Table dialog box appears.

2 Optional: Choose from one of Photoshop's preset palettes in the Table pull-down menu.

3 Optional: Click OK if you have found the exact palette you want to use.

TIPS

Can I access the color table at the same time I convert to indexed color?

Yes. Choose Image ➪ Mode ➪ Indexed Color. The Indexed Color dialog box appears. From the Palette pull-down menu, choose Custom. The Color Table dialog box appears. From here you can take any of the steps shown in this exercise.

How can I load the color table used by another image?

Open the file containing the color table you want to borrow. Choose Image ➪ Mode ➪ Color Table. When the image's color table appears, click the Save button and name the file. In Windows, the required .ACT extension is automatically added by Photoshop. On Mac, the letters CLUT (for Color Lookup Table) appear in the icon.

Do I need to access the Eyedropper before picking colors from the image?

No. The cursor automatically changes to an Eyedropper icon whenever the Color Picker dialog box is visible and the cursor is simultaneously over the current image.

Can I use the color table to create special effects?

Yes. The easiest and most effective trick is to convert the image to grayscale and then back to indexed color. The color table will then consist entirely of shades of gray. Now, substitute the same color for a whole range of grays. You'll end up with a bizarre pop-art effect.

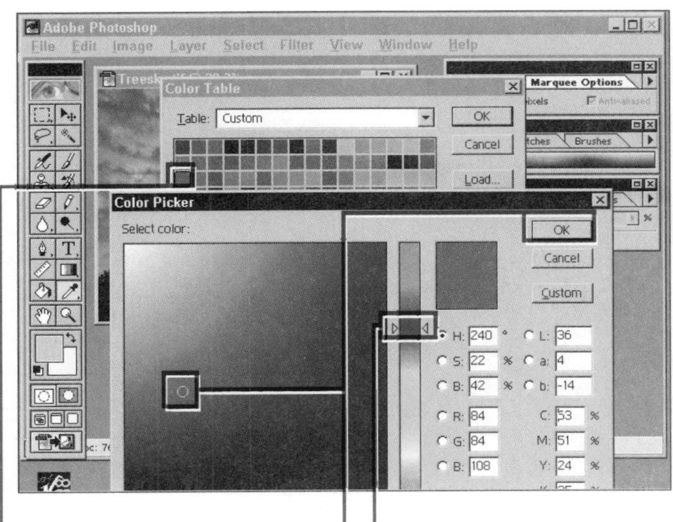

4 Optional: To change an individual color in the color table, click the color you want to change.

■ The standard Color Picker dialog box appears.

5 Drag the spectrum slider to indicate the base color.

6 Click in the Select Color box to indicate brightness and saturation.

7 Click OK.

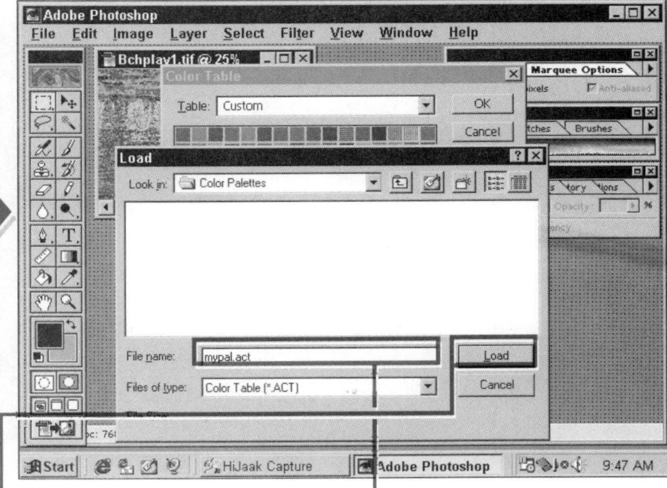

8 To load a specific, presaved palette (such as one required by Director or one you have previously customized), click the Load button.

9 Click the name of the file you want to load, which then appears in the File Name field.

10 Click the Load button.

CORRECT TONAL VALUES WITH THE LEVELS COMMAND

The Levels command enables you to make layer-wide changes (or image-wide changes, if used on an adjustment layer) in the intensity of shadows, midtones, and highlights by dragging the corresponding slider. You can also make more precise changes by entering exact numbers in the corresponding Input Levels fields.

The Levels dialog box can also be used to control overall image contrast by dragging the Shadow and Highlight sliders to specify output and input levels. The Shadow slider controls the maximum density; the Highlight slider controls maximum brightness. Here, too, you can enter exact figures instead of using the slider.

Activating the Preview check box enables you to see the effect on the image of any changes you make in the output. Finally, Highlight, Midtone, and Shadow Eyedroppers let you set levels visually. Do this by selecting the Shadow Eyedropper, and then clicking its tip on the darkest part of the image. Select the Highlight Eyedropper, and then click its tip on the part of the image you want to be absolute white. Use the Midtone Eyedropper to indicate the pixel that should be fifty percent gray.

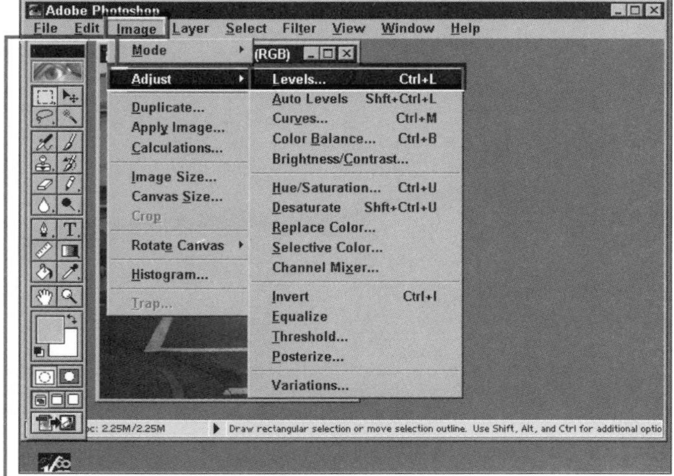

1 Choose Image ➪ Adjust ➪ Levels (or press ⌘/Ctrl+L).

■ The Levels dialog box appears.

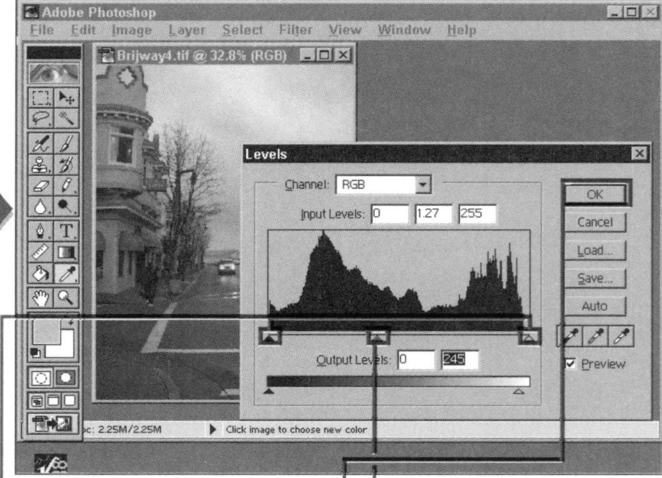

2 Drag the Highlight slider to the point where brightness should be maximum.

3 Drag the Shadow slider to the point below which everything should turn to black.

4 Drag the Midtone slider to adjust the brightness of midtones.

5 If you are satisfied with the results, click OK. If you want to adjust contrast, go to the next figure.

TIPS

I have a hard time using the Eyedroppers accurately. What am I doing wrong?

Zoom in on the image (about 200 percent) and use the Navigation palette to help you move to the exact pixels you want to pick for the darkest, median, and brightest points.

Is it true I can do color balancing with the Levels dialog box?

Yes, to some extent. The Highlight Eyedropper "white balances" any pixel you click on. If that pixel really should have been white, you will get a fairly accurate overall color balance. Of course, if you pick a point that wasn't originally white, you may throw the color balance way off.

Is there any way to apply the same settings to a whole series of images?

Yes. Make the adjustments to a typical image until you're satisfied with the result. Next, click the Save button. When the Save dialog box appears, follow normal file-saving procedures. Open the next image in the series and load the saved Level settings. The settings thus retrieved will automatically apply to the image. Just be warned that if you apply the same settings to a whole group of images, you're likely to get undesirable results unless all of the images were shot at the same time and place and with the same lighting.

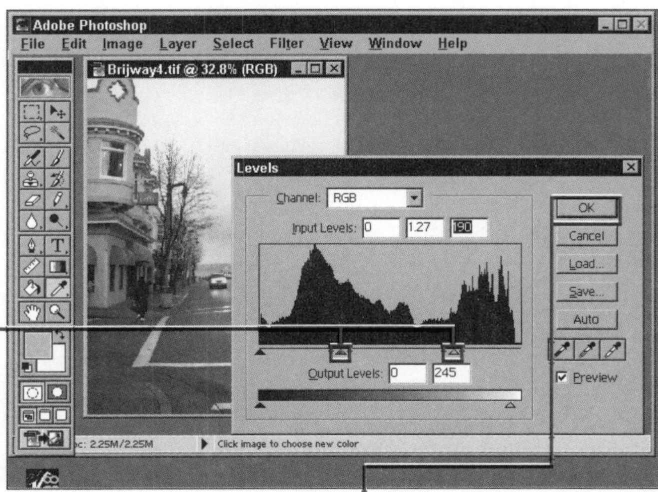

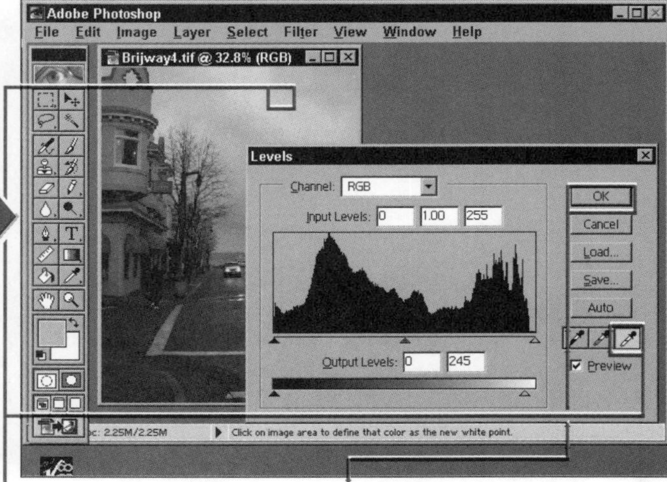

CHANGE THE CONTRAST OF THE IMAGE

6 Drag the Highlight slider to lower the white point.

7 Drag the Shadow slider to raise the black point.

8 Click OK when satisfied with the result.

Note: It is a good idea to save the image before making tonal adjustments. This way you can return to the original state by choosing File ⇨ Revert.

9 To adjust highlights, click the Highlight Eyedropper.

10 Click a white point in the image.

11 Repeat to pick the midtone point.

12 Repeat to pick the black point.

13 When satisfied, click OK.

CORRECT TONAL VALUES WITH THE CURVES COMMAND

The Curves command presents many more options for controlling tonal values, in more precise fashion, than any of the other image adjustment controls. You can control tonal values for any point on the curve of any color in the current color model. In other words, you can use the Curves command for color correction of specific areas as well as brightness and contrast correction. The Curves command affects either the current layer or, if used in an adjustment layer, all layers below.

As with the Levels command, you can try automatically adjusting tonal values and color balance by simply clicking the Auto button. You can immediately preview the results of this or any other curves adjustment by checking the Preview box. If you don't like what you see, press Opt/Alt to change the Cancel button to Reset.

Because the Curves command is so appropriate for correcting specific tonal ranges, it helps to know exactly where the tonal ranges occur on the curve. If you place the pointer on the image and click, a circle appears on the portion of the curve that would affect that tone in the image. Drag the circle to establish that point.

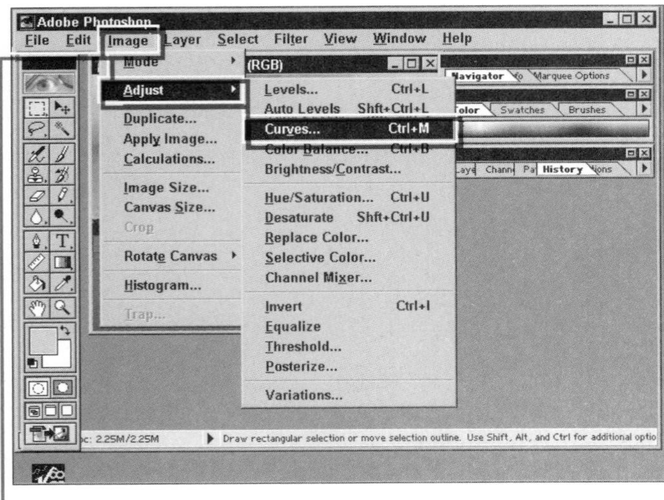

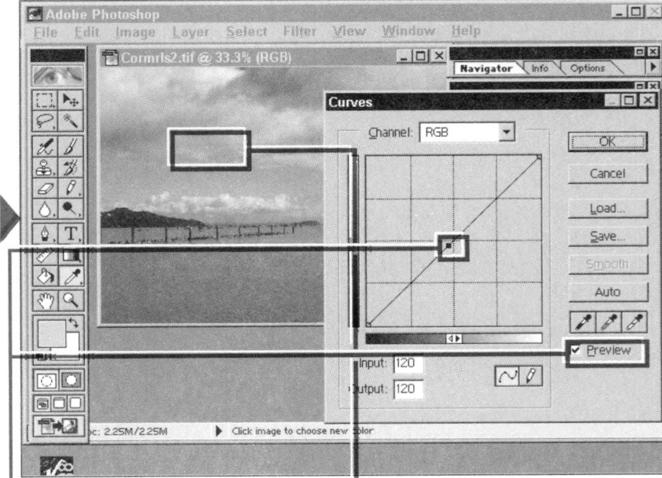

1 Choose Image ⇨ Adjust ⇨ Curves.

■ The Curves dialog box appears.

2 Click to check the Preview box.

3 If you want to maintain a current value, click to place an anchor point at the appropriate point on the curve.

■ A solid dot appears to indicate the anchor point.

4 Place the cursor over an area in the image where you want to change values and click and hold.

TIPS

Are there other possibilities for using the Curves dialog box?

Yes. The Curves dialog box is often used to change color balance in a specific portion of the spectrum and to create special effects.

Can I apply the same curves to a series of images?

Use the Save and Load buttons. Set the curves for a typical image, and then save the file by clicking the Save button and following normal procedures for saving a file. Open the other images to which you want to apply that curve and click the Load button. Follow normal file-loading procedures, and the chosen curve will automatically be applied to the current image.

What is the quickest and most direct route to adjusting for acceptable image quality?

The Shadow and Highlight Eyedropper method is the most direct. See the fourth figure in this layout for the proper procedure.

If I use the Eyedropper or Auto methods, can I still make adjustments to specific parts of the range?

Yes. And, in practice, you'll often want to lighten or darken the midtones by dragging the middle (or near middle) of the curve. This is usually a better idea than using the Midtone Eyedropper, because the Eyedropper will change the color balance to 50 percent gray at that point — which may shift the entire color balance of the image.

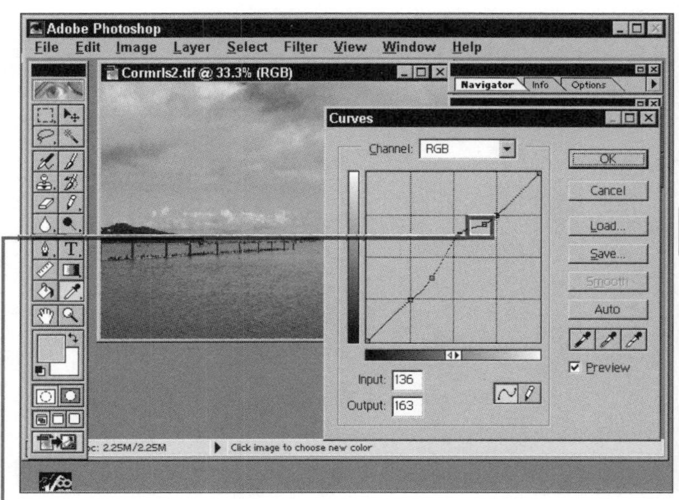

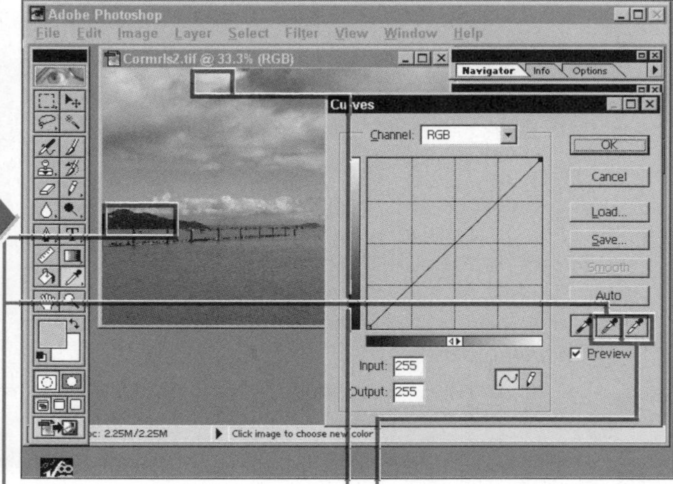

Note: The hollow circle that appeared to indicate the tonal value disappears when you release the mouse button. Note its position.

5 Click to place an anchor point at the approximate location of the circle.

6 Drag the point you placed in Step 5 up to lighten, down to darken.

Note: To delete an anchor point you no longer need, select the point and press Delete or simply drag the point off the edge of the window.

7 Select the Shadow Eyedropper.

8 Click in the area of the image you want to be 100 percent black.

9 Select the Highlight Eyedropper.

10 Click in the area you want to represent absolute white.

■ The tonal range between highlight and shadow is automatically adjusted.

CORRECT SOME COLOR VALUES WITH THE CURVES COMMAND

In addition to providing a way to modify tonal value in a particular area for all colors simultaneously, the Curves command lets you modify the same characteristics for each color channel. This method is especially useful when you want to exaggerate color in a particular part of the spectrum for a mood effect. Also, many make this their primary method for color correction (rather than relying on the Color Balance command). For that matter, it's worth experimenting with other possibilities for special effects.

If your goal is correction of the overall color balance of the image, using the Curves command isn't the easiest method to do so. You may want to try Image ➪ Adjust ➪ Variations or Image ➪ Adjust ➪ Color Balance. You may also be able to achieve certain effects with the Image ➪ Adjust ➪ Hue/Saturation command.

All the adjustments made here can be made on an adjustment layer or on only the active layer within the current selection.

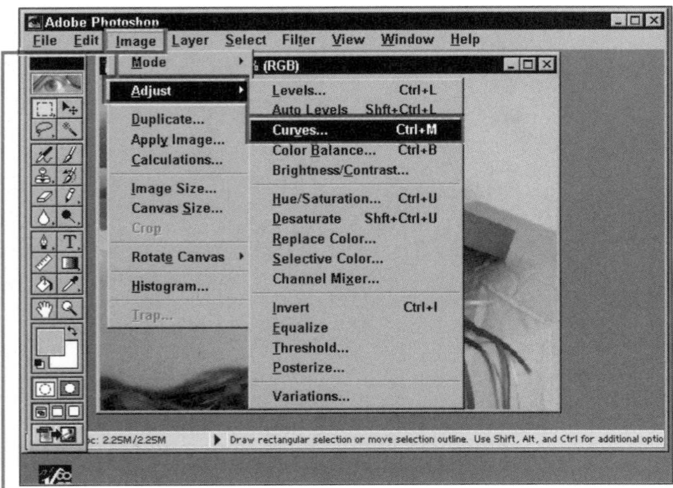

1 Choose Image ➪ Adjust ➪ Curves.

■ The Curves dialog box appears.

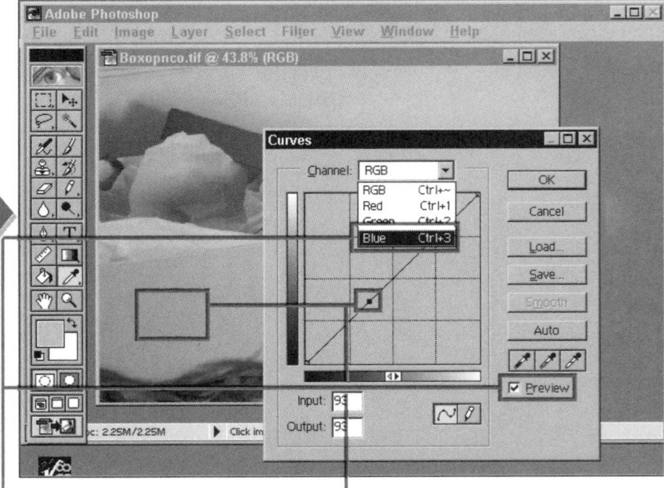

2 Check the Preview box so that you can see your results the instant you make an adjustment.

3 Choose the Color channel you want to modify.

4 Click and hold in the area of the image in which you want to modify color balance.

5 Click to place an anchor point where the circle was.

TIPS

What if I want to make exactly the same degree and area of correction to multiple (but not all) color channels?

Press Shift and choose the channels you want to simultaneously modify. You have to do this in the Channels palette first while keeping an eye on RGB values so you can see what you're doing when you go to the Curves dialog box to make the change to more than one channel.

Why don't I get a single color preview when I choose a single color channel?

Every change you make in a single color channel affects the overall color balance, so you get a much more accurate idea of the effect of your changes.

What if I want to change the overall color balance of the image?

You can do it with the Curves command, but unless you want to emphasize some part of the spectrum in a limited number of color channels, the other methods (Levels, Color Balance, Variations) will save you time and confusion.

Note: To make a smooth adjustment where the curve peaks in the chosen area, drag the control point up to brighten, down to darken, and click OK.

6 Place two anchor points on either side of the last anchor point.

■ These hold the rest of the curve more in line while you move the center point.

7 Use this method to make adjustments in other color channels until you re satisfied.

8 Click OK.

Note: You can also use the arbitrary method for making a color correction.

9 Click to select the Pencil tool.

10 Draw a line parallel to the diagonal line to indicate the brightness range you want modified.

11 Click the Smooth button.

Note: Variations of this method are used to create special effects.

CREATE SPECIAL EFFECTS COLOR CHANGES WITH CURVES

In a sense, using the Curves dialog box to alter part of the color spectrum is a special effect. For instance, by adding a little pink to the sky, you could change the time of day to sunset. In this case, the special effects I'm referring to are far less subtle and much more freeform.

You can use the control-point method to create special effects, but these will always display smooth transitions. Most find it easier and faster to use the Freehand or Pencil tool to draw the curve. Adobe calls this the *arbitrary* method.

By now, you should know how to invoke the Image ➪ Adjust ➪ Curves command, so the following figures take you straight to the dialog box. The result of certain attempts at special effects is highly experimental. Remember to press Opt/Alt and click Reset whenever you want to start over. If you come up with an effect that might work on several images, remember that you can save the curve and load it from any image.

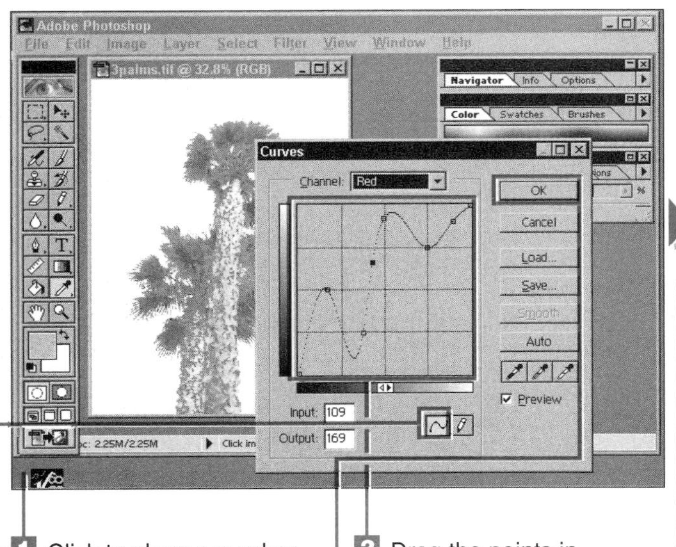

1 Click to place a number of points along the diagonal line.

Note: Where you place the points, and how many, is arbitrary. To subtract a point, select it and press Delete.

2 Drag the points in alternating directions. The wider the curves, the more pronounced the effect.

3 When you re satisfied with the result, click OK.

■ This shows the result of the curve using the points method on an otherwise well-balanced landscape photo.

TIPS

Is there any way to *white balance* (remove any tint caused by the color of ambient light) all the photos shot in a particular time and location?

Get a Kodak 50 percent gray card from your local photo store and set it near your subject in one of the photos. Make sure it's not shaded. Shoot one photo, take the card away, and finish the shoot. Bring the test image into Photoshop and use Curves or Levels to correct exposure (if necessary). Next choose the Neutral (Gray) Eyedropper and click the gray card. The image will now be white balanced. Click the Save button and save the settings. Bring the other photos into Photoshop by the same methods and settings. Open the Curves dialog box, click the Load button, retrieve the original settings file, and then click OK to preserve the result.

Is there any way to make the grid smaller so it is easier to judge the exact distance between points?

Press Opt/Alt and click on the grid. Each time you do this, the grid switches between the default 4×4 grid and a 10×10 grid.

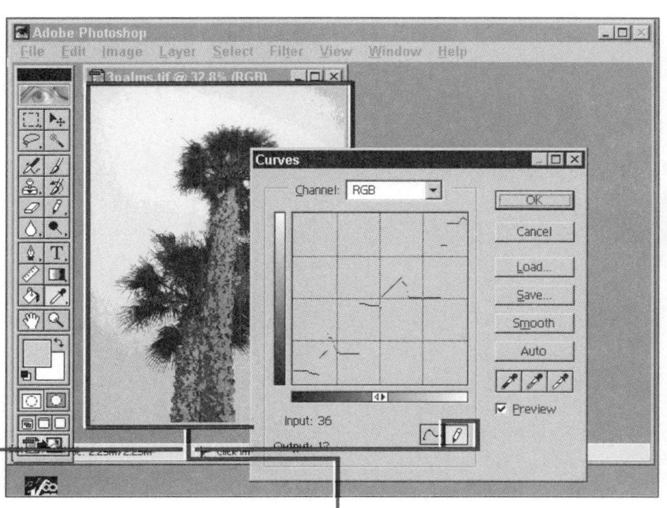

4 Click to select the Arbitrary (Pencil) Curves tool.

Note: Experiment with drawing lines in random directions at various angles and lengths.

■ If the Preview box is checked, you will see the results in the image window.

■ This time, the result is more posterized, with hard edges.

Note: If you click the Smooth button, the hard edges disappear, and you'll get a much different effect. The more times you click the Smooth button, the less pronounced the effect will be.

5

CORRECTING MISTAKES

This chapter deals with the tools, commands, and techniques in Photoshop that are used to correct mistakes in an image.

The tools you use for retouching are, aside from the Clone tool, the same tools you would use to create an original image from scratch. The Photoshop tools used primarily for retouching include the brushes (Paintbrush, Airbrush, and Pencil); the Rubber Stamp (also called the Clone tool); and the Smudge and Blur tools.

Paintbrush

The Paintbrush has an associated Options palette, shown here.

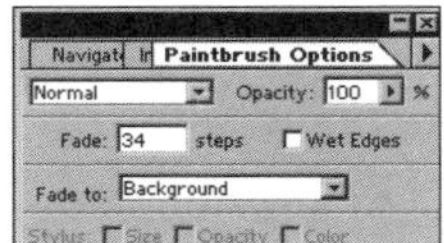

Paintbrush Tool Modifiers

Icon	Shortcut	Modifier: Result
	B	Shift: Produces straight line at any 15-degree angle from the origin of the stroke ⌘/Ctrl: Switches to the Move tool Opt/Alt: Switches to the Eyedropper tool

Paintbrush Options

Component	Function
Apply Mode pull-down menu	Causes the foreground color to be applied according to the method assigned to that Apply (Blend) mode.
Opacity field and slider	Changes the transparency of the brush stroke according to the percentage entered in the field. You may enter this information numerically or by dragging a slider that pops up when you click the button.
Fade steps field	Causes the brush to fade over a specific number of steps, each step being equal to the width of the current brush. The brush stroke will graduate evenly from its foreground color to the fade-out color specified by the Fade to pull-down menu choice.
Wet Edges check box	If checked, causes the edges of the stroke to blend with surrounding pixels in a manner reminiscent of watercolors.
Fade to pull-down menu	Choice determines whether the stroke will fade to the background color or to 100 percent transparency.

Component	Function
Stylus Size check box	If checked, pressure-sensitive stylus increases the size of the brush (up to the maximum size of the current brush) as pressure is applied.
Stylus Opacity check box	If checked, stroke becomes less transparent as pressure is applied.
Stylus Color check box	If checked, stroke fades to background color as pressure is applied.

Airbrush

The Airbrush has an associated Options palette, which is almost identical to the brush options, shown in this figure.

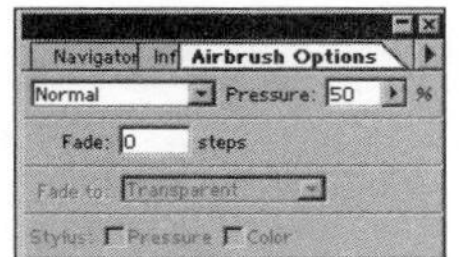

Airbrush Tool Modifiers

Icon	Shortcut	Modifier: Result
	J	Shift: Produces straight line at any 15-degree angle from the origin of the stroke ⌘ /Ctrl: Switches to the Move tool Opt/Alt: Switches to the Eyedropper tool

Airbrush Options

Component	Function
Pressure field and slider	Has exactly the same function as the Opacity field for the Paintbrush

Pencil

The Pencil distinguishes itself from the other brush tools in two respects: 1) Its strokes are always hard-edged, regardless of the brush chosen. 2) It can be set to automatically erase. The Pencil has an associated Options palette, as shown in this figure. The only Pencil option that differs from the Paintbrush options is the Auto Erase check box.

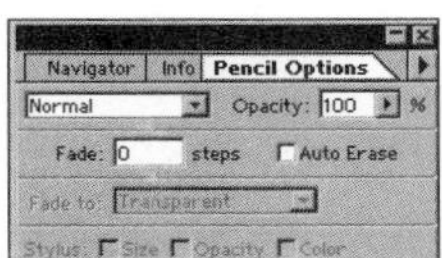

CONTINUED

CORRECTING MISTAKES CONTINUED

Pencil Tool Modifiers

Icon	Shortcut	Modifier: Result
	N	Shift: Produces straight line at any 90-degree angle from the origin of the stroke ⌘/Ctrl: Switches to the Move tool Opt/Alt: Switches to the Eyedropper tool

Pencil Options

Component	Function
Auto Erase check box	Makes it possible to paint the background color over any areas that already have been sketched with the foreground color

Rubber Stamp (Clone) Tool

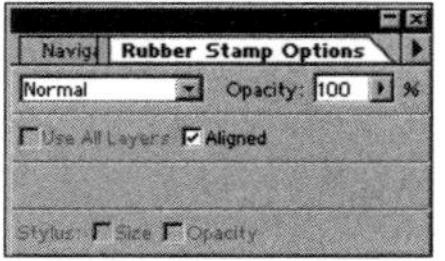

The Rubber Stamp (Clone) tool uses the currently chosen brush to paint a copy of the image it finds in a specific location of the image at a specified place. This specified place may be either a specific brush-sized area that is painted no matter where you lay the brush down (if the aligned box is checked in the Options dialog box), or a specific distance and angle from the brush that is always maintained, no matter where you start the stroke. The Rubber Stamp tool has an associated Options palette that is shown here.

Rubber Stamp Tool Modifiers

Icon	Shortcut	Modifier: Result
	S	Shift: Produces straight line at any 15-degree angle from the origin of the stroke ⌘/Ctrl: Switches to the Move tool Opt/Alt: Places the pickup point for cloning

Rubber Stamp Options

Component	Function
Apply Mode pull-down menu	Causes the foreground color to be applied according to the method assigned to that Apply (Blend) mode. See the Color Section for a visual description of what each Apply mode does.
Opacity field and slider	Changes the transparency of the brush stroke according to the percentage entered in the field. You may enter this information numerically or by dragging a slider that pops up when you click the button.
Stylus Size check box	If checked, pressure-sensitive stylus increases the size of the brush (up to the maximum size of the current brush) as pressure is applied.
Stylus Opacity check box	If checked, means stroke becomes less transparent as pressure is applied.

Blur Tool

The Blur tool has an associated Options palette, as illustrated in the following figure. Note: The letter-key shortcut for the Blur, Sharpen, and Smudge tool is *R*. Repeated pressing of this key cycles through the three tools.

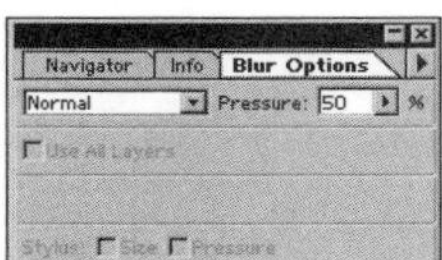

Blur Tool Modifiers

Icon	Shortcut	Modifier: Result
	R	Shift: Produces straight line at any 15-degree angle from the origin of the stroke ⌘/Ctrl: Switches to the Move tool Opt/Alt: Switches to the Layer Picker (double-headed arrow tool

CONTINUED

CORRECTING MISTAKES CONTINUED

Blur Tool Options

Component	Function
Apply Mode pull-down menu	Causes the foreground color to be applied according to the method assigned to that Apply (Blend) mode. See the Color Section for a visual description of what each Apply mode does. Apply modes for this tool are limited to Normal, Darken, Lighten, Hue, Saturation, Color, and Luminosity.
Pressure field and slider	Changes the transparency of the brush stroke according to the percentage entered in the field. You may enter this information numerically or by dragging a slider that pops up when you click the button.
Use All Layers check box	If checked, causes the blur stroke to affect all underlying layers.
Stylus Size check box	If checked, pressure-sensitive stylus increases the size of the brush (up to the maximum size of the current brush) as pressure is applied.
Stylus Pressure check box	If checked, stroke becomes less transparent as pressure is applied.

Smudge Tool

The Smudge tool has an associated Options palette, as shown in this figure. Note: The letter-key shortcut for the Blur, Sharpen, and Smudge tool is *R*. Repeated pressing of this key cycles through the three tools.

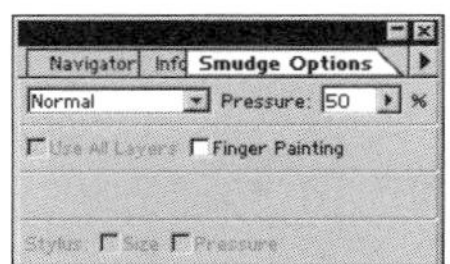

Smudge Tool Modifiers

Icon	Shortcut	Modifiers and result
	R	Shift: Produces straight line at any 15-degree angle from the origin of the stroke ⌘/Ctrl: Switches to the Move tool Opt/Alt: Switches to the Eyedropper tool

Smudge Tool Options

Component	Function
Apply Mode pull-down menu	Causes the foreground color to be applied according to the method assigned to that Apply (Blend) mode. See the Color Section for a visual description of what each Apply mode does.
Pressure field and slider	Changes the transparency of the brush stroke according to the percentage entered in the field. You may enter this information numerically or by dragging a slider that pops up when you click the button.
Use All Layers check box	If checked, causes the blur stroke to affect all underlying layers.
Finger Painting check box	If checked, causes the tool to smudge using the foreground color, rather than whatever color happens to be immediately under the pointer.
Stylus Size check box	If checked, pressure-sensitive stylus increases the size of the brush (up to the maximum size of the current brush) as pressure is applied.
Stylus Pressure check box	If checked, stroke becomes less transparent as pressure is applied.

USE THE EYEDROPPER TO PICK UP COLOR

You can access the Eyedropper tool in one of three ways: Press I, click the Eyedropper tool icon in the toolbox, or (when using the Airbrush, Paintbrush, Pencil, Paint Bucket, or Gradient tool) press Opt/Alt to make an Eyedropper cursor appear in place of the standard cursor.

The Eyedropper enables you to pick up the foreground color from any pixel or group of pixels in the current (active) layer. That makes it easy to match surrounding colors when "painting out" blemishes in the image.

Using the Eyedropper is easy enough, but remember that there are options for this tool. (The behavior of the Eyedropper, no matter how it's ultimately accessed, is determined in the Eyedropper Options palette.) The options let you decide whether you want to stick with the default single-pixel sample or whether to average the foreground color via a 3×3 or 5×5 matrix of pixels. (Hint: To pick up background color, press X to swap the background color for the foreground color, pick up, and then press X again. Or press Opt/Alt and click with the Eyedropper to select the background color directly.)

1 Click the Eyedropper.

2 Choose Window ➪ Show Options.

3 Or, click the Options tab (or double-click the Eyedropper) to open the Options palette.

4 Choose the sampling method from the Sample Size pull-down menu.

Note: If pickup colors don't seem to quite match, check to see if sampling is set at Point Sample.

5 While working with Airbrush, Paintbrush, Pencil, Bucket Fill, or Gradient tool, press Opt/Alt.

■ The cursor changes to the Eyedropper.

6 Click the color to be picked up.

■ Color is shown in Foreground Color box

USE OFFSET CLONING

The problem with trying to retouch an image by matching colors is that often the area you want to retouch is heavily detailed and subtly shaded.

In the image of the flower used in this example, the Rubber Stamp tool (also known as the Clone tool) is used to create another flower, using colors and textures from the rest of the image. This is called *offset cloning*.

You may find it desirable (especially if you're using a mouse) to change brush sizes frequently. The square bracket keys cycle up ( ]) and down ([ ) the brushes in the palette.

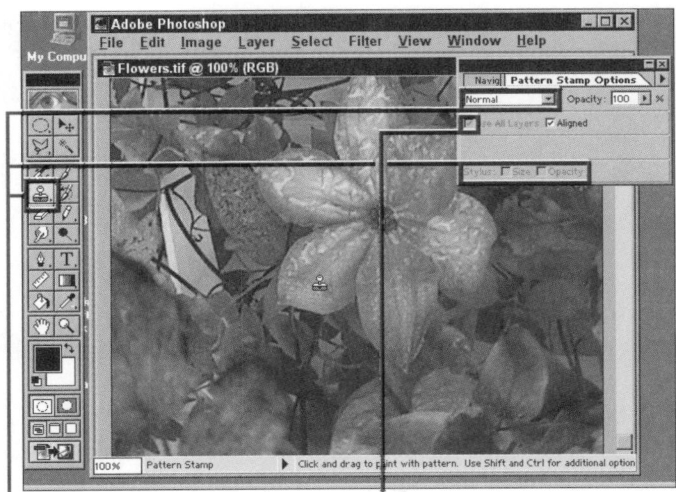

1 Double-click the Rubber Stamp tool.

2 Select Normal from the Mode pull-down menu.

3 Click Size, Opacity, or both to dictate behavior of pressure-sensitive pen.

4 Optional: Click to clone from all layers.(You can now clone from the image as if it were flat without flattening it!)

5 Press Opt/Alt and click the pixel you wish to start your clone stroke from.

6 Paint in the area you wish to clone from.

Note: When you release and start cloning again, the pickup point moves relative to the source point if you have the option set on Aligned. It's a good idea to blend the retouched area by cloning repeatedly from different pickup points.

USE ALIGNED CLONING

There may be times when you want to replace a whole section of the image with another section of the image. This technique is often used for such things as placing an extra car in an otherwise empty parking space or for duplicating a window to fill the space in what would have otherwise been a blank wall.

You could use cut and paste to place those objects. Often, however, it's easier to blend the objects with their old surroundings by painting them in. You can do this easily with *aligned cloning*. Click the Aligned check box to institute (checked) or turn off (unchecked) aligned cloning.

When Aligned is checked, you will be able to reproduce an entire area of the image in another area of the image.

Note: The Rubber Stamp Options pull-down menu found in Photoshop 4 no longer exists. There is no Impressionist or Pattern mode. The Reversion mode has been replaced by the History Brush.

1 Double-click the Rubber Stamp tool.

■ The Rubber Stamp tool Options palette appears and the Rubber Stamp tool is active. Change any settings that seem appropriate.

2 Click the Aligned check box if unchecked.

3 Optional: Click to clone from all layers.

4 Press Opt/Alt and click in the center of the area you wish to clone from.

■ The Rubber Stamp tool displays a white arrow until Opt/Alt is released.

5 Paint in the area in which you wish to clone part of the image.

Note: When you release and start cloning again, the pickup point moves. Blend the retouched area by cloning repeatedly from different pickup points.

AUTOMATIC SPOTTING WITH THE DUST & SCRATCHES FILTER

Some scanned images may be marred by tiny dust and scratches. Removing these scratches with brushes is time-consuming. Fortunately, Photoshop provides a nearly instant fix for most of these imperfections: Choose Filter ➪ Noise ➪ Dust & Scratches.

The Dust & Scratches dialog box sports a pair of sliders called Radius and Threshold. *Radius* refers to the width of the largest blemish. As a rule, don't try to remove lines and blobs more than a few pixels across or you will see blurring in the overall image. *Threshold* is a reference to the contrast between the blemish and its surrounding pixels. (The higher the number, the higher the contrast has to be before the filter will have an effect.) The hardest blemishes to resolve tend to be those in light areas of the picture.

The best use of the Dust & Scratches filter usually involves compromise: Get rid of all the blemishes, and you may start losing file detail. Get rid of most of them, and the time you spend retouching by hand is greatly reduced. Finally, you can always run the filter again within selected areas.

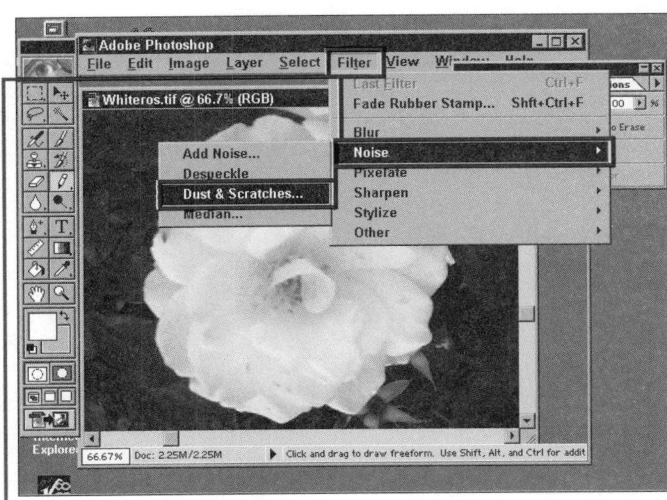

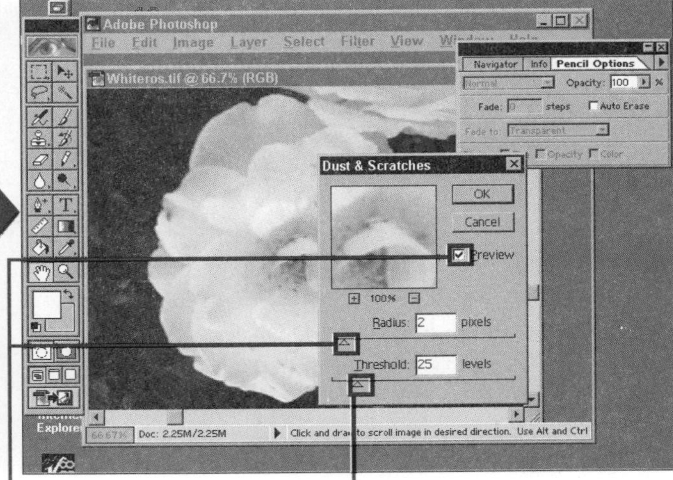

1 Choose Filter ➪ Noise ➪ Dust & Scratches.

■ The Dust & Scratches dialog box is displayed.

2 Click to check the Preview box.

3 Drag the Radius slider until most of the dust and/or scratches disappear.

Note: If you set Radius too high, the image will start to lose sharpness.

4 Drag the Threshold slider until the least contrasting scratches disappear.

AUTOMATIC SPOTTING WITH THE GAUSSIAN BLUR FILTER

Sometimes dust, scratches, and tiny detail take too many forms and shapes to be effectively eliminated with the Dust & Scratches filter. Usually, this will mean retouching by hand.

However, if the garbage is in an even-toned, nontextured area, you may be able to simply blur that area enough to hide the problem. The filter of choice, because it enables you to control the exact amount of blur, is Filter ➪ Blur ➪ Gaussian Blur. This technique works best when photos have been shot against a highly out-of-focus background, seamless paper studio backdrops, or bare sky.

In most cases, you want to employ this technique within a selection. You may want to skip ahead to Chapter 7 to polish your ability to make those selections. Most of the time, however, simply drawing a freehand selection with the Lasso or Polygon Lasso works just fine.

Note: If you blur an area to eliminate small defects or artifacts, you may want to match the grain in the rest of the image by using one of the noise filters.

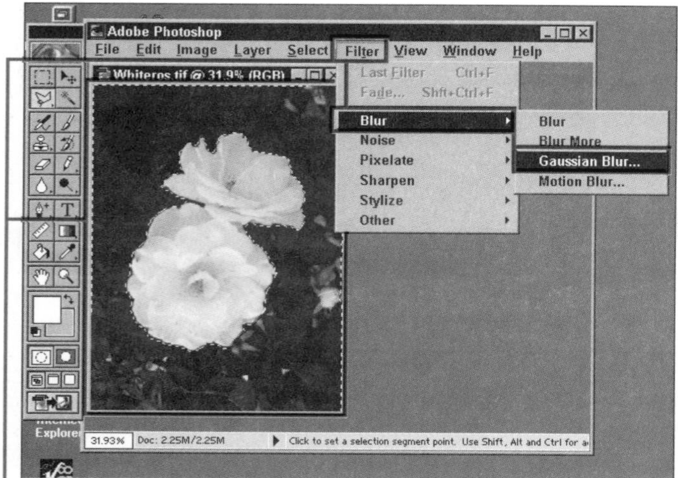

1 Select the area to be blurred.

2 Choose Filter ➪ Blur ➪ Gaussian Blur.

■ The Gaussian Blur dialog box appears.

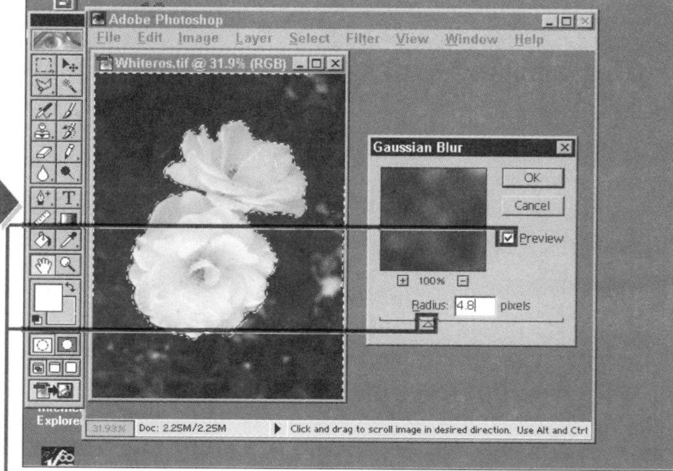

3 Check the Preview box.

4 Drag the Radius slider until the pixels blend together.

Note: Don't feather the edges of the selection. If you see a border when you hide the selection, you blurred too much. Go back in the History palette just prior to using the Gaussian Blur filter and try again, or retouch by hand.

CORRECT BLENDING DEFECTS

Some retouching can be done effectively with the Smudge and Blur tools. These tools are especially appropriate for fixing the jagged edges that occur in some parts of an image when it is enlarged. They also work well for tiny scratches or for small seams in a montage.

The Smudge and Blur tools work especially well when the defect is less than 2 pixels wide. This is because both of these tools work by blending pixels. These tools change the picture of the grain and texture painted by the original pixels, so make sure your brush is no more than 3 pixels wide and follow the defect with care. Also be sure to zoom in very tight (about 200 to 400 percent).

When choosing between the Blur and Smudge tools, keep in mind that each makes pixels appear to blend together. The Blur tool works by lowering the contrast between neighboring pixels. The Smudge tool actually pushes pixels around, so that they exchange places. You can use it to push light pixels into a dark area or vice versa.

When you've finished retouching with either tool, try matching the surrounding grain pattern by using the Add Noise filter (Filter ➪ Noise ➪ Add Noise).

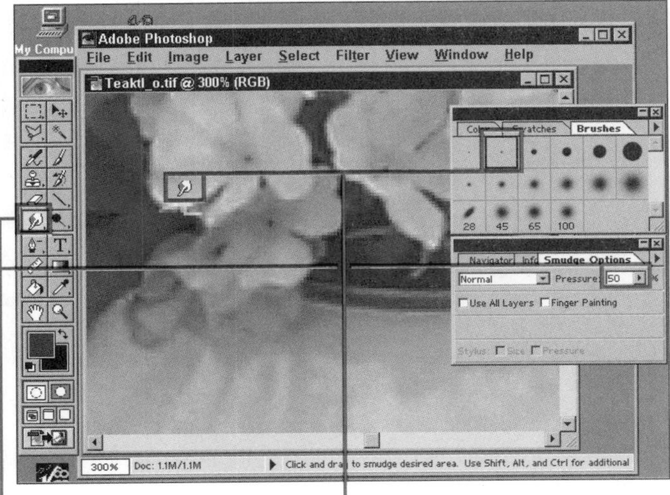

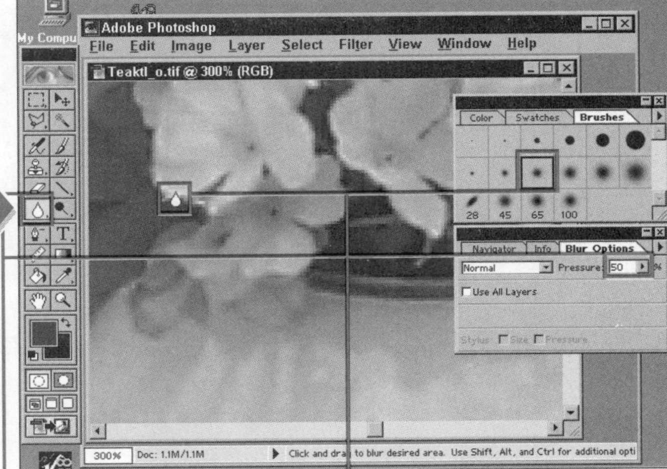

RETOUCHING WITH THE SMUDGE TOOL

1 Double-click the Smudge tool.

2 Set pressure at about 50 percent (the default).

3 Choose Window ➪ Show Brushes.

4 Choose a small, slightly feathered brush.

5 Stroke the edge where you want to blend pixels.

RETOUCHING WITH THE BLUR TOOL

1 Double-click the Blur tool.

2 Click and drag to set pressure at about 50 percent (the default).

3 Choose Window ➪ Show Brushes.

4 Choose a small, slightly feathered brush.

5 Stroke the edge where you want to blend pixels.

HAND-SPOTTING WITH THE BRUSHES

Sometimes retouching has to be done by hand. If your time is precious, this should be a last resort. If you need to eliminate a spare person, a rock, a sunspot, or dust specks on a tweed jacket, hand-spotting is one of the solutions.

Which tool you use will depend mostly on what the problem is. The Pencil is best for making exact pixel matches because there's no soft edge, for example.

The main thing to remember when retouching by hand is to keep it subtle. Pay particular attention to blending the retouching seamlessly with surrounding pixels. If a large area needs to be retouched, you may be better off using a clone of another image or another part of the picture. Zoom in far enough to exaggerate the pixel structure, so you can follow the pattern — but not so close that you can't stay oriented.

The initial figure in the example below has several problems: The door needs to be cropped out. The chair (at lower left) is distracting. There's white paper and garbage on the ground. The retouching technique outlined here makes these problems disappear.

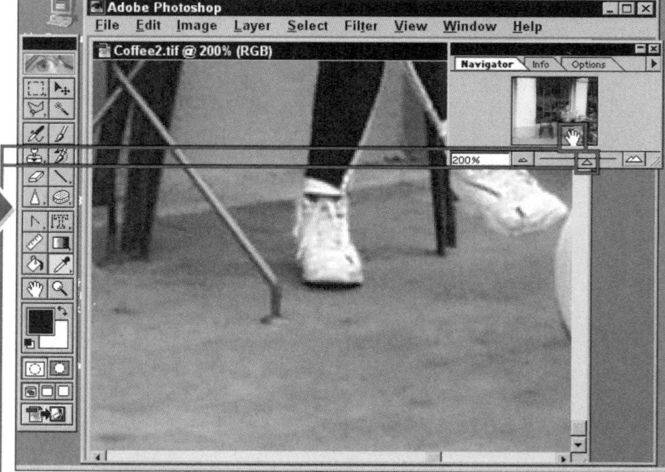

1 Choose the crop tool.

2 Drag the marquee to exclude the door.

3 Drag the marquee handles to adjust the marquee.

4 Double-click inside the marquee to crop.

5 Choose Window ➪ Show Navigator.

6 Drag the slider to Zoom in to 200 percent to see detail.

7 Drag the window to inspect retouched areas.

TIPS

What is the best way to retouch textured areas of a picture, such as a tweed coat?

Use the Clone tool with the Alignment box unchecked. Find an area of the image that contains the texture you want in the right shade and color and clone from there.

What if I can't find an area to clone that's as light or dark as the area I want to retouch?

You can compensate to some degree by judiciously using the Burn and Dodge tools. Keep the exposure slider at a very low setting and do your burning and dodging carefully. If you overdo it, go back a few strokes in the History palette.

What is the best tool for retouching pimples, wrinkles, and other skin blemishes?

It's usually easier and more effective to work with the Clone tool so that you duplicate skin texture in the retouched areas. Be sure to clone from several different spots around the retouched area so that the retouching blends smoothly.

Isn't it really tough to retouch grainy pictures?

You may be able to match the grain with some of the Add Noise filters. Using harder (not really soft) brushes and full opacity will help to preserve grain. Also, see the preceding tip.

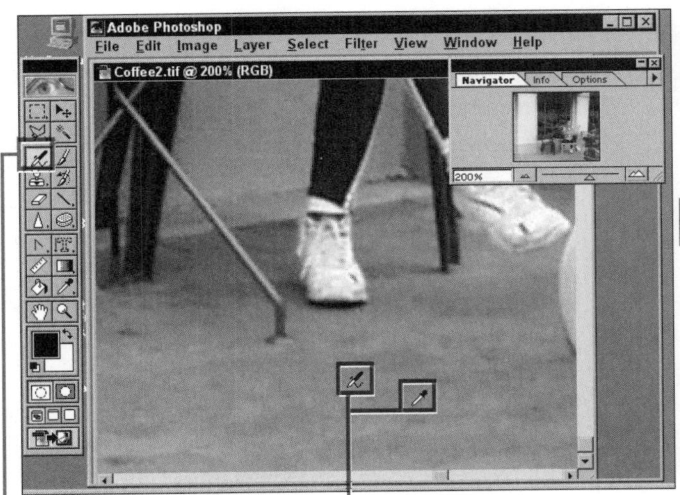

8 Choose the Airbrush, Paintbrush, or Pencil tool.

9 Choose Window ⇨ Show Brushes.

10 Choose a 3-pixel brush from the Brushes palette.

11 Press Opt/Alt and click in area close to spot to pick up color.

12 Paint into spot.

■ The finished retouched image. Can you see a single sign of retouching?

SECTION III

6 MAKING SELECTIONS

The Art of Making Selections 128
Make Polygon Selections 130
Automate Selection with the Magic Wand 131
Automate Selection with the Magnetic Lasso 132
Magnetic Lasso Options and Keyboard Shortcuts 134
Use the Color Range Command 135
Use Quick Mask Mode 136
Make Compound Selections 138
Edit Selections 140
Modify Selections 142
Modify Selections with Grow and Similar 144
Make Wholesale Selection Changes 146
Blend Selections 148
Magical Erasing with the Magic Eraser 150
Erase Backgrounds 152

ISOLATING PARTS OF THE IMAGE

7 WORKING WITH PATHS

Making and Using Paths 154
Draw a Path 158
Draw Complex Paths 160
Draw Freehand Paths 162
Convert Selections to a Path 163
Automate Path Tracing with the Magnetic Pen 164
Edit and Reshape a Path 166
Make and Use a Clipping Path 168
Export and Save Paths 169
Paint a Path 170

8 WORKING WITH MASKS

Making and Using Masks 172
Save and Load Selections 180
Edit Masks 182
Edit Masks with Brushes 184
Edit Masks with Fills 186
Edit Masks with Quick Mask Mode 188
Make Texture Masks 190
Use Texture Masks 192
Make a Mask from a Color Channel 194
Make a Threshold Mask 196
Make a Layer Mask 198

SECTION III

9 WORKING WITH LAYERS

Using Layers 200
Create a New Layer 210
Stack and Reorder Layers 212
Show and Hide Layers 213
Merge Layers 214
Use Transparency with Layers 216
Delete Layers 217
Change the Size of Layers 218
Use Layer Blend Modes 220
Effects of the Layer Blend Modes 221
Stretch Layers, Selections, and Paths 222
Make Multiple Freehand Transformations 224
Make Numerically Precise Transformations 226
Link Layers 228
Make and Use a Clipping Group 229
Make and Use Adjustment Layers 230
Make a Layer Mask 232
Make and Use Layer Effects 234

10 CHANNEL OPERATIONS

Using Channel Operations 238
Split Out the Channels 244
Make a Separate Channel for Spot Colors 245
Merge Channels to Create Special Effects 246
Merge Channels from Different Files 248
Use the Apply Image Command 250
Use the Calculations Command 252

ISOLATING PARTS OF THE IMAGE

11 TEXT AND TEXT EFFECTS

Using Text 254
Using the Type Tools 258
Edit a Type Layer 260
Use the Type Selection Tool 262
Use Transparency and Blend for Type Effects 264
Enter Vertical Type 266

6

The Art of Making Selections

If image adjustments are the heart of Photoshop and filters its brains, then selections are the soul of Photoshop. Selections make it possible to create irregularly shaped layers, isolate any part of the image, and blend images along their edges to make them continuous.

Selections can be used to isolate the effect of almost any Photoshop command, and they can be used to graduate the effect of almost any Photoshop command.

Things to Remember About Selections

Whereas selections enable you to manipulate Photoshop's effects to their full extent, there are a few things you should remember about them:

- Any selection can be turned into a mask.
- Any mask can be turned into a selection.
- A selection is a mask, except it's only temporary and can't be reused unless it's first turned into a mask. This happens automatically when you save the selection.
- The edges of any selection can be blurred by a command known as *feathering*. You can set the amount of feathering for any selection tool.
- A selection has to be accurate to be effective (in other words, to be believable).
- Almost all accurate selections require that you use a mixture of tools and techniques.
- There is no single recipe for making accurate selections. Almost every situation is a unique case.
- Settings in a selection tool's Options palette remain in effect until they are purposely changed or until you reset the tool.
- You can also make selections with the brushes by painting into a channel, by creating a path, or by using Quick Mask. Often, these are the best tools for creating the selection you want.

The Right Tool for the Job

Each Photoshop selection tool or Select menu command gives you access to a different technique for making selections. The following table describes each tool, along with the types of images most likely to benefit from use of that tool.

Photoshop's Selection Tools

Icon	Name	What It Does
	Marquee	Makes a rectangular or square (when pressing Shift) selection. Good for making buttons and filling areas that will be used as backgrounds for text. Also very useful as preliminary selection to be refined by editing.
	Elliptical Marquee	Makes oval or circular (when pressing Shift) selections. Good for same purposes as Marquee tool, where desired shape is closer to an oval. Excellent for vignettes and radial blurs.
	Single Row Marquee	Makes a horizontal selection one pixel wide from edge to edge.
	Single Column Marquee	Makes a vertical selection one pixel wide from edge to edge.
	Magic Wand	Selects all pixels within a given lightness (not color) range. Good starting point for isolating items from solid-color backgrounds.
	Lasso	Makes a completely freehand selection. The most useful tool for editing rough selections.
	Polygon Lasso	Makes straight-edged, many-sided selections. Ideal for many manufactured objects and for making rough selections quickly.
	Magnetic Lasso	Shrinks to fit or expands to fit, depending on value of first pixel selected.
	Select All	Selects everything in the image. It's the easiest way to copy everything onto a new layer or to drag an image from one file to another.
	Color Range	Selects everything in the image that falls within the same brightness range as the target pixels. Great for selecting complex shapes, such as lace and hair, from solid or near-solid backgrounds.

Another method of making a selection, outside of using one of the preceding tools, is by painting in a mask in Quick Mask mode. Because this can be one of the most powerful methods of making selections (and of saving them as permanent mask channels), be sure to read the section "Using Quick Mask Mode," later in this chapter.

Moving and Feathering Selections

The following applies to all selections, regardless of the tool used:

- To move the selection marquee, but not its contents, drag from inside the selection or exactly on its border.
- To move the selection marquee in exact increments, use arrow keys to move marquee 1 pixel per press or Shift+Arrow key to move 10 pixels per press.
- ⌘/Ctrl+Drag cuts the selection from the background and *floats* it (places the selection into a temporary layer that hovers or "floats" above the surface of the image).
- ⌘/Ctrl+Opt/Alt+Drag copies the contents (pixels) inside the marquee without cutting a hole in the image.
- Changing the feathering in the Options dialog box must take place before you make the selection.
- You can increase feathering after the selection is made, but you can't decrease it below the amount shown in the Options dialog box.
- To decrease the feathering, change the amount in the dialog box. This won't take effect until you make the next selection. If you need to decrease feathering on the current selection, you're out of luck.

MAKE POLYGON SELECTIONS

The Polygon Lasso tool makes straight-line selection marquees between successive clicks. It's a lifesaver when you have to select the straight edges of buildings, boxes, and computer monitors. Later in this chapter, the section "Making Compound Selections" demonstrates how handy the Polygon Lasso is for quickly making rough selections that can be refined later.

Using the Polygon Lasso is easy. Click to select the tool, click to designate the pixel where the marquee will start, move the cursor to stretch the line, and click to end the line and start the next segment. Double-click to end the Polygon Lasso selection, and the selection will close between the first and last points clicked.

You don't need to select the Polygon Lasso tool to make a Polygon Lasso selection. Pressing Opt/Alt while drawing with the Lasso tool makes it possible to stretch a straight line. Likewise, pressing the Opt/Alt key while using the Polygon Lasso tool toggles to the Lasso tool. Thus, you can combine both techniques into a single selection.

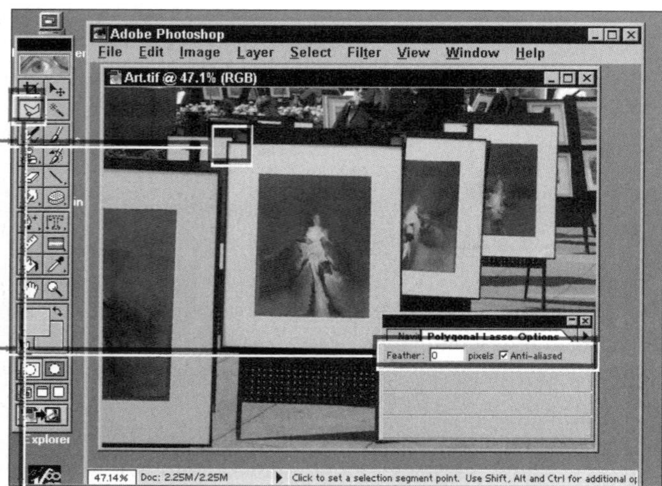

1. Choose the Polygon Lasso tool.
2. Set Options in the Options palette.
3. Click to set start point of each straight-line segment.
4. Move the cursor without dragging to stretch straight line to next connect point.
5. Double-click when ready to close the selection or click on first point.
6. To start a polygon selection, press Opt/Alt at the pixel where the straight line is to start.
7. Move cursor without dragging to stretch the straight line.
8. Click to set end of the straight line.

Note: If you have released the Opt/Alt key, you can resume freehand or Magnetic Lasso selection; otherwise, continue making Polygon Lasso selections.

AUTOMATE SELECTION WITH THE MAGIC WAND

Sometimes I think the Magic Wand tool should be called the *Maddening Wand*. It automatically selects all the pixels that fall within a specified contrast range surrounding the click point. This can either save you lots of hours or waste lots of your time. Which one depends on your knowing when the Magic Wand is appropriate, on getting a good feel for specifying the contrast range (more a matter of practice than anything else), and on understanding how to edit a selection once it's been made.

Simply using the Magic Wand is a matter of choosing the tool and clicking somewhere in the image. If the resulting marquee doesn't include enough of the area you want, increase the Tolerance setting in the Magic Wand Options palette.

Hint: Try using the Magic Wand in conjunction with the Magnetic Lasso. Select a large area, such as the sky or a building, with the Magic Wand. Then choose the Magnetic Lasso and press Shift to select the exact edges you had in mind.

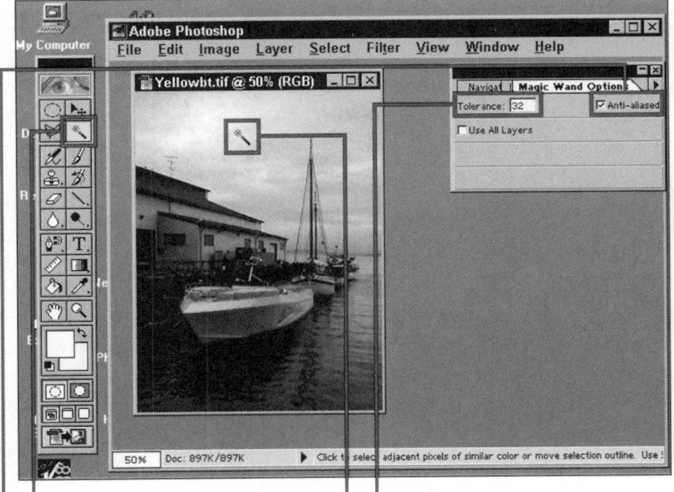

1 Choose the Magic Wand tool and double-click to bring up Magic Wand Options palette.

2 Check the Anti-aliased check box.

3 Specify a tolerance (a number between 1 and 255).

4 Click on a pixel that represents the middle of the tonal range you want to select.

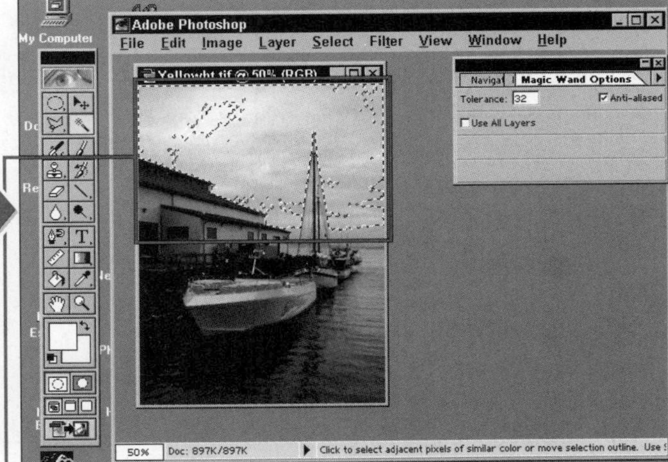

■ Most of the desired edges will be selected.

5 You can add to the selection by pressing Shift and clicking in an area outside the selection.

Note: Unless your subject was photographed on a plain and contrasting background, you will almost certainly have some edges to edit.

AUTOMATE SELECTION WITH THE MAGNETIC LASSO

Photoshop still lacks a "shrink-to-fit" tool or a command to eliminate the "holes" in a selection — features that have been around in some other programs for years. Nonetheless, it does take a step forward in automated selection making with the addition of the Magnetic Lasso and Magnetic Pen tools. Both work in exactly the same way, except one draws a selection marquee, whereas the other creates a path.

The Magnetic Lasso makes it easy for you to create a selection that precisely follows the shape of an object. If there's enough contrast between the pixels in the object and the surrounding background, and if you keep the cursor within a specified number of pixels of the desired edge, it works quite nicely.

That's not to say it works perfectly. Often there won't be enough contrast, or you'll slip away from your goal. You can press the Backspace key to back up to a previous control point (yes, even the Magnetic Lasso uses control points) and try again.

1 Choose the Magnetic Lasso tool and double-click to bring up the Magnetic Lasso Options palette.

2 Specify feathering and anti-aliasing.

3 Set Lasso Width to between 1 and 40.

4 Enter number of pixels selection can travel before auto-inserting a control point.

5 Enter a percentage for edge contrast.

Note: Edge contrast refers to the difference in lightness between pixels that form one shape versus the pixels in the background.

6 Click the Pressure check box if you want stylus pressure to determine Lasso width.

TIPS

Can I move or edit the control points?

No. They merely serve to anchor the selection to a given pixel so that if you back up you don't deselect the edge preceding the control point.

What do I do when the selection starts following an edge I don't want it to follow?

This can happen a lot if you're working in an area of low contrast. When it does happen, just move the cursor backward (you don't need to drag). To eliminate unwanted control points, press Delete/Backspace.

How many ways are there to close the selection?

The most popular is to click on the start point. If you want to close from the current point to the start point and have the in-between edges automatically selected, double-click. If you want to close the shape with a straight line between the first and last points, press Opt/Alt and then double-click.

7 Click to start the selection.

8 Move the cursor along the desired edge of the selection within the distance set by path.

9 Click to set the control point to change direction.

10 To close the selection between the first and last points with a straight line, press Opt/Alt and then double-click.

11 To continue the selection, press Shift and draw as before.

Note: This two-part selection technique is especially useful with the Magnetic Lasso tool. Otherwise, it's difficult to control the behavior of the tool when you need to pan, scroll, or zoom to complete the selection.

Magnetic Lasso Options and Keyboard Shortcuts

Much of your success in using the Magnetic Lasso tool will depend on how well you understand and use the keyboard shortcuts and settings options. The following tables outline the keyboard shortcuts and options for using the Magnetic Lasso tool.

Magnetic Lasso Keyboard Shortcuts

Keyboard Shortcut	Resulting Effect
Click	Sets a corner point to redirect outline when contrast changes between bordering pixels
Click on 1st point	Closes the path and brings up a marquee
Double-click or Return/Enter	Closes the path (marquee between first and last point automatically follows contrasting borders)
Opt/Alt+Double-click	Straight line between first and last points closes the path
]	Increases pen width
[	Decreases pen width
Delete/Backspace	Enables you to back up to reset the direction of the line
⌘+D/Escape	Deselects everything
Opt/Alt+drag	Switches to Lasso
Opt/Alt+move (mouse up)	Switches to Polygon Lasso

Magnetic Lasso Option Settings

Option	Purpose
Feather	Blurs the edges of the selection so edges become gradually more transparent over the range of pixels specified.
Anti-aliased	Mixes lighter colored pixels with those on the edges of a selection to make the line look smoother. Can create a light-colored halo if selection is subsequently placed on a darker background.
Lasso Width	The number of pixels surrounding the cursor that will be considered first in determining changes in contrast.
Frequency	Specifies the number of pixels between automatically placed control points.
Edge Contrast	The percentage of change in brightness to be used in determining when a group of pixels should be considered as an edge. Lower the number to select subtle edges; raise it to avoid selecting noise or texture.

USE THE COLOR RANGE COMMAND

As you have seen in the exercise earlier in this chapter for the Magic Wand command, there may be times when you want to select more of a given area than the Magic Wand can cover in a single stroke. Imagine the spaces between the leaves of a tree when you are trying to set the tree apart from the sky. Another good example might be a model's hair. You could still use the Magic Wand to make these selections by pressing Shift to add to the selection and then clicking additional areas.

Actually, this is not a bad technique for something like the sky in the preceding Magic Wand illustrations, but some subjects would have you Shift-clicking all day. Enter the Color Range command.

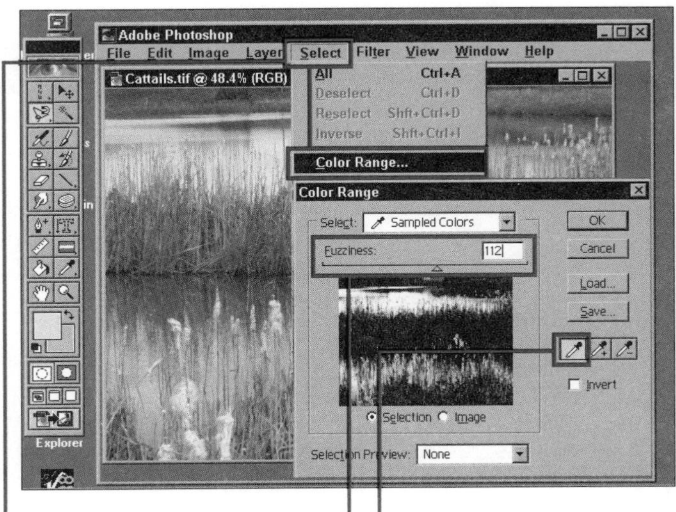

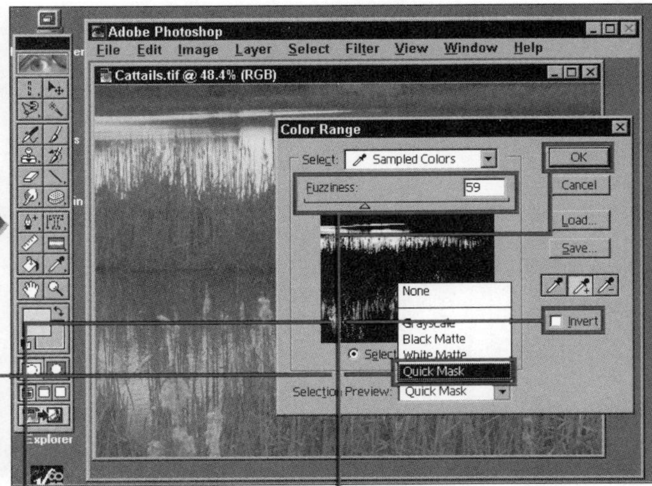

1 Choose Select ⇨ Color Range.

■ The Color Range dialog box appears.

2 Click the Eyedropper in the area to be selected.

3 Drag the fuzziness slider to increase size of the selection (tonal range).

4 To interactively test how well the selection has been made, click the Invert check box.

5 Choose Quick Mask from the Selection Preview pull-down menu.

Note: If colors in the selection vary, you may want to add colors to the range. Click+Eyedropper or - Eyedropper and click in the image.

6 Drag the fuzziness slider until most of the area you want selected is in the mask color.

USE QUICK MASK MODE

The most intuitive and accurate way to edit a selection is by painting in Quick Mask mode. To enter this mode, you click the Quick Mask icon. Quick Mask shows your selection as a red-orange overlay. To change this color to one that contrasts more obviously with the colors in your image, double-click the Quick Mask icon to reveal the Quick Mask Options dialog box. Then click the Color Box to bring up the standard Color Picker and click OK.

To quickly clean up a selection like the one made in the previous exercise, "Use the Color Range Command," click the Quick Mask icon and change the mask color to one that is unlike anything in your image. Press D to select the default foreground and background colors, press X to switch the foreground color to white, press B to select the brush, and paint out any mask color that doesn't belong there. If you miss an edge, press X to switch the foreground color to black and paint the masking color back in. Many tools work while in Quick Mask, including the Pencil, Eraser, and Paint Bucket selection tools, and the Blur tool.

1 Starting with an active selection marquee, click the Quick Mask icon or press Q.

2 Click to select default foreground/background colors (or press D).

3 Click the curved double-arrow (or press X) to switch to white as foreground color.

4 Click the Paint Brush icon (or press B) to choose the Paint Brush.

5 Paint white where the mask infringes on areas that should not be selected.

6 Paint black in areas where the mask doesn't meet desired selection border.

7 Press X to switch foreground and background colors.

Note: Paint in gray when you want the mask to be partly effective or to indicate atmospherics. Lighter grays make the mask more transparent.

What if I find it easier to paint the entire mask in Quick Mask mode?

This will certainly be the case at times. You will find this to be true much more often if you are using a pressure-sensitive digitizing pad, because painting will seem so much more natural and you won't have to switch brush sizes constantly.

Is there any other way to make the mask color contrast more obviously with the image?

Yes. Choose Window ➪ Show Channels and pick a single-color channel that contrasts the most sharply with the area to be selected (masked). Paint to correct your mask; then switch back to Normal mode (click the Normal mode icon and save the selection).

Is there another way to check to make sure I haven't missed painting out any areas?

Before you scroll to the next section of the image, press Q to toggle Quick Mask mode off. If you see a little marquee inside the target marquee, press Q again and paint white over that area.

■ This selection is completely cleaned up as a result of painting in Quick Mask mode. Compare it to the previous screen.

Note: When cleaning up or editing images in zoomed-in windows, move one full window at a time from left to right, move down one window, move right to left, and then move down one window, repeating until you are sure you have covered the entire image.

CLEAN UP LARGE AREAS WITHIN AN UNSELECTED AREA

1 Choose the Polygon Lasso tool.

2 Click to make a selection.

3 If necessary, click the curved double-headed arrow (or press X) to make white the background color.

4 Press Delete.

MAKE COMPOUND SELECTIONS

Often a single selection tool just doesn't do the job. Even more frequently, a single selection tool isn't the quickest way to get the job done. You can, for instance, use the Polygon Lasso tool to select a building in an image, the Magic Wand to select the sky, and a rectangular marquee to select most of the foreground, and then pick up the odd shapes with the Lasso tool.

Making compound selections is also the first step in learning to change the shape of selections by editing them. Pressing Shift adds the selection made by the current tool to an existing selection, Opt/Alt subtracts the current tool's shape, and ⌘/Ctrl leaves whatever portion of the previous and current selections both have in common.

In this exercise, compound selections are used to speed the selection of the desired area while improving accuracy.

The quickest way to make freehand selections is to select most of the inside of the subject, and then zoom in and work around the edges. You start by selecting the largest area with the fastest tool.

1 Click to select the Rectangular Marquee icon (or press M/Shift+M until it cycles into view).

2 Drag to select the first rectangle.

3 Press Shift and drag to add other overlapping rectangles as necessary.

4 Choose the Polygon Lasso tool.

5 Press Shift and click just inside the subject s profile until nearly the whole item is selected.

TIPS

Can I draw a perfect circle or square and add it at the same time?

Believe it or not, it's possible (but it takes some practice). Press Shift before you drag to add the elliptical or rectangular marquee selection. While dragging, release and then press Shift. The marquee will be constrained to a square or circle.

Isn't it likely that I'll have to subtract as well as add?

Yes. When you have to subtract, press the Opt/Alt key instead of the Shift key. Otherwise, the process is the same.

Are there other key modifiers that help in making selections?

Yes. You can draw a geometric selection from the center by pressing Shift+Opt/Alt while dragging.

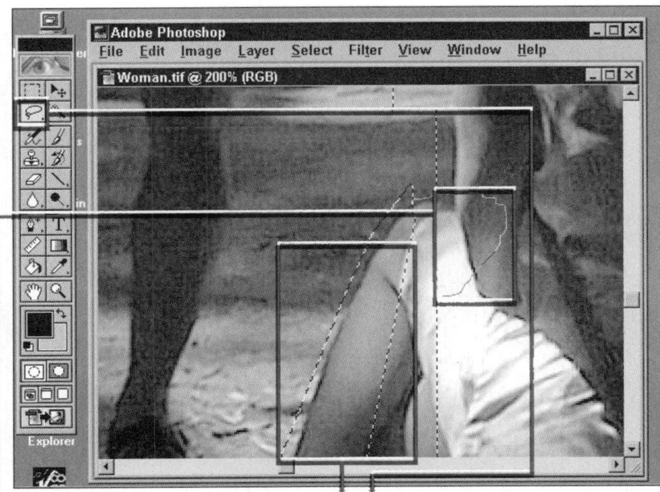

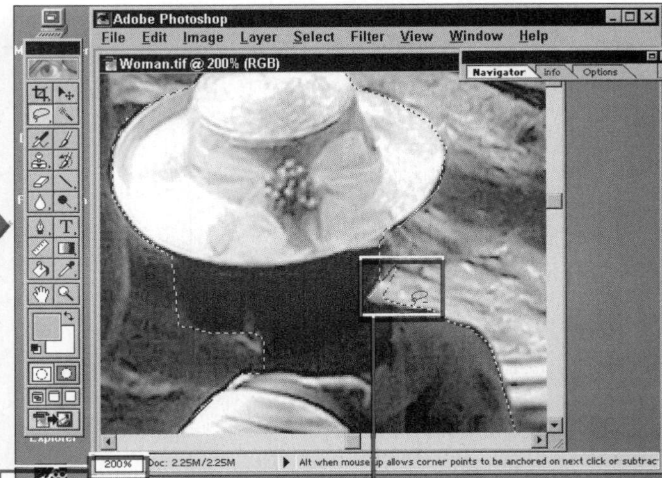

6 Zoom in to 200 percent so you can pick edges accurately.

7 Select the more irregular outline with the Magnetic Lasso or the Lasso tool.

8 Click to select the Lasso tool (or press L until it appears).

9 Drag to carefully select the outlines of the leg.

Note: If you miss a bit, press Opt/Alt and drag the Lasso to subtract from the selection. In this manner, you can make even the most demanding selections accurately by hand.

10 Zoom in very tight.

11 Press Opt/Alt to subtract wherever the selection goes out-of-bounds.

Note: You can use Shift to add to or Opt/Alt key to subtract from any selection, with any selection tool.

EDIT SELECTIONS

As you probably already know, especially if you've just worked through the preceding exercise, you often find a need to change the shape of a selection. You do this by using another selection. If you followed the preceding exercise, you may have already figured out how to edit a selection; if not, this section should clarify the process.

There are three basic ways to edit a selection, aside from working in Quick Mask mode (see "Use Quick Mask Mode," earlier in this chapter):
1) Adding to a selection: Choose preferred selection tool, press Shift, and then drag.
2) Subtracting from a selection: Choose preferred selection tool, press Opt/Alt, and then drag.
3) Intersecting a selection: Choose preferred selection tool, press Shift+Opt/Alt, and then drag.

You can also use the same keys to add, subtract, and intersect saved selections, channel masks, and selection commands.

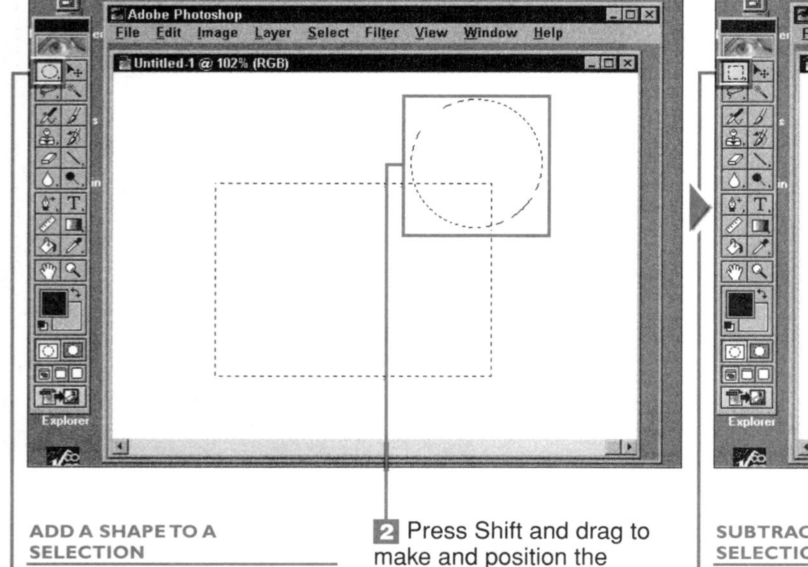

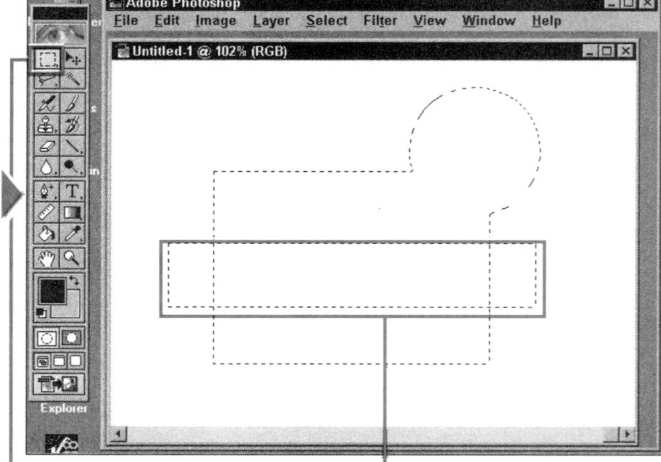

ADD A SHAPE TO A SELECTION

1 Click to select the selection tool that will make the shape you want to add.

2 Press Shift and drag to make and position the shape.

■ The shape is added to the existing shape. If the two shapes didn't touch, you will have two separate marquees.

SUBTRACT A SHAPE FROM A SELECTION

1 Click to select the selection tool that will make the shape you want to subtract.

2 Press Opt/Alt and drag to make the shape.

■ The shape is subtracted from the existing shape, leaving a gap, indent, or hole.

TIPS

When the marquee sits right over the seam, how can I tell how an edge affects the blending of the selection with the rest of the image?

You can hide the marquee. Just press ⌘/Ctrl+H. The only danger is that the selection is still in effect and you can't see it. Be sure you press ⌘/Ctrl+D to drop the selection the second you're through with it — or press ⌘/Ctrl+H again to make the selection visible.

These edits have been demonstrated with geometric tools. Will the Lasso and Magic Wand tools behave in the same way?

Absolutely. The geometrics were used only because the result would be more obvious.

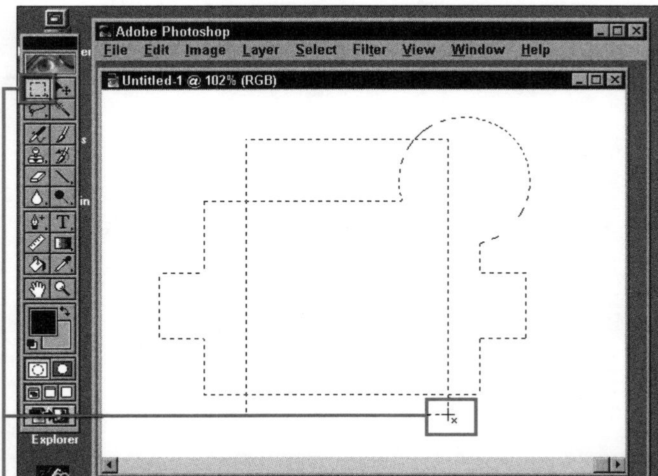

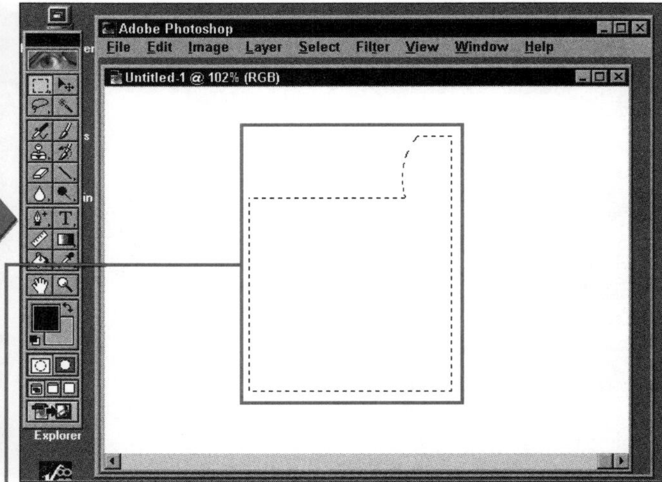

INTERSECT A SELECTION WITH A SELECTION

1 Click to select the selection tool want.

2 Press Opt/Alt+Shift and drag to make and position the shape.

■ Any shape that resulted from the intersection of the two selections remains a selection. If the two shapes didn't touch, you have no selection.

■ Here is the result of the intersection in the previous figure.

MODIFY SELECTIONS

In addition to the selection tools, there are commands for making selections and for modifying selections that have already been made. This exercise is specifically concerned with the four commands found under the Select ➪ Layout menu: 1) Border: Makes a selection around the edge of the current selection border that's as wide as the number of pixels you specify — up to 64 pixels wide. 2) Smooth: Rounds the "corners" or sharp turns in a selection by a radius of any number of pixels up to 16. 3) Expand: Increases the size of the selection marquee by any number of pixels, up to 16. Sharp corners will be rounded in the process. 4) Contract: Decreases the size of the selection marquee by any number of pixels, up to 16. Rounded corners will be sharpened in the process.

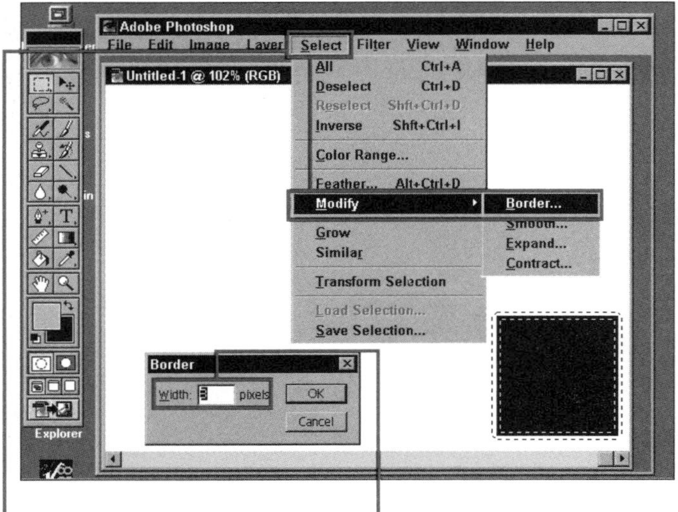

MAKE A SELECTION FRAME AROUND THE CURRENT SELECTION

1 Choose Select ➪ Modify ➪ Border.

■ The Border dialog box appears.

2 Enter the number of pixels (up to 64) desired for the frame width.

3 Click OK.

■ The original selection is dropped and the border selection appears.

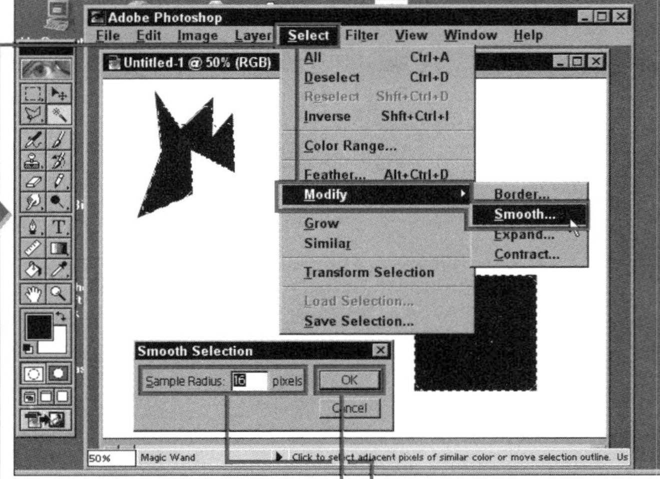

SMOOTH THE CURRENT SELECTION'S SHARP TURNS

1 Choose Select ➪ Modify ➪ Smooth.

■ The Smooth Selection dialog box appears.

2 Enter the number of pixels (up to 16) desired for the rounding radius.

3 Click OK.

■ The original selection is dropped and the smoothed selection appears.

TIPS

Can I use Select ➪ Modify ➪ Smooth to actually smooth marquees created by an unsteady hand?

Yes, but you may find that the smoothing causes the selection of pixels you didn't want to have selected. Take a look at the smoothed path around the starburst in the second screen on this page.

The limit for the options Smooth, Expand, and Contract is 16 pixels. What if I want more?

Divide the number you want by 2 until you get below 16, and enter that number in the dialog box. Then repeat the command as many times as it takes to get back to the number you want. If you want an odd number, repeat until you're within a few pixels, and then reissue the command and enter the exact number of pixels you want to add to the last border.

How do I make a rounded-corner rectangle or polygon selection?

Well, there's no command for such. Nevertheless, it's easy to do: Make a selection with straight edges. Choose Select ➪ Modify ➪ Smooth and enter the desired corner radius.

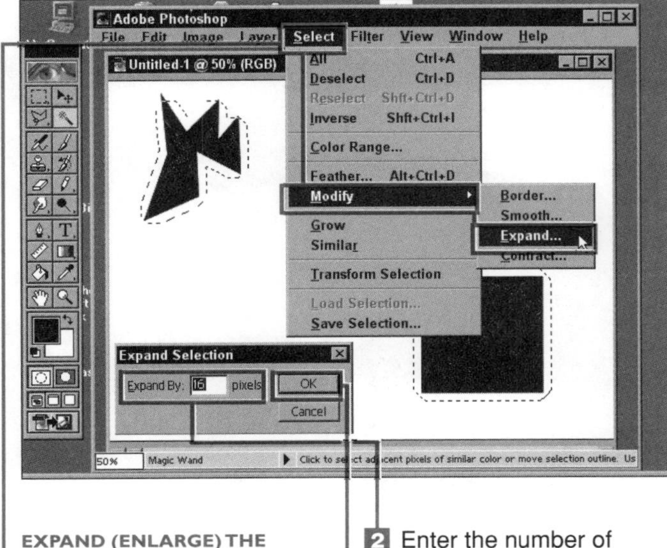

EXPAND (ENLARGE) THE CURRENT SELECTION'S SIZE

1. Choose Select ➪ Modify ➪ Expand.

■ The Expand Selection dialog box appears.

2. Enter the number of pixels (up to 16) desired for the size increase.

3. Click OK.

■ The original selection is dropped, and a larger selection, appears.

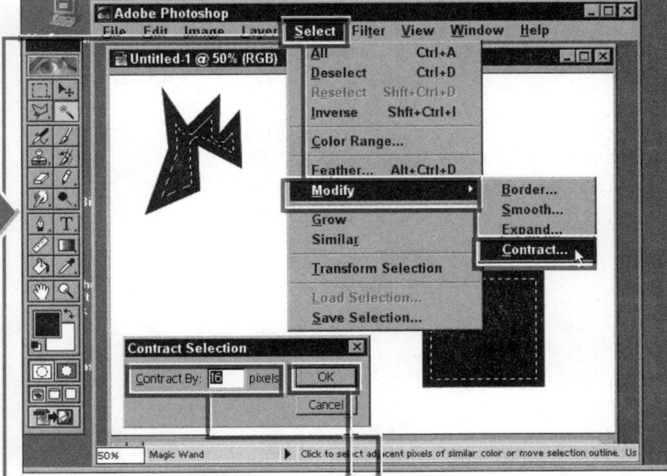

CONTRACT (SHRINK) THE CURRENT SELECTION'S SHARP TURNS

1. Choose Select ➪ Modify ➪ Contract.

■ The Contract Selection dialog box appears.

2. Enter the number of pixels (up to 16) desired for the size decrease.

3. Click OK.

■ The original selection is dropped and the reduced selection appears.

MODIFY SELECTIONS WITH GROW AND SIMILAR

We've looked at Select ➪ Modify ➪ Border, Smooth, Expand, and Contract. Two additional commands on the Select menu, Grow and Similar, can change the borders of the current selection to include more of the image.

Choosing Select ➪ Grow immediately expands the current selection by the same grayscale range as exists in the current selection's Magic Wand Tolerance options — so long as the pixels within that range are contiguous.

Choosing Select ➪ Similar immediately selects all shades that fall within the same range of tones as those in the original, regardless of any tolerance settings and whether the newly selected pixels are contiguous.

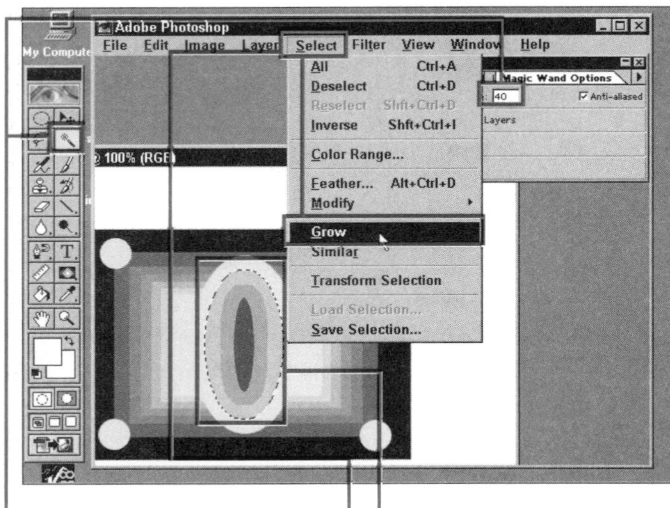

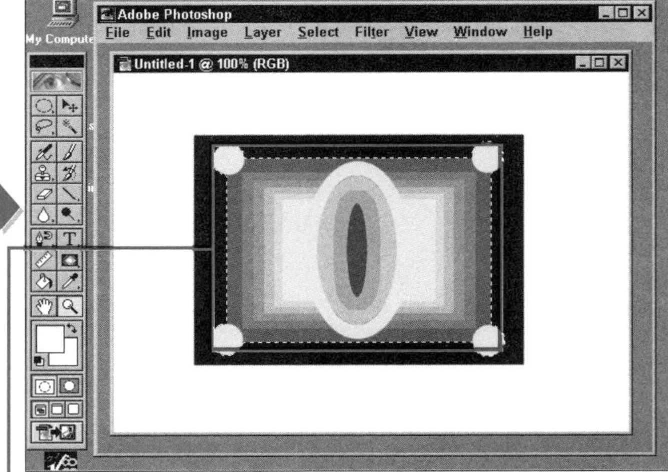

MAKE A SELECTION GROW

1 Double-click the Magic Wand tool to choose it and bring up its Options palette.

2 Set a tolerance (between 1 and 255) in the selection tool s Options palette.

3 Make a selection.

4 Choose Select ➪ Grow.

■ The selection will instantly grow to double the previously chosen tool tolerance.

■ The selection after the Grow command has been issued.

TIPS

How do I keep the Grow command from making the selection grow too much?

Open the Magic Wand Options palette and set the tolerance level to a fairly low number (try 8). Now issue the Grow command. If the selection doesn't grow enough, press ⌘/Ctrl+F to repeat the command at the same setting until the selection includes everything you want. If you go one step too far, press ⌘/Ctrl+Z to go back a step. If you're still not dead on, drop the selection and try again at a lower tolerance setting.

What is the best use for the Similar command?

Selecting all the instances of a particular color — for instance, the colors in lace or in particular interface elements. Suppose you wanted to place a frame around all the Web page buttons: Select a button, choose Select ➪ Similar, and then choose Select ➪ Border.

Are selections made with the Grow and Similar commands anti-aliased?

Only if the Anti-aliased box is checked in the Magic Wand Options palette.

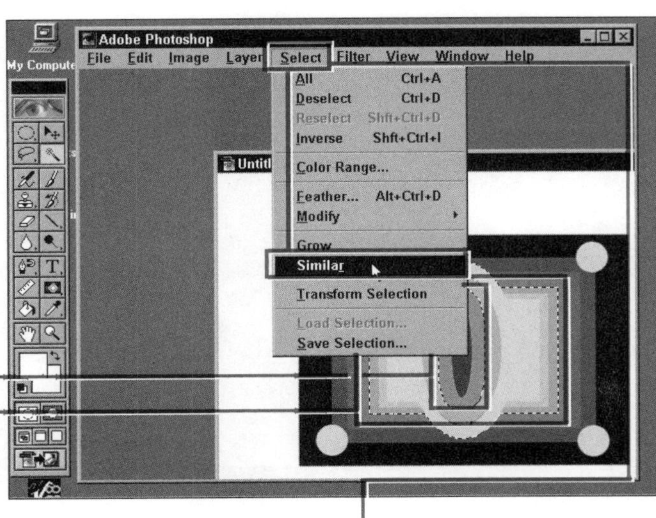

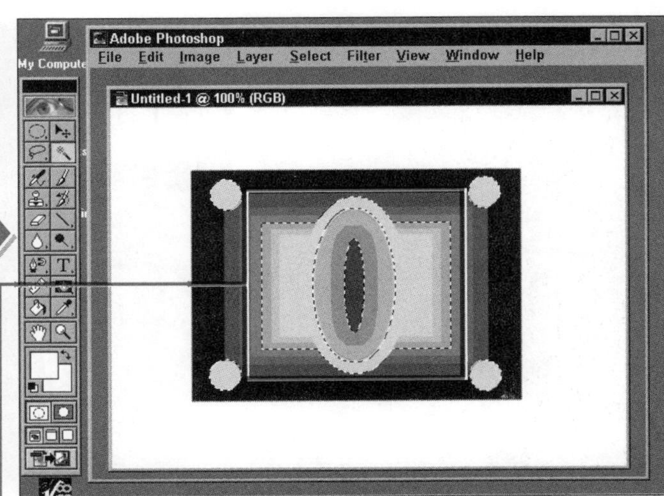

SELECT SIMILAR SHADES

1 Make a selection.

2 Press Shift and make as many more selections as necessary to include the tones you want selected.

3 Choose Select ➪ Similar.

■ The selection instantly grows to include all the shades in the image that were included in your original selection.

■ Here s the selection after the Similar command has been issued.

MAKE WHOLESALE SELECTION CHANGES

SELECT ALL, SELECT NONE, AND SELECT INVERSE

So far, this chapter has focused on the sophisticated commands that enable you to make highly refined and accurate selections. However, there's also a need for some selection commands that don't even require you to make a selection, never mind acquiring a talent for it.

Choosing Select ➪ All (⌘/Ctrl+A) places a rectangular marquee around the entire layer. You can then float the image, make it into another layer, drag it into another file, or use any of the transformation commands on it.

Choosing Select ➪ None might be the most valuable selection command of all. It lets you get rid of all the selections and adjustments you made so you can start all over again.

Choosing Select ➪ Inverse makes it easy to choose everything in the image except what's already been chosen. Best of all, you only need to make one selection. This is usually the easiest way to separate an object from its surroundings.

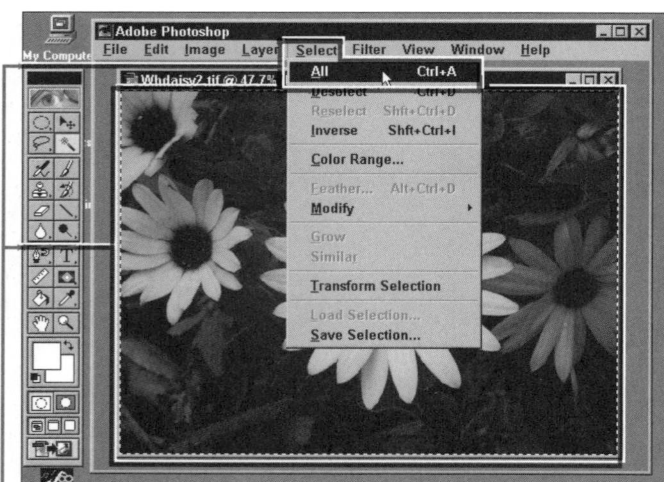

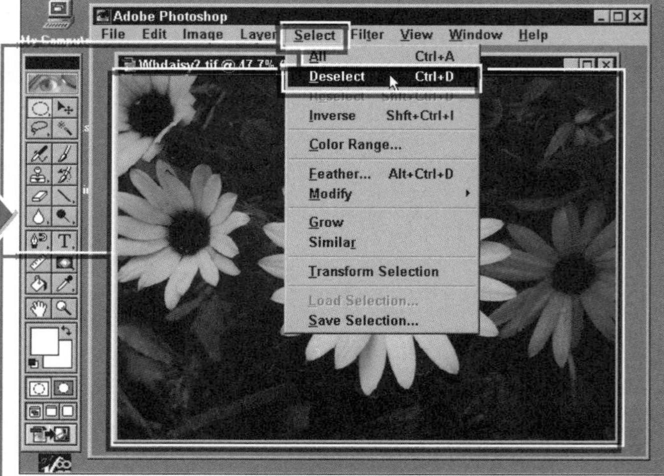

SELECT THE ENTIRE LAYER

1 Choose Select ➪ All.

■ A selection marquee covers the entire window, indicating the whole layer is selected. Any preexisting selections disappear.

Note: If you are zoomed in, you may not see any of this marquee, as it is outside the borders of the workspace window.

CANCEL (DROP) ALL CURRENT SELECTION(S)

1 Choose Select ➪ Deselect.

■ You won't see a selection marquee anywhere.

Note: It's a good idea to execute this command just before you do anything that's intended to affect the whole layer. You might have forgotten to unhide a selection marquee or might have made selections too subtle to allow the marquee to be visible.

TIPS

Is it true that Select All is the fastest way to make a new layer?

I haven't made a scientific survey, but I'd bet it is. Press ⌘/Ctrl+A, press ⌘/Ctrl+C, and press ⌘/Ctrl+V. Presto! You've copied the current layer without ever having to pull down a menu or drag a layer name bar.

What's all this about hiding selections?

Thought you'd never ask. It's tough to find a spot to show something invisible in a book such as this, so let me elaborate here: If you want to hide the edges of a selection so you can see how smoothly the effect of a command blends, press ⌘/Ctrl+H.

Can you give me an example of why I'd want to invert a selection?

Inverting is a great way to throw the background out of focus or to knock out the background entirely (just press the Delete/Backspace key). If you knock out the background, you can put a new background on a layer beneath the current one.

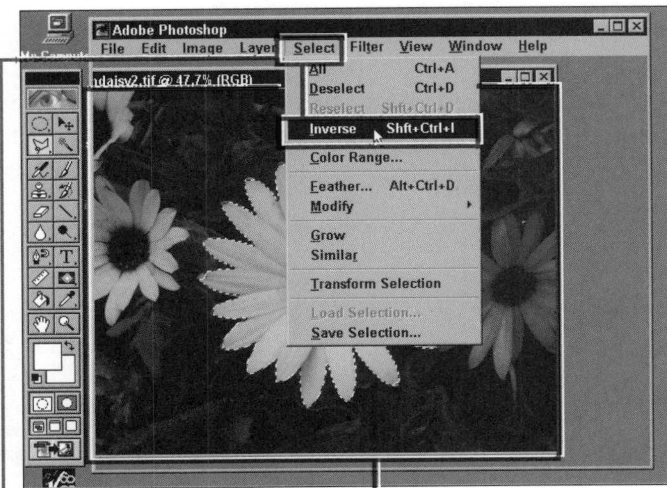

REVERSE (INVERT) THE SELECTION

Note: Selecting everything except what's already selected is called reversing or inverting the selection.

1 Choose Select ➪ Inverse.

■ You should instantly see the marquee surround all of the previously unselected image.

■ Here's how the selection appears after inversion.

Note: In this example, I've used Image ➪ Adjust ➪ Brightness/Contrast to darken the other flowers and foliage so that the foreground daisy stands out more.

BLEND SELECTIONS

ANTI-ALIASING AND FEATHERING

The secret to making realistic composite photos lies in subtly and gradually making the edges of selections transparent (in imitation of persistence of vision). There are two methods for doing this: *anti-aliasing* and *feathering*.

Anti-aliasing is simply a matter of alternating the edge pixels with pixels of a lighter shade, which creates an optical illusion that makes the edges seem smoother. Photoshop feathers a selection's edges by applying a bell-curve grayscale gradient for a specified number of pixels on either side of the selection marquee.

Because a selection is really a temporary mask, and the density of a gray in a mask determines the degree of the mask's transparency, feathering can be used to "fade" almost any image adjustment, brush stroke, or filter effect. Feathering is also useful in collage compositions, creating cross-fades between some or all of the composition's images.

Caution: If you set feathering for a selection tool in its Options palette, every selection you make thereafter will be feathered. This can cause you to inadvertently select unwanted pixels.

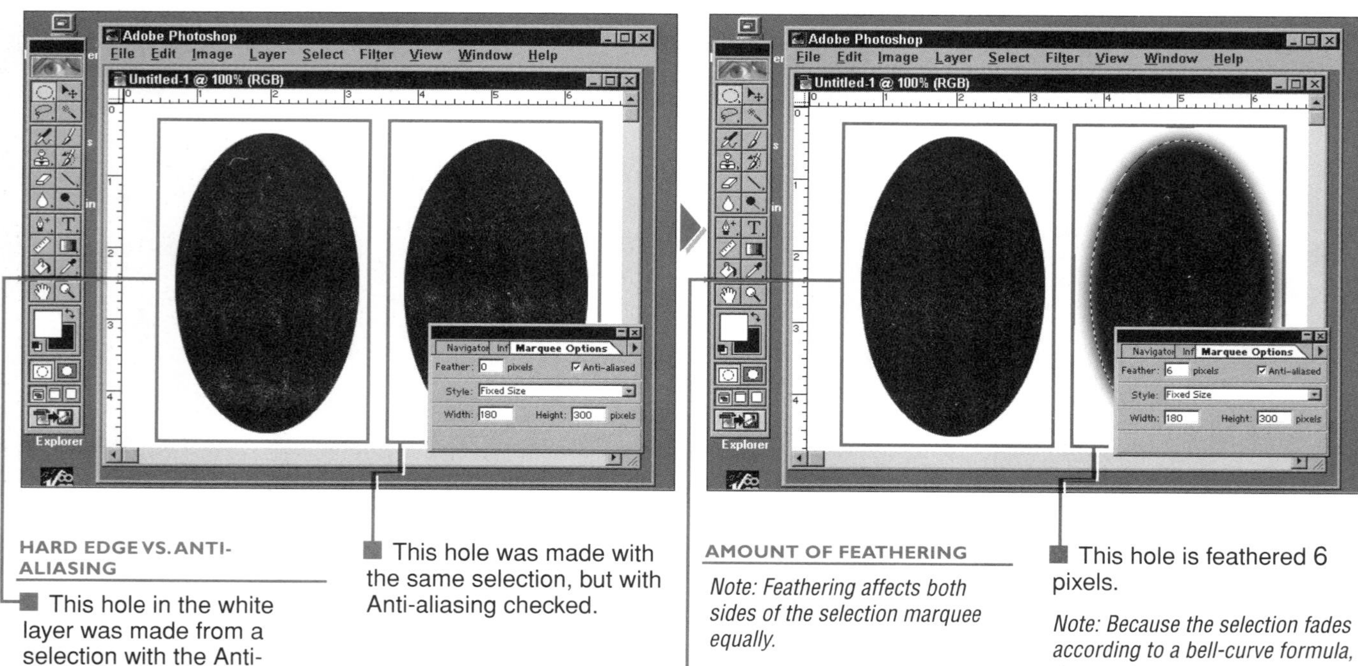

HARD EDGE VS. ANTI-ALIASING

■ This hole in the white layer was made from a selection with the Anti-aliasing box unchecked. Notice the jagged edges.

■ This hole was made with the same selection, but with Anti-aliasing checked.

AMOUNT OF FEATHERING

Note: Feathering affects both sides of the selection marquee equally.

■ This hole is feathered only 1 pixel.

■ This hole is feathered 6 pixels.

Note: Because the selection fades according to a bell-curve formula, the total effect is actually about four times greater than the number of pixels specified.

TIPS

Is there a way to feather the selection less than 1 pixel?

If you are doing this for a composite, the answer is yes. Before making any selection, cut the image you want to cut out and paste it into another file of the same size. Double the size of the image, make the selection, and feather it 1 pixel. Invert the selection and press the Delete key to cut out the background. Reduce the image to its original size and drag it back to the original file. The feathering now takes place in half the space. This is possible because a 1-pixel feather actually affects a 4-pixel radius.

Is there a difference between setting feathering in a tool's Options dialog box and choosing the Select ⇨ Feather command?

Yes. Any setting you make in the Options palette will affect all subsequent selections, but not any current selection. Any degree of feathering you specify in the Feather command's Feather Selection dialog box will affect the current selection, regardless of which tool(s) you used to make that selection.

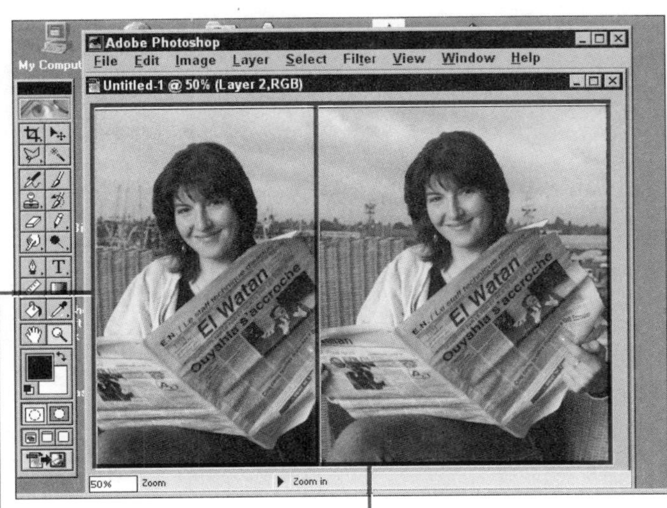

SOFTENING EDGES IN COMPOSITES

■ The edges in this image were cut out with the selection edges anti-aliased.

■ This image used very slightly feathered edges (1 pixel) and blends more naturally with the background.

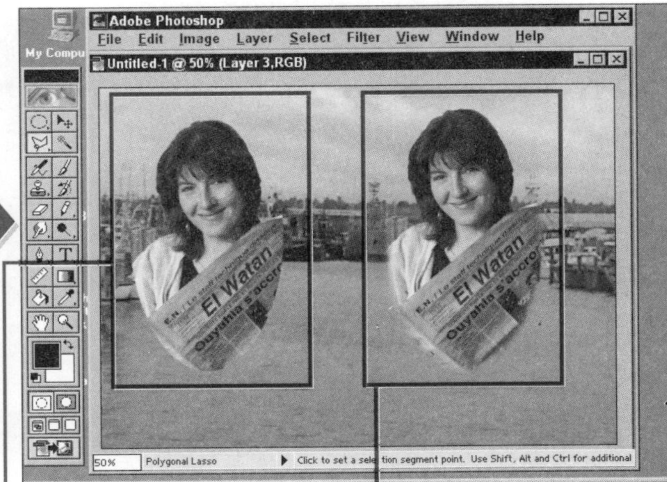

FADING EDGES FOR COLLAGE

■ This image is cut out with anti-aliasing turned on. Edges are smooth, but the transition between photos is abrupt.

■ This image is heavily feathered, making a smooth transition between images.

MAGICAL ERASING WITH THE MAGIC ERASER

The magician says, "Presto!," and the rabbit disappears. The new Photoshop 5.5 Magic Eraser is nearly as magical as the ol' rabbit in the hat trick, but its trick is making solid-color, evenly-lit areas of the image disappear, not a cute, white bunny.

Like the Magic Wand or the Paint Bucket, you set a tolerance between 1 and 255. The tones you're erasing don't actually have to be identical, they just need to fall within the brightness range you specify in the Tolerance field.

There are three checkbox options in the Magic Eraser Options palette: Use All Layers, Anti-aliased, and Contiguous. If All Layers is checked, the erasure will take place on all visible tones that fall within specified tones, regardless of layer. Checking Antializing ensures that edges will be smooth. Check Contiguous if your foreground subject has lots of "holes"— that is, spaces where the background shows through.

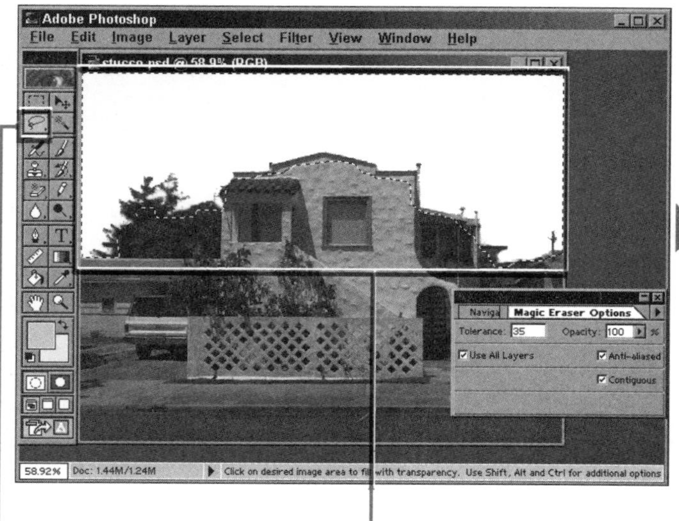

1 Open an image you want to erase.

2 Chose the Lasso tool.

3 Select the area around the sky. Be sure to include edges with holes.

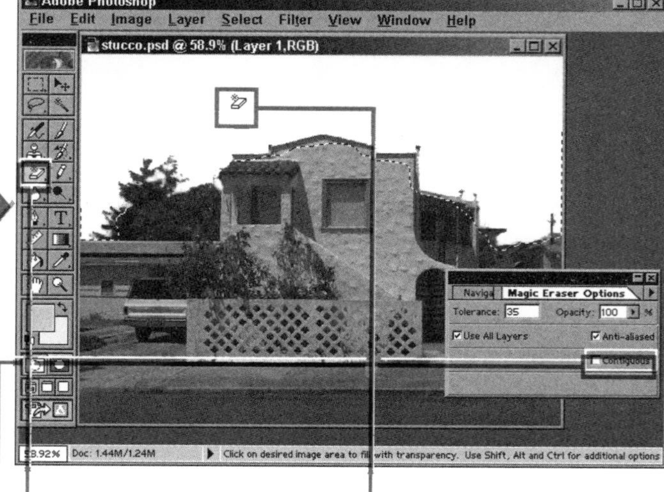

4 Choose the Magic Eraser.

5 Uncheck Contiguous.

6 Chose a 5x5 sample size.

7 Click a color in the middle of the range you want to erase.

■ The sky goes blank. If you erased wanted edges, Tolerance was set too high.

TIPS

Should I always check Antialias?

No. Sometimes the antialiased pixels will contain unexpected colors that create a "halo" around your foreground object.

When should I use the Contiguous option?

When you want to make sure that nothing besides the clicked area is erased. You'll find that there are times when it's better to make several clicks.

How do I know how much Tolerance to specify?

The same way you get to Carnegie Hall: *practice*. If I'm erasing an evenly-lit seamless background, I start at around 10. If it's a cloudless sky, something around 30 seems to work.

Note: You may need to do some edge cleanup. Inspect edges closely.

8 Choose the Zoom tool.

9 Drag with the Marquee to zoom-in on suspect areas.

10 Choose the Hand tool.

11 Scroll to inspect and retouch.

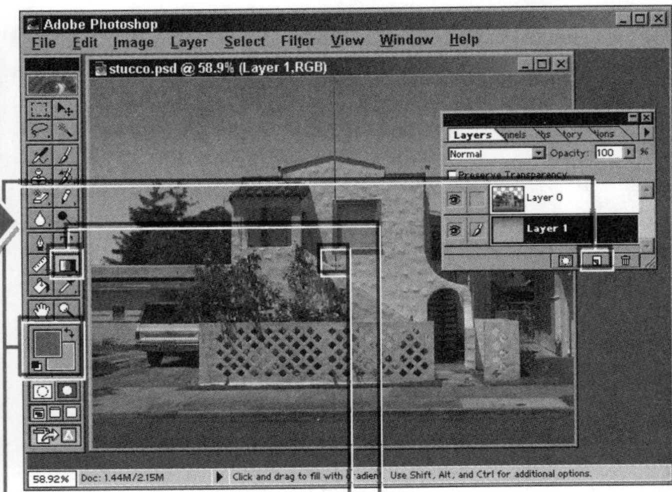

REPLACE THE BACKGROUND

12 Click the New Layer button in the Layers palette.

13 Choose colors for the background.

14 Choose the Gradient tool.

15 Drag to show direction of gradient fill.

ERASE BACKGROUNDS

The Background Eraser is the other new eraser tool in Photoshop 5.5. You can set it up so that you can just paint out the background. This is also an excellent tool for retouching the results of the Extract Image command.

The cursor for the Background Eraser is a circle with a cross in the center. It works by erasing all the colors within a specified range of the color that the center of that cross passes over. Unlike the Magic Eraser, the Background Eraser works only on the currently active layer.

Note, however, that the Background Eraser erases to the background, so if you want it to erase a single-layer image to transparency rather than the background color, you must change the name of the background layer.

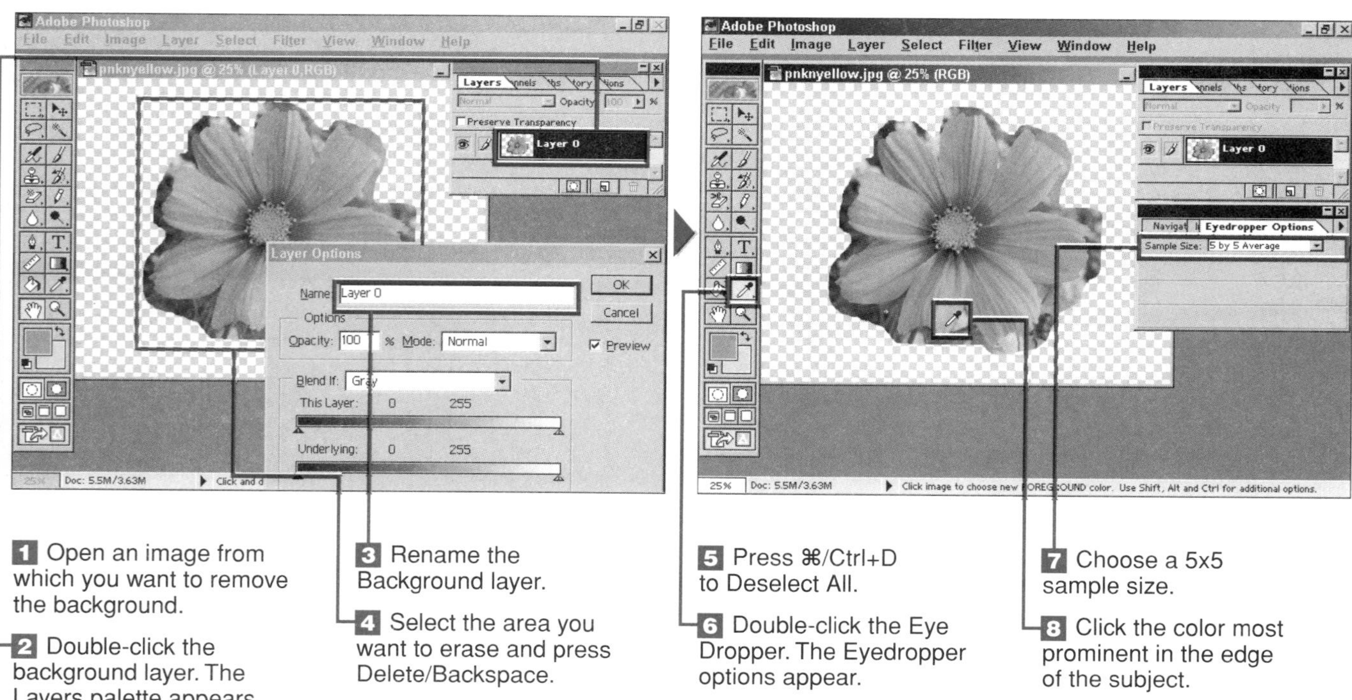

1 Open an image from which you want to remove the background.

2 Double-click the background layer. The Layers palette appears.

3 Rename the Background layer.

4 Select the area you want to erase and press Delete/Backspace.

5 Press ⌘/Ctrl+D to Deselect All.

6 Double-click the Eye Dropper. The Eyedropper options appear.

7 Choose a 5x5 sample size.

8 Click the color most prominent in the edge of the subject.

TIPS

What do the choices in the top left pull-down menu mean?

The choices are Contiguous (erases all colors within range the color sampled click); Discontiguous (erases all colors within range as cursor is dragged); and Find Edges (favors not erasing colors on the other side of an obvious edge).

What about the choices in the Sampling menu?

The choices are Continuous (samples continuously as the mouse is dragged); Once (samples only once when the mouse is first clicked); and Background (erases only the Background color wherever it's found).

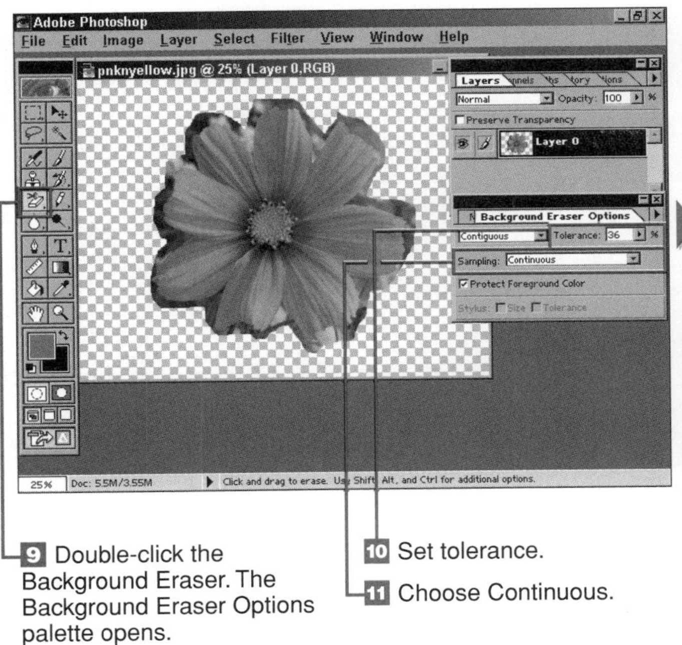

9 Double-click the Background Eraser. The Background Eraser Options palette opens.

10 Set tolerance.

11 Choose Continuous.

12 Check Protect Foreground Color.

13 Drag around subject. The background will erase to the edge of the subject.

14 Continue until done. Press ⌘/Ctrl+Z to Undo if you linger too long or set tolerance too high.

MAKING AND USING PATHS

Photoshop practically gives you a complete illustration program in its Pen tools feature, accessible through a toolbar slot pop-out menu. There are seven tools in all, each with its associated Options palette for setting that tool's behavior parameters. Here I give you a quick overview of each Pen tool.

The Burn Tool

The Burn tool is used to darken relatively small areas of the image. It usually works best when used in a way that mimics a traditional darkroom technique — repeatedly stroking with a highly feathered brush set at a low exposure percentage.

The Pen Tool

The Pen tool is the tool you'll use most often for drawing smooth, efficient paths. Click to start a line segment, move the cursor and click to end the line segment, and drag to curve and shape the line. Releasing the button enables you to make the next line segment. If you make a mistake, press Delete/Backspace. The first figure shows the Pen Options palette.

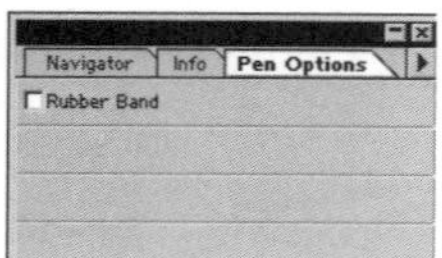

Pen Tool Shortcuts

Icon	Shortcut	Result
	Cursor over point	Deletes Point arrow
	Cursor over path	Adds point
	Shift	Forces a straight line at 45-degree angles from last point
	⌘/Ctrl	Switches to Direct Selection tool (arrow)
	Opt/Alt	Switches to Convert Point tool
	⌘/Ctrl, then ⌘/Ctrl+Opt/Alt	Switches to Select Path arrow

Pen Tool Options

Component	Function
Rubber Band	Enables you to preview the path following the entry of the last point as the cursor moves. Path doesn't become permanent until you click a new point.

The Magnetic Pen Tool

The Magnetic Pen tool acts almost exactly like the Magnetic Lasso: It automatically makes a path that follows the edges closest to the cursor that contrast most sharply with one another. The Magnetic Pen Options palette is shown in the following figure.

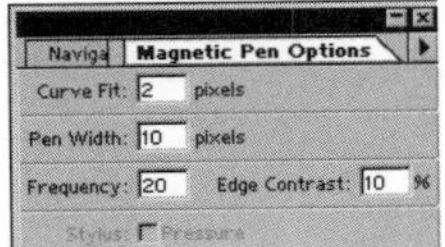

Magnetic Pen Tool Shortcuts

Icon	Shortcut	Result
	Cursor over point	Deletes Point arrow
	Cursor over path	Adds point
	⌘/Ctrl	Switches to Close Path if drawing or switches to Direct Selection tool (arrow) if editing
	Opt/Alt	Switches to Convert Point tool
	⌘/Ctrl, then ⌘/Ctrl+ Opt/Alt	Switches to Select Path arrow

Magnetic Pen Tool Options

Component	Function
Curve Fit	Enter a value between 1 and 10. Lower numbers enter more control points, making the curve fit the path more accurately. Careful: Too much accuracy may reflect any lack of precision on your part and cause too many points to be entered, resulting in a rougher, less accurate selection.
Pen Width	Enter a number between 1 and 40. This is the pixel width of the path that will be scanned for a contrasting edge. If there are several possible edges within close range of your cursor, keep this number as low as possible. Note: Pressing [while Magnetic Pen is in use decreases pen width by 1 pixel. Pressing] increases pen width by 1 pixel.
Frequency	Enter a number between 1 and 100 to determine the speed with which new points are placed. A high number causes more points to be placed over a given path length in a given amount of time.
Edge Contrast	Enter a percentage between 1 and 100 to determine the level of contrast between adjacent pixels before they are considered an edge.
Stylus Pressure	If checked, an increase in stylus pressure shrinks the lasso width.

MAKING AND USING PATHS CONTINUED

The Freeform Tool

The Freeform tool lets you draw a path freehand. Best used by those with a steady hand and a pen tablet; otherwise, you end up with too many control points. The Freeform Pen Options palette is pictured here.

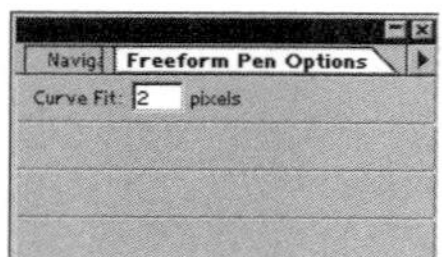

Freeform Tool Shortcuts

Icon	Shortcut	Result
[icon]	Cursor over point	Deletes Point arrow
	Cursor over path	Adds Point arrow
	⌘/Ctrl	Switches to Close Path if drawing or switches to Direct Selection tool (arrow) if editing
	Opt/Alt	Switches to Convert Point tool
	⌘/Ctrl, then ⌘/Ctrl+Opt/Alt	Switches to Select Path arrow

Freeform Tool Options

Component	Function
Curve Fit	Enables you to control the frequency of control points along the freeform path. The higher the number, the more distant the points are from one another.

The Add Point Tool

The Add Point tool adds a control point whenever you click an existing path.

Add Point Tool Shortcuts

Icon	Shortcut	Result
[icon]	Cursor over point	Deletes Point arrow
	⌘/Ctrl	Switches to Direct Selection arrow
	Opt/Alt	Switches to Select Path arrow

The Delete Point Tool

The Delete Point tool removes a control point whenever you click on an existing point or an existing path.

Delete Point Tool Shortcuts

Icon	Shortcut	Result
[icon]	Cursor over point	Deletes Point arrow
	Cursor over path	Brings up Selection arrow
	⌘/Ctrl	Switches to Direct Selection tool
	Opt/Alt	Switches to Select Path arrow

The Direct Selection Tool

The Direct Selection tool, or arrow, selects a control point and shows any attached direction points (handles). If a + appears alongside, all control points are selected, and dragging moves the entire path rather than a single point or handle. You can select several points at once by dragging a marquee around them.

Direct Selection Tool Shortcuts

Icon	Shortcut	Result
[icon]	None	

The Convert Point Tool

The Convert Point tool lets you convert any type of control point to any other. Click once to remove all handles, drag from the control point to make a smooth curve, and drag handles to make an asymmetrical curve or cusp point (handles not diametrically opposed).

Convert Point Tool Shortcuts

Icon	Shortcut	Result
[icon]	Cursor over point	Brings up Direct Selection arrow
	Opt/Alt	Switches to Direct Selection tool

DRAW A PATH

Before you can use paths, you need to learn how to draw one. Actually, you can turn any mask or selection into a path. You can also import any Adobe Illustrator path into Photoshop. So you don't *really* have to learn how to *draw* a path. But if you do, you're more likely to understand how to edit and use paths.

If you're used to working in Adobe Illustrator, Macromedia FreeHand, or CorelDRAW! you're already familiar with how to draw a path, so you can skip this exercise. If you're not used to drawing paths, you may find it a bit unnatural, except for the method Photoshop 5 provides by including the Freehand Pen. This tool's so easy to use that I won't dwell on it here. After choosing it, you draw as you would with a pencil.

The two most important things to remember about drawing paths are 1) click-click makes a straight line and 2) click and drag makes a curve. The best thing about drawing paths is that you can correct all your mistakes without ever having to use an eraser.

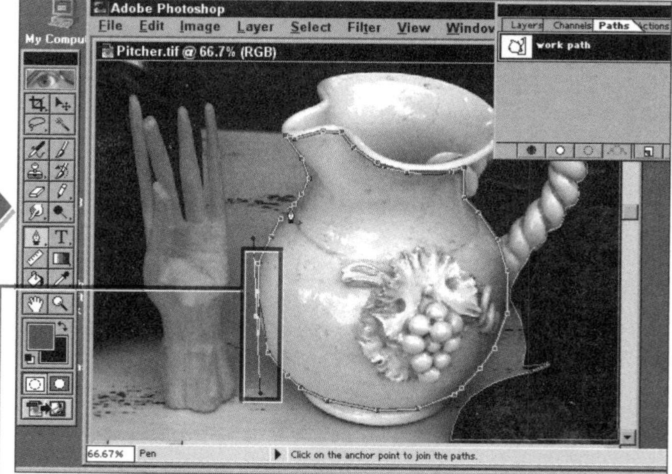

1 Choose Window ⇨ Show Paths if the Paths palette isn't already visible.

2 Choose the Pen tool.

3 Click to start the path and again at each point where a straight segment ends.

4 To start a curve, click to end the previous segment, and then drag to indicate the direction and distance of the upcoming curve.

5 Click and drag to shape the next curve segment.

Note: At this point, you want to go back to making straight line segments. This means you have to switch to the Convert Anchor Point tool, found on the Pen tools fly-out menu. You can also Opt/Alt+click the last anchor point to start a new vector.

TIPS

Why bother to draw with the Pen tools when I can draw with the Freehand Pen?

If you want paths that are perfectly smooth and as simple as possible, it is faster and easier to draw with the Pen tools. The Freehand Pen tends to lay down a control point every time you get a bit shaky.

What have you found to be the most efficient way to draw the path of highly irregular shapes?

I draw a "quick and dirty" rough path around the object, and then drag the major points into exact alignment. Next I use the Add Point tool to insert any needed control points, drag them into place, and edit the curve until it fits.

How can I use paths to make geometric shapes?

Choose View ➪ Show Grid and then choose View ➪ Snap to Grid, which lets you easily place anchor points at exact distances from one another. This is a great way to make rounded-corner buttons, rectangular banners, and other functional graphics.

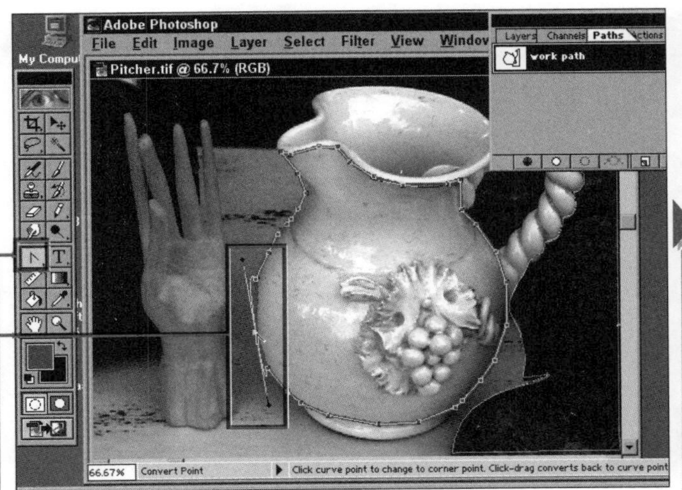

6 Choose the Convert Anchor Point tool.

7 Drag the lower direction point until it points in the direction of the next straight line segment.

Note: A better method may be to drag the direction point atop the control point; otherwise, you might bend the desired straight line slightly.

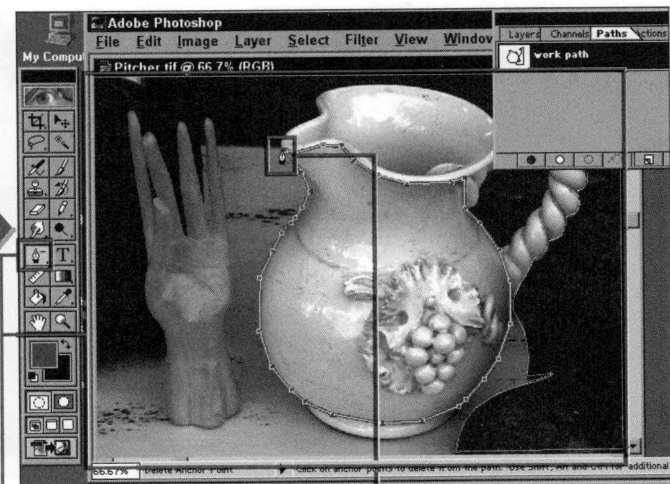

8 Choose the Pen tool.

9 Click each straight-line point.

■ The path now surrounds all but the right edge of this image.

10 Place the Pen tool cursor directly over the first point.

■ A circle appears next to the Pen tool cursor to indicate that you are about to close the path.

11 Click to close the path.

DRAW COMPLEX PATHS

The preceding exercise orients you to the simpler and more common methods for making a path and introduces you to using paths to trace over a photo. In actual practice, you'll find it's rare for a path to have such simple requirements. You want to master making paths that suddenly change the direction and severity of curves.

But what if you want to make a path that incorporates a combination of straight and curved lines or smooth and asymmetrical curves? You'll find that it's a good idea to learn how to use modifier keys with the Pen tools. Flip back to the beginning of this chapter to find tables containing information on what the Pen tool modifiers do.

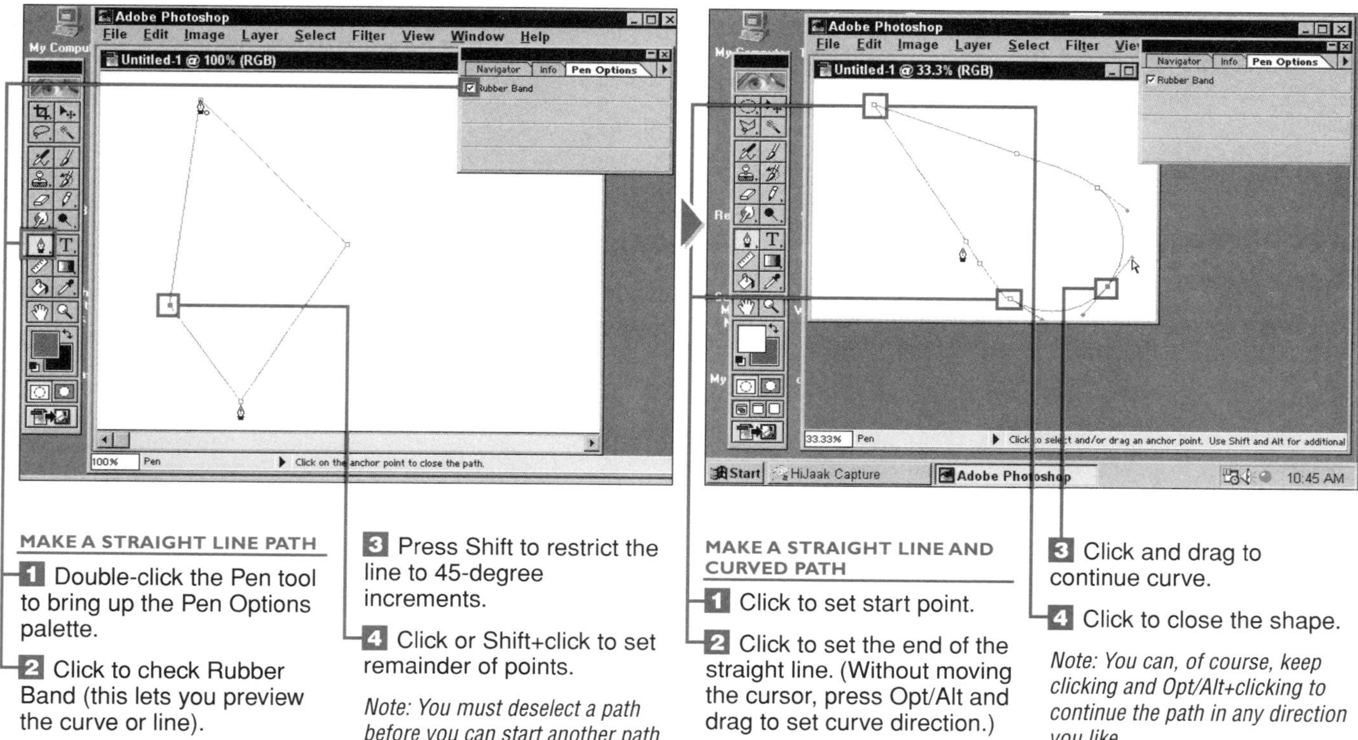

MAKE A STRAIGHT LINE PATH

1 Double-click the Pen tool to bring up the Pen Options palette.

2 Click to check Rubber Band (this lets you preview the curve or line).

3 Press Shift to restrict the line to 45-degree increments.

4 Click or Shift+click to set remainder of points.

Note: You must deselect a path before you can start another path.

MAKE A STRAIGHT LINE AND CURVED PATH

1 Click to set start point.

2 Click to set the end of the straight line. (Without moving the cursor, press Opt/Alt and drag to set curve direction.)

3 Click and drag to continue curve.

4 Click to close the shape.

Note: You can, of course, keep clicking and Opt/Alt+clicking to continue the path in any direction you like.

TIPS

Why aren't you having me change tools from the Pen tools fly-out menu?

It can be very confusing to change tools from the Toolbox while drawing because success depends so much on exactly when you press a modifier key or switch tools. Also, if you have the Rubber Band box checked, the line will seem to go wild while you're reaching out to pick the tool.

How do I make an open Path?

You have to make it in an illustration program, such as Adobe Illustrator, Macromedia FreeHand, or CorelDRAW! Then import or paste the path into Photoshop. You'll find detailed instructions on how to do this later in the chapter.

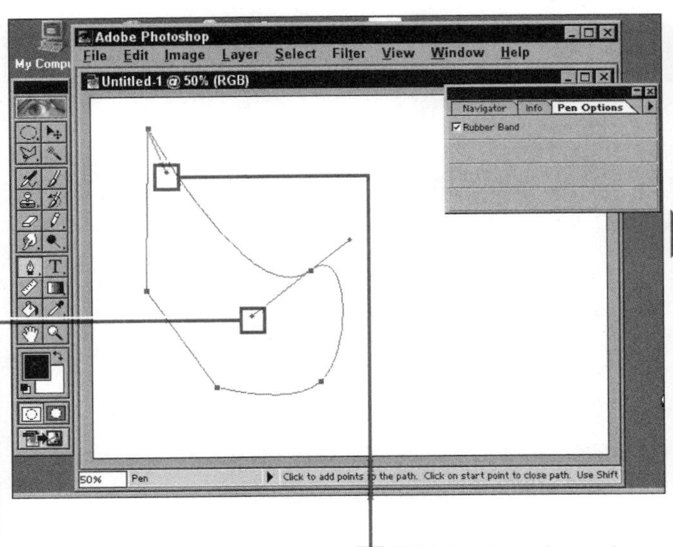

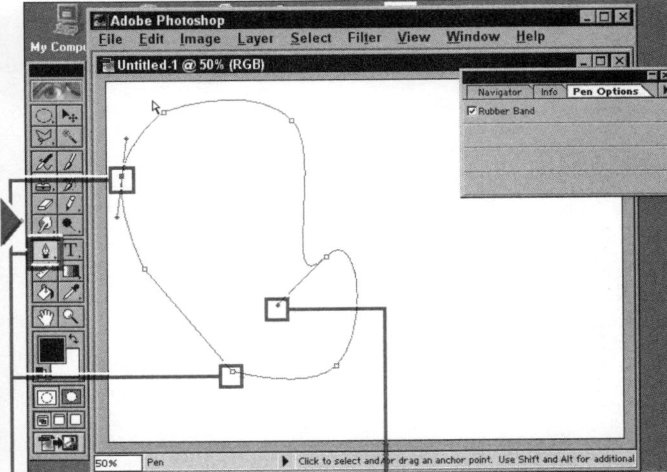

MAKE A MORE COMPLEX PATH

1 Start the shape.

2 Press ⌘/Ctrl to convert the Pen tool to the Selection arrow and drag the outgoing control point to reshape the curve.

3 Click to close the path and immediately drag down to influence the position of the direction point.

MAKE A COMPLEX PATH THAT STARTS WITH A CURVE

1 Choose the Pen tool.

2 Set the direction point.

3 Click and press Opt/Alt and click again to convert the point to a corner point.

4 Click and drag to set the direction of the incoming curve, press Opt/Alt, and click the direction arrows to shape the outgoing and incoming curves.

DRAW FREEHAND PATHS

Using the Freeform Pen tool is quite easy: Choose the tool and draw. The problem isn't drawing the paths. It's drawing them accurately enough that you don't have to spend the rest of the week editing them.

First, unless you have the utmost patience, get a pressure-sensitive tablet, take a deep breath, and draw with a steady hand. Second, experiment with the Curve Fit setting in the Freeform Pen Options palette.

You get the most accurate tracing at over 100 percent zoom, because the Curve Fit settings apply to screen pixels. If you have to pan to complete the path, you risk accidentally dropping it. Pause drawing and press the spacebar to get the Hand icon. Then you can drag the screen view, release the spacebar, and continue drawing. Doing this successfully requires a little practice and training, though.

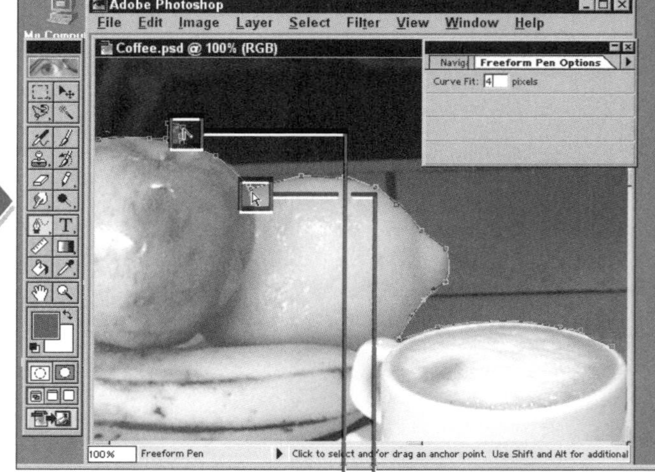

1 Double-click the Freeform Pen tool to bring up its Options palette.

2 Enter the number of pixels.

3 Trace the edge of the outline.

4 Press the spacebar and drag to pan when the Hand icon appears.

5 Continue tracing until you return to the origin point.

6 Release the spacebar to close the path.

Note: This figure is a composite. You won't see both types of cursors on screen at one time.

7 To move a point, press ⌘/Ctrl to switch to the Direct Selection tool and then drag.

8 To change the nature of a control point, press Opt/Alt to switch to the Convert Point tool.

CONVERT SELECTIONS TO A PATH

One of the easiest ways to create a path that follows a shape precisely is to convert a selection to a path. You need to be aware that this method isn't a panacea, either. Feathered selections and selections made from channels aren't likely to follow the edge you had in mind because the edge of the mask isn't well-enough defined.

On the other hand, converting a selection is a very fast process, especially if it's used in conjunction with Magic Wand selections. If you want the path to accurately follow the selection marquee, be sure to turn off feathering (check the Options dialog box for the selection tool you used before making the selection). On the other hand, you can get a smoother path if you try feathering slightly.

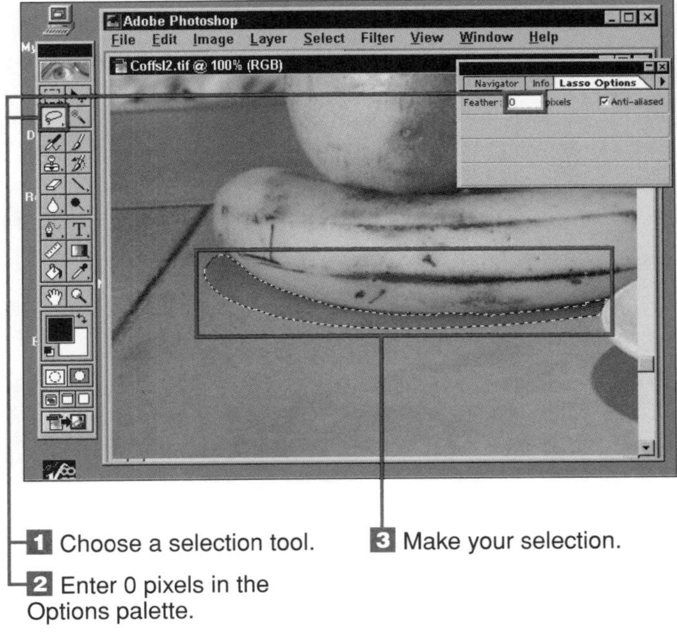

1 Choose a selection tool.

2 Enter 0 pixels in the Options palette.

3 Make your selection.

4 Choose Window ⇨ Show Paths.

■ The Paths palette appears.

5 Click the Make Path from Selection icon.

Note: The selection is made according to the setting in the Make Work Path dialog box.

■ This is a path made from the same selection after feathering.

AUTOMATE PATH TRACING WITH THE MAGNETIC PEN

Using the Magnetic Pen tool is almost exactly like using the Magnetic Lasso tool. The theory is that if you drag the pen close to an edge in the image, it automatically traces a path exactly along that edge. This actually works pretty well if you have sharp edges and strong contrasts, few and minor changes in direction along the edge, and fairly consistent contrast differences along the edge. Otherwise, the tool goes berserk. Frankly, you'll often save time by hand-tracing with the Pen tool or making selections with the Magic Wand and then converting the selection to a path.

The trick to using the Magic Pen tool efficiently is to move without dragging. Click to place a start point, and move the cursor along the edge without dragging. When you reach a point where the contrast or direction of the edge changes, click to set a point, and then continue moving until the need arises to set another point.

If you go too far and the path starts to go crazy, press Delete/Backspace to delete any points that have been set down. Move backward until you're at a point where you can resume. Lots and lots of practice makes, well, better, if not perfect.

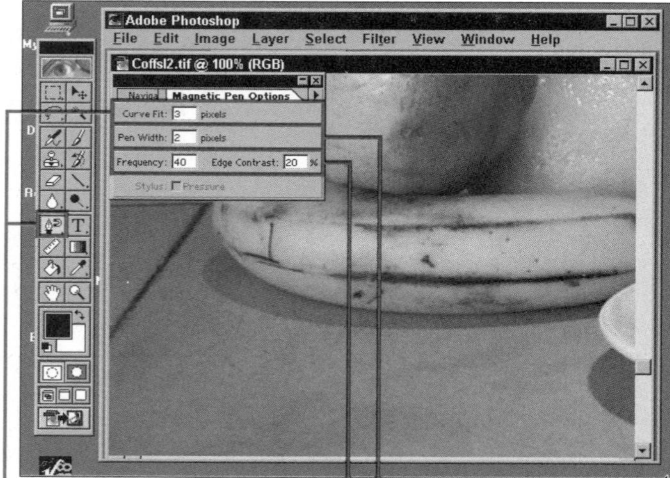

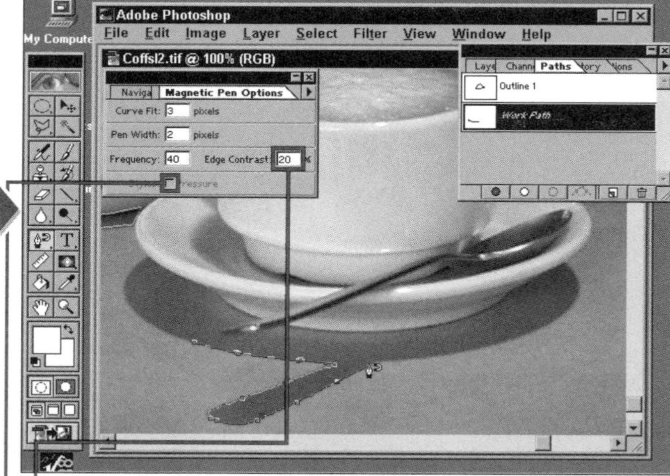

1 Double-click to bring up the Magnetic Pen Options palette.

2 Specify the number of pixels to determine how smooth the path should be.

3 Specify the number of pixels on either side of the cursor that will be scanned for a contrasting edge.

4 Enter the number of pixels between automatic insertion of control points.

5 Specify how much contrast must change before the Magnetic Pen considers something an edge.

6 If you are using a pressure pen, click to toggle pressure sensitivity on/off.

Note: Until you've had some practice, turning pressure sensitivity off will make your life easier. Start using it after you've gotten used to the effect of the other settings.

TIPS

Is this tool more trouble than it's worth?

That depends. If the image has pronounced and obvious edges, it can speed your work quite a bit. On the other hand, it's good that they didn't call this the Magic Pen tool. It's not a panacea.

Why isn't this tool more help in selecting really tough shapes, such as those with fuzzy edges, thin threads, and low contrast?

Because it's not as accurate as the human eye. Also, remember that paths are straight, smooth lines. If a shape has fuzzy edges, transparent areas, and shadows, you're going to need to work with grayscale masks. (See Chapter 8 for information on masks.)

Can you close the path without clicking on the last point?

There are two ways to do this. If you double-click, the path automatically closes while attempting to follow any edges it finds along the way. If you press Opt/Alt and click on the first point, the path closes in a straight line between the first and last points.

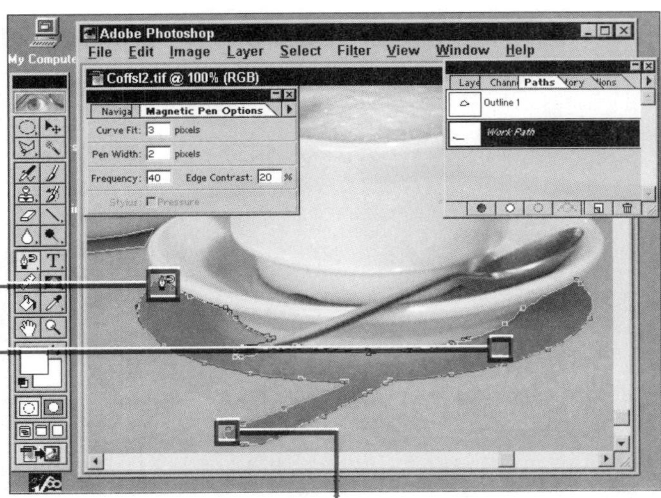

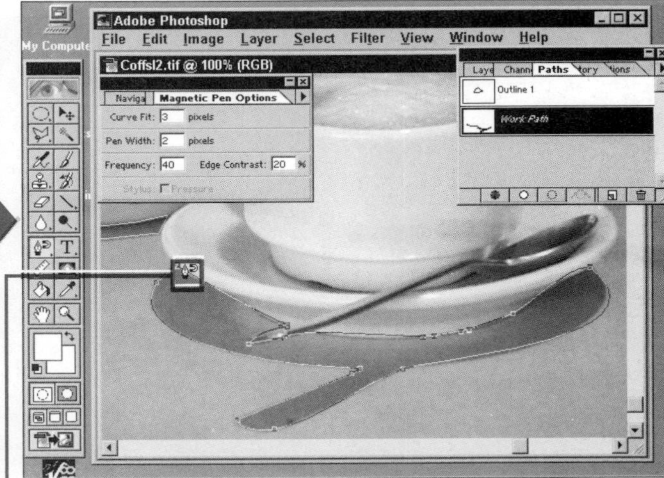

7 Click to set the start point.

8 Release the mouse button and move the cursor along the edge.

■ The path automatically begins to attach itself to the edge.

9 Click the mouse whenever the path changes direction.

10 If the path starts to wander while you're tracing, move backwards and press Delete/Backspace.

11 To close the path, click the start point.

■ You will probably have editing to do. See "Edit and Reshape a Path," next in this chapter.

EDIT AND RESHAPE A PATH

The paths in Photoshop are vector-based and use Bezier curves, which are curves that can be controlled by attached levers called *direction points*. Direction points are attached to control points. A *control point* can have zero (corner point), one (combination curve-line point), or two direction points (sometimes called *handles* or *levers*).

A control point that has two levers can be either a smooth curve (the direction points are equidistant and opposed by 180 degrees), an asymmetrical curve (the direction points are opposed by 180 degrees, but their distance to the control point is unequal), or a cusp point (the two direction points are not directly opposed).

Knowing the structure of curve types makes it easy to understand how to edit them. Not enough curves to provide the wrinkles you need? Just add points and adjust their handles. Too many wrinkles? Subtract points. Need to change a corner point to a curve? No problem. Just add and position the needed control points. The changes made to the shape in the following figures cover all this.

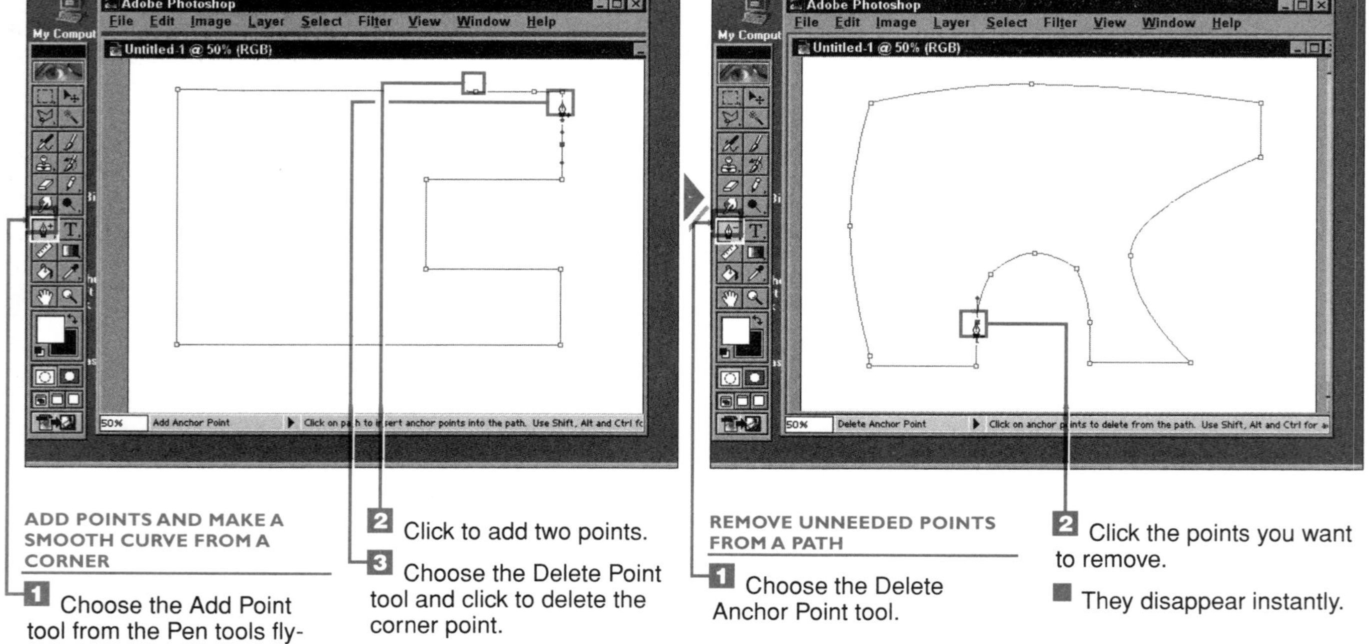

ADD POINTS AND MAKE A SMOOTH CURVE FROM A CORNER

1 Choose the Add Point tool from the Pen tools fly-out menu.

2 Click to add two points.

3 Choose the Delete Point tool and click to delete the corner point.

REMOVE UNNEEDED POINTS FROM A PATH

1 Choose the Delete Anchor Point tool.

2 Click the points you want to remove.

■ They disappear instantly.

TIPS

How do I edit a path?

Mysteriously, Photoshop doesn't give users any way to transform a path. Transformations are overall edits, such as scaling (resizing), rotating, stretching, and skewing.

Is there really no way to create an open path? What if I want to stroke a path that isn't closed

Well, you'll have to cheat. Before you finish the path, choose Window ➪ Show Paths. Then choose New Path from the Paths palette menu. The current path will be saved without closing it. You can also double-click the work path layer in the Paths palette to prompt a save.

Can I join two open paths?

Yes. Choose the Pen tool. Click the end point of one of the open paths and, if the join will be a curve, drag to indicate the direction. Then click an end point of the other open path. Drag if necessary to complete the curve.

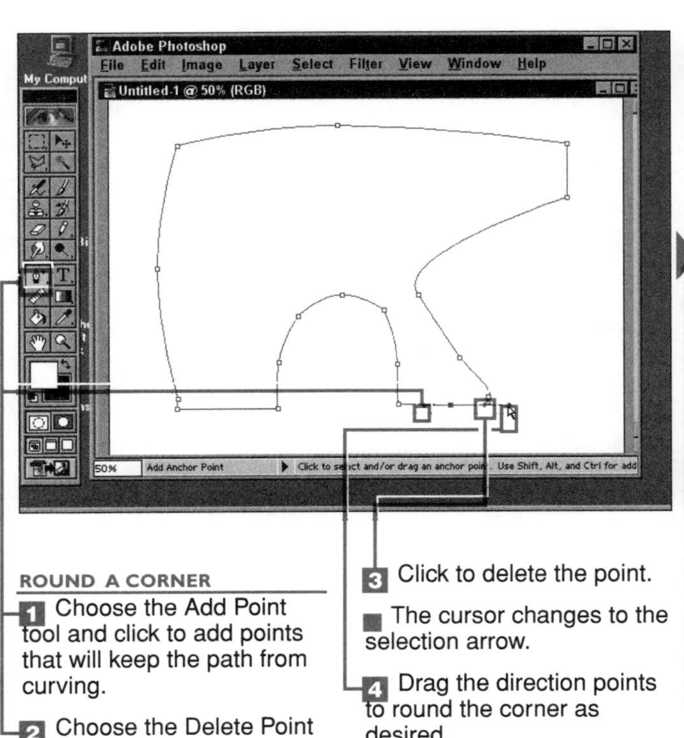

ROUND A CORNER

1 Choose the Add Point tool and click to add points that will keep the path from curving.

2 Choose the Delete Point tool.

3 Click to delete the point.

■ The cursor changes to the selection arrow.

4 Drag the direction points to round the corner as desired.

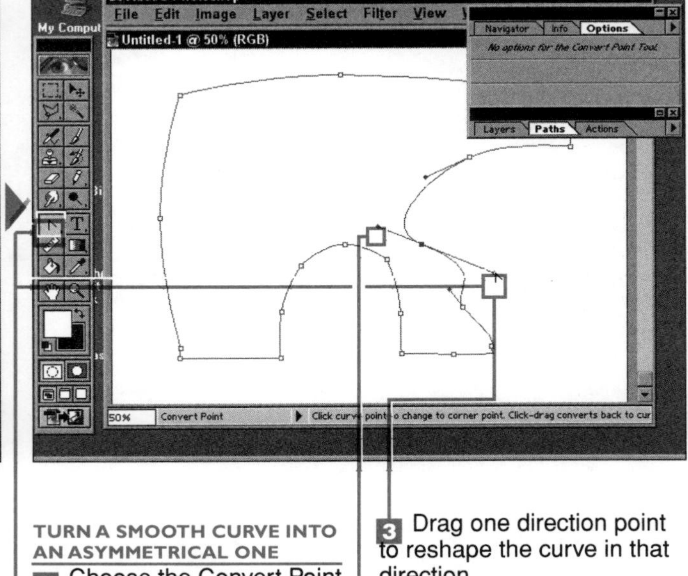

TURN A SMOOTH CURVE INTO AN ASYMMETRICAL ONE

1 Choose the Convert Point tool.

2 Drag from the control point you want to change.

3 Drag one direction point to reshape the curve in that direction.

4 If necessary, drag the opposite direction point to reshape the curve in that direction.

MAKE AND USE A CLIPPING PATH

Clipping paths are nothing more than ordinary Bezier paths that have been designated as clipping paths. Clipping paths trim the image outside the path to give it a nonrectangular shape in a publication. A clipping path has no effect in Photoshop; you must export the image to a PostScript-based illustration or page-makeup program, such as QuarkXPress, Adobe Illustrator or PageMaker, Macromedia FreeHand, or CorelDRAW!

You can designate any path in the Paths palette as a clipping path. Highlight the path you want to use and choose Clipping Path. The Clipping Path dialog box lets you choose any of the named paths (not working paths).

When you export the file to EPS format, the clipping path goes with it (you can designate it as a clipping path as you're saving in EPS format). PageMaker and some other programs also recognize clipping paths saved to TIFF format.

1 Make a path by any method.

2 Save the path by double-clicking the path's name bar.

■ The Save Path dialog box appears.

3 Enter a new name for the path or accept the default.

4 Click OK.

MAKE THE PATH INTO A CLIPPING PATH

5 Choose Clipping Path.

6 Enter a flatness value if you want to change the curved path to a series of polygons.

Note: Until you're experienced, you can leave this option blank and let the output device decide what flatness to apply.

7 Click OK.

EXPORT AND SAVE PATHS

The lovely thing about Bezier paths is that they're very space efficient and can be understood by lots of vector-based programs. OK, that's two lovely things. Their space efficiency makes them a good way to keep your saved selections while dumping alpha channels in favor of file size (but you will lose virtually all softness or opacity you may have in your masks). You can also use the Photoshop Export command to save just the paths in Adobe Illustrator format. Fortunately, almost all illustration programs can read Adobe Illustrator files.

Saving a path takes so little disk space that you could save dozens of them without noticing much difference in overall file size. If you make a lot of selections that you just might want to use later, convert them to paths and save them. Converting them back to selections is much easier than making the selection all over again.

To export paths to Illustrator, choose File ⇨ Export to Illustrator. The Export Paths dialog box is typical of all file-saving dialog boxes except that you can choose to export a specific path, all paths, or the document boundaries.

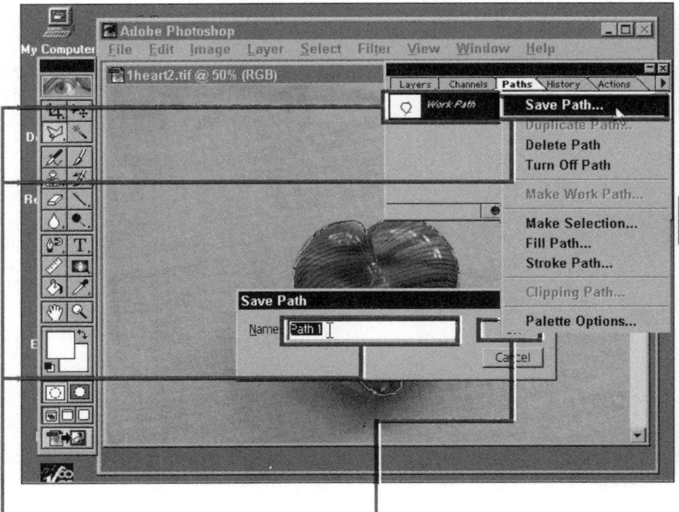

SAVE A PATH IN THE SAME PHOTOSHOP FILE

1 Click to select the work path.

2 Choose Save Path.

3 Enter a name for the path or just accept the default.

4 Click OK.

Note: You can also place paths into other Photoshop files by making the path active and then dragging it into the open window of the target file.

EXPORT A PATH TO ILLUSTRATOR

1 Choose File ⇨ Export ⇨ Paths to Illustrator.

2 Choose the path you want to export.

3 Navigate to the directory in which you want to save, and name the file.

4 Click OK. (You can only save to one format: .AIS.)

PAINT A PATH

Once you've created a path in Photoshop, you can paint it by stroking the path itself or by filling the space inside the path. This is very much like filling or stroking a selection, but with important differences.

The most important difference is the versatility with which you can stroke a path, compared to stroking a selection. When you stroke a path, the stroke uses the foreground color, and you can specify the width. When you stroke a selection, you can choose which brush and brush style to use. Furthermore, all the settings currently in effect for that brush are applied.

When you fill a path, your only options are to anti-alias the outline and to feather the edges of the fill. Nonetheless, this is a very useful command. You can use it to shade and feather channel masks, for instance.

You can also use paths and selections in combination with one another. If you fill a path and a selection overlaps it, only that part of the path inside the selection will be filled. You can use this technique to paint a variety of shapes, using only a single mask.

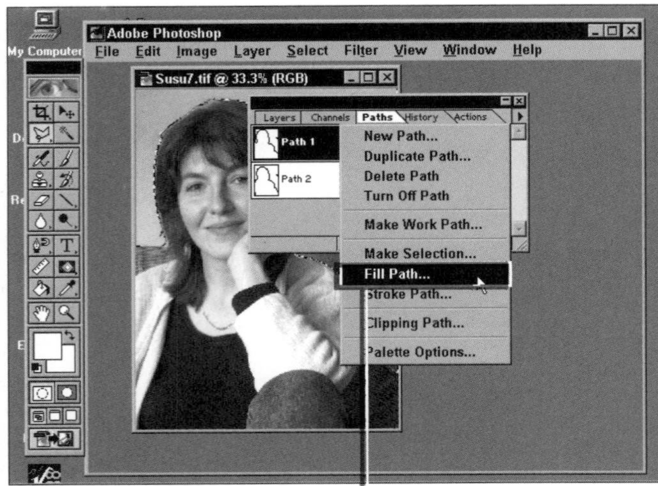

PAINT INSIDE A PATH

1 Choose Window ➪ Show Paths to reveal the Paths palette.

2 Choose Fill Path.

■ The Fill Path dialog box appears.

Note: You can choose Foreground, Background, Black, or White from the Use pull-down menu, and you can use any of the Apply (Blend) modes.

3 Enter a number for Feather Radius to soften edges of the fill.

4 Click to toggle anti-aliasing of the border.

5 Click OK.

TIPS

Please elaborate on why I would want to use Fill Path in making alpha channel masks?

You can store dozens of selection shapes as paths and then recall and fill or stroke them in any sequence or arrangement you like.

Should I just save every selection I make as a path, even if I can't imagine ever using it again?

It is probably a good idea. You can always turn a path back into a selection and modify that in much less time than it would take to make the whole selection all over again. Even if what you need is a hand-painted grayscale mask, starting with a selection that's already been made will save you time.

What if I want to transform a path?

Select the path or any sequence of points in the path. Choose Edit ➪ Transform Points. You can use any of the Photoshop transformations, including entering a transformation numerically.

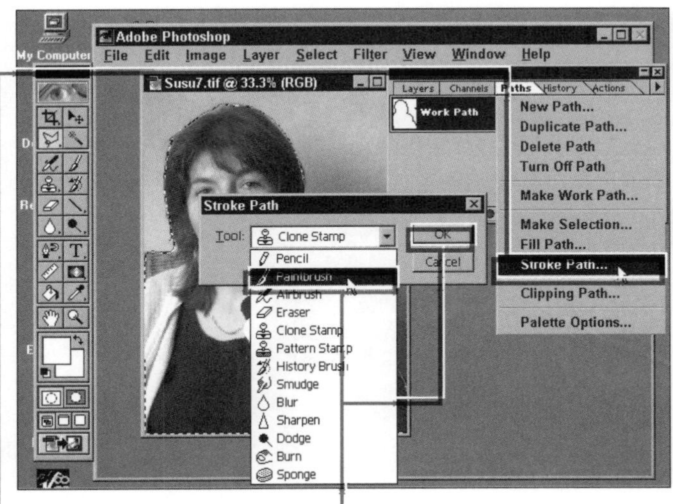

Note: To stroke a path, be sure the Paths palette is in view. If not, choose Window ➪ Show Paths.

1 Choose Stroke Path.

■ The Stroke Path dialog box appears.

2 Choose a brush type.

3 Click OK.

■ The path is stroked according to settings previously made for the brush. Notice that because this is an angled brush, some parts of the path are thicker.

■ Also notice the color fades from the foreground to the background as it travels the path.

MAKING AND USING MASKS

Masks are one of the most powerful tools Photoshop has to offer. Masks make it possible to restrict any of Photoshop's commands, tools, or filters to the unmasked portion of the current layer. Selections and masks are essentially the same, with two distinctions: 1) A selection doesn't become a mask until it is saved to an alpha channel. An alpha channel is one that is not needed for recording a file's color information and that isn't a composite channel. 2) Masks are more editable than selections (although both are highly editable), because masks are actually bit-mapped images that can be modified by any of Photoshop's tools and commands.

To visualize the basics of how masks work, take a look at the first figure, which shows a mask made by saving a selection. The image is that of the alpha channel resulting from saving a selection made with the Lasso tool and then editing it with the Elliptical Marquee tool. The selection made with the Lasso tool was feathered by 20 pixels, so the mask, white on the inside, fades to black on the outside. The selection made with the Elliptical Marquee tool is unfeathered and was subtracted from the first selection, so it cuts a sharp-edged hole into the center of the mask.

Prior to saving, the selection from which the mask in the first figure was made would behave just as the mask would: The black areas would totally block the effect of any Photoshop command or tool. The white areas would be affected 100 percent by those same commands. The gray areas would be partially affected, in direct proportion to their brightness. On the theory that a picture is worth more than a paragraph, look at the following figure.

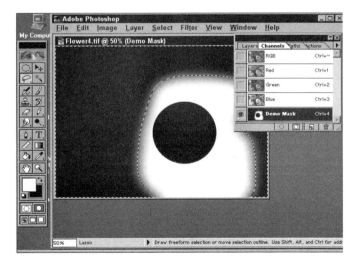

The tools and commands described in this chapter include the following:

- The Channels palette
- Quick Mask mode and options
- The Feather Selection dialog box
- The Save Selection dialog box
- The Load Selection dialog box

The Channels palette

The Channels palette, shown in this figure, is the centerpiece of Photoshop's masking operations.

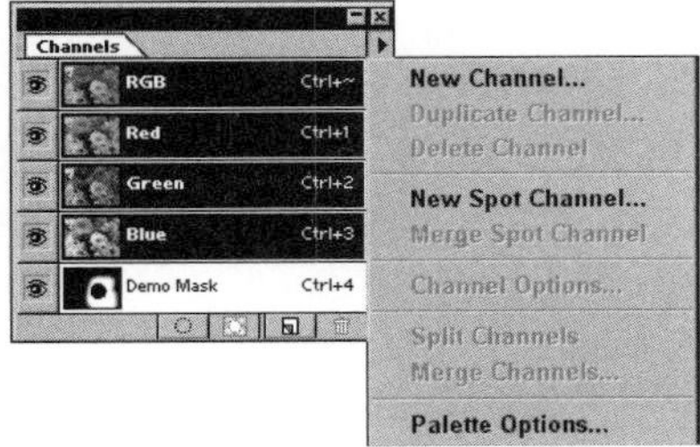

Channels Palette Contents

Component	Function
Visibility icon	Indicates what an option is, providing the user with a cue as to what the option does and when to use it.
Composite channel	Actually not an independent channel, but a composite of the color channels. In other words, this channel shows a preview of what the final result of any channel manipulations will be.
Channel name bar	Click to select. When selected (highlighted), the image from this channel appears in the workspace and can be edited with the full power of Photoshop 5.
Color channels	The three or four (depending on the color mode in which you are operating) independent channels that make up the primary colors in your image. Each of these channels can be edited independently of one another.
Alpha (mask) channel	A grayscale bitmap that indicates areas to be masked. Black is 100 percent opaque, white is 100 percent transparent, grays are translucent.
Make Selection icon	Drag a channel to this icon to turn its image into a selection, or select the channel and then click the icon.
Make Mask icon	Click to turn the current selection into a new alpha channel. To put it another way, clicking this icon saves the current selection.
New Channel icon	Creates a new, empty channel. You may then use any of Photoshop's tools or commands to place an image in that channel. Often used to create an empty channel into which a mask will be painted. You can also duplicate a channel by dragging its name bar to this icon.
Delete Channel icon	Drag a channel to this icon to delete it, or select the channel and then click the icon to delete it.
Channels palette menu button	Pops up the Channels palette menu.
Channels palette menu	Through this menu you can access the commands listed in the table that follows.

CONTINUED

MAKING AND USING MASKS CONTINUED

Channels Palette Menu Commands

Command	Result
New Channel	Creates a new, empty channel. You may then use any of Photoshop's tools or commands to place an image in that channel. Often used to create an empty channel into which a mask will be painted.
Duplicate Channel	Duplicates the currently selected channel as an alpha channel.
Delete Channel	Deletes the currently selected channel.
New Spot Channel	Creates a new spot color channel. This is a new feature in Photoshop 5. If a selection is active, the spot color will appear inside the selection. If not, you can paint the spot color into the channel.
Merge Spot Channel	Merges the selected spot channel with the primary channels.
Channel Options	The dialog box that appears after choosing this command depends on the type of channel selected. If a color channel is selected, the command is unavailable. There are different Options dialog boxes for spot channels and alpha channels. (See the text that follows for specifics.)
Split Channels	Creates a new file window for each channel.
Merge Channels	Brings up a Merge Channels dialog box. By default, reunites color channels that have been split.
Palette Options	Enables you to pick from small, medium, or large thumbnail sizes.

Options for Alpha Channels

An alpha channel is a channel that is not needed for recording a file's color information and that isn't a composite channel. The Channel Options dialog box that appears when an alpha channel is selected enables you to specify color, opacity, and what the colors indicate in the alpha channel.

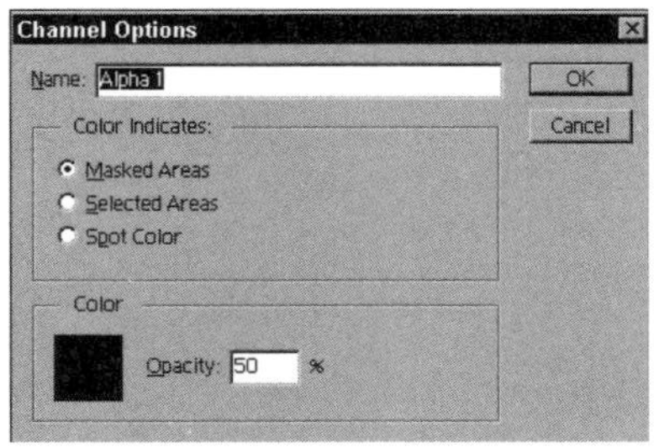

Channel Options Dialog Box Contents

Component	Function
Name field	Area in which you enter a name for the channel.
Color Indicates radio buttons	Mutually exclusive choices indicate whether colors in the channel represent masked or unmasked areas or spot colors. If the Spot Color option is chosen, the alpha channel changes to a spot color channel.
Color Swatch	Takes you to your operating system's Color Picker. If you are choosing spot color, you probably want to choose from an industry-standard spot color palette, such as those from Pantone, ANPA, DIC, and Focaltone.
Opacity/ Solidity field	Enter a number between 1 and 100 to indicate the percentage of opacity or the solidity of the spot color.
OK button	Applies the current settings.
Cancel button	Closes the dialog box without applying any setting changes to the image.

Options for Spot Channels

Adding a new Spot channel to an image is a new feature in Photoshop 5. When you select New Spot Color in the Channels palette menu, the New Spot Channel dialog box appears.

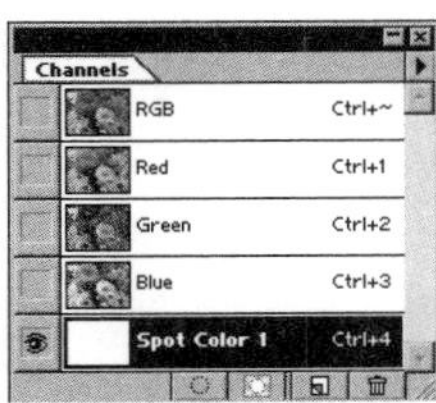

Spot Channel Options Dialog Box Contents

Component	Function
Name field	Enter any name of your choice. Use a name that will help you identify this channel's purpose.
Color Swatch	Takes you to your operating system's Color Picker. If you are choosing spot color, you probably want to choose from an industry-standard spot color palette, such as those from Pantone, ANPA, DIC, and Focaltone.
Solidity field	Enter a number between 1 and 100 to enter the percentage of solidity of the spot color.

Quick Mask Mode

Quick Mask mode is handy when creating masks for a couple of reasons:

- It lets you edit a selection using any of the Photoshop tools without forcing you to first save the channel.
- It lets you edit a mask while viewing it superimposed over the image. You can choose a contrasting color for the mask and the degree of opacity to be used.

You can also edit an alpha channel mask in Quick Mask mode. To do so, select the channel in the Channels palette, click the Make Selection icon at the bottom of the Channels palette, and then click the Quick Mask mode icon.

CONTINUED

MAKING AND USING MASKS CONTINUED

Quick Mask Mode Shortcut and Modifier

Icon	Shortcut	Modifiers and Result
	Q	Opt/Alt+click Quick Mask Mode button to invert the selected and unselected areas

The Quick Mask tool, which has an associated Options palette, is depicted here. Double-click the Quick Mask button to bring up the Quick Mask Options dialog box.

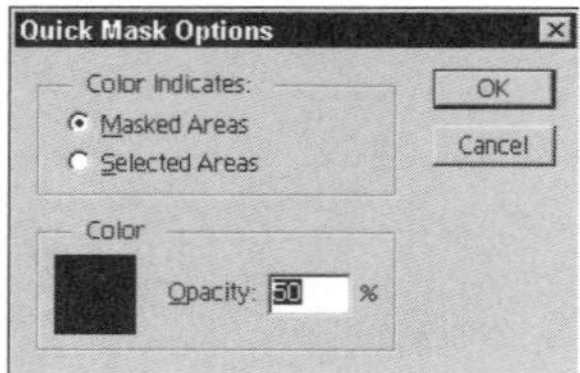

Quick Mask Dialog Box Contents

Component	Function
Color Indicates radio buttons	Choose a radio button to indicate whether colored area represents the masked or unmasked areas of the image.
Color Swatch	Click here to access your operating system's Color Picker. You can choose any color as a color for the mask. It is best to choose a color that is not present (or, at least, not prevalent) in the image you are masking.
Opacity field	Enter a number between 0 and 100 to indicate the percentage of opacity of the masking color. Note: This doesn't determine the opacity of the mask itself. The mask opacity is determined by the shade of gray used to paint or fill the mask.

Feather Selection dialog box

The Feather Selection dialog box, shown here, appears when you feather an existing selection. To feather an existing selection, choose Select ➪ Feather (Opt/Alt+⌘/Ctrl+D).

Feather Selection Option

Component	Function
Feather Radius field	Enter a number of pixels to indicate the width of feathering. Feathering (graduating the edges of the mask from black to white or, to put it another way, from opaque to transparent) is always centered on the selection marquee.

Two techniques are available for feathering different parts of a selection to different degrees:

- Make two selections. After making the first, which should not encompass what will be the edge of the second selection, feather it (as detailed in the previous table). Press Shift and make a second selection that does encompass the edge you want to feather to a different degree. Now, specify a different number of pixels for feathering.
- Set a given degree of feathering in the selection tool's Options dialog box Feather field. Make a selection. Double-click the selection tool a second time to bring up its options and set a different pixel width for feathering. Now press Shift and add to the first selection. Once again, the second selection must fall outside the first selection.

Save Selection dialog box

When you save a selection by choosing Select ⇨ Save Selection from the menu bar, the Save Selection dialog box shown in the following figure appears.

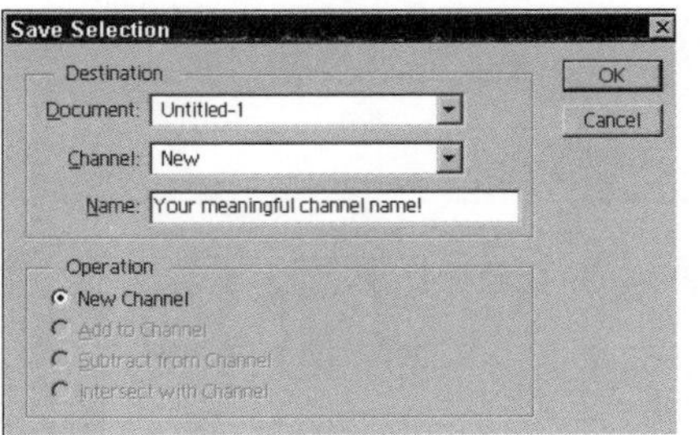

Save Selection Options

Component	Function
Document pull-down menu	Lets you choose the document into which you want to store the current selection. This is one way you can transfer channels between files: Open both files, turn the channel into a selection, save the selection, and choose the other open document as the destination using this menu. You can only choose a currently open document as a destination.
Channel pull-down menu	Lets you either create a new channel for this selection or merge this selection with the mask in an existing channel. The method of merging is determined by your choice of Operations radio buttons (the specific buttons are described below).
Name field	Enter any name that will help you remember the purpose of this channel.
New Channel operation	Creates a new channel for the current selection.

CONTINUED

MAKING AND USING MASKS CONTINUED

Save Selection Options

Component	Function
Add to Channel operation	Adds the current selection to the mask stored in an existing channel (be sure you have chosen the desired target channel from the Channel pull-down menu).
Subtract from Channel operation	Removes the current selection from the mask stored in an existing channel (be sure you have chosen the desired target channel from the Channel pull-down menu).
Intersect with Channel operation	Leaves only the area shared in common between the current selection and the mask stored in an existing channel (be sure you have chosen the desired target channel from the Channel pull-down menu).

Load Selection dialog box

When you load a selection by choosing Select ➪ Load Selection from the menu bar, the Load Selection dialog box appears, as illustrated here.

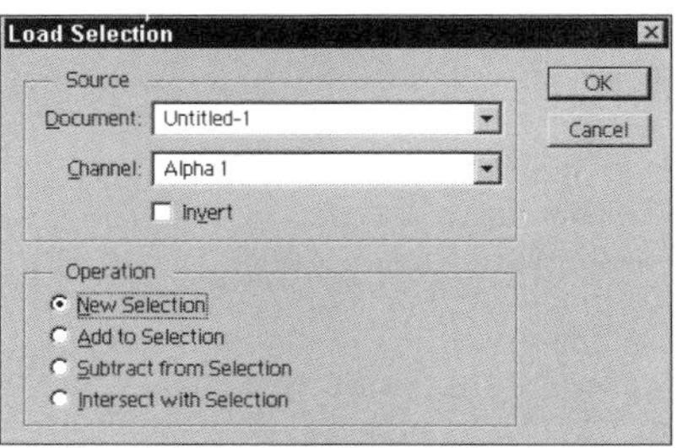

Load Selection Options

Component	Function
Document pull-down menu	Lets you choose the document from which you want to load the current selection.
Channel pull-down menu	Lets you choose to either load a new channel as the current selection or merge a current selection with the mask loaded from an existing channel. The method of merging is determined by your choice of Operations radio buttons (the specific buttons are described below).

Component	Function
Invert check box	Makes an inverted selection when the selection is retrieved. In other words, everything that wasn't selected will be selected and vice versa.
New Selection operation	Creates a new selection from the channel chosen in the Channel pull-down menu.
Add to Channel operation	Adds the mask stored in an existing channel (be sure you have chosen the desired target channel from the Channel pull-down menu) to the current selection.
Subtract from Channel operation	Removes the mask stored in an existing channel (be sure you have chosen the desired target channel from the Channel pull-down menu) to the current selection.
Intersect with Channel operation	Leaves only the area shared in common between the current selection and the mask stored in an existing channel (be sure you have chosen the desired target channel from the Channel pull-down menu).

SAVE AND LOAD SELECTIONS

Making accurate and workable selections takes time, so you'll want to save your selections. Remember, you may want to reuse a selection for purposes other than those originally intended. Also, it's much quicker to make a new selection by adding or subtracting from an old one than to start from scratch.

As soon as you save a selection, you've made a grayscale, alpha channel mask. Masks keep subsequent processing from affecting anything in the masked area.

Masks are grayscale images that cover the entire workspace. White areas are unmasked (100 percent transparent), black areas are fully masked (100 percent opaque). Gray areas are transparent in inverse proportion to their percentage of gray: If an area is 10 percent gray, it is 90 percent transparent. Almost anything you do to the image when that mask is active (such as making a brush stroke, adjusting the image, or running a filter) will have only 90 percent of its unmasked effect.

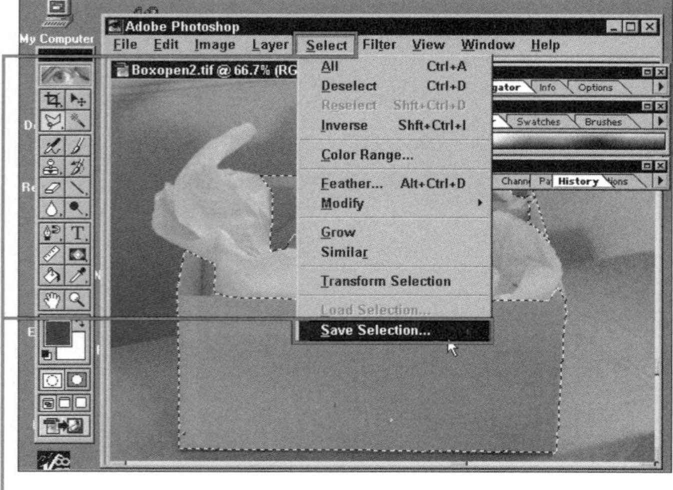

SAVE A SELECTION

1 Choose Select ⇨ Save Selection.

■ The Save Selection dialog box appears.

2 Enter a name for your channel mask.

3 If you want the current selection to be added to, subtracted from, or intersected with an existing channel, choose the target channel.

4 Click the appropriate radio button. Here a new channel is being specified for the current selection.

5 Click OK.

TIPS

When I save a selection, can I modify the resulting mask?

Yes — this is one of Photoshop's most powerful capabilities. You can paint into a mask, fill it with a gradient, or blur it with a filter. All such alterations result in differences in the way the mask interacts with subsequent processing commands. See "Edit Masks" in this chapter.

When I need to mask (select) a group of items, should I select each individually?

If you do so, you'll be able to add all the individual masks together to outline the whole group. You'll also be able to adjust and filter each item individually.

Should I save every selection I make?

This is a good idea, unless you're 100 percent sure you'll never need it again. It's far quicker to load a mask than to make a new selection. More importantly, the selection will remain consistent each time you use it for a different purpose, so you won't get weird borders.

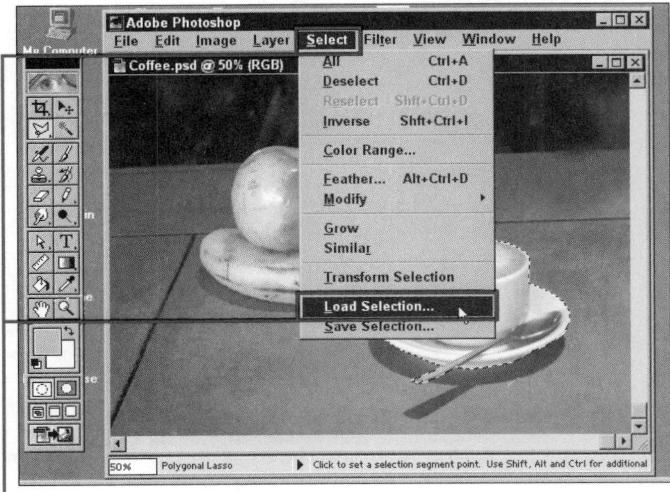

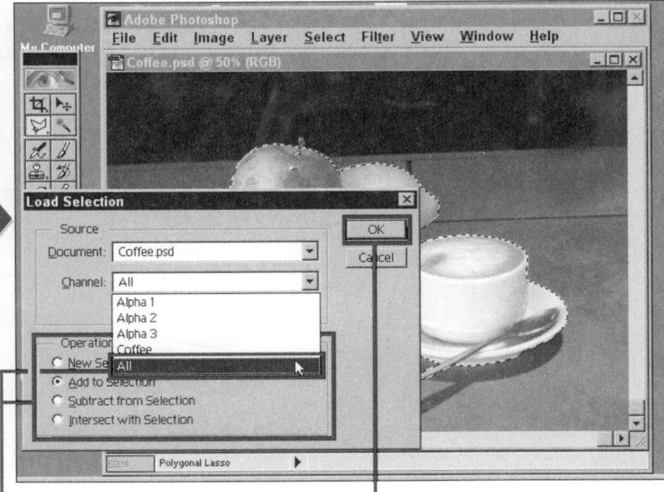

RETRIEVE (LOAD) A SELECTION

1 Choose Select ➪ Load Selection.

■ The Load Selection dialog box appears.

2 Choose the selection.

3 To added to, subtracted from, or intersected the current selection with an existing channel, click the appropriate radio button.

4 Click OK

EDIT MASKS

As noted in the last exercise, any time you save a selection, you create a mask. That mask is a grayscale painting you can edit, using any of Photoshop's tools and commands. When you darken the mask, it becomes more opaque, and this results in Photoshop's processing having less effect.

This and the following exercises show you the three most commonly used editing techniques: painting the mask with a brush (in this case, an airbrush, but any can be used), blurring edges to control feathering, and filling the mask with a gradient.

You also learn to use selections to "mask the mask." You can even load a selection from another mask while you're editing a mask. The steps that follow assume you have already made a mask.

This exercise demonstrates the use of a combination of a blur filter and a selection to make a sharp edge that graduates into the image. This effect is useful for making rounded-edge buttons or for creating the illusion that part of the image is raised from the rest of the image.

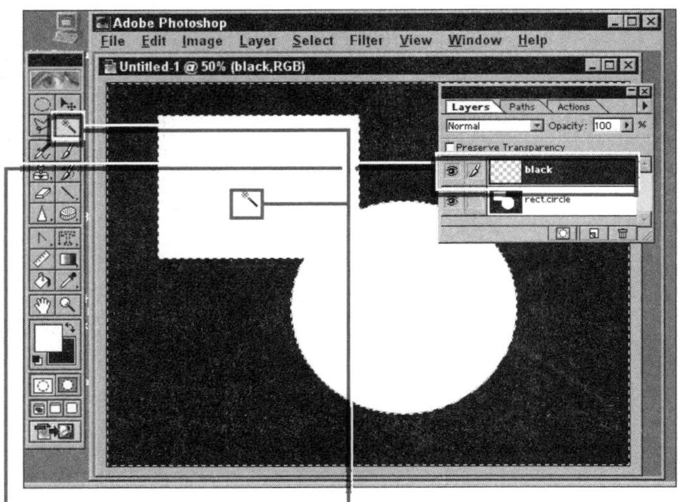

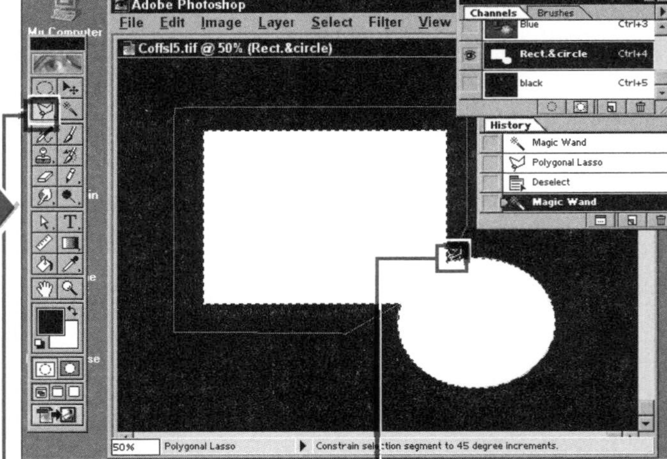

1 Choose Window ➪ Show Channels.

■ The Channels palette appears.

2 Click to choose the mask you want to edit.

3 Choose the Magic Wand tool.

4 Click inside the white portion of the mask to create a selection around the mask.

Note: To feather only part of this shape, subtract the part of the selection you want to leave unaffected.

5 Choose the Polygon Lasso tool and select what you want to subtract from the image.

6 Press Opt/Alt to subtract from the selection and click at several points to eliminate the rectangular part of the mask.

7 Double-click to close the selection.

TIPS

Why would I want to use this technique?

On occasion you may need to partially blend an effect into its surroundings while limiting the blending to a restricted area. As mentioned, this is also an excellent technique for creating the illusion of a rounded edge when making 3D buttons or picture frames.

Can I save a selection made in a mask?

You can save a selection made in a mask in exactly the same way as saving any other selection.

Are there useful variations of this technique?

There are endless variations. The two most useful are 1) limiting the blur to a specific area, and 2) blending an effect smoothly with the surrounding area by creating the blur without using a selection.

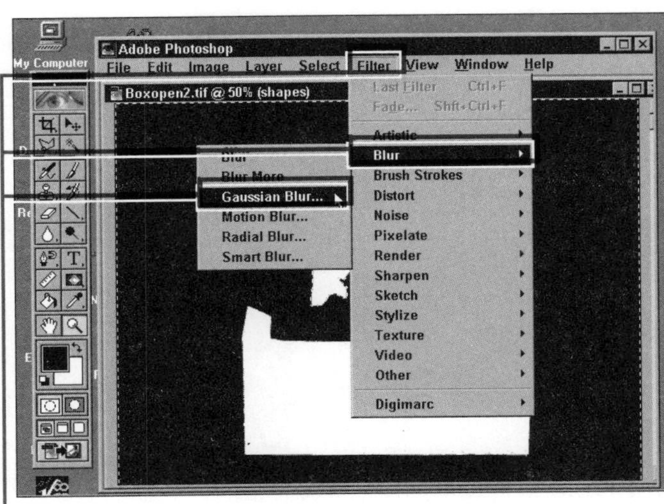

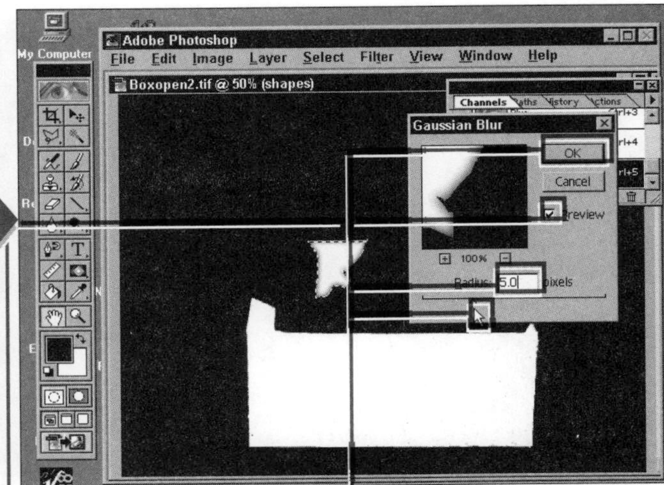

8 Choose Filter ➪ Blur ➪ Gaussian Blur.

■ The Gaussian Blur dialog box appears.

9 Check the Preview check box.

■ You should be able to see the effect of your blurring in the workspace.

10 Drag to the desired level of blur, or

11 Enter a specific pixel radius for the blur.

23 When satisfied, click OK.

EDIT MASKS WITH BRUSHES

On occasion you may find it easier or more intuitive to simply paint into a mask rather than trying to select edges perfectly. For instance, you may want to select a large portion of the image with the Magic Wand to isolate a contrasting main subject. However, this almost always leaves holes in the selection. Fortunately, you can save the selection as a mask and then simply paint out the holes with any of Photoshop's brushes.

You can also use brushes to fine-tune the edges of selections. For instance, if an edge is a bit jagged, you can try smoothing it with the Blur brush.

Finally, you can simply paint into blank space to create texture or atmospheric effects, such as smoke or raindrops. When you load a selection from such a mask, any subsequent fill or filter will be effective only in the transparent or semitransparent areas of the mask.

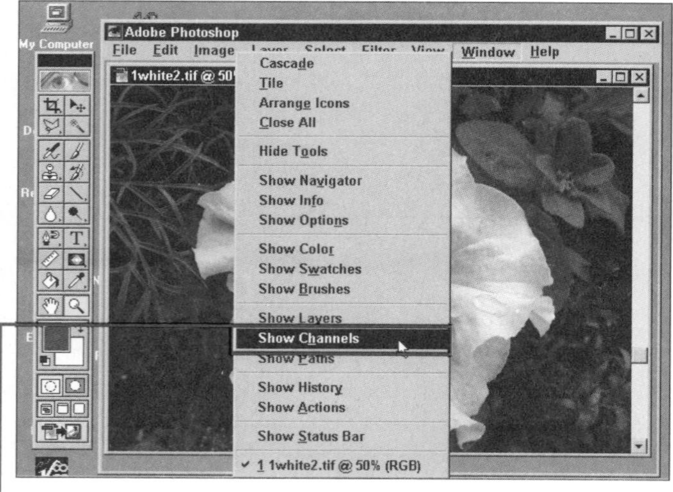

PLACE THE MASK INTO THE WORKSPACE

1 Choose Window ➪ Show Channels.

■ The Channels palette appears.

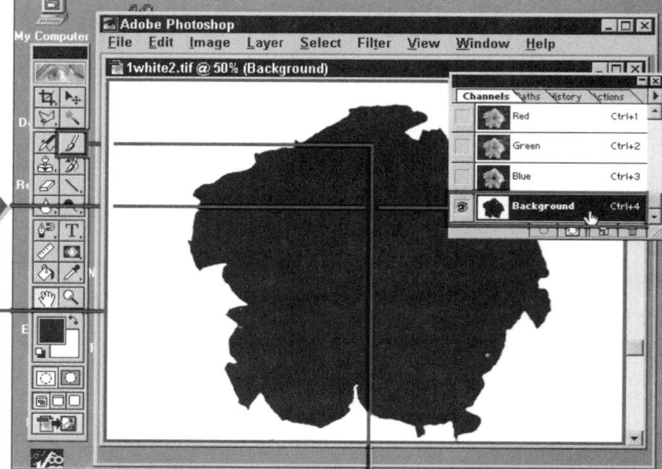

2 Choose the mask you want to edit from the alpha channels.

■ The mask appears in the workspace.

3 Click to choose a brush.

Note: The paintbrush and airbrush are the most commonly used, but you can use any of the tools in this space.

TIPS

Wouldn't it be simpler to simply select and fill the areas with holes?

That's often a better solution, but not always. You'll have to decide which works best for you in any given situation. As a rule, it's better to paint out holes in small, tight areas.

How do I paint a texture mask and how is it used?

Rough textures, such as graffiti or raindrops, are fairly easy. Choose New Channel from the Channels palette menu and select the newly created channel so that it appears in the workspace. Then paint in your texture, using the Paintbrush, Cloner, Airbrush, or other appropriate tools.

How do I know how transparent a given portion of the mask is?

Select the color with the Eyedropper. Click the foreground color to bring up the Color Picker. Check the brightness percentage in the HSB fields. The percentage of transparency is the inverse of the percentage of brightness.

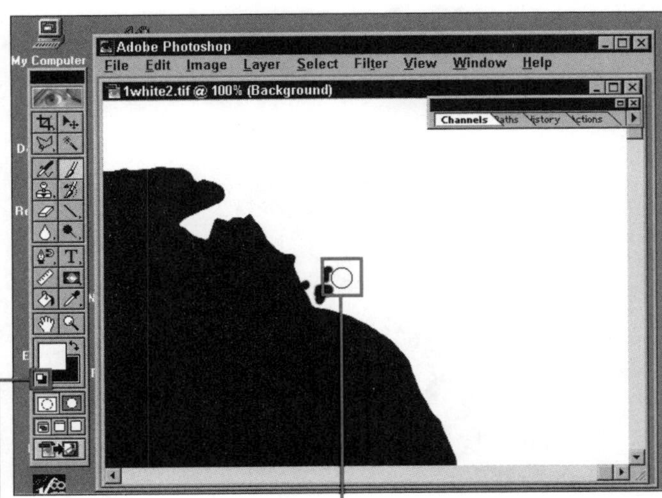

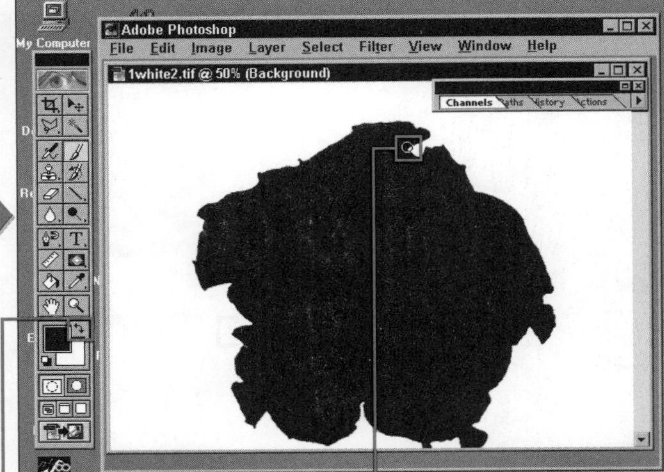

4 Click to switch to default foreground and background colors (white and black) or press D.

5 Drag to paint out the black holes.

■ If you accidentally paint into an area that should remain unmasked, you have two options. You can Undo (or back up in the History palette if you went several strokes too far).

■ Or, you can click to switch foreground color to black.

EDIT MASKS WITH FILLS

The fastest way to clean up a mask is by using a combination of selections and fills. For instance, to get rid of a large area full of holes or partially masked areas that should be solid, simply surround the area with a quick Lasso selection and fill it with white.

Another type of fill that's useful in masking is the gradient fill. These are especially good for blending transitions between images in a collage. They're also useful for shading areas that will be adjusted for brightness or color or for areas that will be filtered with a special effect.

Remember, too, that you can combine masks, which means you could make a mask from a gradient and combine it with other masks specific to individual shapes within the image. The effect of the gradient would then be consistent with the position of the object in the overall image.

Note: This exercise assumes that you know how to call up the Channels palette. If this isn't the case, refer to the previous exercise.

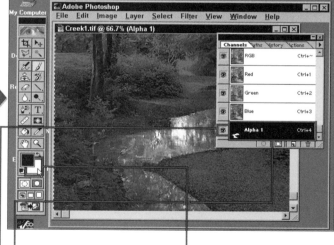

1 Drag the chosen mask to the Make Selection icon.

■ A selection appears in the workspace. Your gradient is restricted to the area within the selection.

2 Click to restore Default colors.

3 Click to make an orange mask visible over the image.

4 Click to make the mask the active workspace.

Note: You can still see the full color image under the orange mask.

5 Click to change the Background color.

■ The Color Picker dialog box appears.

TIPS

Can I also paint with the orange mask showing?

Yes. Actually, it's the best way to correct edges by hand. (Unfortunately, space considerations prevent this from being demonstrated here.)

How would I use this particular gradient fill?

This fill was made so the reflection of city buildings could be seen in a body of water (load the mask as a selection, open and flip the image of the skyline, press ⌘/Ctrl+A and ⌘/Ctrl+C, and choose Edit ➪ Paste Into) and at the same time to mask the effect of a ripple filter.

What other types of fills might prove useful?

You can use a solid fill to restrict the effect of an adjustment, filter, or subsequent brush strokes to the transparency of the filter. You could also achieve the same effect by choosing Filter ➪ Fade (Last adjustment or filter), but the mask works better when you have to do several operations at the same level of intensity.

Any other useful fills?

You can fill with a pattern to create a texture mask.

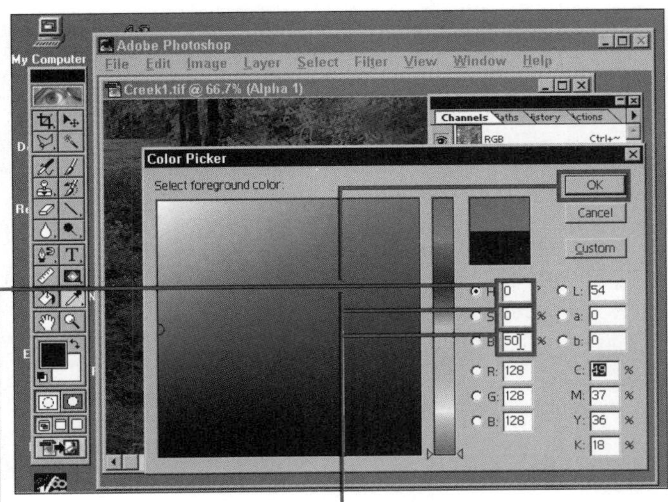

Note: This gradient will run between black and 50 percent gray, so change the background color to 50 percent gray.

6 Enter 0 for Hue (you can press Tab to jump from one field to the next).

7 Enter 0 for Saturation.

8 Enter 50 for Brightness.

9 Click OK.

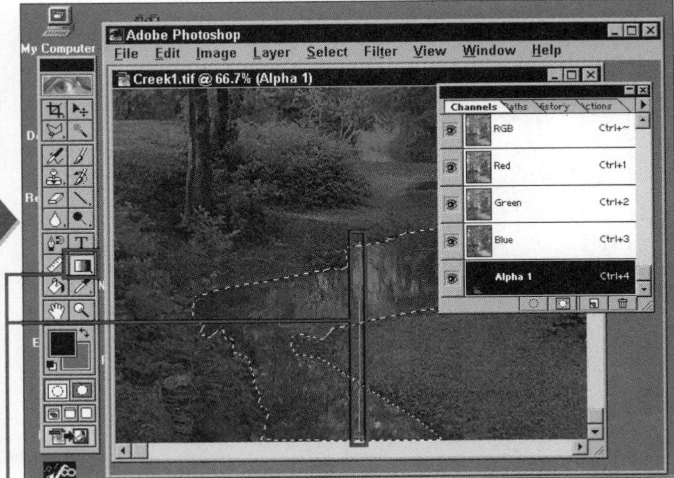

10 Choose the Gradient tool.

11 Drag from top to bottom.

■ The mask area fills with a gradient between black and 50 percent gray. You see this effect in orange. To see the full effect in the mask, click the eye icon and make sure the mask is chosen.

EDIT MASKS WITH QUICK MASK MODE

One of the easiest ways to edit a mask is to load it as a selection and then edit it in Quick Mask mode. Quick Mask mode lets you use all the editing methods described in the three previous layouts to modify a selection mask.

Quick Mask mode has two main benefits over the other mask-editing methods: 1) You can edit the mask before you even save the selection (if, indeed, you ever save it). 2) You can always see the edits in precise registration with the image, because the mask is represented as a 50 percent transparent solid color overlay.

You edit the mask just as if it were grayscale: Black masks, white unmasks, grays create varying degrees of transparency. Furthermore, all the Photoshop tools and commands are applicable in the same ways. Also, you can create selections while in Quick Mask mode to limit the extent of your edits. It's important to note that Quick Mask can be set to show "selected areas" or "masked areas" — each of which is the inverse of the other.

Note: This exercise assumes you know how to retrieve a previously stored selection. To refresh your memory, see "Save and Load Selections," earlier in this chapter.

1 Load the selection for the mask you want to edit.

■ In this example, a selection appears in the workspace. Note that the selection leaves some holes in some areas of the mask.

2 Click or press Q to switch to Quick Mask mode.

■ A red mask appears over the masked portion of the image.

■ The image as it appears in Quick Mask mode. Even in this grayscale version, you can see light areas in the branches and on the ribs of the roof that the mask doesn t cover.

3 Zoom in to about 200%.

■ You will likely see small defects in the mask, which you can correct by painting over, erasing, or blurring.

TIPS

What if I want the mask color to indicate the unmasked area?

You can specify this in the Quick Mask Options dialog box. Double-click the Quick Mask icon, click the Selected Areas radio button, and then click OK.

Can I change the color of the Quick Mask so that it shows up better against my red subjects?

Easily. Double-click the Quick Mask icon, and the Quick Mask Options dialog box appears. Click in the color box, and the standard Color Picker dialog box appears. You can then choose from any of the 16.8 million colors.

Why do I sometimes see unwanted blotchiness in the image after filling a masked area?

The mask wasn't really clean. This often happens after using "automatic" masking methods such as third-party masking plug-ins, "blue screen" compositing plug-ins, or the Select ➪ Color Range command. The blotchiness occurs because the masking algorithm finds certain colors to be masked inside the area that should be masked. Moral: Examine each mask after saving the selection, and make any necessary edits by hand.

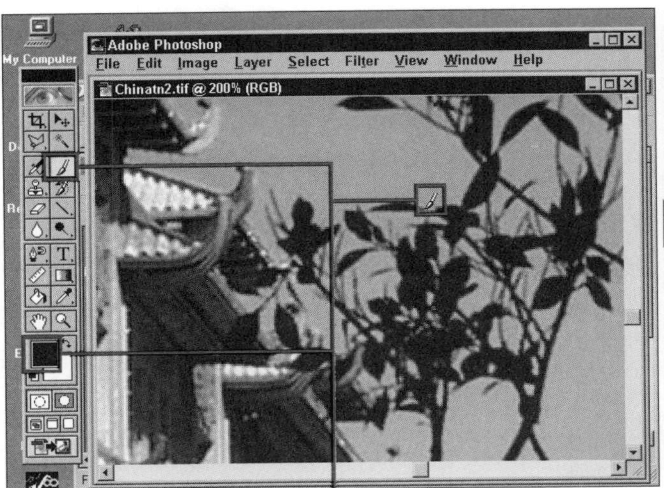

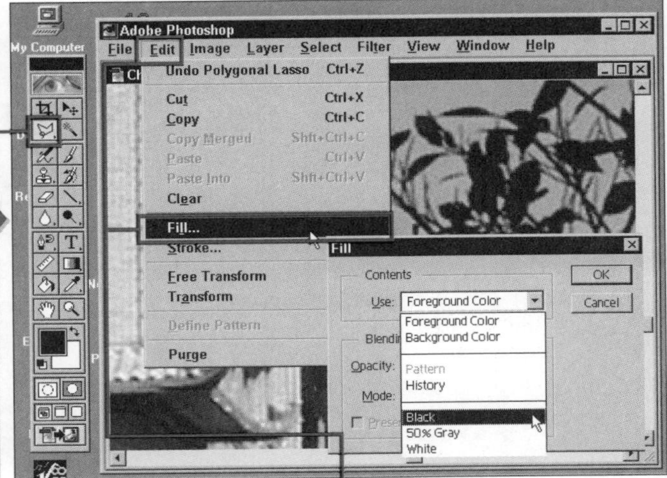

Note: Just as when editing the mask itself, you edit the Quick Mask by choosing black to create opacity (solid red, in this case), white to clear the mask, and gray for any level of transparency in between.

4 Choose the brush with which you want to retouch.

5 Choose the shade of gray to paint with.

6 Paint on or erase the mask.

7 To mask large areas uniformly, select the area.

8 Choose a selection tool.

9 Make the selection.

10 Choose Edit ➪ Fill and then Black from the Fill dialog box s pull-down menu.

■ Any holes in the mask are filled. To clear large areas of mask, follow the preceding steps, but choose Edit ➪ Fill ➪ White.

MAKE TEXTURE MASKS

Texture masks provide one way to superimpose a texture on an image. You can fill colors, patterns, or images through this mask and even move the mask between fills to create highlights and patterns there.

All it takes to make a texture mask is to create a new channel, make that channel active, and then paste a textured image into it. Alternatively, you could fill the channel with a pattern. In either case, the texture of the mask will be monochromatic because the channel is monochromatic.

When working with masks, you will be working in channels, so it's a good idea to keep the Channels palette visible (choose Window ➪ Show Channels).

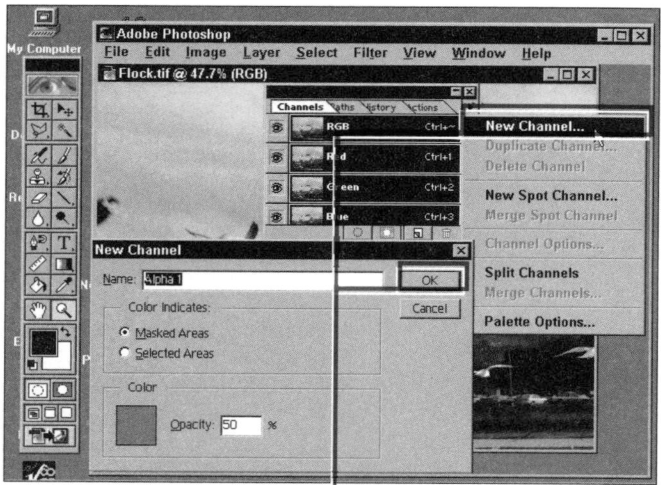

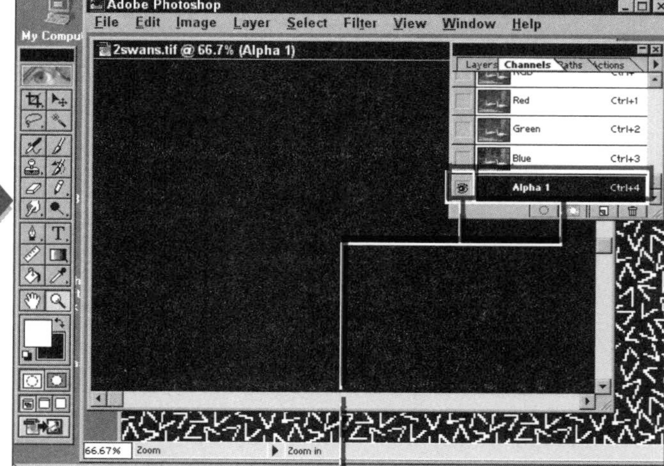

1 Open the file to which you want to add the texture mask and the image that contains the texture. Both must be the same size.

2 Choose Window ➪ Show Channels.

3 Choose New Channel.

4 If you choose the command from the Channels palette menu, the Channel Options dialog box appears. For the time being, accept the defaults and click OK.

Note: Either way, the workspace goes black because the new channel that has been created is the active channel. If you want to activate this channel later:

5 Click the channel name bar.

6 Click the eye icon to turn off all other channels.

TIPS

Can you give me some good sources for textures?

You can make your own by painting on a black or white background. Another good source is fabrics and papers. You can scan those on a flatbed scanner or photograph them and scan the film. Photographs of textures such as concrete, sand, pebbles, and wood grain are also valuable.

How about some specific examples of how textures might be used?

Using a texture mask, you can simulate the texture of cracked plaster, sand, or watercolor paper; make a photo appear to be lighted through a gauze curtain; or create the appearance of falling raindrops or snowflakes.

Couldn't I use several of these masks in conjunction with one another?

In fact, it's a good idea to copy the mask's channel, make it active, and then invert it (⌘/Ctrl+I). Now you have both positive and negative versions of the texture. Load one of the channels as a selection, press the right and down arrow keys a couple of times to offset the selection, and then save it to the original channel. Now you can fill these two masks with different colors to create highlights and shadows.

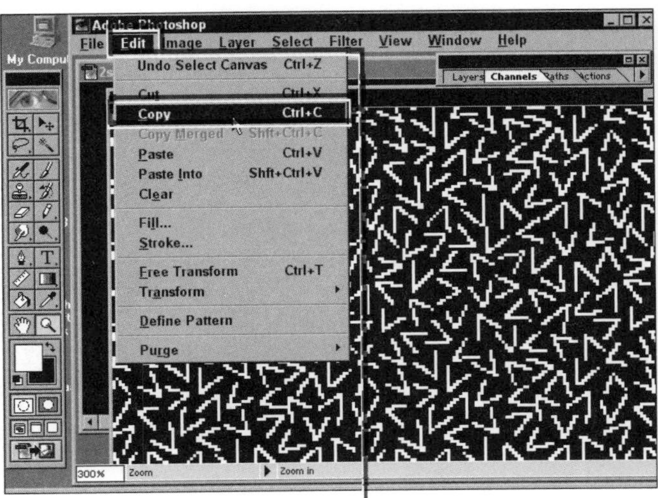

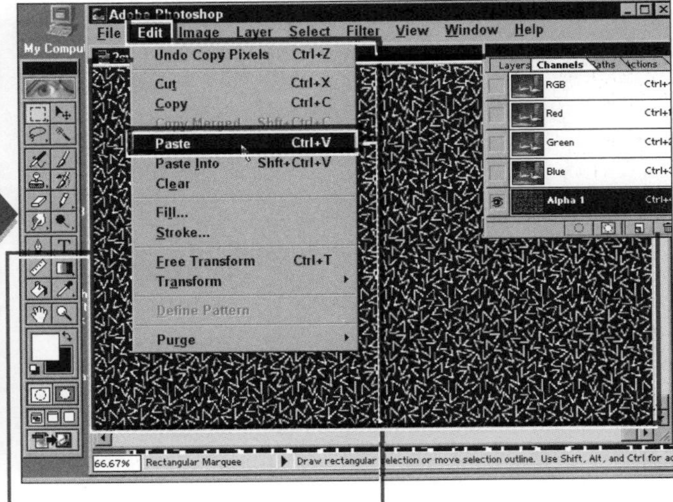

■ Now you need to copy the texture image and paste it into the new channel. Make sure the texture image window is active.

7 Choose Select ➪ All or press ⌘/Ctrl+A.

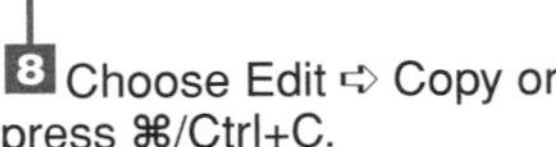

8 Choose Edit ➪ Copy or press ⌘/Ctrl+C.

9 Click to switch windows to the target image.

10 Choose Edit ➪ Paste or press ⌘/Ctrl+V.

■ The texture appears in the new channel.

8

USE TEXTURE MASKS

Once you've made a texture mask, it is possible to use it to achieve many different effects — so many, in fact, that the possibilities are limitless.

Because Photoshop doesn't discriminate between different uses for alpha channels, all the suggestions in this section apply to all types of channel masks.

The same options that apply to the use of any type of mask can also add versatility to your texture masks. Think about layers. You could use the mask selection to cut out portions of layers so one texture is superimposed on another. Or, you could copy the same layer, apply the texture to each in different ways, and then use different transparencies, combine modes, and offsets for each layer. Mind boggling, eh?

1 Open a file that contains a texture mask. If the Channels palette isn't visible, choose Window ➪ Show Channels.

2 Drag the texture channel to the Make Selection icon.

■ The selection appears in the workspace.

Note: If you want to add, subtract, or intersect channels to this selection, choose Select ➪ Load Selection, choose the next channel you want to combine, and click the radio button for the desired operation.

TIPS

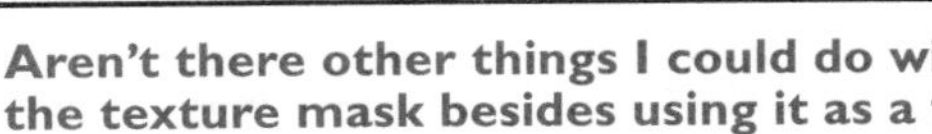

Aren't there other things I could do with the texture mask besides using it as a fill?

You can apply virtually any Photoshop command to the texture selection. For instance, you could paint with random colors. You could also make the texture mask into a layer mask (see "Make a Layer Mask," later in this chapter).

What are Blend modes and why do they matter?

Blend modes affect what happens to an underlying image when you add almost anything to it, such as adding a fill or brush stroke or merging another layer.

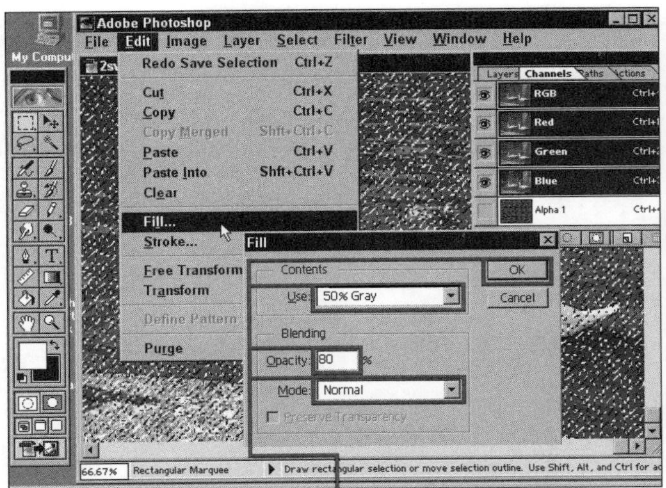

■ Now you apply a Photoshop command to the texture mask. The most common would be Fill, but you could paint over the selection, apply an image adjustment, or run a filter by using the same procedure.

4 Choose a fill type from the Use pull-down menu.

5 Enter a percentage for opacity.

6 Choose a Blend mode

7 Click OK.

■ This shows the result of applying a 50 percent gray fill at 80 percent opacity, using the Multiply Combine mode with the texture mask as a selection.

MAKE A MASK FROM A COLOR CHANNEL

Any image you can see in Photoshop 5 can be (or can contribute to making) a mask, by copying any of its existing channels. The copy then appears as an alpha channel. You can, of course, then use any of Photoshop's tools and commands to modify the resulting alpha channel mask. Although this procedure can be used with any color model, it works best with device-dependent varieties such as RGB and CMYK. (Remember, it's always best to save conversion to CMYK until the very last step.)

Suppose, for instance, that you want to knock out a wild-haired author from her background. First, you'd make a mask of the channel with the most contrast between hair and background. Then, boost the contrast. Finally, paint and fill the interior details to create an open mask.

Of course, before you can do any of this, you need to know how to copy a channel to an alpha channel. The short answer is to drag the color channel to the New Channel icon at the bottom of the Channels palette.

1 Open the file you wish to mask, and then choose Window ➪ Show Channels.

2 Click each channel to see which has greatest contrast between the desired mask edge and background.

3 Drag the channel with the most contrast to the New Channel icon — or choose Duplicate Channel from the Channels palette menu.

4 Choose Image ➪ Adjust ➪ Brightness/Contrast.

■ The Brightness/Contrast dialog box appears. Watch the image to make sure you don't eliminate subtleties in the edge.

5 Click to check the Preview box.

6 Drag the sliders until you see a clean contrast between mask edge and background; then click OK.

TIPS

What if I can't adjust the contrast properly for all edges of the selection?

This happens when the background changes color or when one side of the subject is in deep shadow and the other is in highlight. You can usually solve the problem by selecting each area separately and then making contrast adjustments for each of the areas.

Can I use adjustments other than Brightness/Contrast?

In fact, it may be easier to fine-tune your adjustments with the Image ⇨ Adjust Curves or Image ⇨ Adjust Levels commands. This is especially true when the areas that contrast with the edge are more subtle than those shown here.

What if I get specks when I select a large area with the Magic Wand?

That's pretty common. Choose the Lasso, press Shift (to add to the selection), and make a selection around the holes or specks so they're included in the overall selection. Now, when you fill, the specks will be covered.

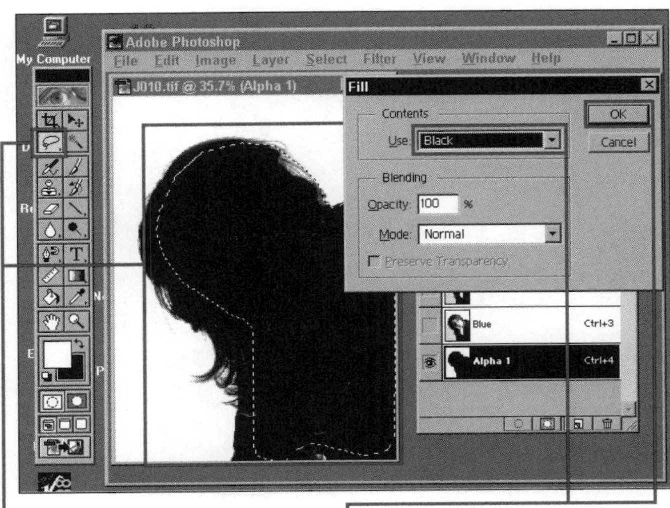

7 Choose a Lasso selection tool.

8 Select the area to be masked.

9 Choose Edit ⇨ Fill.

10 Choose Black from the Use pull-down menu.

11 Click OK.

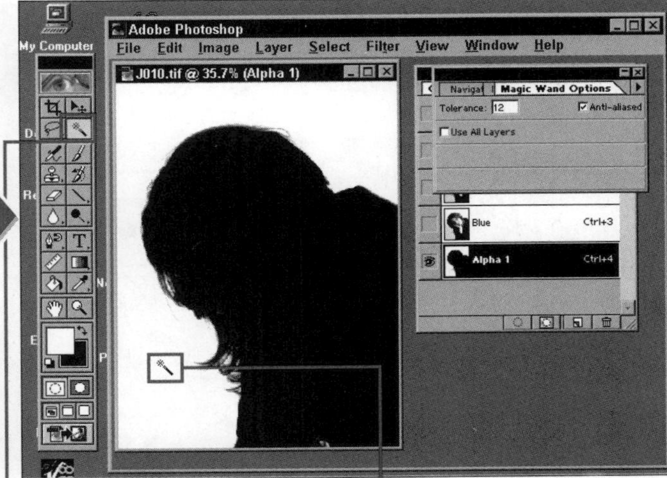

■ There may also be masked (gray) areas in the portion of the mask you wish to make unmasked.

12 Choose a selection tool that will surround the area to be unmasked.

13 Select the area to be unmasked.

14 Choose Edit ⇨ Fill.

15 Choose White from the Use pull-down menu.

16 Click OK.

8

MAKE A THRESHOLD MASK

If you want to mask a subject that's been shot against a fairly solid background, and if that subject has a reasonably hard-edged silhouette, one of the easiest methods of doing so is to make what I call a *threshold mask*. This is nothing more complicated than copying a channel and choosing Image ⇨ Adjust ⇨ Threshold to turn all the shades above a certain threshold to white and all those below it to black.

Threshold masks usually work best if the object you want to mask is a solid color. The channel you should duplicate as a mask is the one that's closest in color to that of the subject. For instance, the flower in these examples is bright fuchsia, so there's considerably more contrast in the red channel.

One of the problems with making threshold masks is that you can't see the edge. Also, the edge quality will be very "hard" with no anti-aliasing.

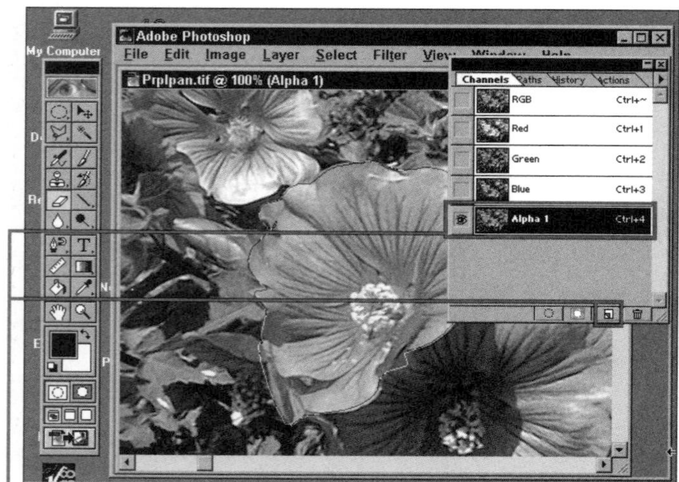

1 Open the image you want to mask and choose Window ⇨ Show Channels.

2 Drag the channel with the most contrast between the object you want to mask and its background to the New Channel icon.

■ The channel is be duplicated as an alpha channel, and you should see the mask in the workspace.

3 Choose Image ⇨ Adjust ⇨ Threshold.

■ The Threshold Level dialog box appears.

TIPS

The masks are often a little bit off or have jagged edges. How can I check and correct for this?

Edit in Quick Mask mode. Drag the mask channel to make a selection and click the Quick Mask icon. Press D to restore the default foreground and background colors. Next, use the Paintbrush to retouch the edges.

Can you recommend which type of brushes to use for cleaning up masks?

The block eraser is best for cleaning up larger areas. If you want a soft-edged mask for soft-edged objects, use the Blur tool.

What if the block eraser is too big for retouching?

The block eraser is always the same size, no matter how far you zoom in. So if you want a smaller block eraser, zoom in tighter. Remember, the block eraser always uses the background color.

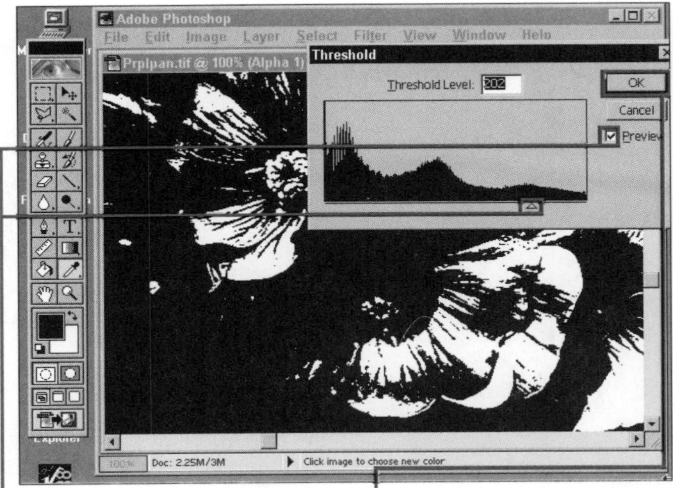

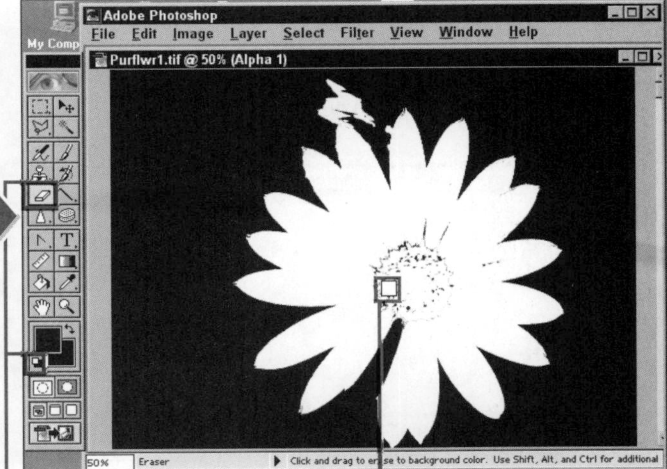

4 Click to check the Preview box.

5 Drag the slider until your subject is (mostly) white and its surroundings mostly black.

6 Click OK.

7 Choose the Eraser. Double-click it to show Eraser Options and choose Block from the Type menu.

8 Click to restore default colors (or press D).

9 Erase unwanted blacks from unmasked (subject) area.

10 Press X to switch foreground and background colors and erase unwanted whites from background.

8

MAKE A LAYER MASK

Layer masks aren't masks made from a layer but masks that are attached to a specific layer. Unlike file layers, which can be numerous, only one mask can be assigned per layer.

The easiest way to mask a layer is to make a selection, press ⌘/Ctrl+C, and choose Edit ➪ Paste Into. A new layer is automatically made and the selection shape is the shape of the layer mask. Of course, you can edit that mask by all the methods described in this chapter.

You can also make a mask for any existing layer: In the Layers palette, click the name of the layer you want to activate. Make a selection on the image in the workspace (or in a color channel, if that makes the edges easier to distinguish). Next, while the target layer is still active, click the Make Mask icon at the bottom of the layers palette. Presto! The layer mask's thumbnail appears to the right of the image thumbnail in the Layers palette.

1 Open both the file to which you want to add the layer and the file you want to use as a masked layer.

2 With the layer file window active, press ⌘/Ctrl+A to select the entire image.

3 Press ⌘/Ctrl+C to copy the selection.

4 Click the target window, and then make the selection to paste into.

5 Choose Edit ➪ Paste Into.

■ The clipboard image appears inside the selected area, and the selection marquee disappears.

■ A new layer appears in the Layers palette.

■ A mask thumbnail automatically appears to the right of the new layer s image thumbnail.

TIPS

What advantages does using a layer mask provide over other methods of eliminating unwanted images in a layer, such as using the eraser?

You can mask an area in an adjustment layer so that only that portion of the overall image will be affected by the adjustment. If you already have a mask that suits your purpose, you can turn it into a layer mask by converting it to a selection and then clicking the Add Layer Mask icon. Also, you can edit the layer mask in as many ways as you like and save each of the edits as a new alpha channel mask. Layer masks can also be edited at any time during the process of working on an image.

What if I want to blur the object that's in a layer mask?

Only that part of the blur that's inside the mask will show. Use the Gaussian Blur filter to blur the mask slightly. Then, when you blur the masked object, the edges will be softened as well.

What happens to a layer mask if I make a new selection on that layer and then click the Add Layer Mask icon?

The cursor will turn into a "Cancel" sign and you will be unable to execute the command.

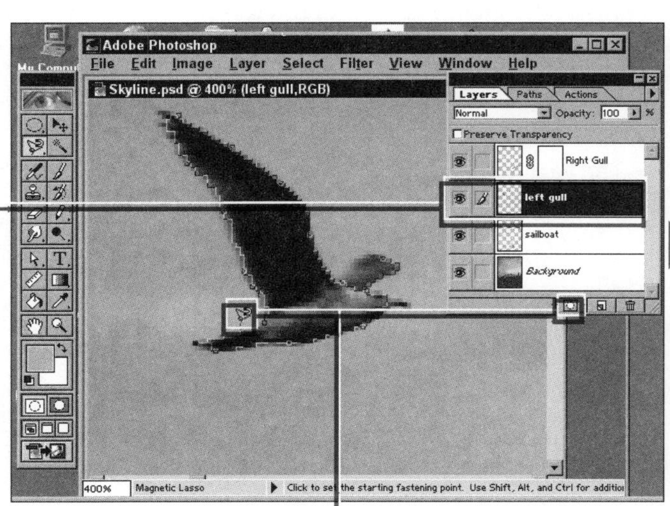

MAKE A LAYER MASK FROM A SELECTION

1 Choose Window ➪ Show Layers to make sure the Layers palette is visible.

2 Click to activate the layer you want to mask.

3 Select the shape you want to mask.

4 Click the Add Layer Mask icon.

■ The layer mask appears here.

■ The masked portions of the layer are invisible to the underlying layers.

USING LAYERS

Layers are, in my opinion, Photoshop's strongest feature. They make it possible to show a client (or you) several variations or interpretations of a composition. They make it much easier to seamlessly combine several images and to test or combine special effects from multiple processes into the same image. They make it possible to deal with part of the image independent of the rest of the image. Finally, they enable you to move, scale, rotate, stretch, slant, or give perspective to an image. You can mask layers. You can change their stacking order and their transparency. You can assign each layer its own Blend mode so that it creates a special effect in combining with the layer beneath it.

Yet despite all this power, there is nothing you can do with layers that Photoshop won't let you do without them. Layers, however, provide ease of use, convenience, and interactivity. They also let you experiment without endangering the whole file, as almost all Photoshop commands apply only to the active layer, as shown in the first figure. Of course, if the active layer is an adjustment layer, all adjustments affect all layers; but you can always toss out the adjustment layer, and the rest of the image stays intact.

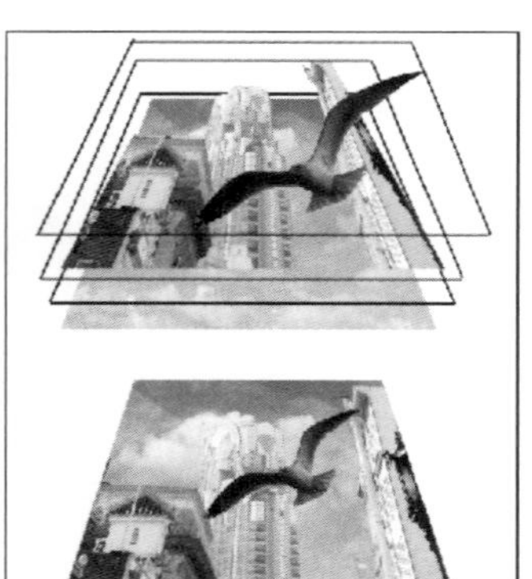

Layers palette

The Layers palette provides control over layers. You can rearrange the stacking order of layers by dragging the name bar of any given layer to a new location in the Layers palette, as illustrated in the following figure, so long as that location is in between any two existing layers. To place a layer above the top layer, drag it to a position between the top and second layers, and then drag the top layer below the new second layer. To place a layer below the bottom layer, drag it to a position between the bottom and second layers, and then drag the bottom layer to a position above the new second layer.

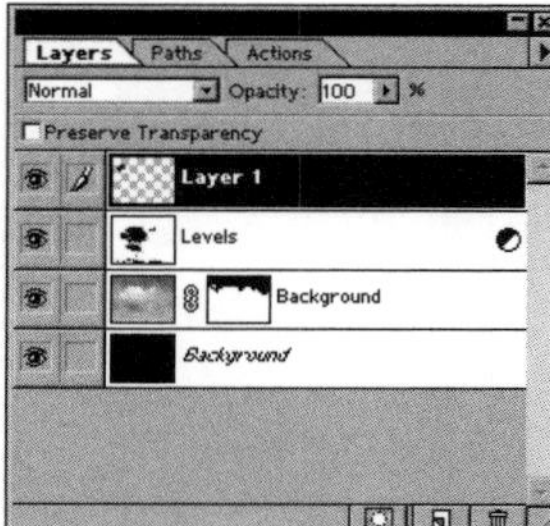

Layers Palette Contents

Component	Function
Blend modes pull-down menu	Setting a Blend mode for an active layer affects all underlying layers. See the color section for a visual indication of the effect of all Blend modes.
Preserve Transparency check box	Check this box to keep tools and commands in this layer from affecting transparent areas.
Layer Visibility box	When Eye icon is visible, the layer is visible. Click to toggle hiding and revealing of the layer.
Linked/Masked/ Paint box	Can contain one of three icons: brush, which indicates the layer is active; chain link, which means the layer is linked to another one or more layers; or mask, which indicates the mask is active.
Layer thumbnail	You can change these to any of three sizes with the Layer Palette Options dialog box.
Make Layer Mask icon	Masks the layer with the current selection. If no selection is active, creates a new, blank mask.
Make New Layer icon	Creates a new layer when clicked. Duplicates any layer that is dragged onto it.
Delete Layer icon	Deletes the active layer or any layer or layer mask that's dragged onto it (it prompts you whether to apply or discard).
Mask Lock icon	Click to toggle capability to move mask or image independently.
Mask icon	Click to activate and edit mask.
Adjustment Layer symbol	Indicates that this is an adjustment layer. Default layer name indicates the type of adjustment layer.
Layer name	Double-click to rename a layer in the Layer Options palette. Also, a double-click here will turn a "background" (flat) layer into one that can have transparency.
Layer bar	Click to make a layer active. Double-click to bring up Layer Options palette.
Opacity slider	The Opacity slider appears when you drag the Opacity pull-down menu. Click and drag to change opacity percentage or type a number between 1 and 100.
Layers palette menu	Click and drag to choose menu options.

CONTINUED

USING LAYERS CONTINUED

Layers palette menu

Many of the commands that can be found in the Layers menu (discussed next) are duplicated on the Layers palette menu, as shown here, where they may be handier if the Layers palette is open. Of course, many of these commands are duplicated by the functions of the icons at the bottom of the Layers palette, which are even handier.

New Layer...
New Adjustment Layer...
Duplicate Layer...
Delete Layer
Layer Options...
Merge Down
Merge Visible
Flatten Image
Palette Options...

Layers Palette Menu Contents

Command	Shortcut	Function
New Layer	Shift+⌘/Ctrl+N	Creates a new, empty, transparent layer after bringing up the Duplicate Layer dialog box.
New Adjustment Layer		Creates a new adjustment layer after bringing up the Duplicate Layer dialog box.
Duplicate Layer		Duplicates the active (selected) layer after bringing up the Duplicate Layer dialog box.
Delete Layer		Eradicates the active (selected) layer.
Layer Options	Double-click layer name	Brings up the Layer Options dialog box.
Merge Layers/Linked		Merges all the layers in the image. If layers are linked, command reads Merge Linked and links only those layers.
Merge Visible		Merges only those layers whose Eye icon is present.
Flatten Image		Merges all layers with the background. It is wise to use this command whenever you want to reduce the file to its smallest possible size. (After applying this command, it is no longer be possible to edit layers independently.)
Palette Options		Enables you to choose from small, medium, or large thumbnail sizes.

Layers menu

Several commands that affect layers can be accessed only from the menu bar in the Layers menu. Those that aren't duplicated in the Layers palette menu are listed in the following table.

Layers Menu Contents

Command	Shortcut	Function
New ➪ Background		Creates a new background layer, which will be filled with the current background color.
New ➪ Layer via Copy		Copies the contents of the current selection to a new layer. The area outside the selection will be transparent in the new layer.
New ➪ Layer via Cut		Copies the contents of the current selection to a new layer and simultaneously deletes the content of that selection from the original layer.
Adjustment Options		Brings up the Adjustment Layer Options dialog box.
Effects ➪ Various		This menu includes the commands for creating the following effects: drop shadows, inner shadows, outer glow, inner glow, bevel, and emboss.
Effects ➪ Copy Effects		Copies the effects in the active layer to memory so that they can be applied to another layer(s) with the Paste Effects or Paste Effects to Linked commands.
Effects ➪ Paste Effects		Pastes effects copied by the Copy Effects command to the selected layer.
Effects ➪ Paste Effects to Linked		Pastes copied effects to multiple layers, which must first be linked to one another.
Effects ➪ Clear Effects		Clears all the effects assigned to a layer. If you want to remove individual effects, make sure the target layer is active, and then reselect the individual effect from the Layers ➪ Effects submenu. The check mark will disappear.
Effects ➪ Global Angle		Sets the angle for all effects according to the number you enter (any integer between 0 and 360).
Effects ➪ Create Layer		Creates a new layer that contains only the effects assigned to the current layer. At the same time, it removes the effect from the active layer.
Effects ➪ Hide All Effects		Hides all the effects currently assigned to the active layer.

CONTINUED

USING LAYERS CONTINUED

Layers Menu Contents

Command	Shortcut	Function
Type ➪ Render Layer		Renders the type as a bitmapped image, which can then be altered by any of Photoshop's image-editing commands and tools. Type that has been rendered can no longer be edited as type — that is, you can't insert letters, change the kerning, or switch fonts and font sizes.
Type ➪ Horizontal		Causes type to be entered in normal, left-to-right fashion.
Type ➪ Vertical		Switches type to a vertical orientation, with letters entered one under the other.
Add Layer Mask ➪ Reveal All		Adds an empty (completely transparent) layer mask. You can edit this mask by any of the methods detailed in Chapter 10.
Add Layer Mask ➪ Hide All		Adds a completely opaque layer mask. You can edit this mask by any of the methods detailed in Chapter 10.
Add Layer Mask ➪ Reveal Selection		Saves the current selection to a mask for the active layer.
Add Layer Mask ➪ Hide Selection		Saves the current selection as an inverted mask for the active layer.
Enable/Disable Layer Mask		Toggles the layer mask off and on.
Group With Previous/Linked	⌘/Ctrl+G	Groups the active layer (and any linked to it) with the layer just below it (or the one at the bottom of a linked stack). Grouping causes all the grouped layers to be masked by the layer mask assigned to the bottom layer in the group.
Ungroup	Shift+⌘/Ctrl+G	Removes the grouping of a stack of layers.
Arrange ➪ Bring to Front	Shift+ ⌘/Ctrl+]	Brings the active layer to the top of the stack.
Arrange ➪ Bring Forward	⌘/Ctrl+]	Brings the active layer one level closer to the top of the stack.
Arrange ➪ Send Backward	⌘/Ctrl+[	Moves the active layer one level lower in the stack.

Layers Menu Contents

Command	Shortcut	Function
Arrange ➪ Send to Back	Shift+ ⌘/Ctrl+[	Places the active layer at the bottom of the stack.
Align Linked		Aligns all the linked layers to one another along their tops, vertical centers, bottoms, left sides, horizontal centers, or right sides.
Distribute Linked		Evenly distributes linked layers between the first linked layer and the last. Distribution is measured between your choice of tops, vertical centers, bottoms, left sides, horizontal centers, or right sides.
Merge Down/Linked		If no layers are linked, merges all layers below the active layer.
Matting ➪ Defringe		Automatically replaces a selection's fringe pixels (those left from cutting the image from another background) with those of the color(s) that currently surround the selection. A dialog box lets you enter the pixel width that Photoshop should examine for defringing.
Matting ➪ Remove Black Matte		Automatically removes black pixels found on the borders of a selection.
Matting ➪ Remove White Matte		Automatically removes white pixels found on the borders of a selection.

Layer Options

Layer options can be applied to any nonadjustment layer. Access the Layer Options dialog box when you want to change the name of a layer, change its Blend mode, or alter its transparency, as shown in the figure below. Use one of the following methods:

- Choose Layer ➪ Options from the menu bar.
- Choose Layer ➪ Options from the Layers palette menu.
- Double-click the layer name bar in the Layers palette.

Remember, the opacity and mode settings for tools and layers interact with one another. So if you have a layer opacity of 30 percent and a brush opacity of 50 percent, the opacity of the paint will be only 15 percent.

CONTINUED

USING LAYERS CONTINUED

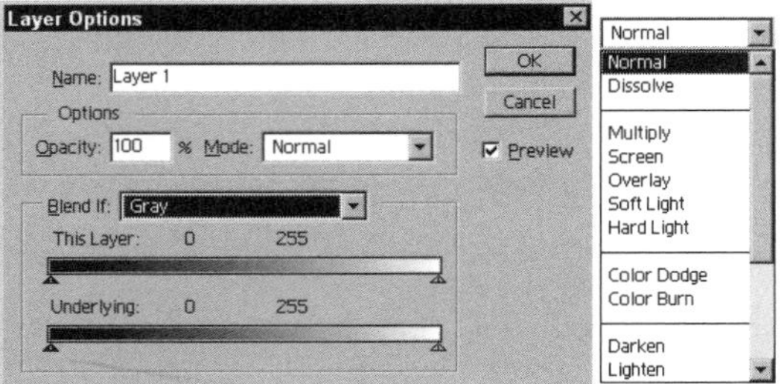

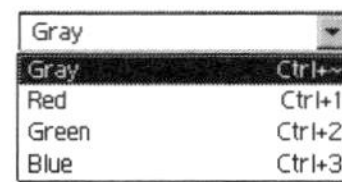

Layer Options Dialog Box Contents

Component	Function
Name field	Enter a meaningful name that will help you remember the purpose of this layer. You can rename this layer at any time by entering a new name.
Opacity field	Enter a number between 0 and 100 to indicate the percentage of overall transparency for this layer.
Mode pull-down menu	Lets you specify a Blend mode that will determine how this layer interacts with layers below it. See the color section for a picture of how each Blend mode works.
Preview check box	If checked, instantaneously shows preview.
Blend if pull-down menu	Determines whether Blend modes are applied to all channels (gray) or only to individual color channels.
Source Layer brightness bar	Indicates gray level at which sliders are set for source (current) layer.
Source Layer Shadow slider	Drag to indicate darkest pixels that will be blended with underlying layers. You can split this range to indicate pixels that will be partially affected by pressing Opt/Alt while dragging either the left or right half of the slider.
Source Layer Highlight slider	Drag to indicate brightest pixels that will be blended with underlying layers. You can split this range to indicate pixels that will be partially affected by pressing Opt/Alt while dragging either the left or right half of the slider.
Target Layer brightness bar	Indicates gray level at which sliders are set for underlying layers.
Target Layer Shadow slider	Drag to indicate darkest pixels in underlying layers that will be blended with the source layer. You can split this range to indicate pixels that will be partially affected by pressing Opt/Alt while dragging either the left or right half of the slider.

Component Function

Target Layer Highlight slider	Drag to indicate brightest pixels in underlying layers that will be blended with the source layer. You can split this range to indicate pixels that will be partially affected by pressing Opt/Alt while dragging either the left or right half of the slider.
Cancel/Reset button	Pressing Opt/Alt switches the Cancel button to Reset, which returns the settings to their last saved state.

New Layer dialog box

The New Layer dialog box, depicted here, is, for the most part, a subset of the Layers palette menu. This dialog box appears only if you choose New Layer from the menu bar. Those methods of creating a new layer afforded by the Layers palette don't bring up this dialog box, but you can always bring up the Layer Options dialog box after the fact by double-clicking the layer name bar in the Layers palette. There are two settings unique to this palette: Group With Previous Layer and Fill with. The uses for these settings are explained in the following table.

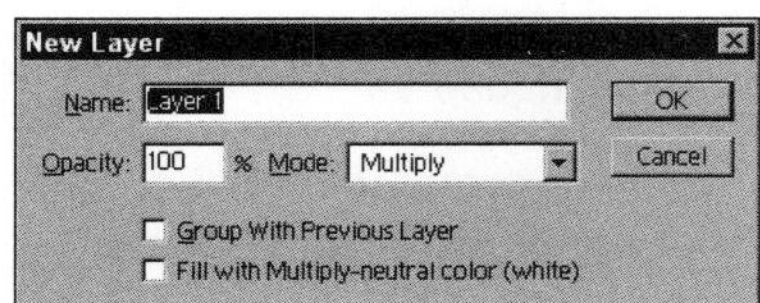

New Layer Dialog Box Contents

Component	Function
Name field	Enter a meaningful name that will help you remember the purpose of this layer. You can rename this layer at any time by entering a new name.
Opacity field	Enter a number between 0 and 100 to indicate the percentage of overall transparency for this layer.
Mode pull-down menu	Lets you specify a Blend mode that will determine how this layer interacts with layers below it. See the color section for a picture of how each Blend mode works.
Group With Previous Layer check box	If checked, the new Layer is grouped with the layer immediately below it.
Fill with Multiply-neutral color (white) check box	Fills the layer with a color that is unaffected by the current Blend mode (usually black, white, or gray).

Duplicate Layer dialog box

The Duplicate Layer dialog box, shown in the following figure, can only be reached if the Duplicate Layer command is chosen from the menu bar. When the command is chosen in this way, the duplicated (copied) layer can be sent to a document other than the current document. To do this, you must make sure that the target document is also open in Photoshop. You then choose the name of the target document from the Document pull-down menu. You can also choose New from this menu, and Photoshop will automatically create a new document that contains only the layer to be duplicated.

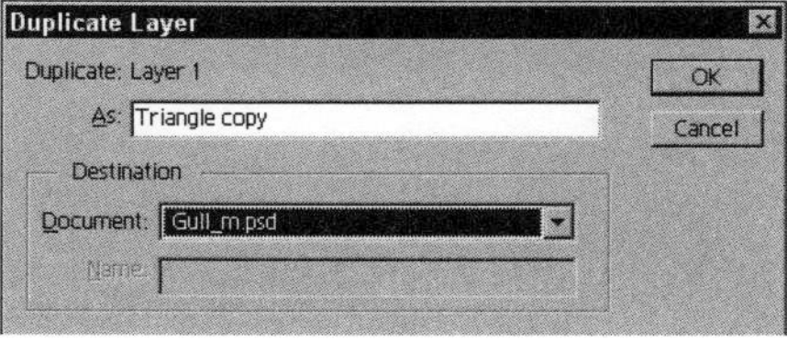

CONTINUED

USING LAYERS CONTINUED

Duplicate Layer Dialog Box Contents

Component	Function
As field	The word *copy* is added automatically to the name of the layer being duplicated. If you want, you can enter a new name in this field.
Destination pull-down menu	Lets you choose the current document, a new document, or any open Photoshop document as the target for the duplicated layer.
Destination Name field	Lets you assign a name to the new document. This field is unavailable unless you are targeting a new document.

New Adjustment Layer dialog box

The New Adjustment Layer dialog box , shown here, appears whether you choose the command from the menu bar or from the Layers palette menu. It is here that you name the layer, choose its adjustment type, set its opacity, and set its Blend mode.

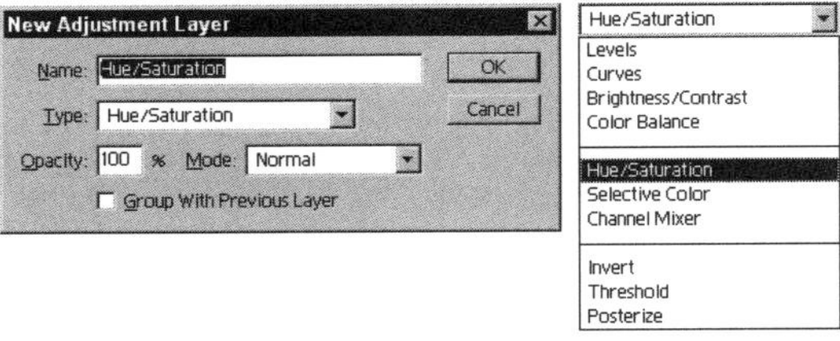

New Adjustment Layer Dialog Box Contents

Component	Function
Name field	The name of the adjustment type is automatically entered. You can enter a name of your choice, if you like.
Type pull-down menu	Enables you to choose any of the adjustment types, which correspond to image adjustments on the Image ⇨ Adjust menu.
Opacity field	Determines the percentage of effect that the adjustment layer will have on underlying layers.
Mode pull-down menu	Enables you to choose a Blend mode for the adjustment.

Component	Function
Group With Previous Layer check box	If checked, groups the new adjustment layer with the layer immediately below, thus restricting the effect of the adjustment to an unmasked portion of the bottom layer's layer mask. Remember, you can also assign a layer mask to the adjustment layer itself.

Adjustment Options

Each type of adjustment, listed in the Type pull-down menu in the New Adjustment layer dialog box and shown in the following figure, has its own Adjustment Options dialog box. The corresponding options are Levels, Curves, Brightness/Contrast, Color Balance, Hue/Saturation, Selective Color, Channel Mixer, Invert, Threshold, and Posterize.

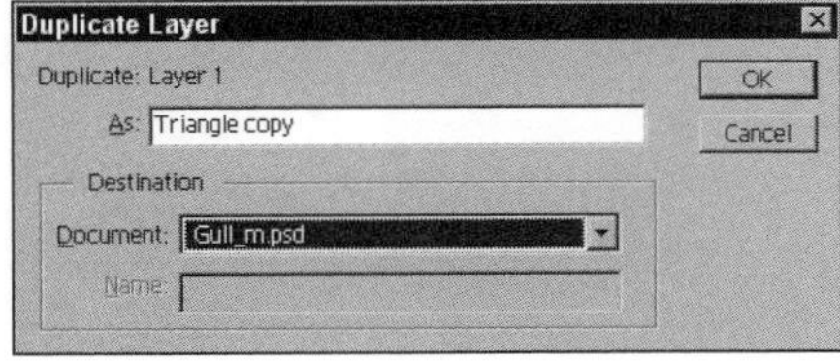

CREATE A NEW LAYER

Several methods exist for creating a new layer. Which you use depends partly on whether the new layer is to be empty (transparent) or should contain a new image.

If you want an empty layer, the easiest way to create a new one is to click the New Layer icon at the bottom of the Layers palette. If you want to create a new layer from an image in another file, open the other file and drag the image (or a layer from that image) into the current file. It will automatically appear as an independent layer in the Layers palette.

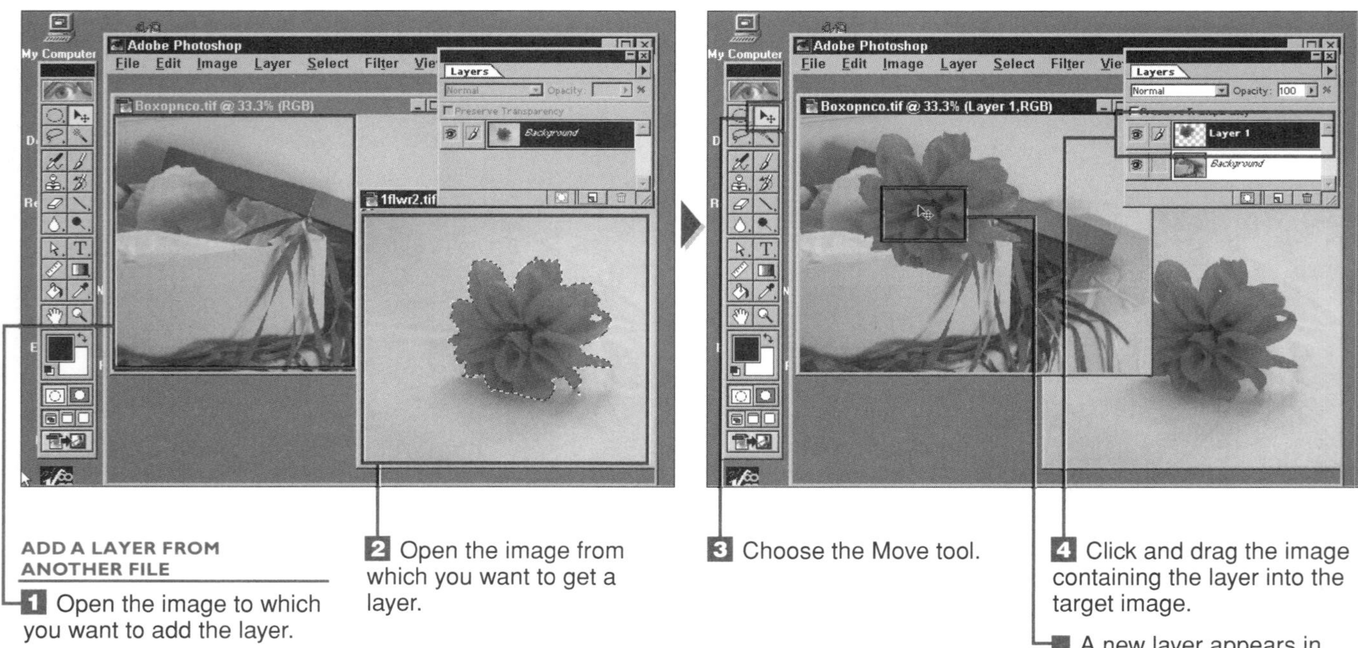

ADD A LAYER FROM ANOTHER FILE

1 Open the image to which you want to add the layer.

2 Open the image from which you want to get a layer.

3 Choose the Move tool.

4 Click and drag the image containing the layer into the target image.

■ A new layer appears in the target image's Layers palette.

TIPS

Why would I want to create a layer that contains nothing?

So that you can create original work on it. Of course, this work could be simple, such as painting color into an area so you can try using a Blend mode without having the experiment endanger the original.

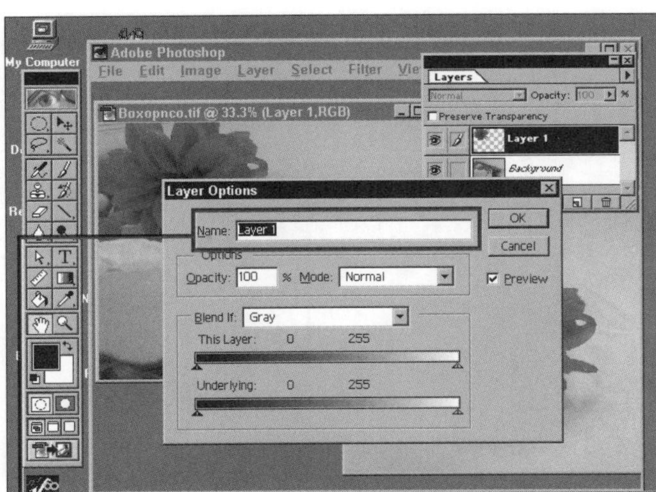

5 To set options for the new layer, double-click the layer name bar or choose Layer Options from the Layers palette menu.

6 To make the layer thumbnail larger so you can more easily distinguish layers, choose Palette Options from the Layers palette menu.

7 Click the size thumbnail you prefer.

8 Click OK.

STACK AND REORDER LAYERS

One of the benefits of layers is that you can change their stacking order easily, enabling you to decide which objects should appear to be in the foreground and which should appear farther back on overlapping layers. Because the visible portions of layers can be any size smaller than the overall image (or, of course, the same size), the ability to stack layers also makes it easier to see which layers you may want to remove, mask, or partially erase.

This exercise shows you how to reorder layers, using the Layers palette, and gives you some shortcuts to speed things along:

Opt/Alt+] or [moves up (]) or down([) one layer at a time.

Shift+Opt/Alt+] or [takes you to the top (]) or the bottom ([) of the stack.

⌘/Ctrl+Opt/Alt+Click takes you directly to the layer you clicked.

Pressing Control+click (Mac) or right-clicking when using the Move tool over any layer brings up a context-sensitive menu of the layers under the cursor.

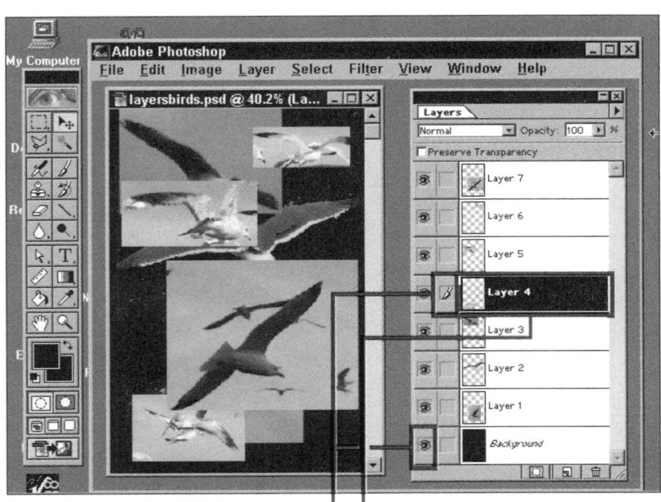

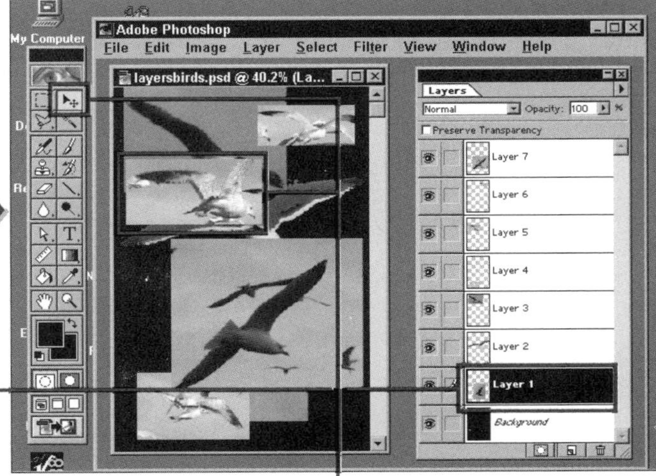

■ The eleven layers in this image were all dragged in from other open files. The artist's objective is to make a composition that shows a field of egrets (and one duck).

■ Each layer is automatically numbered as it's created.

■ All layers are visible.

■ Paintbrush icon and highlight indicate the active layer.

MOVE A LAYER BETWEEN TWO TARGET LAYERS

1 Drag the layer name bar into the target position.

MOVE THE LAYER IN RESPECT TO THE OVERALL IMAGE

1 Choose the Move tool (or press V).

2 Drag the image in the workspace.

SHOW AND HIDE LAYERS

In Photoshop, showing or hiding a layer is simply matter of clicking the Eye icon in the Layers palette. If you can see the Eye icon, you can see the layer.

At times, you may want to show some layers and hide others for these reasons: 1) To see and work on all of a layer without changing its stacking order. 2) To change the apparent distance of objects from the viewer. 3) To merge or link a select number of layers.

If operations are slowing down because you have too many layers, you can remove layers from the file without changing them. Create a new file (⌘/Ctrl+N), and enter dimensions large enough for the biggest layer. Drag the layers you want to set aside to the new file, and then (in the original file) drag them to the trash. Name and save the new file. When you're ready, you can open the original file and drag the layers back — unscathed.

Note: In Photoshop 5, hiding a layer also protects it from editing, even if it is the active layer.

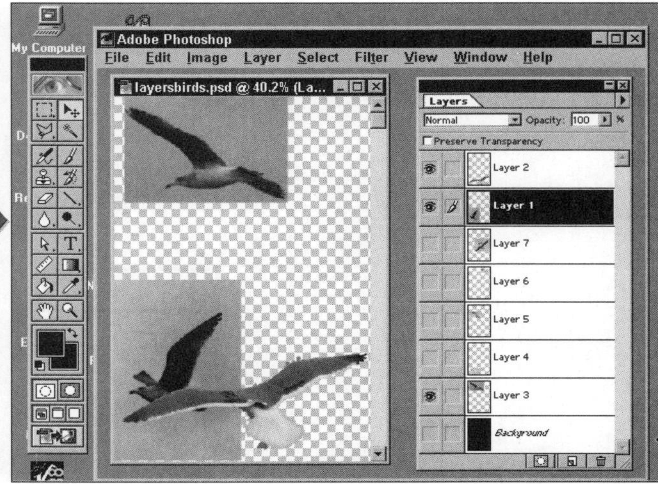

HIDE A LAYER

1 Click the layer's Eye icon.

Note: To turn the layer back on, click the Eye icon again.

■ By turning off all but three of the layers, you can easily position and size the standing egrets in relation to one another.

MERGE LAYERS

The more layers, the more memory you need to store them; so it pays to merge layers whenever you're sure you no longer need to keep them separate.

Also, there may be times when you'll want to merge layers so that you can use them as a single element. For instance, you might want to create a whole field of grass by selecting a grassy area and then copying the selection to a new layer. You could then copy the new layer several times and move the individual copies until they cover the whole field. Your image will have seams, so just merge all those grass layers into one and then paint out the seams with the Clone tool.

You can merge layers in one of several ways: merge all the visible layers, merge all the linked layers, merge with the layer immediately below, or just flatten the whole file. You'll have to flatten an image before you can put it on the Net or read it into other image-editing applications.

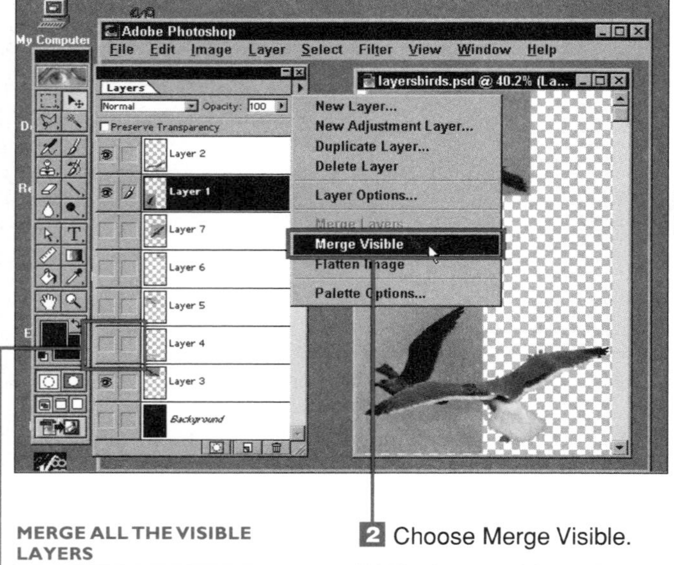

MERGE ALL THE VISIBLE LAYERS

Note: If the Layers palette isn't on screen, choose Window ⇨ Show Layers.

1 Click to hide layers you don't want to merge.

2 Choose Merge Visible.

■ The layers with the Eye icons visible become one layer, with the name of the layer that was active when you issued the command.

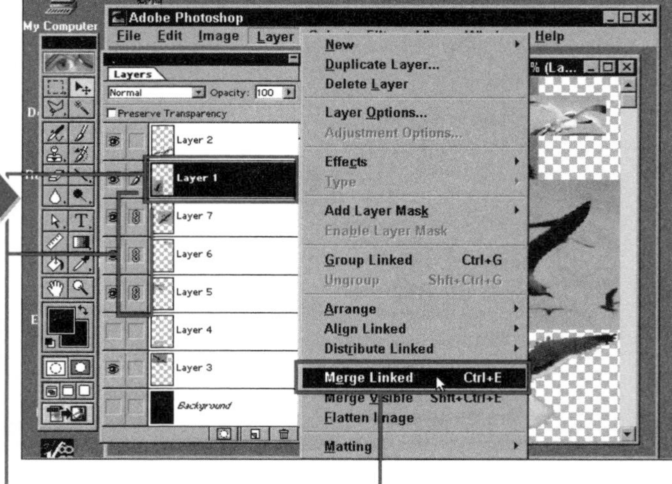

MERGE SOME LAYERS, VISIBLE OR NOT

1 Choose the layer to link to.

2 Click to toggle linking.

3 Choose Merge Linked from the Layers palette menu.

■ The layers with the link icons become one and have the name of the active layer.

TIPS

Why are there so many different ways to merge layers?

Photoshop is a thoroughly professional program; as such, it tries to be adaptable to any working style and set of requirements. Some images are composed of hundreds of layers, but keeping them all active at once is rarely practical.

How much memory does a layer use?

It depends on the layer. If the layer consists of a full-color photograph that covers the entire image, it will be quite large. Adjustment layers, on the other hand, use virtually no extra memory.

What if I want to move a layer while I'm painting? Is there a way to choose the Move tool without losing the current brush?

Press ⌘/Ctrl. The Move tool stays in effect until you release the key. It's very much like pressing the spacebar to pan and scroll with the Hand tool.

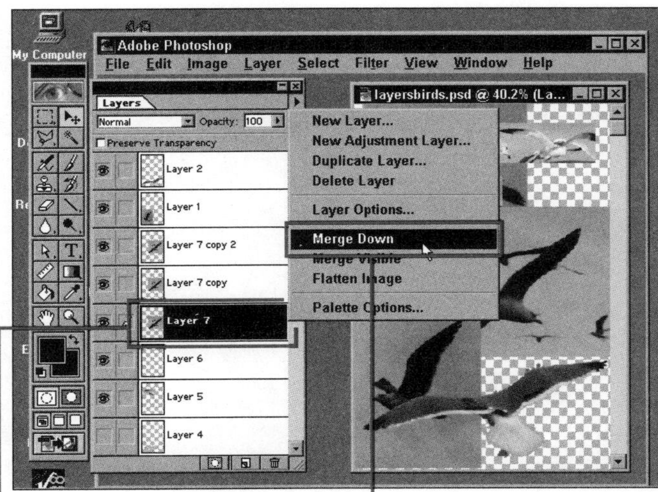

MERGE THE ACTIVE LAYER WITH A LAYER BELOW IT

1 Choose the layer you want to merge with the layer below it.

2 Choose Merge Down from the Layers palette menu.

■ The merged layer bears the name of the active layer.

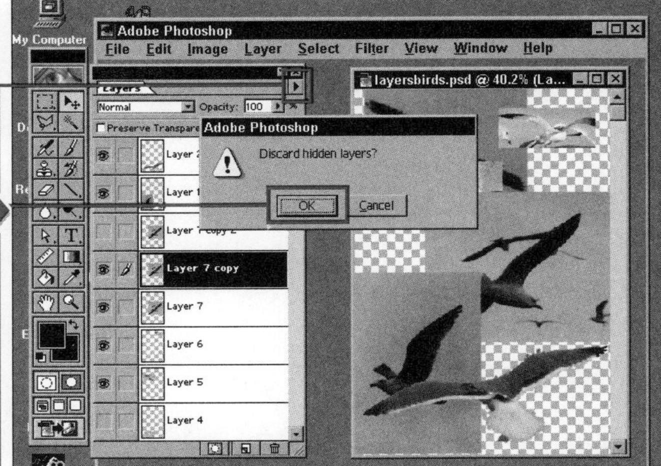

MERGE ALL VISIBLE LAYERS INTO ONE FLATTENED FILE

1 Choose Flatten Image from the Layers palette menu.

2 Click OK to discard hidden layers.

Note: If you press cancel, no layers will be merged.

Note: This command has exactly the same effect as Merge Visible.

USE TRANSPARENCY WITH LAYERS

You can change the transparency of any layer at any time using one of the following methods: 1) In the Layers palette, enter a number between 1 and 100 in the Opacity field. 2) Click the slider button and drag the Opacity slider. 3) Double-click the layer name bar to bring up the Layer Options palette. Enter a number between 1 and 100 in the Layer Options dialog box.

Why change the opacity of layers? Often, you'll want to combine images by erasing a portion of the layer. By making overlapping layers transparent, you can position them so that their new, irregular borders will blend accurately. Partially transparent layers are also useful in making collages and in creating double-exposure effects. Finally, changing the transparency of a layer also changes the apparent effect of a special effects filter or Blending mode.

Note: You can transform several layers at the same time by linking them.

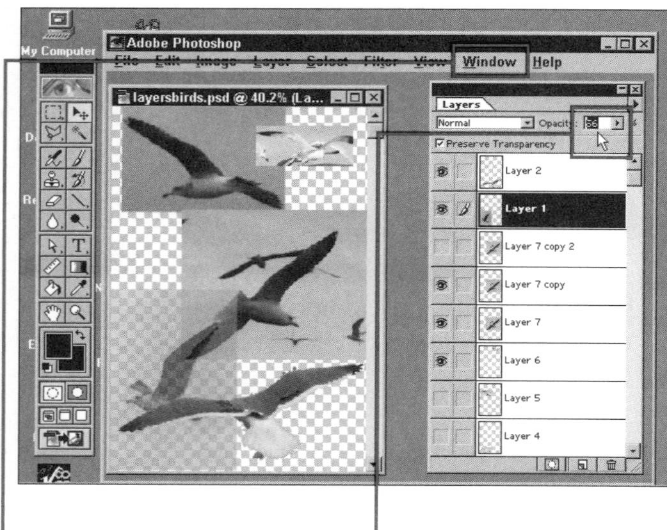

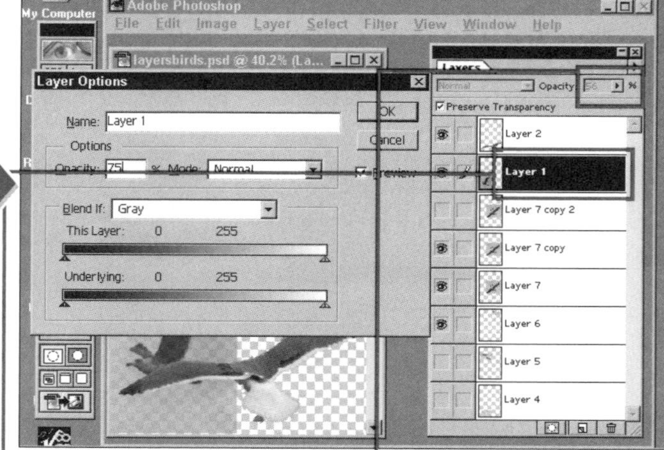

CHANGE THE TRANSPARENCY

1 Choose Window ⇨ Show Layers.

2 Enter a number between 1 and 100 (0 percent is transparent) in the Opacity field (or drag the Opacity slider).

CHANGE THE TRANSPARENCY IN THE LAYER OPTIONS DIALOG BOX

1 Double-click the layer name bar.

2 Enter a number between 1 and 100 (100 percent is opaque) in the Opacity field.

Note: If you want to see all variations in transparency, turn off all other layers (including the background).

DELETE LAYERS

It's a good thing it's so easy to get rid of layers when you no longer need them. Once you realize how easy it is, you won't mind making several versions of the image within the same file.

Extra layers are also a great way to experiment without endangering your work. Make a layer copy, alter the image to test an idea, make several other layers with slightly different versions, compare them, and throw out the layers that don't make it.

The main repository for deceased layers is the Trash Can icon at the bottom of the Layers palette. You can delete layers by dragging them to that icon. You can also delete the active layer by either clicking the Trash Can icon or choosing Layer ⇨ Delete Layer. You can retrieve a deleted layer as long as it's still in the History palette, but once you've pushed it out or closed the file, the layer is gone.

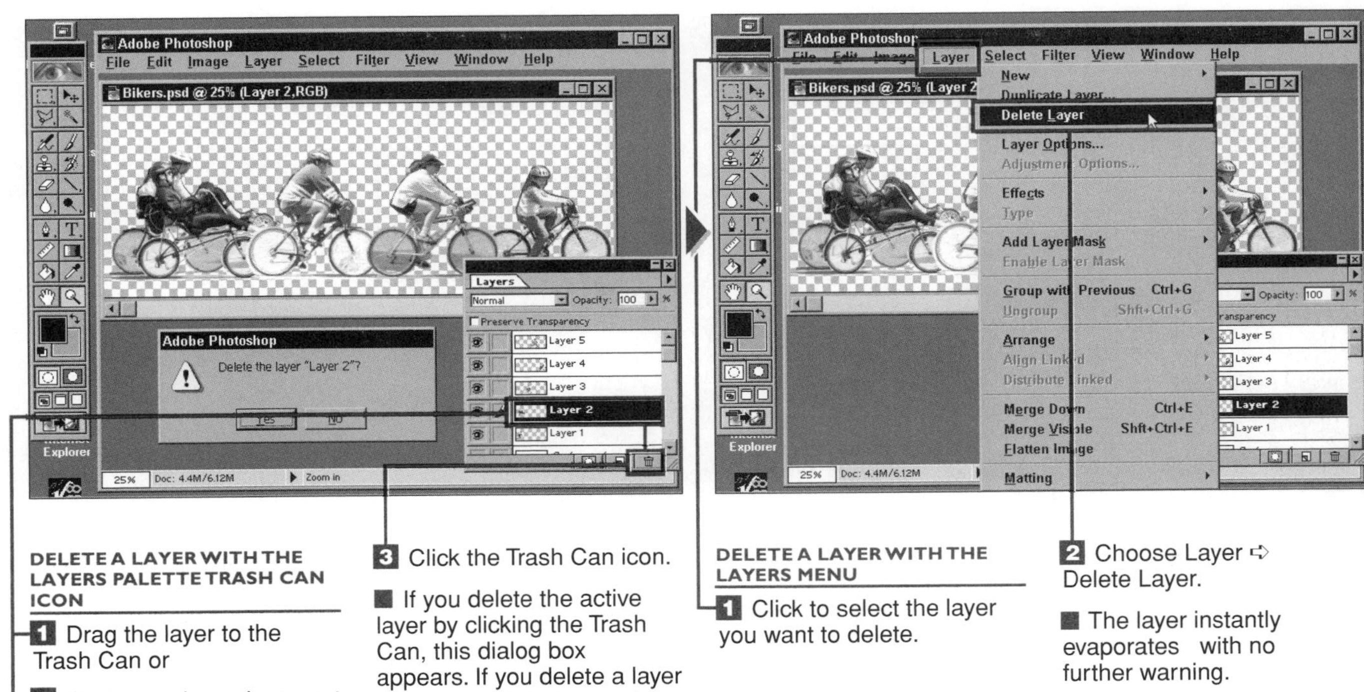

DELETE A LAYER WITH THE LAYERS PALETTE TRASH CAN ICON

1 Drag the layer to the Trash Can or

2 Click to activate the target layer and

3 Click the Trash Can icon.

■ If you delete the active layer by clicking the Trash Can, this dialog box appears. If you delete a layer by dragging it to the trash, you receive no warning.

DELETE A LAYER WITH THE LAYERS MENU

1 Click to select the layer you want to delete.

2 Choose Layer ⇨ Delete Layer.

■ The layer instantly evaporates with no further warning.

CHANGE THE SIZE OF LAYERS

Layers (and the contents of an active selection on an active layer) can be transformed in a number of ways with the commands Scale, Rotate, Distort, Skew, Perspective, Flop, and Flip.

By far the most common transformation is scaling. *Scaling* a layer differs from the Image ➪ Image Size command in that the scaling is always done within the confines of the overall image and always uses bipolar interpolation.

As is the case with all other types of transitions, scaling can be accomplished by several methods: 1) In precise mathematical increments. 2) By dragging control handles. 3) In Free Form mode, where you can combine several types of transformation in the same operation. Free form transformations are handled in a separate spread so you can see how all the types of transformations work at once.

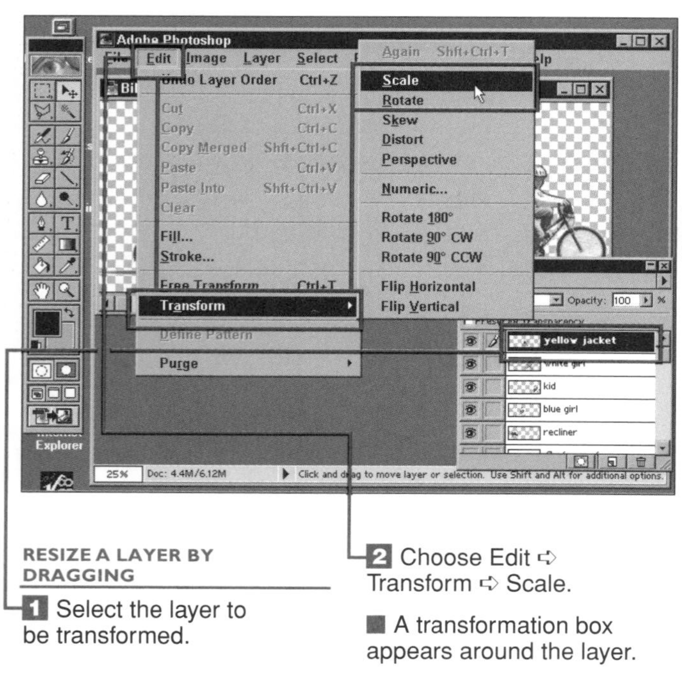

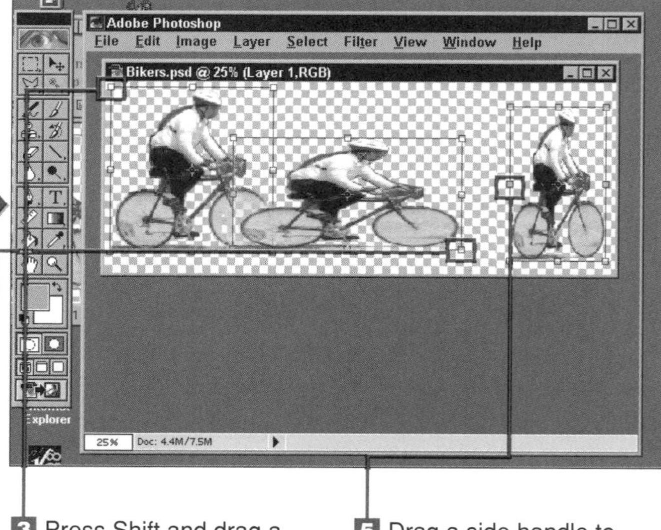

RESIZE A LAYER BY DRAGGING

1 Select the layer to be transformed.

2 Choose Edit ➪ Transform ➪ Scale.

■ A transformation box appears around the layer.

3 Press Shift and drag a corner to maintain the original proportions.

4 Drag a corner to scale to fit an area without regard to height and width proportions.

5 Drag a side handle to scale the image in only one direction.

Note: Photoshop transforms layers and selections, using the interpolation method specified in Preferences.

Besides saving time, is there any other advantage to combining several types of transformations into a single operation?

Both the Free transformation command and the Numeric transformation dialog box let you specify all the transformation settings before any of the transformations are made. Working this way gives you a big quality advantage, because pixels only have to be recalculated once. Of course, if you only need to make one type of transformation, the individual methods produce the same result.

What if I start to make a transformation and need to get out of it?

Press Escape or ⌘+Opt+. (Mac only). Until then, you will be unable to do anything else.

If I choose a conventional unit of measure, such as inches or centimeters, for transformation, will the image be that size on paper?

Not unless you have already set the resolution of your file to match that of your printing device.

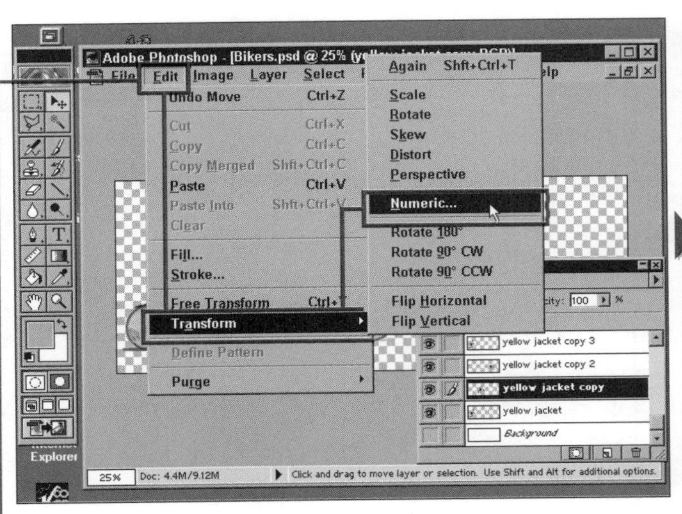

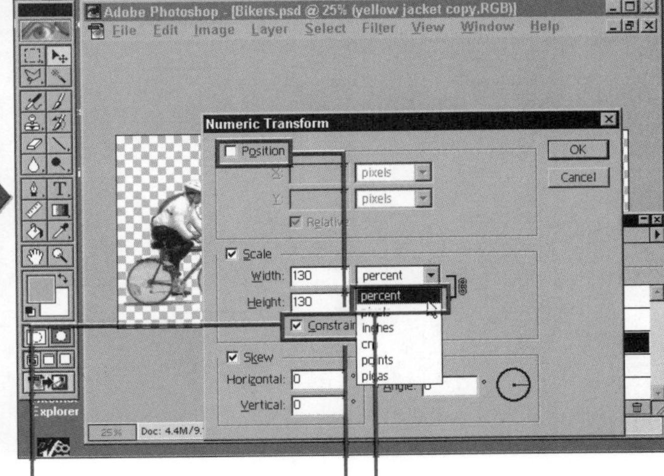

SCALE A LAYER (OR THE CONTENTS OF A SELECTION) TO EXACT DIMENSIONS

1 Choose Edit ⇨ Transform ⇨ Numeric.

■ The Numeric Transformation dialog box appears.

2 Check the Constrain Proportions check box.

Note: If the check mark is on, you need only enter one dimension.

3 Choose the unit of measurement.

4 If you don't want to perform other transformations, uncheck the other transformation types.

USE LAYER BLEND MODES

Just as Photoshop enables you to place parts of images on as many layers as your memory and hard drive can hold, it offers limitless possibilities as to how those layers can influence one another. You can change the opacity of any layer, thus making it translucent and creating a double-exposure effect. You can mask various parts of various layers so they can become intertwined parts of the whole.

Perhaps the most powerful adjustments are the Layer Blend modes (also often called Apply modes). Blend modes are various methods of mixing the pixels in the active layer with those in underlying layers. Each of these methods creates a different visual effect.

To access a Blend mode, choose Window ⇨ Show Layers and use the Mode pull-down menu to choose the desired mode.

Photoshop features nineteen Blend modes, seventeen of which work with any type of layer. The last two work only with floating layers.

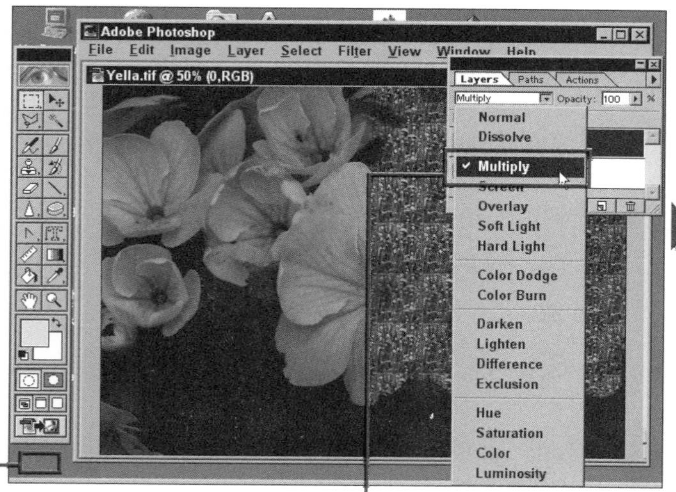

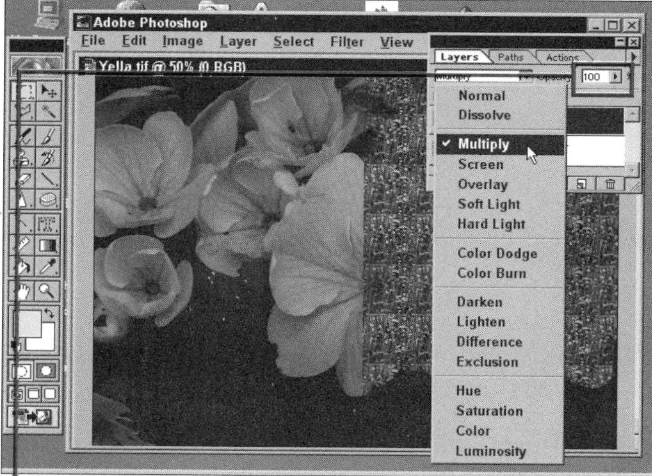

Note: For Layer modes to work, you must have more than one layer.

■ Here, a texture layer has been created to illustrate the interaction between blended layers.

1 Choose the desired mode from the Mode pull-down menu on the Layers palette.

■ The effect will be immediately visible in the workspace window.

2 Enter a percentage to modify the intensity of the effect.

■ This shows the effect of using the Multiply Blend mode on these two layers. Notice how the texture almost seems to be projected onto the surface of the flowers.

EFFECTS OF THE LAYER BLEND MODES

Photoshop's Layer Blend modes are found in the Mode pull-down menu in the Layers palette. To access a Blend mode, choose Window ➪ Show Layers and use the Mode pull-down menu to choose the desired mode. Each mode produces a different effect on the active layer:

- **Normal:** The active layer covers the layer beneath it.
- **Dissolve:** Has no effect unless feathered or softened edges occur in the layer or unless the layer is less than opaque. Increase overall effect by lowering opacity.
- **Multiply:** Best mode for texturing existing surfaces or for building density in overexposed photos. Same as cramming two slides into the projector at once. The composite picture is darker.
- **Screen:** Same as a double exposure. The pixels of one layer lighten the pixels of the other. The composite picture is lighter.
- **Overlay:** Uses layer's pixels to multiply shadows and brighten highlights of the midtones only. Extreme highlights and shadows not affected.
- **Soft Light:** Soft, diffuse lightening and darkening of pixels.
- **Hard Light:** Increases contrast, exaggerates the multiplication of the darkest and lightest tones.
- **Color Dodge:** The current layer's brightest pixels lighten the underlying layer.
- **Color Burn:** The current layer's darkest pixels darken the underlying layer.
- **Darken:** Shows the darkest pixels of the combined layers.
- **Lighten:** Shows the lightest pixels of the combined layers.
- **Difference:** The brightest pixels in one layer are subtracted from the brightest pixels in the other, creating a partial negative.
- **Exclusion:** A softer, less-contrast version of Difference.
- **Hue:** Only the hue values are mixed with the underlying layer.
- **Saturation:** Only the saturation values are mixed with the underlying layer.
- **Color:** The colors (hue and saturation) in the blend layer are applied to the shading (luminosity) of the target layer.
- **Luminosity:** Only the brightness values are mixed with the underlying layer.
- **Behind:** (For floating selections only.) Fills clear portions of the active layer with the contents of the floating layer.
- **Clear:** (For floating selections only.) The floating selection becomes a hole in the selected layer.

STRETCH LAYERS, SELECTIONS, AND PATHS

Photoshop lets you stretch selections and layers in several ways through the Skew, Distort, and Perspective commands, all available under the Edit ➪ Transform submenu.

Skew offsets opposite sides of the bounding box so that the image seems to lean.

Distort lets you change a layer by pulling one of the corner handles without moving the others; pressing Opt/Alt enables you to drag opposing handles simultaneously.

Perspective lets you distort by moving both of the corner handles on a given side the same degree.

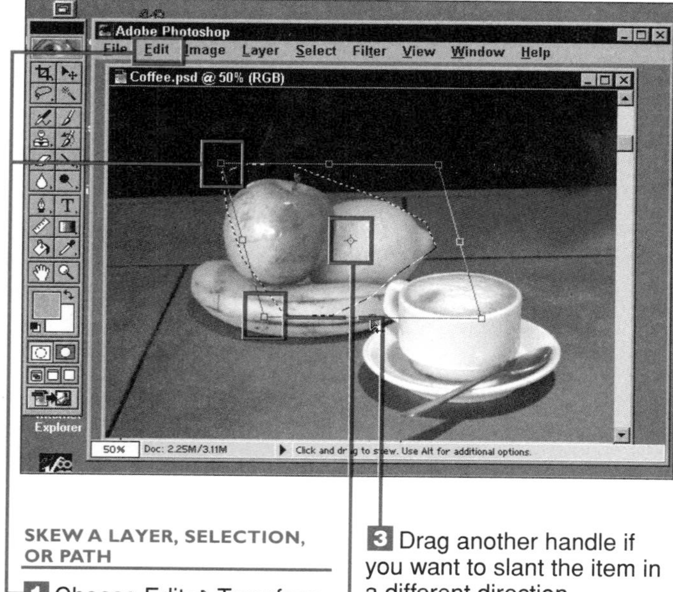

SKEW A LAYER, SELECTION, OR PATH

1. Choose Edit ➪ Transform ➪ Skew.
2. Drag any handle to slant the item.
3. Drag another handle if you want to slant the item in a different direction.
4. Double-click inside the box to render.

STRETCH A SINGLE CORNER

1. Choose Edit ➪ Transform ➪ Distort.
2. Drag any corner handle.
3. Drag other corners if needed.
4. Double-click to render.

TIPS

I've been trying to transform the whole image and it doesn't work. Any idea why?

Probably because you're trying to transform the background layer and that's illegal. Here are two workarounds: 1) Select the entire layer and then transform the selection (you'll see the background color wherever the transformation has moved the image away from the edges). 2) Double-click the background layer and rename it in the Layers Options dialog box. It is now a standard image layer.

Can I slant in two different directions?

You can repeat the reshaping, using different handles, as many times as you like until you're ready to render (calculate the pixel modifications and make them permanent) the item.

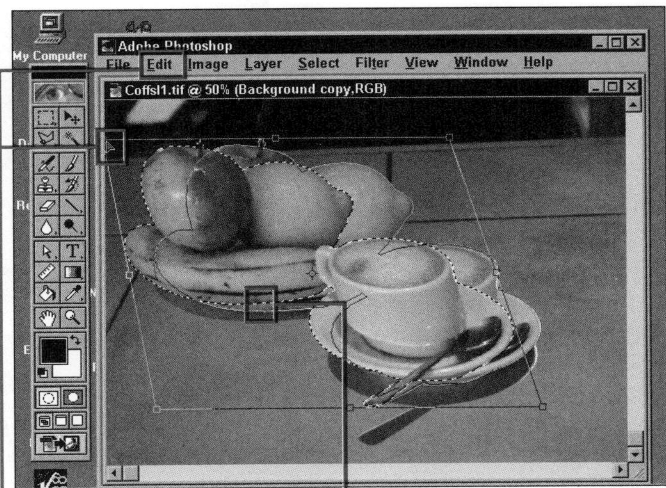

STRETCH BY MOVING TWO CORNERS EQUIDISTANTLY IN OPPOSITE DIRECTIONS

1 Choose Edit ➪ Transform ➪ Distort.

2 Press Opt/Alt and drag a corner.

■ The opposite corner moves the same distance in the opposite direction.

3 Double-click to render.

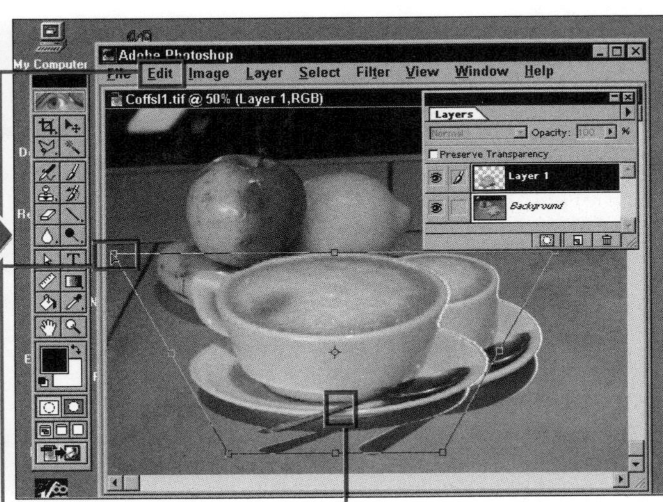

CHANGE THE APPARENT POINT OF VIEW OF A SELECTION LAYER, OR PATH

1 Choose Edit ➪ Transform ➪ Perspective.

2 Drag a corner handle.

■ The opposite handle on the same side moves the same distance from the center.

3 Double-click to render.

MAKE MULTIPLE FREEHAND TRANSFORMATIONS

The fastest, most intuitive method for making transformations — and the one with the highest fidelity — is to choose Edit ⇨ Free Transform. Unless, that is, you know you need to make only one specific type of transformation to the layer, selection, or path.

Using Free Transform is the fastest and easiest method because you issue only one command and then use modifier keys and cursor location to control the type of transformation made with a single drag movement. The reason its the method with the highest fidelity is that all of the reshaping is done before rendering. Any time the program has to make interpolation calculations, it has to decide which pixels to drop and which to duplicate. Each successive interpolation increases the errors, which degrades the image.

The Edit ⇨ Free Transform command allows all types of transformations (except flips and flops): scaling, rotating, skewing, distorting, and changing perspective.

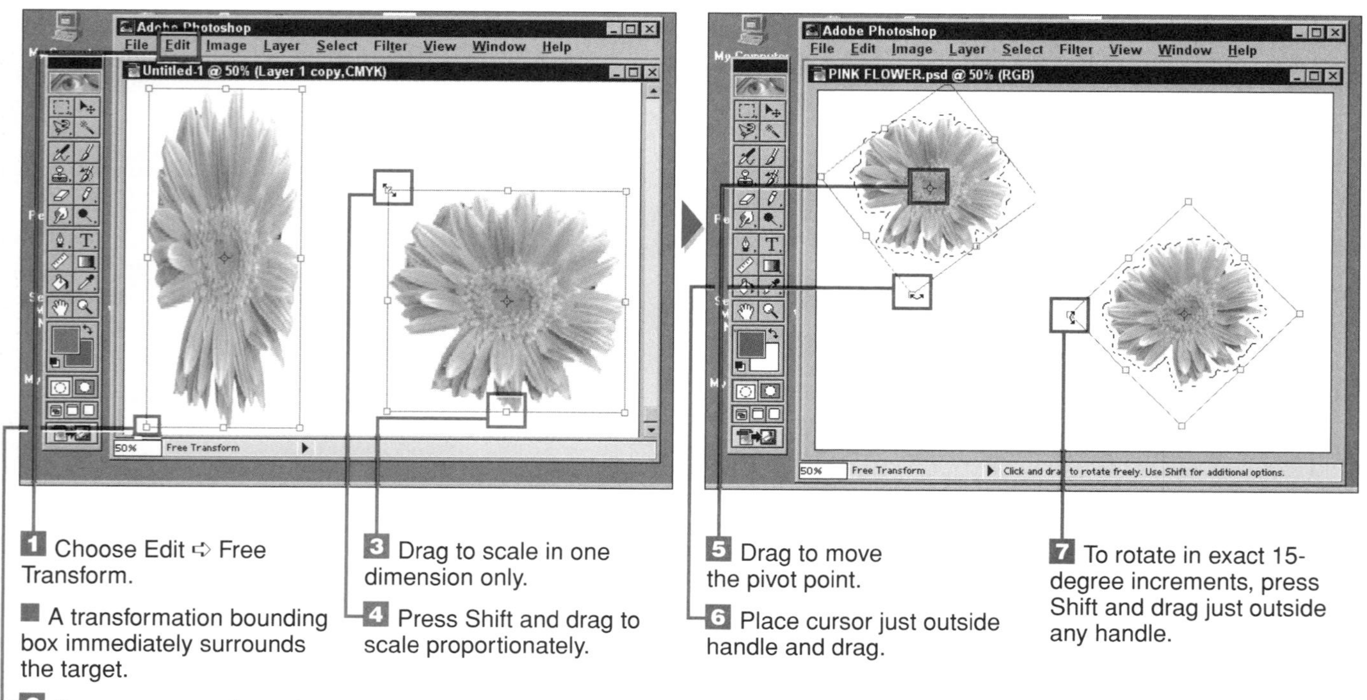

1 Choose Edit ⇨ Free Transform.

■ A transformation bounding box immediately surrounds the target.

2 Drag any corner to scale disproportionately.

3 Drag to scale in one dimension only.

4 Press Shift and drag to scale proportionately.

5 Drag to move the pivot point.

6 Place cursor just outside handle and drag.

7 To rotate in exact 15-degree increments, press Shift and drag just outside any handle.

Do I have to use the Edit ➪ Free Transform command to perform several types of transformations before I render the item?

Not really. If you have trouble remembering the modifier keys to use with Free Transform, you can just choose Edit ➪ Transform as many times as you like before you double-click to render. You still get the benefit of rendering just once.

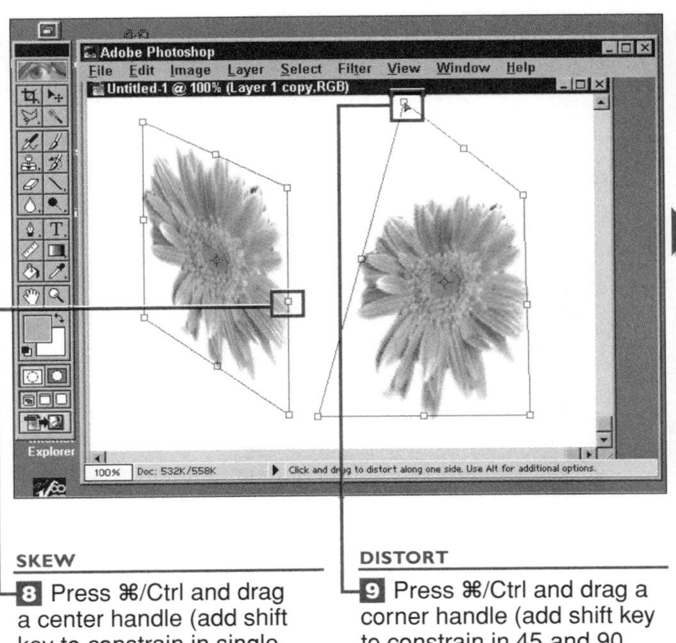

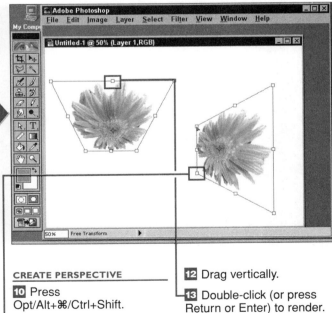

SKEW

8 Press ⌘/Ctrl and drag a center handle (add shift key to constrain in single direction or Opt/Alt for a constrainted tilt).

DISTORT

9 Press ⌘/Ctrl and drag a corner handle (add shift key to constrain in 45 and 90 degrees).

Note: In both cases, the cursor arrow turns gray.

CREATE PERSPECTIVE

10 Press Opt/Alt+⌘/Ctrl+Shift.

11 Drag horizontally or

12 Drag vertically.

13 Double-click (or press Return or Enter) to render.

MAKE NUMERICALLY PRECISE TRANSFORMATIONS

If you want a layer, selection, or path to have a perfectly precise location, size, orientation, or slant, choose the Edit ➪ Transform ➪ Numeric command. You'll get a dialog that enables you to use numbers to specify each of these types of transformations. You can also perform any or all of them at once.

The Numeric Transform dialog box is divided into areas for each transformation type: Position, Scale, Skew, and Rotate. The Transformation Type check box determines which of these will be rendered when you click OK. In other words, to make sure you don't accidentally perform an unwanted transformation, uncheck the appropriate box.

You can reset this (or any other Photoshop dialog box) to the last-used setting by pressing Opt/Alt, whereupon the Cancel button becomes the Reset button.

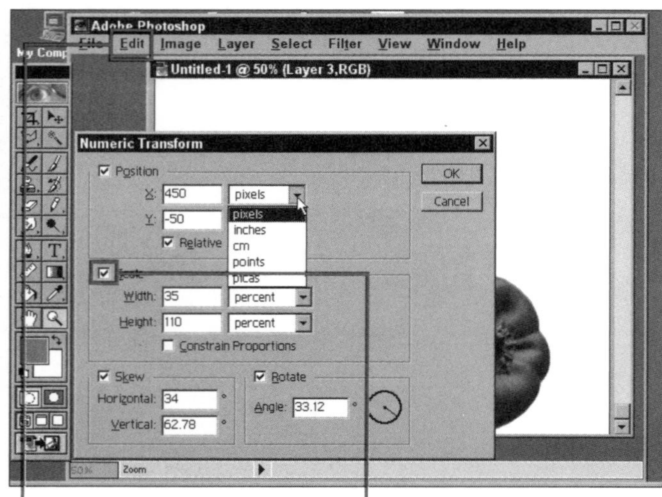

1 Choose Edit ➪ Transform ➪ Numeric.

■ The Numeric Transform dialog box appears.

2 To change the position of the active layer, selection, or path, check the Position check box and enter X, Y values.

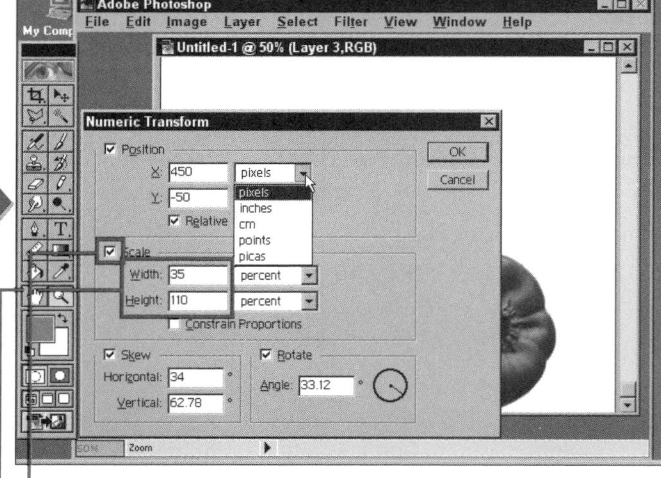

3 To resize the item, click to check.

4 Enter width and height.

Note: If you check Constrain Proportions, you need enter only one dimension. The other is entered automatically.

TIPS

What are the advantages of performing transitions numerically?

Precision and fidelity. If you want to transform several items so that they have the same characteristics, the dialog box will remember the numbers you last entered. So you activate each item in succession, choose the Edit ➪ Transform ➪ Numeric command, and click OK. Of course, if your targets are all on individual layers, you can simply link the layers. Then all will transform, using any of the transformation methods. However, all object will maintain their position in relationship to one another and will rotate about the center of the object on the active layer.

How many decimal points can I use?

As many as you like, but Photoshop 5 will round it off to two.

Can I enter negative numbers in any field?

Yes, except for Scale. A negative number positions left of center or up from center. If you enter a negative number for the rotation angle, you'll rotate the item counterclockwise.

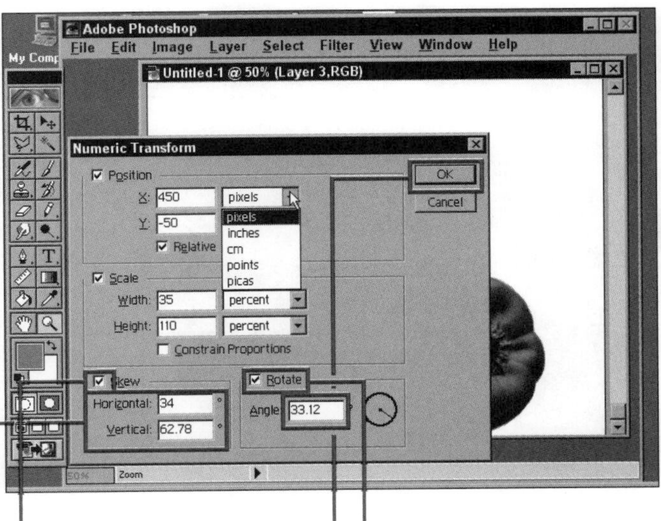

5 To slant the item, click the Skew check box.

6 Enter degrees of slant from the opposite edge

7 To rotate the item, click the Rotate check box.

8 Enter a number with up to two decimal points (or drag to indicate angle).

9 Click OK.

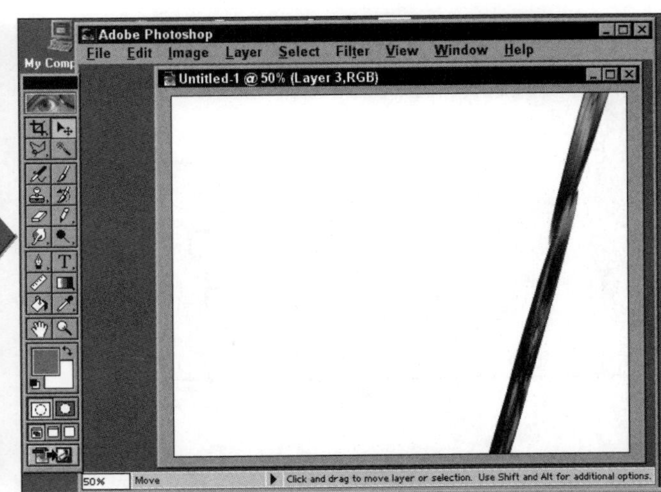

■ Here is the result produced by the numbers entered in the preceding example.

LINK LAYERS

The capability to link layers so that all react to a command in the same way is another Photoshop time-saver. Conceivably, you could end up with dozens of layers. What if you need to rotate ten of them to the same degree, or what if you want to merge them into one? In case you didn't already guess, the solution is to link them.

Linking layers is easy. Just click the box in the second column of the Layers palette. If a Link icon appears, that layer is linked to the active layer. There are no menu commands for linking layers, so this is one of the rare instances where Photoshop 5 provides you with only one way of doing things.

You can have multiple links in an image file. However, if you change the links to one of the linked layers, all the formerly associated links are dropped.

There are three possibilities for affecting layers: move them, merge them, or transform them. Other Photoshop 5 commands simply don't work on multiple image layers.

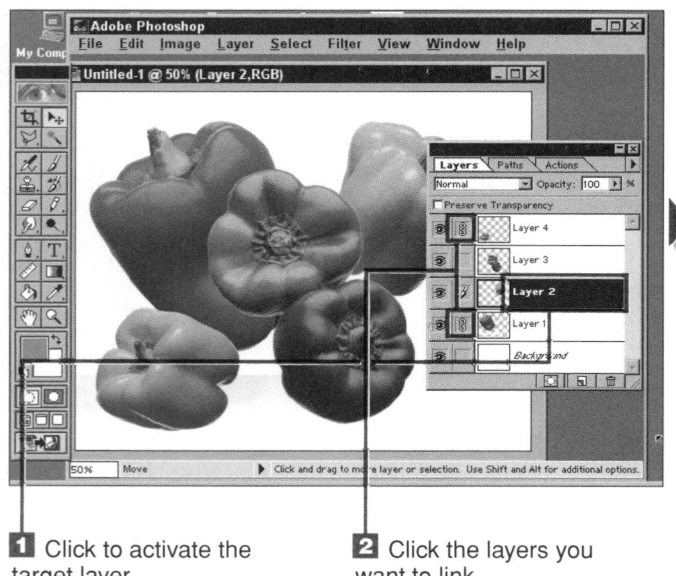

1 Click to activate the target layer.

2 Click the layers you want to link.

Note: Linked layers need not be in any stacking order.

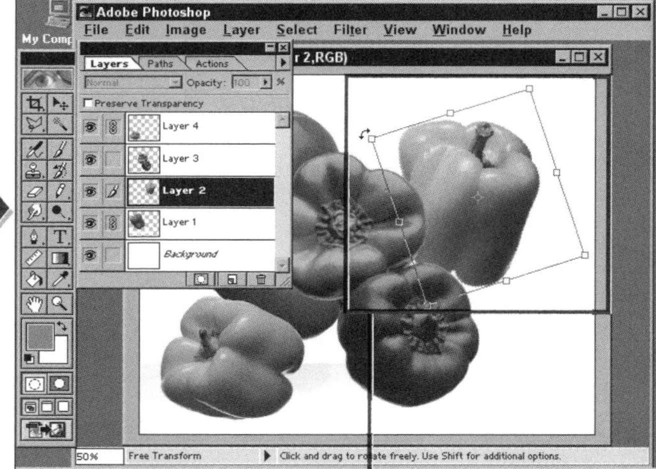

3 Merge or transform the linked layers.

■ Here, the result of rotating linked layers is shown.

MAKE AND USE A CLIPPING GROUP

A clipping group uses the silhouette (transparency mask) of the active layer as a cutout for the visible layers in a group. For the clipping group to be effective, you need an item that has been isolated on a layer by lifting it from a selection on another layer or by erasing portions of the layer it's on. In other words, you want the object's silhouette to be surrounded by transparency.

You can get a similar effect by adding a mask to a layer; however, more steps are involved, especially if the mask shape you want is already present as a transparent background layer. Clipping groups are often confused with clipping paths, but they have no relationship. Clipping paths are used to place an irregularly shaped, bit-mapped graphic into a DTP document in such a way that the program knows how to wrap text around the object.

You can ungroup layers by selecting one layer of the group and pressing Shift+⌘/Ctrl+G or by clicking the dotted line between grouped layers.

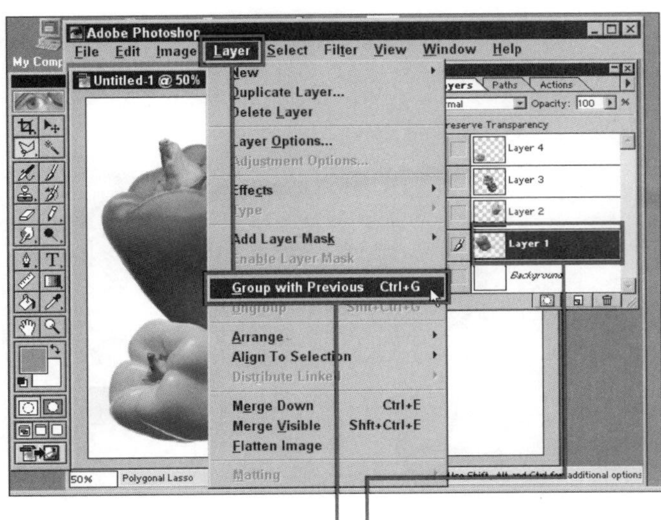

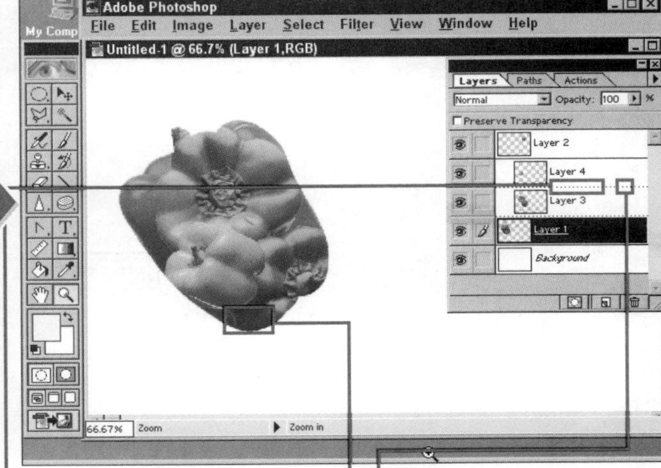

MAKE A CLIPPING GROUP WITH THE MENU COMMAND

1 Drag to arrange layers so that the image you want masked is above the image that will become the mask.

2 Click to choose the layer or layers you want masked.

3 Choose Layer ➪ Group With Previous (or press ⌘/Ctrl+G).

MAKE A CLIPPING GROUP WITH THE LAYERS PALETTE

1 Drag to arrange all the layers you want masked above the mask layer.

2 Press Opt/Alt and click the border between layers.

■ The cursor changes to overlapping circles and the border between grouped layers is dotted.

■ The lower layer's image shows through the mask, but grouped layers are trimmed to fit inside.

MAKE AND USE ADJUSTMENT LAYERS

You can apply Image ➪ Adjust commands simultaneously to all visible layers below the active layer when you use adjustment layers. In this exercise you see how to choose each type of adjustment layer.

The adjustments available in adjustment layers include Levels, Curves, Brightness/Contrast, Hue/Saturation, Selective Color, Channel Mixer, Invert, Threshold, and Posterize.

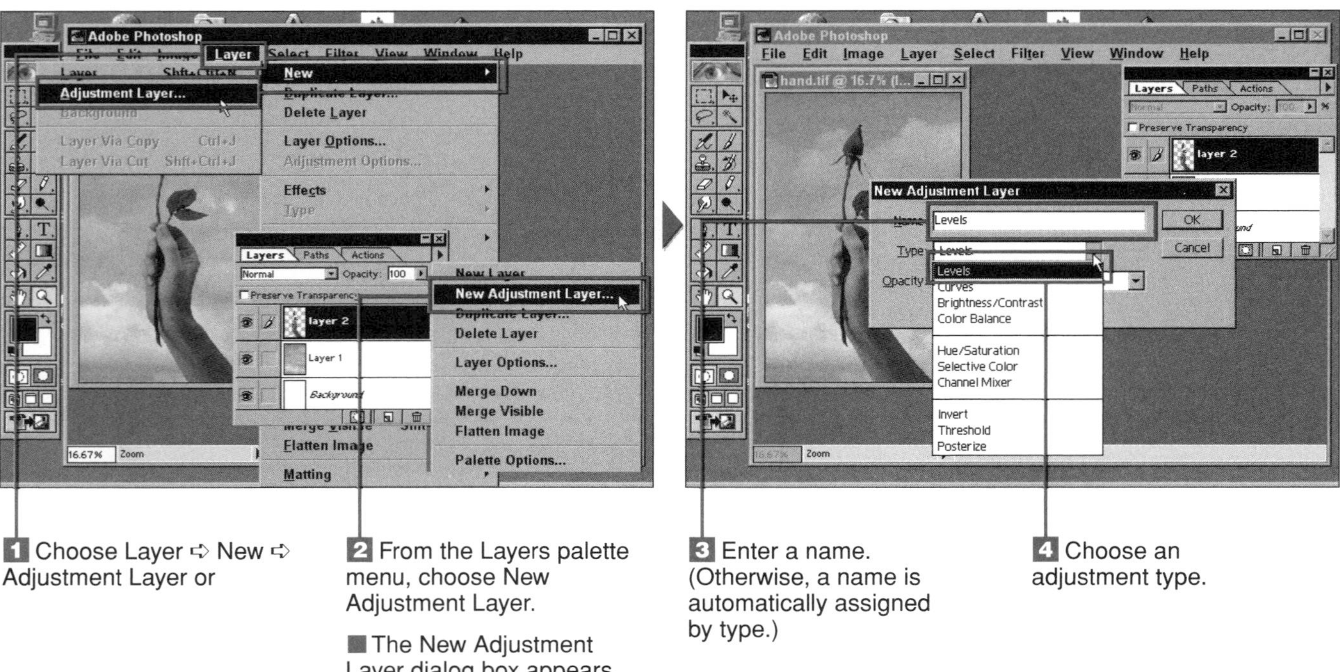

1 Choose Layer ➪ New ➪ Adjustment Layer or

2 From the Layers palette menu, choose New Adjustment Layer.

■ The New Adjustment Layer dialog box appears.

3 Enter a name. (Otherwise, a name is automatically assigned by type.)

4 Choose an adjustment type.

TIPS

Is there any way to skip some layers while affecting all the others below the adjustment layer?

Only if you can drag that layer to a position above the adjustment layer. If all the layers you want to affect overlap, you may have trouble doing this. You could, however, add a mask to the adjustment layer to cancel the adjustment over the area (including the whole layer) you don't want affected.

Can you elaborate on what the Group With Previous check box does?

It makes the adjustment layer affect the layers below it without affecting the other layers. Of course, you could just make that the active layer and then make an image adjustment.

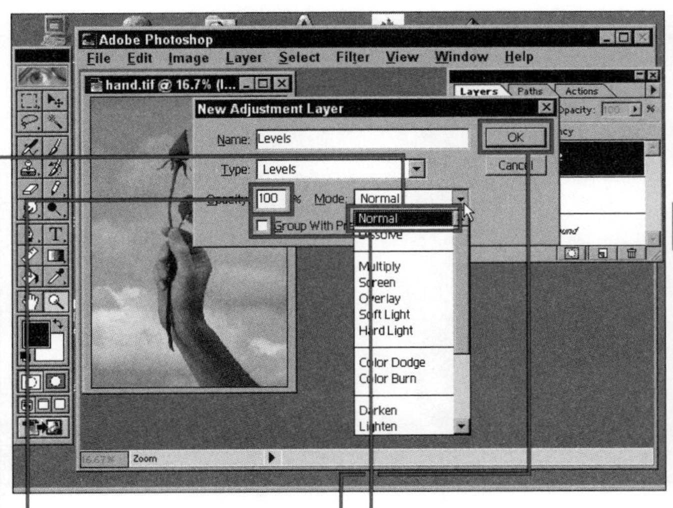

5 Enter the percentage of the effect you want for the adjustment.

6 Choose a Blend mode for the effect.

7 Click the Group With Previous check box.

8 Click OK.

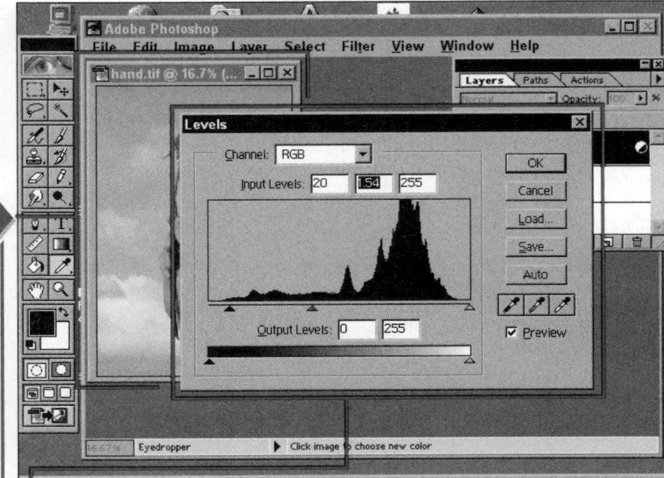

■ The dialog box for your chosen adjustment type appears.

■ The background image shows you the effects of these adjustments.

Note: If you double-click the mask (thumbnail) part of the adjustment layer in the Layers palette, you can rename it, change what you call the Blend mode, and adjust the Blend If sliders. Double-click the layer itself to bring up the appropriate adjustment window.

MAKE A LAYER MASK

Each layer can have one mask associated with it. Like a channel mask, a layer mask can dictate specific areas of the layer as transparent, semitransparent, or graduating from transparent to opaque. The difference is that layer masks can be altered and turned on and off without affecting the pixels on that layer or anything else in the rest of the image. Of course, if you merge the layer with another or flatten the image, the layer mask becomes integrated with the final product and no longer accessible.

Layer masks can be made in several ways. The simplest is to click the Layer Mask icon at the bottom of the Layers palette. If a selection is active, the mask reveals the contents of the selection (the rest of the layer is transparent). If there is no selection, the mask reveals all of the layer. You can also use the Layer menu: Choose Layer ➪ Add Layer Mask ➪ Reveal All/Selection or Hide All/Selection.

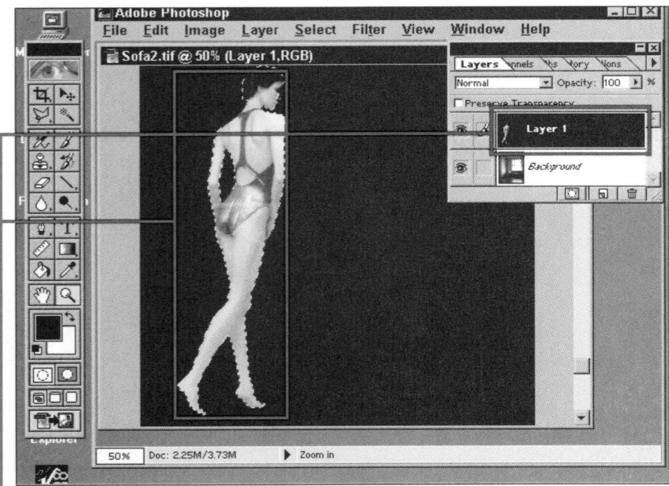

MAKE A LAYER MASK FROM A SELECTION

1 Click to activate the layer to which you want to add a mask.

2 Select the area of the layer you want to mask.

Note: Be sure to invert the selection if you've selected the portion of the image you want kept clear. Or invert the mask itself after the fact.

3 Click the Layer Mask icon or

4 Choose Layer ➪ Add Layer Mask ➪ Hide/Reveal selection.

■ The image appears with the masked portion transparent. In other words, you can see the underlying layer through the masked area.

TIPS

Is there any way to defringe (matte) a layer mask?

Edit the layer mask in the Channels palette. Use the Magic Wand to select the interior of the mask. Choose Select ➪ Modify ➪ Contract, and enter the number of pixels to defringe the mask. Click OK, and then invert the selection and fill it with black. If you want to soften the edge, feather the selection before filling it.

How do I delete a layer mask?

Drag the layer mask to the Trash Can icon at the bottom of the Layers palette — or choose Layer ➪ Remove Layer. A dialog box appears asking if you want to apply the mask before it's removed. To remove the mask and leave the layer intact, click Discard.

How do I link a layer mask so that it stays registered with the layer when I move it?

Layer masks are linked by default, but it's good to check that the link is still in effect before you move the layer. If the layer mask is linked, you should see a Link icon between the Layer icon and the Layer Mask icon. You can turn linking on and off by clicking the icon.

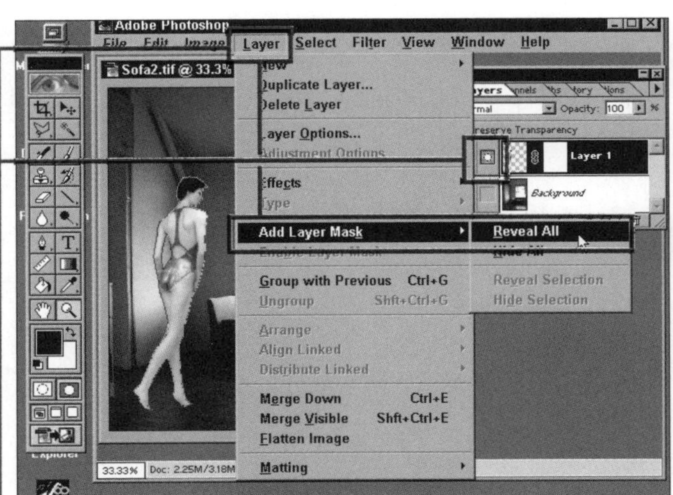

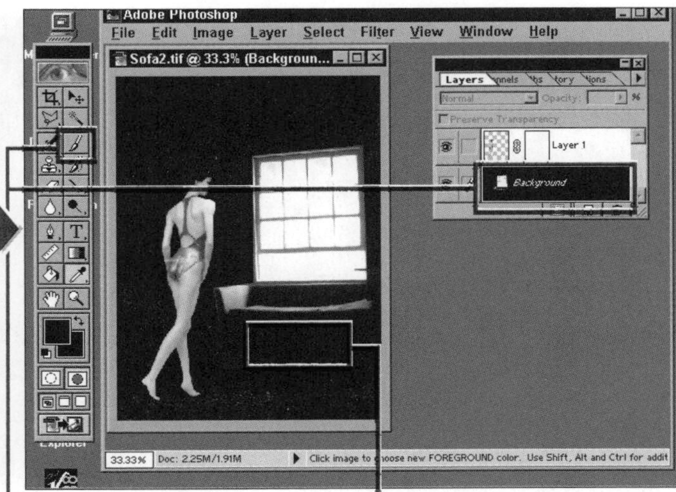

MAKE A NEW, SOLID MASK

1. Click the Layer Mask icon (press Opt/Alt before clicking to Hide All) or
2. Choose Layer ➪ Add Layer Mask ➪ Reveal All/Hide All.

■ The Layer Mask icon (either solid white or black) and the Layer Mask link appear.

EDIT THE LAYER MASK

1. Click to activate the layer mask.
2. Use any of Photoshop s image-editing tools to alter the mask.

■ Here we painted with a black brush. You could fill a selection, run a filter, or do many other things to alter this mask.

MAKE AND USE LAYER EFFECTS

Layer effects are new to Photoshop 5. Meant mostly to enhance the appearance of text layers (see Chapter 11 for information on making text layers), layer effects can also be applied to any irregular shape (if it has a transparent background).

The following effects are available: Drop Shadow, Inner Shadow, Outer Glow, Inner Glow, and Bevel and Emboss. You can apply multiple effects to a single layer. An *f* icon appears on the right side of the layer name bar when a layer effect has been applied. Normally, layer effects are linked to the layer so that if you move the layer, you move the effect. You have the option to move the effect to its own layer. You can also clear, copy, and paste effects.

DROP SHADOW

This effect gives the appearance that the subject of the layer is floating above any visible lower layers and seems to be casting a shadow below it. You can vary the size, offset angle, color, blurring, and intensity of the shadow.

1 Choose Layer ➪ Effects ➪ Drop Shadow.

■ The Effects dialog box appears with Drop Shadow chosen as the type.

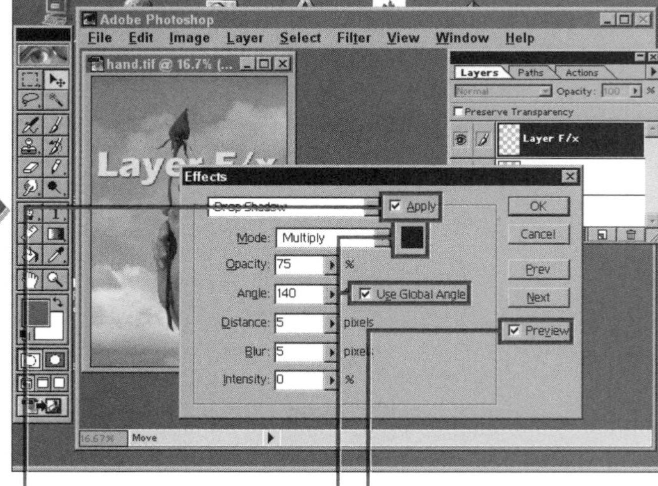

2 Click the Apply check box.

Note: You must clear the check mark if you use the Type pull-down menu to go to another choice, unless you want the Drop Shadow effect added to the next effect.

3 Click the Preview check box.

4 Click the color sample to bring up Color Picker.

5 Click the Use Global Angle check box.

TIPS

Will the ability to choose Blending Modes give me a wider variety of effects?

Yes, especially when you consider how you can combine them with all the other adjustments on screen.

Will the effect render faster if I turn Preview off?

Slightly. The difference will add up if you create this effect as part of an action that will be applied to numerous layers. As this is usually done because you want a consistent look, the ability to preview adds little value.

Why doesn't Photoshop just impose a blur automatically, based on distance?

A hard edge will make the letter (or other layer edge) look more three-dimensional. The combination of blurring and distance, on the other hand, make the layer seem to float at different distances from the background.

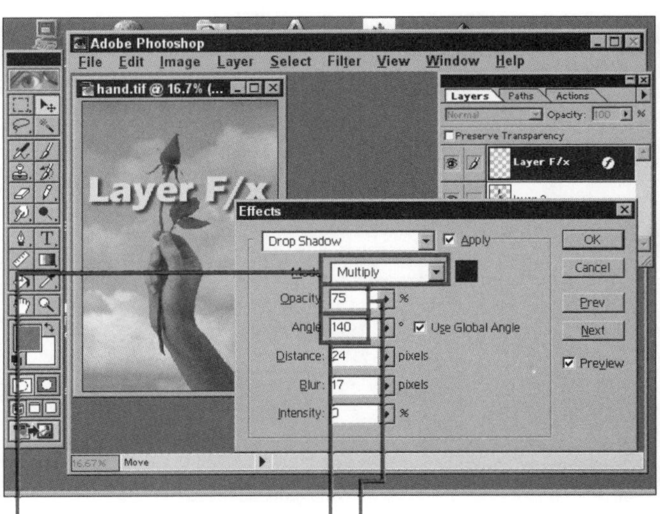

6 Choose a mode from the pull-down menu.

Note: If you click the button, you can drag a slider to indicate the figures for Opacity, Angle, Distance, Blur, and Intensity.

7 Enter a number between 1 and 100 for percentage of opacity.

8 Enter a number between 0 and 360 (positive or negative) for the lighting angle (direction shadow will be cast).

9 Enter the number of pixels that should be blurred from the shadow's edge.

10 Enter a percentage of intensity.

11 Click OK.

CONTINUED

9

MAKE AND USE LAYER EFFECTS
CONTINUED

INNER SHADOW

This effect makes the layer look recessed because the shadow falls inside the layer rather than being cast on the background.

The use of Blend modes will have a more pronounced visual effect than for the other types because the blending is taking place within the layer itself.

Note: Be sure you have turned off the Apply check mark from any previously made effect for this layer, unless you want that effect added to the Inner Shadow effect.

1 Choose Layer ⇨ Effects ⇨ Inner Shadow or

2 Choose Inner Shadow from the pull-down menu.

■ The Effects dialog box appears with Inner Shadow chosen as the type.

3 Click the Apply check box.

■ You must turn the check mark on if you turned it off after experimenting with another effect.

4 Click the Preview check box.

5 Click the color sample to bring up Color Picker.

6 Click the Use Global Angle check box.

TIPS

Why did you have me uncheck Use Global Angle?

Because the shadow falls inside the layer and the effects are often performed on layers, the exact angle you'll want to use likely depends on the shape and orientation of the letters. Also, this isn't an effect that's often used in conjunction with one of the other effects, so setting a global angle is probably not important.

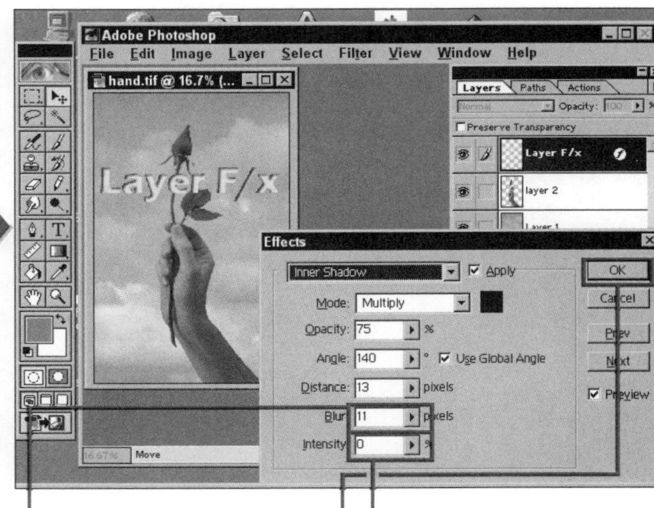

7 Chose a mode from the pull-down menu.

Note: If you click the button, you can drag a slider to indicate the figures for Opacity, Angle, Distance, Blur, and Intensity.

8 Enter a number between 1 and 100 for percentage of opacity.

9 Enter a number between 0 and 360 (negative or positive) for the lighting angle.

10 Enter the number of pixels that should be blurred from the shadow's edge.

11 Enter a percentage of intensity (the strength of the effect).

12 Click OK.

10 Using Channel Operations

Channel operations are those functions created by causing one Photoshop channel to interact with another according to a specific mathematical formula. Many of the special effects in Photoshop are due to preprogrammed channel operations. Channel operations can make use of any combination of Photoshop's channels, whether they are color channels or alpha channels.

Although all masks are channels, not all channels are masks. First, there's the composite channel, which isn't really a channel but a screen image that represents the combination of all the individual color channels. Then there are the individual color channels, the number of which varies from color model to color model. For instance, the RGB model has three color channels: Red, Green, and Blue; the CMYK model has four color channels: Cyan, Magenta, Yellow, and blacK. Bitmap, grayscale, duotone, and indexed-color images have only one channel.

In addition, any Photoshop file (except bitmap images) can have a total of up to 24 channels. Those that are not color channels are called alpha channels.

The Channels Palette

The Channels palette, shown here, is accessed by choosing Window ➪ Show Channels. Every channel in a particular image will appear in the Channels palette.

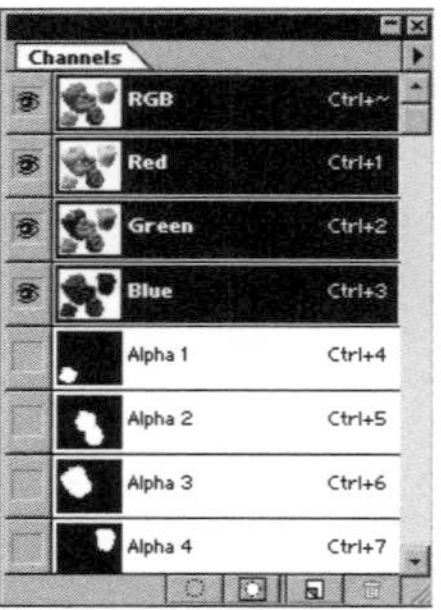

Channels Palette Contents

Component	Function
Selection icon	Click to make selection from active channel (load channel), or drag channel to icon to make selection from channel.
Mask icon	Click to make mask channel from active channel, or drag channel to icon to make mask (alpha) channel from channel.
New Channel icon	Click to make new (blank) channel, or drag channel to icon to duplicate (copy) a channel.

Component	Function
Trash icon	Click to delete the currently active channel, or drag any channel to icon to delete it.
Palette menu button	Drag to open menu and choose menu item (see the following section, "Channels Palette Menu").

Channels Palette Menu

The Channels palette menu, shown in the following figure, is a pop-out menu accessed by clicking the right arrow in the upper-right corner of the palette. The Channels palette menu offers a list of additional channel commands.

New Channel...
Duplicate Channel...
Delete Channel
New Spot Channel...
Merge Spot Channel
Channel Options...
Split Channels
Merge Channels...
Palette Options...

Channels Palette Menu Contents

Component	Function
New Channel	Creates a new, empty channel and brings up the New Channel dialog box.
Duplicate Channel	Makes a copy of the currently active channel and brings up the Duplicate Channel dialog box.
Delete Channel	Deletes the active channel.
New Spot Channel	Creates a new channel for a spot color. Spot colors are specific colors from ink makers' swatchbooks (ANPA, DIC, Focoltone, Pantone, Toyo, and Trumatch are supported by Photoshop 5). If you specify a channel to print in one of these colors, you'll get an exact match from the printers. Useful for printing solid text and logos that must meet corporate specs.
Merge Spot Channel	Converts the spot channel to the current color mode and merges it with the existing color channels. This command automatically flattens the image. The merged channels will be affected by solidity settings made in the New Spot Channel Options dialog box.

CONTINUED

USING CHANNEL OPERATIONS CONTINUED

Channels Palette Menu Contents

Component	Function
Channel Options	Enables you to rename the layer, choose the masking color, and indicate whether it covers masked, unmasked, or spot color areas of the image. You can also set the opacity of the mask color. (Double-clicking the channel also brings up this dialog box.)
Split Channels	Automatically exports each channel to a separate file. Command is inactive if only one channel exists in the file.
Merge Channels	Active only if channels have been split and the window for each of the split channels is still open. Merges all the split channels back into one channel. Enables you to reassign channels through several dialogs boxes (see "Merge Channels," later in this chapter).
Palette Options	Enables you to choose the size of the thumbnail.

New Channel

The New Channel dialog box, depicted here, appears when you select the New Channel command from the Channels palette menu. Use this dialog box to select the type of channel you wish to create.

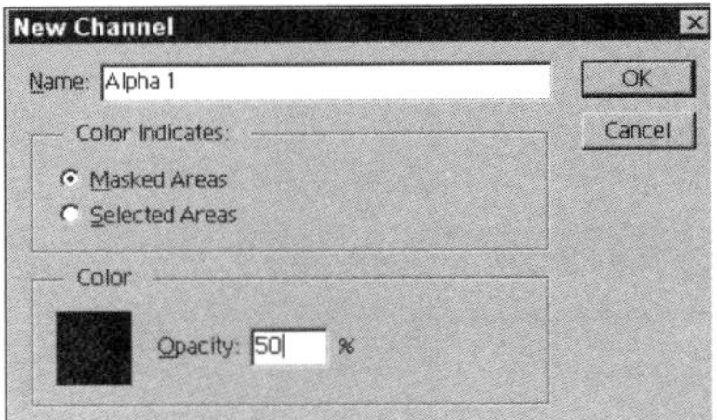

New Channel Dialog Box Contents

Component	Function
Name field	Enter new name for channel or accept default.
Color Indicates radio buttons	Click to choose whether the mask color indicates masked or unmasked (selected) areas of the channel.
Color swatch	Click to bring up the Color Picker dialog box. You can change color any time you like.
Opacity field	Enter desired percentage of transparency for the masking color.

Duplicate Channel

The Duplicate Channel dialog box, as shown here, appears when you select Duplicate Channel from the Channels palette menu. Use this dialog box to select the name and destination for your duplicated channel.

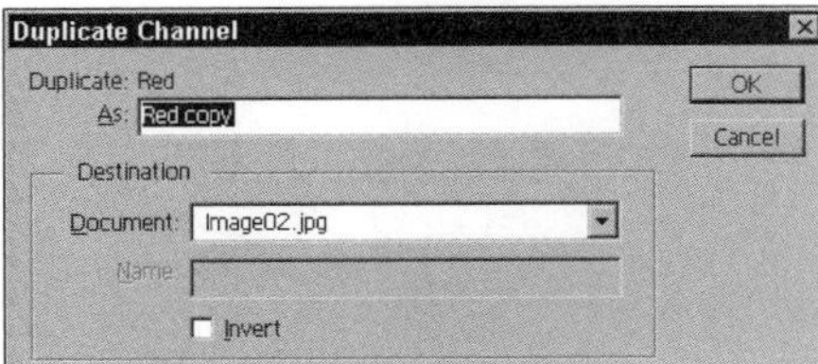

Duplicate Channel Dialog Box Contents

Component	Function
Duplicated channel	Enter a name for the copied channel.
Duplicated As name field	Enter a name that is meaningful to you for the duplicate channel or accept the automatically entered name.
Destination Document pull-down menu	Choose the destination file for the duplicated channel (the current document is the default). All documents that are open are listed on this pull-down menu, or you can choose New if you want to send the channel to a new document.
Name field	Enter the name for the new document. This field is grayed if you're duplicating to an existing document.
Invert check box	If checked, the image in this channel is inverted (made a negative).

Saving alpha channels to a new file is a great way to keep selections for a particular file in a different file. This way they're always available, but you don't have to increase your file size (and therefore your need for system memory).

New Spot Channel

The New Spot Channel dialog box, shown here, appears when you select New Spot Channel from the Channels palette menu. Each spot color channel prints on a separate color plate. In this dialog box, you can select the color and solidity (the opacity of the ink) of the channel.

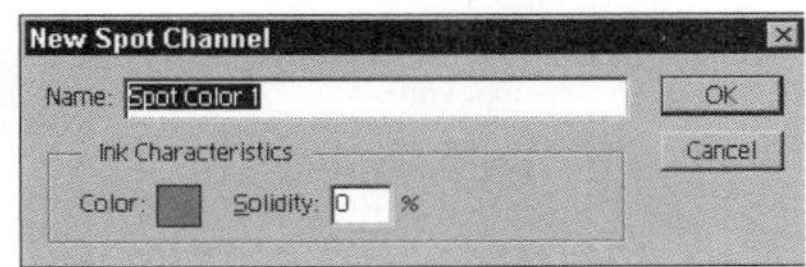

New Spot Channel Dialog Box Contents

Component	Function
Name field	Accept the default name for the new color channel, or enter your own.
Color swatch	Click to bring up Color Picker. When the Color Picker appears, be sure to click the Custom button so you can pick the spot color from one of Photoshop's swatch booklets.
Solidity field	Enter a percentage of coverage (roughly equivalent to transparency) for this spot color. The number you enter here affects the influence the spot color has if this channel is merged into the color channels. (See note that follows.)

CONTINUED

USING CHANNEL OPERATIONS CONTINUED

Note: The idea here is to tell the imagesetter what percentage of a particular ink you want on that plate. How it affects the merge is less important, since the purpose of the feature is for spot color, which will not be merged. If you play with this feature, you will notice that Photoshop 5 always puts 100 percent black in the channel but displays a rendition of the spot color in its specified percentage. The percentage info is not displayed (as opacity or percentage of gray) in the channel itself.

Channel Options

The Channel Options dialog box is accessed by selecting the Channel Options command from the Channels palette menu, as shown in the following figure. Choose this command to change the settings assigned to a spot color or mask channel.

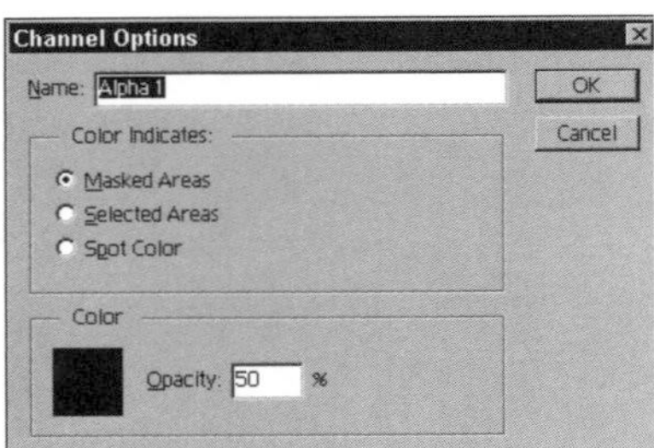

Channel Options Dialog Box Contents

Component	Function
Name field	Accept the default name for the new color channel, or enter your own.
Color Indicates radio buttons	Click to indicate whether you want the color to be a spot or mask color and whether the mask color will cover selected or unselected areas of the layer.
Color swatch	Click to bring up the Color Picker so you can change the mask or spot color.
Opacity field	Enter the opacity of the masking color (the number will be translated as the solidity if this is to be a spot color).

Merge Channels

The Merge Channels dialog box appears by selecting the Merge Channels command in the Channels palette menu, depicted here. This command enables you to merge several images into a single multichannel image.

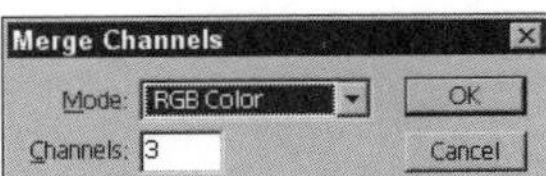

Merge Channels Dialog Box Contents

Component	Function
Mode pull-down menu	Drag to choose a color mode from the pull-down menu.
Channels field	Enter the number of channels (this can be no more than the number of currently open grayscale files of exactly the same pixel dimension).

Channel Palette Options

The Channel Palette Options dialog box, shown in the following figure, enables you to choose the size of the thumbnail image that appears in the Channels palette.

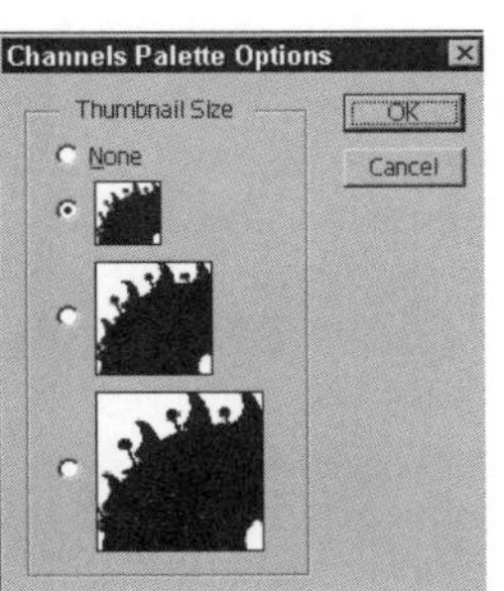

Channels Palette Options Dialog Box Contents

Component	Function
Thumbnail Size radio buttons	Click to choose size of channel thumbnail.

SPLIT OUT THE CHANNELS

Photoshop 5 places each channel in an image file — whether color, spot, or alpha — into a separate file. This is a good thing. Each of the channels is a grayscale channel, so if you need a black-and-white photo that looks more dramatic, one of these images might just do the job. The Red channel even looks a little like a photograph shot on infrared film.

You can do many things with split-out channels. Most important, you can edit any flaws in the individual channels and then recombine them all. Or, you could run different special effects in each channel and then recombine them.

You could also delete everything but the alpha channels, merging them into a new file so you end up with a separate file that contains all the masks for your file. Then you could delete all the masks from the original, thereby cutting the file size down significantly. If you need one of those masks later, just merge it back with the original.

One common use for this feature is for transportation purposes. You can put a 3MB or larger RGB file on three floppy disks by splitting the file into three grayscale files — one per disk — and then reassembling them to re-create the color file.

To split out your channels, choose Split Channels from the Channels Palette menu.

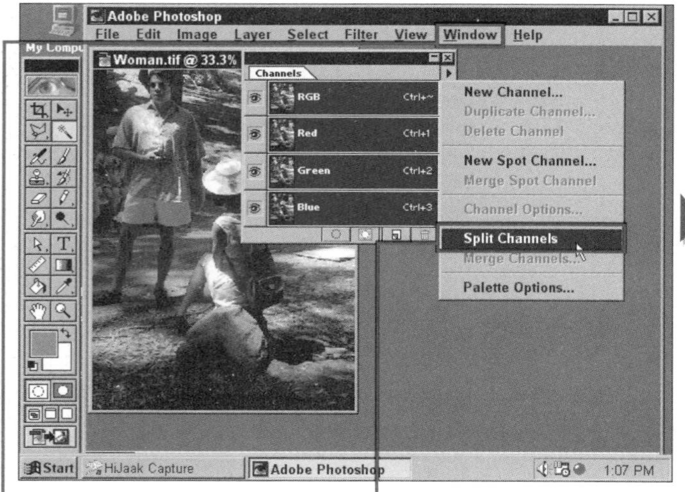

1 Choose Window ⇨ Show Channels.

■ The Channels palette appears.

2 Choose Split Channels.

Note: Each channel is written out to a separate file (but not saved to disk — that's up to you).

■ The individual channels appear in a window of their own.

Note: You can merge these channels into a new file or merge them with other grayscale files (as long as all have exactly the same dimensions in pixels).

MAKE A SEPARATE CHANNEL FOR SPOT COLORS

Photoshop 5 introduces a new kind of color channel — *spot color channels*. Now you can create a specific channel for printing a specific spot color over the continuous tone image. This could be a spot color (from a color-matching swatchbook, such as one of the Pantone or Toyo books) to match a particular shade at a particular spot in the image. (Think of this as the electronic version of, say, matching the paint color on a car for touch-ups).

More often, you'll use spot colors to overprint type or a logo. Spot color is usually used to introduce a brilliant blue, purple, orange, or fluorescent (which can't be produced accurately with process color), or it can be used for a varnish or metallic ink.

When this file is printed, the traditional color separation is made for the C, M, Y, and K channels. Separate plates are then made for the spot color channels. These spot color plates are then used to overprint colors on the full-range print.

Making a spot color channel isn't tricky at all. Unless you want a blank channel, first select the area you want overprinted in the spot color. Choose New Spot Channel from the Channels palette menu. When the New Spot Channel dialog box opens, pick a color.

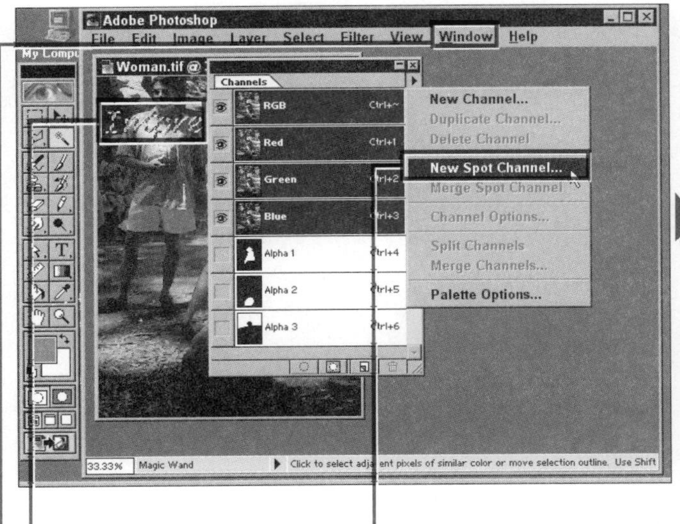

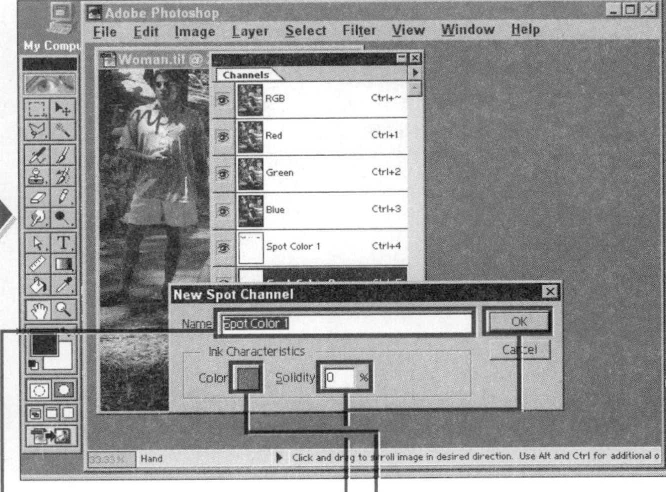

1 Unless you want a new, blank channel, select the area you want the spot color to cover.

2 Choose Window ⇨ Show Channels.

3 Choose New Spot Channel.

■ The New Spot Channel dialog box appears.

■ The new channel automatically appears and is activated in the Channels palette.

4 Accept the default or enter a new name for the spot color channel.

5 Click the color swatch to bring up the Color Picker.

6 Click the Custom button and choose your color.

7 Enter a percentage of solidity for the spot color and click OK.

MERGE CHANNELS TO CREATE SPECIAL EFFECTS

This exercise shows you how to merge channels. The most common reason for splitting and merging channels is so that each channel can be edited individually without having to worry about messing up the original image. However, this exercise adds a few extra steps so you can see the dramatic results that can be produced by merging channels.

You can merge channels from any files you like. If you specify more channels than are in the color model, the remaining channels become alpha (mask) channels. When you merge channels, Photoshop looks for all the open grayscale files that have the same number of vertical and horizontal pixels. If you're off by one pixel, the files won't merge.

This exercise turns a photograph into a uniquely rendered poster by treating each split channel with an artistic filter. You can experiment with using any Photoshop process on the individual channels.

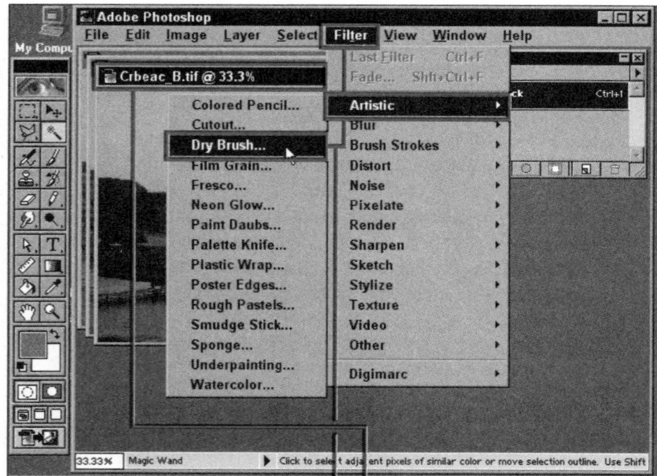

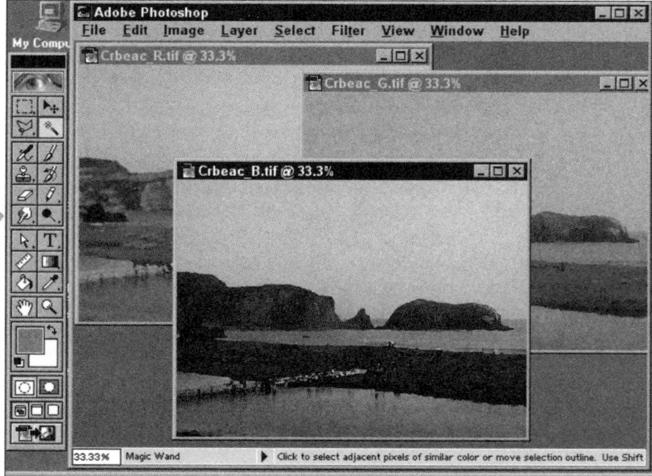

Note: Use the Split Channels command to create a separate grayscale file for each active channel.

Note: Each of the files can be processed separately.

1 Activate the window you want to process.

2 Choose the processing command (or edit the document any way you like).

■ Here you see the result of running a different artistic filter on each of the grayscale files.

TIPS

Can you suggest processes for each channel that are most likely to be effective?

Run the Image ➪ Adjust ➪ Auto Levels or Image ➪ Adjust ➪ Equalize commands on each channel. Other effects that can prove interesting (well, heck, just about anything you do can prove interesting — or psychedelic) is to run a different distortion filter or a different texture filter on each channel document.

Is there an everyday use for Merge Channels?

The most common use is improving the Blue channel from low-end scanners and overcompressed JPEG files. This is the channel in which mistakes and artifacts are most likely to appear. Often, the image can be improved by using a combination of the Gaussian Blur filter and the Unsharp mask filter on the Blue channel.

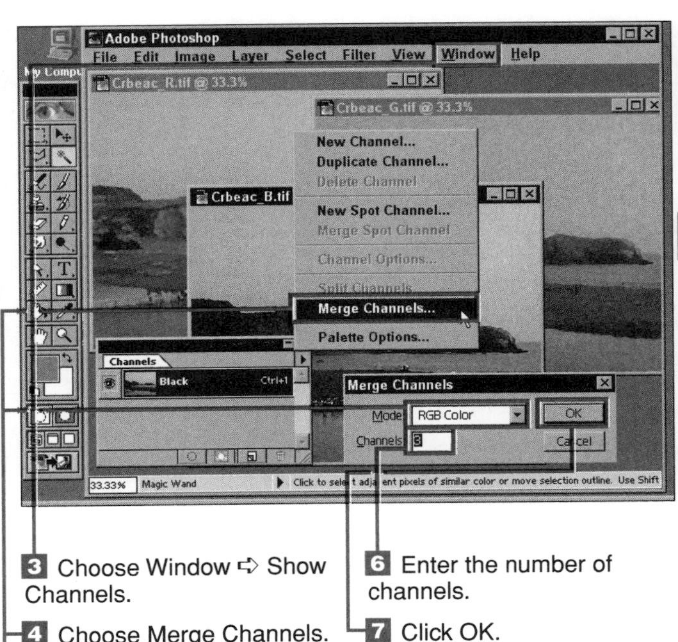

3 Choose Window ➪ Show Channels.

4 Choose Merge Channels.

5 Choose the target color mode.

6 Enter the number of channels.

7 Click OK.

■ Here is the result of running three separate artistic filters, one in each of the channels, and then merging them.

MERGE CHANNELS FROM DIFFERENT FILES

You can merge any number of channels into a single file, as long as they're all grayscale and all the same size. This is one way to import masks and spot color channels from other files. Merging can be handy for compositing, special effects, spot color compositions, and generic masks (such as those for vignettes and picture frames).

If you want to merge more files than a particular color model has channels (three for RGB and LAB, four for CMYK), you have to select Multichannel from the Mode pull-down menu in the Merge Channels dialog box. You won't have a color model in the merged file, so after merging, you need to choose Image ⇨ Mode ⇨ *color model*. When the image converts, Photoshop 5 makes a composite channel of the first three or four (depending on mode) channels.

If these aren't the channels you want to use as the first three, simply use the Channels palette to drag the correct channels into position.

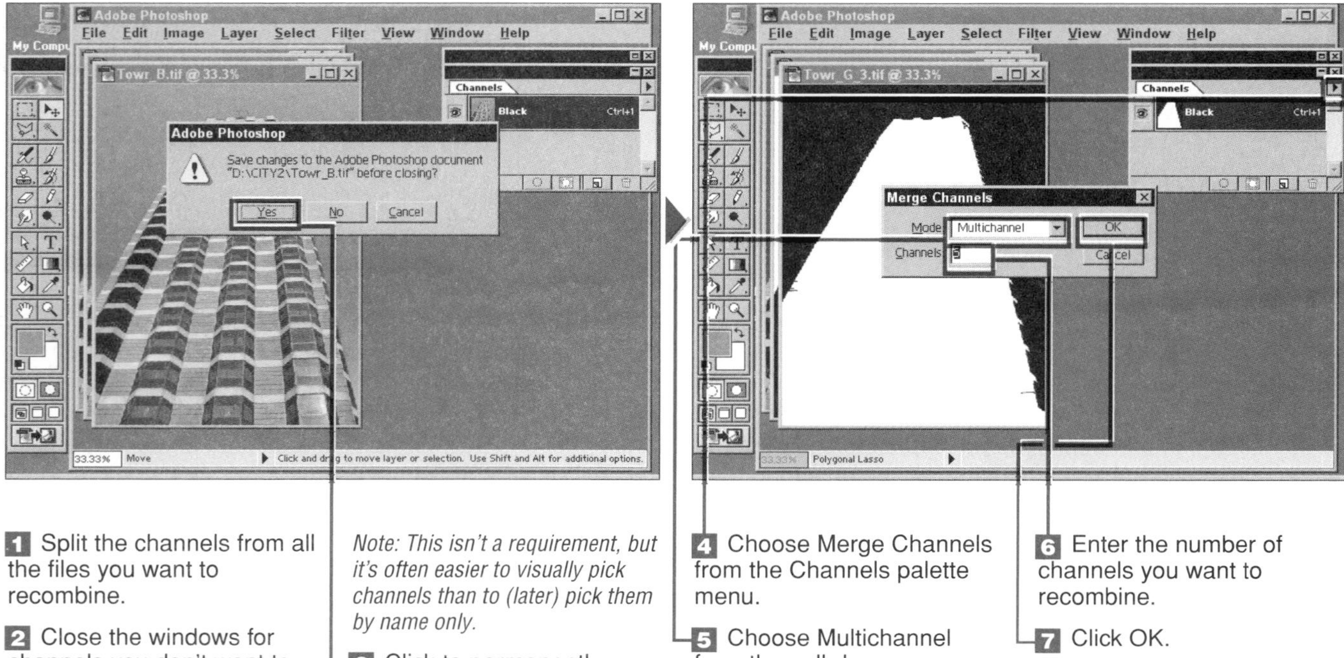

1 Split the channels from all the files you want to recombine.

2 Close the windows for channels you don't want to use in the new file.

Note: This isn't a requirement, but it's often easier to visually pick channels than to (later) pick them by name only.

3 Click to permanently dump unwanted channels.

4 Choose Merge Channels from the Channels palette menu.

5 Choose Multichannel from the pull-down menu.

6 Enter the number of channels you want to recombine.

7 Click OK.

TIPS

Couldn't collections of masks made from the silhouettes of shapes be used to create drawings?

Yes, indeed. You can convert the mask to a selection, convert the selection to a path, save the path as an EPS file, and read that file into (almost) any illustration program. Remember, paths can also be converted to selections, so you could collect masks from any number of files, turn them all into paths, and save them in a single, tiny file.

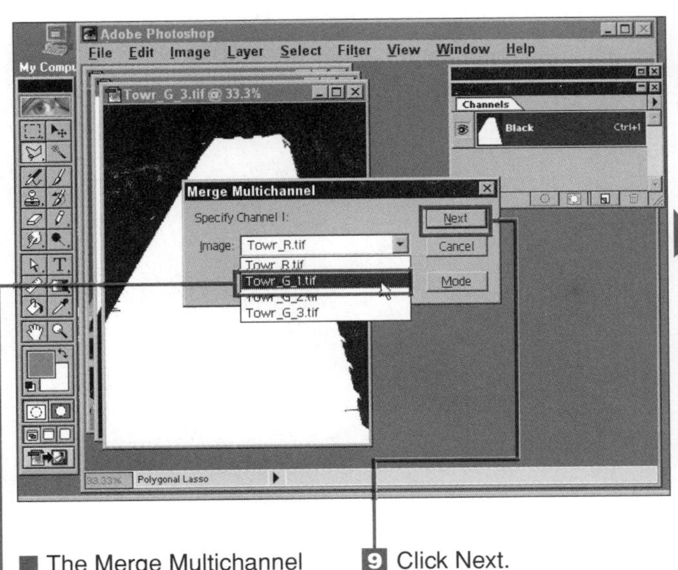

■ The Merge Multichannel dialog box appears.

8 Choose the channel you want to merge.

9 Click Next.

10 Repeat Steps 8 and 9 until you've chosen all the files you want to merge.

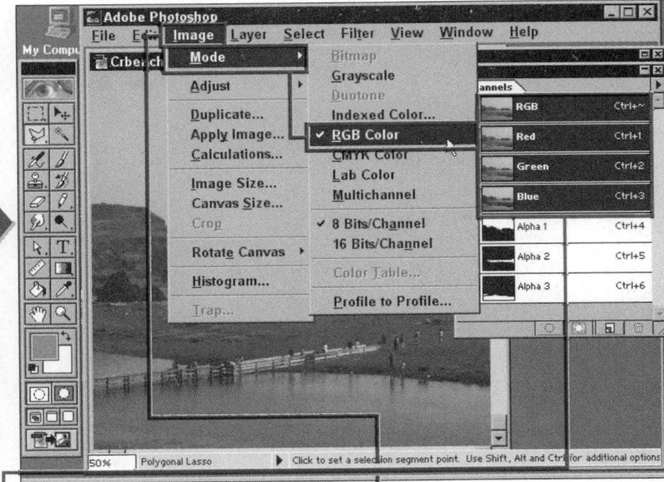

PLACE THE FILE BACK IN RGB MODE

11 Drag channels into proper order.

12 Choose Image ➪ Mode ➪ RGB.

■ A composite channel appears at the top of the Channels palette.

■ The image appears in full color.

USE THE APPLY IMAGE COMMAND

For years, real Photoshop geeks prided themselves on knowing their CHOPS — short for CHannel OPerations. This referred to the amazing effects you could apply if you fully understood the mathematics behind combining channels.

Today, you can perform almost all CHOPS by using the Blend modes in the Layers palette. There are, however, still ways you can apply one channel to another and use Blend modes (Multiply, Add, Screen, for example) in the process. These are the Image ⇨ Apply Image and Image ⇨ Calculations commands — the simplest being the Apply Image command.

Through the Apply Image dialog box, you can combine channels, either in the current file or from another open file of the same dimensions, and store them in the current channel of the active file (document). You can achieve an infinite number of effects in this way: texturing, intensification of colors, framing — you name it.

Coming up with the exact effect you want requires some experimentation. Fortunately, by checking the Preview box, you can see any effect before committing to it.

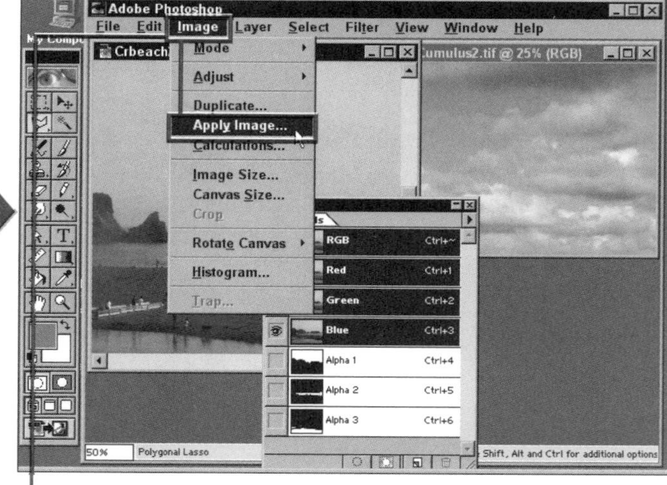

1 Open the target file and the file from which you want to apply either the whole image or a channel.

2 Make your target image active (click its title bar).

3 Choose Window ⇨ Show Channels to display the Channels palette.

Note: Showing the Channels palette makes it easier to decide which channels you want to combine, and from which images.

4 Choose Image ⇨ Apply Image.

■ The Apply Image dialog box appears.

TIPS

Wouldn't this be an even faster way to collect alpha channels into a separate file?

I haven't timed the difference, but it's certainly an alternative method.

If I don't get the transparency right for the blend, or I want to lower it, can I use the Filter ⇨ Fade command?

Actually, this is the best way to deal with transparency, because it gives you a way to visualize the result interactively. Also, the huge Apply Image dialog box is no longer covering your image.

How might I use this command to texture an image?

Use a scanned photograph of the texture you have in mind, use one of the many texture files available in CD-ROM libraries, or use one of the texture-generating plug-in filters such as Real Texture or Terrazo from Xaos Tools. Make a file the same size as the target file, and apply any of its channels in any of the Blend modes. Or, you could apply one of its channels and use another as a mask.

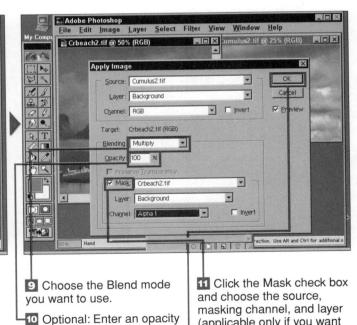

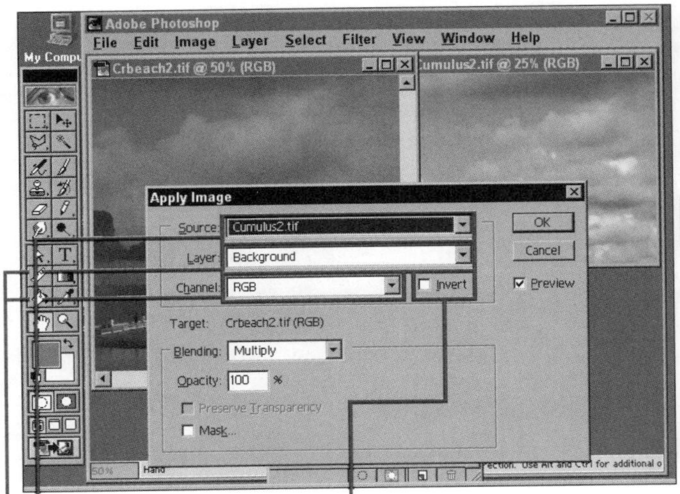

5 Choose the document containing the image to apply.

6 Choose the layer that holds the image.

7 Choose the channel to apply.

Note: To apply the entire layer, choose the composite (RGB/CMYK/LAB) channel.

8 Optional: Click to invert (make negative) the source channel.

9 Choose the Blend mode you want to use.

10 Optional: Enter an opacity for the Blend mode.

11 Click the Mask check box and choose the source, masking channel, and layer (applicable only if you want to use a layer mask).

12 Click OK.

USE THE CALCULATIONS COMMAND

The Image ⇨ Calculations command is similar to the Image ⇨ Apply Image command. Both commands require that you blend images between open files having the same pixel dimensions.

The big difference is that the result of the application of channels or images doesn't take place in the composite channel. You can choose whether the result appears as a layer mask (only if you're working with an active layer that has a layer mask), a new channel within the current file, or an alpha channel in an entirely new file. Furthermore, the target image may or may not be the active image and can even be a brand new image. To put it another way, you mix two different channels from up to two different sources into one, which may or may not be a new file.

Blending options are the same as for the Apply Image command. You can see the visual effect of all Blend modes, regardless of which tool is used to apply them, in the "Color Section" of this book.

You can also apply a mask with the Calculations command, but the mask always applies to the first source and protects the second source. The white portions of the mask show the result of the calculations, and the black portions show only the second source image.

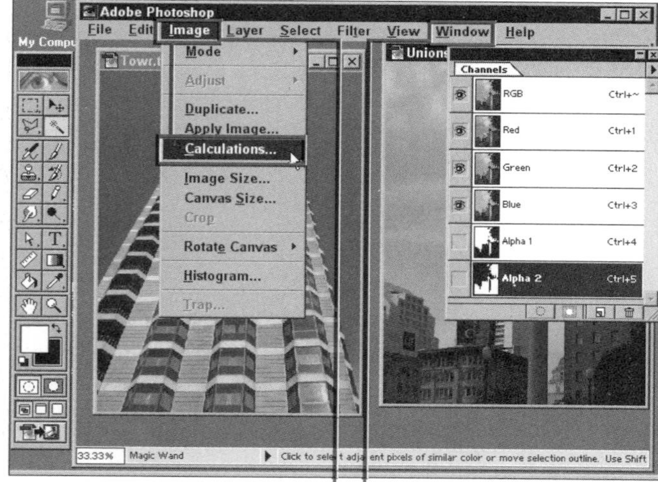

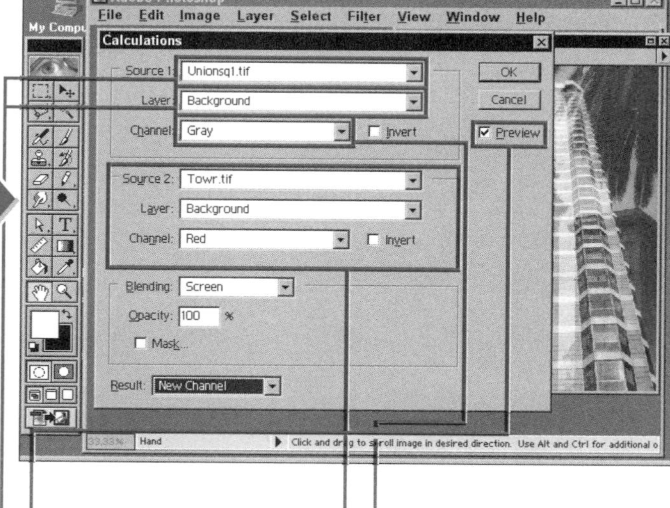

1 Open one or two files from which you want to combine channels.

2 Choose Window ⇨ Show Channels to see which channels you want to blend.

3 Choose Image ⇨ Calculations.

■ The Calculations dialog box appears.

4 Click the Preview check box.

5 Choose from list of open files of the same size.

6 Choose the image layer you want calculated.

7 Choose the color channel you want calculated.

8 Repeat for Source 2 fields.

TIPS

Is there any way to get rid of the Calculations dialog box so that I can see what I'm doing in the preview window?

Just use its title bar to drag it out of the way. On the Mac, if you hold Option while you choose the Image ➪ Calculations, the type in the dialog box will be smaller, making the dialog box smaller.

What is the Gray channel? I don't see it in the Channels palette.

Because it's not there. If you choose Gray, Photoshop makes the blend from a grayscale version of the composite channel.

Are any of the Blend modes in the Apply Image and Calculations dialog boxes unique to channel calculations?

Yes, Add and Subtract. These modes add and subtract the brightness values of the two source channels with the result that Add lightens and Subtract darkens. The offset value divides the sum or difference. The Scale value is then added to the result. Add the ability to set transparency, and you have total control over the intensity of the result.

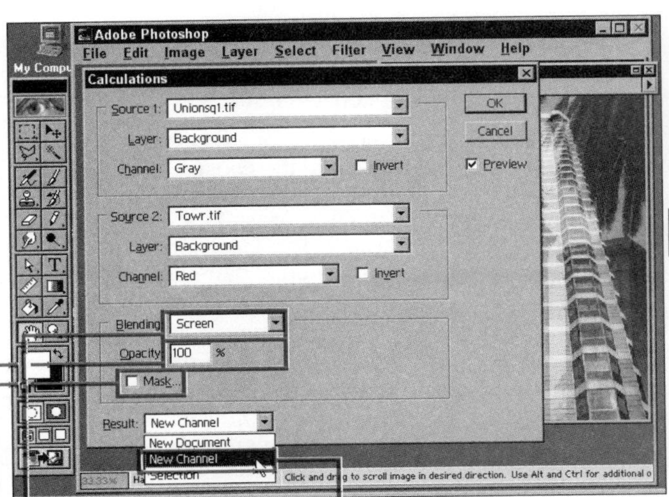

8 Choose a blend mode.

9 Enter a number for the opacity of the blend.

10 Click to check if you want to use any of the mask channels in either source to limit the effect of the blend.

11 Choose layer for the blend.

12 Choose the channel to be used as a mask.

■ The effect of the channel operation on the target channel.

Note: An unlimited number of these effects are available, depending on the number and type of channels in the target and source and depending on which Blend modes you use.

USING TEXT

As of Photoshop 5, text control is far more powerful than it has been in previous versions. When you enter text, it's automatically placed on its own layer. You can control leading (the space between lines) and kerning (the space between letters), change the baseline shift (where to place the bottoms of letters after the initial capital letter), and control tracking (the spacing between letters in a word or line of type). You can edit the text or change any of these specs at any time, as long as the text is maintained on its own layer. You can also change the color of text after it's been entered, but you can't mix colors in the same entry. You can, however, mix text styles in the same entry.

Full type layer features, such as post-entry editing, are available only when editing in Color modes that support layers. This excludes multichannel, bitmap, or indexed-color modes, as these models don't support layers. You can still enter text, but when you click OK in the text dialog box, it is merged directly into the underlying bitmap.

The Text Tools

Drag from the Text tool in the Tools palette to access the Text Tools pop-out menu, shown in the following figure. Then drag across until the tool of your choice is highlighted. To choose a tool from the keyboard, press T to select the currently chosen text tool. Press Shift+T to cycle through the four tools in succession.

Text Tools Pop-Out Menu Contents

Component	Function
Type tool	Enters solid-color text in a horizontal line.
Type Mask tool	Enters a selection in the shape of the chosen typeface in a horizontal line. Type Mask tools are excellent for filling letters with textures, patterns, gradients, colors, or images.
Vertical Type tool	Enters a selection in the shape of the chosen typeface in a vertical line, each letter right-side up under the other.
Vertical Type Mask tool	Enters solid-color text in a vertical line, each letter right-side up under the other.

The Type Layer

The Type Layer is found in the Layers palette, which is accessed by selecting Windows ➪ Show Layers and selecting the Layers palette tab, depicted here.

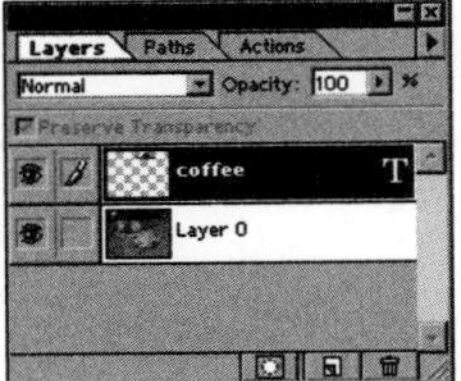

Layers Palette Contents

Component	Function
Show/Hide icon	Click to toggle.
Active Layer icon	Click to show or hide the layer. If layer is hidden, the eye icon is not visible.
Layer thumbnail	Shows a thumbnail of the image that resides on this layer.
Layer name bar	Click layer name bar to activate a layer, double-click to bring up the Text Options dialog box. Press ⌘/Ctrl+click to make a selection from the type outline.
Type Layer identifier icon	Indicates that this is a type layer.

The Type Tool

The Type Tool dialog box, shown here, appears when you click the Type Entry cursor to place text or when you double-click the layer name bar of a text layer.

Type Tool Dialog Box Contents

Component	Function
Font pull-down menu	All the fonts in your system are listed on this menu. Click the button to drop the menu and drag to choose a font. On choosing a font, any text that's highlighted in the entry area (or subsequently entered) will be displayed in that font.
Style pull-down menu	Lists all the style variations for the chosen font. These vary from font to font.

CONTINUED

USING TEXT CONTINUED

Type Tool Dialog Box Contents

Component	Function
OK button	Click to implement the text entry settings.
Size entry field	Enter any whole number.
Size pull-down menu	Click the button to choose between points and pixels.
Kerning entry field	Each unit is equal to 1/1,000 of an em space. Enter 100 units to equal 1 point in a 10-point font. This is grayed out (unavailable) when Auto Kern is checked.
Color swatch	Click to bring up the Color Picker dialog box. You can choose any standard or custom color.
Leading entry field	Define the space between baselines. Measured in points or pixels, depending on which you picked in the Size pull-down menu. To change leading for existing type, highlight the type and then enter a new number for leading.
Tracking entry field	Tracking is used to space letters evenly between the start and stop of a highlighted word or phrase. Like leading, tracking is measured in em spaces. This field is grayed (unavailable) unless you have some text selected (highlighted).
Baseline entry field	Enter a number to shift the default baseline for a font by that number of points. Enter a minus number to shift the baseline down. You can shift the baseline for part of a word or phrase by highlighting only those letters that you want to shift.
Align Left button	Aligns type from the left of the insertion point.
Align Center button	Aligns type from the center of the insertion point.
Align Right button	Aligns type from the right of the insertion point.

Component	Function
Preview check box	When this box is checked, type will appear in the workspace window as soon as you type it. If you don't like what you see, you can change the color or specs before clicking OK.
Auto Kern check box	If this box is checked, kerning (spacing between letters) is done automatically according to the type design specifications for the chosen font.
Anti-Aliased check box	If this box is checked, the edges of text will be smoothed. You may want to turn this off if you are selecting text to be used as a transparent GIF on the Web.
Rotate check box	Available only for vertical type. Enables you to toggle between vertical text reading with letters upright and vertical text with letters running down (as on the spine of a book).
Type magnification buttons	Click to zoom in and out on text.
Fit in Window check box	When this box is checked, all text will be visible within the text entry window, regardless of how you may have sized it.

USING THE TYPE TOOLS

Photoshop 5 has four Type tools, divided into two categories: *Type* tools and *Type Selection* tools. Each of these is divided into horizontal and vertical varieties. (Type Selection tools are treated separately in another exercise.)

Type tools automatically fill text with the current foreground color and places the text on its own layer. Photoshop 5 now even lets you edit that text after it's been entered — as long as you don't merge or flatten its text layer. Text entered with a Type tool is also readily available for layer effects, so you can automatically bevel its edges, make drop shadows, and do embossing.

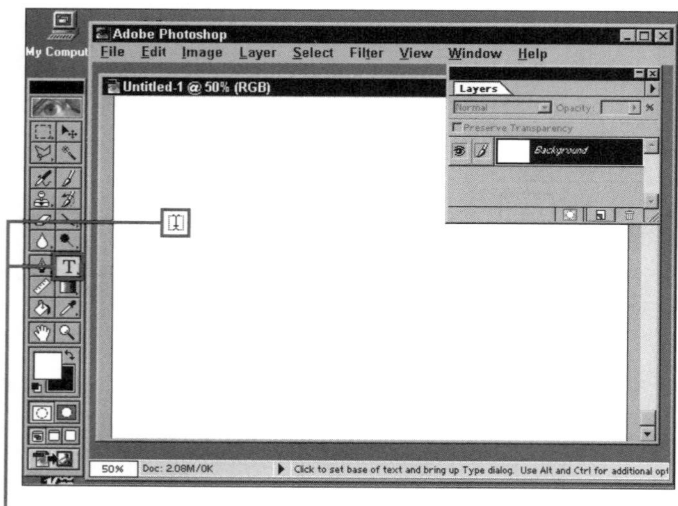

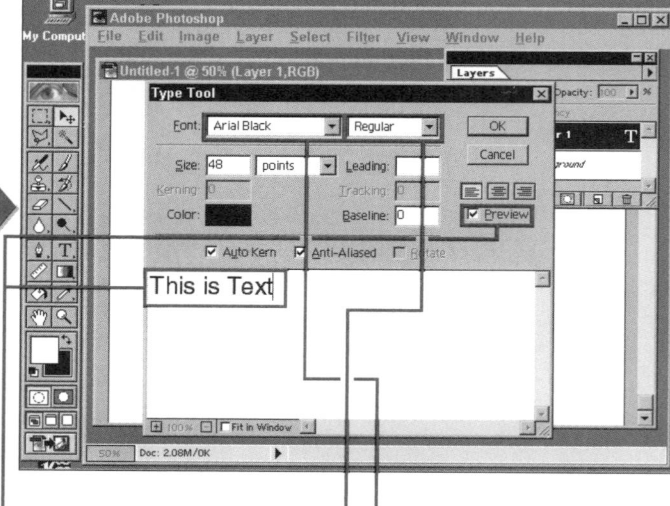

1 Click to select the Type tool.

■ The cursor shape changes to indicate a text insertion point.

2 Click to indicate starting point for entering text.

Note: If justification is set to Left, all text aligns at the left margin; If set to Center, text aligns equidistant on both sides; If set to Right, it aligns to the right.

■ The Type Tool dialog box appears.

3 Enter the words you want to overlay on your image.

4 Check Preview.

5 Highlight any letters the style or spacing of which you want to change.

6 Choose a font.

7 Choose the font style.

TIPS

How do I get type to be a specific size on paper?

Use a vector graphics program, such as Adobe Illustrator, CorelDRAW!, or Macromedia FreeHand. Or use a page makeup program such as Adobe PageMaker or QuarkXPress. You can place your Photoshop document as an image into any of these programs and use the typesetting capabilities of the program to specify type for print. If you are trying to size the type in Photoshop, make sure your inch dimensions and dpi are correct, and then use point sizes.

How do I know what point size to choose? Will the text print at that point size?

Choose the point size that makes the lettering the right size in relationship to the image on which you're overlaying it.

Then why bother to set type in Photoshop?

Photoshop is ideal for setting type destined to be used onscreen and for setting type to be treated with artistic effects or integrated into an image as part of a collage.

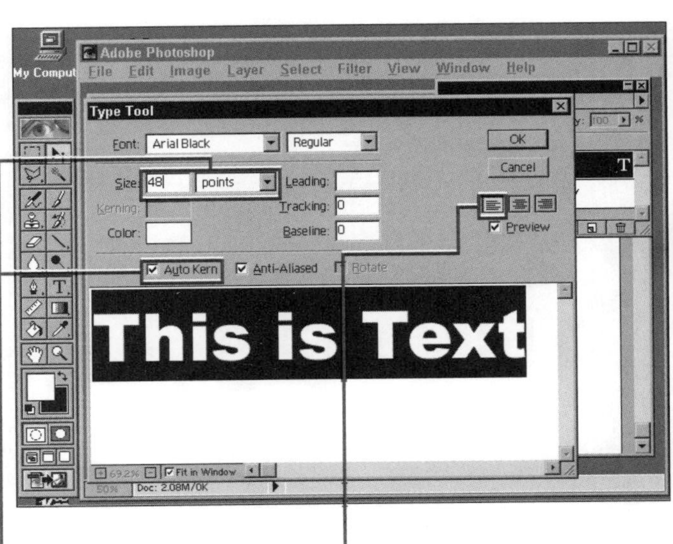

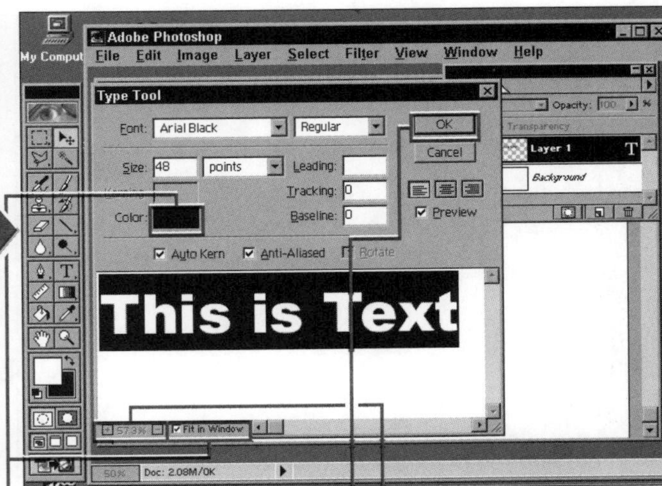

8 Enter size and choose unit of measurement.

9 Click to toggle automatic kerning. Uncheck if you want to enter spacing specifications manually.

Note: You must insert the blinking text insertion bar between the letters you wish to kern.

10 Click to set justification.

11 Click to change color.

12 Click to toggle, making all text visible within the text entry window.

13 Click + to zoom in, - to zoom out.

14 Click OK when satisfied.

EDIT A TYPE LAYER

In Photoshop 5, for the first time, you can correct misspellings or even change the entire content of a paragraph without having to delete a text layer and start all over.

To edit text, you have to show the Layers palette (choose Window ⇨ Show Layers or press Opt/Alt+F7 if you haven't changed the default function key assignments). You can only edit text that has been entered with the Type tool. Text entered with the Type Selection tool is bitmapped and cannot be edited.

When you double-click to edit, the Type Tool dialog box reopens. You simply make any changes you like and then click OK to implement them. In this spread, you even see how to mix type styles and to change the baseline so that you can have drop caps and super- or subscripts.

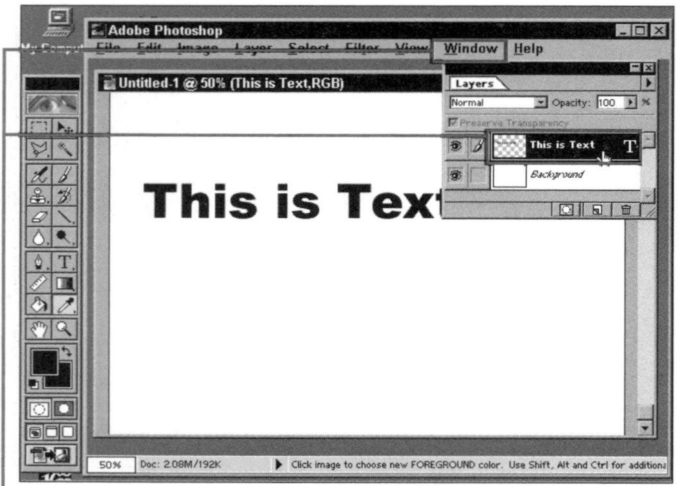

1 Choose Window ⇨ Show Layers or press Opt/Alt+F7.

2 Double-click the layer bar of the layer whose text you want to edit.

■ The Type Tool dialog box appears, with the contents of the current layer in the Type window.

3 Highlight any text you want to edit.

Note: Changes in almost all settings affect only the highlighted letters.

Note: However, if you alter the color setting, all the text in the work window changes to the same color.

TIPS

Is there a way to change the color of part of the text in the Type Tool dialog window?

Not officially, but there's an easy workaround, as long as your text is still on its own layer: Change your foreground color to the one you want for the new color of your text. Activate the layer, click to check the Preserve Transparency check box, drag a selection marquee around the letters whose color you want to change, and then choose Edit ➪ Fill ➪ Foreground color. Another workaround is to duplicate the layer for as many times as you want different text colors. Then select and delete all but the text you want in each color.

What advantage does setting type in Photoshop have that can't be had in vector programs?

The big advantage is transparency. Although illustration programs are just beginning to introduce transparency, all you have to do to get it in Photoshop is drag the slider that controls the transparency of the layer. Another advantage is the availability of patterned and textured fills.

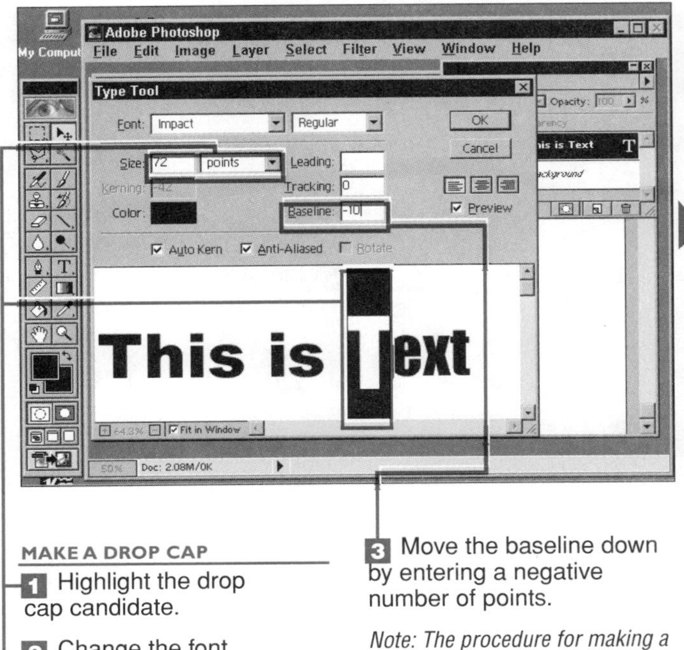

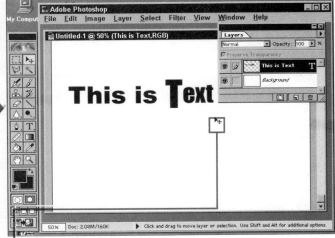

MAKE A DROP CAP

1 Highlight the drop cap candidate.

2 Change the font size as needed.

3 Move the baseline down by entering a negative number of points.

Note: The procedure for making a superscript is virtually the same. Raise the baseline by entering a positive number.

4 To move the text, choose the Move tool and drag.

Note: If the Type Tool dialog box is out of the way, and the Preview box is checked, you will see the result of your changes immediately.

Note: The changes aren't permanent, because you can always edit them. If you merge type layers, your ability to edit them is lost.

USE THE TYPE SELECTION TOOL

If you want to fill type with the image in a layer, paint colors into type, or fill type with a pattern or texture, the Type Selection tool saves you a time. This tool makes a selection marquee that's the size, shape, and spacing you specify in the Type Selection dialog box. You can then use that selection in the same way as any other selection in Photoshop.

Unlike the Type tool, the Type Selection tool doesn't automatically create its own layer; however, if you want the text you create or fill to be on its own layer, that's no problem. Just create a new, empty layer (click the New Layer icon at the bottom of the Layers palette) and enter the type you want to have appear as a selection. This gives you the advantage of being able to control the transparency of the text and of being able to throw out the layer if you goof.

The big disadvantage of text entered with the Type Selection tool is that it can't be edited (except, of course, by painting over it).

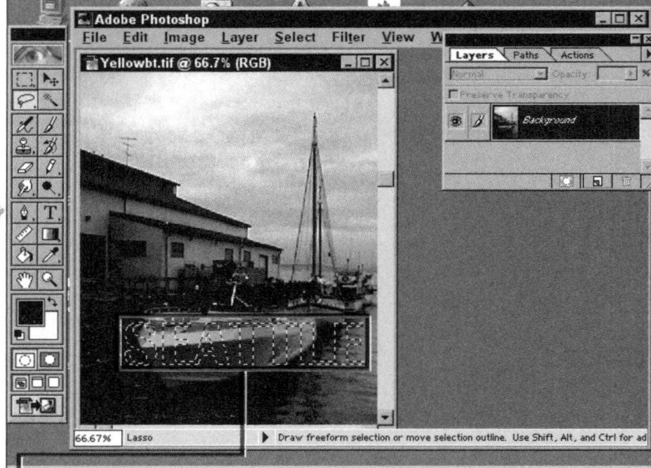

1 Choose the Type Selection tool or the Vertical Type Selection tool.

2 Click the point where you want the marquee to start.

■ The Type Tool dialog box appears.

3 Enter size, leading, and baseline for your type.

4 Click OK.

5 Place the cursor anywhere inside the marquee and drag the marquee to the desired position.

6 Press ⌘/Ctrl+J to cut out the contents of the image and place the text on its own layer.

TIPS

What's the difference between type on a layer and any other irregular shape on a layer?

If the type was made with the Type Selection tool, there is no difference. Anything you can do to any image on any layer can be done to type created in this way.

What if I created the type with the Type tool and then wanted to treat it like any other graphic on an independent layer?

No problem. Create a new, empty layer, and then merge the type layer with the empty layer. To do that, link the type layer and the new layer, and then choose Merge Linked from the Layers palette menu.

Can I make use of the transparency slider and the Blend modes just as with any other layer?

You can do anything with a type layer that you can do with any other layer. Transparency and Blend modes enable you to do some things with type that are especially cool, however — for example, superimposing two different fonts and then blending them.

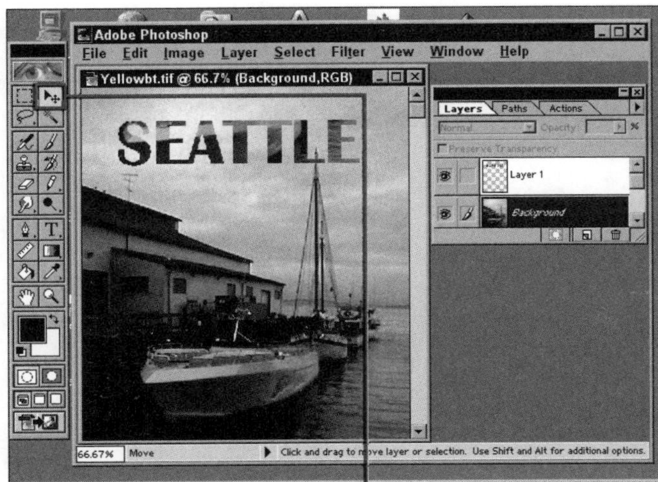

Note: Though it seems the text has disappeared, a look at the Layers palette reveals a new layer.

7 Choose the Move tool and drag to place the text where you want it.

Note: Now that this text is on its own layer, you can enhance it with any of the layer effects. You can also paint on or fill the text and automatically confine the effect to the shape of the text.

8 Click to check Preserve Transparency.

9 Paint the text or choose Edit ➪ Fill to change the color of the text or to fill it with a pattern.

USE TRANSPARENCY AND BLEND FOR TYPE EFFECTS

Used to be de rigueur for all Photoshop books to devote a chapter or two (or even the whole book) to special type effects. Nowadays, the new Layer Effects feature (covered in Chapter 9) makes child's play of creating some of the most useful type effects. However, there are a few worthwhile tricks that layer effects still can't touch.

The most interesting of these derive from the fact that layers can be blended, made semitransparent, and can be transformed. Blending and transparency work the same way for text layers as for normal layers; however, you can't use Distort and Perspective when transforming text layers.

Note: To transform a text layer to a normal layer, choose Layer ➪ Type ➪ Render Layer. You can now treat this type layer just as any other. (You'll no longer be able to edit the text.)

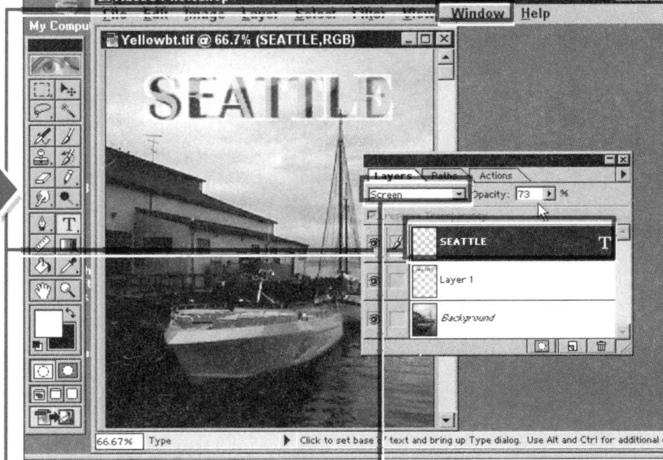

PLACE ONE FONT ATOP OR INSIDE ANOTHER

1 Choose the Type tool.

2 Click the insertion point at the exact beginning of the existing type.

3 Change the font to something different, but with similarly proportioned letters.

4 Adjust the point size and tracking until the letters are superimposed.

BLEND THE NEW TEXT WITH THE UNDERLYING TEXT

5 Show the Layers palette (Choose Window ➪ Show Layers).

6 Click to activate the layer of the text you want to blend.

7 Choose a Blending Mode.

8 Adjust Transparency.

TIPS

Can I use layer effects on the rendered text layers?

Absolutely — any and all of them. You could also make things even more interesting (or messy — take your pick) by running layer effects on the individual layers before you do the blending and transparency. You could then run the layer effects again after the layers have been combined.

What do I do when I take it too far and things get really ugly?

Open the History palette and back up to the last step in which you liked the result. Then delete all that followed and either quit making changes or take a different path.

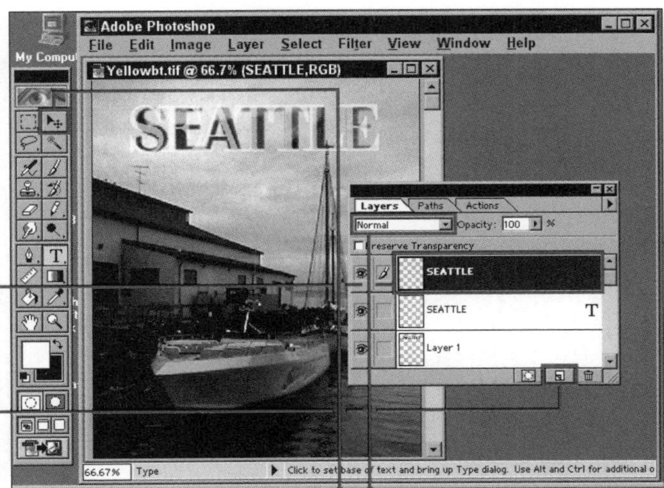

CREATE AN OFFSET DUPLICATE OF A LAYER

9 Drag the original layer to the New Layer icon.

10 Double-click the new layer's name bar and change the text color.

11 Choose a Blend mode and adjust the transparency slider to your taste.

12 Choose the Move tool and press the arrow keys to offset this layer slightly from the original.

DISTORT THE TEXT

13 Activate each text layer and choose Layer ➪ Type ➪ Render Layer for each.

14 Click to link all three layers that now contain rendered text.

15 Choose Edit ➪ Transform ➪ Distort.

16 Drag the transformation handles to get the shape you want, and then double-click inside the Transform box to render.

ENTER VERTICAL TYPE

Everything you've seen so far about entering type and type selections pertains to entering vertical type. If you want vertical type, the big difference is that you usually start by choosing either the Vertical Type tool or the Vertical Type Selection tool.

Actually, you don't even have to do that. If you enter normal type by using the Type tool, you can make the layer active and then choose Layer ⇨ Type ⇨ Vertical. The type will change to vertical, and then you can edit it later and rotate the letters if you like.

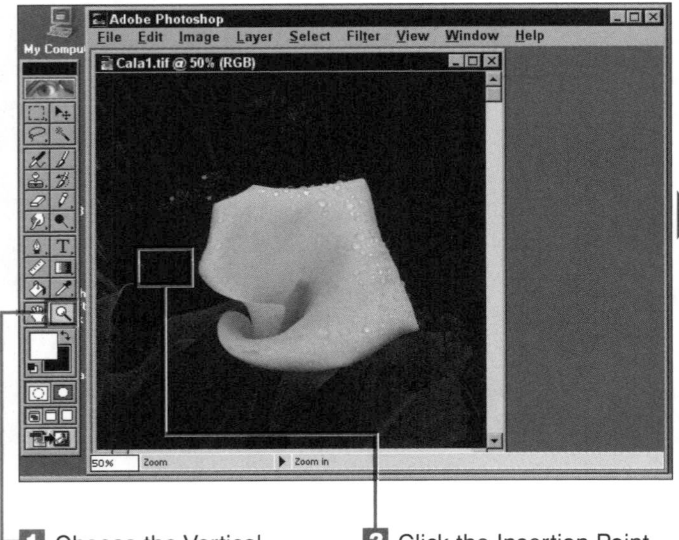

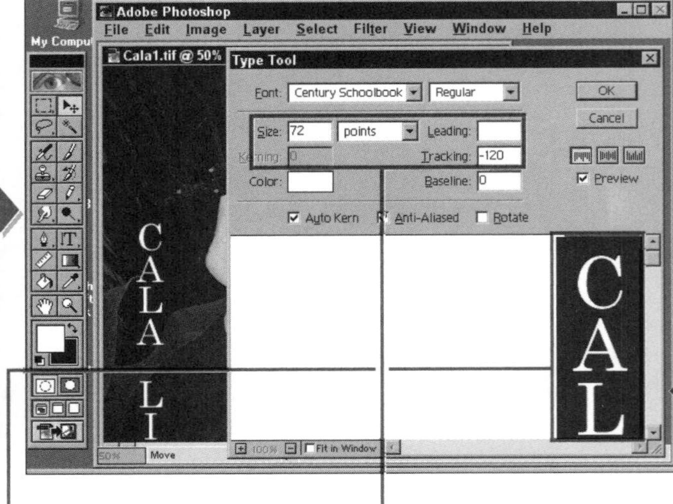

1 Choose the Vertical Type tool.

2 Click the Insertion Point cursor to designate the start and baseline for the type.

■ The Type Tool dialog box appears.

3 Enter your type and highlight it.

■ Assuming the Preview box is checked, you will see your type appear in the workspace.

4 Adjust size, kerning, and tracking until the type fits the desired layout.

TIPS

Can I still use the alignment icons when entering vertical text?

Yes. The type will appear equidistant from the insertion point if the alignment is specified as Center and will appear from the bottom up if the alignment is specified as Right. Although you can use the Move tool to place your type precisely where you want it, these choices will help you position type more quickly.

What if I need to shorten the line of type without rotating it?

Use the leading and tracking adjustments in the Type Tool dialog box. If that doesn't do the job, you'll have to choose a smaller size of type. Of course, if your type line is too long because there are too many words, you need to use more than one line of type or change your copy.

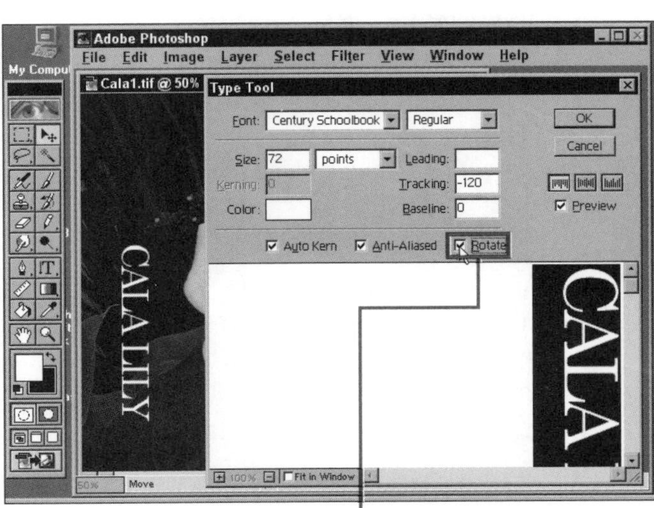

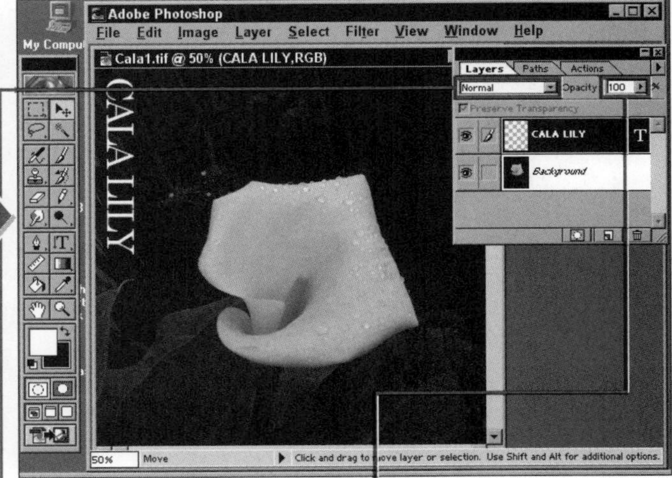

Note: In this case, the line of type is still too long. It can be shortened by rotating the letters.

5 Click the Rotate check box.

■ The letters turn on their right sides, taking far less space.

6 To change the blending of the type and underlying layers, choose a Blend mode.

7 Enter a number for the opacity.

SECTION IV

12 USING PHOTOSHOP'S BRUSHES

The Photoshop Brushes 272
Choose the Right Brush 278
Set Airbrush Options 280
Set Paintbrush Options 281
Set Pencil Options 282
Set Eraser Options 283
Save and Load Brush Palettes 284
Create Custom Brush Shapes 286
Create a Brush from Type 288
Create a Brush from a Postscript Image 289
Paint from a Snapshot 290
Get Even More Painterly with the Art History Brush 292

13 APPLYING DARKROOM EFFECTS

Correcting Details 294
Create Simple Tonal Effects 298
Suck Up Color with the Sponge Tool 302
Match Color with the Paintbrush Tool 303
Add Color Tone to the Image 304
Hand-color a Monotone Image 308
Control Focus: Blurring and Sharpening 310
Eliminate Artifacts from Compressed Images 322
Eliminate More Artifacts 324

14 WORKING WITH TEXTURES

Creating Textures with Photoshop 326

Apply Texture Filters 331
Apply Craquelure Texture 332
Apply Grain Texture 333
Create Mosaic Tiles 334
Create a Patchwork 335
Create Stained Glass 336
Apply Texturizer Textures 337
Create New Textures from Photos 338
Create Seamless Pattern and Texture Tiles 340

15 USING THE ARTISTIC FILTERS

Painterly Filter Effects 342
Create a Painting by Filtering Specific Areas 362
Texturize an Image with a Sketch Filter 364
Apply the Colored Pencil Filter 366
Apply the Cutout Filter 367
Apply the Dry Brush Filter 368
Apply the Film Grain Filter 369
Apply the Fresco Filter 370
Apply the Neon Glow Filter 371
Apply the Paint Daubs Filter 372
Apply the Palette Knife Filter 373
Apply the Plastic Wrap Filter 374
Apply the Poster Edges Filter 375
Apply the Rough Pastels Filter 376
Apply the Smudge Stick Filter 377
Apply the Sponge Filter 378
Apply the Underpainting Filter 379
Apply the Watercolor Filter 380
Apply the Accented Edges Filter 381
Apply the Angled Strokes Filter 382
Apply the Crosshatch Filter 383
Apply the Dark Strokes Filter 384
Apply the Ink Outlines Filter 385
Apply the Spatter Filter 386
Apply the Sumi-e Filter 387
Apply the Bas Relief Filter 388
Apply the Chalk & Charcoal Filter 389
Apply the Charcoal Filter 390
Apply the Chrome Filter 391
Apply the Conté Crayon Filter 392
Apply the Graphic Pen Filter 393
Apply the Halftone Pattern Filter 394
Apply the Note Paper Filter 395
Apply the Photocopy Filter 396
Apply the Plaster Filter 397
Apply the Reticulation Filter 398
Apply the Stamp Filter 399
Apply the Torn Edges Filter 400
Apply the Water Paper Filter 401

16 USING THE DISTORT FILTERS

Warping and Morphing 402
Distort with the Diffuse Glow Filter 410
Distort with the Displace Filter 411
Distort with the Glass Filter 412
Distort with the Ocean Ripple Filter 413
Distort with the Pinch Filter 414
Distort with the Polar Coordinates Filter 415
Distort with the Ripple Filter 416
Distort with the Shear Filter 417
Distort with the Spherize Filter 418
Distort with the Twirl Filter 419

SECTION IV

Distort with the Wave Filter 420
Distort with the ZigZag Filter 421
Apply a Third-Party 3D Surface Filter 422

17 USING THE NOISE, PIXELATE, AND STYLIZE FILTERS

Breaking Up Is Easy to Do 424
Apply the Add Noise Filter 433
Apply the Despeckle Filter 434
Apply the Dust & Scratches Filter 435
Apply the Median Filter 436
Apply the Color Halftone Filter 437
Apply the Crystallize Filter 438
Apply the Facet Filter 439
Apply the Fragment Filter 440
Apply the Mezzotint Filter 441
Create a Texture with the Mezzotint Filter 442
Apply the Pointillize Filter 444
Apply the Diffuse Filter 445
Apply the Emboss Filter 446
Apply the Extrude Filter 447
Apply the Find Edges Filter 448
Apply the Glowing Edges Filter 449
Apply the Solarize Filter 450
Apply the Tiles Filter 451
Apply the Trace Contour Filter 452

Apply the Wind Filter 453
Create Your Own Filter Effects: The Custom Filter 454
Save and Load Custom Filters 456
Sharpen with the Custom Filter 457
Create Directional Blurs with the Custom Filter 458
Emboss with the Custom Filter 459

THE PHOTOSHOP BRUSHES

Photoshop has only three brush tools — the Airbrush, the Paintbrush, and the Pencil — unlike some natural media art programs that have dozens or even hundreds.

The Options menus specific to these tools and the Brushes palette provide a lot of variation, however. Between these three tools, you can create brushes to fit your every need.

Airbrush

The Airbrush tool paints with a somewhat softer edge than does the Paintbrush (which is described next). It builds the intensity of the color the longer the brush is kept in the same position (or, if you have a pressure-sensitive pen, the more pressure is applied). To put it another way, if your strokes are made slowly, paint builds up. It's also worth noting the differences between Photoshop's Airbrush and a real, analog air brush:

- No matter how long you pause a stroke, paint won't run.
- Paint never spatters or looks grainy. You could simulate that effect, however, with a tiny dot pattern in your brush.
- It doesn't matter what angle you hold the brush at, even if you are using a pen instead of a mouse.

Paintbrush

The Paintbrush tool (often simply called the Brush tool) paints with an anti-aliased edge, but isn't quite as soft-edged as the Airbrush. It also differs from the Airbrush in that the speed of the stroke doesn't affect the intensity of color.

Pencil

Strokes made by the Pencil tool are always hard-edged. There is no blending of the stroke or anti-aliasing to soften the edges. Look at the shapes in the Brushes palette when you switch from the Paintbrush to the Pencil, and it will be obvious how much harder the edges are. This is the tool to use when you're working on a bitmapped image or one that's been reduced to very high contrast.

Line

The Line tool isn't, strictly speaking, a *brush*. It's included here because it's found on the Pencil tool's pop-out menu in the Toolbox. Use the Line tool when you want to make an absolutely straight line between two points. You can choose any line width and can have arrowheads at either or both ends of the line.

Airbrush Options

To bring up the Airbrush Options palette, as shown in the following figure, double-click the Airbrush in the Toolbox.

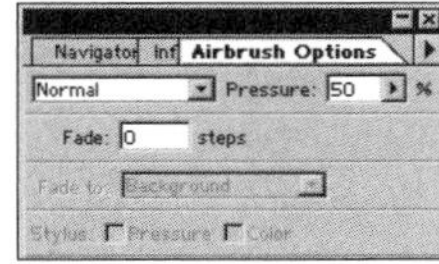

Airbrush Options Palette Contents

Component	Function
Apply Mode pull-down menu	Lets you choose one of the following Apply modes to determine how paint affects the pixels onto which they are applied: Normal, Dissolve, Multiply, Screen, Overlay, Soft Light, Hard Light, Color Dodge, Color Burn, Darken, Lighten, Difference, and Exclusion.
Pressure field	Determines how much of the foreground color is applied over existing pixels. (Perhaps this option would be better named *Transparency*.) Enter any number from 0 to 100 percent.
Pressure slider button	If you'd rather not type in a value in the Pressure field, click this button and drag the pop-up slider that appears. The percentage of pressure (transparency) automatically appears in the Pressure field.
Fade steps field	Determines the number of brush widths over which the brush stroke blends to either transparency or the background color.
Fade to pull-down menu	Determines whether brush stroke blends to transparency or the background color.
Stylus Pressure check box	If checked, makes paint more intense (opaque) as pressure increases.
Stylus Color check box	If checked, changes in stylus pressure will fade strokes between the foreground and background colors.

Paintbrush Options

Access the Paintbrush Options palette, shown in the following figure, by double-clicking the Paintbrush tool in the Toolbox.

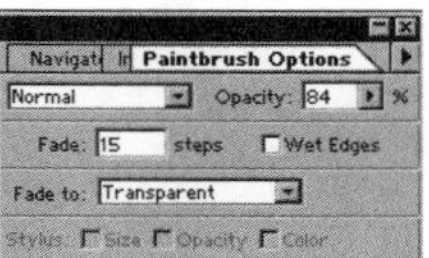

Paintbrush Options Palette Contents

Component	Function
Apply Mode pull-down menu	Enables you to choose one of the following Apply modes to determine how paint affects the pixels onto which they are applied: Normal, Dissolve, Behind, Multiply, Screen, Overlay, Soft Light, Hard Light, Color Dodge, Color Burn, Darken, Lighten, Difference, Exclusion, Hue, Saturation, Color, and Luminosity.
Opacity field	Determines the transparency of the foreground color. Enter any number from 0 to 100 percent.

CONTINUED

THE PHOTOSHOP BRUSHES CONTINUED

Paintbrush Options Palette Contents

Component	Function
Opacity slider button	If you'd rather not type in a value for transparency in the Opacity field, click this button and drag the pop-up slider that appears. The percentage of transparency then appears in the Opacity field.
Fade steps field	Determines the number of brush widths over which the brush stroke blends to either transparency or the background color.
Fade to pull-down menu	Determines whether brush stroke blends to transparency or the background color.
Wet Edges check box	If checked, makes the stroke darker on the edges and more transparent in the center, producing a water or turpentine effect.
Stylus Size check box	If checked, makes paint more intense (opaque) as pressure increases.
Stylus Opacity check box	If checked, more stylus pressure makes paint more opaque.
Stylus Color check box	If checked, changes in stylus pressure will fade strokes between the foreground and background colors.

Pencil Options

The Pencil Options Palette, depicted here, contains the same options as the Paintbrush Options Palette, which have the same effects except for the items noted in the table that follows.

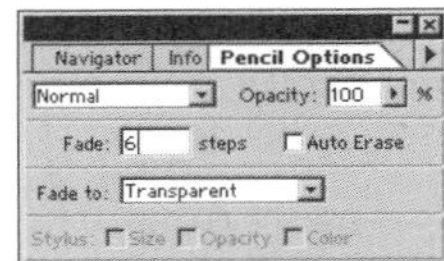

Pencil Options Palette Contents

Component	Function
Apply Mode pull-down menu	Hue, Saturation, Color, and Luminosity are not available as choices on this pull-down menu.
Auto Erase check box	Paints the background color over the foreground color if you start your stroke within an area that contains the foreground color. Paints normally if the stroke is begun in an area of pixels colored with any color other than the foreground color. (Replaces the Wet Edges option in the Paintbrush Options Palette.)

Line Options

The Line Options palette, as shown here, features the same options as the Paintbrush Options palette, except as noted in the table that follows.

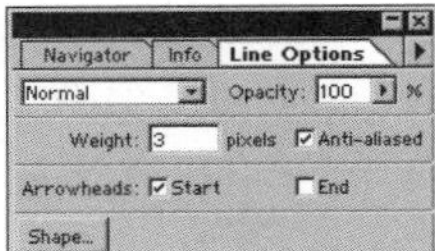

Line Options Palette Contents

Component	Function
Apply Mode pull-down menu	Clear, Hue, Saturation, Color, and Luminosity are not available as options on this pull-down menu.
Weight field	Enter a whole number for the number of pixels wide you want the line to be. 1,000 pixels is the maximum.
Anti-aliased check box	If checked, smoothes the edges of the line. (Replaces the Wet Edges check box in the Paintbrush Options Palette.)
Arrowheads Start check box	If checked, arrowhead is placed at the start point of the line.
Arrowheads End check box	If checked, arrowhead is placed at the end point of the line. Note: Both Arrowheads Start and Arrowheads End boxes may be checked.
Shape button	Brings up the Arrowhead Shape dialog box (see following section).

Arrowhead Shape

The Arrowhead Shape dialog box, as shown in the following figure, appears if you click the Shape button in the Line Options palette. Here you are able to specify width, height, and concavity (curve) of the arrowhead placed at the start and/or end of your line.

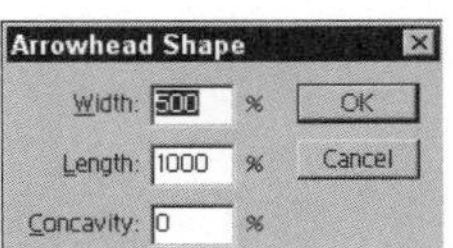

Arrowhead Shape Dialog Box Contents

Component	Function
Width field	Determines percentage of line width of widest part of arrowhead.
Length field	Determines percentage of line length for length of arrowhead, from tip to base.
Concavity field	Determines the curve between the base tips of the arrowhead and the line. You can specify a percentage from 1 to 50. This setting does not affect the curvature of the sides of the arrowhead.

The Brushes Palette and Menu

The Brushes palette displays the default brush shapes and any user-defined brush shapes that may have been previously created and saved. The Brushes palette menu, depicted here with the Brushes palette, is accessed by clicking the right-arrow button.

CONTINUED

THE PHOTOSHOP BRUSHES CONTINUED

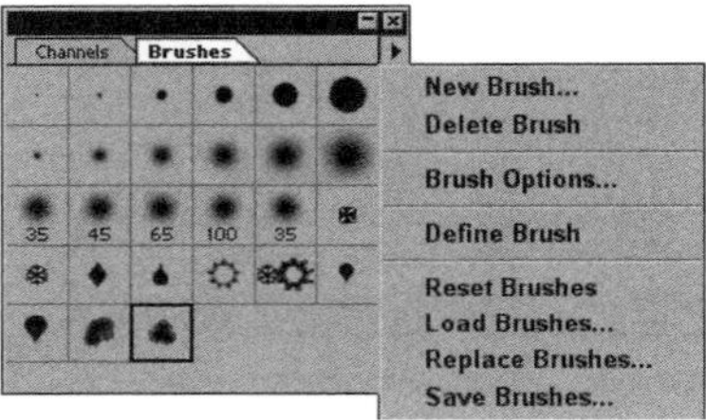

Brushes Palette and Menu Contents

Component	Function
Default brush shapes	These are the standard brush shapes. You can change the size, transparency, and other brush options in the Brush Options dialog box. Double-click a brush to bring up the Brush Options dialog box.
User-defined brush shapes	These are brushes that have been captured with the Define Brush command.
Brushes Palette Menu button	Click this button to choose from the menu.

Brushes Palette Menu Commands

Component	Function
New Brush	Brings up the New Brush dialog box, which is identical to the Brush Options dialog box. When you click OK, however, the settings create a new brush in the Brush palette.
Delete Brush	Select a brush before choosing this command to make it disappear from the grid.
Brush Options	Brings up the Brush Options palette. Lets you control diameter, edge softness, shape of ellipse, and other characteristics.
Define Brush	Before choosing this command, make a rectangular marquee selection around the item you want to define as a brush.
Reset Brushes	Enables you to choose to reset the Brushes palette so that it contains nothing but the default brushes.

Component	Function
Load Brushes	Enables you to add a file of brushes to the current Brushes palette. Operates like any other file loading dialog box.
Replace Brushes	Enables you to replace the brushes in the current Brushes palette with the brushes stored in a brushes file. Operates like any other file loading dialog box.
Save Brushes	Saves the whole set of visible brushes to an ABR file. Operates like any other file saving dialog box.

The New Brush Options

The New Brush Options dialog box, shown here, is accessed when you select New Brush from the Brushes palette menu.

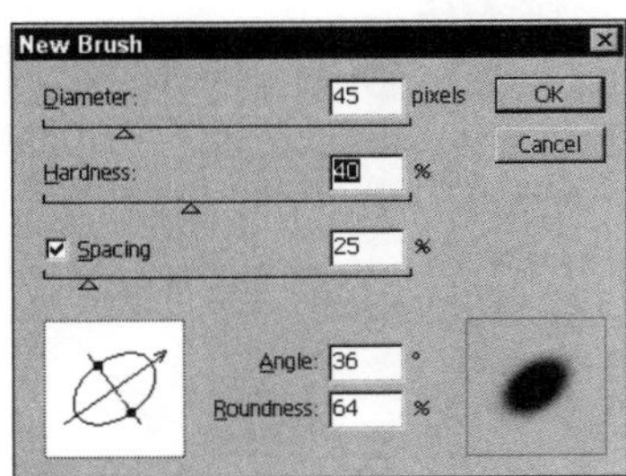

New Brush Options Dialog Box Contents

Component	Function
Diameter slider	Drag to change the overall size of the brush.
Diameter field	Specify the diameter by entering any integer from 1 to 1,000.
Hardness slider	Drag to change the feathering of the edge of the brush.
Hardness field	Enter any percentage of feathering from 0 to 100.
Spacing check box	Check to activate spacing. Otherwise, brush will stroke a continuous line.
Spacing slider	Drag to enter a percentage of brush width to indicate the distance between brush strokes.
Spacing field	Enter any percentage for the brush's width from 0 to 100.
Angle and Roundness adjuster	Drag dots to narrow brush shape. Drag arrowhead to indicate angle of elliptical shape. Angled brushes make calligraphic-type (thick and thin) strokes.
Angle field	Enter a number from 0 to 360 to specify optional numeric entry of exact angle of brush.
Roundness field	Enter a number from 0 to 100 percent to specify optional numeric entry of roundness of brush.
Brush preview	Preview in this area what the brush will look like if you click the OK button.

CHOOSE THE RIGHT BRUSH

The three Photoshop brushes are the Airbrush, Paintbrush, and Pencil. All of these apply the current foreground color, using whatever brush shape you've chosen in the Brushes palette. All also enable you to control the opacity of the colors you apply and to choose a Blend mode for the color you apply. Finally, all three can use custom brush shapes that you create in the Brushes palette.

Of course, differences also exist between the three brushes. (Otherwise, you'd just have one, right?) The Pencil is unique in that it always strokes with hard, aliased edges. Unlike other program's pencils, you can use different sizes and shapes of strokes with this one.

The Airbrush and Paintbrush are so much alike, you won't notice the difference most of the time. Both enable the use of soft-edged brushes; however, the Paintbrush lets you use the Wet Edges option to make colors that mix with underlying colors. The Airbrush can simulate paint buildup (though you can never get it to drip) and paints in user-specified burst intervals and fall-off rates.

Also, the Eraser tool can be set to act pretty much like any of the other brushes.

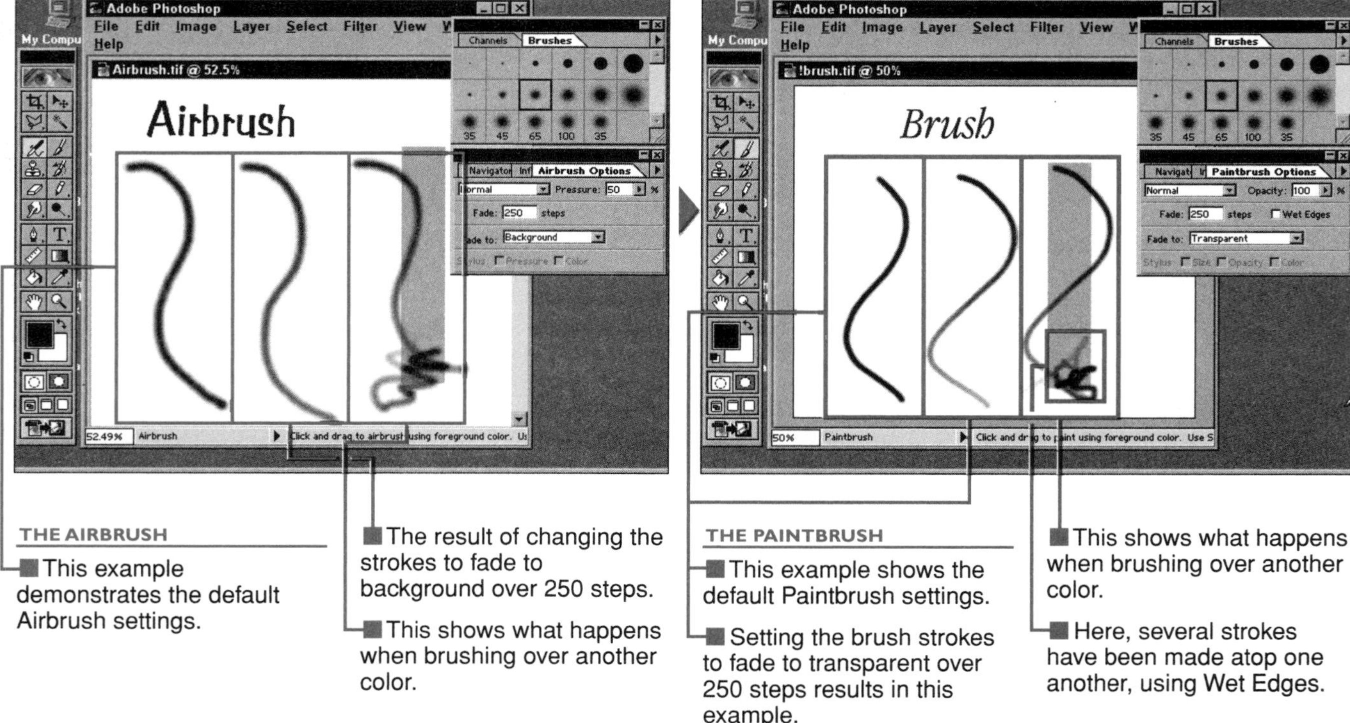

THE AIRBRUSH

■ This example demonstrates the default Airbrush settings.

■ The result of changing the strokes to fade to background over 250 steps.

■ This shows what happens when brushing over another color.

THE PAINTBRUSH

■ This example shows the default Paintbrush settings.

■ Setting the brush strokes to fade to transparent over 250 steps results in this example.

■ This shows what happens when brushing over another color.

■ Here, several strokes have been made atop one another, using Wet Edges.

TIPS

How could you possibly make exactly the same brush stroke for each brush?

A cheap Photoshop trick. Make a path with the Pen tools, and then choose Window ➪ Show Paths. From the Paths palette menu, choose Stroke Subpath. When the Stroke Subpath dialog box appears, choose the tool you want to use for the stroke. All the brushes, focus tools, and darkroom tools are available for autostroking.

How did you change the options for each of the brushes?

The easy way is to double-click the tool to bring up its Options palette. Brush width, shape, and feathering are specified in the Brushes palette, which is discussed later in this chapter.

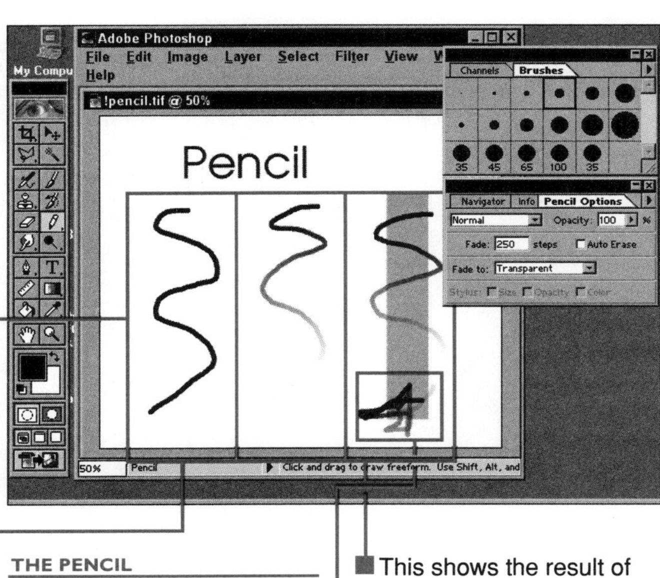

THE PENCIL

■ This example shows the default Pencil settings.

■ Here a larger brush, set to fade to transparent over 250 steps, was used.

■ This shows the result of using the same brush as in Step 2 to stroke over another color.

■ Here several strokes were made atop one another, with Auto Erase checked.

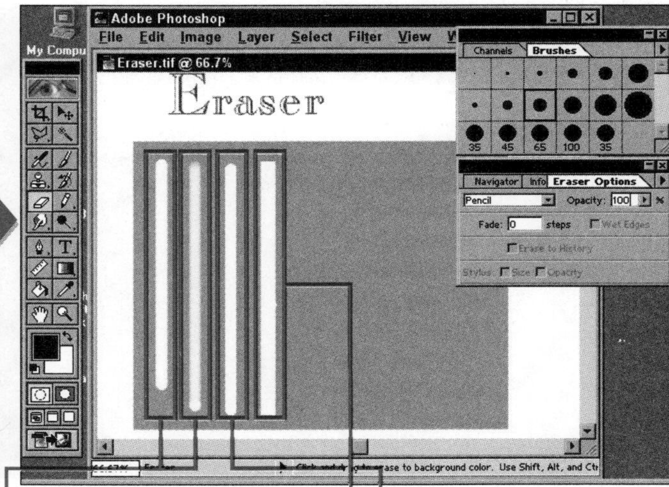

THE ERASER

■ This example demonstrates the default Eraser settings.

■ Setting the strokes to fade to transparency over 250 steps results in this example.

■ Here's how the stroke looks brushed over another color.

■ This results from using the Eraser in Block mode.

SET AIRBRUSH OPTIONS

The exact effect of each of the brushes depends on the settings used in its Options dialog box. The options settings for the Airbrush include Blend mode, Pressure, Fade steps, Fade to, and two pressure-sensitive tablet check boxes: Pressure and Color.

The Airbrush's Pressure setting behaves exactly the same as the Opacity setting for the Paintbrush and has nothing to do with the effect of a pressure-sensitive tablet. Confusingly, the Pressure check box has no effect on opacity. Checking the box means that the size of the brush will increase as you put pressure on the tip of a pressure-sensitive pen. In other words, it is the same setting as the Size check box for the Paintbrush. If you check the Color box and use a pressure-sensitive pen, you can use pressure to mix the foreground and background colors. (Checking the Pressure or Color box has no effect if you use a mouse.)

The Fade to menu offers a choice between Transparent and Background. Choosing Transparent simply fades the intensity of the stroke. Choosing Background creates a gradient stroke over the length of the number of steps specified in the Fade steps field. The value in this field equals the number of brush widths the stroke will travel before it fades.

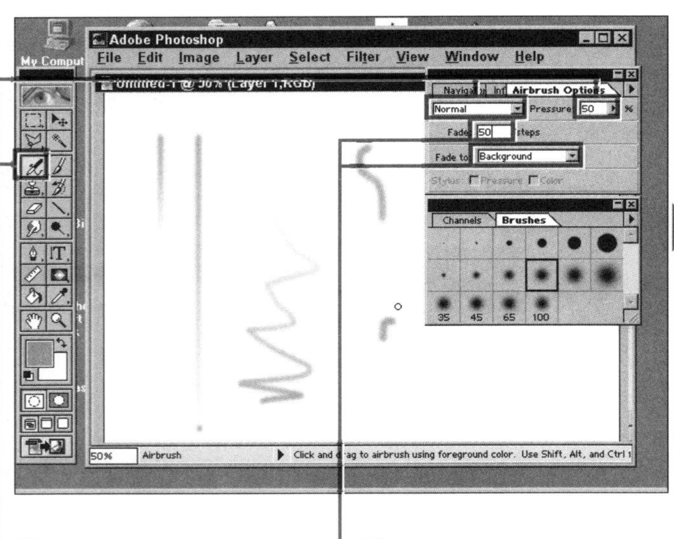

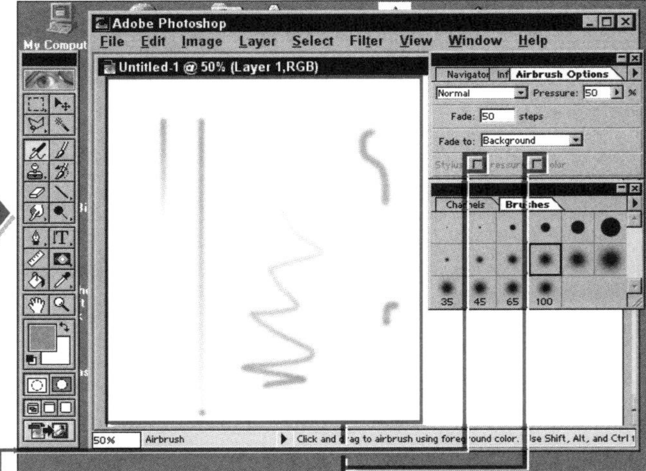

1 Double-click the Airbrush or choose Window ➪ Show Options when the Airbrush is the active tool.

2 Select a mode.

3 Enter a pressure setting or drag the slider.

4 Specify a number in the Fade steps field.

5 Select Transparent or Background in the Fade to field.

6 Check to make pressure-sensitive pen increase the width of the brush stroke as pressure is increased.

7 Check to cause pressure-sensitive pen to blend from foreground to background color with pressure.

8 Experiment with different settings.

SET PAINTBRUSH OPTIONS

The Paintbrush settings are similar to those for the Airbrush. However, an Opacity slider and entry field take the place of the Pressure settings for the Airbrush. A Wet Edges check box makes the stroke darker on the edges and more transparent in the center, producing a water or turpentine effect.

The three Stylus check boxes — Size, Opacity, and Color — rule the behavior of a pressure-sensitive pen tablet. Checking Size causes increased pen pressure to widen the stroke to the size of the chosen brush. Checking Opacity causes increased pen pressure to make the color more opaque. Checking Color causes the stroke to blend from foreground to background color as pen pressure changes.

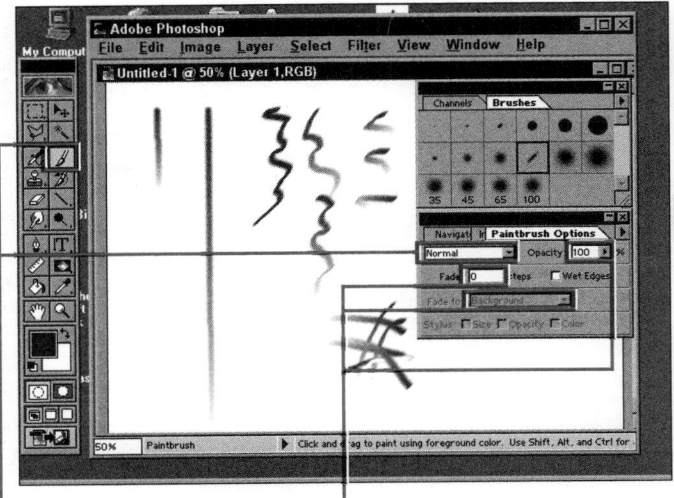

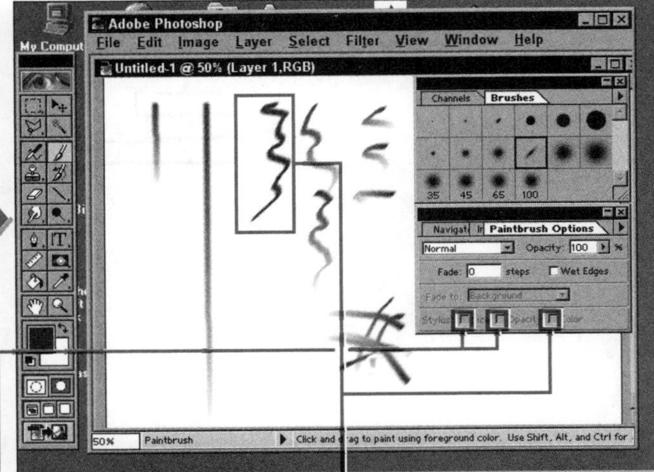

1 Double-click the Paintbrush, or choose Window ➪ Show Options when the Paintbrush is the active tool.

2 Select the Blend mode.

3 Enter an opacity setting or drag the slider.

4 Specify a number in the Fade steps field.

5 Select Transparent or Background in the Fade to field.

6 Check to make pressure-sensitive pen increase size of stroke as pressure is increased.

7 Check to cause stroke to change transparency with pressure.

8 Check to cause pressure-sensitive pen to switch colors with pressure.

9 Experiment with different settings.

SET PENCIL OPTIONS

The Pencil Options are the same as the Paintbrush Options in all but one respect: In place of the Wet Edges check box is an Auto Erase check box.

Auto Erase is useful for quickly refining a monochrome drawing without having to switch to the Eraser tool. Check this box, and the tool paints with the background color over any area where the foreground color already exists. You must start painting with the cursor inside the foreground color for the effect to occur. If you click and drag in any other area, the Pencil paints with the foreground color.

If you combine this capability with the use of a pressure-sensitive pen, and you check the Opacity or Color boxes, you get much more erratic results because Photoshop considers each shade of a color to be an entirely different color.

The first figure in this exercise shows the result of checking the Auto Erase box when using a mouse. The second figure shows what happens when the box is checked while a pressure-sensitive pen is in use.

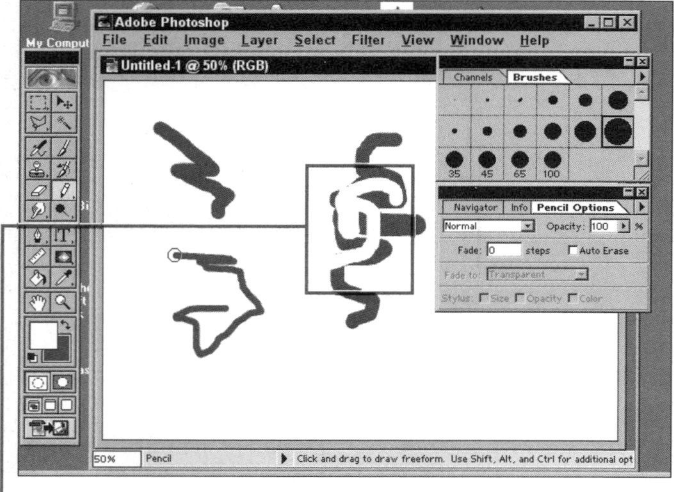

■ Here you can see Pencil strokes made with a mouse while Auto Erase is checked.

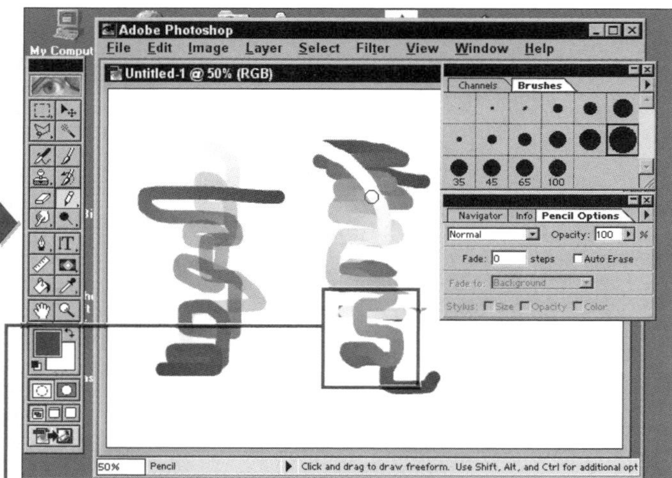

■ Here, Pencil strokes are made with a pressure-sensitive pen while Auto Erase is checked.

SET ERASER OPTIONS

The Eraser options are unusual in that, except in Block mode, the effect of these options is dependent on the options settings for the Airbrush, Paintbrush, or Pencil. All four of these modes can be chosen from the pull-down menu that occupies the position normally used by the Apply Mode pull-down menu. In other words, if you choose Airbrush as the mode for the Eraser, the currently chosen options for the Airbrush are applied. Also, the interface for settings changes to reflect the chosen Eraser mode.

Although the settings may change to reflect the Eraser mode, this doesn't mean they are identical to the options for the corresponding brush. For instance, if you're in Airbrush mode, there is no Background option for the Fade to field. The Eraser always erases to the current background color — unless, of course, you have checked the Erase to History box. In this case, the Eraser will "paint in" whatever state the file was in at the point in the History palette when you checked the History Brush Source box.

Note: If the Eraser is used on a layer, and the Preserve Transparency box on the Layers palette is unchecked, you will be able to see through to the immediately underlying layer.

The two figures on this page show the results of changing various settings for Eraser, as indicated below.

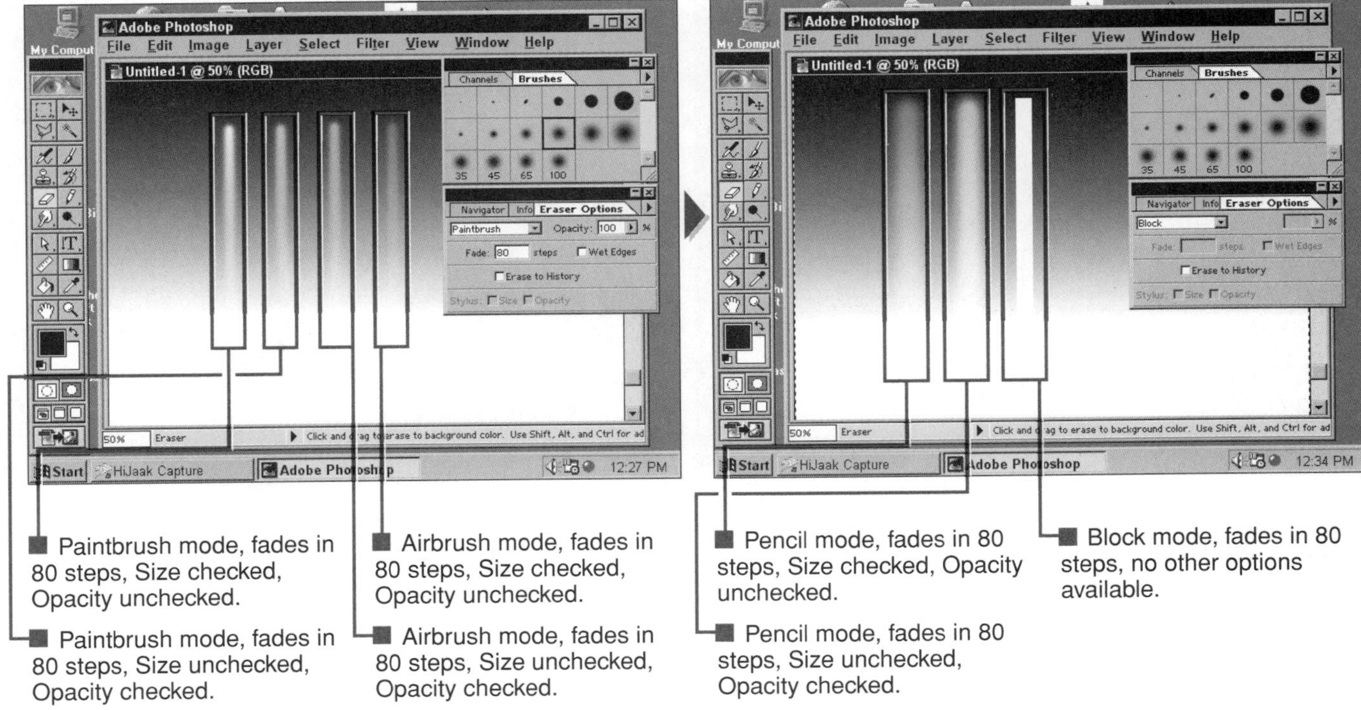

■ Paintbrush mode, fades in 80 steps, Size checked, Opacity unchecked.

■ Paintbrush mode, fades in 80 steps, Size unchecked, Opacity checked.

■ Airbrush mode, fades in 80 steps, Size checked, Opacity unchecked.

■ Airbrush mode, fades in 80 steps, Size unchecked, Opacity checked.

■ Pencil mode, fades in 80 steps, Size checked, Opacity unchecked.

■ Pencil mode, fades in 80 steps, Size unchecked, Opacity checked.

■ Block mode, fades in 80 steps, no other options available.

SAVE AND LOAD BRUSH PALETTES

Photoshop 5 comes with several brush palettes: Assorted, Drop Shadows, and Square. You'll find an even more extensive set of brush shapes on the CD-ROM that accompanies this book. (You'll also see all these brushes pictured on the figure that accompany this exercise.)

When you save brushes, you save all the brushes in your palette to the new file. If you want to save just the new brushes you've made, you have to first delete all the existing brushes one at a time. When you load brushes, you can either add the brushes to those in the current palette, or you can replace the current palette with a new palette by choosing Replace Brushes from the Brushes Palette menu.

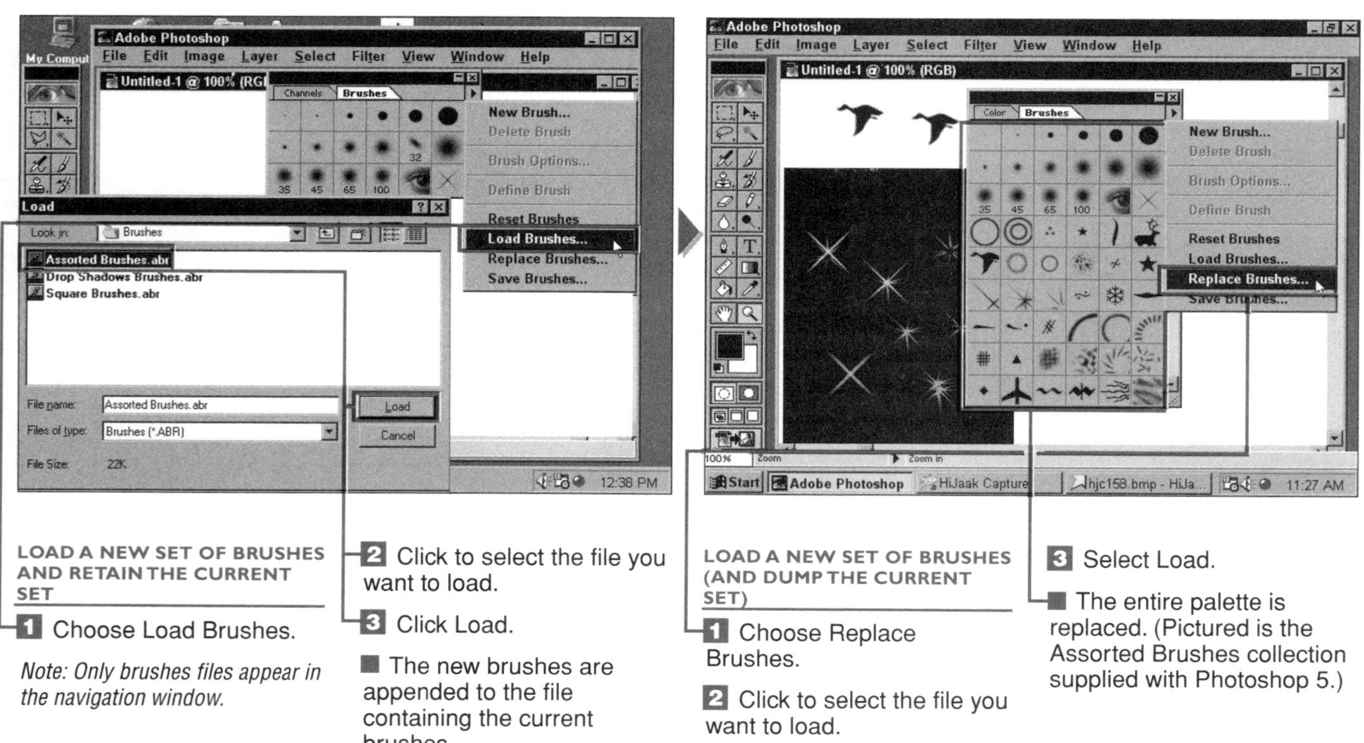

LOAD A NEW SET OF BRUSHES AND RETAIN THE CURRENT SET

1 Choose Load Brushes.

Note: Only brushes files appear in the navigation window.

2 Click to select the file you want to load.

3 Click Load.

■ The new brushes are appended to the file containing the current brushes.

LOAD A NEW SET OF BRUSHES (AND DUMP THE CURRENT SET)

1 Choose Replace Brushes.

2 Click to select the file you want to load.

3 Select Load.

■ The entire palette is replaced. (Pictured is the Assorted Brushes collection supplied with Photoshop 5.)

TIPS

Is there any way to avoid the pain of deleting a horde of brushes one at a time if I want to save a newly created set of brushes into a file exclusive to them?

Good question, and a good idea. If you don't save your new brushes to a clean file, you keep duplicating the existing brushes every time you load a file. Here's the trick: Delete all the brushes in the palette, and then choose Save Brushes. Name the file Clean. Next time you start defining a new set of brushes, start by choosing Replace Brushes. Then load the new "clean" set and add as many new brushes as you'd like. Choose Save Brushes and give the file a new name. Your clean file will stay that way, and you can reuse it any time you want to start a new palette.

Can I transfer a Brushes palette from Mac to Windows and back?

Yes, but for the Windows version of Photoshop to recognize the palette, you have to rename the file in the Windows Explorer to include the extension .ABR (not case-sensitive). The Mac automatically recognizes the file type regardless of extension, so you can make all your files work both ways by giving them all the same extension.

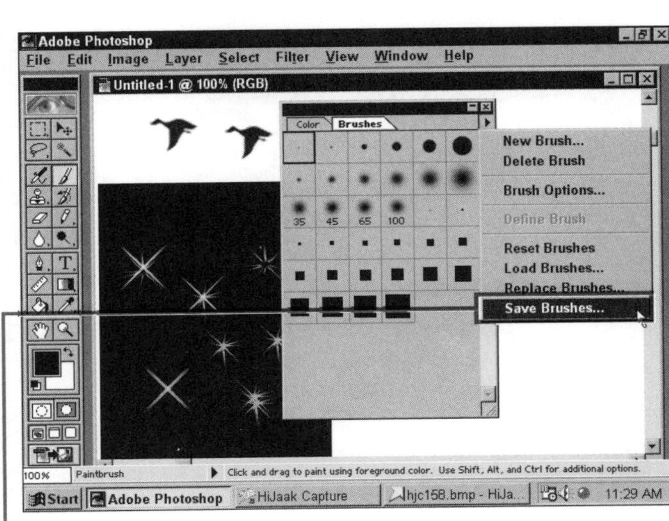

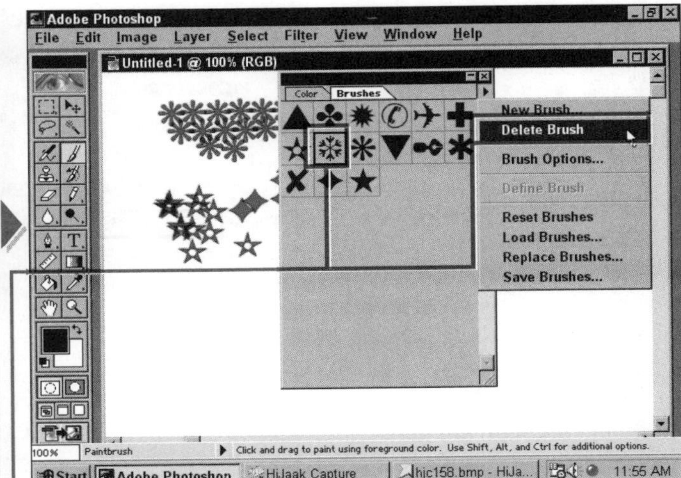

SAVE THE CURRENT SET OF BRUSHES

1 Choose Save Brushes.

2 In the Save dialog box, navigate to the Photoshop 5/Extras/Brushes folder.

3 Enter a name you d like to give this set.

Note: In Windows, the .ABR extension is added automatically.

DELETE BRUSHES

1 Click to select the brush you want to delete.

2 Choose Delete Brush.

Note: A nice shortcut is to hold down the ⌘/Ctrl key (the scissors icon will appear), and click on the brush to delete it.

3 Repeat Steps 1 and 2 until you've removed all the brushes you don't want.

CREATE CUSTOM BRUSH SHAPES

On its own, Photoshop doesn't have any natural media brushes. It does, however, enable you to create brushes from the content of any selection.

This does have some practical limits. It doesn't make much sense to cut out a solid portion of a photo and then use it as a brush, because the brush is grayscale — so all you get is a gray square.

Light colors make translucent brushes, imparting an effect like that of watercolors. You can make speckles and stripes to simulate hairy brushes. You can make starbursts, raindrops, and odd little shapes like confetti to add atmosphere to an image. Finally, you can make silhouette shapes that will act as components for patterns and textures. Basically, you can use any shape or texture as a new brush.

You can't change the size of custom brushes if you're using a mouse. Pressure pen users are luckier — you can make the size of even the largest shape range from a few pixels to over a hundred by just checking the Size box in the chosen tool's Options palette.

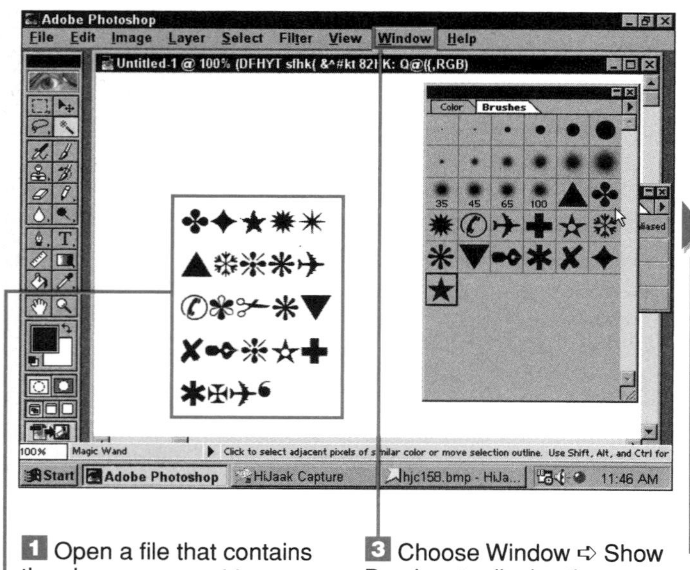

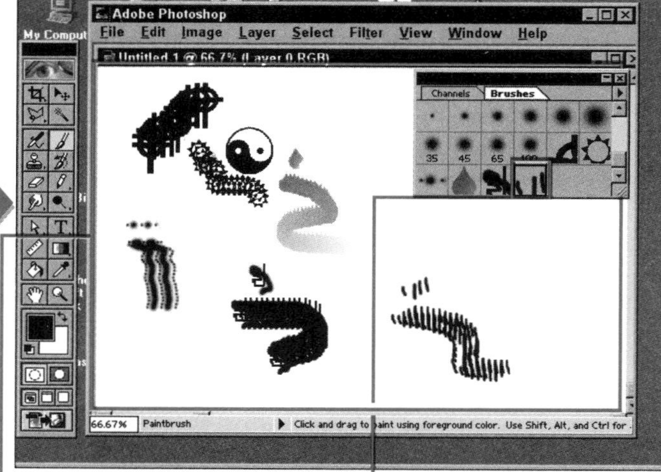

1 Open a file that contains the shape you want to use, or paint some strokes to make a texture brush.

2 Select the area you want to use as a shape.

3 Choose Window ➪ Show Brushes to display the Brushes palette. Choose Define Brush from the Brushes palette menu.

■ The brush immediately appears in the Brushes palette.

■ The result of painting when using these shapes with a pressure-sensitive pen tablet.

TIPS

Do you have any suggestions for cutting the time it takes to create a whole series of brushes?

Here is an idea that has helped me quite a bit if I'm importing and rasterizing a lot of line art. First, I import and rasterize as many files as my RAM can stand. Then I make an Action that reduces the files to a common size (typically about 30 pixels high), fills them with black, and selects the image. Next, while the Action is still recording, I use ⌘/Ctrl+click on the layer name bar to select the imported shape and then choose Define Brush from the Brushes palette menu. Finally, I close the current file and stop recording.

What if the shapes aren't on a transparent background?

Crop each file to its minimum size before running the preceding Action.

What are some good sources for brushes?

Virtually all of the inexpensive clip art collections — just make sure that the files are in EPS format. You can also use raster images, but the shapes don't tend to be as clean and well defined.

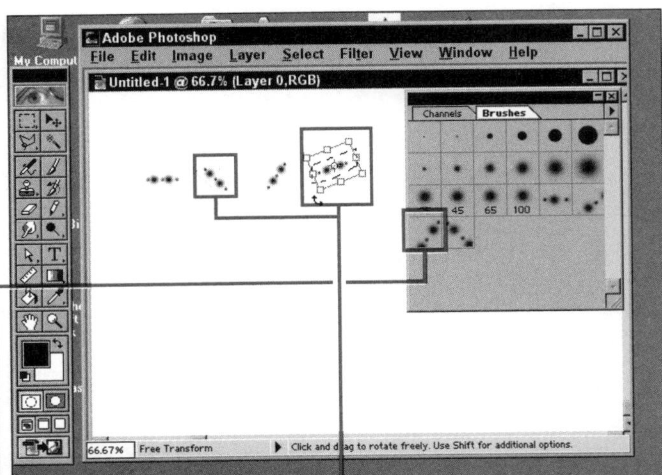

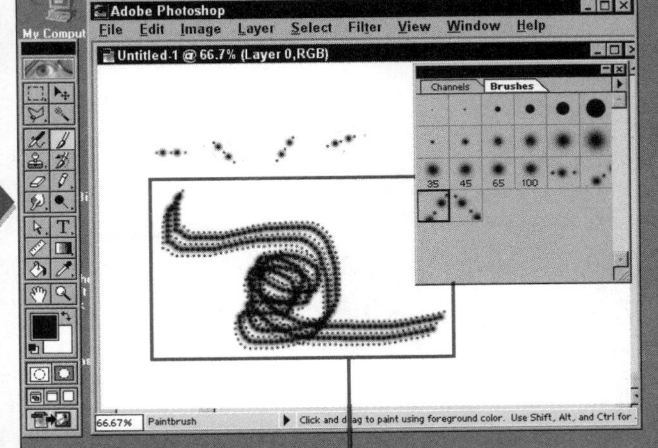

MAKE A BRUSH YOU CAN ROTATE

1 Select the original brush shape.

2 Press ⌘/Ctrl+C and then ⌘/Ctrl+V to copy the shape to a new layer.

3 Press ⌘/Ctrl+T. A transformation box and handles appear around the new layer.

4 Drag outside the transformation box to rotate the new layer as desired.

5 Repeat Steps 1—4 as many times as necessary to make additional rotated brushes.

6 Select each brush in turn and choose Define Brush from the Brushes palette menu.

■ A stroke made while pressing the bracket keys to alter the stroke angle.

CREATE A BRUSH FROM TYPE

One of the easiest ways to capture useful shapes for brushes is to capture text — especially from the many dingbats and symbol libraries available. If you have a fairly sizable type library, you could also make a set of brushes consisting of nothing but asterisks or exclamation points — one from each typeface. And it's very easy to enter type in various sizes and then capture each size as a different brush.

Why might you want to use type as a brush shape? Well, for one thing, letters can produce some interesting effects when they're smeared. You could also use type brushes to hide messages in strange places or to create textures and patterns.

This exercise shows you the procedure for making a brush from type by demonstrating the creation of a series of brushes from one character in a number of fonts.

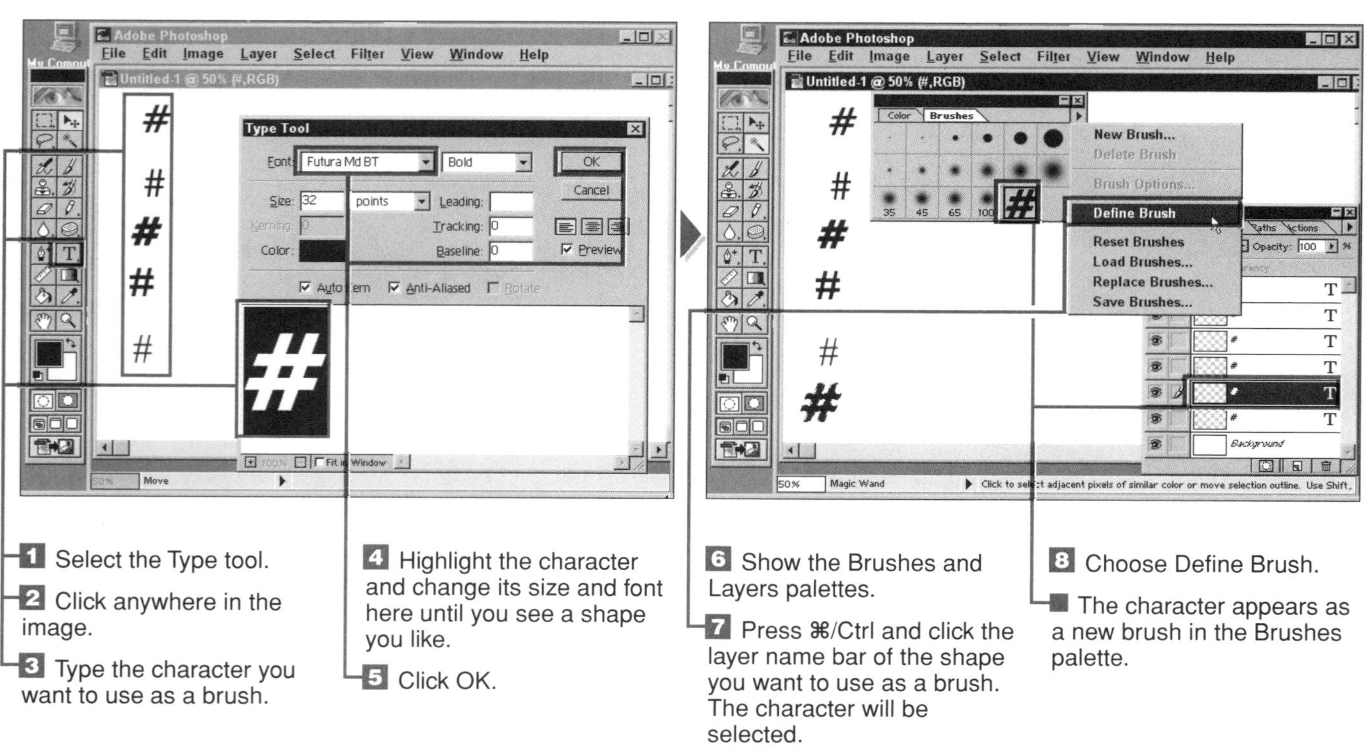

1 Select the Type tool.

2 Click anywhere in the image.

3 Type the character you want to use as a brush.

4 Highlight the character and change its size and font here until you see a shape you like.

5 Click OK.

6 Show the Brushes and Layers palettes.

7 Press ⌘/Ctrl and click the layer name bar of the shape you want to use as a brush. The character will be selected.

8 Choose Define Brush.

■ The character appears as a new brush in the Brushes palette.

CREATE A BRUSH FROM A POSTSCRIPT IMAGE

Many useful brush shapes can be imported from the inexpensive and voluminous libraries of vector clip art made for use in illustration and page makeup programs.

You start by dragging any EPS file or icon from a folder (or the desktop) onto the Photoshop alias or into its workspace. A Rasterize Generic EPS dialog then appears. Specify the pixel height of the brush you want to create and click OK. The image appears in Photoshop in its own file on a transparent background. Press ⌘/Ctrl and click the layer name bar in the new file's Layers palette to select the shape. Choose Define Brush from the brushes palette menu and — bingo! — the brush appears in your palette.

Tip: To make several sizes or rotations of this brush, size the brush to the largest you'll want, choose Define Brush, and then use the Transform ➪ Numeric command to reduce the image to the next largest size and rotation. Capture the brush again and repeat the process for the next size as many times as desired.

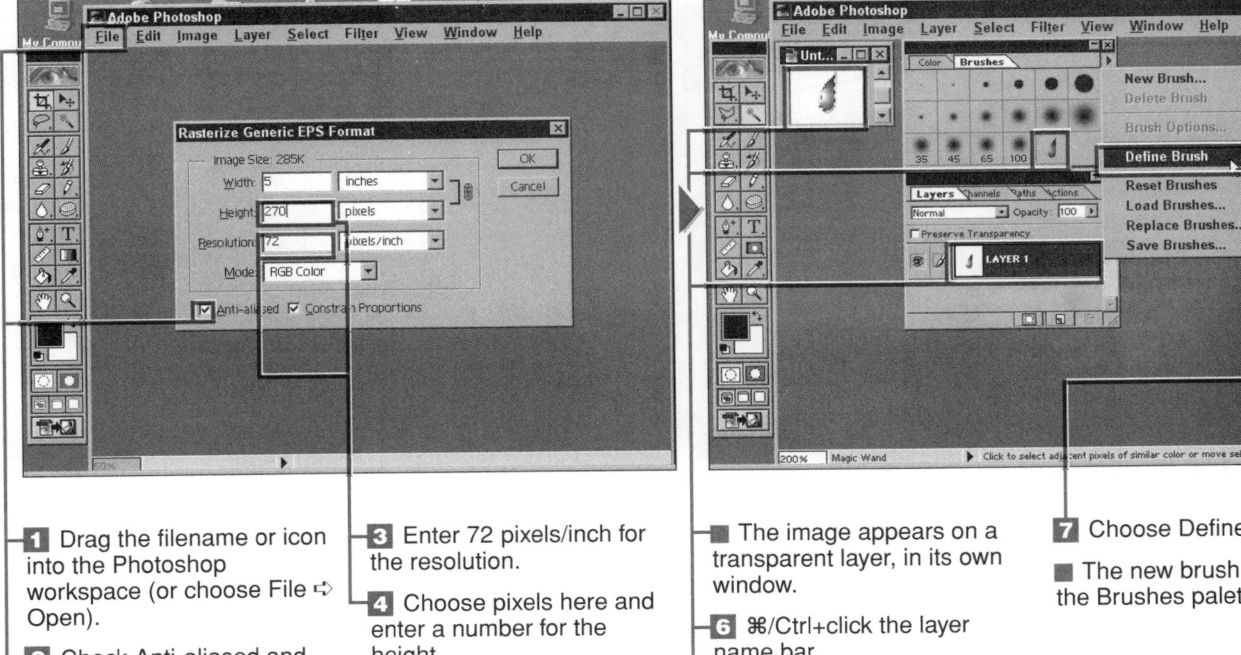

1 Drag the filename or icon into the Photoshop workspace (or choose File ➪ Open).

2 Check Anti-aliased and Constrain Proportions.

3 Enter 72 pixels/inch for the resolution.

4 Choose pixels here and enter a number for the height.

5 Click OK.

■ The image appears on a transparent layer, in its own window.

6 ⌘/Ctrl+click the layer name bar.

■ Nontransparent portions of the layer are selected.

7 Choose Define Brush.

■ The new brush appears in the Brushes palette.

PAINT FROM A SNAPSHOT

Photoshop has a tool introduced in Version 5 that few realize the value of called the History Brush. The History Brush lets you paint in any effect Photoshop can do to an image. That includes all of the filters, all of the third-party filters, all of the Image Controls, any sort of compositing — anything you can imagine.

There are two areas in which I find the History Brush invaluable: Extending the tonal range of the image and turning photos into paintings. To do either of these things, you want to create one or more new layers, run the process(es) that you want to paint into areas on those whole layers, take a snapshot, and then delete the layers (if you're tight on memory or want to speed things up).

Now all you need to do is select the snapshot of the original image, choose the History Brush, and click the box to the right of the layer that you want to paint in. Then, just paint in the effect from that layer.

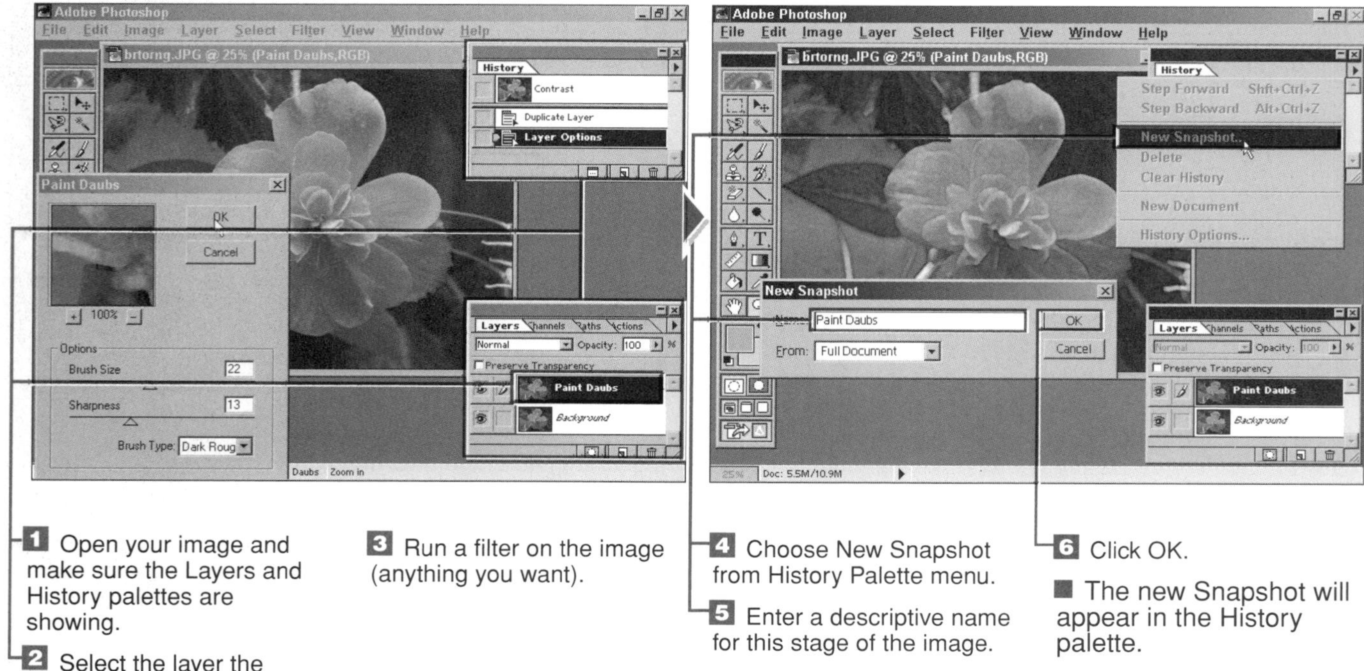

1 Open your image and make sure the Layers and History palettes are showing.

2 Select the layer the image is on and duplicate it.

3 Run a filter on the image (anything you want).

4 Choose New Snapshot from History Palette menu.

5 Enter a descriptive name for this stage of the image.

6 Click OK.

■ The new Snapshot will appear in the History palette.

TIPS

Why aren't I seeing any results when I try to paint?

Make sure the History Brush icon is showing in the box to the left of the Snapshot that you are supposed to be painting from. Also make sure you are painting into an active and visible layer.

What if I want to blend the effects of the History Brush?

No problem. In the History Brush Options palette, drag the opacity setting to a lower level to obtain a less intense effect. If you're using a pressure-sensitive stylus, you can also check the Stylus Opacity box. Then less pressure will mean less effect.

How many snapshots can I paint from?

As many as your computer's memory can handle. It is likely that you'd want to impose several different effects. If you're short on memory, create a snapshot, paint in the needed changes, flatten and save the file. Then open it again and create a new effect with a new Snapshot.

7 Select the History Brush.

8 Click the box to the left of the layer you want to paint from.

9 Click to hide any layers covering the layer you want to paint to.

10 Choose History Brush Options.

11 Paint into the area you want to cover.

12 Eliminate any layers anc snapshots no longer neede and save.

GET EVEN MORE PAINTERLY WITH THE ART HISTORY BRUSH

The Art History Brush is brand new in Photoshop 5.5. Like the History Brush, it paints from a Snapshot, but at the same time, it imposes its own "style."

The brush works by sampling the color from a snapshot at the moment you press the mouse button, then smearing and changing the color of those pixels as you drag. You have a choice of ten stroke styles. The names are somewhat descriptive of how much farther and in what shape the pixels will be smeared as the strokes are moved. The size of these "smears" is dictated by the size of the brush chosen in the Brushes palette.

As you start to become familiar with this brush, it's a good idea to set Tolerance at a very low setting, the Blend Modes at Normal, and Fidelity at a fairly high level. These settings guarantee the lowest number of rude surprises.

1 Choose Window ➪ Show History.

2 Choose the Art History brush.

3 Run a filter.

Note: You could make any overall change to this image at this stage.

■ The changed image appears.

4 Double-click the History brush. The History Brush Options appear.

5 Choose Window ➪ Show Brushes The Brushes palette appears.

6 Click in the Snapshot box to select the snapshot as the source for colors.

What do I do if I set the brush size too large and really mess up the image?

Happens all the time. Sometimes it can even produce some nice effects. All you have to do is pick a smaller brush and paint over the area again. You can keep painting over areas with different brushes until you get the effect you're looking for.

But what if I want photographic detail in some areas?

Use the History (not Art History) brush and paint it back in.

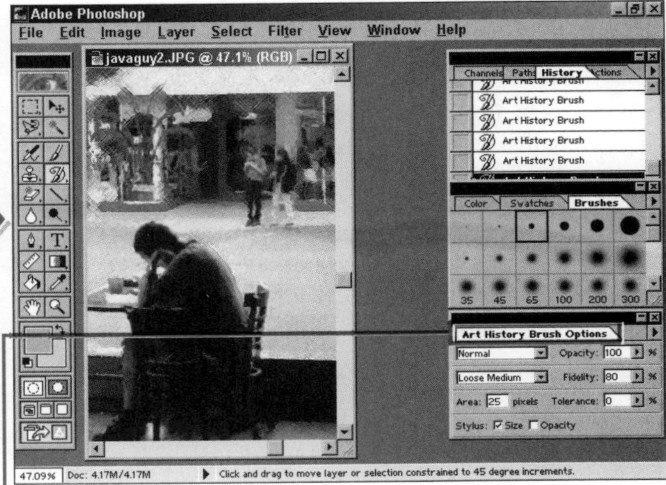

7 Choose a brush size and style. This determines how much area a stroke will cover.

8 For starters, set History Brush Options as shown.

9 Start Painting.

10 To enlarge or reduce the stroke, press the [and] keys.

11 To change the degree to which the strokes cover the current painting, drag the opacity slider in the History Brush Options palette.

13 CORRECTING DETAILS

This chapter covers a variety of techniques for correcting specific details within images. Some of these techniques involve applying a Photoshop command or filter within a masked area (or selection) of the image (or adjustment layer). Others involve corrections made to smaller areas by stroking them with editing tools, which differ from brushes in that they change pixels, rather than apply them.

Techniques for making corrections inside a masked, or selected, area include the following:

- Shortening depth of field
- Sharpening specific edges
- Controlling exposure and gamma over a large area
- Eliminating artifacts from shadow areas

Techniques for using editing tools for correcting small areas with brush strokes include the following:

- Burning (darkening)
- Dodging (brightening)
- Sponging (dulling and brightening colors)
- Color toning (creating a monotint or a duotone)
- Hand coloring a toned image

Burn Tool

The Burn tool is used to darken relatively small areas of the image. It usually works best when employed in the same way as in a traditional darkroom technique, by repeatedly stroking with a highly feathered brush set at a low exposure percentage. The Burn tool has an associated Options palette, as shown in the following figure.

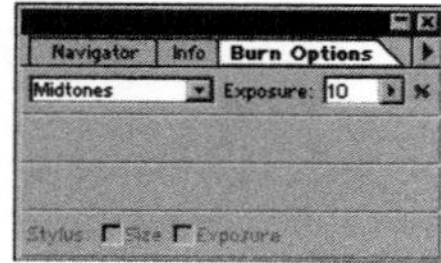

Burn Tool Shortcut and Modifiers

Icon	Shortcut	Modifier: Result
[Burn icon]	0... (Repeat to alternate with Dodge and Sponge.)	Shift: Produces straight line at any 90-degree angle from the origin of the stroke.
		⌘/Ctrl: Switches to the Move tool.
		Opt/Alt: Switches to the Dodge tool.

Dodge Tool

The Dodge tool is the exact opposite of the Burn tool — that is, it lightens those portions of the subject over which the brush passes. It, too, works best by scrubbing at a low exposure setting. The Burn and Dodge tools share an Options palette, which is shown in the first figure.

Dodge Tool Shortcut and Modifiers

Icon	Shortcut	Modifier: Result
	0 Repeat to alternate with Dodge and Sponge.	Shift: Produces straight line at any 90-degree angle from the origin of the stroke.
		⌘/Ctrl: Switches to the Move tool.
		Opt/Alt: Switches to the Burn tool.

Burn and Dodge Options Palette Contents

Component	Function
Tonal Range pull-down menu	Restricts the effect of a stroke to only that portion of the tonal range.
Exposure field and slider	Controls the intensity of the effect to be applied in a single stroke. It is usually best to set this at a low setting (under 10 percent) so that the effect can be blended using multiple strokes.
Stylus Size check box	If checked, pressure-sensitive stylus increases the size of the brush (up to the maximum size of the current brush) as pressure is applied.
Stylus Exposure check box	If checked, stroke becomes more intense as pressure is applied.

Sponge Tool

The Sponge tool is really two tools in one: a color infuser and a color sucker. You switch between the two by choosing Saturate or Desaturate from the pull-down menu in the Sponge Options palette, shown in the following figure. The best pressure setting depends on the application of the moment. If you want to change an area completely to grayscale (perhaps so that you can recolor it by hand), a high (or even 100 percent) setting is in order. After all, you can't overdo it for that application. On the other hand, you can very easily oversaturate. If you do, it is usually best to back off using the History palette (or ⌘/Ctrl+Opt/Alt+Z), rather than trying to correct by switching to Desaturate mode.

Here's a little-known secret about the sponge tool: You can use it when in Grayscale mode to lower the contrast between gray pixels. This sounds as though it would do the same thing as the Blur tool, but the Blur tool concentrates its effect on lowering the contrast between edges.

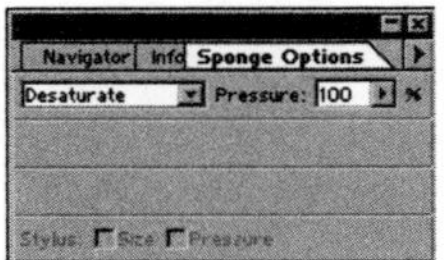

CONTINUED

CORRECTING DETAILS CONTINUED

Sponge Tool Shortcut and Modifiers

Icon	Shortcut	Modifier: Result
	0 Repeat to alternate with Dodge and Burn.	Shift: Produces straight line at any 90-degree angle from the origin of the stroke.
		⌘/Ctrl: Switches to the Move Tool.
		Opt/Alt: No effect.

Sponge Options Palette Contents

Component	Function
Saturate/Desaturate pull-down menu	Saturate intensifies colors, Desaturate mutes them. 100 percent desaturation results in grayscale.
Pressure field and slider	Controls the intensity of the effect to be applied in a single stroke. The default 50 percent setting is usually the best place to start.
Stylus Size check box	If checked, pressure-sensitive stylus increases the size of the brush (up to the maximum size of the current brush) as pressure is applied.
Stylus Pressure check box	If checked, stroke becomes more intense as pressure is applied.

Sharpen Tool

The Sharpen tool accomplishes its particular magic by heightening the contrast between adjacent pixels when the brush passes over them. In other words, it is the opposite of the Blur tool — just as its name implies. Repeated applications (known as *scrubbing*) intensify the effect (as is the case with all the tools mentioned so far). The associated Sharpen Options palette is depicted here.

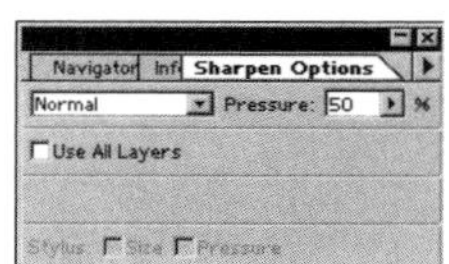

Sharpen Tool Shortcut and Modifiers

Icon	Shortcut	Modifier: Result
	R Repeat to alternate with Blur and Smudge.	Shift: Produces straight line at any 90-degree angle from the origin of the stroke.
		⌘/Ctrl: Switches to the Move Tool.
		Opt/Alt: Switches to the Blur tool.

Sharpen Options Palette Contents

Component	Function
Apply Mode pull-down menu	Brings up a selection of Apply modes: Normal, Darken, Lighten, Hue, Saturation, Color, and Luminosity.
Pressure field and slider	Controls the intensity of the effect to be applied in a single stroke. The default 50 percent setting is usually the best place to start.
Use All Layers check box	If checked, strokes affect visible parts of image on all layers. Otherwise, only the current layer is affected.
Stylus Size check box	If checked, pressure-sensitive stylus increases the size of the brush (up to the maximum size of the current brush) as pressure is applied.
Stylus Pressure check box	If checked, stroke becomes more intense as pressure is applied.

CREATE SIMPLE TONAL EFFECTS

BURNING AND DODGING SMALL AREAS

Two of the oldest darkroom tricks in the business are known as *burning* and *dodging*. Burning and dodging are techniques for correcting or emphasizing the luminosity values over a specific portion of the image. In traditional photographic printmaking, dodging is done by blocking some light from the enlarger over an area with a small piece of cardboard taped to coat-hanger wire. Burning is done by cutting a hole in cardboard (or using your hands as shown in the Burn Tool icon) so exposure can be increased over a small area.

Photoshop has always featured electronic equivalents of these tools. To darken an area, choose the Burn tool. To lighten an area, choose the Dodge tool. Then, wiggle the tool so the affected area blends with its surroundings.

You can also lighten or darken by selecting a specific area and using the image adjustment tools, as discussed next in this chapter.

■ This portrait can be improved by burning and dodging.

1 Choose the Dodge tool from the Toolbox and double-click to open the Options palette.

2 Drag to set exposure at about 10 percent.

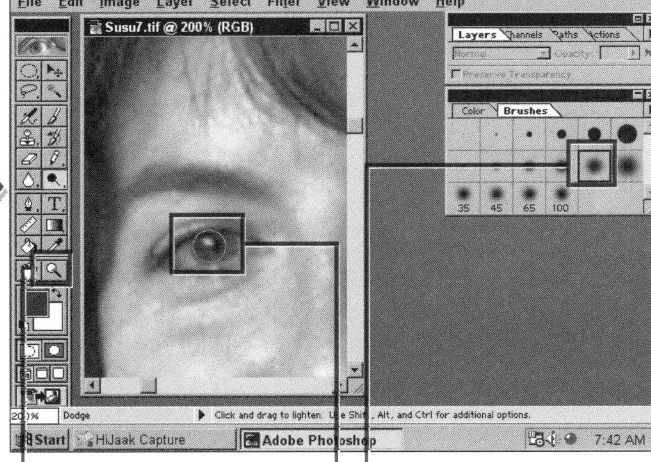

3 Zoom in to see small details. Reselect the Dodge tool.

4 Choose Window ➪ Show Brushes.

5 Choose a brush size slightly smaller than the area you want to dodge.

6 Drag the tool over the area several times until the desired degree of lightening/darkening is achieved.

TIPS

How do I avoid streaking the image, which seems to happen easily?

Here are two tips for avoiding streaks: First make sure you set the exposure low enough to keep the effect of a single drag subtle. Second, choose a feathered brush so that the tool won't have a hard-edged path. Finally, avoid trying to work on too large an area.

Is there any way to correct streaking once it's been noticed?

Just step back in the History palette (⌘/Ctrl+Opt/Shift+Z) until the streaking disappears and then delete the subsequent steps. Now you can resume the operation.

How do I decide whether to use Burn and Dodge or to adjust within a selection?

If the area is more than a few times larger than the largest brush in the brush palette (100 pixels), a selection is probably more appropriate. Adjusting within a selection also promises more exact control over the effect and over shadows, midtones, and highlights.

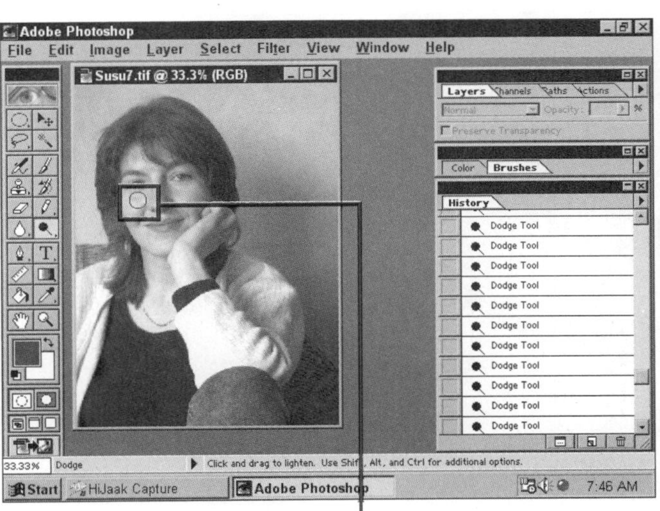

7 To work on larger areas, zoom out so that you can see the entire area.

8 Drag the tool over the area to be affected.

9 Repeat until the desired degree of lightening is achieved.

■ Darkening (burning in) an area is done in the same way, but it darkens the area covered.

10 Choose the Burn tool.

11 Choose a brush size appropriate to the area you want to darken.

12 Drag repeatedly in the area to be affected until the desired effect is achieved.

CONTINUED

CREATE SIMPLE TONAL EFFECTS CONTINUED

BURNING AND DODGING USING A SELECTION

The Burn and Dodge tools are wonderful for making freehand exposure adjustments to small areas of the image, but they can produce disturbingly uneven results over large areas. For larger areas of the image, simply select that area with the selection tools and use the Image ➪ Adjust commands to make the adjustment. Once you've made the selection, you probably want to feather it slightly so that the newly brightened or darkened area doesn't show an obvious border.

The Image ➪ Adjust command that's usually quickest and easiest for the purpose is Brightness/Contrast. Depending on the subject, AutoLevels and Equalize might also be worth a try. Keep the Preview box checked while you're making adjustments.

Of course, there may be times when neither using the Burn or Dodge tools nor adjusting within a selection is the whole answer. Often, once you make the adjustments within the selection, you'll want to use the Burn or Dodge tool on smaller details.

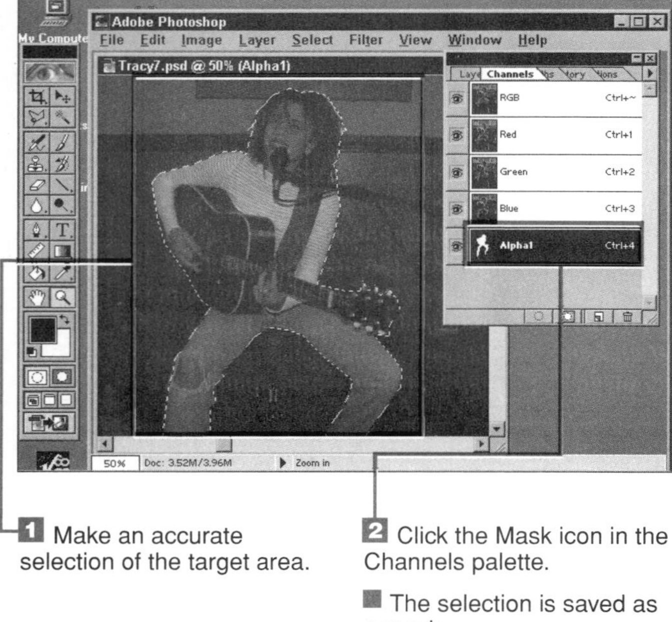

1 Make an accurate selection of the target area.

2 Click the Mask icon in the Channels palette.

■ The selection is saved as a mask.

Note: Saving the selection isn't mandatory, but making accurate selections takes time.

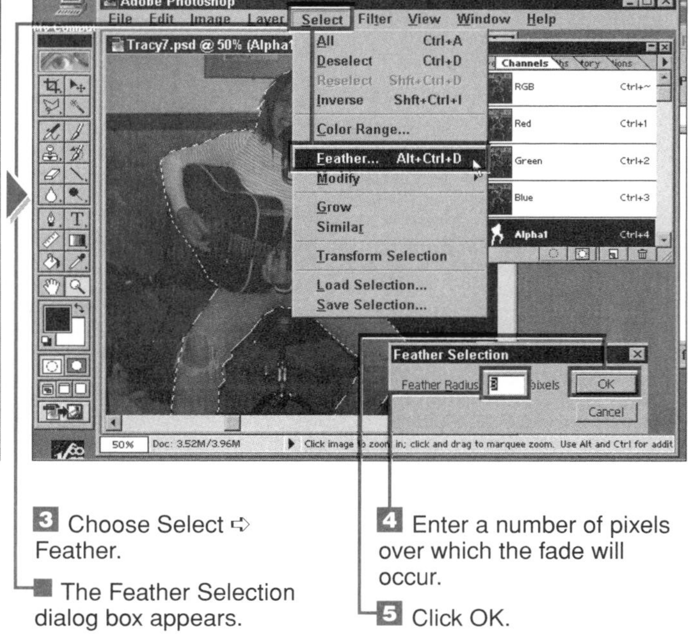

3 Choose Select ➪ Feather.

■ The Feather Selection dialog box appears.

4 Enter a number of pixels over which the fade will occur.

5 Click OK.

How do I avoid making the edge of the selection obvious?

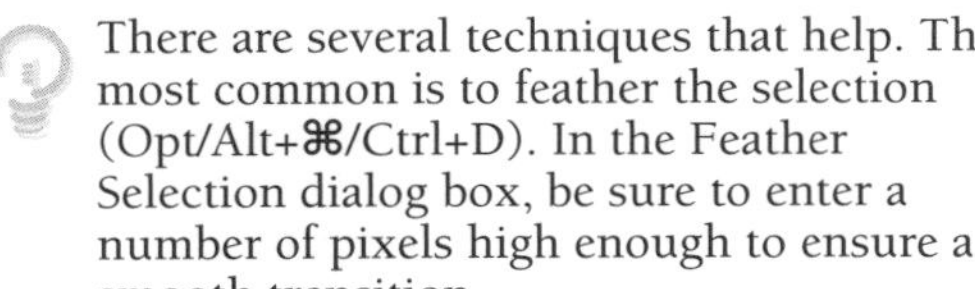

There are several techniques that help. The most common is to feather the selection (Opt/Alt+⌘/Ctrl+D). In the Feather Selection dialog box, be sure to enter a number of pixels high enough to ensure a smooth transition.

At times you may want to feather one part of the selection edge to a different degree than another. Feather the first selection. Now press Shift and add another selection that covers the edge you want to feather to a different degree. Press Opt/Alt+⌘/Ctrl+D again, and this time enter a different number of pixels in the Feather Selection dialog box.

Finally, lighten or darken the area you want to burn or dodge by using the Curves command (⌘/Ctrl+M) to raise and lower only the midtones.

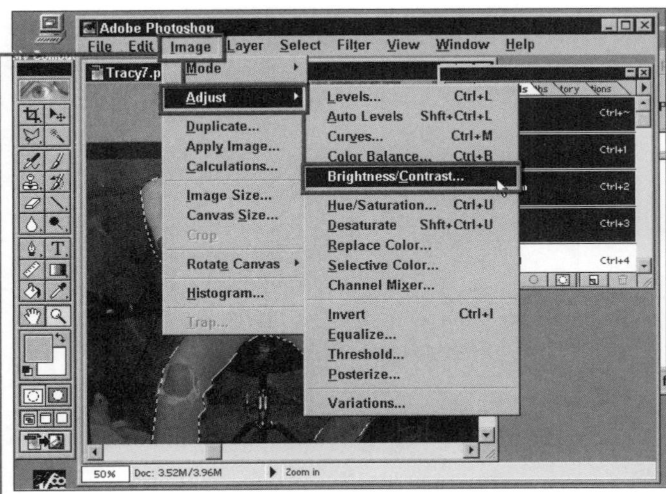

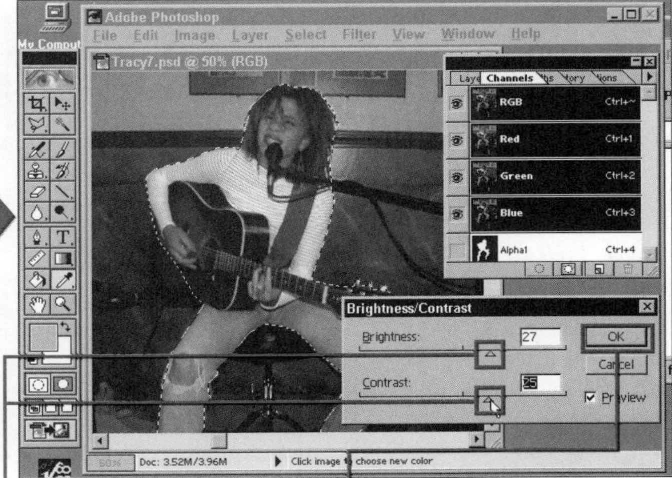

6 Choose Image ⇨ Adjust ⇨ Brightness/Contrast.

■ The Brightness/Contrast dialog box appears.

7 Drag the Brightness level until the luminosity seems correct.

8 Drag the Contrast slider until all the tonal values look natural for the subject.

9 Press ⌘/Ctrl+H to hide the selection border.

10 Click OK to accept the changes.

SUCK UP COLOR WITH THE SPONGE TOOL

The Sponge is the third tool on the Burn and Dodge tool pop-out menu. Choose it by selecting it from the pop-out menu or by pressing the letter O (Shift+O) until you see the Sponge tool appear in place of the Dodge or Burn tools.

The purpose of the Sponge tool is to help you tone down overintense colors or jazz up dull ones by changing the saturation. Tone down too much, and you'll end up with a gray tone. Double-click the Sponge tool to bring up the Options palette. Choose Saturate or Desaturate from the pull-down menu, and set a pressure percentage. Next, choose the appropriate brush size, and drag repeatedly until the adjustment blends properly.

One of the most useful applications for the Sponge tool is toning down blotchiness in skin tones. Take out the redness (or blue in veins) with this tool. Complementary operations would include matching the surrounding skin tones by using the Paintbrush in Color Blend mode and then lightening or darkening with the Dodge or Burn tools (see "Match Color with the Paintbrush Tool" later in this chapter).

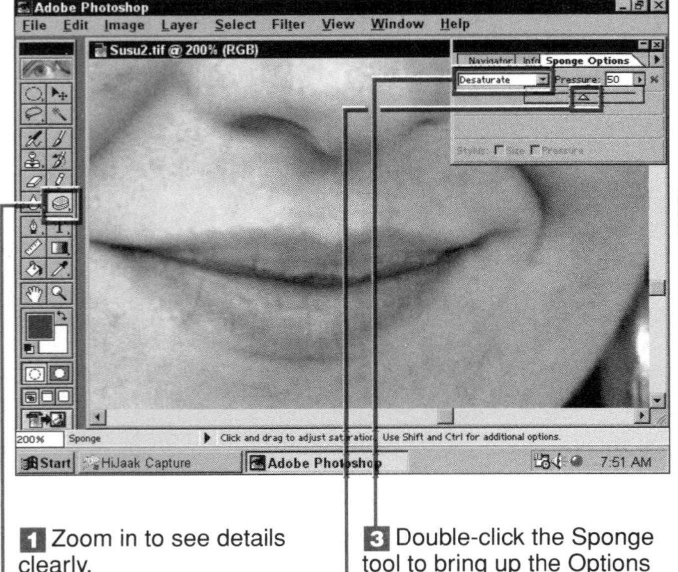

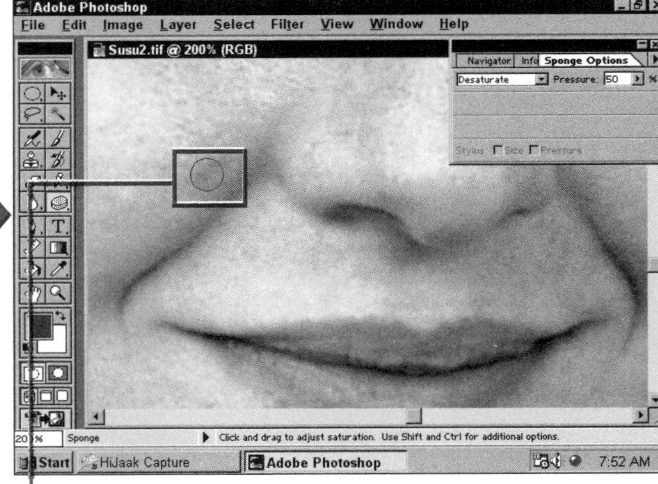

1 Zoom in to see details clearly.

2 Choose the Sponge tool from the Toolbox (or press O).

3 Double-click the Sponge tool to bring up the Options palette and choose Desaturate from the pull-down menu.

4 Drag the Pressure slider to a low percentage.

5 Drag the cursor over the oversaturated area to lower saturation

MATCH COLOR WITH THE PAINTBRUSH TOOL

Usually, the Paintbrush tool is used for painting, but when it is used with Blend modes (available from the Paintbrush Options palette pull-down menu), it can serve a variety of other purposes as well. One of the most popular of these is retouching to change the color of small areas of the image.

You may want to change color to match the surrounding colors, to make the image more colorful (replacing ivory-colored flowers with red ones, for example), or simply to enhance composition in the image. In the example below, the lipstick color is being matched to the outline of the lips.

Tip: Remember when retouching that pressing the square bracket keys cycles you through the brushes, so it's easy to change sizes. Also, if you're working on small areas, zoom in by using the Zoom tool to drag a marquee around the area you will be retouching.

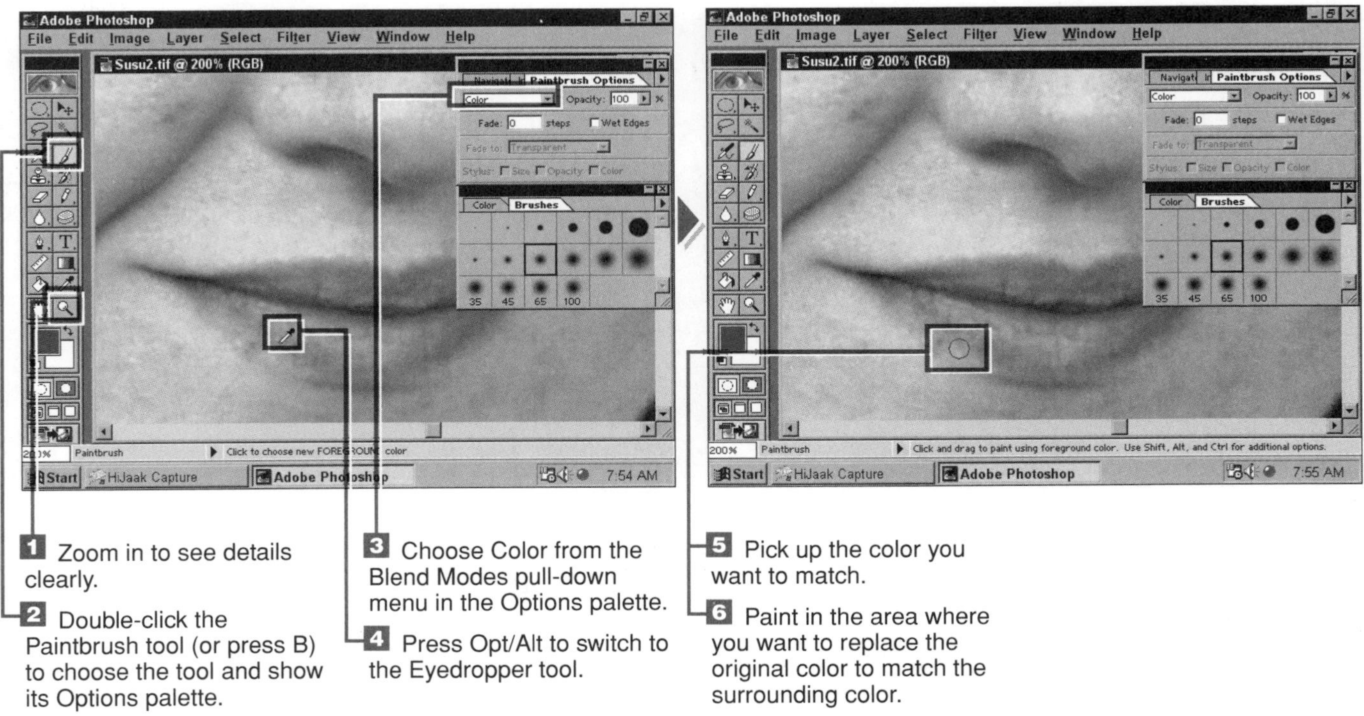

1 Zoom in to see details clearly.

2 Double-click the Paintbrush tool (or press B) to choose the tool and show its Options palette.

3 Choose Color from the Blend Modes pull-down menu in the Options palette.

4 Press Opt/Alt to switch to the Eyedropper tool.

5 Pick up the color you want to match.

6 Paint in the area where you want to replace the original color to match the surrounding color.

ADD COLOR TONE TO THE IMAGE

SINGLE-COLOR TONING

Black-and-white photography is a treasured art form that we are in danger of losing, thanks to the overwhelming popularity of color. You have the power with Photoshop, however, to instantly turn color into monochrome.

You may want to do this for several reasons, and you can use more than one way to do it. First, the reasons: Black-and-white images can strengthen composition and impact. Black-and-white images cost far less to print and load much faster on the Web. Finally, they are the perfect starting point for hand-coloring (which can be done either in Photoshop or with transparent oils).

If you plan to do hand-coloring, the basic pigment color should be the one you want to dominate in the image. This is somewhat less important if you're going to do your coloring in Photoshop, because the coloring technique will recolor the pixels. Still, making your monochrome a particular color could save you from having to hand-color everything.

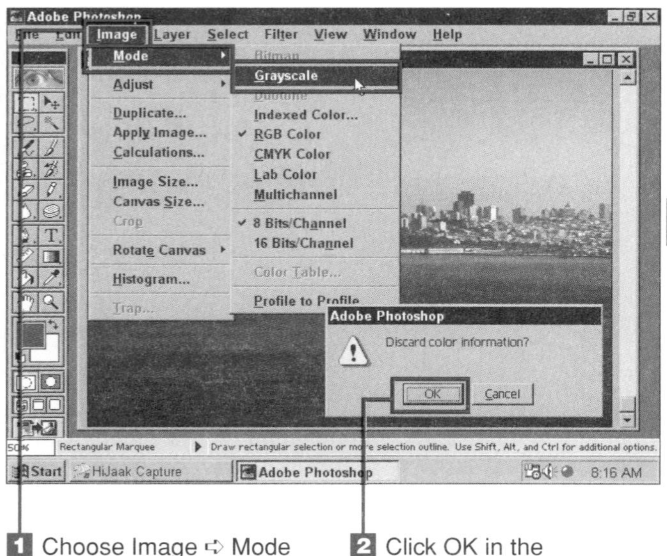

1 Choose Image ➪ Mode ➪ Grayscale.

2 Click OK in the Photoshop warning dialog box.

■ The image becomes black and white. For toning, it has to be converted back to a color mode.

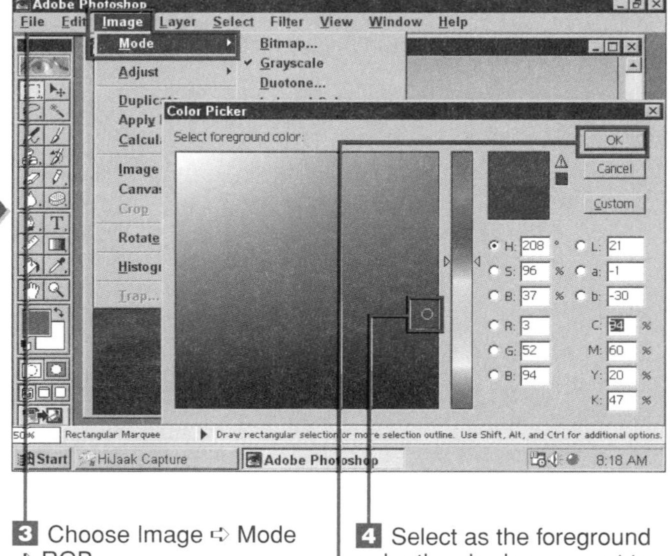

3 Choose Image ➪ Mode ➪ RGB.

4 Select as the foreground color the shade you want to use as the toning color.

5 Click OK.

TIPS

What colors are best for toned prints?

That really depends on the print. Sepia (reddish brown) and blue are the two colors most commonly used, mostly because sepia produces fairly natural-looking skin tones and blue is the color of sky and water. If you're after a special effect, anything goes.

Can I choose to tone an image with a spot color ink?

Definitely. You can choose from such leading spot color systems as Pantone, DIC, Focoltone, Toyo, and Trumatch. You can reach these color books by clicking the Custom button in the Color Picker dialog box.

Are there other ways to tone images?

There are many ways to create toned images from grayscale. One is to use a Hue/Sat adjustment layer: Choose Colorize and click the foreground color box with a preselected color to change the foreground color, or just dial the color in with the sliders. Choosing Image ➪ Mode ➪ Duotone produces a smaller file size (closer to grayscale). Finally, the Channel Mixer can be used to create toned images.

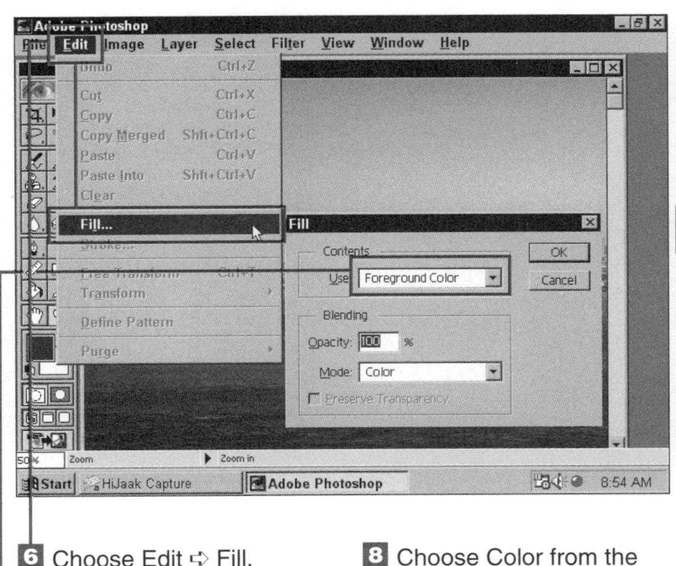

6 Choose Edit ➪ Fill.

7 Choose Foreground Color from the Use pull-down menu.

8 Choose Color from the Mode pull-down menu.

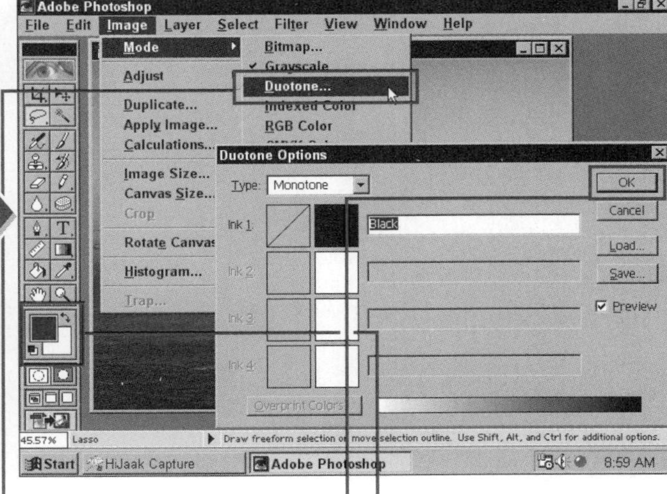

9 Starting from the color image, repeat Steps 1 and 2. The image is now Grayscale.

10 Choose Image ➪ Mode ➪ Duotone.

11 Click the color box.

12 Choose a color as in Step 4.

13 Click OK.

CONTINUED

ADD COLOR TONE TO THE IMAGE CONTINUED

MAKING DUOTONES

You can create duotones from any image, though you must first make sure that image is in Grayscale mode. Then choose Image ⇨ Mode ⇨ Duotone.

Duotones are images printed in two overlaid ink colors. The result is generally a richer tonal range than can be accomplished by printing a standard monotone image with only black ink.

Usually you create duotones because the publication in which you are going to place the image is printed in spot (custom) colors, and you want to use the same inks to print the images. Another reason to create duotones is to jazz up the otherwise grayscale images in a particular print job. However, you can create a duotone just for the effect that mixing specific inks produces, and then change back to RGB and add your own colors.

The Duotone command gives you access to monotone, duotone, tritone, and quadtone, which means you can choose as many as four colors. You can also choose the percentage of ink that will be applied at any 10 percent increment of the tonal range from highlight to shadow.

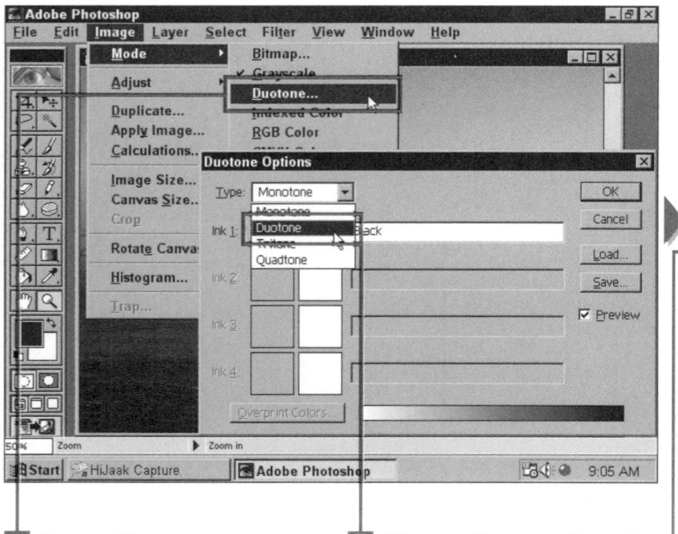

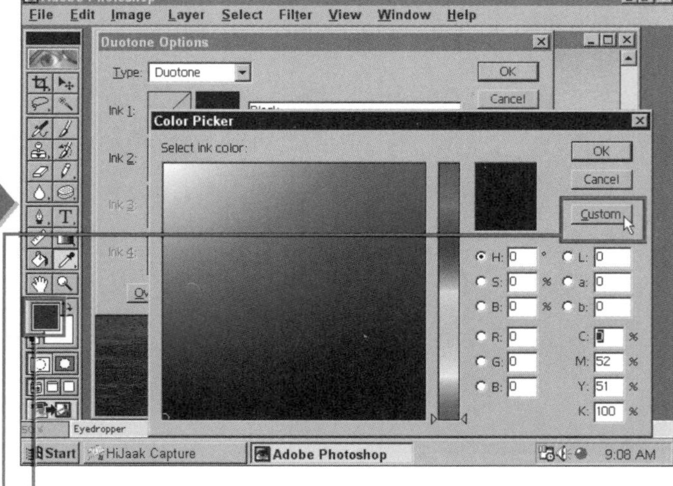

1 Start with or convert to a Grayscale image, and then choose Image ⇨ Mode ⇨ Duotone.

■ The Duotone Options dialog box appears.

2 Choose Duotone from the Type pull-down menu.

3 Click to bring up the Color Picker.

4 In the Color Picker dialog box, click to bring up the Custom Colors dialog box.

Note: You usually want Custom Colors because most duotones are printed in spot color used by other type on the page.

TIPS

Must I choose colors from color books?

No. If the Custom Colors dialog box appears first, click the Color Picker button. If you choose colors from the Color Picker, remember that they can't be printed from spot colors. However, if you're going to hand-color the image, feel free to choose colors from the Color Picker because you'll need to print in CMYK (all colors) anyway.

What if I want to use three or four colors?

The procedures are exactly the same as for a duotone, except you must choose Tritone (three colors) or Quadtone (four colors) from the Type pull-down menu in the Duotone Options dialog box.

What if I want to use more than four specific colors?

You will have to use a different method. You can create as many custom color channels as you want by choosing Image ➪ Mode ➪ Multichannel. You can use Image ➪ Adjust commands on each of many different channels.

5 Choose the Color Book you want to use.

6 Drag the slider to the required color range.

7 Click the color square to choose the second color.

8 Click OK to approve color for Ink 1, and then repeat the two previous steps for Ink 2.

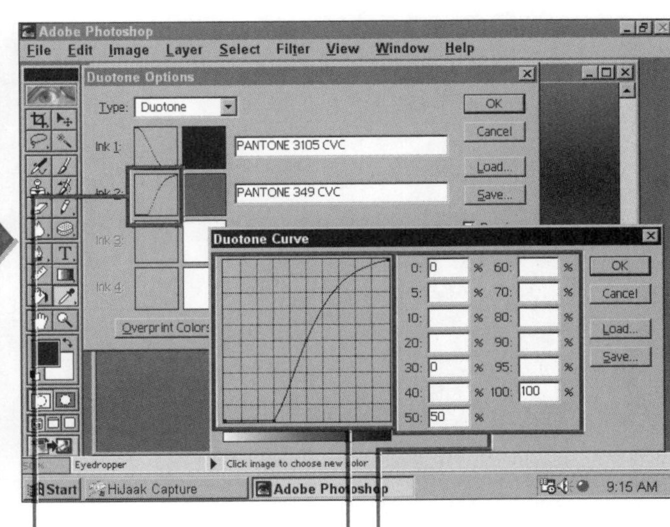

9 To alter the range of tones to which each ink will apply, click the left Ink 2 square.

■ The Duotone Curve dialog box appears. 0 = white, 100 = black.

10 Enter the percentage of ink you want to apply.

11 Or drag the curve to place a point and change the percentage.

HAND-COLOR A MONOTONE IMAGE

You're not stuck with the colors your images were born with. Photoshop provides you with several ways to recolor images. You have seen how to convert an image to grayscale and how to make duotones.

You can also recolor any selection, layer, or channel with the Edit ➪ Fill command or use the Image ➪ Adjust ➪ Replace Color command to replace all of a particular range of colors within the image.

If you want absolute control over the color of every specific area of the image, however, use hand-coloring techniques. You can hand-color any part of a full-color image, using the techniques described in this exercise. If you want a completely hand-tinted photograph, however, start with a grayscale or duotone image. Convert that image back to full color, double-click the Paintbrush tool, and pick Color from the Blend Mode pull-down menu. When you color, the original luminance and saturation stay intact. Only the color changes.

You can employ this same technique with more control by creating a new layer, say, for each basic color, setting the layer to Color mode, and painting. You can later adjust the colors according to what you grouped per layer, and you can adjust opacity.

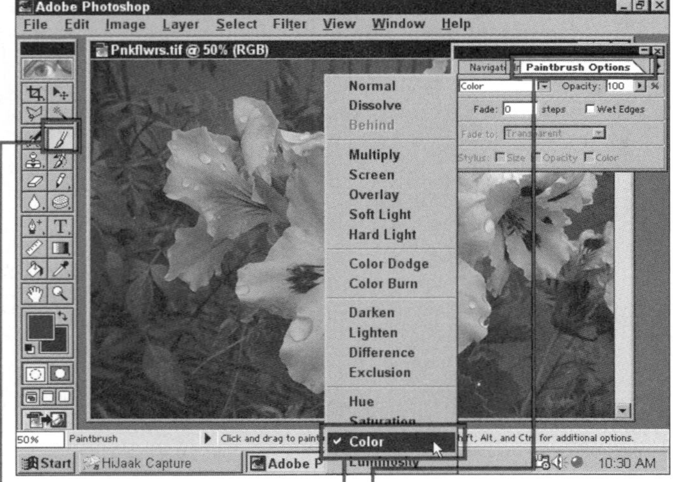

Note: The image used for this exercise was first converted to a duotone. This gives a different effect than working on a color image.

1 Click to choose a brush (Paintbrush, Airbrush, or Pencil).

2 Double-click to bring up the Paintbrush Options palette.

3 Choose Color from the Blend Mode pull-down menu.

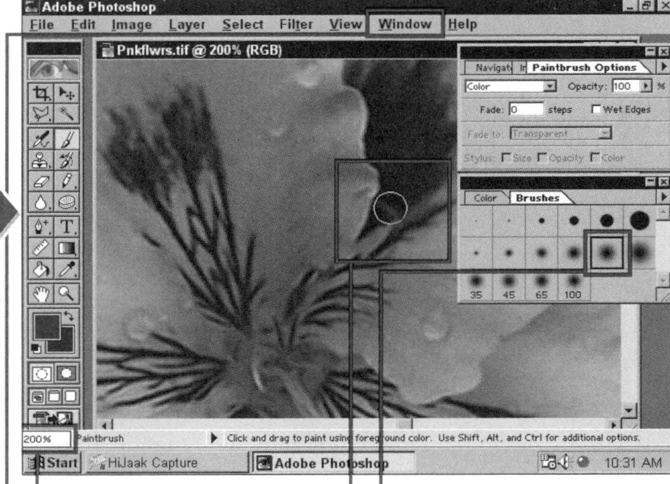

4 Zoom in to about 200 percent so you can easily see the edges you want to stay within.

5 Choose Window ➪ Show Brushes to bring up the Brushes palette.

6 Click to choose the brush size you want to work with.

7 Reselect the Paintbrush tool and paint in the area where you want to change the color.

TIPS

Sometimes boundaries are hard to see after converting to grayscale. Any way to make it easier to see what I want to select?

You make and save selections before converting to gray. You can retrieve the selections by dragging the channel mask to the Selection icon at the bottom right of the Channels palette.

Can the technique of hand-coloring be extended in any way?

Hand-coloring can also mean that you use other Blend modes that will change the colorization in the original. Remember, too, that you can set opacity for your brush, which will affect the intensity of the color you are painting with.

Is there any way to save time over constantly having to choose colors from the Color Picker?

Two suggestions: If you're recoloring an image that was formerly in color, save the image under another name as soon as you convert to monochrome. Then open the original in another window, and use the Eyedropper to pick from the original colors. If you want to stick to more basic colors, choose Window ➪ Show Swatches and pick your colors from that palette.

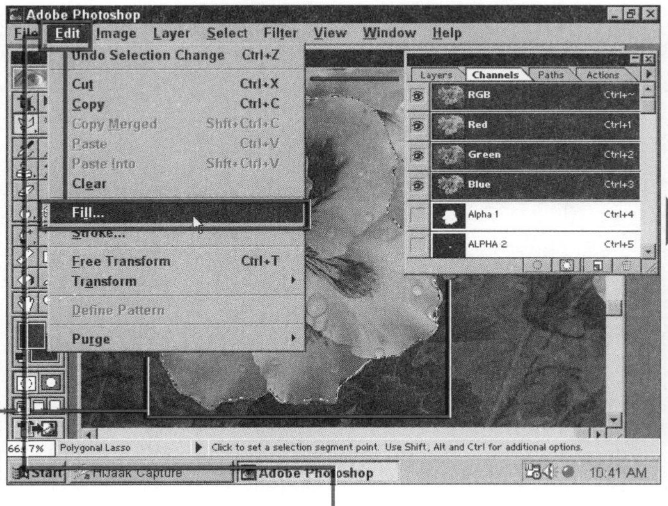

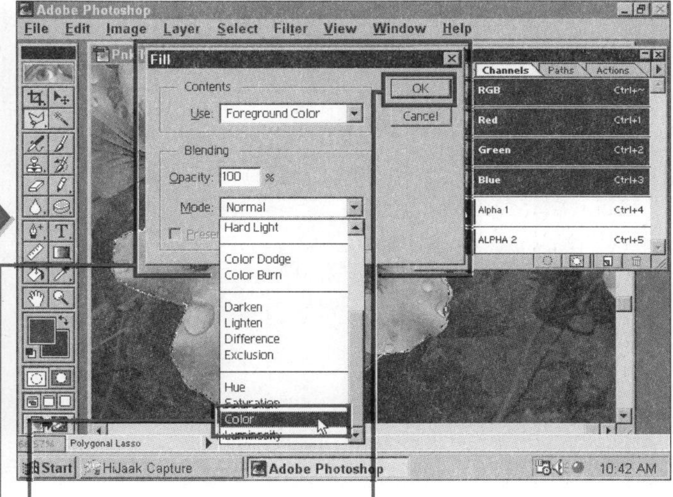

CHANGE COLOR BY FILLING A SELECTION

1 Select the area you want to fill.

2 Choose Edit ➪ Fill.

Note: If you save your selections, you will be able to change colors more quickly when you want to make other interpretations of the image.

3 Choose Color from the Mode menu.

4 Make sure other settings are at their defaults, as shown.

5 Click OK.

■ The selected area is filled with the current foreground color.

CONTROL FOCUS: BLURRING AND SHARPENING

CHANGING DEPTH OF FIELD

Often an image will be more effective if the focus is, literally, on the subject. In conventional photography, this is achieved by keeping the subject in sharp focus while throwing foreground and background objects dramatically out of focus. It is an effect known as *depth-of-field control*.

Depth of field is only controllable in-camera when the right equipment is used: a telephoto lens or a large-format camera, a wide aperture, and a camera that allows for exact focus control. Today's point-and-shoot and digital cameras generally sport wide-angle lenses, small imaging sensors (especially true of digital cameras), and automatic focusing.

Photoshop to the rescue! Thanks to the capability to precisely select any portion of the image (covered in the next chapter) and to Photoshop's Blur and Sharpen filters, you can reinvent depth of field after the fact. This layout shows you how to focus attention where you want it by blurring certain portions of the picture. (Sharpening is covered later in this chapter.)

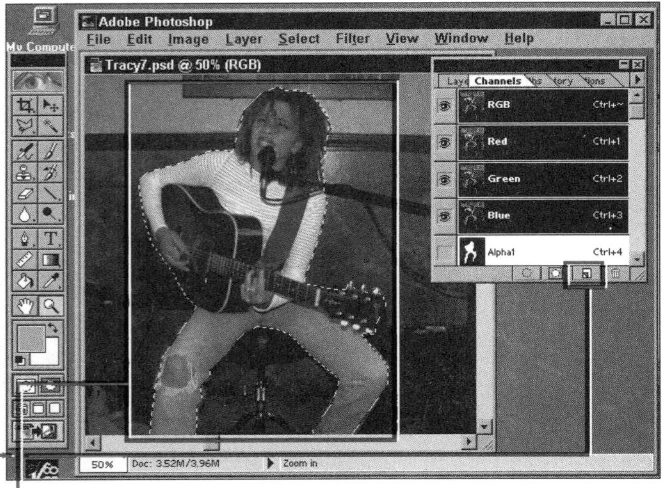

1 Select the object you want to keep in focus.

2 Save the selection as a new layer (you may want to add and subtract from it later).

Note: Refer to Chapter 7 for specific selection techniques, which will vary according to image characteristics and the type of selection needed.

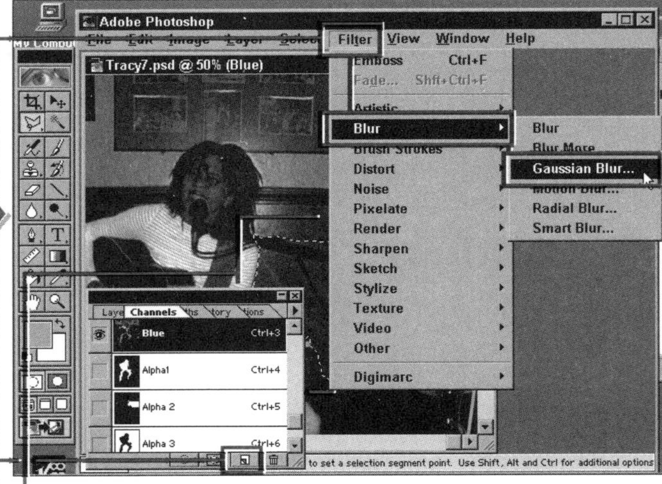

3 Select the objects close to the camera.

4 Save the selection as a new layer.

5 Choose Filter ➪ Blur ➪ Gaussian Blur.

TIPS

Is there a better way if I want to create numerous interwoven planes of focus?

If you have enough memory, which will depend on the size of your image, you can copy the image to the same number of layers as the planes of focus you desire, and then blur each layer to the desired degree of focus. Erase those parts of a given layer not at the desired level of focus. Finally, change the stacking order of the layers so that the closest objects are at the top, the most distant at the bottom.

What if I want to just slightly blur an area to smooth blemishes or give a soft portrait effect?

Although the Gaussian Blur filter seems a likely choice, you can easily overdo it with that filter. You're better off choosing Filter ⇨ Blur ⇨ Blur. The effect will be barely discernible, but you can press ⌘/Ctrl+F repeatedly until you see exactly the effect you want.

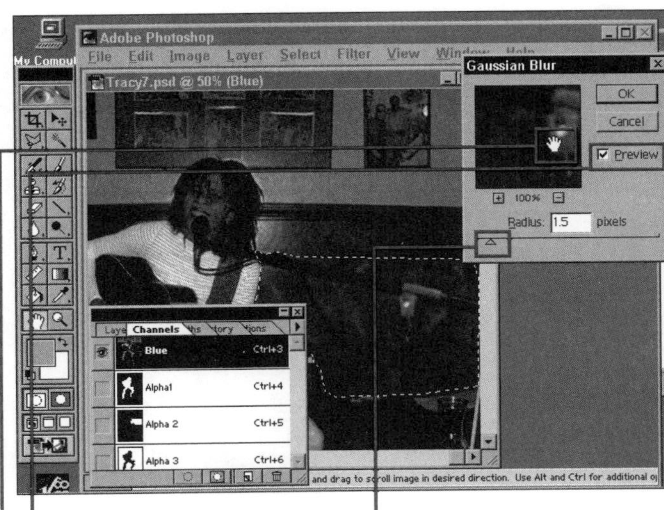

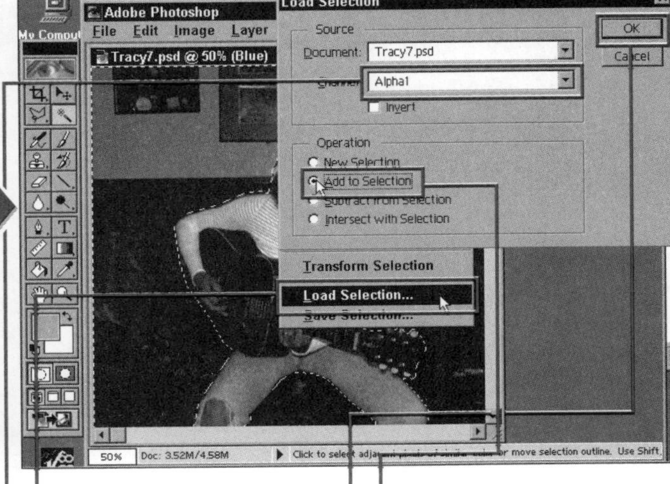

6 Click to check Preview box (if unchecked).

7 Drag in the Preview box to center area that will be defocused.

8 Drag the slider until the item is mildly blurred.

9 Choose Select ⇨ Load Selection.

10 Choose Alpha 1 (the original selection).

11 Click Add to Selection.

12 Click OK.

13 Press ⌘/Ctrl+Shift+I to Invert the Selection.

CONTINUED

CONTROL FOCUS: BLURRING AND SHARPENING CONTINUED

PUTTING IT IN MOTION: MOTION BLUR

Sometimes today's cameras — particularly the automated ones — are just too good: They freeze motion in bright light, whether you want them to or not. That's actually perfectly okay because Photoshop enables you to create as much motion blur as you like. You can even control the angle of that motion blur.

Motion blur is just a directional blur. To apply it to any selection, layer, or channel, all you need to do is choose Filter ➪ Blur ➪ Motion Blur. When the Motion Blur dialog box appears, drag a slider to indicate the degree of the blur, and drag an angle wheel to indicate the directional angle of the blur.

The example in this exercise shows you how to apply a comic-strip type blur that smears the trailing edge of an isolated object. You will be able to modify these selections and settings to create different effects.

1 Carefully select the object you wish to put in motion.

2 Press ⌘/Ctrl+C to copy the selection to the Clipboard.

3 Press ⌘/Ctrl+V to paste the object.

■ The object is now isolated on a new layer.

4 Choose Window ➪ Show Layers.

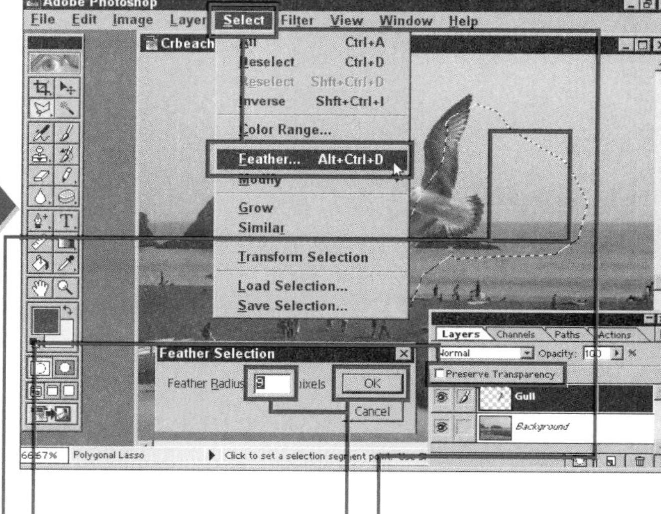

5 Make sure Preserve Transparency is unchecked.

6 Select the portion of the image within which you wish the blur to occur.

7 Choose Select ➪ Feather.

8 Enter a fairly broad range of pixels to graduate the effect.

9 Click OK.

TIPS

How do I blur the selection so that it isn't just blurred inside the selection?

Float the selection, or place it on its own, transparent layer. This also enables you to select only part of the layer, such as the trailing edge, so that the effect will look more natural. Be sure the option Preserve Transparency is unchecked; otherwise, the blur won't extend past the object itself.

How can I best combine the effects of Motion Blur and Wind?

Duplicate the layer containing the Motion Blur effect and run the Wind filter on the two layers. Then adjust the transparency of the two layers so that you get a blend of the two effects.

What if I want more of a streaked comic-strip type blur?

Try choosing Filter ➪ Stylize ➪ Wind to bring up the Wind dialog box. This effect actually streaks the image from either the left or right edge. There's no slider for continuously varying the effect, but you could scale the layer up, run the filter, and then scale it back down if the effect is too dramatic. You have no control over direction, but you can rotate the layer before applying the filter.

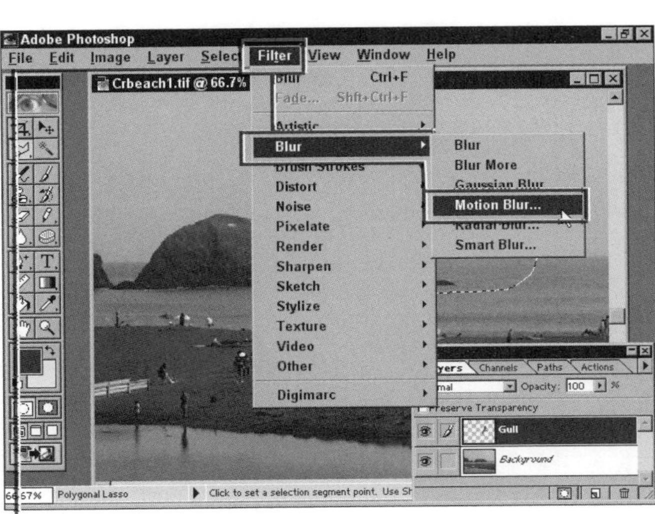

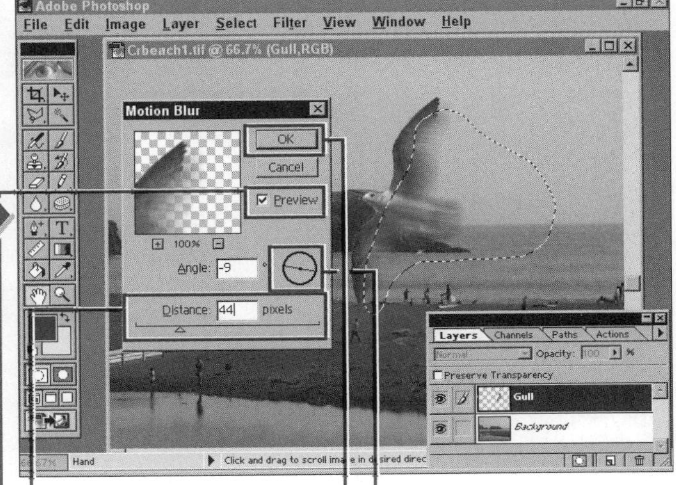

10 Choose Filter ➪ Blur ➪ Motion Blur.

■ The Motion Blur dialog box appears.

11 Drag the Distance slider until you see the degree of streaking you desire.

12 Check the Preview box if it isn't already checked.

13 Drag to indicate the angle of blur.

14 Click OK when you re happy with the result.

CONTINUED

CONTROL FOCUS: BLURRING AND SHARPENING CONTINUED

ZOOMING AND SPINNING: RADIAL BLUR

The Radial Blur filter can produce one effect that can't be produced by any camera setting (although you could do it in the darkroom by spinning the paper during the exposure of an enlargement). The other effect you can create with this filter can be produced in-camera by rapidly zooming the lens during the course of a long exposure.

Once again, Photoshop gives you a great deal more control than you would have in real life. You can use a feathered selection to freeze the center of the blur and graduate the effect. The conventional process is going to blur the center as well as the edges, although the edges are blurred more because they move a greater distance during exposure.

The three quality settings in the Radial Blur dialog box are Draft, Good, and Best. The Good and Best settings produce a fairly smooth diffusion of pixels, but processing takes significantly longer. The Draft mode is quicker, but produces the pixelization seen in the second of the four figures in this exercise.

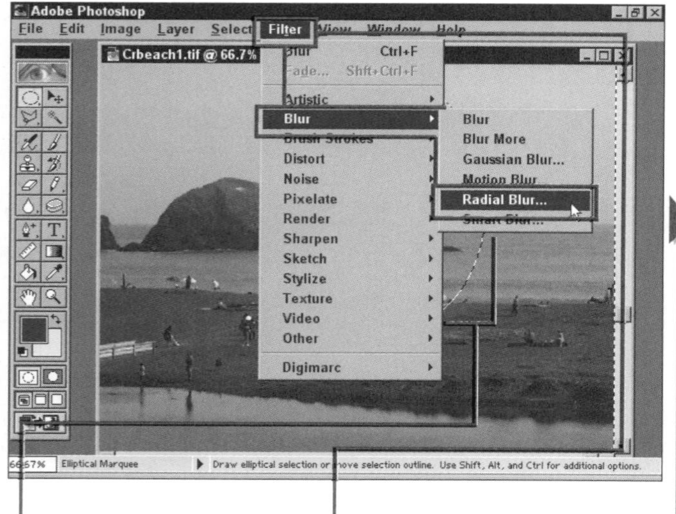

1 Use any of the Selection tools to select an area around or within the subject that you want to keep sharply focused.

2 Feather the selection for about 1/4 of the radius.

3 Press Shift+⌘/Ctrl+I to invert the selection.

4 Choose Filter ➪ Blur ➪ Radial Blur.

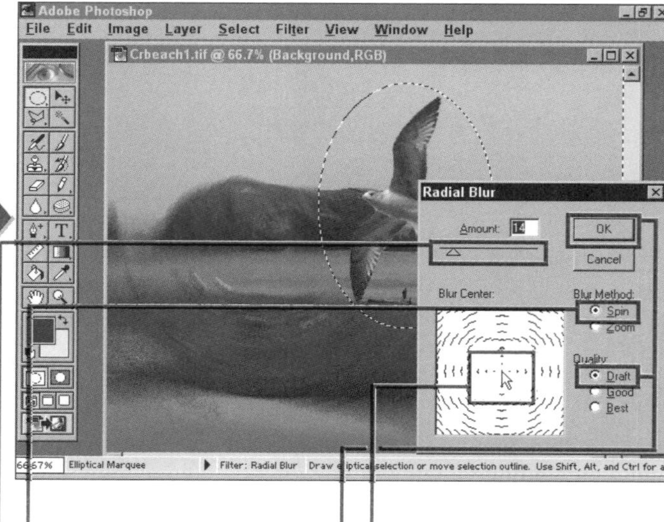

5 Click to set the Blur Method to Spin.

6 Drag the slider to set the distance the image will spin.

7 Drag the center of the Preview window to approximate the center of the spin.

8 Click to set the degree of quality.

9 Click OK.

TIPS

Is there any way to speed the processing of these filters?

The quality you choose affects the speed of the filter: The better the interpolation method, the slower the processing time. Short of that, you just have to spend the money on a dual-processor 400+ MHz machine with lots of memory.

Is there an easy way to control the blending of these effects with the information in the target image?

At last! An opportunity to mention the fact that you can use the Fade command in conjunction with all the Image ⇨ Adjust and Filter commands, as well as many other operations. Just press Shift+⌘/Ctrl+F, and the Fade dialog appears. Drag the slider until you get the desired degree of blending.

Could I use the Spin mode to make the gull's wings flap?

No problem. Select and place the gull on a separate layer. Place an elliptical selection around the gull that extends past the wing tips. Now subtract a selection from the center of the gull, so it'll stay sharp, and apply the Spin mode of the Radial Blur filter.

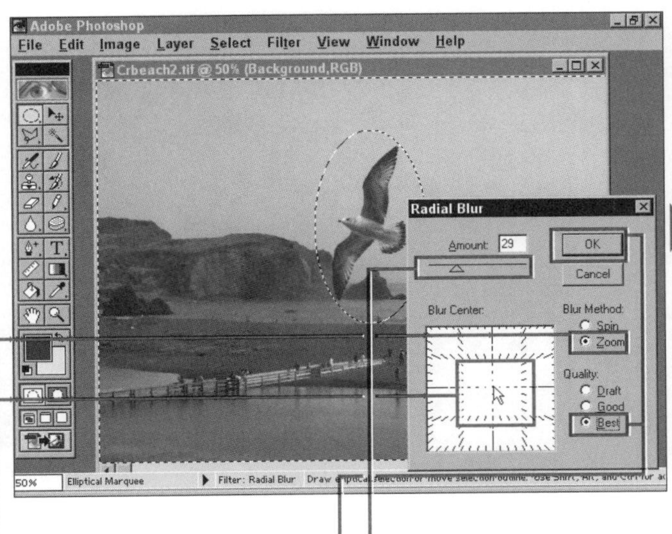

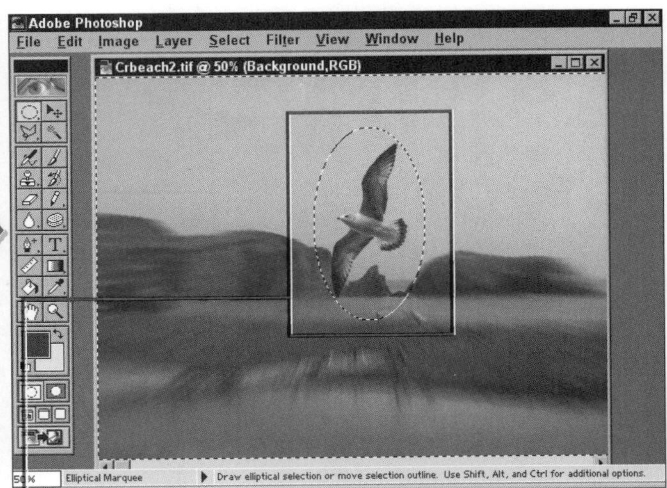

USE THE ZOOM MODE OF THE RADIAL BLUR FILTER

1 Follow Steps 1-4 from the previous example.

2 Click to set the Blur Method.

3 Drag to set the center of the zoom.

4 Drag to set the degree of zoom effect.

5 Click to set the image interpolation quality.

6 Click OK.

■ This is the way the image looks after processing at high quality. Notice that there is no scattering of pixels when compared to the second screen in this spread. Notice how dramatically attention is focused on the bird.

CONTINUED

CONTROL FOCUS: BLURRING AND SHARPENING CONTINUED

SMOOTHING WITHIN EDGES: SMART BLUR

Choosing Filter ⇨ Blur ⇨ Smart Blur enables you to blur lighter or neutral tones in the image while retaining the sharpness of darker edges. This is useful in portraits for keeping the hair, eyelashes, and pupils sharp while smoothing skin defects. It's also a nice way to keep some tonal gradations while "averaging" the neutral tones in preparation for running a special or artistic effects filter.

Four settings appear in the Smart Blur dialog box: Radius, Threshold, Quality, and Mode. Radius is the number of pixels included in the blur. If you set this number too high, the blur will encroach on the sharpness of edges. Threshold is the darkness value assigned to edges. The best results are achieved when the Radius is about half that of the Threshold.

Edge smoothness is controlled by the setting chosen from the Quality pull-down menu. Of course, higher quality affects processing speed. The Mode options enable you to trace edges: white against black or vice versa.

1 Choose Filter ⇨ Blur ⇨ Smart Blur.

■ The Smart Blur dialog box appears.

2 Click here to raise or lower magnification in the Preview window.

3 Drag to change approximate radius, or type in a number.

4 Drag to change approximate threshold value, or type in a number.

TIPS

What on earth would I use the Edge Only or Overlay Edge settings for?

Good question. If the Overlay Edges were black, this could be a nice way to outline a painting. I use the Edge Only option after copying the image to another layer. Then I invert the layer, choose Select ⇨ Color Range, set Fuzziness to a fairly low number (3–6), click the Eyedropper in the white area, and click OK. Finally, I press Shift+⌘/Ctrl+I and click the layer mask icon at the bottom of the Layers palette. Bingo! The original image is seen through the outline.

Can Smart Blur be used to make it easier to create selections?

Yes, especially when it comes to automated selection tools such as the Magic Wand and Magnetic Lasso and Pen, which can be easily thrown off-track by texture irregularities. Make an extra layer, select it, set Smart Blur Threshold and Radius at fairly high numbers, and click OK. Make your automated masks in that layer and save them. Then delete the layer and use the masks wherever they're needed.

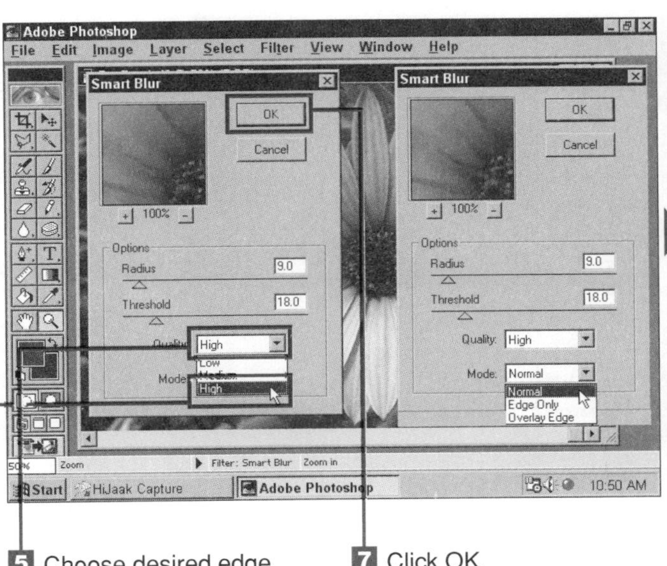

5 Choose desired edge smoothness from the Quality pull-down menu.

6 Choose Edge-Tracing mode from the Mode pull-down menu.

7 Click OK.

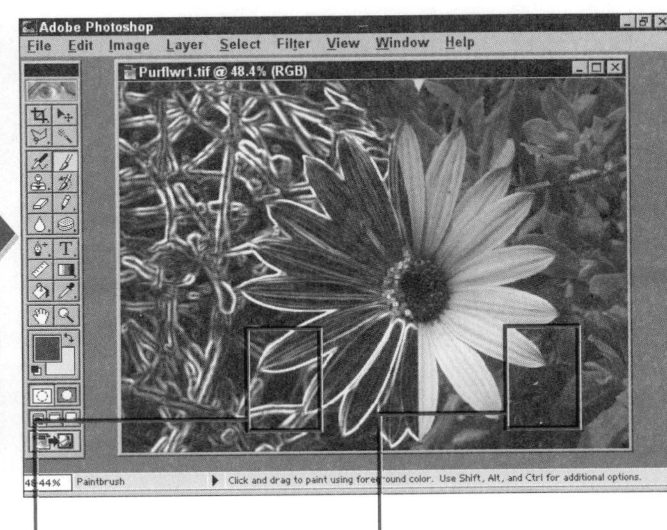

■ The left side of the image shows Edge Only tracing.

■ The right side of the image shows the result of the settings made in the previous screens.

CONTINUED

CONTROL FOCUS: BLURRING AND SHARPENING CONTINUED

USING PRESET SHARPENING FILTERS

Although Photoshop will do a passable job of throwing portions of the image out of focus, there's not much it can do to rescue hopelessly fuzzy ones. On the other hand, if your camera optics aren't up to Carl Zeiss standards or you were a little nervous when you pressed the shutter button, you're in several kinds of luck. Not only can you make the image crisper, but you can also be selective about it.

The preset Sharpen filters are Sharpen, Sharpen More, and Sharpen Edges. Using them involves nothing more than choosing them from the menu. You can, however, intensify their effect by pressing ⌘/Ctrl+F to repeat their application. Watch the image carefully while doing this. The second it becomes too harsh, press ⌘/Ctrl+Z to undo the last application.

Sharpen and Sharpen More work by simply increasing the contrast between adjacent pixels. Sharpen edges increases contrast only where pixels pass a certain contrast threshold.

■ This is the original portrait at 100 percent zoom. As you can see, it s a little soft.

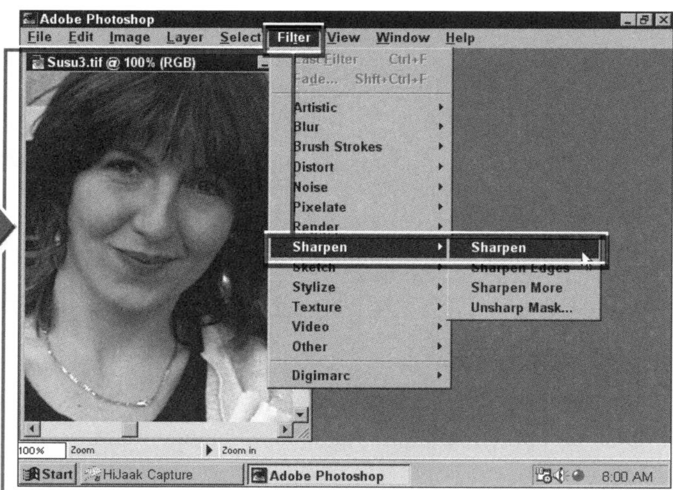

USE THE SHARPEN FILTER

1 Choose Filter ➪ Sharpen ➪ Sharpen.

■ The result appears almost immediately. There is no dialog box for setting options.

TIPS

Can I sharpen only part of the image without having to make a selection?

Photoshop makes this easy. Choose the Eraser and then double-click its icon to bring up the Options palette. Click to check the Erase to History box and drag the Opacity slider to about 50 percent. Now you can scrub areas of the image back to the original.

What if I can't get enough control by repeatedly applying the filter and then undoing?

If the closest you can get is either a bit too hard or a bit too soft, use the Fade Last command. (Fade Last will actually name the last "fade-able" command you executed.) Drag the slider in the resultant dialog box until you see the effect you want.

Is there a way to control the focus of very small areas without resorting to making a zillion selections?

Yes — use the Focus Brushes in the Toolbar. The Sharpen brush sharpens within the area covered by the chosen brush. The Blur tool has the opposite effect. You can intensify either by repeatedly stroking the same area.

■ Here's the same portrait after one pass with the Sharpen More filter. The effect can be a bit much. Notice the jaggies in the model's hair.

2 Choose Filter ⇨ Sharpen ⇨ Sharpen More.

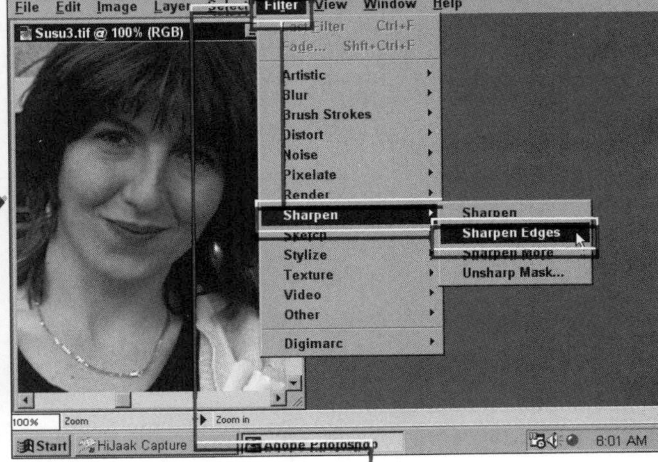

■ Here's the same portrait after one pass with the Sharpen Edges filter. This is a pretty good quick fix. Lashes, hair, and necklace appear to be in sharp focus, but the skin is still soft and realistic looking.

3 Choose Filter ⇨ Sharpen ⇨ Sharpen Edges.

CONTINUED

CONTROL FOCUS: BLURRING AND SHARPENING CONTINUED

CONTROLLING SHARPNESS WITH THE UNSHARP MASK

The Unsharp Mask filter lets you balance the sharpening of edges (where dissimilarly colored pixels meet) and the sharpening or blurring of the rest of the image. Exactly how it works depends on how you set the Amount, Radius, and Threshold settings in the dialog box.

Understanding the Amount setting is easy: Set it for the desired degree of overall sharpening. The other two settings sound similar to settings found on some other filters, but they behave differently. Radius controls the thickness of edges. Higher values produce more overall image sharpness; lower values soften neutral tones and exaggerate the edges. Threshold determines the degree of contrast that must exist between neighboring pixels before they will be sharpened.

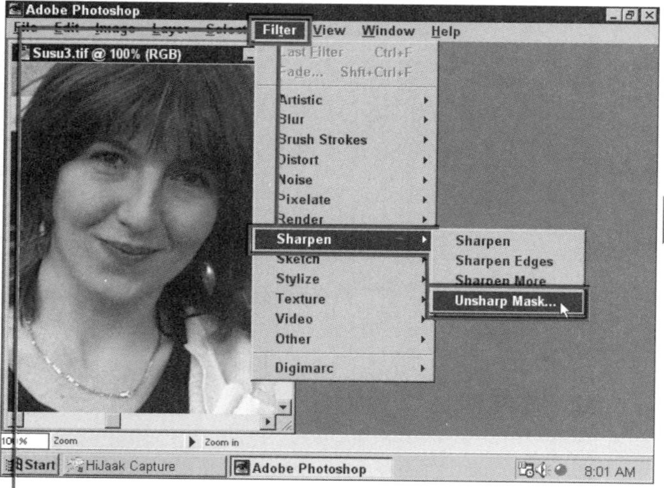

1 Choose Filter ➪ Sharpen ➪ Unsharp Mask.

■ The Unsharp Mask dialog box appears.

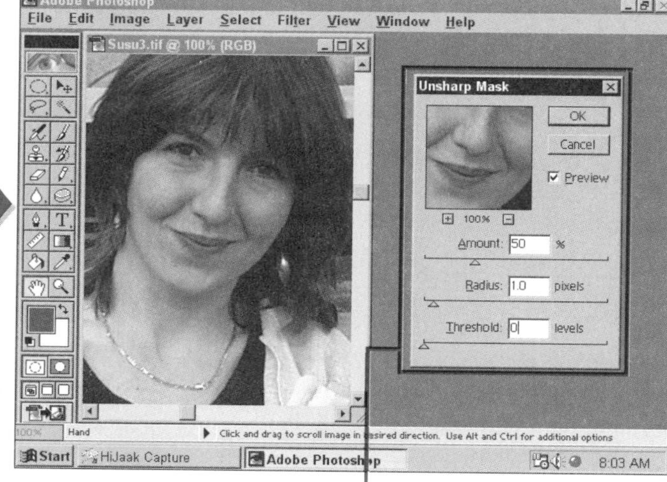

Note: Unlike the other sharpening filters, Unsharp Mask has a Preview window and Preview check box for interactive previewing of the entire image. It's a good idea to preview at 100 percent magnification so you can see the exact settings.

■ These are the default settings. Probably 90 percent of the time they will work best for your situation, in which case you can just click OK.

TIPS 

What is the most frequent application for the Unsharp Mask filter?

Transformations, image resizing, and filters can all cause the image to be resampled. Resampling can scramble some pixels, causing an overall softening of the image. You can usually fix this by running the Unsharp Mask filter.

What's the best way to experiment with this filter?

Keep the settings low and repeat the execution of the filter until you get an effect that's just slightly overdone. Then Undo (⌘/Ctrl+Z) to move back a step.

What settings are usually the most successful?

The answer depends on the contrast and colors in your image as well as the overall resolution of the image. The higher the image resolution, the higher the settings need to be. Having said that, you usually want to keep the numbers low: Amount below 150 percent, Threshold and Radius between 0 and 2. For prepress work (images that are to be screened and printed), it is generally recommended that you slightly oversharpen from what you think looks good on your screen.

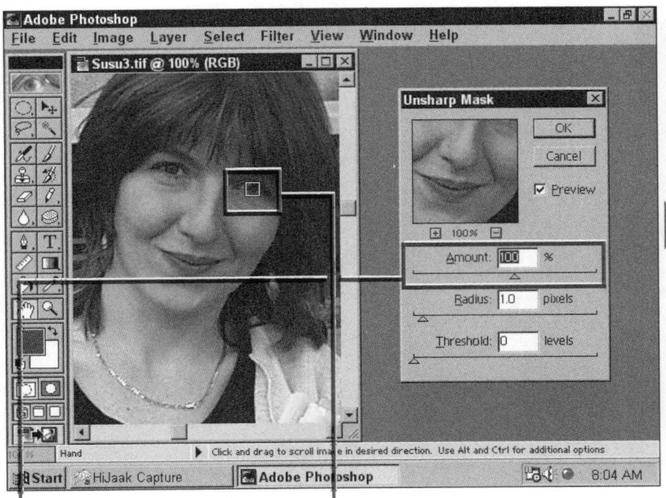

2 Drag to determine the degree of overall sharpening.

■ Note the increase in sharpening in the skin areas.

■ Moving the cursor into the image area produces a square cursor.

3 Click the square cursor to center the Preview window.

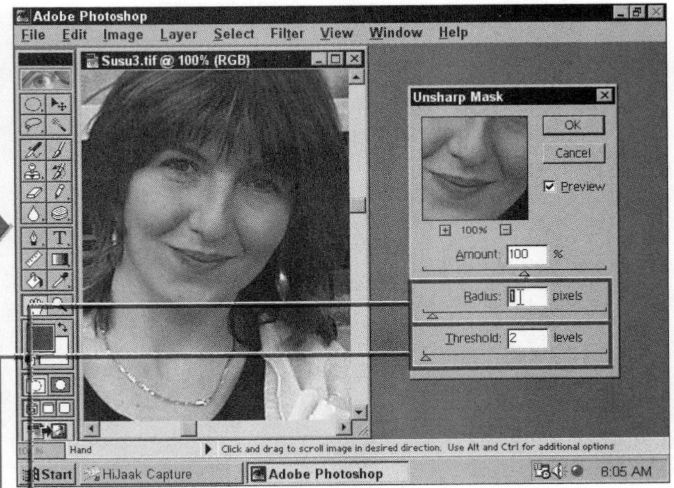

4 Drag the Radius slider to adjust thickness of edges and overall contrast.

5 Drag the Threshold slider to specify brightness contrast between pixels before they are considered edges.

Note: You can also type exact numbers into the Radius and Threshold entry fields.

ELIMINATE ARTIFACTS FROM COMPRESSED IMAGES

The popularity of digital cameras and the Web have resulted in our having to deal with many compressed images. Compression sacrifices accuracy of detail and color for efficiency of storage. The visible results are blotchiness in midtones and shadows and pixelated highlights near edges. These pixel aberrations are called *artifacts*.

This exercise deals with four techniques for minimizing artifacts, all of which involve blurring some aspect of the image: 1) Converting to LAB color and blurring a chosen channel. 2) Adding a blurry layer and applying the Color Blend mode. 3) Blurring the blue channel. 4) Using the Blur brush to smooth any artifacts you may have missed with the other techniques.

You will probably want to use all of these techniques on the same image to get the best effect, although at times one of these techniques will do the job.

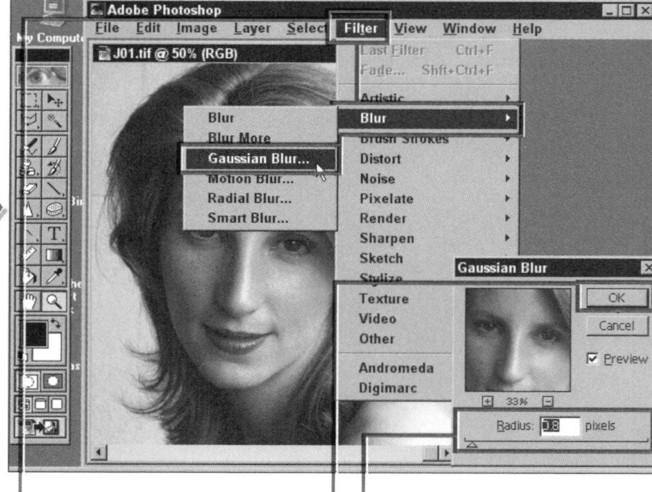

BLURRING A NEW LAYER

1 Drag the background layer to the New Layer icon.

2 Double-click the background layer copy name.

■ The Layer Options palette appears.

3 Enter a new, descriptive name for the layer.

4 Choose Filter ➪ Blur ➪ Gaussian Blur.

Note: You could choose Blur or Blur More, but Gaussian Blur gives you more control.

5 Enter a small pixel radius (or drag the slider).

6 Click OK.

TIPS

What's with using Lab mode for getting rid of artifacts?

Lab is actually Photoshop's native mode, used for converting images from Color mode to Color mode. If the artifacts are the same level of lightness, they can be blended in any channel without affecting sharpness, which is defined by the brightness (L) channel.

In RGB mode, why does blurring the blue channel help to eliminate artifacts?

The blue channel tends to exhibit more artifacts than the other channels, so if you blur the blue channel slightly, you'll kill many artifacts without having much effect on overall sharpness.

Should I use the Unsharp Mask filter after performing all these steps?

Sometimes it helps, and sometimes it takes you right back to where you started. Don't try it until you've saved your work. This way you can choose File ➪ Revert if you're not happy with the results.

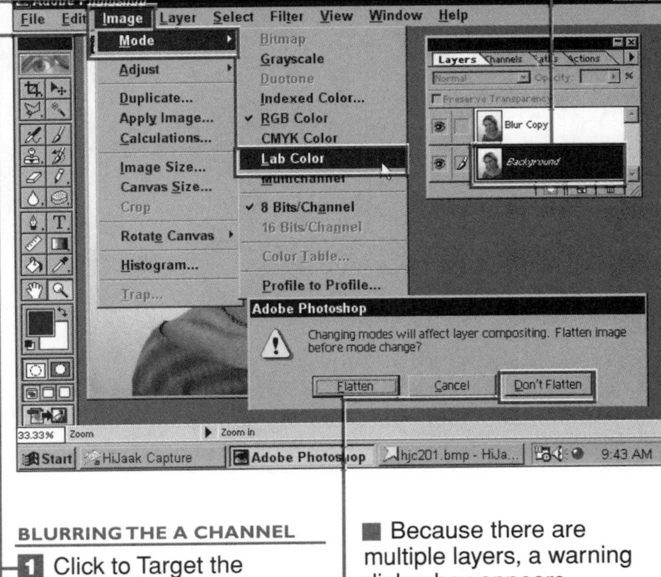

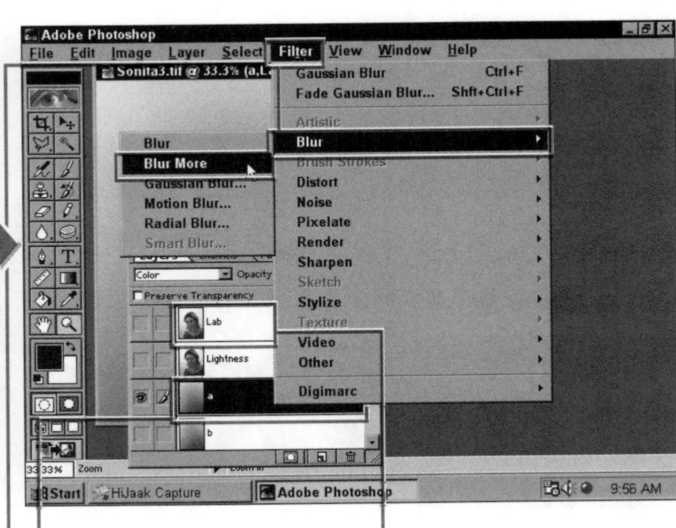

BLURRING THE A CHANNEL

1 Click to Target the background layer.

2 Choose Image ➪ Mode ➪ Lab Color.

■ Because there are multiple layers, a warning dialog box appears.

3 Click Don't Flatten.

■ You are now in Lab Color mode.

4 Click to target the A channel.

5 Choose Filter ➪ Blur ➪ Blur More.

6 Click to target the Lab channel.

■ You should now see the results of your efforts up to this point. Unless you want to perform other operations in Lab mode, choose Image ➪ Mode ➪ RGB color.

ELIMINATE MORE ARTIFACTS

This exercise picks up where the preceding exercise left off, demonstrating the latter two of the four techniques mentioned: blurring the blue channel, and using the Blur brush to smooth any artifacts you might have missed with the other techniques.

Blurring the blue channel in an RGB image is often an easy way to eliminate most scanning and digital camera artifacts because the blue channel tends to show artifacts more prominently. At the same time, blurring the blue channel does little to distort our perception of the end result.

BLURRING THE BLUE CHANNEL

Note: Make sure the background layer is still targeted.

1 Click to target the blue channel.

■ The blue channel image appears in the workspace. You can clearly see the edges of artifacts in this channel, so slight blurring will minimize the effect without blurring the overall image.

2 Choose Filter ⇨ Blur ⇨ Blur More (or, if you haven t used another filter in the meantime, press ⌘/Ctrl+F to repeat the Blur More filter).

3 Click to target the RGB channel.

■ You now see the result of what you have done. At this point, virtually all artifacts should have disappeared. You may still have some streaking near highly contrasting edges. If so, continue on.

TIPS

Why can't I just blur the whole image and then use the Sharpen Edges filter.

Because you'll probably end up with something that looks worse than the image you started with. Some of the most bizarre edges may be overemphasized. Try it if you like to go in search of "happy accidents," but be sure to do it on a duplicate copy of your image.

Wouldn't some of the retouching methods help in getting rid of artifacts?

You bet. Often, the really objectionable artifacts are limited to small areas anyway. So you don't need to go through all the steps outlined in these two spreads. Just clone, blur, or use any other retouching technique to get rid of them.

If the artifacts are limited to a few shadow areas and the detail doesn't matter anyway, can't I just blur the whole area with a filter?

Yes, this is another technique that works well in certain situations. Two caveats: Be sure to feather the edges of your selections so that the blurring blends. And be sure to use the Add Noise filter on the same selection to match the grain in the rest of the image.

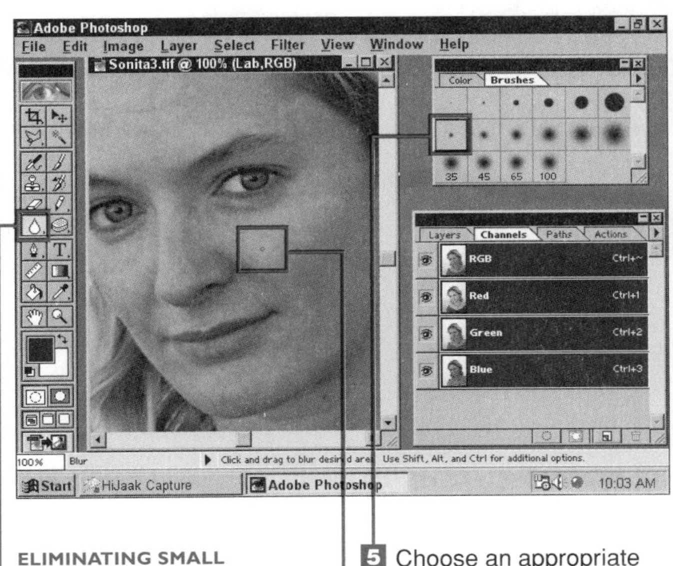

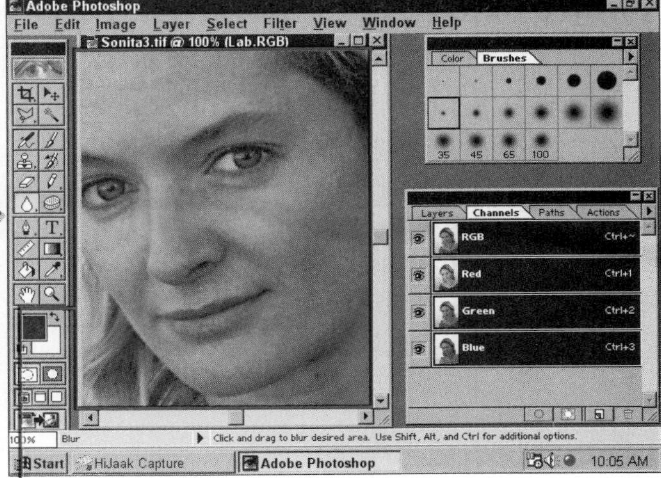

ELIMINATING SMALL ARTIFACTS WITH THE BLUR BRUSH

4 Click to choose the Blur tool.

5 Choose an appropriate brush size with some feathering.

6 Scrub to blend rough borders.

■ This image is now artifact free. Brush retouching required only a few strokes and took only about five minutes.

14 Creating Textures with Photoshop

One of the principal professional uses for Photoshop is creating textures, most often used as backgrounds or combined with other images to give greater depth and a more textured feel. There is also a whole industry of folks who create textures in Photoshop to be used as object surfaces in 3D modeling and animation applications.

Textures can be anything from natural surfaces — such as skin, paper, and concrete — to computer-generated patterns of all sorts. There are a multitude of ways for creating textures: take a texture out of a photograph, scan a surface, use a pattern-making filter, or use a texture-making tool such as Real Texture Tools from CGSD, Terrazzo from Xaos Tools, and the Texture Explorer in Kai's Power Tools.

All these techniques are explored in this chapter. Here I concentrate on the making of textures by using some of Photoshop's resident filters specific to this task. (Many of Photoshop's other filters also create texture-like effects. Refer to the color section in this book to see their effects.)

Topics covered in this chapter include the following:

- Using texture filters
- Using Craquelure texture
- Using Grain texture
- Making mosaic tiles
- Making a patchwork quilt
- Making stained glass
- Using the Texturizer textures
- Creating new textures from photos
- Making seamless pattern and texture tiles

Craquelure Filter

Craquelure is a stucco-like texture that is also useful for making artwork resemble old, cracked paintings. Its dialog box, shown in the following figure, is accessed by selecting Filter ➪ Texture ➪ Craquelure.

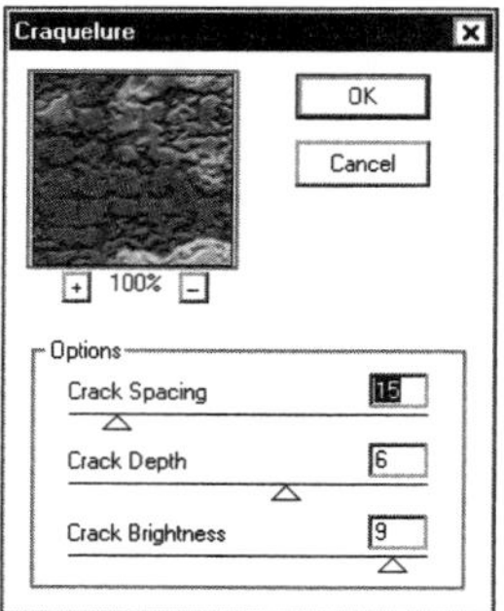

Craquelure Filter Dialog Box Contents

Component	Function
Crack Spacing slider and field	Drag left to narrow or right to widen the width of the cracks. You can also enter a number directly into the field.

Component	Function
Crack Depth slider and field	Drag left to heighten or right to deepen the cracks. Cracks get darker in color, and highlights and shadows on the edges of the cracks become more pronounced as cracks get deeper. You can also enter a number directly into the field.
Crack Brightness slider and field	Drag left to brighten or right to darken the cracks. You can also enter a number directly into the field.

Grain Filter

The Grain filter dialog box, depicted here, actually lets you choose between film grain and several other similar effects: Soft, Sprinkles, Clumped, Contrasty, Enlarged, Stippled, Horizontal, Vertical, and Speckle. Sliders control the intensity and contrast of the effect. To access the Grain filter, select Filter ⇨ Texture ⇨ Grain.

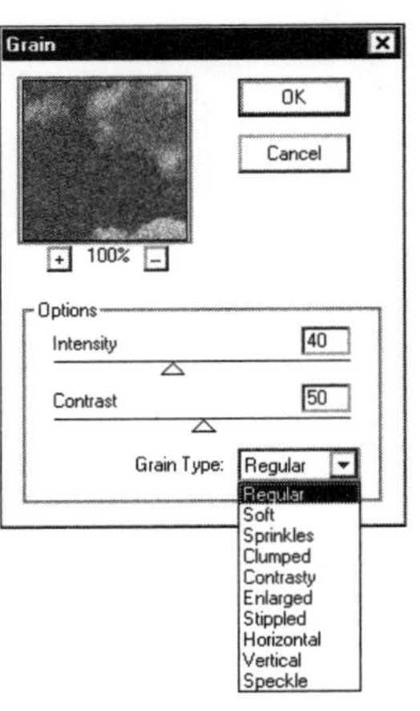

Grain Filter Dialog Box Contents

Component	Function
Intensity slider	Drag left to minimize or right to maximize the size of the grain clumps. You can also enter a number (between 0 and 100) directly into the field.
Contrast slider	Drag left to narrow or right to widen the width of the clumps. You can also enter a number (between 0 and 100) directly into the field.
Grain Type pdm	Choose between any of ten different grain patterns.

Mosaic Tiles Filter

The Mosaic Tiles texture gives images a cool effect, similar to the Craquelure filter and reminiscent of cobblestone. To access the Mosaic Tiles filter dialog box, as shown here, select Filter ⇨ Texture ⇨ Mosaic Tiles.

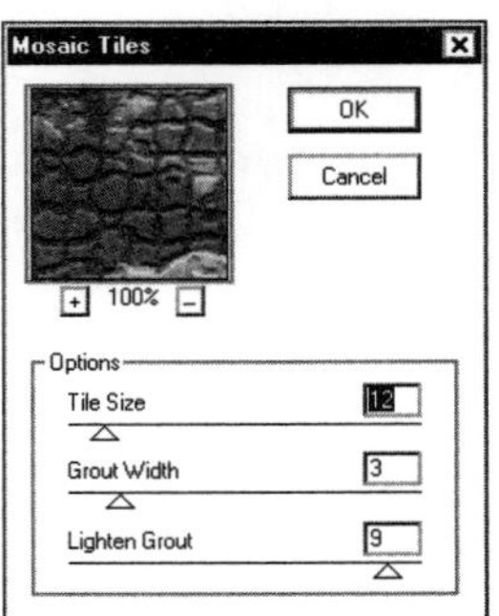

CONTINUED

CREATING TEXTURES WITH PHOTOSHOP CONTINUED

Mosaic Tiles Filter Dialog Box Contents

Component	Function
Tile Size slider and field	Drag left to narrow or right to widen the width of the tiles. You can also enter a number directly into the field.
Grout width slider and field	Drag left to heighten or right to deepen the space between the tiles. The grout (area between tiles) gets darker in color, and highlights and shadows on the edges of the cracks become more pronounced as the cracks gets deeper. You can also enter a number directly into the field.
Lighten Grout slider and field	Drag left to brighten or right to darken the grout. You can also enter a number directly into the field.

Patchwork Filter

If you ever need to create a view through a screen or a net, the Patchwork filter might do the trick. This texture makes an image look similar to a mosaic with tiny square tiles. To access the Patchwork filter dialog box, as shown in the following figure, select Filter ➪ Texture ➪ Patchwork.

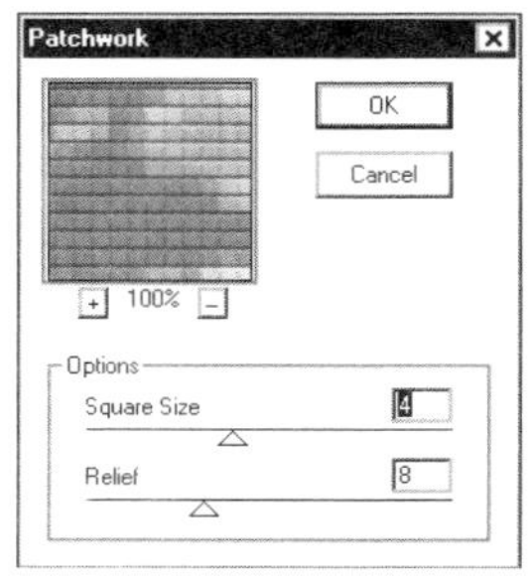

Patchwork Filter Dialog Box Contents

Component	Function
Square Size slider and field	Drag left to shrink or right to enlarge the size of the tiles. You can also enter a number directly into the field.
Relief slider and field	Drag left to heighten or right to deepen the space between the tiles. The grout (area between tiles) gets darker in color and highlights and shadows on the edges of the cracks become more pronounced as cracks get deeper. You can also enter a number directly into the field.

Stained Glass Filter

The Mosaic Tiles and Patchwork effects may not look much like their namesakes, but Stained Glass resembles the real thing. Each cell is a solid color, and the individual pieces of "glass" are of different sizes and shapes. To access the Stained Glass filter, as shown here, select Filter ➪ Texture ➪ Stained Glass.

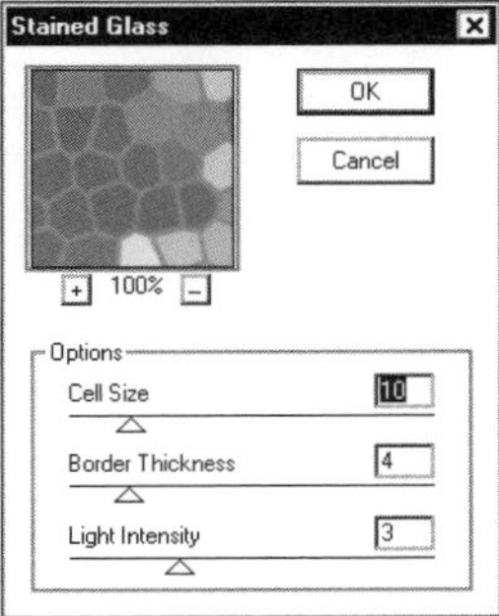

Stained Glass Filter Dialog Box Contents

Component	Function
Cell Size slider and field	Drag left to shrink or right to enlarge the size of the panes of colored glass. You can also enter a number directly into the field.
Border Thickness slider and field	Drag left to shrink or right to enlarge the width of the space between the panes of glass. You can also enter a number directly into the field.
Light Intensity slider and field	Drag the slider or enter a number to determine which panes of colored glass should appear dark and which should appear light. (Zoom out and experiment with this one.)

Texturizer Filter

At the bottom of the Filter ⇨ Texture menu is Texturizer, which comes with premade textures Canvas, Burlap, and Sandstone. The following figure shows the Texturizer filter dialog box.

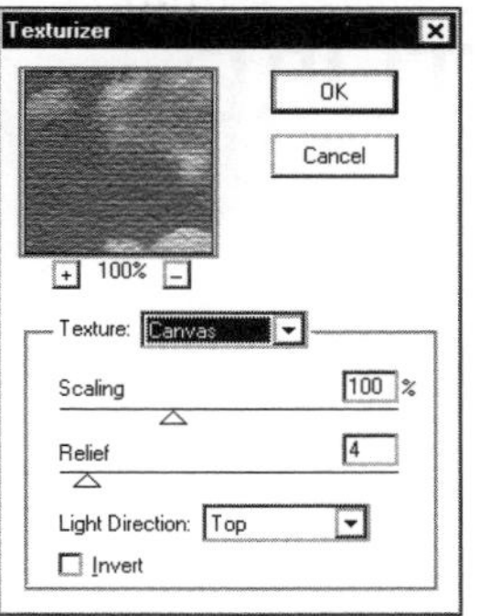

Texturizer Filter Dialog Box Contents

Component	Function
Texture pull-down menu	You can load any texture of your own from this menu or use one of the three built-in textures: Burlap, Canvas, or Sandstone.
Scaling slider and field	Enlarges or reduces the percentage of magnification of the texture file.
Relief slider and field	Makes the texture appear to be more or less pronounced by increasing the contrast between highlights and shadows in the texture file.
Light Direction pull-down menu	Changes the apparent direction of the light falling on the texture pattern. Choices are Bottom, Bottom Left, Top Left, Top, Top Right, Right, and Bottom Right.
Invert check box	If checked, reverses the highlight and shadow areas of the texture.

CONTINUED

CREATING TEXTURES WITH PHOTOSHOP CONTINUED

Offset Filter

Use the Offset filter to shift your image horizontally or vertically. To access the Offset filter dialog box, depicted here, select Filter ➪ Other ➪ Offset.

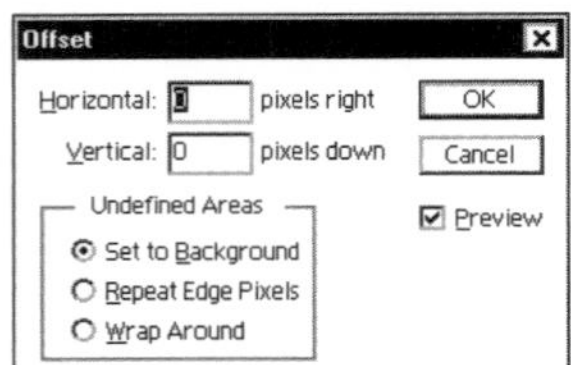

Offset Filter Dialog Box Contents

Component	Function
Horizontal offset field	Enter any number to shift the selected image that number of pixels to the right.
Vertical offset field	Enter any number to shift the selected image that number of pixels down.
Set to Background radio button	If selected, fills area vacated after the shift with the background color.
Repeat Edge Pixels radio button	If selected, fills area vacated after the shift by repeating the row of pixels at the outermost edges of the selection in the direction of the offset(s). Usually creates a streaked look.
Wrap Around radio button	If selected, fills area vacated after the shift with the pixels that were moved outside the selection by the shift.
Preview check box	If checked, results occur immediately in the workspace (file window).

APPLY TEXTURE FILTERS

The Photoshop built-in texture filters impose a textured pattern on the active image layer. There are six texture filters available by selecting Filter ⇨ Texture: Craquelure, Grain, Mosaic Tiles, Patchwork, Stained Glass, and Texturizer.

Texturizer enables you to use any pattern you can make in a grayscale file. Settings for the individual filters in this group are covered later in this chapter.

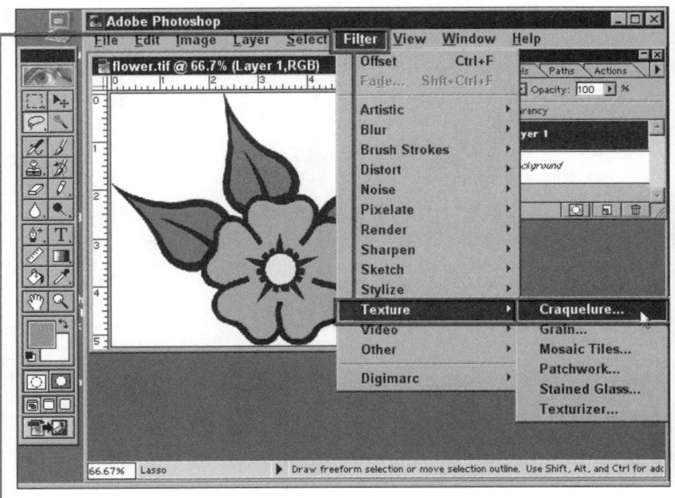

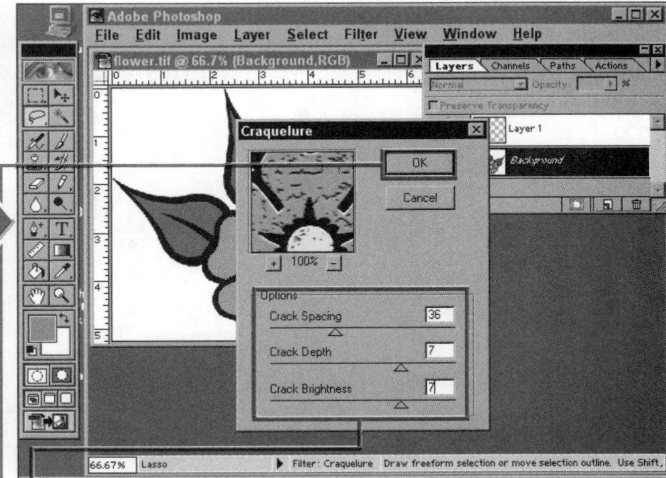

1 Choose Filter ⇨ Texture ⇨ Craquelure, Grain, Mosaic Tiles, Patchwork, or Stained Glass.

■ The dialog box for the filter you choose appears.

2 Adjust the sliders in the dialog box.

3 Click OK when you're satisfied with what you see in the preview windows.

Note: The following exercises show you how to adjust the sliders for each of the five filter dialog boxes, as well as the result of such changes on the same image.

APPLY CRAQUELURE TEXTURE

Craquelure is a stucco-like texture that is also useful for making artwork look like old, cracked paintings. This filter, like many other texture filters, tends to obscure fine details, such as single-pixel lines.

The Crack Spacing slider adjusts the spacing between cracks from almost invisible to very widely spaced. For an ancient oil-on-canvas look, try a medium-low setting. Crack Depth has to do with the width of the shadow cast into the cracks. Crack Brightness controls the difference between the brightness of the main surface and that of the cracks in between.

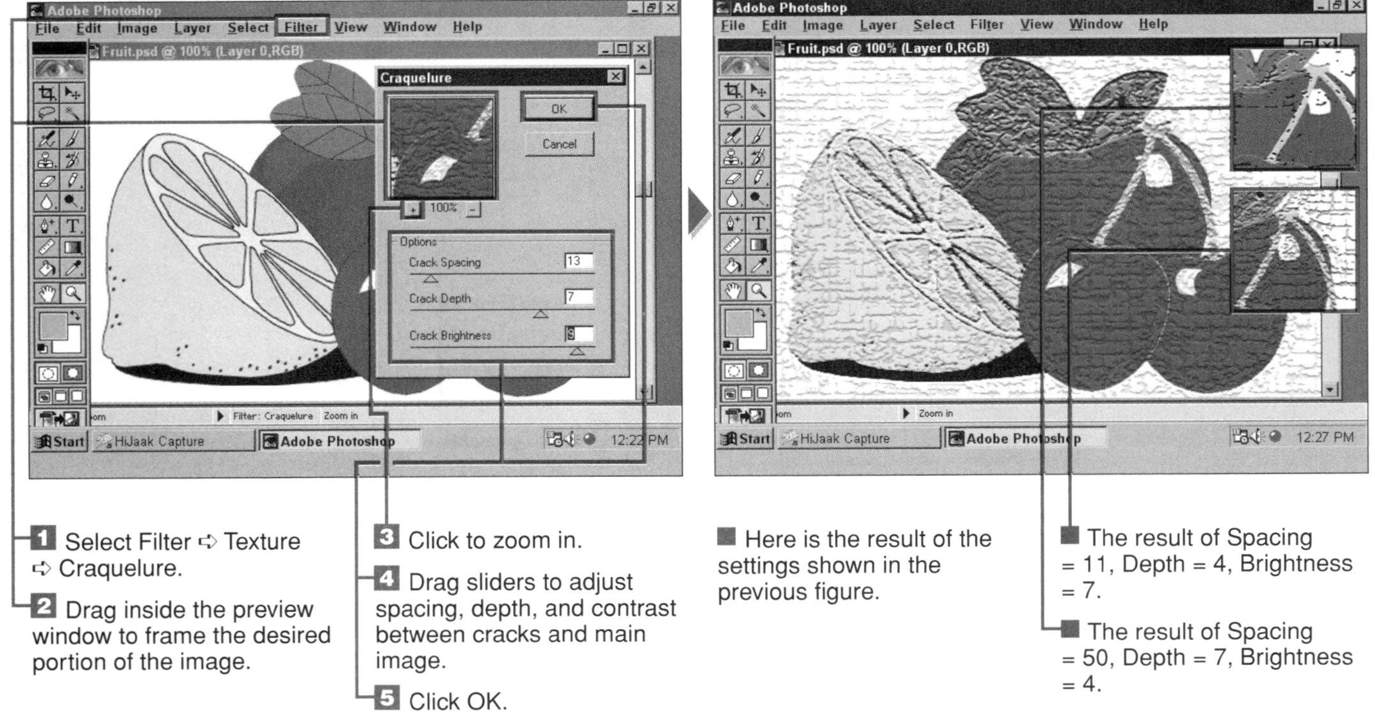

1 Select Filter ➪ Texture ➪ Craquelure.

2 Drag inside the preview window to frame the desired portion of the image.

3 Click to zoom in.

4 Drag sliders to adjust spacing, depth, and contrast between cracks and main image.

5 Click OK.

■ Here is the result of the settings shown in the previous figure.

■ The result of Spacing = 11, Depth = 4, Brightness = 7.

■ The result of Spacing = 50, Depth = 7, Brightness = 4.

APPLY GRAIN TEXTURE

The Grain texture actually lets you choose between film grain (an excellent way to match film grain in images composited from different photos with different grain patterns) and several other grainy effects: Soft, Sprinkles, Clumped, Contrasty, Enlarged, Stippled, Horizontal, Vertical, and Speckle. Sliders control the intensity and contrast of the effect.

Most of the names for these grain types are self-descriptive. It's worth mentioning, however, that Sprinkles gives the look of a high-contrast overenlargement (photos have the look of being shot in adverse conditions). Clumped produces a sort of plaster texture. Stippled makes a high-contrast, grainy monochrome in the foreground color. Speckle has virtually no effect on solid colors but can give the look of an impressionist painting to photos.

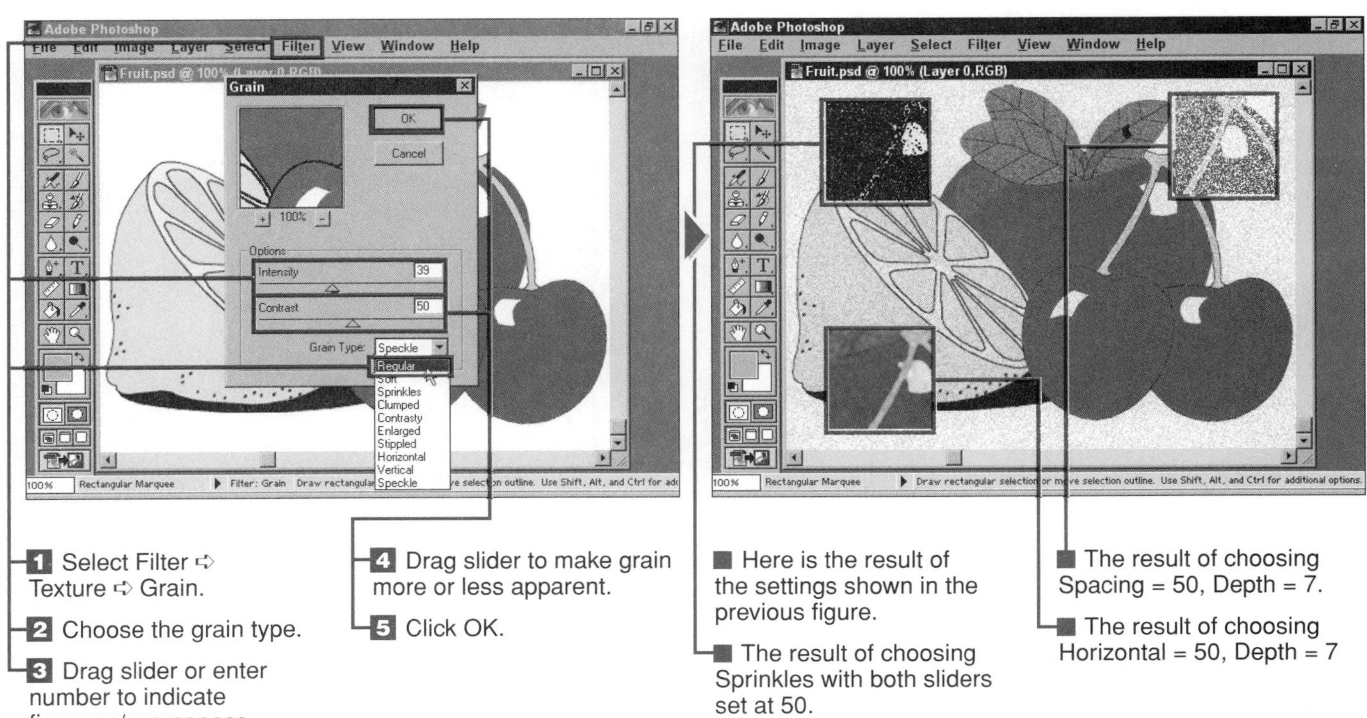

1 Select Filter ➪ Texture ➪ Grain.

2 Choose the grain type.

3 Drag slider or enter number to indicate fineness/coarseness of grain.

4 Drag slider to make grain more or less apparent.

5 Click OK.

■ Here is the result of the settings shown in the previous figure.

■ The result of choosing Sprinkles with both sliders set at 50.

■ The result of choosing Spacing = 50, Depth = 7.

■ The result of choosing Horizontal = 50, Depth = 7

CREATE MOSAIC TILES

The Mosaic Tiles texture looks more like an image that's been broken into irregular pieces and then glued back together than the traditional mosaic made of solid-color tiles.

The space between the tiles isn't white or light gray, as real grout would likely be, either. It's just a darker version of the same color that's in the image, which imparts a cool effect, reminiscent of cobblestone.

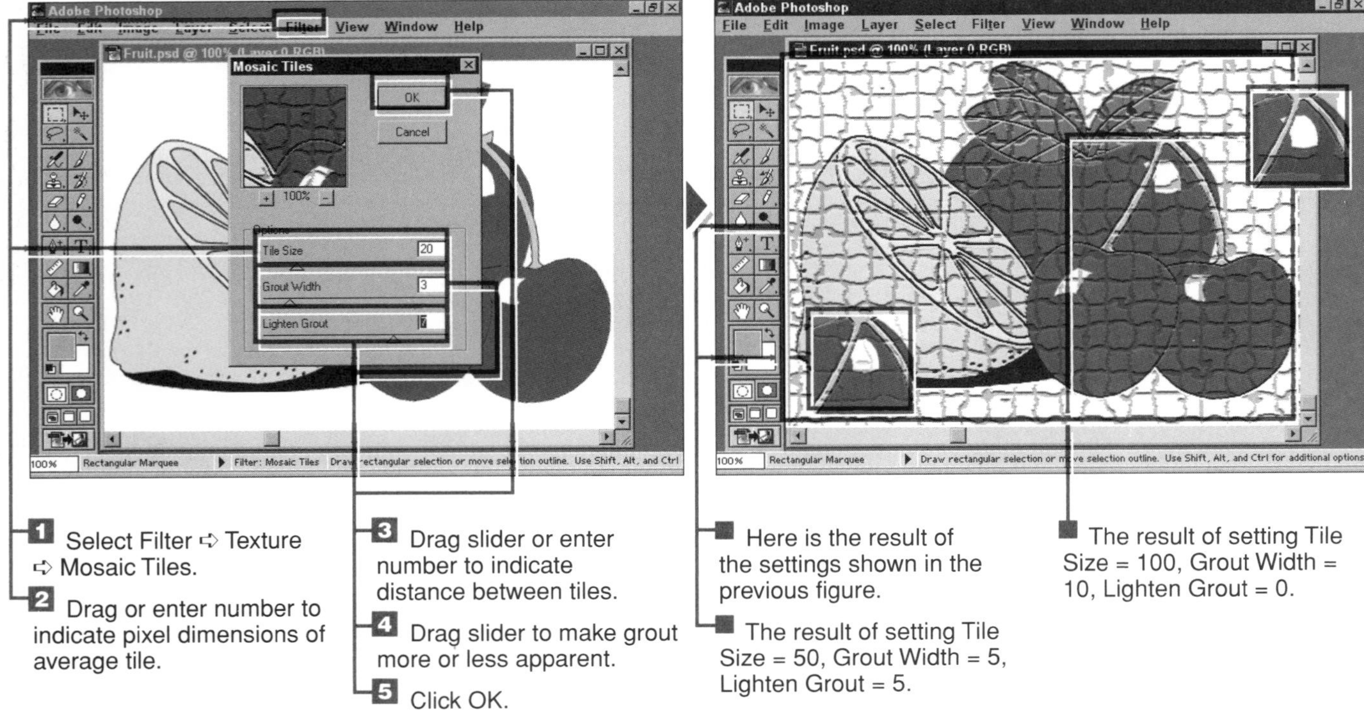

1 Select Filter ➪ Texture ➪ Mosaic Tiles.

2 Drag or enter number to indicate pixel dimensions of average tile.

3 Drag slider or enter number to indicate distance between tiles.

4 Drag slider to make grout more or less apparent.

5 Click OK.

■ Here is the result of the settings shown in the previous figure.

■ The result of setting Tile Size = 50, Grout Width = 5, Lighten Grout = 5.

■ The result of setting Tile Size = 100, Grout Width = 10, Lighten Grout = 0.

CREATE A PATCHWORK

The Patchwork texture looks as much like a patchwork quilt as the Mosaic Tiles texture looks like suede. The weird thing is that it makes the image look like a traditional mosaic — except that it's made of itty-bitty tiles, even at the largest tile size. Also, notice that the horizontal grout is always darker than the vertical grout.

If you ever need to create a view through a screen or a net, this might do the trick — at least if the rendition doesn't have to be too literal.

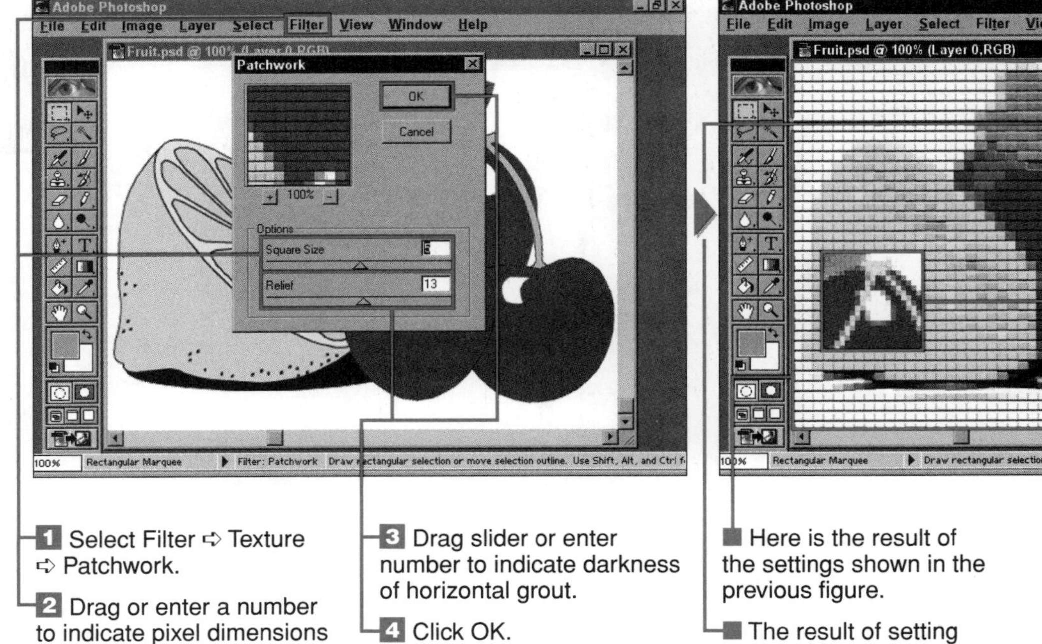

1 Select Filter ➪ Texture ➪ Patchwork.

2 Drag or enter a number to indicate pixel dimensions of squares.

3 Drag slider or enter number to indicate darkness of horizontal grout.

4 Click OK.

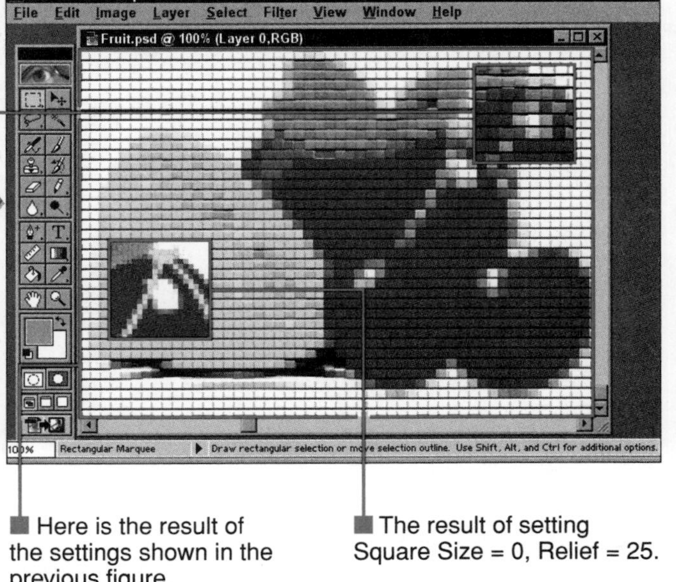

■ Here is the result of the settings shown in the previous figure.

■ The result of setting Square Size = 10, Relief = 25.

■ The result of setting Square Size = 0, Relief = 25.

CREATE STAINED GLASS

Mosaic Tiles and Patchwork may not look much like their namesakes, but Stained Glass resembles the real thing. Each cell is a solid color, and the individual pieces of "glass" are of different sizes and shapes.

Of course, some stained glass, especially the medieval variety, is also painted, so in real stained glass, each pane doesn't have to be a solid color.

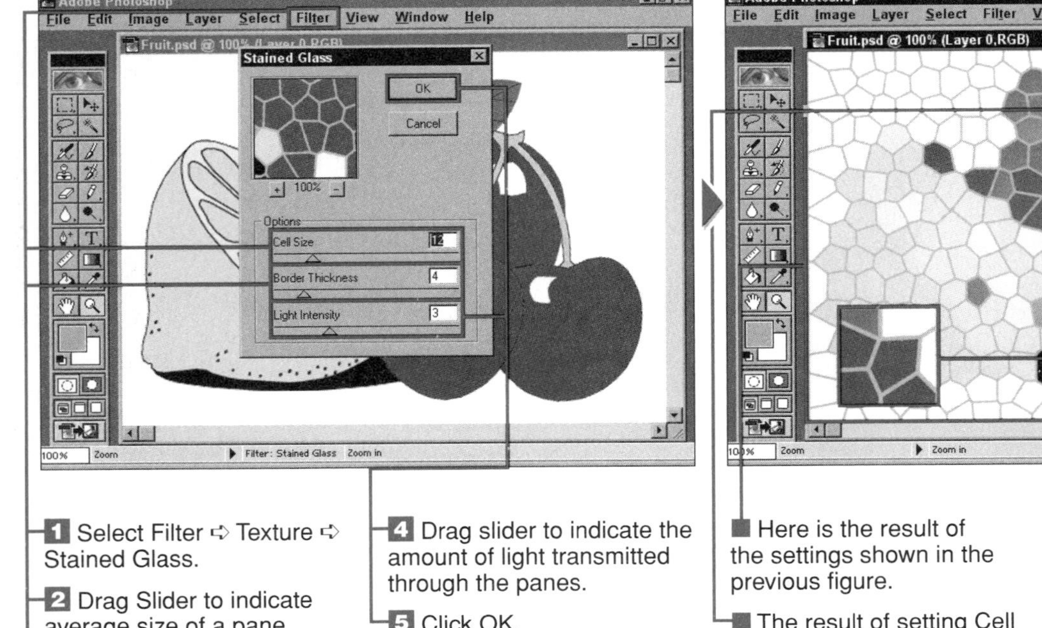

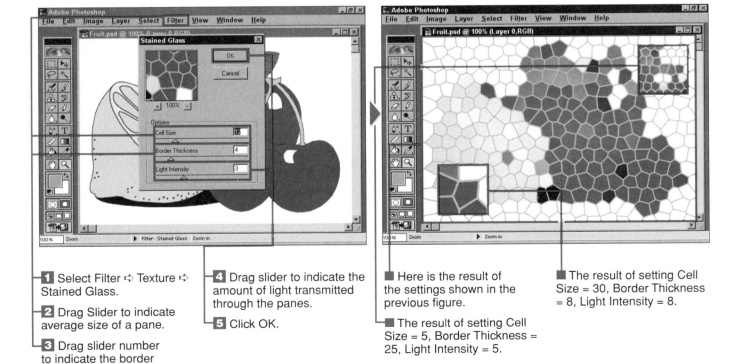

1 Select Filter ➪ Texture ➪ Stained Glass.

2 Drag Slider to indicate average size of a pane.

3 Drag slider number to indicate the border thickness.

4 Drag slider to indicate the amount of light transmitted through the panes.

5 Click OK.

■ Here is the result of the settings shown in the previous figure.

■ The result of setting Cell Size = 5, Border Thickness = 25, Light Intensity = 5.

■ The result of setting Cell Size = 30, Border Thickness = 8, Light Intensity = 8.

APPLY TEXTURIZER TEXTURES

Some of the most useful textures are those that make your images look as though they were painted or projected on the surfaces conventional to the fine arts: linen, canvas, watercolor paper. At the bottom of the Filter ⇨ Texture menu is Texturize, which comes with premade textures that mimic canvas, burlap, and sandstone. A Load Texture item on the same menu enables you to load any seamless texture tile.

On the Photoshop 5 CD are texture files for bumpy leather, hard linear grain, regular paper, and soft linear grain. In addition, you can photograph or scan any texture, turn it into a seamless tile (see "Create Seamless Pattern and Texture Tiles" later in this chapter), save it as a grayscale file, and then load it into Texturizer. You can also make textures by using any of the methods described elsewhere in this chapter, including taking them from the collections of companies such as Artbeats or making them from any of the texture-producing third-party plug-ins.

You can scale these textures to suit the overall size of the image you're producing. You can also adjust the apparent depth of the texture and change the angle of lighting in 45-degree increments.

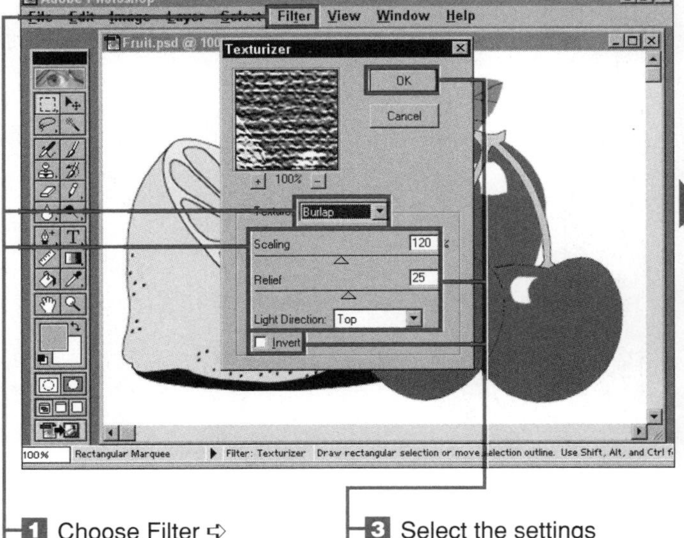

1 Choose Filter ⇨ Texture ⇨ Texturizer.

2 Choose one of the standard textures.

3 Select the settings shown here.

4 Check to invert the selection.

5 Click OK.

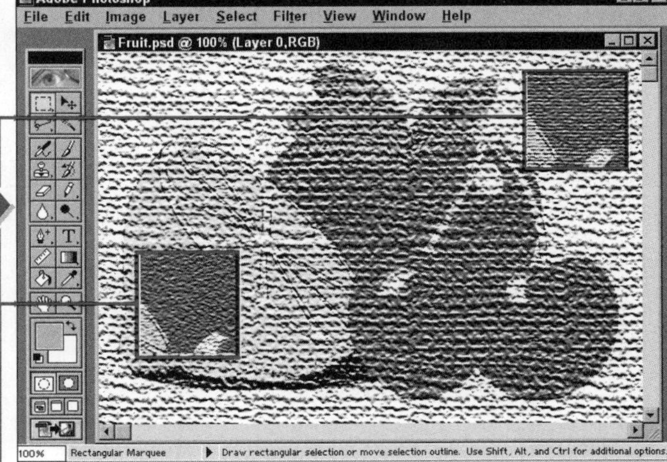

■ Here is the Burlap texture, using the settings shown in the previous figure.

■ The Sandstone texture.

■ The Canvas texture.

Note: You can also choose Load Texture from the Texture pull-down menu to use any Photoshop-format grayscale file as the texture map.

CREATE NEW TEXTURES FROM PHOTOS

You can readily make a texture image of just about anything under the sun. It helps if you have a macro lens or a close-up lens and a tripod. If you don't have a sophisticated studio and strobe lights available to you, shoot outdoors so that the amount of light falling on the surface is even, yet there is good contrast between highlights and shadows (you want to see the texture, remember). Use a tripod, and make sure the camera back is parallel to the subject surface. Finally, transfer the image to a data file.

You have to process the digitized image in Photoshop, which this layout shows you how to do. Texturizer requires a grayscale Photoshop-format image. When you use the result in Texturizer, Photoshop repeats the texture as often as necessary to fill the current image. If your target images are bigger than your textures, you want to make a seamless tile (see "Create Seamless Pattern and Texture Tiles" later in this chapter).

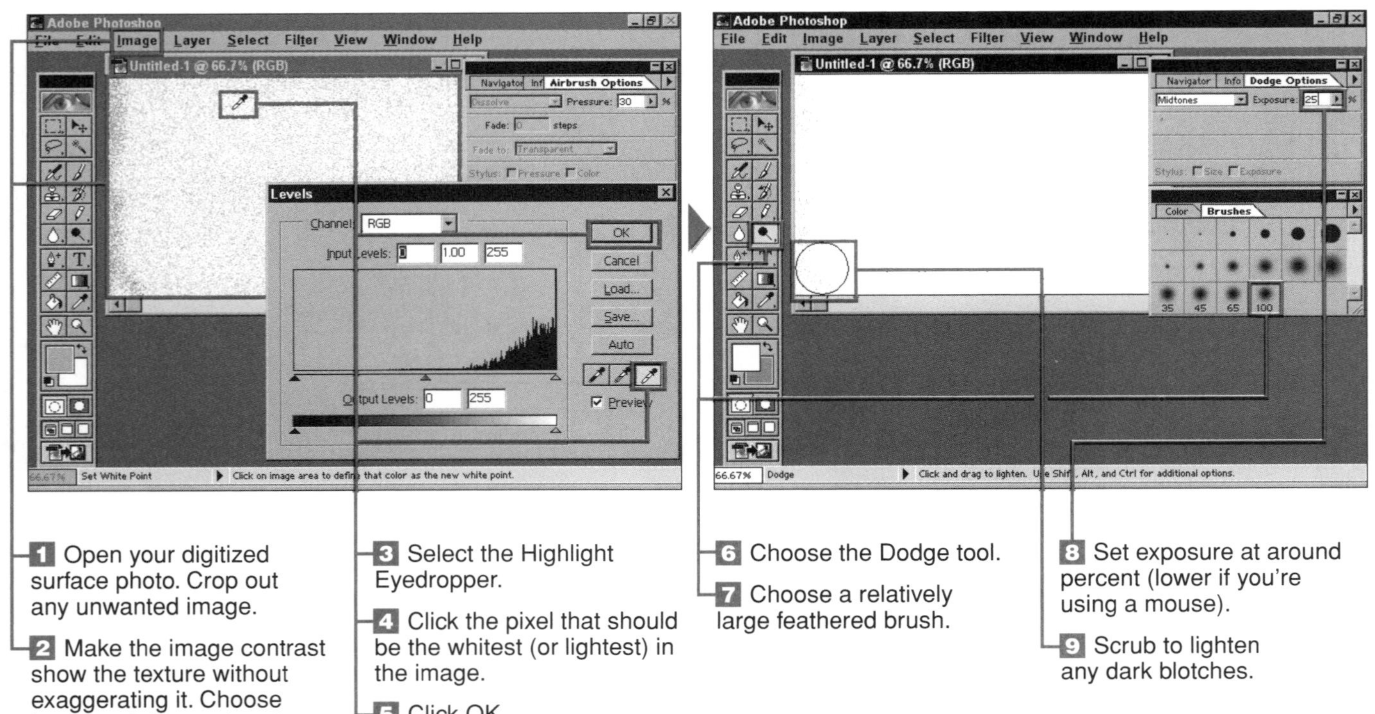

1 Open your digitized surface photo. Crop out any unwanted image.

2 Make the image contrast show the texture without exaggerating it. Choose Image ⇨ Adjust ⇨ Levels.

3 Select the Highlight Eyedropper.

4 Click the pixel that should be the whitest (or lightest) in the image.

5 Click OK.

6 Choose the Dodge tool.

7 Choose a relatively large feathered brush.

8 Set exposure at around percent (lower if you're using a mouse).

9 Scrub to lighten any dark blotches.

TIPS

Why am I setting only the Highlight dropper in the Levels dialog box?

This is usually the adjustment that works best with the least amount of fiddling. No hard and fast rule says you can't make other adjustments; in fact, experimentation is encouraged. Remember that you're after a grayscale file that maps the texture, not color or other photographic details. Also, you don't want contrast to be significantly higher than is natural to the texture of the surface of the material you're recording (unless, of course, you're after a special effect).

Why does the image get more uneven when I try to burn and dodge?

It takes practice to do this well. Keep your exposure setting low (5 percent might be good), so that each stroke makes only a mild adjustment. Use a highly feathered brush, so that the strokes tend to blend together. Use the History palette to go back several strokes if you suddenly notice you've made a mess.

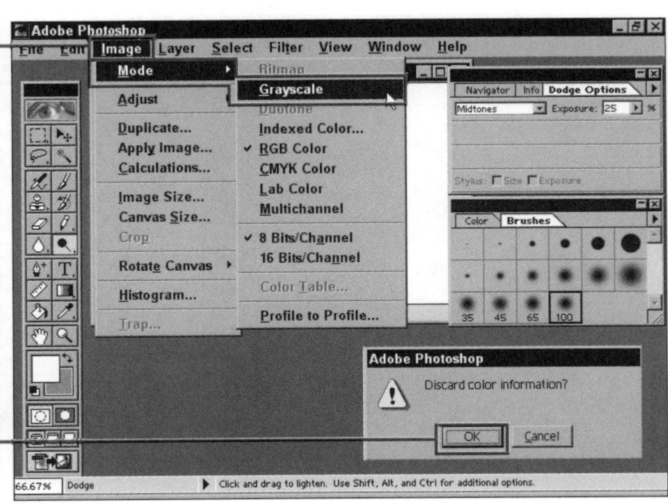

10 Choose Image ⇨ Mode ⇨ Grayscale.

11 Click OK.

■ The image loses all color.

Note: Don't waste space in this file with extra layers. Choose Layers ⇨ Flatten Image, if necessary.

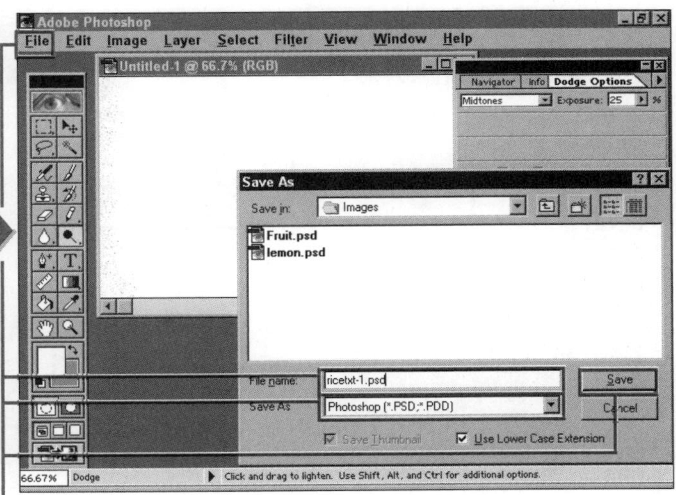

12 Choose File ⇨ Save As.

13 Choose Photoshop from the Save As pull-down menu.

14 Enter a name.

15 Click Save.

Note: To use this texture, choose Filter ⇨ Texture ⇨ Texturizer and choose Load Texture from the Texture pull-down menu.

CREATE SEAMLESS PATTERN AND TEXTURE TILES

Making a tile is nearly a no-brainer. Choose the marquee tool and press ⌘/Ctrl+C to copy the contents to the clipboard. Press ⌘/Ctrl+N to open a new file, and immediately click the OK button in the resulting dialog box (the default file size for a new file is the size of the clipboard contents). Press ⌘/Ctrl+V to paste the contents of the clipboard into the new file that opens. Flatten the image (Layer ➪ Flatten Image) and, if it's to be a paper texture (a texture for Texturizer), make sure it's grayscale (choose Image ➪ Mode ➪ Grayscale). Finally, choose File ➪ Save As, choose Photoshop (PSD) file format, and give the file a name.

Now, here's a problem: You'll get an obvious edge between the tiles. Sometimes that's OK, but most of the time, it isn't. To make seamless tiles, you need to select an exact size rectangle and choose Filter ➪ Other ➪ Offset. Wrap the contents halfway across, both side to side and top to bottom. You then use the Clone tool to eliminate the seam. Finally, reverse the overlap and save the tile.

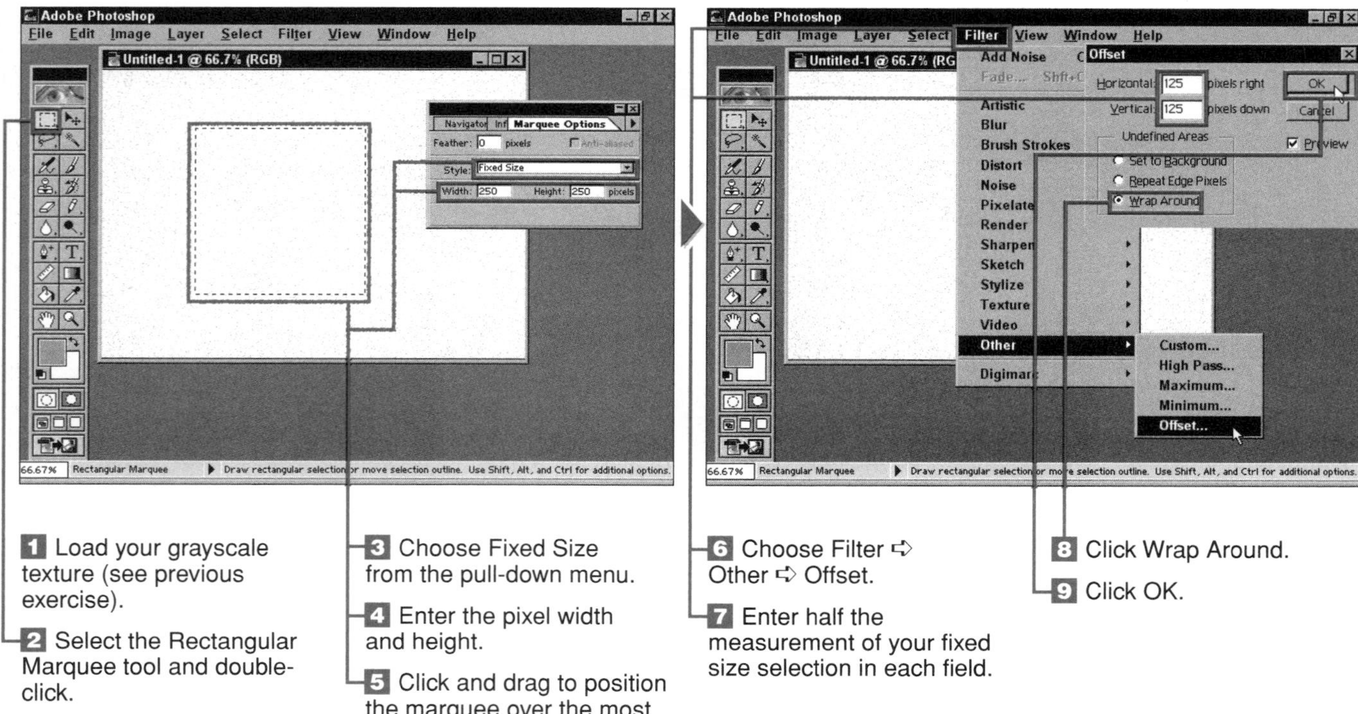

1 Load your grayscale texture (see previous exercise).

2 Select the Rectangular Marquee tool and double-click.

3 Choose Fixed Size from the pull-down menu.

4 Enter the pixel width and height.

5 Click and drag to position the marquee over the most uniform part of the texture.

6 Choose Filter ➪ Other ➪ Offset.

7 Enter half the measurement of your fixed size selection in each field.

8 Click Wrap Around.

9 Click OK.

TIPS

What is the best way to test my seamless tile?

Open a new file of sufficient dimensions to hold several repetitions of the tile, both vertical and horizontal. Open your tile file and press ⌘/Ctrl+A to Select All. Then choose Define Pattern from the Edit menu. Finally, activate the window of the new, empty file, and choose Edit ➪ Fill ➪ Pattern.

What do I do if the tile doesn't look right?

This will be the case if the pattern is unevenly lighted or if the shapes that make up the pattern are a different size or color in one section of the selection than in others. Try selecting a smaller portion of the texture so that you have a better chance at an even pattern. At least try selecting a different area of the texture that has a more even pattern.

What if I still can't get an even pattern?

Cheat. Duplicate the file (or the layer) so that you don't destroy the original. Next, use the Clone tool to copy areas of texture into other areas of texture until it's all evened out. You can even up lighting by burning and dodging and you can use the Color Apply mode with your brush to even up color.

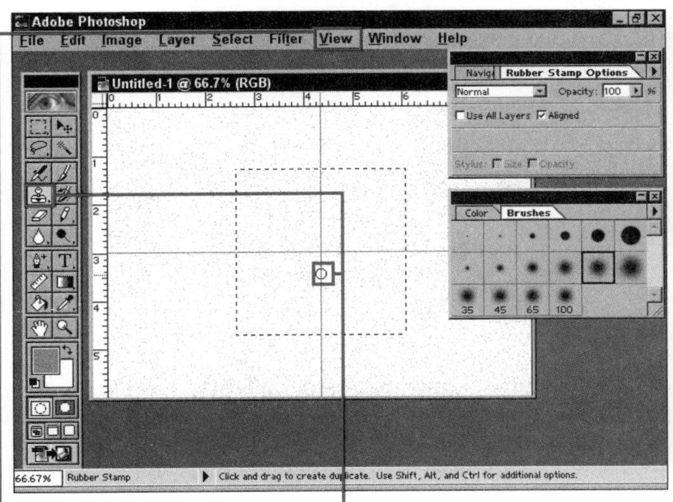

Note: You may or may not be able to see a seam that quarters your selection.

10 Choose View ➪ Show Rulers and drag guidelines to divide your selection vertically and horizontally.

11 Choose the Rubber Stamp.

12 Use Opt/Alt+click to set an origin.

13 Stroke down and across guidelines to cover the seam.

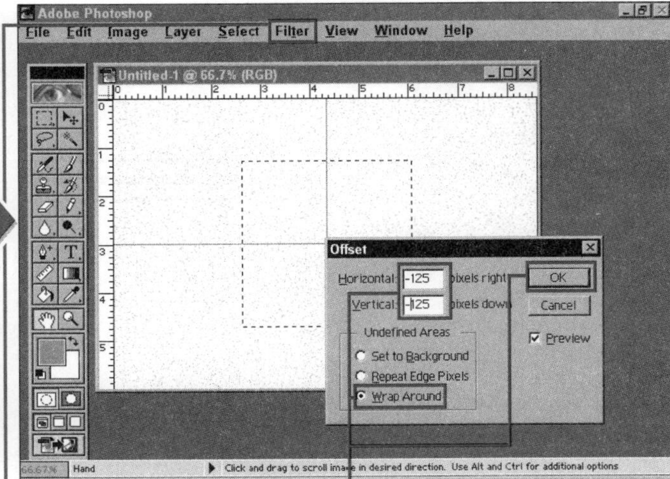

14 Repeat Steps 12—13, starting from different origins so texture appears even across the seam.

15 Choose Filter ➪ Other ➪ Offset.

16 To unwrap (reverse) your offset, insert a - (minus sign) in front of the numbers you first entered.

17 Make sure Wrap Around is still chosen.

18 Click OK.

15 Painterly Filter Effects

Photoshop's built-in Artistic filters make it easy to convert photos and scans into something vaguely resembling a traditional painting. That's not to say, by any means, that Photoshop automatically knows how to paint well. The better artist you are, the more useful these tools will be. On the other hand, sometimes it's enough just to be able to put some texture in part of an image, make a background or button-surface look hand-painted, or use the various filters in conjunction with selections to vary the texture in an image.

Of course, any filter or other Photoshop tool could be labeled *artistic*. In this chapter, you look at those filters that fall under the Artistic, Brush Strokes, and Sketch submenus.

Colored Pencil Filter

The effect of the Colored Pencil filter looks similar to a cross-hatched rubbing made with sharpened pastels. The Colored Pencil dialog box is shown in the following figure.

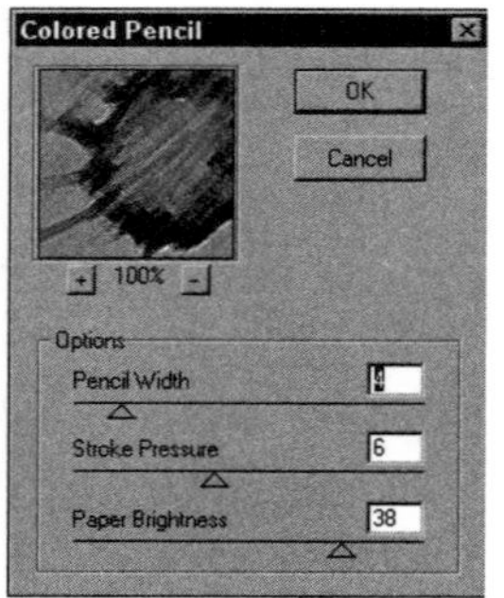

Colored Pencil Filter Dialog Box Contents

Component	Function
Pencil Width slider and field	Drag to determine a pixel width for the crosshatched strokes, or enter a number from 1 to 24.
Stroke Pressure slider and field	Drag to determine the area colored by the cross-hatched strokes, or enter a number from 0 to 15.
Paper Brightness slider and field	Drag to make the unstroked sections brighter (right) or darker (left), or enter a number from 0 to 50.

Cutout Filter

The Cutout filter reduces the number of colors in an image to the number of colors you specify in the dialog box, as shown in the following figure, and then smoothes the edges.

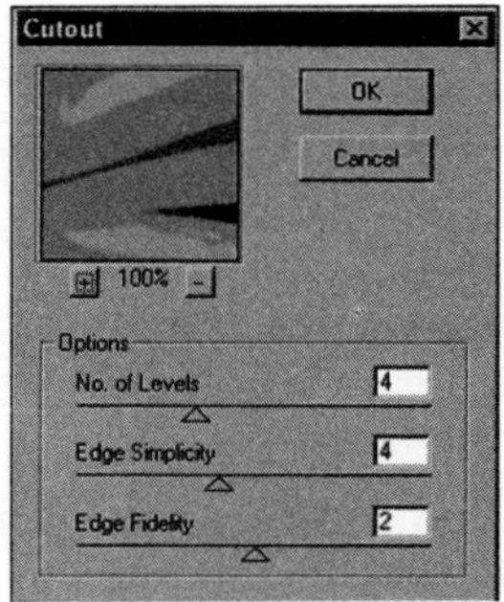

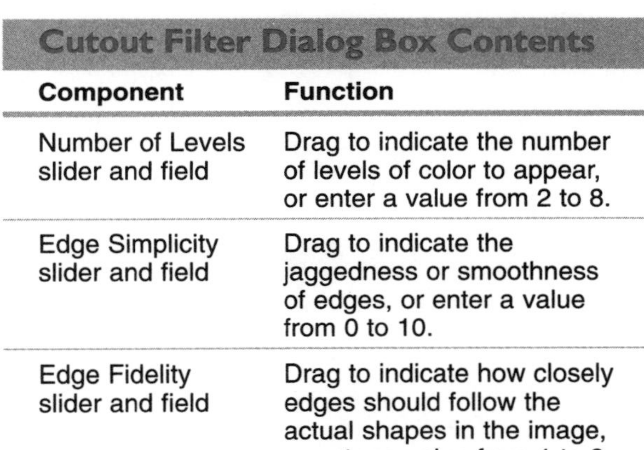

Cutout Filter Dialog Box Contents

Component	Function
Number of Levels slider and field	Drag to indicate the number of levels of color to appear, or enter a value from 2 to 8.
Edge Simplicity slider and field	Drag to indicate the jaggedness or smoothness of edges, or enter a value from 0 to 10.
Edge Fidelity slider and field	Drag to indicate how closely edges should follow the actual shapes in the image, or enter a value from 1 to 3.

Dry Brush Filter

The Dry Brush filter produces an effect similar to that of the Cutout filter. However, with the Dry Brush filter the edges are softer, you can have more levels (up to 10) of detail, and you can add a level of stroke texturing as shown in the following figure.

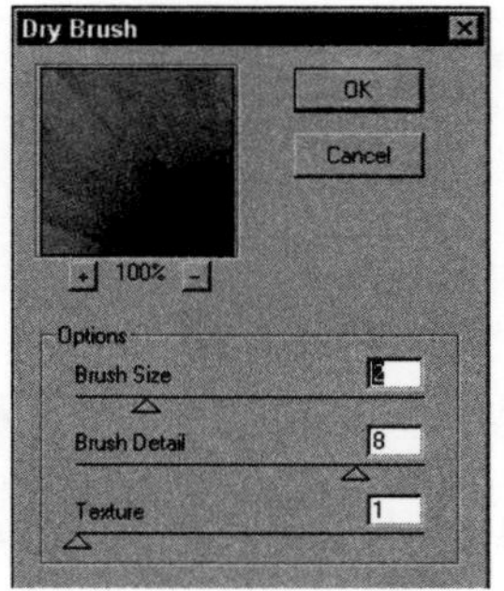

Dry Brush Filter Dialog Box Contents

Component	Function
Brush Size slider and field	Drag to indicate the width of strokes, or enter a value from 1 to 10.
Brush Detail slider and field	Drag to indicate the amount of color and detail to be retained, or enter a value from 0 to 10.
Texture slider and field	Drag to indicate the amount of texturization, or enter a value from 1 to 3.

Film Grain Filter

The Film Grain filter is really more of a photo effect or darkroom filter than an artistic one, but it is contained within the Artistic filters menu. It is one of the few filters that does exactly what you expect of it; that is, it produces an effect that looks like the grain in photographic film. The Film Grain filter dialog box is shown in the following figure.

PAINTERLY FILTER EFFECTS CONTINUED

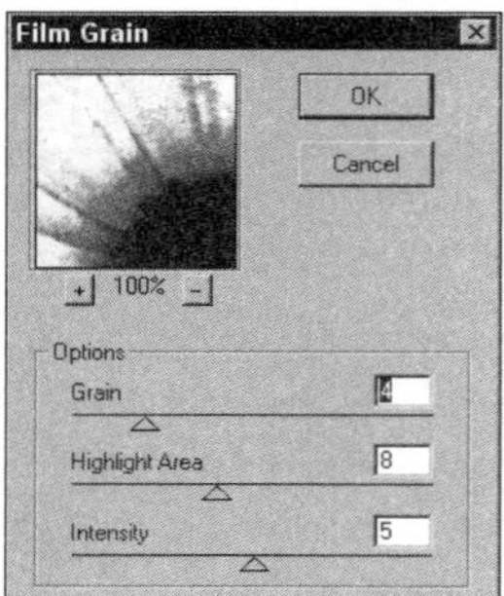

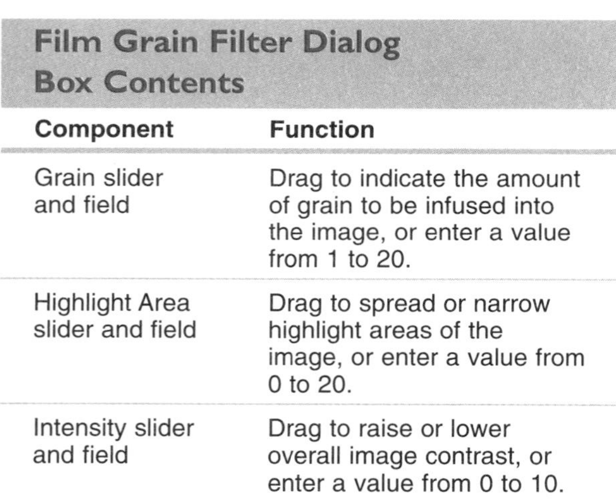

Film Grain Filter Dialog Box Contents

Component	Function
Grain slider and field	Drag to indicate the amount of grain to be infused into the image, or enter a value from 1 to 20.
Highlight Area slider and field	Drag to spread or narrow highlight areas of the image, or enter a value from 0 to 20.
Intensity slider and field	Drag to raise or lower overall image contrast, or enter a value from 0 to 10.

Fresco Filter

The Fresco filter, the dialog box for which is shown in the following figure, is meant to imitate the effect of painting on wet plaster.

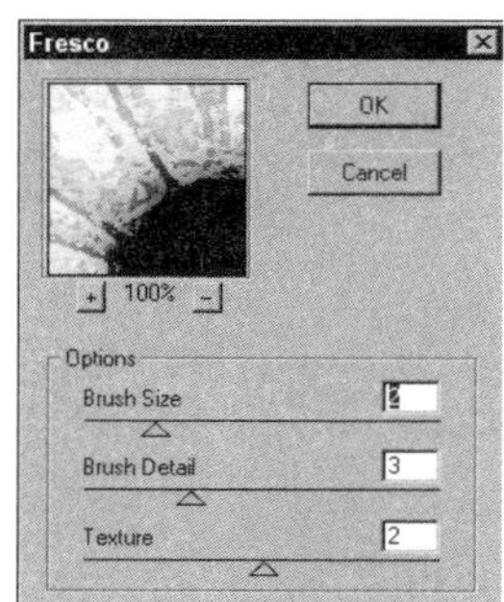

Fresco Filter Dialog Box Contents

Component	Function
Brush Size slider and field	Drag to indicate the width of strokes, or enter a value from 0 to 10.
Brush Detail slider and field	Drag to indicate the amount of color and detail to be retained, or enter a value from 0 to 10.
Texture slider and field	Drag to indicate the amount of texturization, or enter a value from 1 to 3.

Neon Glow Filter

The Neon Glow filter gives everything in an image a bluish, fuzzy tint. The dialog box for this filter is shown in the following figure.

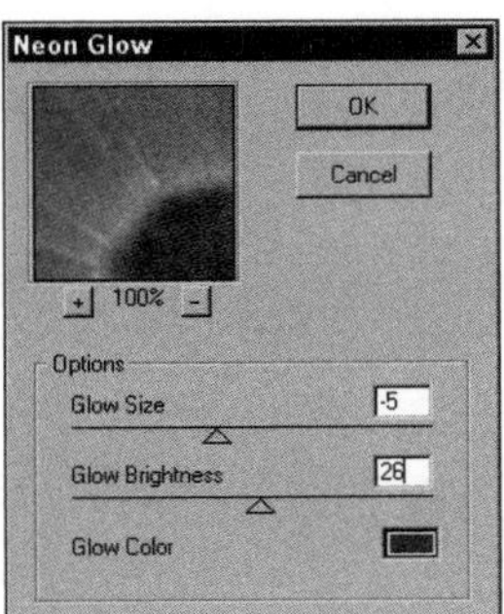

Neon Glow Filter Dialog Box Contents

Component	Function
Glow Size slider and field	Drag right to spread the highlight area (which glows in the color chosen in the Glow swatch), or enter a value from –24 to 24.
Glow Brightness slider and field	Drag to brighten or darken the glow area, or enter a value from 0 to 50.
Glow Color swatch	Click to bring up the Color Picker.

Paint Daubs Filter

The basic idea of the Paint Daubs filter, the dialog box for which is shown in the following figure, is as follows: The strokes created imitate those made by a brush dipped into heavy paint and then applied by tapping the end of the brush on the canvas.

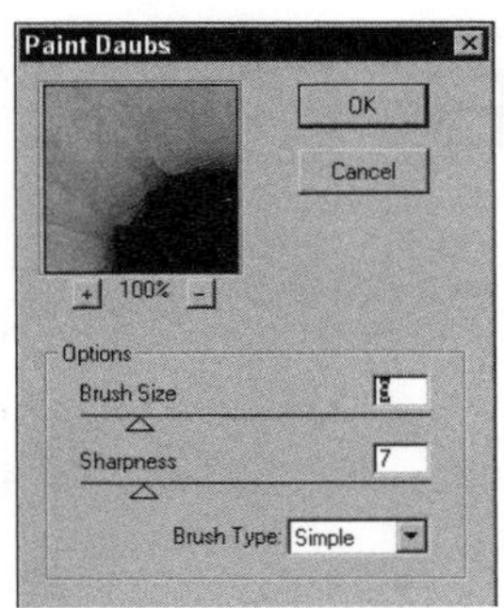

Paint Daubs Filter Dialog Box Contents

Component	Function
Brush Size slider and field	Drag to increase or decrease areas of flat color, or enter a value from 1 to 50.
Sharpness slider and field	Drag to harden or soften borders between colors, or enter a value from 0 to 40.
Brush Type pull-down menu	Choose between the options Simple (default), Light Rough, Dark Rough, Wide Sharp, Wide Blurry, or Sparkle.

Palette Knife Filter

The Palette Knife filter is really just another way to flatten colors into broad strokes. You can vary the softness of edges and the amount of apparent detail in the strokes through the associated dialog box, depicted in the following figure.

CONTINUED

PAINTERLY FILTER EFFECTS CONTINUED

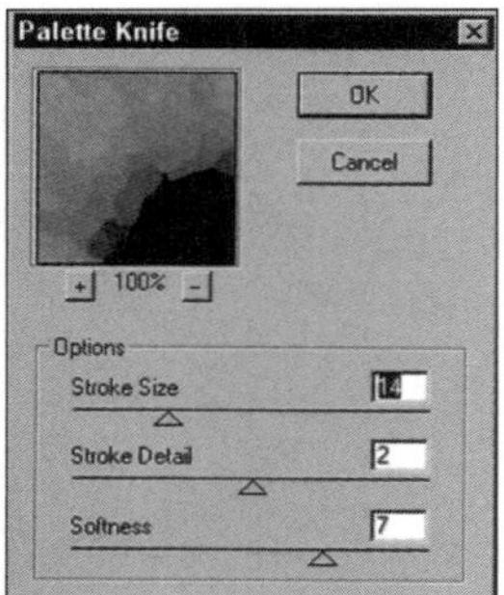

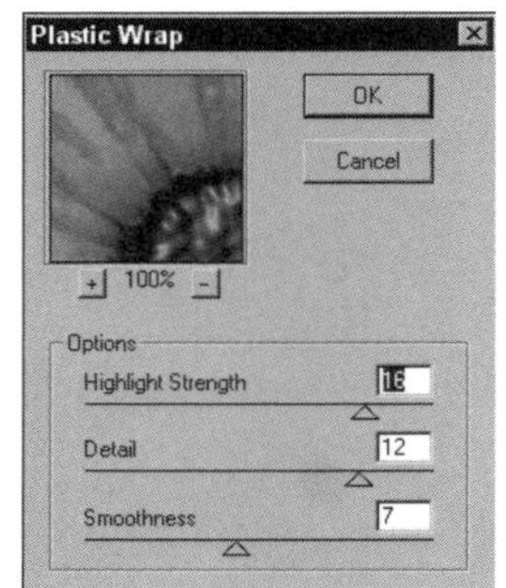

Palette Knife Filter Dialog Box Contents

Component	Function
Stroke Size slider and field	Drag to increase or decrease areas of flat color, or enter a value from 1 to 50.
Stroke Detail slider and field	Drag to increase or decrease the number of flat colors, or enter a value from 1 to 3.
Softness slider and field	Drag to harden or soften the borders between colors, or enter a value from 0 to 10.

Plastic Wrap Filter Dialog Box Contents

Component	Function
Highlight Strength slider and field	Drag to increase or decrease size of highlights, or enter a value from 0 to 20.
Detail slider and field	Drag to increase or decrease areas of flat color, or enter a value from 1 to 15.
Smoothness slider and field	Drag to harden or soften the edges of areas of flat color, or enter a value from 1 to 15.

Plastic Wrap Filter

The Plastic Wrap filter can create a three-dimensional look to an image, which is useful for giving depth and roundness to textured areas of a photo. The following figure shows the Plastic Wrap filter dialog box.

Poster Edges Filter

With the Poster Edges filter, colors are flattened and then outlined with dark edges. The Poster Edges filter is shown in the following figure.

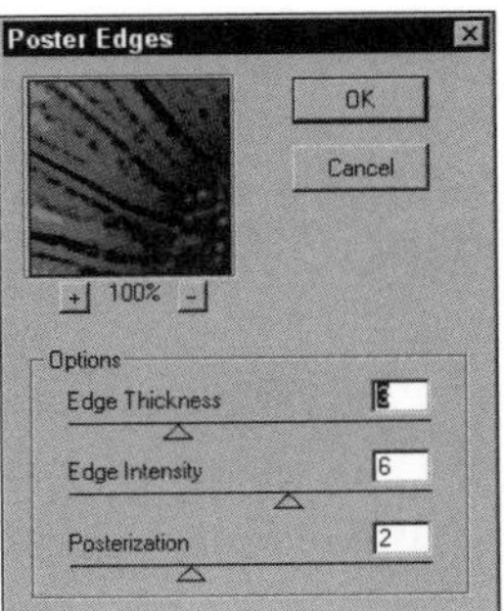

Poster Edges Filter Dialog Box Contents

Component	Function
Edge Thickness slider and field	Drag to indicate average width of black stroke that defines edges between highly contrasting colors, or enter a value from 0 to 10.
Edge Intensity slider and field	Drag to indicate darkness and brightness of edges, or enter a value from 0 to 10.
Posterization slider and field	Drag to specify levels of color, or enter a value from 0 to 6.

Rough Pastels Filter

The look of this filter is a bit like oil pastels, but with all the strokes moving in a parallel direction. Unfortunately, the associated dialog box, as depicted in the following figure, doesn't have an angle control, which would enable you to make the result more natural by filtering selected areas one at a time.

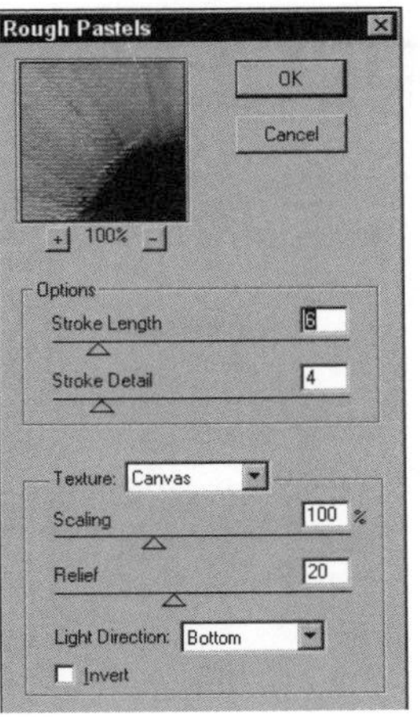

Rough Pastels Filter Dialog Box Contents

Component	Function
Stroke Length slider and field	Drag to indicate length of cross-hatched strokes, or enter a value from 0 to 40.
Stroke Detail slider and field	Drag to indicate number of colors to be interpreted, or enter a value from 1 to 20.
Texture pull-down menu	Choose from Burlap, Canvas, or Sandstone, or load a user-defined texture file.
Scaling slider and field	Drag to resize the texture image.
Relief slider and field	Drag to change emphasis of highlights and shadows in texture.
Light Direction pull-down menu	Choose from Top, Top Right, Right, Bottom Right, Bottom, Bottom Left, Left, Top Left.
Invert check box	Inverts the highlights and shadows in the texture.

CONTINUED

PAINTERLY FILTER EFFECTS CONTINUED

Smudge Stick Filter

The Smudge Stick filter is a little like Rough Pastels, but without the texture. The image is highly posterized (you have no direct control over the number of levels of color) and is smeared in diagonal strokes as seen in the following figure.

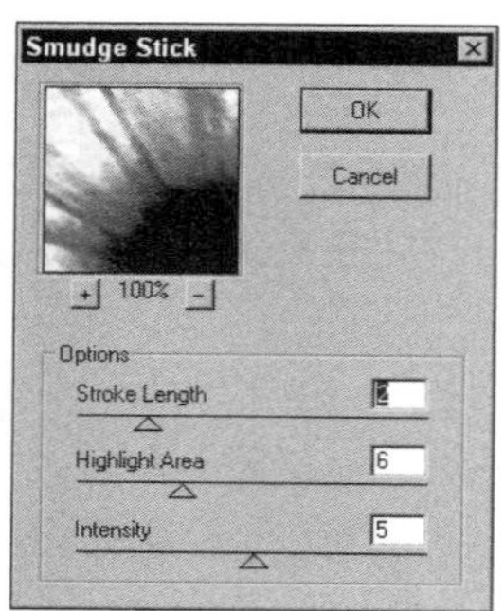

Smudge Stick Filter Dialog Box Contents

Component	Function
Stroke Length slider and field	Drag to specify distance pixels are smudged, or enter a value from 0 to 10.
Highlight Area slider and field	Drag to increase or decrease size of highlight area, or enter a value from 0 to 20.
Intensity slider and field	Drag to indicate overall contrast, or enter a value from 0 to 10.

Sponge Filter

With the Sponge filter, colors are flattened and posterized, and darker blotches are imposed in a seemingly random pattern to give the image a look as if it has been dabbed with a wet sponge. The associated dialog box is shown in the following figure.

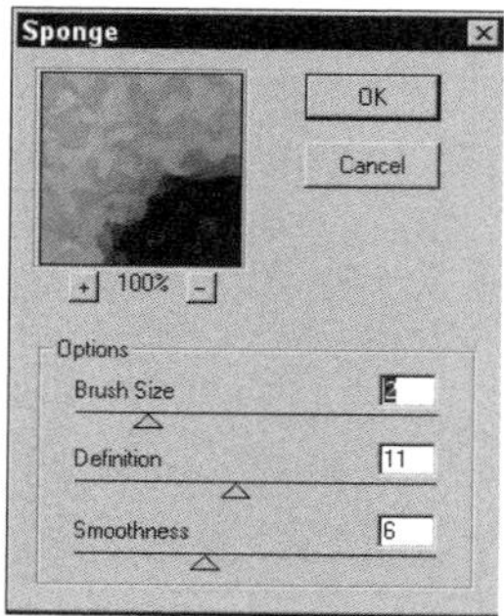

Sponge Filter Dialog Box Contents

Component	Function
Brush Size slider and field	Drag to increase or decrease size of the color blotches, or enter a value from 0 to 10.
Definition slider and field	Drag to specify the amount of detail that can be discerned, or enter a value from 0 to 25.
Smoothness slider and field	Drag to indicate the degree to which edges between colors blend, or enter a value from 1 to 15.

Underpainting Filter

The Underpainting filter, the dialog box for which is shown in the following figure, does a credible job of making an image look as if it was washed onto a textured surface with highly thinned paints. This is a basic technique for starting an oil painting and is a good first step in combining Artistic filters that are increasingly detailed or textured.

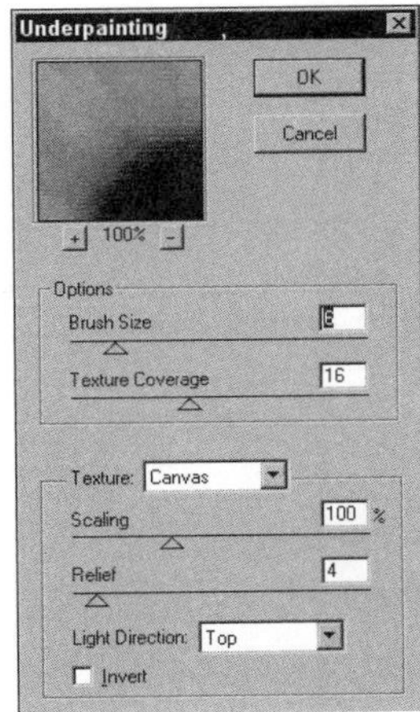

Underpainting Filter Dialog Box Contents

Component	Function
Brush Size slider and field	Drag to increase or decrease size of broad areas of color, or enter a value from 0 to 40.
Texture Coverage slider and field	Drag to increase or decrease the amount of the image in which texture shows through paint colors, or enter a value from 0 to 40.
Texture pull-down menu	Choose from Burlap, Canvas, or Sandstone, or load a user-defined texture file.
Scaling slider and field	Drag to resize the texture image.
Relief slider and field	Drag to change emphasis of highlights and shadows in texture.
Light Direction pull-down menu	Choose from Top, Top Right, Right, Bottom Right, Bottom, Bottom Left, Left, Top Left.
Invert check box	Inverts the highlights and shadows in the texture.

Watercolor Filter

The Watercolor filter's job is to make your image look painted with watercolors. The following figure shows the associated dialog box.

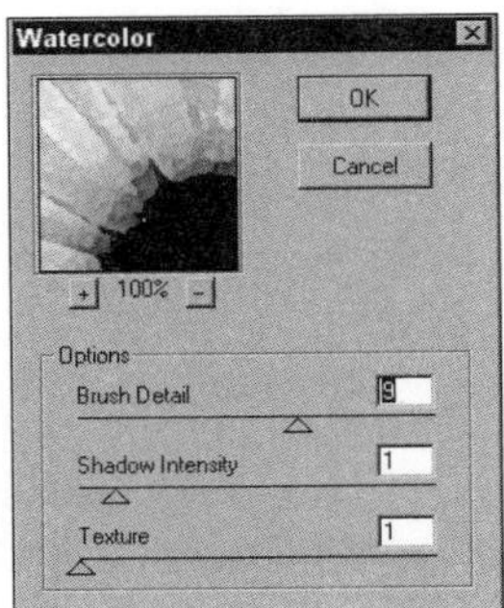

Watercolor Filter Dialog Box Contents

Component	Function
Brush Detail slider and field	Drag to indicate the degree of detail you want to see in the image, or enter a value from 1 to 14. Interacts with Shadow Intensity.

CONTINUED

PAINTERLY FILTER EFFECTS CONTINUED

Component	Function
Shadow Intensity slider and field	Drag to specify the size of areas that will go to black, or enter a value from 0 to 10.
Texture slider and field	Indicates level of texturization, with a value from 1 to 3.

Accented Edges Filter

The Accented Edges filter, the dialog box for which is shown in the following figure, reduces colors and outlines the edges with a uneven dry-brush stroke.

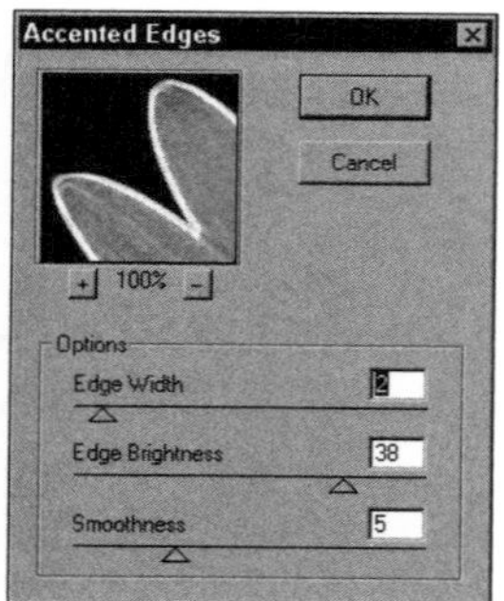

Accented Edges Filter Dialog Box Contents

Component	Function
Edge Width slider and field	Drag to specify the average thickness of accented edges, or enter a value from 1 to 14.
Edge Brightness slider and field	Drag to change brightness of edges from black to white, or enter a value from 0 to 50. Adjustment also determines the number of accented edges.
Smoothness slider and field	Drag to specify the degree to which the edges blend with their surroundings, or enter a value from 1 to 15.

Angled Strokes Filter

The Angled Strokes filter creates an effect similar to the Rough Pastels filter, but you can control the main direction of the strokes as shown in the following figure. Strokes are automatically angled in different directions in contrasting areas of the image, giving the image the appearance of having been created with a very dry, very thick oil brush.

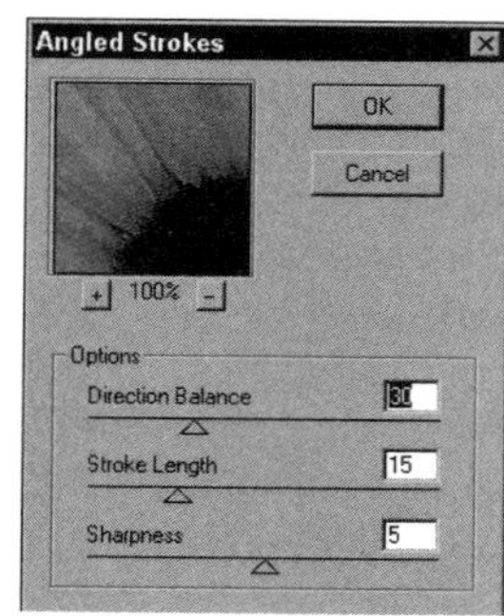

Angled Strokes Filter Dialog Box Contents

Component	Function
Direction Balance slider and field	Drag to change the direction of the strokes, or enter a value from 0 to 100.
Stroke Length slider and field	Drag to lengthen or shorten relative distance over which the stroke travels, or enter a value from 3 to 50.
Sharpness slider and field	Drag to indicate anti-aliasing of edges of strokes, or enter a value from 0 to 10. Eventually strokes blend to more of a palette knife effect.

Crosshatch Filter Dialog Box Contents

Component	Function
Stroke Length slider and field	Drag to change the relative distance over which the stroke travels, or enter a value from 3 to 50.
Sharpness slider and field	Drag to indicate anti-aliasing of edges of strokes, or enter a value from 0 to 10. Eventually strokes blend to more of a palette knife effect.
Strength slider and field	Drag to specify overall contrast after strokes are applied, or enter a value from 1 to 3.

Crosshatch Filter

The Crosshatch filter creates cross-stroked color etching. The associated dialog box is shown here.

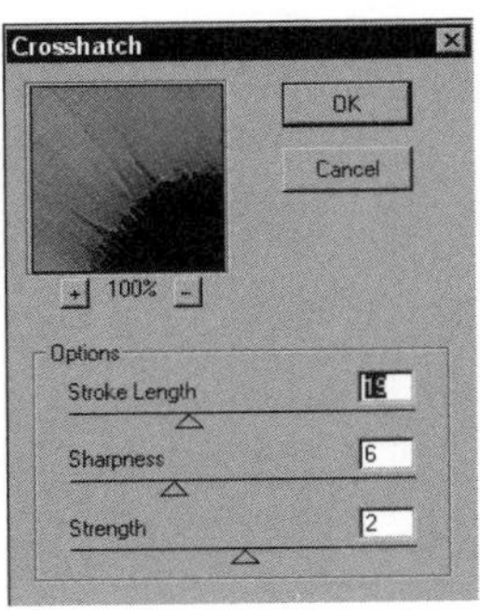

Dark Strokes Filter

The Dark Strokes filter, the dialog box of which is shown in the following figure, makes angular smudged strokes and greatly heightens the difference between highlights and shadows, whereas midtones are left more or less alone.

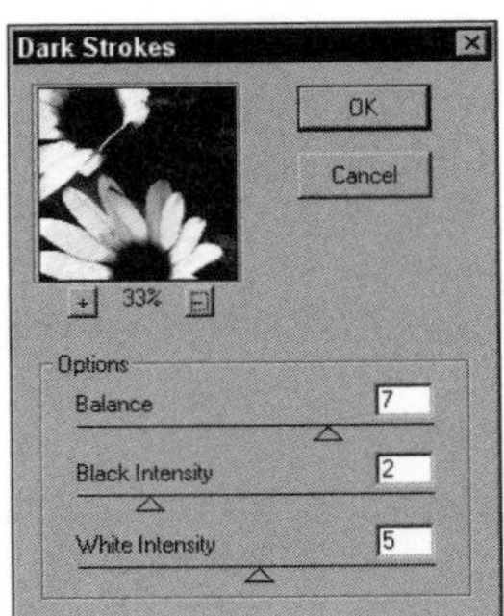

CONTINUED

PAINTERLY FILTER EFFECTS CONTINUED

Dark Strokes Filter Dialog Box Contents

Component	Function
Balance slider and field	Drag to change the distribution of black and white strokes, or enter a value from 0 to 10.
Black Intensity slider and field	Drag to increase or decrease the shadow contrast (amount of black visible in the image), or enter a value from 0 to 10.
White Intensity slider and field	Drag to increase highlight contrast (amount of white visible in the image), or enter a value from 0 to 10.

Ink Outlines Filter

The Ink Outlines filter is a great filter for making images look as though they were painted into inked sketch lines. Similar to the Dark Strokes filter, it darkens the background and increases saturation and contrast as illustrated here.

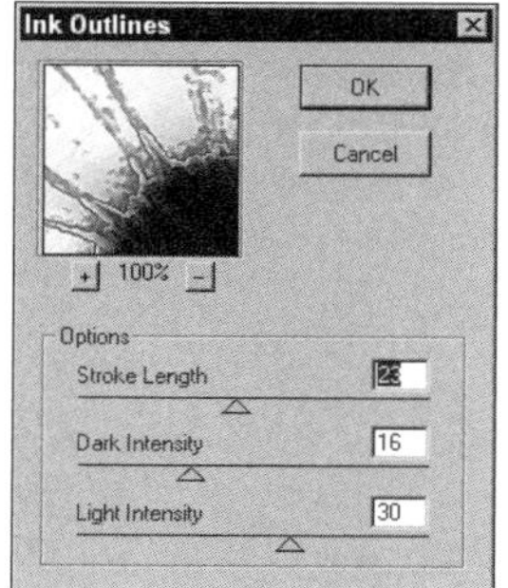

Ink Outlines Filter Dialog Box Contents

Component	Function
Stroke Length slider and field	Drag to influence boldness, thickness, and continuity of black outlines, or enter a value from 1 to 50.
Dark Intensity slider and field	Drag to increase or decrease shadow contrast (amount of black visible in the image), or enter a value from 0 to 50.
Light Intensity slider and field	Drag to increase or decrease highlight contrast (amount of highlights visible in the image), or enter a value from 0 to 50.

Spatter Filter

The Spatter filter creates an effect that looks like something between spraygun painting and pointillism. (How far in between depends on where you set the filter dialog box sliders, shown in the following figure.) This can be an excellent filter for giving a softening effect to an image.

Spatter Filter Dialog Box Contents

Component	Function
Spray Radius slider land field	Drag to increase diameter of paint spatters, or enter a value from 0 to 25.
Smoothness slider and field	Drag to indicate degree of blending of spats with surrounding colors, or enter a value from 1 to 15.

Sumi-e Filter

The Sumi-e filter produces an effect similar to the Dark Strokes filter, but with significantly softer edges and colors. The strokes created are diagonal daubs whose size and intensity can be varied over a wide range as illustrated in the following figure.

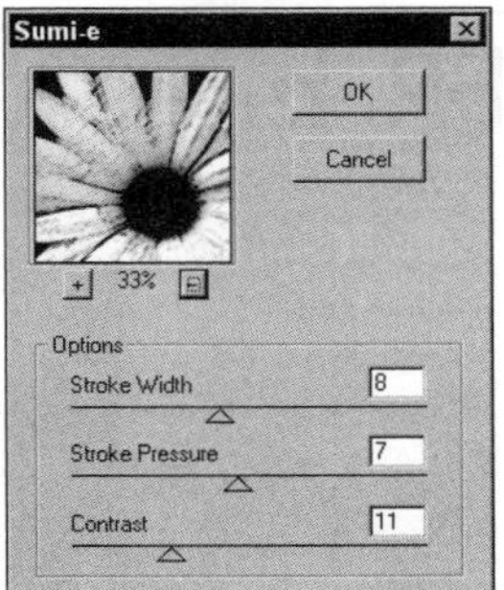

Sumi-e Filter Dialog Box Contents

Component	Function
Stroke Width slider and field	Drag to specify average width of stroke, or enter a value from 3 to 15.
Stroke Pressure slider and field	Drag to indicate number and darkness of strokes, or enter a value from 0 to 15.
Contrast slider and field	Drag to increase or decrease overall image contrast, or enter a value from 0 to 40.

Bas Relief Filter

The Bas Relief filter creates a grayscale embossed effect (grayscale if you leave colors at default; otherwise, whatever colors are there for foreground and background). The associated dialog box is shown in the following figure.

CONTINUED

PAINTERLY FILTER EFFECTS CONTINUED

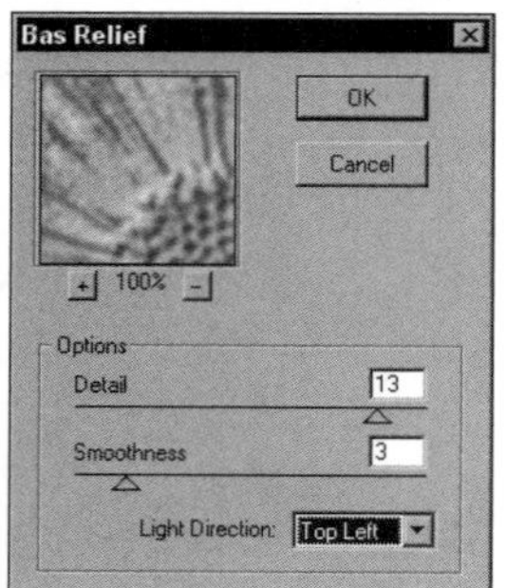

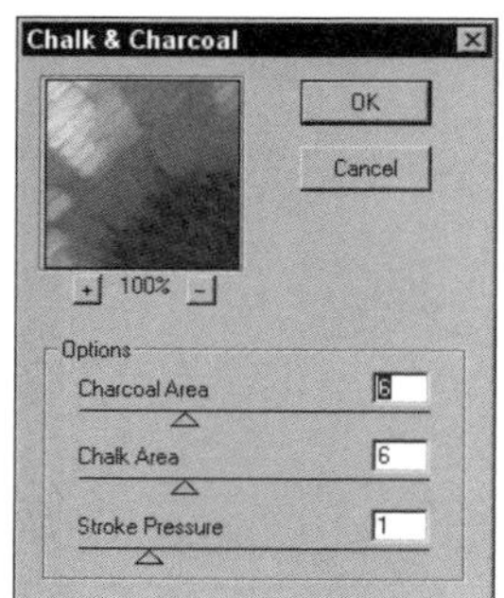

Bas Relief Filter Dialog Box Contents

Component	Function
Detail slider and field	Drag to increase or decrease the number of ridges that will be apparent in the relief, or enter a value from 1 to 15.
Smoothness slider and field	Drag to increase or decrease the degree of blending between edges, or enter a value from 1 to 15.
Light Direction pull-down menu	Choose from Top, Top Right, Right, Bottom Right, Bottom, Bottom Left, Left, Top Left.

Chalk & Charcoal Filter Dialog Box Contents

Component	Function
Charcoal Area slider and field	Drag to specify predominance of foreground color, or enter a value from 0 to 20.
Chalk Area slider and field	Drag to specify predominance of background color, or enter a value from 0 to 20.
Stroke Pressure slider and field	Drag to change overall contrast of image, or enter a value from 0 to 5.

Chalk & Charcoal Filter

The Chalk & Charcoal filter creates a duotone version of the Rough Pastels filter. The angular strokes are a mixture of chalk (foreground color) and charcoal (background color) smudges, a technique illustrated by the following figure.

Charcoal Filter

As with the Chalk & Charcoal filter, the Charcoal filter also uses the foreground and background colors of the image (as do all the Sketch submenu filters), but the strokes are finer and crosshatched. Borders between colors are more emphasized, which gives the result a more authentic feel of charcoal on newsprint. The following figure shows the Charcoal filter dialog box.

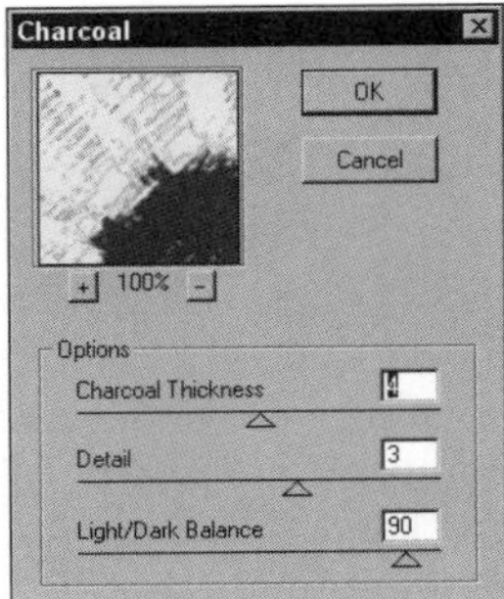

Charcoal Filter Dialog Box Contents

Component	Function
Charcoal Thickness slider and field	Drag to change the average thickness of foreground color strokes, or enter a value from 1 to 7.
Detail slider and field	Drag to increase or decrease the detail of strokes in lighter-toned areas, or enter a value from 0 to 5.
Light/Dark Balance slider and field	Drag to indicate threshold, or enter a value from 0 to 100.

Chrome Filter

The Chrome filter, the dialog box of which is shown here, is basically the same as a grayscale version of the Plastic Wrap filter. It can produce some lovely impasto effects when used with the Texturizer filter (in fact, all the Sketch filters are useful for creating texture effects with any of the filters that can use a grayscale texture).

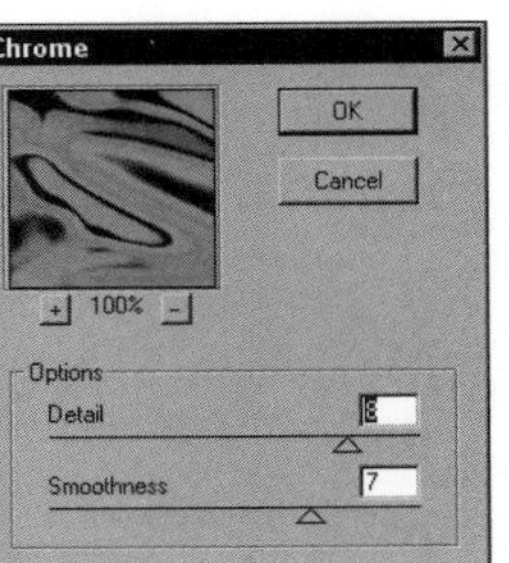

Chrome Filter Dialog Box Contents

Component	Function
Detail slider and field	Drag to specify amount of detail that can be discerned, or enter a value from 0 to 10.
Smoothness slider and field	Drag to dictate the degree to which edges between colors blend, or enter a value from 1 to 10.

Conté Crayon Filter

The Conté Crayon filter can produce interesting results when you're reducing an image to a few duotones (made up of the foreground and background colors of the image). The associated dialog box is shown in the following figure.

CONTINUED

PAINTERLY FILTER EFFECTS CONTINUED

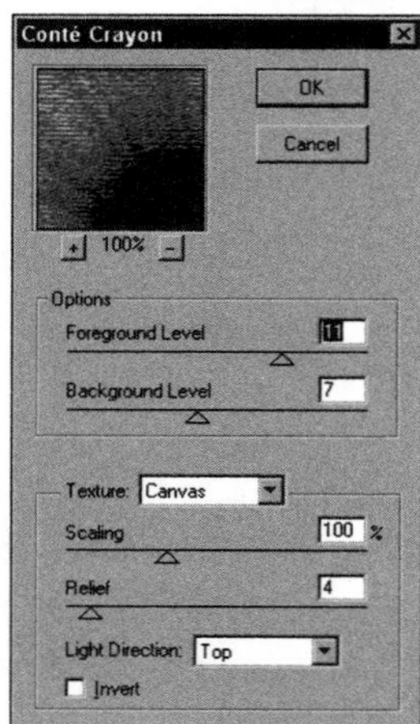

Conté Crayon Filter Dialog Box Contents

Component	Function
Foreground Level slider and field	Drag to increase or decrease intensity of foreground color, or enter a value from 1 to 15.
Background Level slider and field	Drag to increase or decrease the intensity of background color, or enter a value from 1 to 15.
Texture pull-down menu	Choose from Burlap, Canvas, or Sandstone, or load a user-defined texture file.
Scaling slider and field	Drag to resize the texture image.
Relief slider and field	Drag to change emphasis of highlights and shadows in texture.
Light Direction pull-down menu	Right, Right, Bottom Right, Bottom, Bottom Left, Left, Top Left.
Invert check box	Inverts the highlights and shadows in the texture.

Graphic Pen Filter

The Graphic Pen filter produces something that looks like a pen-and-ink etching made with unidirectional strokes. The associated dialog box is shown in the following figure.

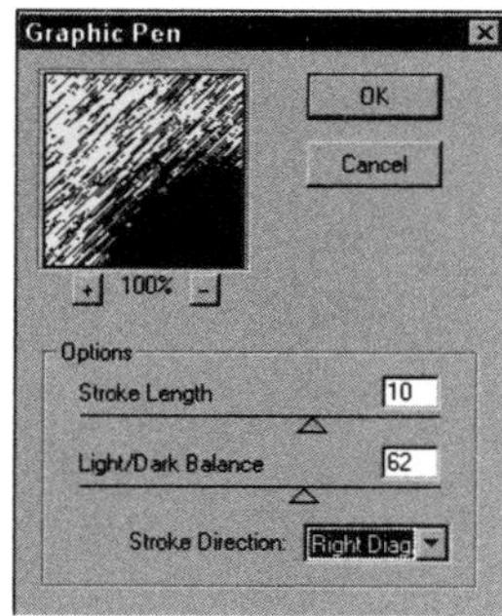

Graphic Pen Filter Dialog Box Contents

Component	Function
Stroke Length slider and field	Drag to change the relative distance over which the stroke travels, or enter a value from 3 to 50.

Component	Function
Light/Dark Balance slider and field	Drag to specify threshold, or enter a value from 0 to 100.
Stroke Direction pull-down menu	Choose from any 45-degree direction: Vertical, Right Diagonal, Horizontal, Left Diagonal.

Halftone Pattern Filter

The Halftone Pattern filter, the dialog box of which is shown in the following figure, produces a halftone pattern atop the image.

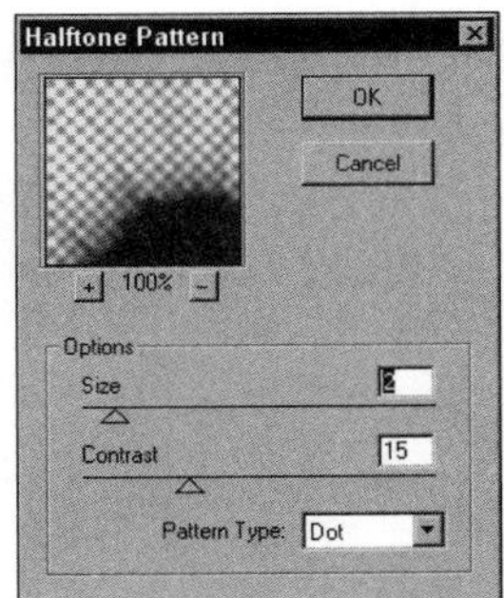

Halftone Pattern Filter Dialog Box Contents

Component	Function
Size slider and field	Drag to specify dot size, or enter a value from 1 to 12.
Contrast slider and field	Drag to change overall contrast, or enter a value from 0 to 50.
Pattern Type pull-down menu	Choose between Circle, Dot, Line.

Note Paper Filter

The effect of the Note Paper filter is a textured two-color (foreground/background) high-contrast rendition of the image on textured paper. You can control the graininess of the paper texture, but not the texture pattern as shown in the following figure.

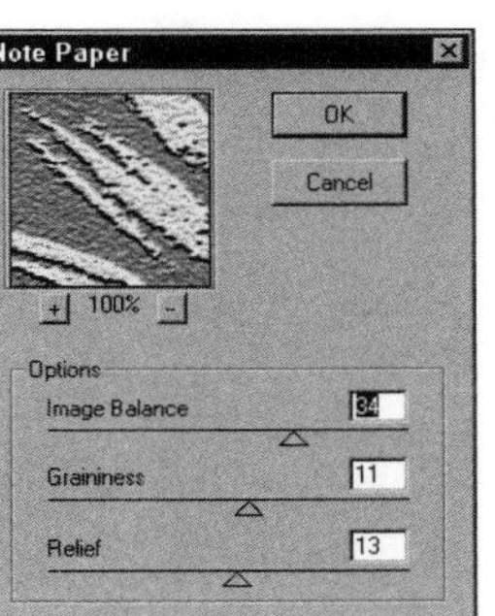

Note Paper Filter Dialog Box Contents

Component	Function
Image Balance slider and field	Drag to specify threshold, or enter a value from 0 to 50.
Graininess slider and field	Drag to increase or decrease amount of texture in the image, or enter a value from 0 to 20.
Relief slider and field	Drag to increase or decrease intensity of edge highlights and shadows, or enter a value from 0 to 25.

CONTINUED

PAINTERLY FILTER EFFECTS CONTINUED

Photocopy Filter

The Photocopy filter makes the image look as though it was copied on a copy machine incapable of producing grays. The following figure shows the Photocopy filter dialog box.

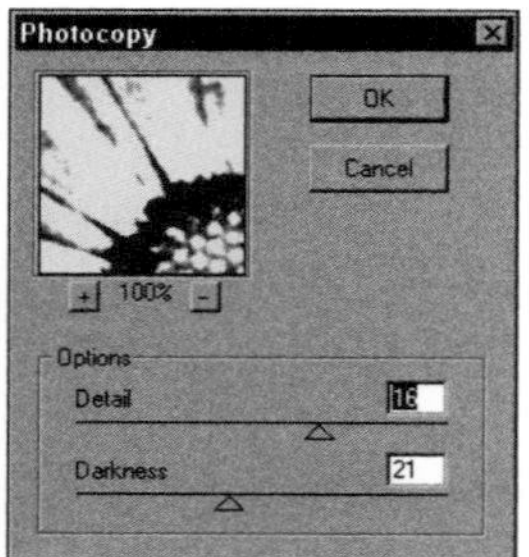

Photocopy Filter Dialog Box Contents

Component	Function
Detail slider and field	Drag to indicate threshold, or enter a value from 1 to 24.
Darkness slider and field	Drag to change brightness and contrast, or enter a value from 1 to 50.

Plaster Filter

The Plaster filter reduces the image to a few tones below an adjustable threshold in shades of the background color and embosses the shapes over a solid foreground color. The associated dialog box is shown in the following figure.

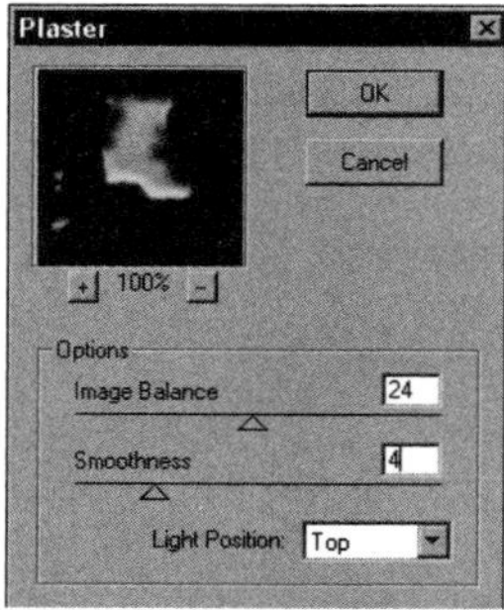

Plaster Filter Dialog Box Contents

Component	Function
Image Balance slider and field	Drag to specify threshold, or enter a value from 0 to 50.
Smoothness slider and field	Drag to adjust the degree to which edges between colors blend, or enter a value from 1 to 15.
Light Position pull-down menu	Choose from Top, Top Right, Right, Bottom Right, Bottom, Bottom Left, Left, Top Left.

Reticulation Filter

The Reticulation filter imitates what happens when photographic film is overheated during processing and film grain clumps together in worm-like forms. The effect, which you apply through the dialog box shown in the following figure, can produce interesting results when used as a texture.

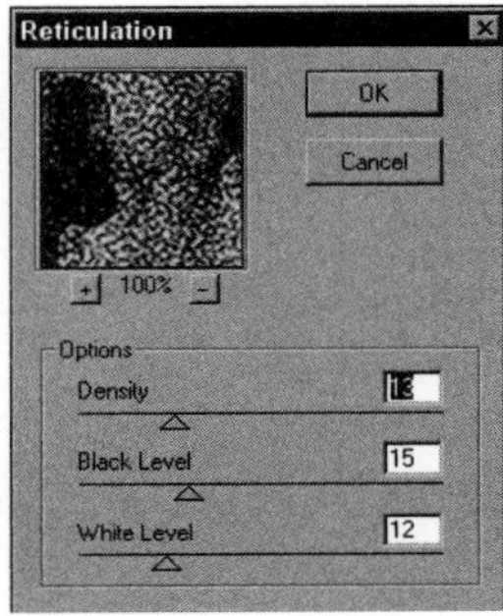

Reticulation Filter Dialog Box Contents

Component	Function
Density slider and field	Drag to increase or decrease the population of grain clumps, or enter a value from 0 to 50.
Black Level slider and field	Drag to indicate threshold for black, or enter a value from 0 to 50.
White Level slider and field	Drag to indicate threshold for white, or enter a value from 0 to 50.

Stamp Filter

The Stamp filter carves the image out in much the same way as rubber is carved to make a rubber stamp; thus, its name. You can control the smoothness of lines and the point at which black and white divide through the Stamp filter dialog box shown in the following figure.

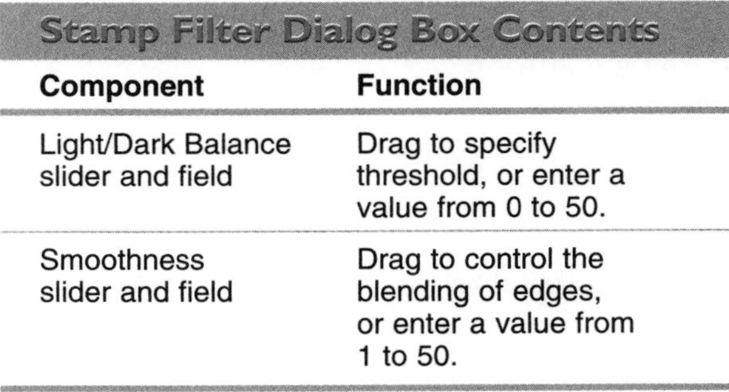

Stamp Filter Dialog Box Contents

Component	Function
Light/Dark Balance slider and field	Drag to specify threshold, or enter a value from 0 to 50.
Smoothness slider and field	Drag to control the blending of edges, or enter a value from 1 to 50.

CONTINUED

PAINTERLY FILTER EFFECTS CONTINUED

Torn Edges Filter

The Torn Edges filter is a Threshold filter that converts everything in the image to the exact foreground or background color. The following figure shows the Torn Edges filter dialog box.

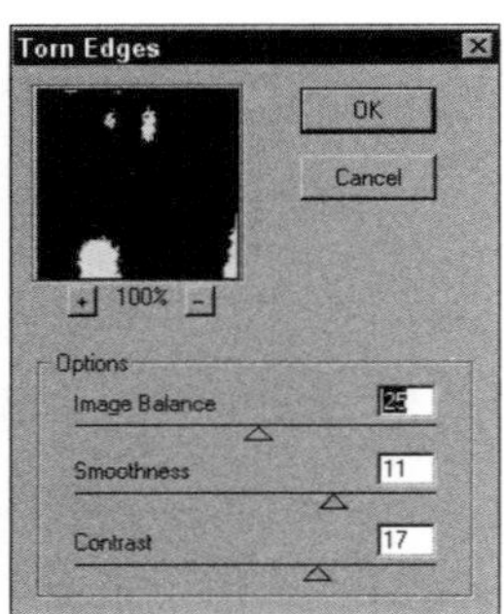

Torn Edges Filter Dialog Box Contents

Component	Function
Image Balance slider and field	Drag to specify threshold, or enter a value from 0 to 50.
Smoothness slider and field	Drag to increase or decrease graininess of edges, or enter a value from 1 to 15.
Contrast slider and field	Drag to change the overall image contrast, or enter a value from 1 to 25.

Water Paper Filter

The Water Paper filter, the dialog box of which is shown in the following figure, is the only Sketch filter that works in full color. It makes your image look like an ink image painted on fibrous paper and soaked in water.

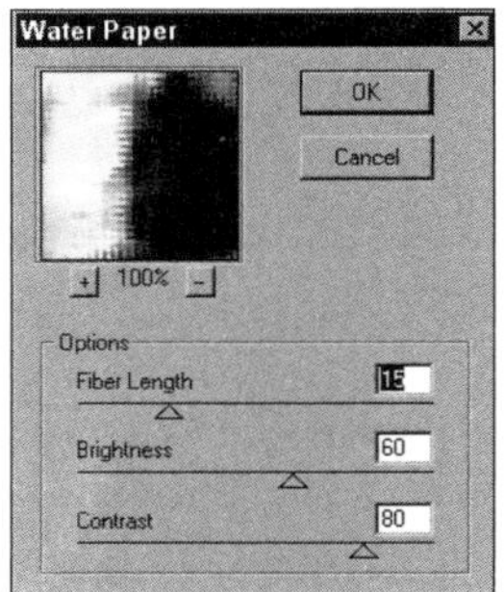

Water Paper Filter Dialog Box Contents

Component	Function
Fibre Length slider and field	Drag to increase or decrease length of the threads in the texture weave, or enter a value from 3 to 50.
Brightness slider and field	Drag to change overall image brightness, or enter a value from 0 to 100.
Contrast slider and field	Drag to change overall image contrast, or enter a value from 0 to 100.

CREATE A PAINTING BY FILTERING SPECIFIC AREAS

Most of the time, using a single filter to create a painting makes for flat, dull-looking images. Besides, a filter that flatters one area of the picture may really not be that flattering to another area.

A much better plan is to isolate specific areas of an image so that you can create a variety of textures and effects. You can then use a filter (or a different setting for the same filter) that works best for each area.

The process is pretty simple. Select each area of focus (or texture) separately, and save the selection. Name each selection for the area it represents. Once you've done that, choose Window ➪ Show Channels and, one at a time, drag each channel to the Make Selection icon. Feather a particular selection (Opt/Alt+⌘/Ctrl+D) if it seems appropriate. Then run the filter you've chosen for that area.

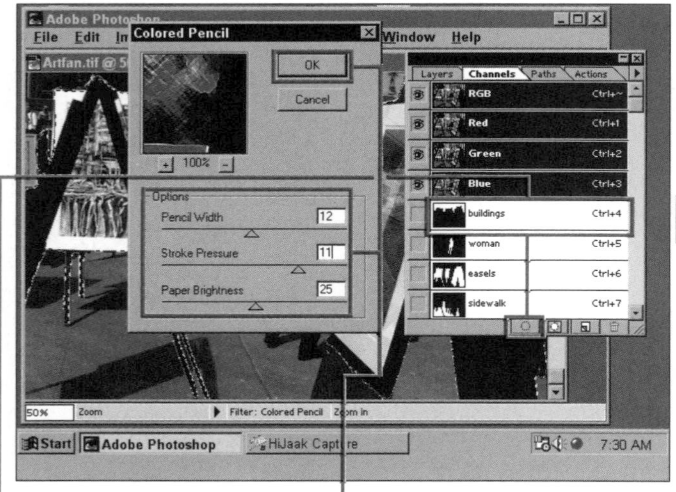

Note: The following steps assume that you have selected each target area, saved each selection under a separate name, and then selected Windows ➪ Show Channels.

1. Drag a channel to the Make Selection icon.
2. Choose a filter that will texture the foreground.
3. Adjust settings.
4. Click OK to run the filter.
5. Activate the selection for the background area (see Steps 1—3).
6. Choose a filter that will soften (throw out of focus) the background.
7. Make adjustments.
8. Click OK to run the filter.

How do I get rid of seams that show up between selected areas?

Try feathering selections slightly before running the filters. Usually, this ends up in a pleasant overlapping of the two effects. Sometimes you'll need to use the Rubber Stamp tool to mend seams. You can also select objects with plenty of extra room inside the selection, mask them more precisely with a layer mask on their own layer, and then interactively fine-tune the seams later.

Are the Artistic filters the only ones I can treat this way?

No. You apply any filter using a selection as a mask. The only limitation is whether you like the result.

What about using this technique to fade the same filter to different degrees?

Fading is the best way to vary the look while keeping the character and direction of filter strokes consistent throughout the painting. Some purists would say that this is the only way to do it. Just choose Filter ➪ Fade (Last Command) and then enter a specific level of fade.

9 Select the area that is the secondary point of interest.

10 Choose a filter that mimics paint strokes, and texture this area in the most appropriate way.

11 Make adjustments.

12 Click OK to run the filter.

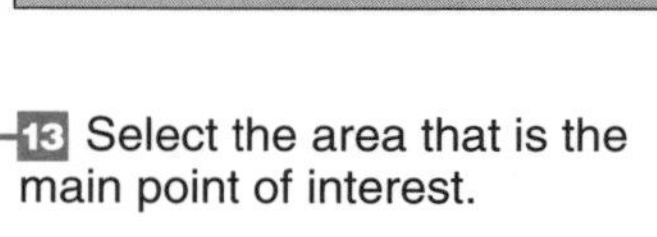

13 Select the area that is the main point of interest.

14 Choose a filter that will paint and texture this area in the most appropriate way.

15 Make adjustments.

16 Click OK to run the filter.

Note: This example is a combined screen, created so you can see the result of the filter in the background painting.

TEXTURIZE AN IMAGE WITH A SKETCH FILTER

Regardless of how expertly you use the Artistic filters to paint an image, the result can still look flat, because most natural media has a texture to give it some of its appealing feel and character. Oil paint, for instance, can go on thicker or thinner, forming little ridges. Sometimes you can even see the underlying texture of the canvas. Watercolors, on the other hand, tend to soak into the paper, but the paper itself has a texture.

You can use both the Texturizer and Lighting Effects filters in combination with one of the two-color Sketch filters to create textures that look like techniques for applying heavy paints, such as oils and acrylics. In traditional painting, this thick application of layers of paint is called *impasto*.

Here's a way to create an impasto texture: Open the image to which you want to apply impasto. Run one of the Sketch filters over it (each produces a different stroke style) and save the result to a unique name. Reopen the original file and apply the new file to it as a Texturize filter.

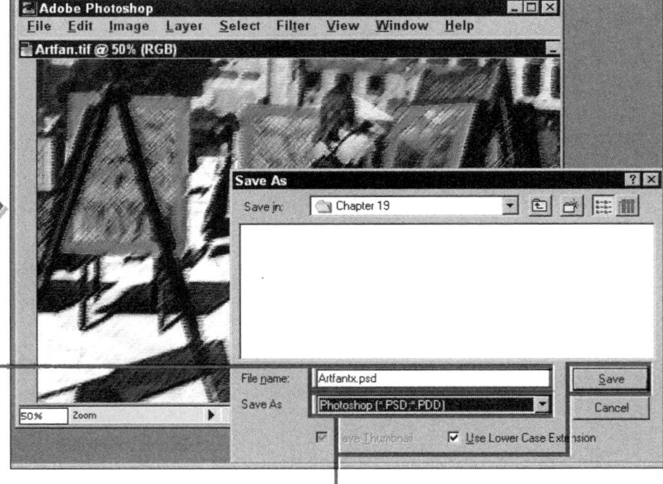

1. Choose Filter ➪ Sketch ➪ Specific filter name.

Note: I chose Chalk & Charcoal for this example because I wanted a subtle, palette-knife-type patina.

2. Adjust the filter s controls. Higher contrast and a more defined stroke produce more complex textures.
3. Click OK to render the filter.
4. Choose File ➪ Save As.
5. Give the file a new name that indicates it is to be used as a texture.
6. Choose Photoshop (.PSD) from the pull-down menu.
7. Click Save.

TIPS

Are any of the Sketch filters more likely to produce pleasing results?

Yes. Bas Relief, Chrome, and Note Paper have produced excellent results for me.

Can I create a texture with more than one Sketch filter?

You can simply keep using different Sketch filters on the same image and save the result as a grayscale or RGB PSD file. Then change the result using Texturizer, or any of the other filters that enable you to import a texture.

Can I use any of the filters other than Sketch for this purpose?

You can try this with any filter — even those from third-party manufacturers. The Mezzotint filters from Andromeda can produce some especially interesting results. Because most of these filters produce a color image, you want to choose Image ➪ Mode ➪ Grayscale and Layer ➪ Flatten Image before saving the file under a new name for use as a texture.

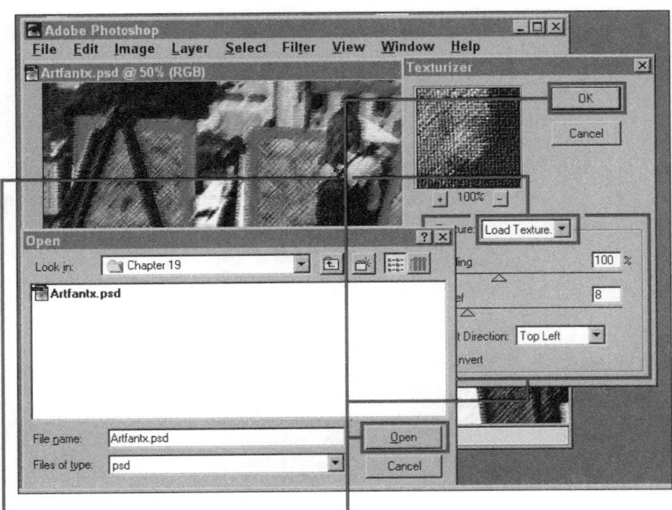

8 Close the file you just renamed and reopen the original file.

9 Choose Filter ➪ Texturize ➪ Texturizer.

10 Choose Load Texture.

11 Choose the texture file you just created and click Open.

12 Make adjustments.

13 Click OK.

■ Here is the result of the preceding steps for this exercise.

APPLY THE COLORED PENCIL FILTER

Many of the Photoshop Artistic filters have slightly misleading names. The Colored Pencil filter is one such example. The effect really looks like a crosshatched rubbing made with sharpened pastels rather than a drawing created with colored pencils.

Nevertheless, the Colored Pencil filter offers three variable effects, Pencil Width, Stroke Pressure, and Paper Brightness. Paper Brightness determines the gray level of the background on which the rubbing is made. Stroke Pressure controls the intensity (brightness) of the strokes. Pencil Width determines whether the crosshatched strokes appear to be made with a newly sharpened pencil or a fat, worn crayon.

1 Choose Filter ⇨ Artistic ⇨ Colored Pencil.

2 Drag the Pencil Width slider to indicate thickness of stroke.

3 Drag the Stroke Pressure slider to indicate brightness of stroke.

4 Drag the Paper Brightness slider to change whiteness of the paper or background.

5 When you're happy with what you see in the Preview window, click OK.

■ Wait a few moments, and you'll see something that looks approximately like this figure.

APPLY THE CUTOUT FILTER

The Cutout filter reduces the number of colors in an image to the number of colors you specify in the dialog box and then smoothes the edges. I find this an extremely useful filter for preparing an image to be hand-painted in a natural-media paint program such as Fractal Designs Painter, Dabbler, or Painter Classic.

Three adjustments can be made in the Cutout filter dialog box: No. of Levels determines how many colors are used in the final image. Edge Simplicity determines how smooth or jagged the borders are between adjacent colors. Edge Fidelity determines accuracy in tracing the original image's shapes.

In determining the number of colors to be used in the result, No. of Levels also determines the number of shapes (or the simplicity) you see in the result. You can set a maximum of eight levels.

1 Choose Filter ⇨ Artistic ⇨ Cutout.

2 Drag the No. of Levels slider to indicate degree of posterization.

3 Drag the Edge Simplicity slider to control border smoothness.

4 Drag the Edge Fidelity slider to adjust edge tracing relative to original shape.

5 When you're happy with what you see in the Preview window, click OK.

■ Wait a few moments, and you'll see something that looks approximately like this figure.

APPLY THE DRY BRUSH FILTER

The Dry Brush filter produces an effect similar to that of the Cutout filter. However, with the Dry Brush filter, the edges are softer, you can have more levels (up to ten) of detail, and you can add a level of stroke texturing.

Brush Size determines the width of the stroke, which translates to the individual areas of color. Brush Detail determines the smoothness of the edges. Texture gives the strokes less or more of an impasto texture.

1 Choose Filter ➪ Artistic ➪ Dry Brush.

2 Drag the Brush Size slider to determine width of brush stroke.

3 Drag the Brush Detail slider to indicate levels of color.

4 Drag the Texture slider to intensify apparent thickness of paint.

5 When you're happy with what you see in the Preview window, click OK.

■ Wait a few moments, and you'll see something that looks approximately like this figure.

APPLY THE FILM GRAIN FILTER

The Film Grain filter is really more of a photo-effect or darkroom filter than an artistic one, but it is contained within the Artistic filters menu. It is one of the few filters that does exactly what you expect of it; that is, it produces an effect that looks like the grain in photographic film. In fact, this filter is very useful (as is the Grain filter in the Texture filter group) when you need to match sections of a composite image that were photographed on different film emulsions or enlarged to different degrees. It is also useful for making photos look as though they were shot on fast film at low light levels and then overdeveloped to bring up the underexposed image. In traditional photography, this always produces excess grain.

In the Film Grain filter dialog box, Grain controls the size or coarseness of the grain. Highlight area adjusts the brightness of highlights. Intensity controls the contrast between the grain pattern and the image, which results in determining how widely the grain is distributed.

1 Choose Filter ⇨ Artistic ⇨ Film Grain.

2 Drag the Grain slider to determined the size of grain.

3 Drag the Highlight Area slider to determine the brightness of highlights.

4 Drag the Intensity slider to spread or reduce the overall occurrence of a grain pattern.

5 When you're happy with what you see in the Preview window, click OK.

■ Wait a few moments, and you'll see something that looks approximately like this figure.

APPLY THE FRESCO FILTER

The Fresco filter is meant to imitate the effect of painting on wet plaster. Highlights become wet and fuzzy, whereas darker colors become deeper and sharper. Saturation and contrast are both increased over the original image.

The Fresco filter's controls are identical to those for the Dry Brush filter. Brush Size determines the width of the stroke, which translates to the individual areas of color. Brush Detail determines the smoothness of the edges. The Texture control makes the background seem more or less like the plaster that is the traditional substrate for a Fresco painting.

1 Choose Filter ⇨ Artistic ⇨ Fresco.

2 Drag the Brush Size slider to determined width of the brush stroke.

3 Drag the Brush Detail slider to indicate levels of color.

4 Drag the Texture slider to intensify apparent thickness of paint.

5 When you're happy with what you see in the Preview window, click OK.

■ Wait a few moments, and you'll see something that looks approximately like this figure.

APPLY THE NEON GLOW FILTER

Neon Glow in Purgatory would be a better name for this filter, which changes everything to a bluish, fuzzed-out netherworld.

The Neon Glow filter controls let you adjust glow size, glow brightness, and glow color. Glow size really determines how unfocused the image becomes.

Glow brightness determines the intensity and spread of the glow color. Glow color is the only color (other than the already chosen foreground color) you can choose in this duotone effect. Clicking the Glow Color Swatch brings up the standard Color Picker to let you choose any color.

1 Choose Filter ⇨ Artistic ⇨ Neon Glow.

2 Drag the Glow Size slider to determine the degree to which the glow color will blur.

3 Drag the Glow Brightness slider to determine how intensely the glow color will appear.

4 Click the Glow Color Swatch to choose a color from the Color Picker.

5 When you're happy with what you see in the Preview window, click OK.

■ Wait a few moments, and you'll see something that looks approximately like this figure.

APPLY THE PAINT DAUBS FILTER

The Paint Daubs filter has a menu of seven different brushes, each of which creates a very different look. The basic idea is that the strokes imitate those made by a brush dipped into heavy paint and then applied by tapping the end of the brush on the canvas.

The three controls are Brush Size, Sharpness, and Brush Type. Brush Size controls the spread of areas of different color (which most brush types tend to fade or blend into one another). Sharpness makes the borders between colors more or less distinct. The Brush Types are Simple, Light Rough, Dark Rough, Wide Sharp, Wide Blurry, and Sparkle. Each of these is shown, in order from left to right and top to bottom, in the second figure below.

1 Choose Filter ➪ Artistic ➪ Paint Daubs.

2 Drag the Brush Size slider to determine the size of the brightest areas.

3 Drag the Sharpness slider to determine the sharpness of borders.

4 Choose a brush type for the effect.

5 When you're happy with what you see in the Preview window, click OK.

■ Wait a few moments, and you'll see something that looks approximately like this figure.

Note: The effects of the six brushes, from left to right: Simple, Light Rough, Dark Rough, Wide Sharp, Wide Blurry, and Sparkle.

APPLY THE PALETTE KNIFE FILTER

The Palette Knife filter is really just another way to flatten colors into broad strokes. You can vary the softness of edges and the amount of apparent detail in the strokes. The effect is a pleasing variation that doesn't appear anything like the impasto effect of actually smearing on thick paint with a palette knife.

However, if you desired, you could use one of the other brushes in a texture channel and then use Lighting Effects to create an impasto effect.

1 Choose Filter ➪ Artistic ➪ Palette Knife.

2 Drag the Stroke Size slider to determine the size of the brightest areas.

3 Drag the Stroke Detail slider to determine the number of colors (areas of color).

4 Drag the Softness slider to determine the sharpness of borders.

5 When you're happy with what you see in the Preview window, click OK.

■ Wait a few moments, and you'll see something that looks approximately like this figure.

■ *An impasto effect was created by using the Glowing Edges filter on a copy of this file, putting the result into an alpha channel, and then using that as the texture channel for the Lighting Effects filter.*

APPLY THE PLASTIC WRAP FILTER

The Plastic Wrap filter is one of my favorite Photoshop filters because it can actually lend a three-dimensional look to an image, which is useful for giving depth and roundness to such textured areas of a photo as the leaves of a tree. You can also make the image look as though you've smothered everything in Saran Wrap.

Plastic Wrap's three controls are Highlight Strength, Detail, and Smoothness. Highlight Strength controls the apparent shininess of the plastic wrap. Detail controls the number of wrinkles and bumps in the plastic wrap. Smoothness controls the abruptness of the transition between the highlights (plastic) and the underlying color.

1 Choose Filter ⇨ Artistic ⇨ Plastic Wrap.

2 Drag the Highlight Strength slider to determine the shininess of effect.

3 Drag the Detail slider to determine how tightly the wrap should adhere.

4 Drag the Smoothness slider to soften or harden the transition between plastic highlights and image details.

5 When you're happy with what you see in the Preview window, click OK.

■ Wait a few moments, and you'll see something that looks approximately like this figure.

APPLY THE POSTER EDGES FILTER

The Poster Edges filter imparts an effect reminiscent of the technique of artist Toulouse-Lautrec. Colors are flattened and then outlined with dark edges. This is another filter than works extremely well when you use one of the texturizing methods described in Chapter 14.

Poster Edge's three controls are Edge Thickness, Edge Intensity, and Posterization. Edge Thickness controls the thickness of the edge outlines, Edge Intensity controls how dark the edges become, and Posterization reduces the number of colors in the image to between zero and six levels.

1 Choose Filter ➪ Artistic ➪ Poster Edges.

2 Drag the Edge Thickness slider to determine the thickness of edge outlines.

3 Drag the Edge Intensity slider to determine the darkness of edge outlines.

4 Drag the Posterization slider to increase or reduce the number of colors in the image.

5 When you're happy with what you see in the Preview window, click OK.

■ Wait a few moments, and you'll see something that looks approximately like this figure.

APPLY THE ROUGH PASTELS FILTER

The Rough Pastels filter is dependent on the use of a texture file. Of course, you can use Canvas, Sandstone, or Burlap — but none of these is a conventional material on which to paint pastels. Make your own watercolor paper texture, or use the one provided on the CD-ROM that accompanies this book (see Appendix B for more about all the goodies on the CD-ROM). The look of this filter is a bit like oil pastels, but with all the strokes moving in a parallel direction. If the filter had an angle control, you could make the result more natural by filtering selected areas one at a time.

Rough Pastels has seven controls, including the capability to include a texture file and to control lighting direction on the texture. The controls are Stroke Length and Stroke Detail, Texture, Texture Scaling, Texture Relief, Light Direction, and an Invert check box. Stroke Length controls the distance over which strokes are smeared. Stroke Detail controls the width of the stroke. You choose the texture from a pull-down menu or load one, and then move sliders to control the size and depth of the texture pattern. Finally, you choose the direction of light from a pull-down menu.

1 Select Filter ➪ Artistic ➪ Rough Pastels.

2 Drag to right to increase stroke length.

3 Drag to right to set the width of a stroke.

4 Choose texture or load a custom texture file.

■ Here is the result of applying the settings in Steps 2-4.

APPLY THE SMUDGE STICK FILTER

The Smudge Stick filter is a little like Rough Pastels without the texture. The image is highly posterized (you have no direct control over the number of levels of color) and is smeared in diagonal strokes.

Smudge Stick takes you back to the conventional three controls: Stroke Length, Highlight Area, and Intensity. Stroke Length, as you know if you've been reading from the beginning of the chapter, is self-descriptive. Highlight Area controls the brightness of highlights. Intensity controls saturation and contrast.

1 Choose Filter ⇨ Artistic ⇨ Smudge Stick.

2 Drag the Stroke Length slider to adjust length of smear.

3 Drag the Highlight Area slider to control highlight brightness.

4 Drag the Intensity slider to change contrast and saturation.

5 When you're happy with what you see in the Preview window, click OK.

■ Wait a few moments, and you'll see something that looks approximately like this figure.

APPLY THE SPONGE FILTER

The Sponge filter is useful for creating a faux finish over backgrounds. Colors are flattened and posterized, and then darker blotches are imposed in a seemingly random pattern. I have used Sponge to excellent effect in conjunction with the Poster Edges filter. I use the Magic Wand to select spaces between the Poster Edges and then treat them with the Sponge filter, using different settings for each selection. Combining filter effects in this way is much easier and faster if you use Actions to assign several filters to a set of function keys.

The Sponge filter dialog box contains the following three controls: Brush Size, Definition, and Smoothness. Brush Size enlarges or reduces the sponge blobs. Definition lightens and darkens the blobs. Smoothness anti-aliases the edges of the blobs.

1 Choose Filter ➪ Artistic ➪Sponge.

2 Drag the Brush Size slider to adjust blotch size.

3 Drag the Definition slider to intensify blotches.

4 Drag the Smoothness slider to smooth blotch edges.

5 When you're happy with what you see in the Preview window, click OK.

■ Wait a few moments, and you'll see something that looks approximately like this figure.

APPLY THE UNDERPAINTING FILTER

The Underpainting filter does a credible job of making an image look as if it was washed onto a textured surface with highly thinned paints. This is a basic technique for starting an oil painting and is a good first step in combining increasingly detailed or textured Artistic filters.

Because Underpainting works with texture maps, its dialog box contains seven controls. The first two control brush size and texture coverage. Texture coverage dictates how light the paint must be before the texture shows through.

1 Choose Filter ⇨ Artistic ⇨ Underpainting.

2 Drag the Brush Size slider to adjust size of solid color areas.

3 Drag the Texture Coverage slider to determine threshold for texture bleed-through.

4 Choose settings in this area to adjust the texture.

5 When you're happy with what you see in the Preview window, click OK.

■ Wait a few moments, and you'll see something that looks approximately like this.

APPLY THE WATERCOLOR FILTER

The Watercolor filter's job is to make your image look as if it were painted with watercolors. Colors are posterized and then made to bleed into one another with soft edges. Darker colors below a certain threshold (which you can't control) get much darker (you can control how much darker). The result looks a lot like the Fresco filter, but with softer borders between colors.

The Watercolor filter dialog box contains three controls: Brush Detail, Shadow Intensity, and Texture. Brush Detail dictates the range of color reduction. Shadow Intensity lowers or raises contrast. Texture doesn't use the standard art surfaces but controls edge smoothness.

1 Choose Filter ➪ Artistic ➪ Watercolor.

2 Drag the Brush Detail slider to adjust color reduction.

3 Drag the Shadow Intensity slider to determine shadow contrast.

4 Drag the Texture slider to control edge smoothness.

5 When you're happy with what you see in the Preview window, click OK.

■ Wait a few moments, and you'll see something that looks approximately like this figure.

APPLY THE ACCENTED EDGES FILTER

The Accented Edges filter reduces colors and outlines the edges with a jagged dry-brush stroke. You can vary the width of this stroke to the extent that the edge can almost become the image. Altering brightness and smoothness also greatly changes the effect and texture of the image. The example shown has all three sliders set near the middle of their range.

The Accented Edges dialog box contains three controls: Edge Width, Edge Brightness, and Smoothness. Edge Width controls the thickness of the brush-stroked border between colors. Edge Brightness adjusts the border color from white to black. Smoothness anti-aliases and blurs the edge stroke.

1 Choose Brush Strokes ➪ Artistic ➪ Accented Edges.

2 Drag the Edge Width slider to adjust the width of the outline brush stroke.

3 Drag the Edge Brightness slider to whiten/blacken the outline stroke.

4 Drag the Smoothness slider to anti-alias the border stroke.

5 When you're happy with what you see in the Preview window, click OK.

■ Wait a few moments, and you'll see something that looks approximately like this figure.

Note: If you want to make outlined edges in a variety of colors within the same image, choose Image ➪ Adjust ➪ Posterize and set the number of colors that suits your image. Select each area of color with the Magic Wand and choose Edit ➪ Stroke.

APPLY THE ANGLED STROKES FILTER

The Angled Strokes filter creates an effect similar to the Rough Pastels filter, but you can control the main direction of the strokes. Strokes are automatically angled in different directions in contrasting areas of the image, giving the image the appearance of having been created with a very dry, very thick oil brush.

The three dialog box controls for this filter are Direction Balance, Stroke Length, and Sharpness. Direction Balance changes the overall angle of the strokes. Stroke Length shrinks and stretches the strokes. Sharpness softens the edges of the strokes by anti-aliasing them.

1 Choose Brush Strokes ➪ Brush Strokes ➪Angled Strokes.

2 Drag the Direction Balance slider to change the principal direction of the brush stroke angle.

3 Drag the Stroke Length slider to lengthen or shorten the brush stroke.

4 Drag the Sharpness slider to anti-alias the strokes.

5 When you're happy with what you see in the Preview window, click OK.

■ Wait a few moments, and you'll see something that looks approximately like this figure.

APPLY THE CROSSHATCH FILTER

The Crosshatch filter creates cross-stroked color etching. You could easily turn this image into a pen-and-ink etching by converting to grayscale and using the Threshold, High Pass, or other Image ⇨ Adjust commands. Pump the Strength control up to 3, and you'll get something that looks almost like a basket weave.

The Crosshatch filter dialog box contains three controls: Stroke Length, Sharpness, and Strength. Stroke Length determines how far the stroke will smear before it fades out. Sharpness can increase the apparent effect but, if you're not careful, can also cause objectionable pixelization. Strength makes the effect more or less obvious, chiefly by broadening the stroke (actually, the "bristles").

1 Choose Brush Strokes ⇨ Brush Strokes ⇨ Crosshatch.

2 Drag the Stroke Length slider to change the stroke distance.

3 Drag the Sharpness slider to harden or soften the strokes.

4 Drag the Strength slider to narrow or widen the strokes.

5 When you're happy with what you see in the Preview window, click OK.

■ Wait a few moments, and you'll see something that looks approximately like this figure.

Note: Try selecting different areas of an image, feathering each selection, and then using different Strength settings in each area. You can use this trick to create an enhanced illusion of depth between foreground, midplane, and background.

APPLY THE DARK STROKES FILTER

The Dark Strokes filter makes angular smudged strokes and greatly heightens the difference between highlights and shadows, whereas midtones are left more or less alone. This filter can make for very dramatic and classical looking portraits if you double the size of the image, run the filter, and then reduce the image to its original size.

The Dark Strokes filter dialog box controls are Stroke Length, Dark Intensity, and Light Intensity. Stroke Length controls how much contrast must exist between edges before a stroke is made.

1 Choose Brush Strokes ⇨ Brush Strokes ⇨ Dark Strokes.

2 Drag the Balance slider to change the midpoint of midtones.

3 Drag the Black Intensity slider to lighten or darken shadows.

4 Drag the White Intensity slider to lighten or darken highlights.

5 When you're happy with what you see in the Preview window, click OK.

■ Wait a while, and you'll see something that looks approximately like this figure.

APPLY THE INK OUTLINES FILTER

The Ink Outlines filter is great for making images look as though they were painted into inked sketch lines. This filter outlines images in a much more predictable manner than the other edge effects created by Photoshop filters.

Also, it darkens the background and increases saturation and contrast in a manner very similar to the Dark Strokes filter.

The Ink Outlines filter dialog box controls are Stroke Length, Dark Intensity, and Light Intensity. These last two controls work just like the controls of the same name in the Dark Strokes filter dialog box. Stroke Length controls how much contrast must exist between edges before a stroke is made. For that reason, it also controls the number of outline strokes.

1 Choose Brush Strokes ⇨ Brush Strokes ⇨ Ink Outlines.

2 Drag the Stroke Length slider to change the number and length of outline strokes.

3 Drag the Dark Intensity slider to lighten or darken shadows.

4 Drag the Light Intensity slider to lighten or darken highlights.

5 When you're happy with what you see in the Preview window, click OK.

■ Wait a few moments, and you'll see something that looks approximately like this figure.

APPLY THE SPATTER FILTER

The Spatter filter creates an effect that is somewhere between a spraygun painting and pointillism. How far in between depends on where you set the sliders. This can be an excellent filter for giving a softening effect to an image. Just apply the filter, and then choose the Filter ⇨ Fade command to diminish the effect of the filter.

Applying the Spatter filter is fairly straightforward, and the two sliders in the filter's dialog box make it easy to experiment with variations. The Spray Radius slider controls the size of the spray dots. The Smoothness slider anti-aliases the spray dots so that the colors blend more smoothly.

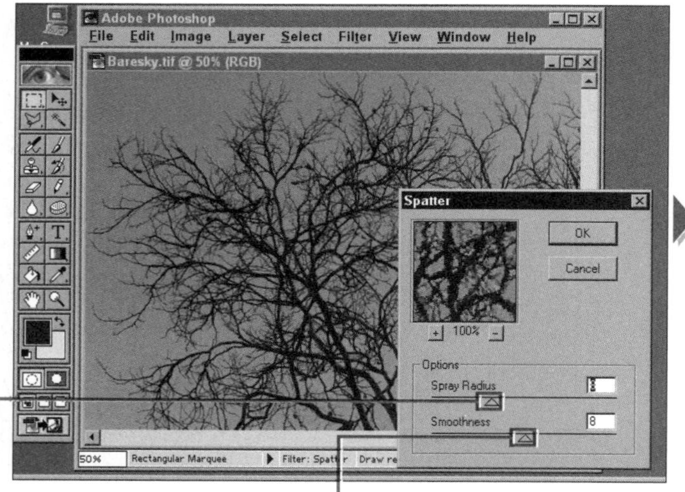

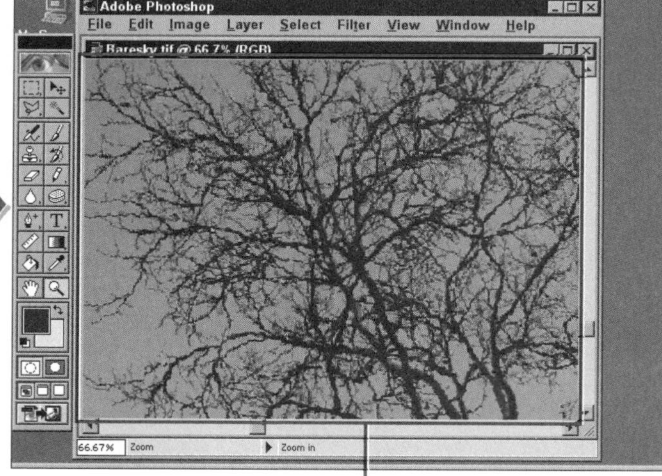

1 Choose Filter ⇨ Brush Strokes ⇨ Spatter.

2 Drag the Spray Radius slider to increase/decrease the radius of a splat (pixel clump).

3 Drag the Smoothness slider to blend or sharpen the dots. Sharper dots heighten the spatter effect.

4 When you're happy with what you see in the Preview window, click OK.

■ Wait a few moments, and you'll see something that looks approximately like this figure.

APPLY THE SUMI-E FILTER

The Sumi-e filter produces an effect similar to the Dark Strokes filter, but with softer edges and colors. You could think of it as a cross between the Watercolor and Dark Strokes filters. The strokes are diagonal daubs whose size and intensity can be varied over a wide range. There is no control over the direction of strokes; they are all diagonal from top right to bottom left.

The Sumi-e filter dialog box controls are Stroke Width, Stroke Pressure, and Contrast. Stroke Width controls the distance over which details in the image are smeared. Stroke Pressure controls the density and intensity of the strokes. Contrast controls the width of the black strokes.

1 Choose Brush Strokes ⇨ Brush Strokes ⇨ Sumi-e.

2 Drag the Stroke Width slider to increase or decrease the area over which colors are blended.

3 Drag the Stroke Pressure slider to increase or decrease blackness of the stroke.

4 Drag the Contrast slider to increase or decrease width of black strokes.

5 When you're happy with what you see in the Preview window, click OK.

■ Wait a few moments, and you'll see something that looks approximately like this figure.

APPLY THE BAS RELIEF FILTER

The Bas Relief filter creates a grayscale embossed effect (grayscale if you leave colors at the default; otherwise, whatever colors are there for foreground and background). Its effect is interesting on its own and can be adjusted to give the impression of more or less depth and detail.

This filter is also a wonderful way to give a color image the look of impasto oils: Run the filter, convert the image to grayscale, flatten it if necessary, and then save it under a new file name. Reload the original file and run the Texturizer filter using the Bas Relief–treated file as the texture.

The Bas Relief filter dialog box controls are Detail, Smoothness, and Light Direction. Detail controls the number of colors that are blended to make a relief plane. Smoothness controls the softness of edges. Light Direction lets you choose 45-degree angles of lighting from a pull-down menu.

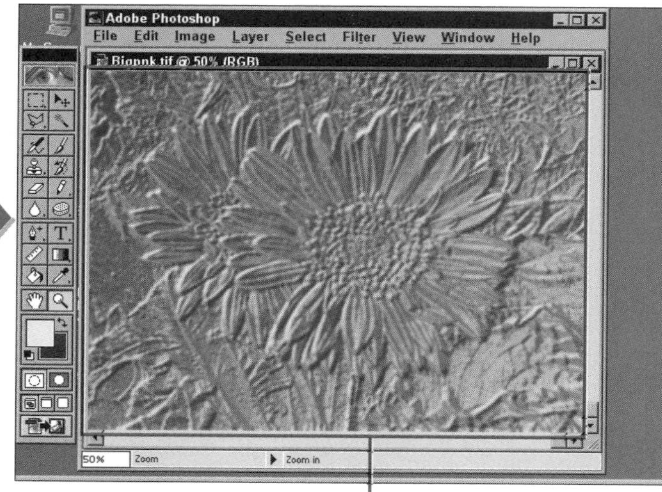

1 Choose Brush Strokes ⇨ Sketch ⇨ Bas Relief.

2 Drag the Detail slider to increase or decrease the area of a shape or depth plane.

3 Drag the Smoothness slider to sharpen or blur the edges of planes.

4 Choose the lighting direction.

5 When you're happy with what you see in the Preview window, click OK.

■ Wait a few moments, and you'll see something that looks approximately like this figure.

APPLY THE CHALK & CHARCOAL FILTER

The Chalk & Charcoal filter creates a duotone version of the Rough Pastels filter. The strokes are a mixture of chalk (foreground color) and charcoal (background color) angular, smudgy strokes. These strokes cover only as much area as the Stroke Pressure setting allows. The remaining area is seen as a light gray.

The Chalk & Charcoal filter dialog box controls are Charcoal Area, Chalk Area, and Stroke Pressure. Charcoal Area controls the threshold below which the image are covered with strokes in the foreground color. Chalk Area controls the threshold above which the image is covered with strokes in the background color. This happens because the default foreground color is black and the default background color is white. Pressure controls the width of the strokes and the degree to which they bleed into one another.

1 Choose Brush Strokes ⇨ Sketch ⇨ Chalk & Charcoal.

2 Drag the Charcoal Area slider to increase or decrease the area stroked with the foreground color.

3 Drag the Chalk Area slider to increase or decrease the area stroked with the background color.

4 Drag the Stroke Pressure slider to narrow or widen the strokes.

5 When you're happy with what you see in the Preview window, click OK.

■ Wait a few moments, and you'll see something that looks approximately like this figure.

APPLY THE CHARCOAL FILTER

As with the Chalk & Charcoal filter, the Charcoal filter also uses the foreground and background colors of the image (as do all the Sketch submenu filters), but the strokes are crosshatched and finer. Borders between colors are more emphasized, which gives the result a relatively authentic look of charcoal on newsprint.

The Charcoal filter dialog box controls are Charcoal Thickness, Detail, and Light/Dark Balance. Charcoal Thickness controls the width of the stroke, but the range is so narrow that the effect is quite subtle. Detail controls the number of colors within a given shape. Light/Dark balance determines the point at which highlights become entirely white (untouched paper).

Hint: You can get an even more interesting effect by running the Ink Outlines filter first.

1 Choose Brush Strokes ➪ Sketch ➪ Charcoal.

2 Drag the Charcoal Thickness slider to increase or decrease the thickness of the crosshatched strokes.

3 Drag the Detail slider to increase or decrease the number of shapes that can be distinguished.

4 Drag the Light/Dark Balance slider to control image contrast.

5 When you're happy with what you see in the Preview window, click OK.

■ Wait a few moments, and you'll see something that looks approximately like this figure.

APPLY THE CHROME FILTER

The Chrome filter is basically the same as a grayscale version of the Plastic Wrap filter. It can produce some lovely impasto effects when used with the Texturize filter (in fact, all the Sketch filters are useful for creating texture effects with any of the filters that can use a grayscale texture). Another way to use the Chrome filter effectively is to copy the layer containing the original filter and combine the two, using one of the Blend modes. The Color and Overlay modes are particularly appealing.

The Chrome filter dialog box controls are Smoothness and Detail. Detail determines the levels of color that are blended together. Smoothness softens the edges between shades of gray.

1 Choose Brush Strokes ⇨ Sketch ⇨ Chrome.

2 Drag the Detail slider to increase or decrease the number of recognizable shapes.

3 Drag the Smoothness slider to increase or decrease the smoothness of the transitions from highlights to shadows.

4 When you're happy with what you see in the Preview window, click OK.

■ Wait a few moments, and you'll see something that looks approximately like this figure.

APPLY THE CONTÉ CRAYON FILTER

The Conté Crayon filter can produce interesting results when you're reducing an image to a few duotones (made up of the foreground colors and background color of the image). You could use the result on its own (to make a fast-loading Web graphic, for instance) or for all sorts of interesting effects using background colors.

The Conté Crayon filter dialog box controls are Foreground Level, Background Level, and the standard set of Texture controls and pull-down menus — which you already know how to use if you've read the chapter up to this point. The midtones in Conté Crayon are always reduced to about 50 percent gray. The highlights are then reinterpreted as the background level and the shadows as the foreground level (remember, the default foreground color is black).

1 Choose Brush Strokes ➪ Sketch ➪ Conté Crayon.

2 Drag the Foreground Level slider to increase or decrease the range of shades to be painted in the foreground color.

3 Drag the Background Level slider to increase or decrease the range of shades to be painted in the background color.

4 Choose and adjust the settings of a texture.

5 When you're happy with what you see in the Preview window, click OK.

■ Wait a few moments, and you'll see something that looks approximately like this figure.

APPLY THE GRAPHIC PEN FILTER

The Graphic Pen filter produces something that looks like a pen-and-ink etching made with unidirectional strokes. The best candidates for this filter (as is the case for most of the Sketch filters) are those images with good contrast between sharp, well-defined edges that aren't too close together. Knowing this, you may want to use image and retouching commands on the image before applying the Graphic Pen filter (or any of the other Sketch filters). This filter can produce some especially nice results using colors other than black and white as the foreground and background colors.

The Graphic Pen filter dialog box controls are Stroke Length, Light/Dark Balance, and the Stroke Direction pull-down menu (which contains the options Right Diagonal, Horizontal, Left Diagonal, and Vertical). Light/Dark balance establishes the threshold for highlights and shadows.

1 Choose Filter ➪ Brush Strokes ➪ Sketch ➪ Graphic Pen.

2 Drag the Stroke Length slider to increase or decrease the length of the black ink stroke.

3 Drag the Light/Dark Balance slider to increase or decrease the range of shades to be painted in the background color.

4 Choose a pen stroke direction.

5 When you're happy with what you see in the Preview window, click OK.

■ Wait a few moments, and you'll see something that looks approximately like this figure.

APPLY THE HALFTONE PATTERN FILTER

The Halftone Pattern filter produces a halftone pattern atop the image. By duplicating layers and using different foreground and background colors with different Blend modes for the layers, you can create any number of postmodern-type stylizations.

This filter offers three types of halftone patterns: Dot (which imitate the standard printer halftone pattern), Circle (a concentric pattern that can create some very interesting texture effects), and Line (which looks a bit like TV scan lines).

The Halftone Pattern filter dialog box controls are Size and Contrast. Size controls the size of the pattern element (circle, dot, or line). Contrast controls the overall contrast of the image and, therefore, how much of it is seen underlying the pattern.

1 Choose Brush Strokes ⇨ Sketch ⇨ Halftone Pattern.

2 Drag the Size slider to increase or decrease the size of the pattern element.

3 Drag the Contrast slider to increase or decrease the overall contrast of the underlying image.

4 Choose a pattern type.

5 When you're happy with what you see in the Preview window, click OK.

■ This shows the results of the Dot pattern type.

■ This shows the results of the Circle pattern type.

APPLY THE NOTE PAPER FILTER

The Note Paper filter creates an effect that makes me wonder how it came by its name. Application of this filter results in a textured, two-color, high-contrast rendition of the image on textured paper. You can control the graininess of the paper texture, but not the texture pattern.

The Note Paper filter dialog box controls are Image Balance, Graininess, and Relief. Image Balance is a threshold control that determines which parts of the image become the foreground and which the background. Graininess determines how pronounced the paper texture will be. Relief controls the intensity of the highlights and shadows that separate the edges of shapes.

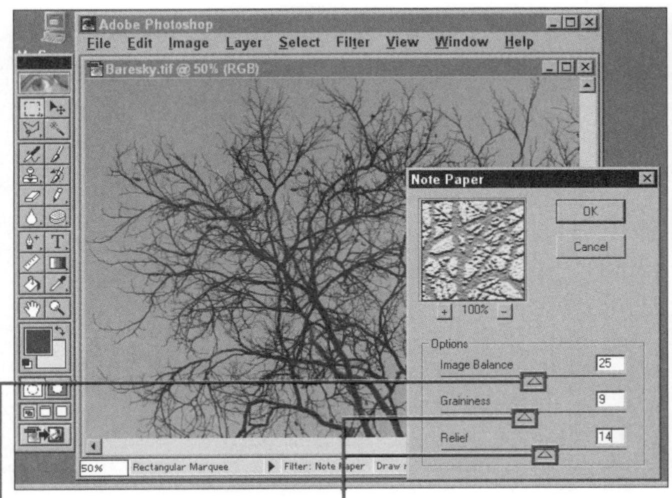

1 Choose Brush Strokes ➪ Sketch ➪ Note Paper.

2 Drag the Image Balance slider to change the foreground/background threshold.

3 Drag the Graininess slider to change the definition of edge shadows and highlights.

4 Drag the Relief slider to adjust the brightness of highlights and shadows.

5 When you're happy with what you see in the Preview window, click OK.

■ Wait a few moments, and you'll see something that looks approximately like this figure.

APPLY THE PHOTOCOPY FILTER

The Photocopy filter makes the image look as though it was copied on a copy machine incapable of producing grays. This filter is similar to the Threshold filter in that all color below a certain level goes to black in the background and all color above a certain level goes to the foreground. The Photocopy filter results in softer edges and a few more apparent shades of gray, however. Because it is such a pleasing version of a Threshold filter, this can be an excellent filter to use in combination with some of the other Sketch filters

The Photocopy filter dialog box controls are Detail and Darkness. Applied to the test image, moving the Detail slider didn't have much effect. The results it produces would be subtle on any image. The Darkness slider controls the intensity of the foreground color.

1 Choose Brush Strokes ⇨ Sketch ⇨ Photocopy.

2 Drag the Detail slider to change the shadow threshold.

3 Drag the Darkness slider to decrease or increase the intensity of the foreground color (shadow).

4 When you're happy with what you see in the Preview window, click OK.

■ Wait a few moments, and you'll see something that looks approximately like this figure.

APPLY THE PLASTER FILTER

The Plaster filter reduces the image to a few tones below an adjustable threshold in shades of the background color and embosses the shapes over a foreground color that is solid. You can easily reverse the effect by switching the foreground and background colors before running the filter. What this all has to do with plaster beats me, but the effect is interesting nevertheless. Just how interesting will depend on the image to a greater than usual degree. This filter becomes even more interesting when it is used on a duplicate layer together with a Blend mode.

The Plaster filter dialog box controls are Image Balance, Smoothness, and Light Position. Image Balance changes the threshold for the background color and determines what is seen as a shape versus what is seen as flat foreground color. Smoothness softens the transition between the embossed shape and the background color. Light Position lets you choose the direction of highlights and shadows on the embossed shapes.

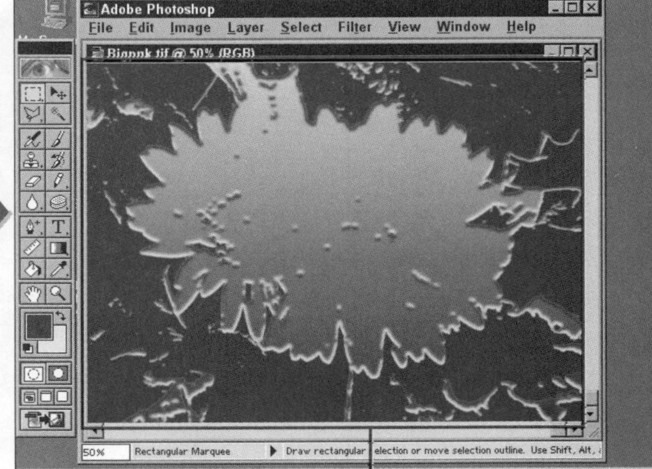

1 Choose Filter ⇨ Brush Strokes ⇨ Sketch ⇨ Plaster.

2 Drag the Image Balance slider to change the shadow threshold.

3 Drag the Smoothness slider to sharpen or smooth the border between foreground color and embossed shapes.

4 Choose a lighting position.

5 When you're happy with what you see in the Preview window, click OK.

■ Wait a few moments, and you'll see something that looks approximately like this figure.

APPLY THE RETICULATION FILTER

The Reticulation filter imitates what happens when photographic film is overheated during processing and film grain clumps together in worm-like forms. Oddly, the effect can produce interesting results when used as a texture. Blurred slightly with the Gaussian Blur filter, it makes great watercolor paper. Used on a duplicate layer applied with a Blend mode, you can get some nicely reticulated color photos, too.

The Reticulation filter dialog box controls are Density, Black Level, and White Level. Density actually dictates the number of grain dots. Black Level controls at what gray point the image turns black. White Level controls at what gray point the image turns white.

1 Choose Brush Strokes ➪ Sketch ➪ Reticulation.

2 Drag the Density slider to change the number of dots.

3 Drag the Black Level slider to delineate the black threshold.

4 Drag the White Level slider to delineate the white threshold.

5 When you're happy with what you see in the Preview window, click OK.

■ Wait a few moments, and you'll see something that looks approximately like this figure.

APPLY THE STAMP FILTER

The Stamp filter carves the image out in much the same way as rubber is carved to make a rubber stamp — thus its name. You can control the smoothness of lines and the point at which black and white divide. This is an excellent filter for making channel masks, by the way, especially because you can visually control the softness of the edges.

The Stamp filter dialog box controls are Light/Dark Balance and Smoothness. As you've probably already guessed, Light/Dark Balance moves the threshold (dividing point) up and down the grayscale. Smoothness hardens or softens the border between black and white.

1 Choose Brush Strokes ➪ Sketch ➪ Stamp.

2 Drag the Light/Dark Balance slider to change the dividing point between black and white.

3 Drag the Smoothness slider to sharpen or blur edges.

4 When you're happy with what you see in the Preview window, click OK.

■ Wait a few moments, and you'll see something that looks approximately like this figure.

APPLY THE TORN EDGES FILTER

The Torn Edges filter is a Threshold filter that converts everything in the image to the exact foreground or background color. The difference between the Torn Edges filter and similar filters is that the borders between foreground color and background color give the impression that the shapes have been torn from newsprint. (Actually, the edges are just grainy.)

There are three controls in the Torn Edges filter dialog box: Image Balance, Smoothness, and Contrast. Image Balance selects the dividing line (threshold) between foreground and background (usually black and white). Smoothness dictates the graininess of the edges. Contrast would seem the same as Image Balance but really has to do with how much detail is seen in the grainy border areas.

1 Choose Filter ➪ Sketch ➪ Torn Edges.

2 Drag the Image Balance slider to select the dividing tone between what is translated to foreground or background color.

3 Drag the Smoothness slider to increase or decrease graininess of torn edges.

4 Drag the Contrast slider to increase or decrease detail (or clumping) in grainy areas.

5 When you're happy with what you see in the Preview window, click OK.

■ Wait a few moments, and you'll see something that looks approximately like this figure.

APPLY THE WATER PAPER FILTER

The Water Paper filter is the only Sketch filter that works in full color. It makes a kind of watercolor painting of your image, but it looks more like an ink image painted on fibrous paper and soaked in water. Highlights flare into shadows, and lots of blurring occurs. The three sliders in the filter's dialog box give quite a bit of control over what stays recognizable and what blurs beyond recognition.

The Water Paper filter dialog box controls are Fiber Length, Brightness, and Contrast. Fiber Length controls blurriness, which actually becomes more or less pronounced as a result of the settings you use for Brightness and Contrast. Brightness and Contrast are used in the same way as the controls in the Image ⇨ Adjust Commands.

1 Choose Water Paper ⇨ Sketch ⇨ Water Paper.

2 Drag the Fiber Length slider to change the blurriness and texture of the image.

3 Drag the Brightness slider to increase or decrease image brightness.

4 Drag the Contrast slider to increase or decrease image contrast.

5 When you're happy with what you see in the Preview window, click OK.

■ Wait a few moments, and you'll see something that looks approximately like this figure.

16 WARPING AND MORPHING

This chapter covers the use of filters that act somewhat like funhouse mirrors by enlarging some pixels, shrinking some pixels, and moving still others. There are a variety of reasons for wanting to do this, including that it's just plain fun. More often, though, you may have a more serious reason. For example:

- You may need to composite two images so that one seems to wrap around the other.
- You may need to make a surface look as though it has been blown by the wind or rippled by raindrops.
- You may want an image to follow multiple contours, like the folds in a windblown flag.

Photoshop's twelve Distort filters perform all these functions and more.

Diffuse Glow Filter

The Diffuse Glow filter is unique among the Distort filters in that it doesn't really distort at all. Instead, it "bleeds" the current background color into the lighter (highlight) areas of your image. The Diffuse Glow filter dialog box is shown here.

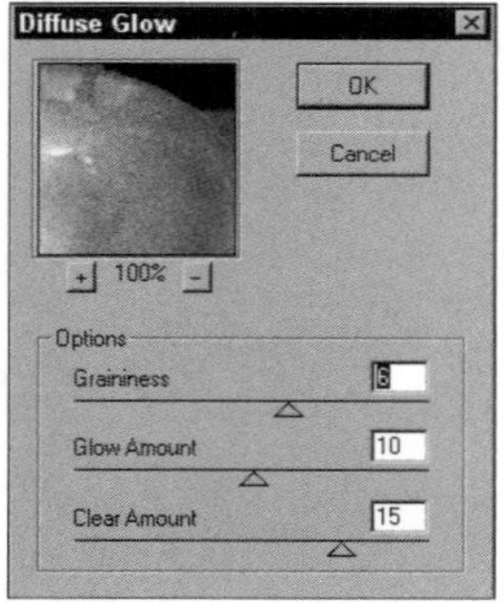

Diffuse Glow Filter Dialog Box Contents

Component	Function
Graininess slider	Increases the overall graininess of the image. Drag right to increase grain. You can't use this control to remove any graininess that is already present in the image.
Glow Amount slider	Infuses the current background color into the area surrounding the highlights. This effect is very different if the background color is darker than the highlights than if it is the same or brighter.
Clear Amount slider	Drag to adjust the radius of the glow.

Displace Filter

The Displace filter enables you to add texture to an image by moving the colors of a certain selection in a direction and distance you specify, as shown in the following figure. It is one of the most powerful filters in Photoshop's arsenal.

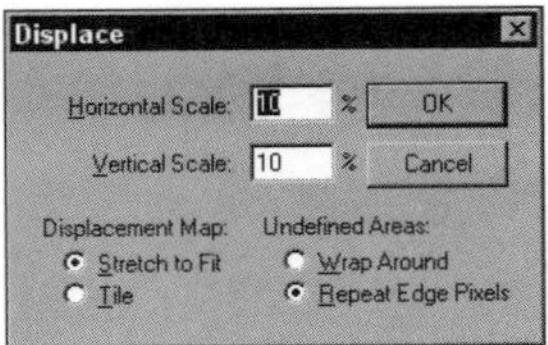

Displace Filter Dialog Box Contents

Component	Function
Horizontal Scale field	Specify a percentage of the image's size by which the displacement should occur in a horizontal direction.
Vertical Scale field	Specify a percentage of the image's size by which the displacement should occur in a vertical direction.
Stretch to Fit radio button	If chosen, the displacement map image file is resized to match the size of the current image's file.
Tile radio button	If chosen, repeats the displacement map image horizontally and vertically as needed to fill a larger image.
Wrap Around radio button	Fills any edge of the image that has been left vacant by a displacement with the part of the image that the displacement has pushed past the opposite border.
Repeat Edge Pixels radio button	Repeats the outermost row of pixels in the edge of the displaced image to the edge of the border.
OK button	When you click the OK button in this dialog box, it doesn't execute the displacement until you use a file loading dialog box to locate the file you want to use as a displacement map.

Glass Filter

The Glass filter, the dialog box of which is shown here, makes your image look as though it's being viewed through textured glass. Some portions of the image are magnified, some reduced, and all are distorted. Its effects are similar to those of the Ocean Ripple filter, described later in this chapter.

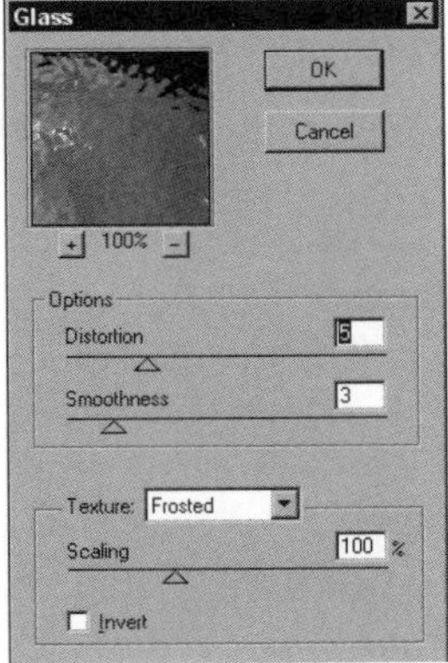

Glass Filter Dialog Box Contents

Component	Function
Distortion slider and field	Drag to the right to increase the bumpiness, or enter a number between 0 and 20.

WARPING AND MORPHING CONTINUED

Glass Filter Dialog Box Contents

Component	Function
Smoothness slider and field	Drag to the right to soften the edges of the texture bumps (that is, to cause them to blend with the image), or enter a number between 1 and 15.
Texture pull-down menu	Choose your own texture file or from one of the built-in textures: Canvas, Frosted, or Tiny Lens.
Scaling slider and field	Drag to enlarge or reduce the texture map tile, or enter a number between 50 and 200.
Invert check box	If checked, inverts the texture map. What was formerly a peak becomes a valley, and vice versa.

Ocean Ripple Filter

The Ocean Ripple filter produces a distortion that's much like the distortion created by the Glass filter, but it creates ripple shapes that are more random in size. The associated dialog box is shown in the following figure.

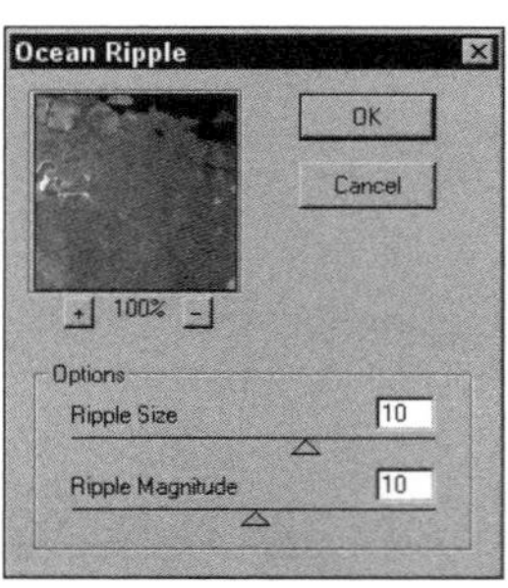

Ocean Ripple Filter Dialog Box Contents

Component	Function
Ripple Size slider and field	Drag to increase the distance between bumps, or enter a number between 1 and 15.
Ripple Magnitude slider and field	Drag to increase the apparent height of the bumps, or enter a number between 0 and 20.

Pinch Filter

The Pinch filter maps an image to the inside of a sphere, making an image appear as if it is printed on a piece of rubber sheeting that has been made to sag in the center. The Pinch filter is a good filter for stretching an object so that it can be blended with a concave or convex surface in a photo composite. The Pinch filter dialog box is depicted here.

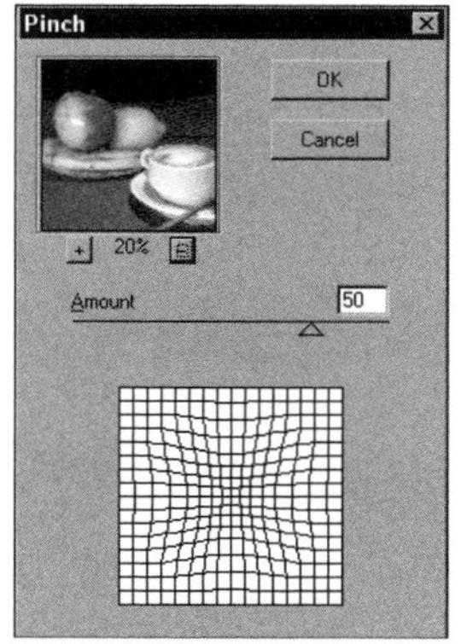

Pinch Filter Dialog Box Options

Component	Function
Amount slider and field	Drag to left of center to make image bulge, to right of center to push center away, or enter a number between –100 and 100.
Preview grid	Preview changes in the Amount field here.

Polar Coordinates Filter

The Polar Coordinates filter can stretch an image over a sphere, with the perspective changing so that you seem to be looking at this object from above, much like viewing Earth from space. The Polar Coordinates filter is often seen as one of the coolest distortion filters, yet one of the most difficult to understand, because you can map an image from rectangular to polar coordinates or from polar to rectangular as shown in the dialog box here. More on the effects of the Polar Coordinates filter later in this chapter.

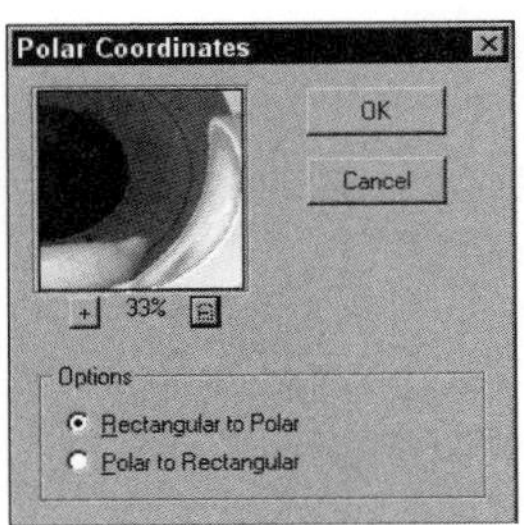

Polar Coordinates Dialog Box Contents

Component	Function
Rectangular to Polar radio button	Pulls all the outer edges into a single dot at the center of the image.
Polar to Rectangular radio button	Moves all the center pixels to the outer edge and pulls all the outer edge pixels to the center.

Ripple Filter

The Ripple filter is nearly identical to the Ocean Ripple filter and produces an effect similar to the Sprayed Strokes filter, but the wavy edges it creates are much lower in frequency and are more rounded. The ripples are regular in frequency (evenly spaced) and can be adjusted for a wide variety of wave heights, as shown in the following figure.

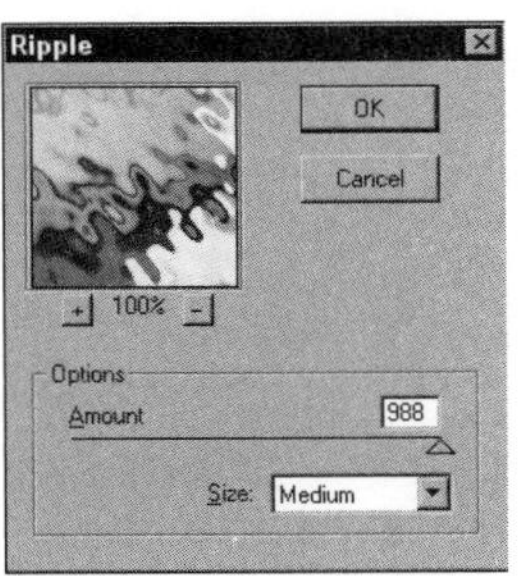

Ripple Filter Dialog Box Contents

Component	Function
Amount slider and field	Drag to adjust the amplitude (width) of individual ripples, or enter an amount between –999 and 999

CONTINUED

WARPING AND MORPHING CONTINUED

Ripple Filter Dialog Box Contents

Component	Function
Size pull-down menu	Use this menu to change the height (or length, if it's easier to visualize them) of the ripples. Choose from small, medium, or large ripples.

Shear Filter

The Shear filter is a powerful and highly useful warping tool that lets you "wrinkle" the surface of anything, producing a skewed image. The associated dialog box is shown here.

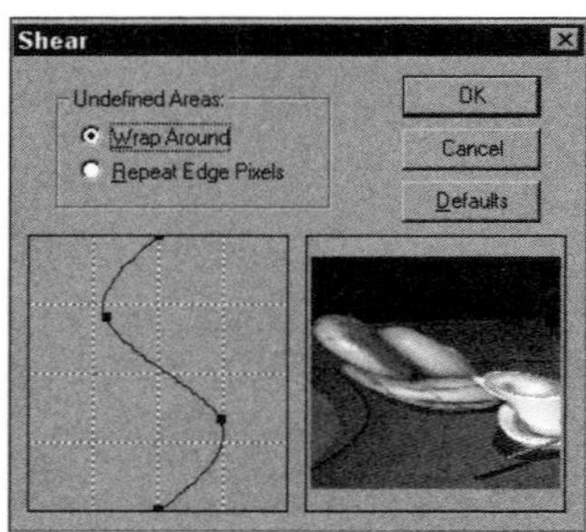

Shear Filter Dialog Box Contents

Component	Function
Wrap Around radio button	Choose to cause pixels pushed off one edge of the image to reappear on the opposite edge.
Repeat Edge Pixels radio button	Choose to extend pixels along a displaced edge to be repeated until they fill the space vacated by the displacement.
Distortion Curve grid	Click anywhere on curve line to enter a point. Drag a point to indicate direction and amount of displacement. You can enter any number of points, and the path can be as straight or wavy as you care to make it.
Preview window	Previews the effect of distorting along the path you've entered. Always shows thumbnail of the entire image within its boundaries.

Spherize Filter

The Spherize filter, the dialog box of which is shown in the following figure, warps the image halfway around a globe, on the outside of a sphere. This is similar to the effect of the Pinch filter, but the image protrudes outward, rather than inward.

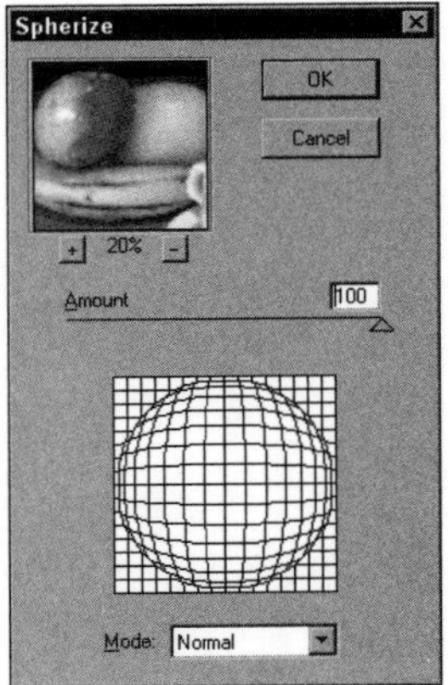

Spherize Filter Dialog Box Contents

Component	Function
Amount slider and field	Drag to left for a concave distortion, to the right for a convex distortion, or enter a value between –100 and 100.
Preview grid	Previews the curvature of the distortion as the amount is changed.
Mode pull-down menu	Choose from Normal, Horizontal, and Vertical. Horizontal and Vertical make the distortion tubular, rather than spherical.

Twirl Filter

The Twirl filter rotates the center of an image, producing a spiral effect, as if the image were being sucked down a giant drain. The following figure shows the Twirl filter dialog box.

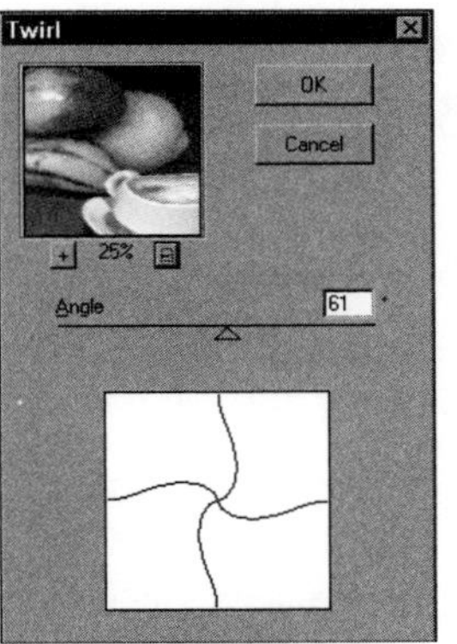

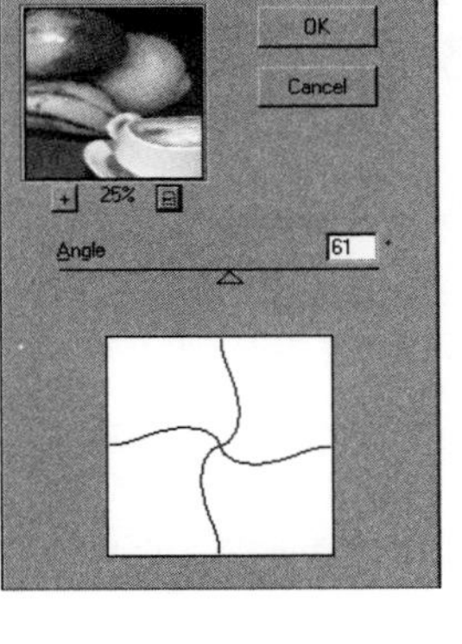

Twirl Filter Dialog Box Contents

Component	Function
Angle slider and field	Drag to determine the rotation and direction of the twist from the center.
Twirl preview	Shows the result of moving the Angle slider.

Wave Filter

The Wave filter contains several options that are among the most complex Photoshop has to offer as shown in the following figure. If you want to “smoosh” the elements of the image to create a watery, marblely, or zigzag texture, this is the filter to use. Think of it is a much more powerful and less predictable version of the Ocean Ripple and Ripple filters.

CONTINUED

WARPING AND MORPHING CONTINUED

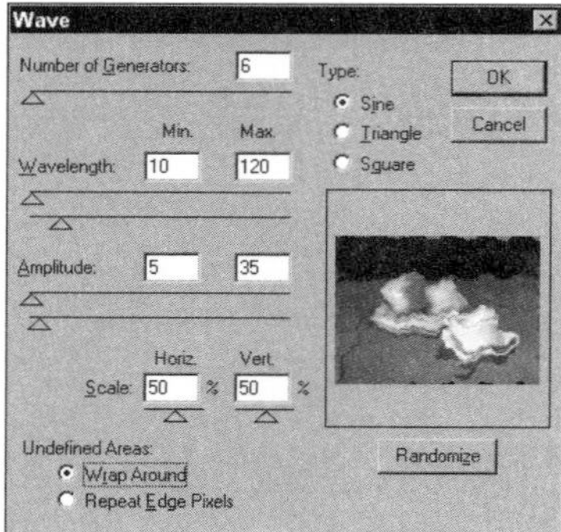

Wave Filter Dialog Box Contents

Component	Function
Number of Generators slider and field	Drag to determine the number of energy centers that will create wave ripples. One generator will create a pond ripple, many will create roiling water.
Wavelength sliders and fields	Drag the arrows to indicate the minimum and maximum height of the individual waves. (The Mac dialog box has only one bar, but adjustments produce the same result.)
Amplitude sliders and fields	Drag the arrows to indicate the minimum and maximum width of the individual waves. (The Mac dialog box has only one bar, but adjustments produce the same result.)
Horizontal scale slider and field	Increases the effect by a percentage in the horizontal direction; drag the slider or enter a value between 1 and 100.
Vertical scale slider and field	Increases the effect by a percentage in the horizontal direction; drag the slider or enter a value between 1 and 100.
Wrap Around radio button	Choose to cause pixels pushed off one edge of the image to reappear on the opposite edge.
Repeat Edge Pixels radio button	Choose to extend pixels along a displaced edge to be repeated until they fill the space vacated by the displacement.
Sine Type radio button	Generates natural-looking, watery ripples.
Triangle radio button	Generates sharply peaked ripples.
Square radio button	Generates square tiles instead of ripples.
Preview window	Always shows 100 percent thumbnail of the image.
Randomize button	Re-randomizes the already random pattern of the waves. Produces a somewhat different effect each time it is clicked.

ZigZag Filter

Rather than create a bunch of alternating points, as in a lightening bolt, the ZigZag filter effect resembles what happens to a quiet pond if you pitch a stone into it: It produces a ripple effect, with a zigzag of color emanating from the center of the image. The associated dialog box is shown in here.

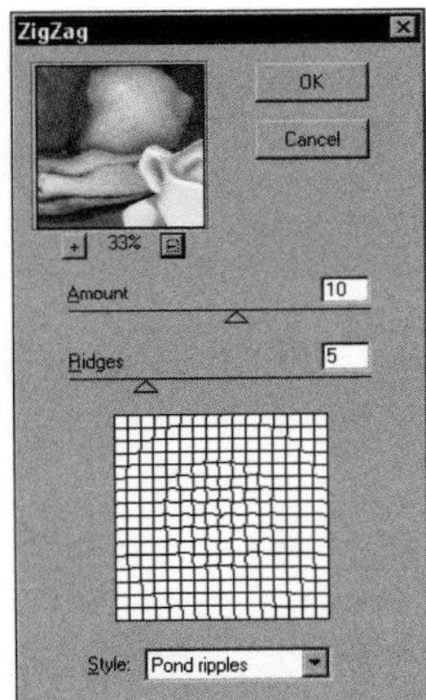

ZigZag Filter Dialog Box Contents

Component	Function
Amount slider and field	Drag to indicate a positive or negative wave height, or enter a number between –100 and 100.
Ridges slider and field	Drag to indicate the number of wave peaks, or enter a value between 0 and 20.
Preview grid	Distorts the grid according to the adjustments of the sliders.
Style pull-down menu	Choose between Around Center, Out from Center, and Pond Ripples.

DISTORT WITH THE DIFFUSE GLOW FILTER

The Diffuse Glow filter is the first filter found under the Distort submenu. It is unique in this group in that it doesn't distort at all. Instead, it "bleeds" the current background color into the lighter (highlight) areas of your image.

There are three controls in the Diffuse Glow dialog box: Graininess, Glow Amount, and Clear Amount. Each of these has an effect on the amount of background color that spreads into the highlights.

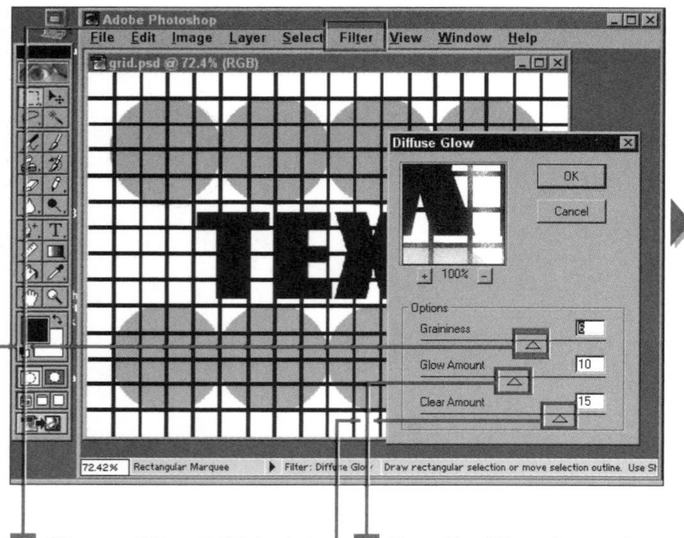

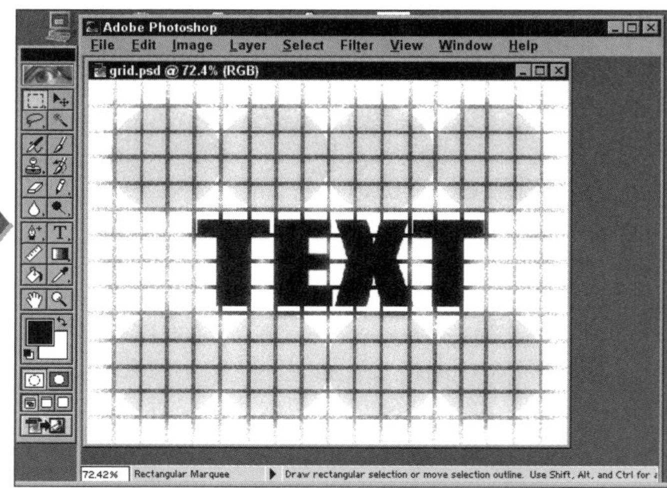

1 Choose Filter ⇨ Distort ⇨ Diffuse Glow.

2 Drag the Graininess slider to enlarge or reduce speckling of scattered highlights.

3 Drag the Glow Amount slider to control spreading of highlights.

4 Drag the Clear Amount slider to control spreading of highlights.

■ This is the result of running the Diffuse Glow filter on the test image. Notice that all the lines and shapes are unmoved.

DISTORT WITH THE DISPLACE FILTER

The Displace filter is one of the most powerful filters on the Distort submenu. It must be used, however, in conjunction with a grayscale texture map. The reason for this is that when the Displace filter is applied, the white tones in the image move the image to a maximum in one direction, whereas the black tones move it to the maximum in the other direction. (Gray tones cause movement proportionate to their lightness or darkness.)

Using the Displace filter can be confusing because the Displace dialog box asks you to make the settings before it asks you to pick a file to use as the displacement map. As soon as you click OK in the Displace dialog box, a conventional File Open dialog box appears, and you simply choose any grayscale Photoshop (PSD) file. It is best to use a single-layer file, because multiple layers use more storage, have slow processing, and can cause unpredictable results.

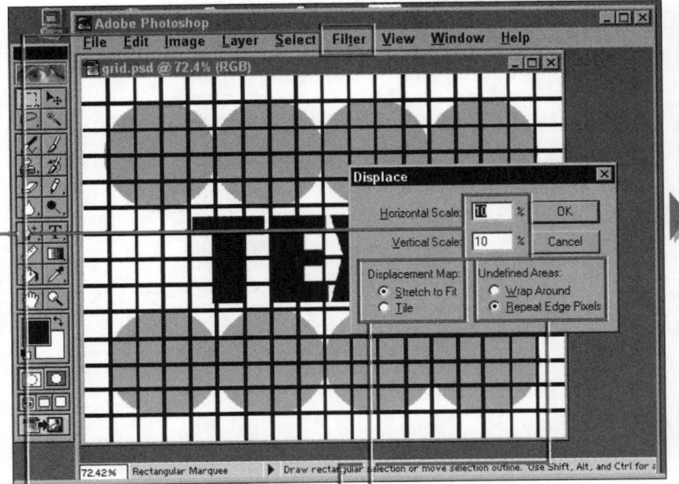

1 Choose Filter ⇨ Distort ⇨ Displace.

2 Enter a number for the percentage of the horizontal and vertical measurement of the image elements to be moved.

3 Click to indicate whether the displacement map should be scaled or tiled.

4 Indicate whether parts of the image left empty should be filled by wrapping the image or repeating edge pixels.

■ Here is the result of running the Distort filter on the test image. The displacement map is shown in the lower-right corner.

DISTORT WITH THE GLASS FILTER

The effects of the Glass filter are easy to see. Put simply, it makes your image look as though it's being viewed through glass. Some portions of the image are magnified, some reduced, and all are somewhat, well, distorted.

The Glass filter is a versatile filter due to its five controls: Distortion, Smoothness, Texture, Scaling, and an Invert check box that inverts the distortion map. Distortion controls the amount of the distortion and Smoothness blends the edges. Texture is a pull-down menu that gives you the choice of three built-in textures (Frosted, Tiny Lens, and Canvas) or lets you load your own grayscale Photoshop-format file. The Invert check box reverses light and dark in the texture map.

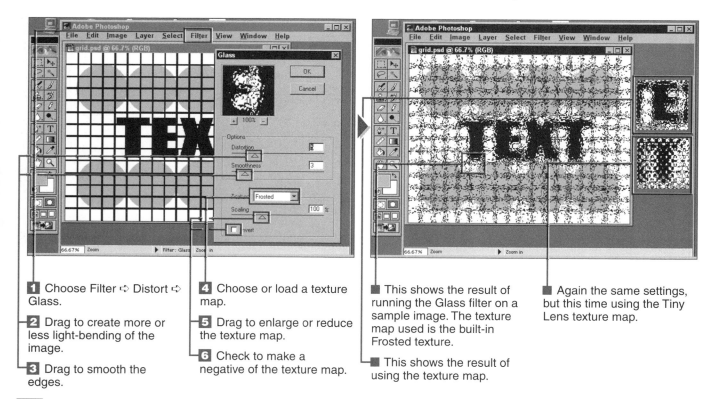

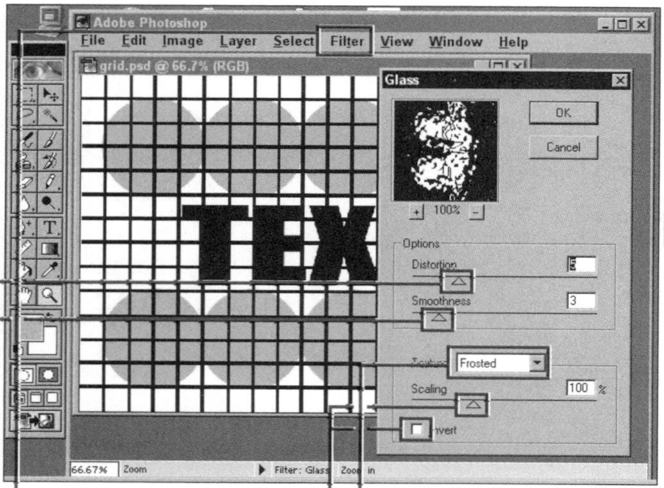

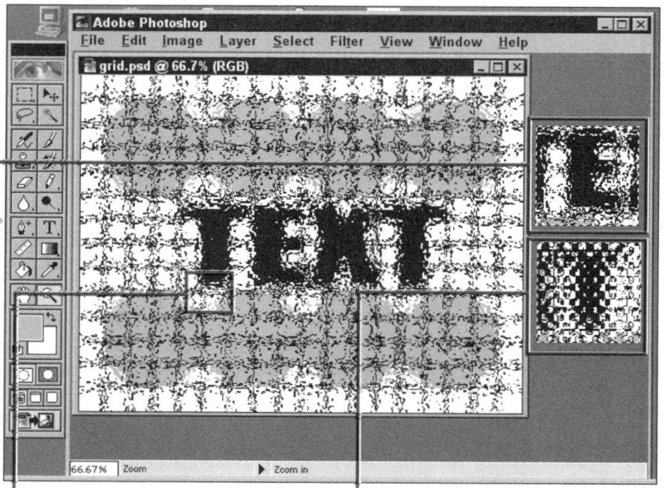

1 Choose Filter ⇨ Distort ⇨ Glass.

2 Drag to create more or less light-bending of the image.

3 Drag to smooth the edges.

4 Choose or load a texture map.

5 Drag to enlarge or reduce the texture map.

6 Check to make a negative of the texture map.

■ This shows the result of running the Glass filter on a sample image. The texture map used is the built-in Frosted texture.

■ This shows the result of using the texture map.

■ Again the same settings, but this time using the Tiny Lens texture map.

DISTORT WITH THE OCEAN RIPPLE FILTER

The Ocean Ripple filter produces a distortion that's much like the distortion created by the Glass filter, but the Ocean Ripple filter creates ripple shapes that are more random in size. The size of the various shapes can also be altered in with the Ocean Ripple filter dialog box.

Note that the Ocean Ripple filter doesn't let you select a displacement map, making this filter easy to use. Two settings appear in the Ocean Ripple dialog box: Ripple Size and Ripple Magnitude. These may sound redundant, but you can think of Magnitude as height to make the distinction clearer.

Ocean Ripple is a good filter for making surfaces look like water or for making images look submerged.

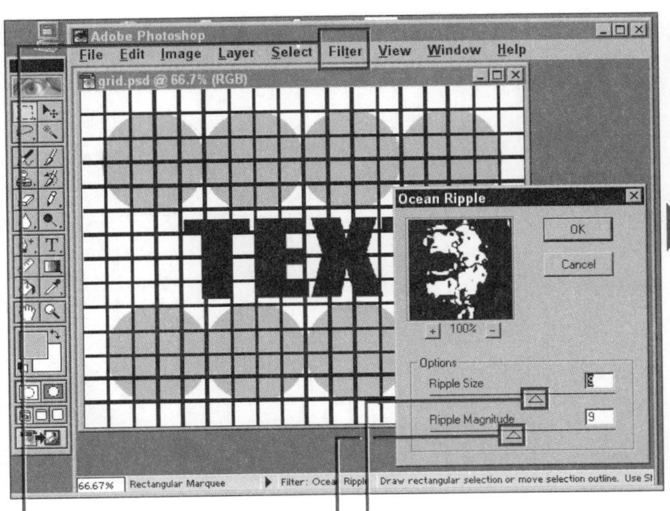

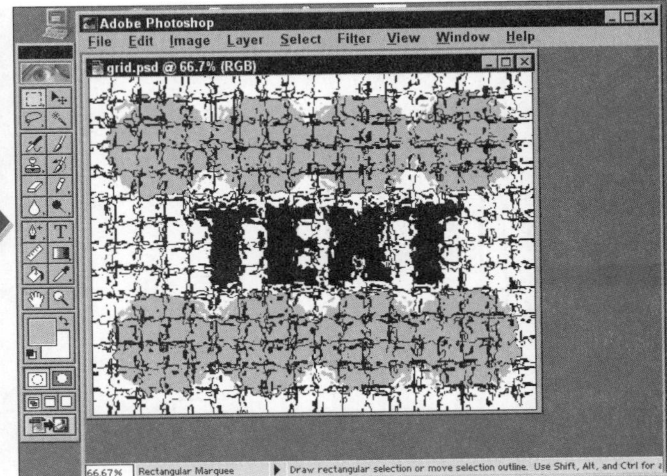

1 Choose Filter ➪ Distort ➪ Ocean Ripple.

2 Drag the Ripple Size slider to indicate the size of shape distortions.

3 Drag the Ripple Magnitude slider to indicate apparent height or thickness of ripples.

■ Here's the result of running the Ocean Ripple filter on the test image.

DISTORT WITH THE PINCH FILTER

The Pinch filter makes an image appear as if it is printed on a piece of rubber sheeting that has been made to sag in the center. You can also make it look as though a big ball is pushing the center of the rubber sheet toward you. This is a good filter for stretching an object so that it can be blended with a concave or convex surface in a photo composite.

The Pinch filter dialog box has only a single setting: Amount. If the pointer is in the center, there is no distortion. Slide to the left, and the distortion expands (blows out), to the right, and it pushes in (sucks in). A preview grid at the bottom of the dialog box shows the exact degree of distortion. There's also a zoomable preview box that shows you how your actual image will look at the distortion setting you're using.

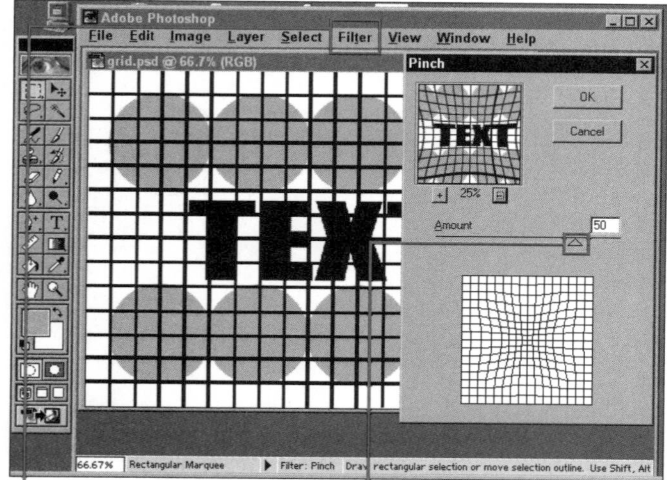

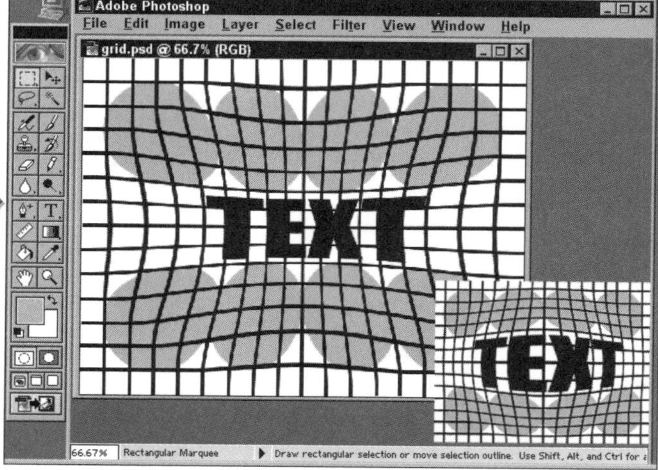

1 Choose Filter ➪ Distort ➪ Pinch.

2 Drag the Amount slider to indicate the depth and spread of the pinch s depression or expansion.

■ This shows the result of running the Pinch filter on the test image. At lower right is the same image with the Amount pointer moved to the left.

Distort with the Polar Coordinates Filter

The Polar Coordinates filter is often seen as one of the coolest distortion filters, yet one of the most difficult to understand. If you exercise the Rectangular to Polar option, for example, it takes the entire upper edge of the image and reduces it to a single pixel, sucking all the other elements into it. If you click the Polar to Rectangular button in the Polar Coordinates dialog box, on the other hand, something entirely different happens. If you look at the second figure in this exercise, you'll get a better idea of how this filter works.

There are no controls for the Polar Coordinates filter, just a pair of mutually exclusive radio buttons: Rectangular to Polar and Polar to Rectangular. What you click is what you get.

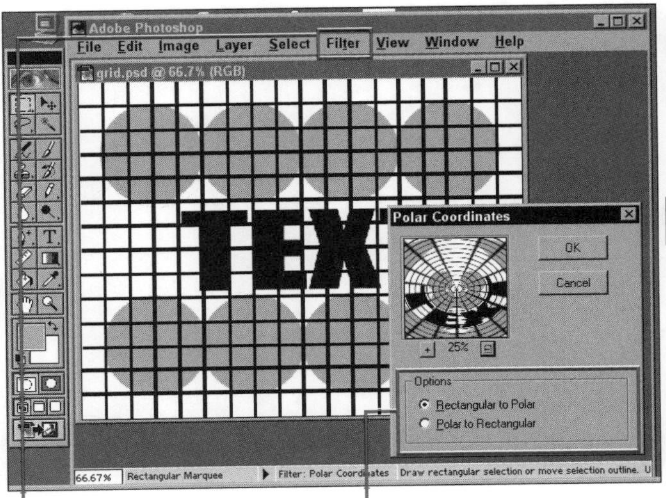

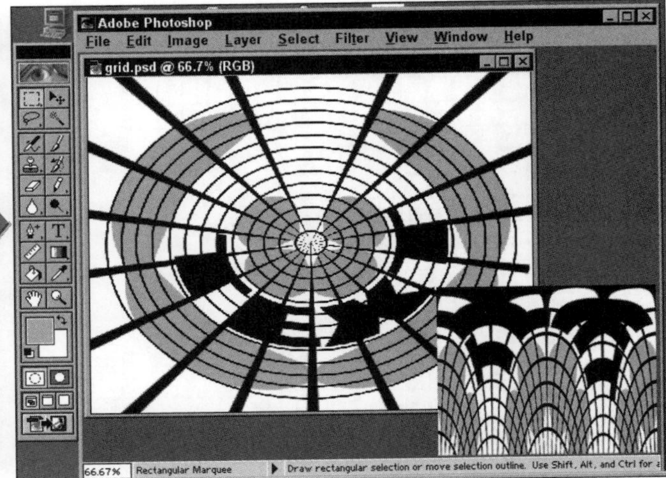

1 Choose Filter ⇨ Distort ⇨ Polar Coordinates.

2 Click to choose an option.

■ Here's the result of running the Polar Coordinates filter on the test image.

Note: At lower right is the same image distorted by clicking Polar to Rectangular.

DISTORT WITH THE RIPPLE FILTER

The Ripple filter is nearly identical to the Ocean Ripple filter and produces an effect similar to the Sprayed Strokes filter, but the wavy edges it creates are much lower in frequency and more rounded. The ripples are regular in frequency (evenly spaced) and can be adjusted for a wide variety of wave heights.

Ripple is a simple filter to use. Only two controls appear in the dialog box: an Amount slider and a Size pull-down menu. The Amount slider pushes the wave in a positive or negative direction. The Size menu offers three choices — Small, Medium, and Large — and these dictate the wave frequency.

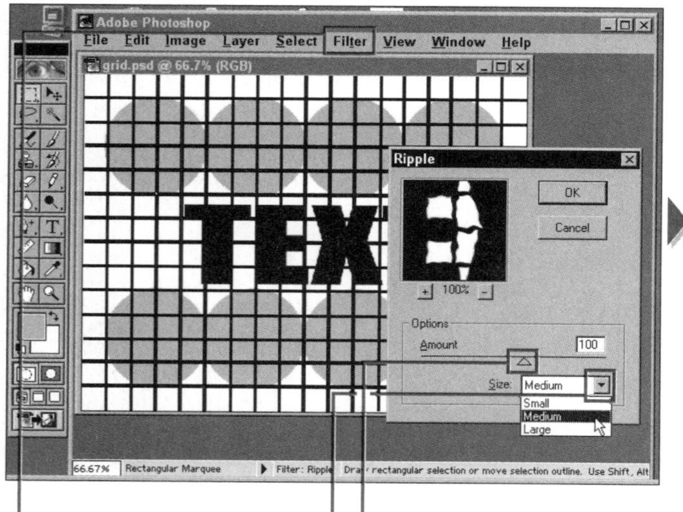

1 Choose Filter ➪ Distort ➪ Ripple.

2 Drag to adjust the Amount slider.

3 Click to choose the size.

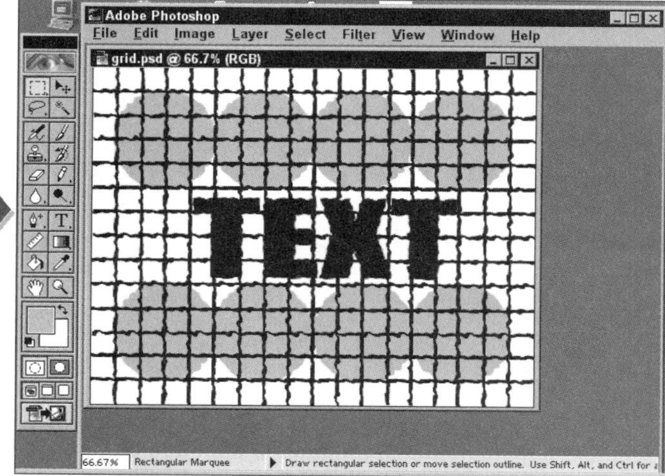

■ This figure shows the result of running the Ripple filter on the test image.

DISTORT WITH THE SHEAR FILTER

The Shear filter is a powerful and highly useful warping tool that lets you "wrinkle" the surface of an image. An easy way to visualize the effect is to think of a photo in which a flat flag is made to appear to be furled in the breeze. You can also warp a texture so it can be blended atop a curved surface — think of a tattooed arm or a woodgrain pencil cup.

The application method for Shear is intuitive. Drag the points of a curve in a grid, and the image warps to match (you create the points by clicking and delete them by dragging them off the edge of the grid). You can immediately see the result in the Preview window.

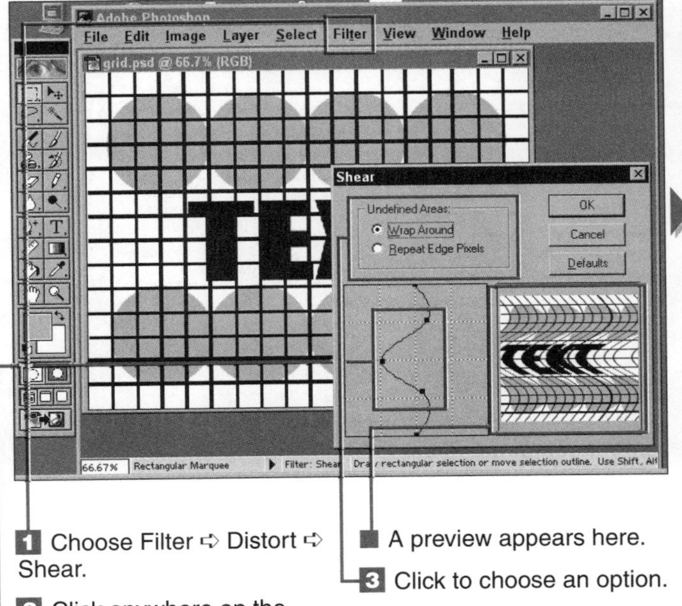

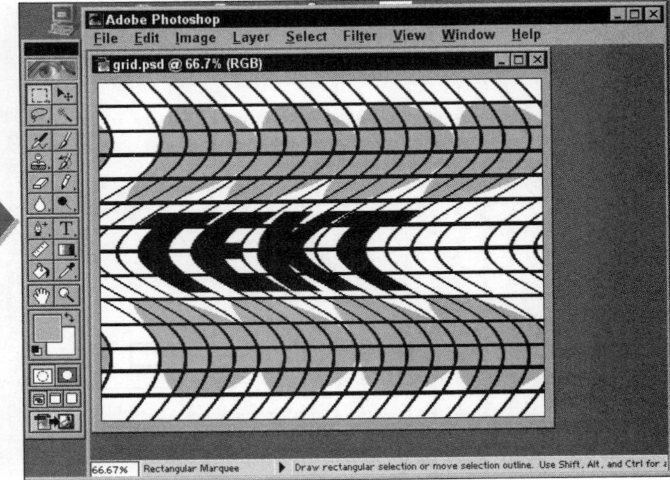

1 Choose Filter ⇨ Distort ⇨ Shear.

2 Click anywhere on the curved line to insert a point, and then drag to warp.

■ A preview appears here.

3 Click to choose an option.

■ This is the result of running the Shear filter on the test image.

DISTORT WITH THE SPHERIZE FILTER

The Spherize filter warps the image halfway around a globe. You can then blend your subject onto a planet and place it in space, or blend it onto a ball and then make a racquet. . . . You get the idea.

The warp effect produced by the Spherize filter can be over any percentage of the surface of a sphere up to 50 percent. In other words, you can't wrap *around* the sphere. There is some overlapping of visual effect with the Pinch filter, but Sphere's warp is perfectly spherical, whereas the Pinch filter effect is a bit more conical. As with the Pinch filter, you can drag to make your warps concave or convex. Also, the Spherize filter can make tubular warps in your choice of horizontal or vertical direction. This makes it an even better candidate for warping a tattoo to match the curve of an arm, for example.

Note: The shape of your sphere depends on the proportions of the layer or selection you are warping. If the shape is square, you get a circle; if not, an ellipse.

Spherize is as easy to use as dragging its single slider to indicate the percentage of the sphere you want to warp over. You can immediately see the result in the Preview window.

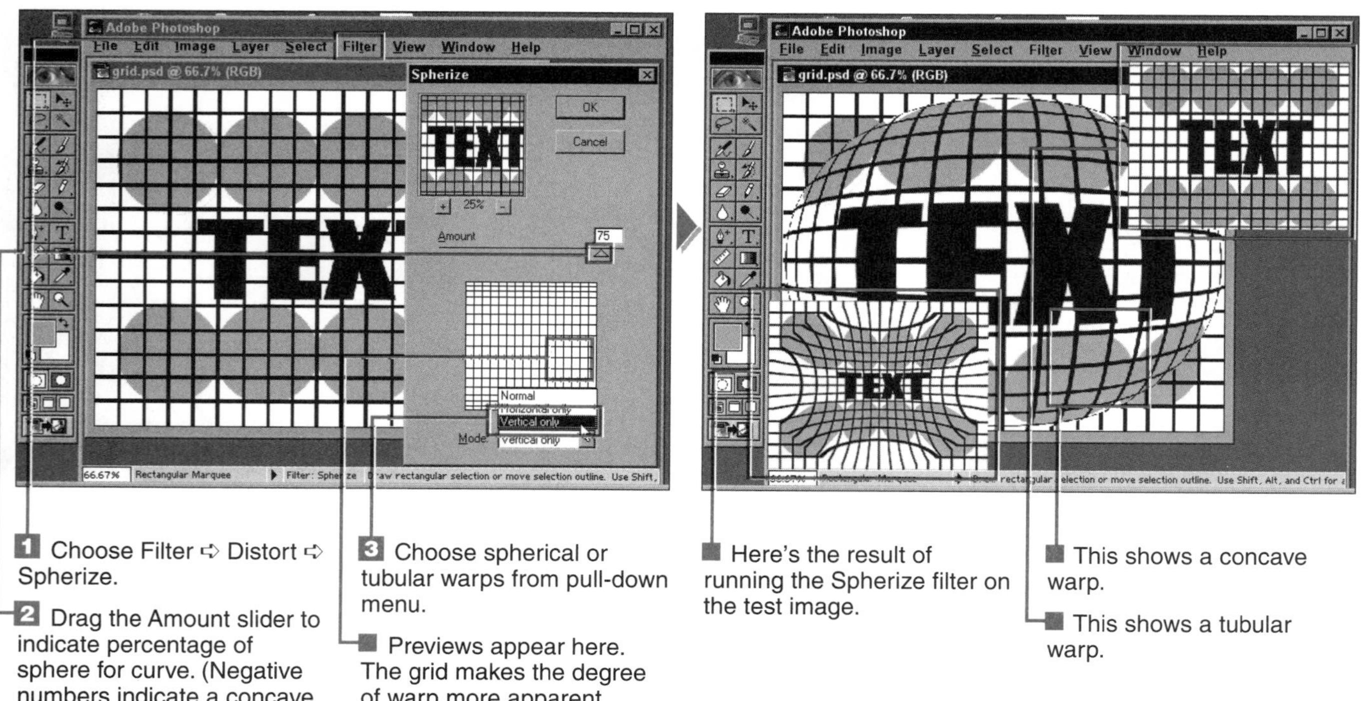

1 Choose Filter ⇨ Distort ⇨ Spherize.

2 Drag the Amount slider to indicate percentage of sphere for curve. (Negative numbers indicate a concave surface.)

3 Choose spherical or tubular warps from pull-down menu.

■ Previews appear here. The grid makes the degree of warp more apparent.

■ Here's the result of running the Spherize filter on the test image.

■ This shows a concave warp.

■ This shows a tubular warp.

DISTORT WITH THE TWIRL FILTER

The Twirl filter twists the image into a spiral, as if it were being sucked down a giant drain. If you need to create a stock photo of money going down the drain, let's say, this is the filter for the job.

The Twirl filter dialog box contains a single slider that lets you spin the image counter-clockwise if you drag to the left of center. There are two Preview windows, one to show the effect on your image, and the other to diagram the effect of the adjustment you've made. Both work in real time (as do all the other Preview windows in Photoshop's built-in filters). There is no Preview check box for the Distort submenu filters, so you won't see the actual effect until you click OK in the Twirl dialog box.

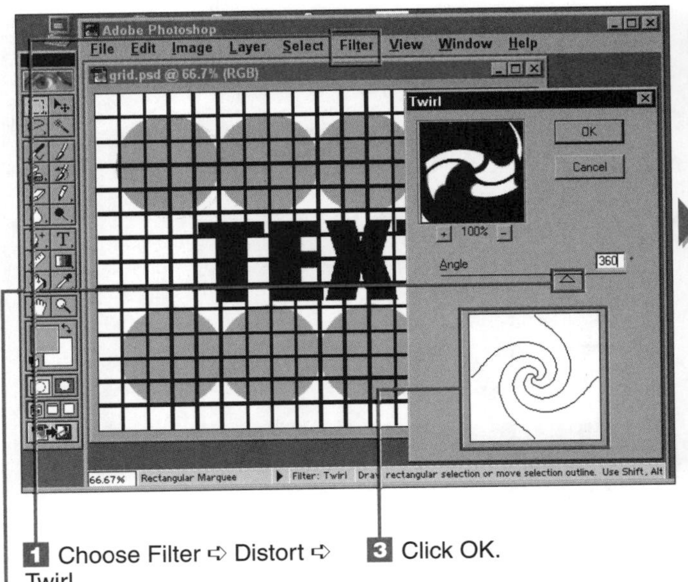

1 Choose Filter ➪ Distort ➪ Twirl.

2 Drag the Angle slider to indicate the direction of the twist and the number of turns.

3 Click OK.

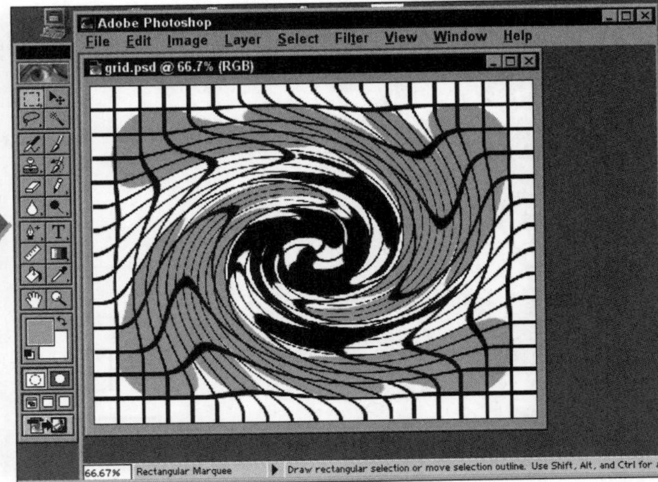

■ This shows the result of running the Twirl filter on the test image.

DISTORT WITH THE WAVE FILTER

The Wave filter options conspire to give you a lot of flexibility in the amount of chaos they can create, but none of them makes much sense. Suffice it to say that if you want to "smoosh" the elements of the image into a watery, marblely, or zigzag texture, this is the filter to use. Think of it is a much more powerful and less predictable version of the Ocean Ripple and Ripple filters.

There are seven controls in the Wave Options palette: Number of Generators, Wavelength, Amplitude, Horizontal and Vertical Scale, Undefined Areas, Type, and Randomize. Number of Generators determines how many times the pattern you set will be applied. Wavelength has two sliders, one each for a minimum and maximum amount. Amplitude has the same two sliders. Scale determines the size of the overall texture in relationship to the size of the image. Undefined Areas determines what happens to edges that were left blank when the image was moved or shrunk to distort it. Type is the most important control. It determines the shape of the wave: Sine produces smooth curves, Triangle results in right-angle peaks and straight edges, and Square creates straight peaks and valleys. When in doubt, click Randomize.

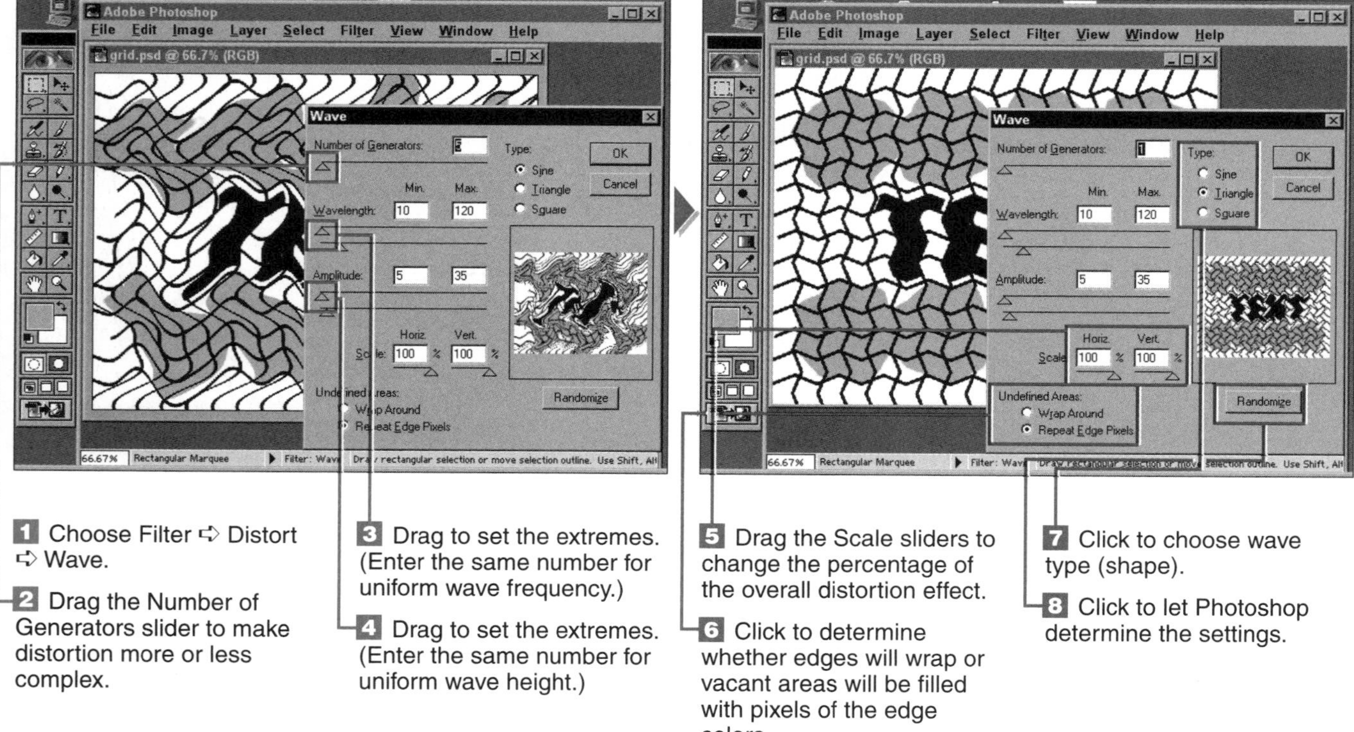

1 Choose Filter ➪ Distort ➪ Wave.

2 Drag the Number of Generators slider to make distortion more or less complex.

3 Drag to set the extremes. (Enter the same number for uniform wave frequency.)

4 Drag to set the extremes. (Enter the same number for uniform wave height.)

5 Drag the Scale sliders to change the percentage of the overall distortion effect.

6 Click to determine whether edges will wrap or vacant areas will be filled with pixels of the edge colors.

7 Click to choose wave type (shape).

8 Click to let Photoshop determine the settings.

DISTORT WITH THE ZIGZAG FILTER

Pitch a stone into a quiet pond, and you'll see the effect of the ZigZag filter. It can be very useful for creating the illusion that waves are emanating from something, whether that's a radio tower or a floating volleyball.

The controls in the ZigZag dialog box are Amount, Ridges, and Style. The Amount slider controls wave size. The Ridges slider determines the number of wave peaks. Style is a pull-down menu containing three style choices: Around Center, Out from Center, and Pond Ripples.

Around Center creates a whirlpool effect. Out from Center creates the illusion that something is bubbling up from under the surface.

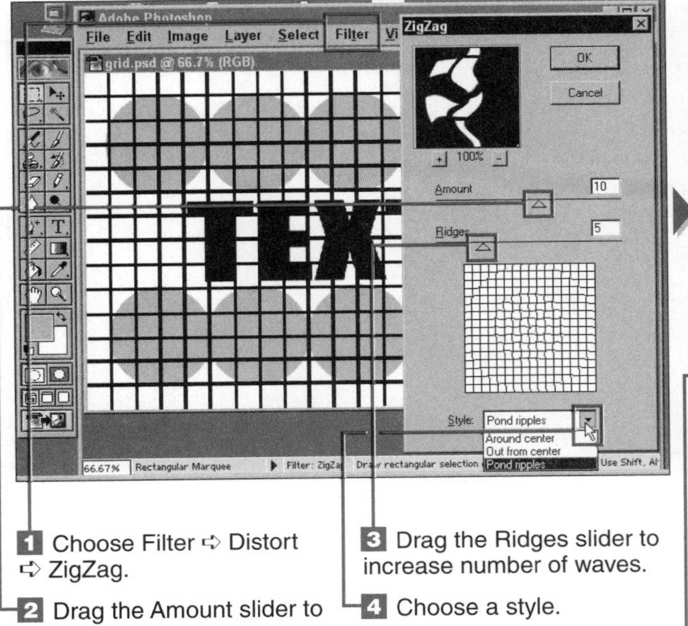

1 Choose Filter ➪ Distort ➪ ZigZag.

2 Drag the Amount slider to increase height of waves.

3 Drag the Ridges slider to increase number of waves.

4 Choose a style.

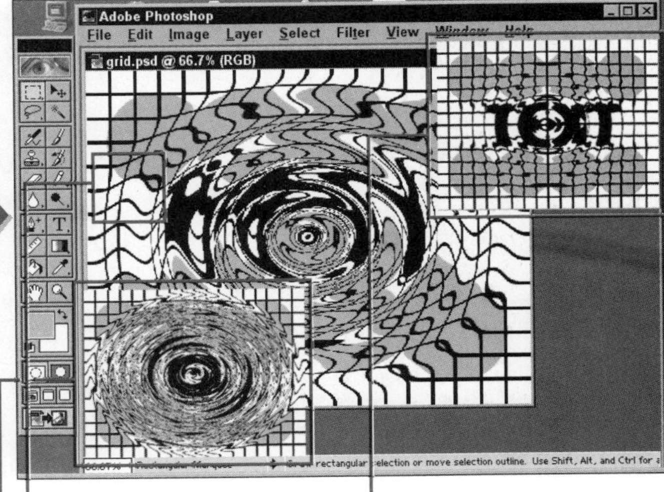

■ Here's the result of running the Twirl filter on the test image.

■ This shows what happens when Around center is chosen.

■ This shows the effect of the Out from center style.

APPLY A THIRD-PARTY 3D SURFACE FILTER

Andromeda Software makes several useful and sophisticated sets of Photoshop-compatible plug-ins. Certainly one of the most useful of these is the Series II 3D Filter, which comes in identical versions for Macintosh and Windows. This filter set enables you to stretch a photo around the surface of a cube, sphere, or tube, or over a plane. You can place your photo at any location and at any scale on the object, turn the object any way you want, give it as much perspective as you like, light the object, and preview it before rendering.

As you might guess, working with the Series II 3D filter is complex enough to take a little getting used to. You can, however, boil it down to four basic processes: 1) Choose the type of surface you want to map to. 2) Scale and orient the surface object. 3) Place the photo on the object. 4) Pick viewpoint and lighting.

Note: To complete this exercise you must first have the Andromeda set of Photoshop plug-ins installed.

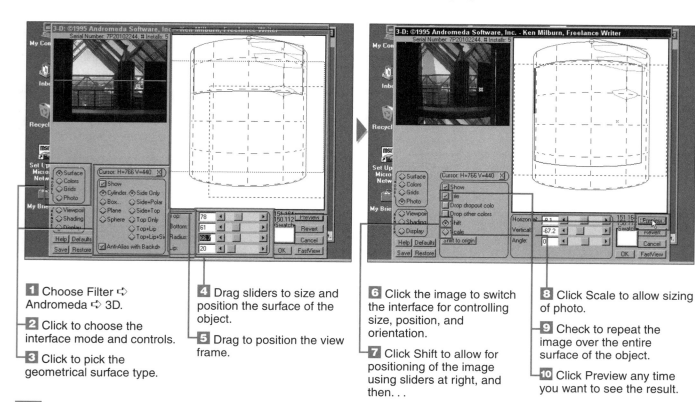

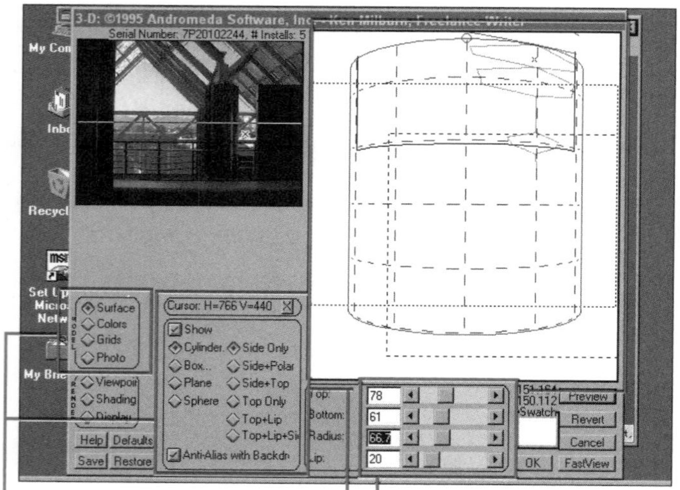

1 Choose Filter ⇨ Andromeda ⇨ 3D.

2 Click to choose the interface mode and controls.

3 Click to pick the geometrical surface type.

4 Drag sliders to size and position the surface of the object.

5 Drag to position the view frame.

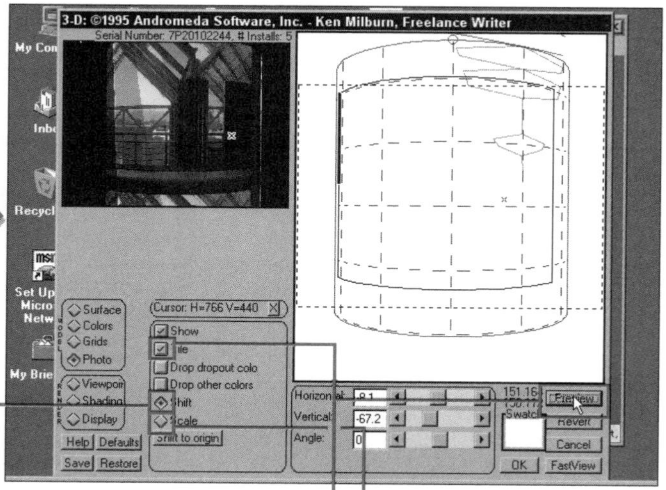

6 Click the image to switch the interface for controlling size, position, and orientation.

7 Click Shift to allow for positioning of the image using sliders at right, and then. . .

8 Click Scale to allow sizing of photo.

9 Check to repeat the image over the entire surface of the object.

10 Click Preview any time you want to see the result.

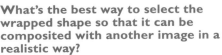

What's the best way to select the wrapped shape so that it can be composited with another image in a realistic way?

The Andromeda filter lets you choose the background color. Pick a nonneutral color that contrasts strongly with colors in the photo. You can then use the Select ⇨ Color Range command to quickly separate the image from the background.

Next, press ⌘/Ctrl+J to lift the image inside the selection to its own layer, and open the file into which you want to composite this image. With both file windows open, drag the 3D model's layer into the target image's window.

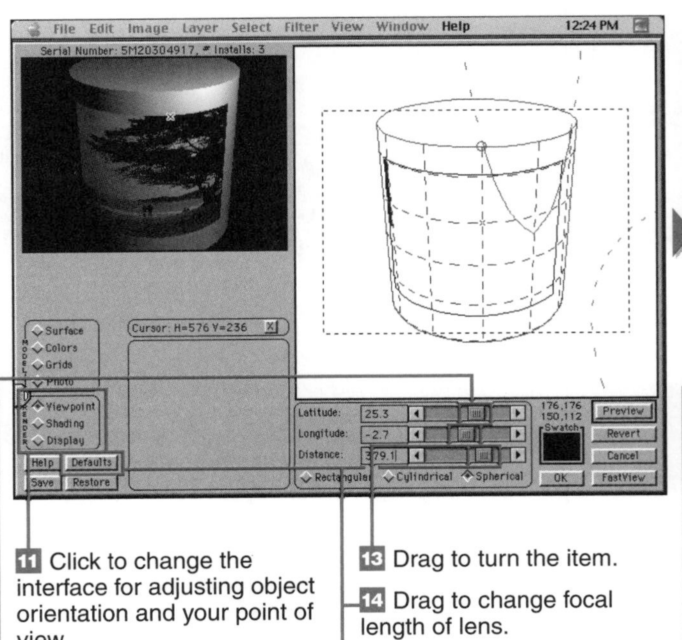

11 Click to change the interface for adjusting object orientation and your point of view.

12 Drag to tip the item.

13 Drag to turn the item.

14 Drag to change focal length of lens.

15 Click Defaults any time you want to reset the entire filter.

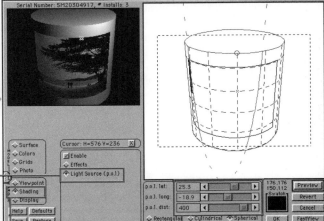

16 Click Shading to change the interface to allow settings for shading and lighting.

17 Click Light Source to change the distance and position of the light.

18 Drag the sliders to position the light vertically or horizontally and to adjust the distance of the light source from the object.

Breaking Up Is Easy to Do

A number of Photoshop's built-in filters are dedicated to fragmenting or stylizing the image in different ways. Four of these are found in the Noise filters submenu: Add Noise, Despeckle, Dust & Scratches, and Median. Another seven appear in the Pixelate filters submenu: Color Halftone, Crystallize, Facet, Fragment, Mezzotint, Mosaic, and Pointillize. The nine filters in the Stylize filter submenu enable you to add interesting stylistic effects: Diffuse, Emboss, Extrude, Find Edges, Glowing Edges, Solarize, Tiles, Trace Contour, and Wind.

Some of these filters *pixelate* an image (add "noise" to it), whereas others remove noise from an image. These filters also serve a variety of practical and artistic purposes, such as matching or creating film grain, retouching scratches, killing moiré patterns (a visible wavy distortion in an image), simulating the look of a halftone, and even imitating the look of a pointillist painting.

Add Noise Filter

The Add Noise filter granulates an image regardless of the image's content. In fact, you can create textures by adding grain to a solid-color image and then use other filters to smear, grow, or move it. The Add Noise filter dialog box is shown in here.

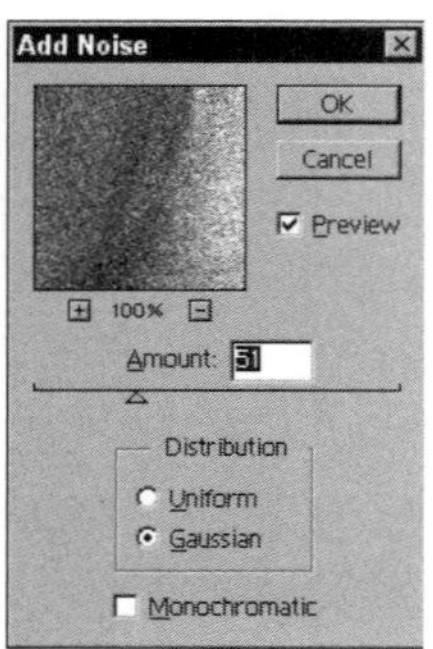

Add Noise Filter Dialog Box Contents

Component	Function
Amount slider and field	Drag the slider right to increase the amount of noise (graininess), left to decrease it. Or, you can specify amount by entering any whole number between 1 and 999 in the Amount field.
Distribution radio buttons	Click Uniform to make an even grain pattern. Click Gaussian if you want the grain pattern to spread in the highlights and clump in the shadows — as it does on film.

Component	Function
Monochromatic check box	If checked, all noise dots are black or white. This does not affect the coloration of the image itself — only of the grain pattern.
Preview check box	If checked, shows the effect of all settings on the image in the workspace.

Dust & Scratches Filter

The Dust & Scratches filter looks for abrupt breaks in the overall pattern of the image and blends those breaks together. (Call it automated retouching.) You can use it on the overall image, but it is likely to blur the image in unpredictable areas. The Dust & Scratches dialog box is shown in the following figure.

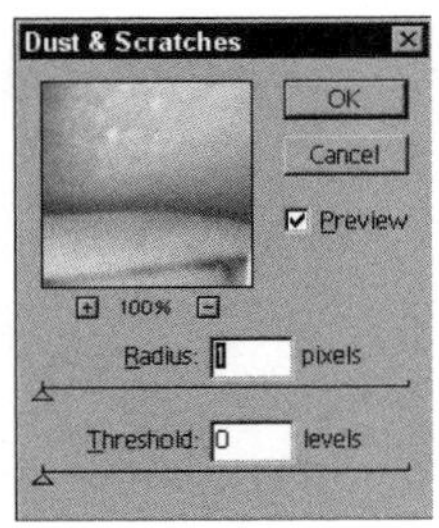

Dust & Scratches Filter Dialog Box Contents

Component	Function
Radius slider and field	Determines the pixel width of the faults that will be eliminated.
Threshold slider and field	Sets the level of contrast that must exist before a clump of pixels will be considered a defect.
Preview check box	If checked, shows the effect of all settings on the image in the workspace.

Median Filter

The Median filter blurs the image but spreads the highlights into the shadows in the process. The result can be an alternative to the Watercolor filter, without the extremely dark shadows Watercolor produces. The Median filter dialog box is depicted here.

CONTINUED

BREAKING UP IS EASY TO DO CONTINUED

Median Filter Dialog Box Contents

Component	Function
Radius slider and field	Drag to determine the radius over which highlight pixels will be pushed into shadow pixels, or enter any number between 1 and 16.
Preview check box	If checked, shows the effect of all settings on the image in the workspace.

Color Halftone Filter

The Color Halftone filter is a pop-art effects filter, not actually usable for making color-separation halftones for color printing. Photoshop does have that capability, but first you need to make the separations and then make a grayscale halftone screen for each separation. The Color Halftone filter dialog box is shown in the following figure.

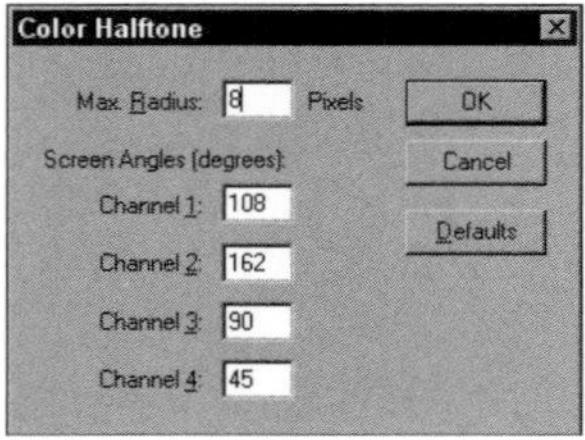

Color Halftone Filter Dialog Box Contents

Component	Function
Max. Radius field	Enter a whole number between 4 and 127 to determine the size of the largest halftone dots.
Screen Angles fields	Experiment with these settings for different effects.
Defaults button	Click to reset all settings to their defaults. (This feature often proves very useful, because it's easy to forget what you did when you were experimenting with the screen angle settings.)

Crystallize Filter

The Crystallize filter averages a clump of pixels into irregular solid-color polygons. The effect is a reduction of colors and a variation on pointillist expressionism as an artistic style. The Crystallize filter dialog box is shown in the following figure.

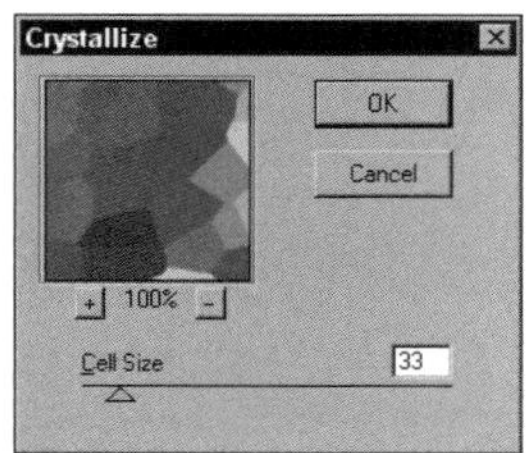

Crystallize Filter Dialog Box Contents

Component	Function
Cell Size slider and field	Determines the size of each crystal. You can directly enter any number between 3 and 300 in the field.

Mezzotint Filter

The Mezzotint filter offers ten variations of a "noisy" special effect. The Mezzotint dialog box is shown here.

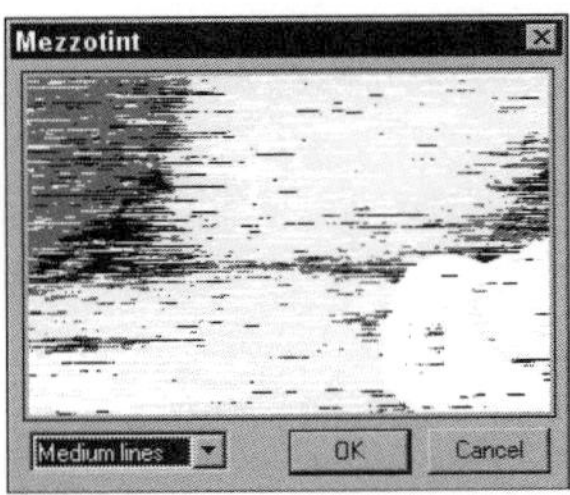

Mezzotint Filter Dialog Box Contents

Component	Function
Type pull-down menu	Choose from the following styles: Fine dots, Medium dots, Grainy dots, Coarse dots, Medium lines, Long lines, Short strokes, Medium strokes, or Long strokes.

Pointillize Filter

The Pointillize filter actually does a fairly credible job of turning your image into a pointillist painting. The Pointillize filter dialog box is shown in this figure.

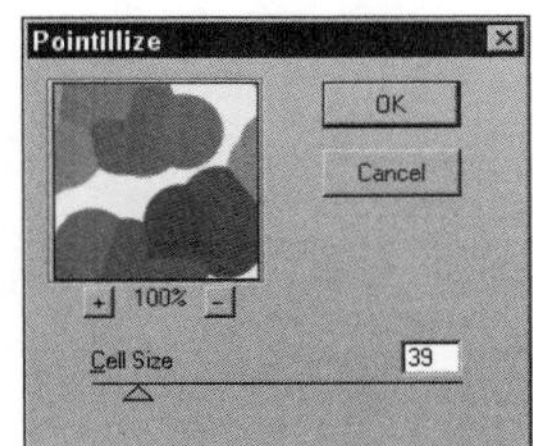

CONTINUED

BREAKING UP IS EASY TO DO CONTINUED

Pointillize Filter Dialog Box Contents

Component	Function
Cell Size slider and field	Determines the size of dots in the pointillist representation of the image. You can enter any number in the field between 3 and 300.

Diffuse Filter

The Diffuse filter makes an image look as though it was sprayed with paint from an aerosol can. It produces a sort of diffused grainy effect. The Diffuse filter dialog box is shown here.

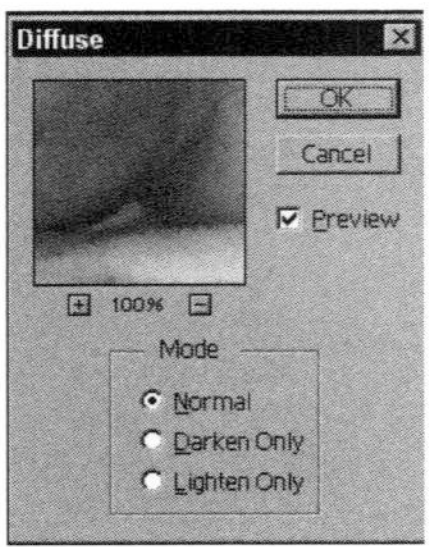

Diffuse Filter Dialog Box Contents

Component	Function
Normal radio button	Click to give a slightly sandy textured or spray-painted effect without shifting tones.
Darken Only radio button	Flattens and roughens shadows, with little or no effect on highlights. Tends to darken shadow areas.
Lighten Only radio button	Flattens and roughens the highlights, with little or no effect on the shadows. Tends to lighten highlight areas. Edges between strongly contrasting areas are less speckled.
Preview check box	If checked, effect is previewed in the workspace window. Greatly slows down the preview in the Preview window.

Emboss Filter

The Emboss filter creates a monochrome image that looks as if the elements in the image are stamped into paper — similar to embossed stationery. The Emboss filter dialog box is shown in the following figure.

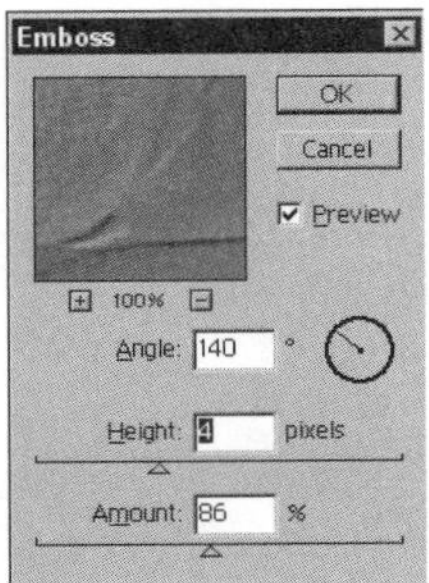

Emboss Filter Dialog Box Contents

Component	Function
Angle field	Enter any number between 0 and 360 to indicate the angle of lighting.
Angle control	Drag dial to indicate "lighting" angle
Height slider and field	Drag to indicate width of highlight and shadows on the edges of shapes, or enter a number between 1 and 10.
Amount slider and field	Also increases or decreases the apparent depth of the embossing.
Preview check box	If checked, shows the effect of all settings on the image in the workspace.

Component Function

Extrude Filter

The Extrude filter makes the image look as though it has been glued to raised blocks. You can also use it to convert the image to solid color 3D blocks or pyramids. The Extrude filter dialog box is shown here.

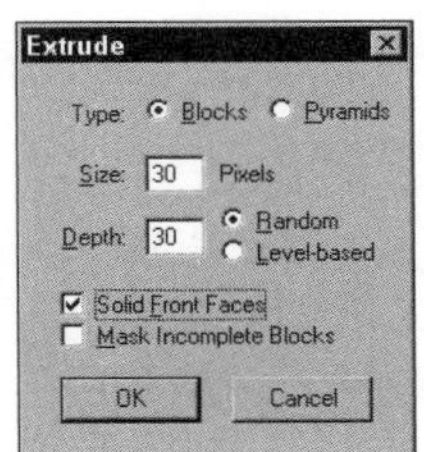

CONTINUED

BREAKING UP IS EASY TO DO CONTINUED

Extrude Filter Dialog Box Contents

Component	Function
Blocks radio button	Click to extrude image onto flat-colored square blocks that radiate away from the center of the image.
Pyramids radio button	Click to extrude image onto pyramids that radiate away from the center of the image.
Size field	Enter a number between 2 and 255 for the number of pixels square for the extruded shape.
Depth field	Enter a number between 2 and 255 for the height in pixels of the extruded shape.
Random radio button	Click to make the apparent height of the extruded shape vary throughout image.
Level-based radio button	Click to make the apparent height of the extruded shape uniform, based on the number entered in the Depth field.
Solid Front Faces check box	Unavailable if the Pyramids button has been chosen. If checked, makes all front faces a solid color. Otherwise, front faces are the same as the original image.
Mask Incomplete Blocks check box	If checked, any blocks that do not fall completely within the selection (or the boundaries of the image) are not extruded or otherwise changed.

Glowing Edges Filter

The Glowing Edges filter traces contrasting edges with a bright line and converts all the other shades in the image to a charcoal shade. The Glowing Edges filter dialog box is shown here.

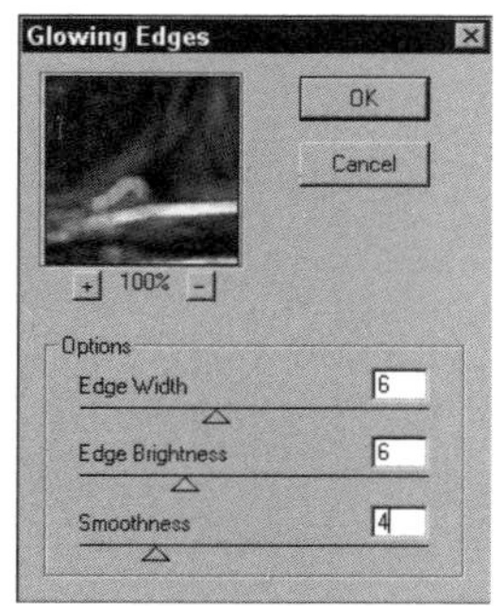

Glowing Edges Filter Dialog Box Contents

Component	Function
Edge Width slider and field	Drag to determine the width of the glowing edges, or enter a number between 1 and 14.
Edge Brightness slider and field	Drag to determine the brightness of the glowing edges, or enter a number between 0 and 20. Edge Brightness and Edge Width will often seem to have the same effect.
Smoothness slider and field	Drag to make glowing edge blend more or less sharply with surrounding image, or enter a whole number between 1 and 15.
Preview check box	If checked, shows the effect of all settings on the image in the workspace.

Tiles Filter

The Tiles filter produces an effect that looks similar to a mosaic, dividing the image up into somewhat irregular square tiles. The Tiles filter dialog box is depicted here.

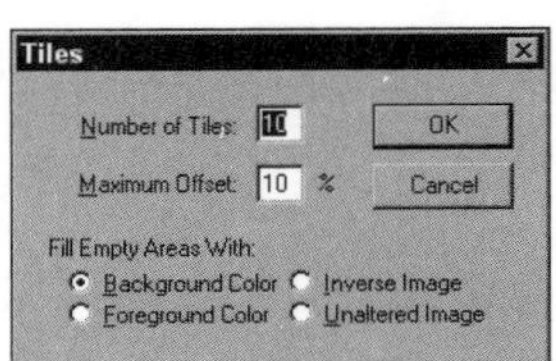

Tiles Filter Dialog Box Contents

Component	Function
Number of Tiles field	Enter a number between 1 and 99 to specify number of tiles. The size of the tiles will be dependent on the size of the image.
Maximum Offset field	Enter any number between 1 and 99 to determine the percentage of the tile size that will be assigned to the space between tiles.
Fill Empty Areas With radio buttons	Choose one of these buttons to determine whether the space between tiles will be filled with the current background color, the current foreground color, the negative of the image, or an offset (but otherwise unchanged) rendition of the original image.

Trace Contour Filter

The Trace Contour filter draws a single-pixel line to trace edges and then drops out all the other colors in the image. The Trace Contour filter dialog box is shown in the following figure.

CONTINUED

BREAKING UP IS EASY TO DO CONTINUED

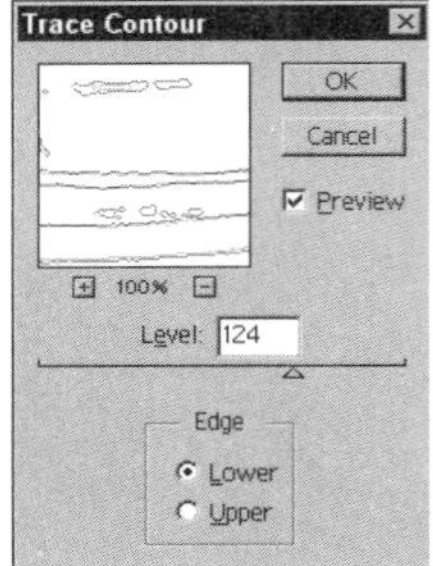

Trace Contour Filter Dialog Box Contents

Component	Function
Level slider and field	Drag to set threshold for definition of edges, or enter a value between 1 and 255.
Edge radio buttons	Determines whether the edge will be traced on the upper or lower side of the threshold (edge) pixel.
Preview check box	If checked, shows the effect of all settings on the image in the workspace.

Wind Filter

The Wind filter is closely related to the Motion Blur filter. This filter produces an effect reminiscent of a comic-strip motion blur, with streaked edges. The Wind filter dialog box is shown here.

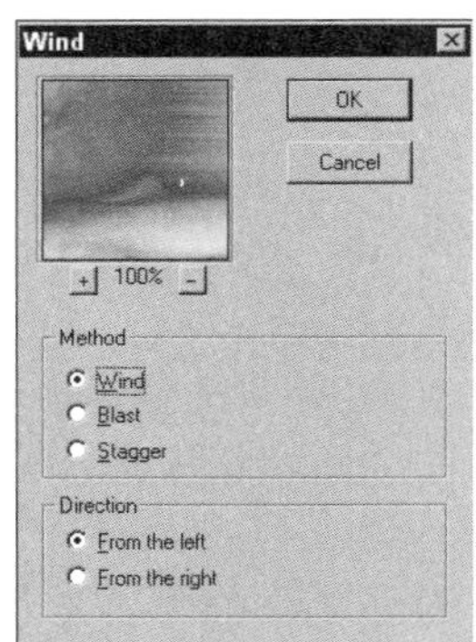

Wind Filter Dialog Box Contents

Component	Function
Wind radio button	Creates a streaking of darker pixels into the lighter areas of the image.
Blast radio button	Same as previous radio button, but the streak is longer.
Stagger radio button	Streaks shadows into highlights in one direction and highlights into shadows in the other. Creates a sort of jarred, jagged effect.
From the left radio button	Specifies that the streak is smudged from the left and tapers to the right.
From the right radio button	Specifies that the streak is smudged from the right and tapers to the left.

APPLY THE ADD NOISE FILTER

The Add Noise filter granulates an image regardless of the image's content. In fact, you can create textures by adding grain to a solid-color image and then use other filters to smear, grow, or move it. You can add grain in a uniform pattern or have it clump according to highlights and shadows, thus simulating the grain of photographic emulsions. The filter can work in color or can switch the appearance (but not the Color mode) of the image to monochrome.

The Add Noise filter is another excellent choice for helping you match the grain pattern in an image after another image is composited into it. You'll also want to match grain patterns after using any of the blur filters.

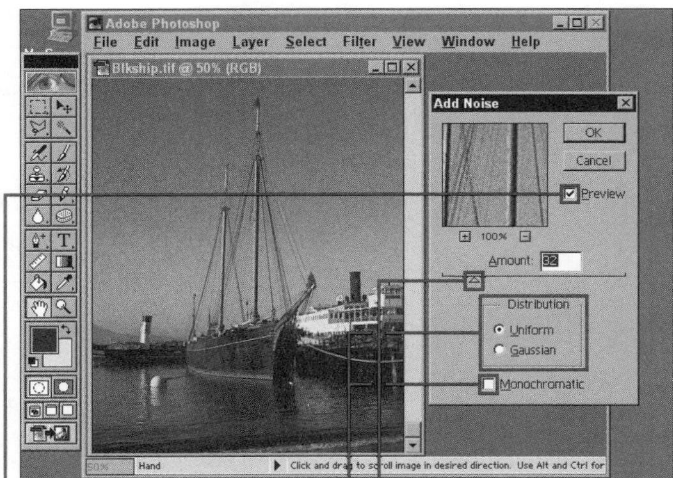

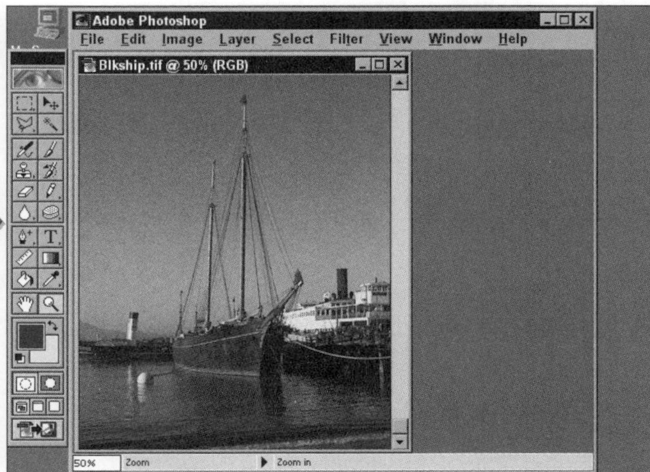

1 Choose Filter ➪ Noise ➪ Add Noise.

2 Check the Preview box to preview all adjustments in the work area.

3 Drag to increase or decrease graininess.

4 Click to choose between even and random grain distribution.

5 Check to render image as grayscale.

■ Here's the result of running the Add Noise filter on this image at the default settings shown in the dialog box.

APPLY THE DESPECKLE FILTER

The Despeckle filter is primarily used to get rid of those unsightly oil-slick patterns that often appear when you scan an already published image. The pattern occurs because the position and size of the dots in the halftone pattern of the printed image are out of register with the dots (pixels) that make up the digitized image.

The Despeckle filter has no adjustments or controls, thus it does not have a dialog box. If the filter doesn't remove all the noise the first time, run it again. Run it too many times, and the image will start to become more and more fuzzy. Careful: If you run the Unsharp Mask filters to cure the softness, you might get the moiré pattern back.

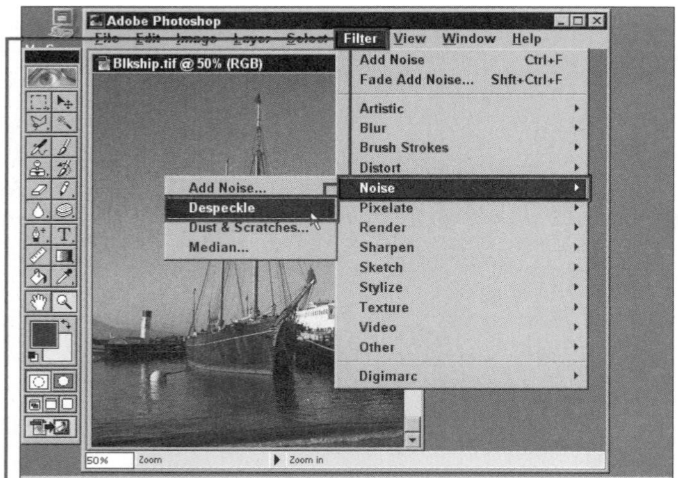

1 Choose Filter ➪ Noise ➪ Despeckle.

■ The pattern, or most of it, disappears.

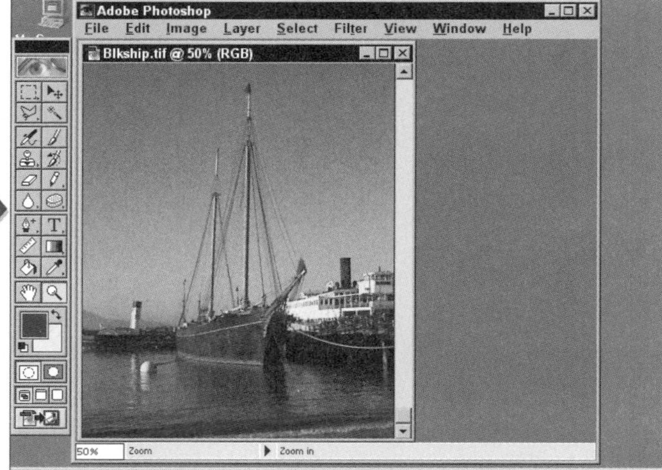

■ This shows the result of running the Despeckle filter on the image from the previous exercise after it had been specked by Add Noise.

APPLY THE DUST & SCRATCHES FILTER

The Dust & Scratches filter looks for abrupt breaks in the overall pattern of the image and blends those breaks together. (Call it automated retouching.) You can use it on the overall image, but it is likely to blur unpredictably in areas of the image.

The Dust & Scratches filter dialog box contains a Preview check box and slider controls for Radius and Threshold. Radius determines the maximum width of a spot or scratch that Photoshop will consider repairing. Increase this setting too much, and the whole picture will appear fuzzy. Threshold determines degree of contrast between defects and surrounding pixels that must exist before Photoshop will attempt a repair.

Note: Dust & Scratches can be used on an image that has no blemishes to produce a chiaroscuro (Rembrandt-like) effect, where highlights spread into shadows.

1 Select the area(s) that need repair.

2 Choose Filter ➪ Noise ➪ Dust & Scratches.

3 Drag to increase radius of defects to be mended.

4 Drag to indicate contrast between pixels that must exist before Photoshop will consider a repair.

■ Here's the result of running the Dust & Scratches filter on an intentionally scratched, dust-laden image.

APPLY THE MEDIAN FILTER

The Median filter blurs the image but spreads the highlights into the shadows in the process. The result can be an alternative to the Watercolor filter, without the extremely dark shadows Watercolor produces.

The effects of this filter are fairly easy to predict, as there's only one control in the filter's dialog box. Try using this filter with the Watercolor Paper texture on the CD-ROM that accompanies this book, which will give you a good idea of what this filter can do. Run the filter and then choose Filter ➪ Texture ➪ Texturizer (see Chapter 14 for more information on working with Textures).

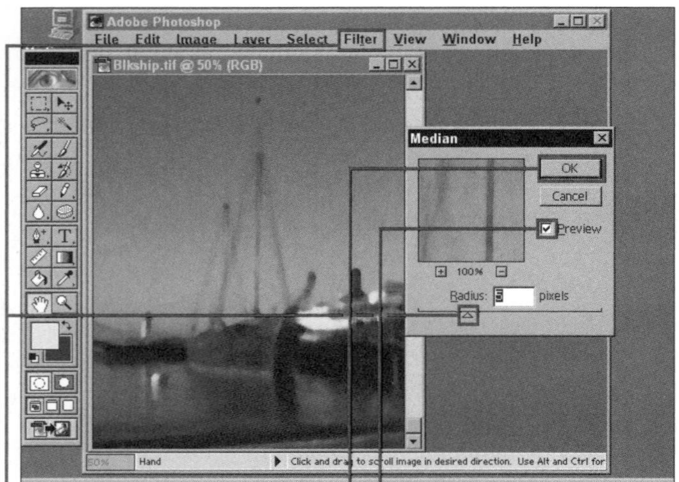

1 Choose Filter ➪ Noise ➪ Median.

2 Drag to increase or decrease the amount of blurring.

3 Check if you want to preview the effect of the Radius setting in the workspace.

4 Click OK to render.

■ This shows what happens to the image when I apply the Median filter with a radius of 5 pixels, select Filter ➪ Texture ➪ Texturizer, load the Watercolor paper texture, and then click OK.

APPLY THE COLOR HALFTONE FILTER

The Color Halftone filter is a pop-art effects filter, not actually usable for making color-separation halftones for color printing. Photoshop does have that capability, but first you need to make the separations and then make a grayscale halftone screen for each separation.

The Color Halftone filter divides the image into dots that you can exaggerate to your liking. There are five controls, one to specify dot size and one each for screen angles for Channels 1 through 4. The settings you use will depend on the overall size of your image and the size at which it will be reproduced. The filter does not have a Preview box.

Be careful about using this filter on images that are to be reproduced by halftone printing methods. If the dots are too small, two out-of-register dot patterns could end up creating a moiré pattern. The bigger the dots in the Color Halftone effect, the safer you'll be.

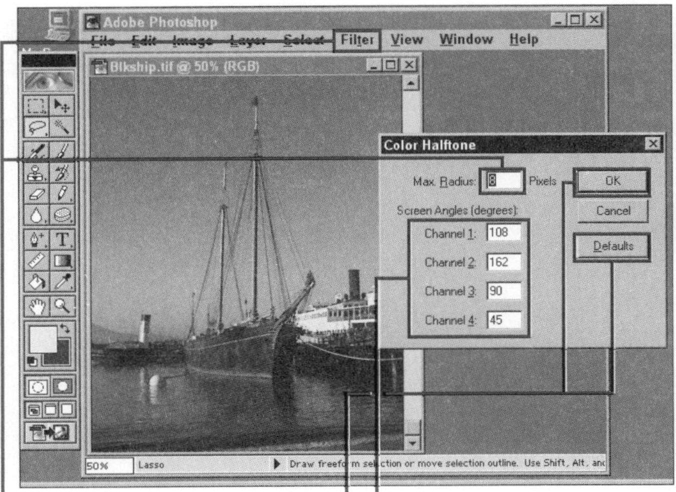

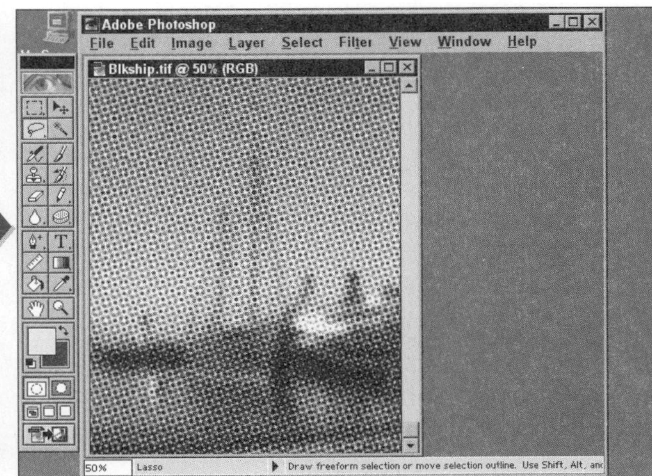

1 Choose Filter ➪ Pixelate ➪ Color Halftone.

2 Enter the radius of the largest dot in number of pixels.

3 Enter a screen angle for all four channels, even if you're in RGB mode.

4 Click OK to render.

5 Click to reset to defaults.

■ Here's the result of running the filter on the test image at the default settings.

Note: The default screen angles usually give the best results, so start by changing the dot size to suit the size of the image you're working on and the effect you want.

APPLY THE CRYSTALLIZE FILTER

The Crystallize filter (Filter ⇨ Pixelate ⇨ Crystallize) averages a pixels into irregular solid-color polygons. The effect is a reduction of colors and a variation on pointillist expressionism as an artistic style.

If you drag the slider far enough to the right, you get a stained glass effect, but with no "leading" between the panes.

By making careful masks for different sections of a scene, you can use this filter to simulate moisture on a pane of glass.

You'll want to make the crystals vary in size and transparency and keep the crystal size relatively small over all.

Only one control appears in the Crystallize filter dialog box — a slider that dictates the size of the polygonal crystal.

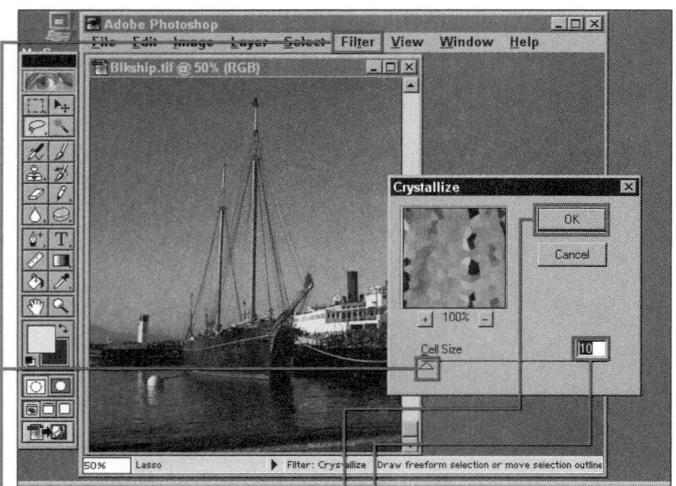

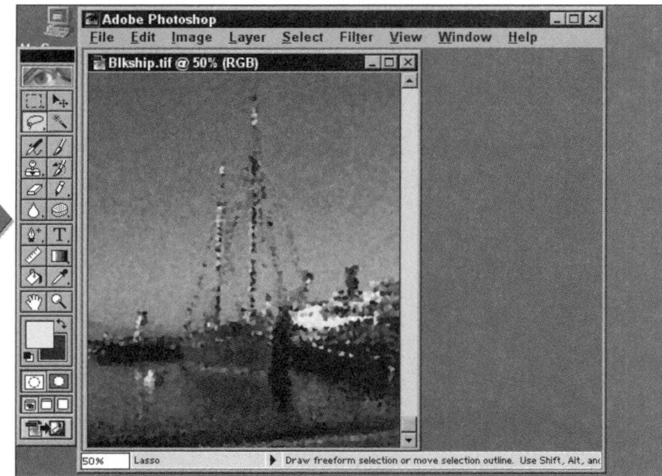

1 Choose Filter ⇨ Pixelate ⇨ Crystallize.

2 Drag to reduce or enlarge size of crystals.

3 Or, enter a number of pixels to indicate Crystal size.

Note: A cell size of 3 is the smallest number that has any effect.

4 Click OK to render.

■ This is the result of running the filter on the test image at the default settings.

Note: If you make the crystals large, you can produce a nice palette knife effect — especially if you then texturize the image by using Lighting Effects and one of the color channels as a texture map.

APPLY THE FACET FILTER

The Facet filter flattens colors and removes anti-aliasing from edges, making them more jagged. This is a single-step filter with no adjustments, thus the filter has no dialog box. (In addition, the effect of the Facet filter is so subtle, you may think that nothing has happened.)

The Facet filter is a good filter to run on images you want to paint over in a natural-media program such as Fractal Design's Painter and Painter Classic. Put the result into one of these programs and then use a brush that moves the existing paint, such as the Palette knife or Turpentine brush.

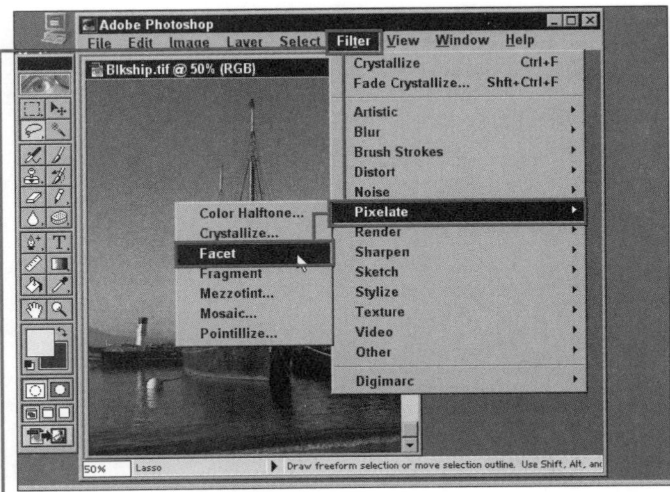

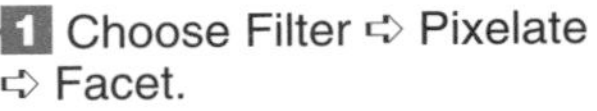

1 Choose Filter ⇨ Pixelate ⇨ Facet.

■ The progress meter runs for a moment (unless you're running a fast Pentium II or G3 processor) and then the image changes very slightly.

■ Here's the test image after running the Facet filter on it. You have to look carefully to notice much of a difference.

Note: You could magnify the effect of this filter by running it several times. Press ⌘/Ctrl+F until you get the result you're after.

APPLY THE FRAGMENT FILTER

The Fragment filter is another one-step Pixelate filter that requires a little imagination to find a use for. The filter causes an image to blur and its elements to duplicate and offset just subtly enough that you'll think you need new glasses.

The Fragment filter does not have any options to control, thus it has no dialog box.

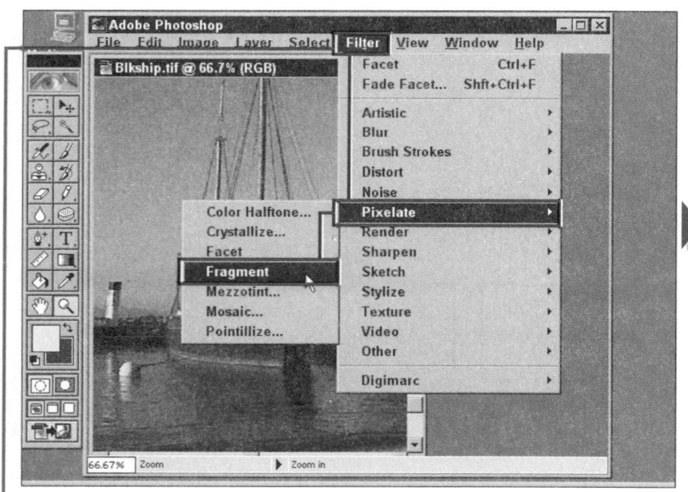

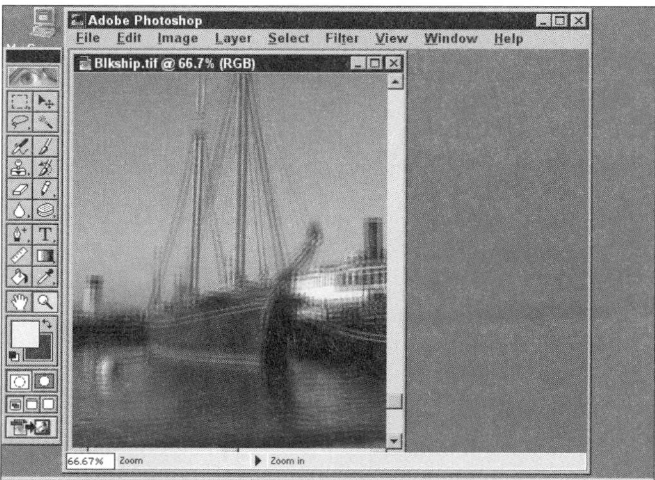

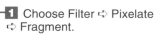

1 Choose Filter ⇨ Pixelate ⇨ Fragment.

■ The progress meter runs for a moment, and then the image appears fragmented.

■ Here's the result of running the Fragment filter.

Note: You might use this as a background for earth-shaking news or as a prelude to the coming of Godzilla.

APPLY THE MEZZOTINT FILTER

The Mezzotint filter offers ten variations of a noise effect. I've found this filter to be of most use in creating texture patterns (see the next exercise in this chapter for more on how to create a texture pattern of your own).

A *mezzotint* is a halftone pattern created by replacing dots with enlarged versions or short lines and strokes. The filter provides options for the type of dots, lines, or strokes you are looking for in a pull-down menu.

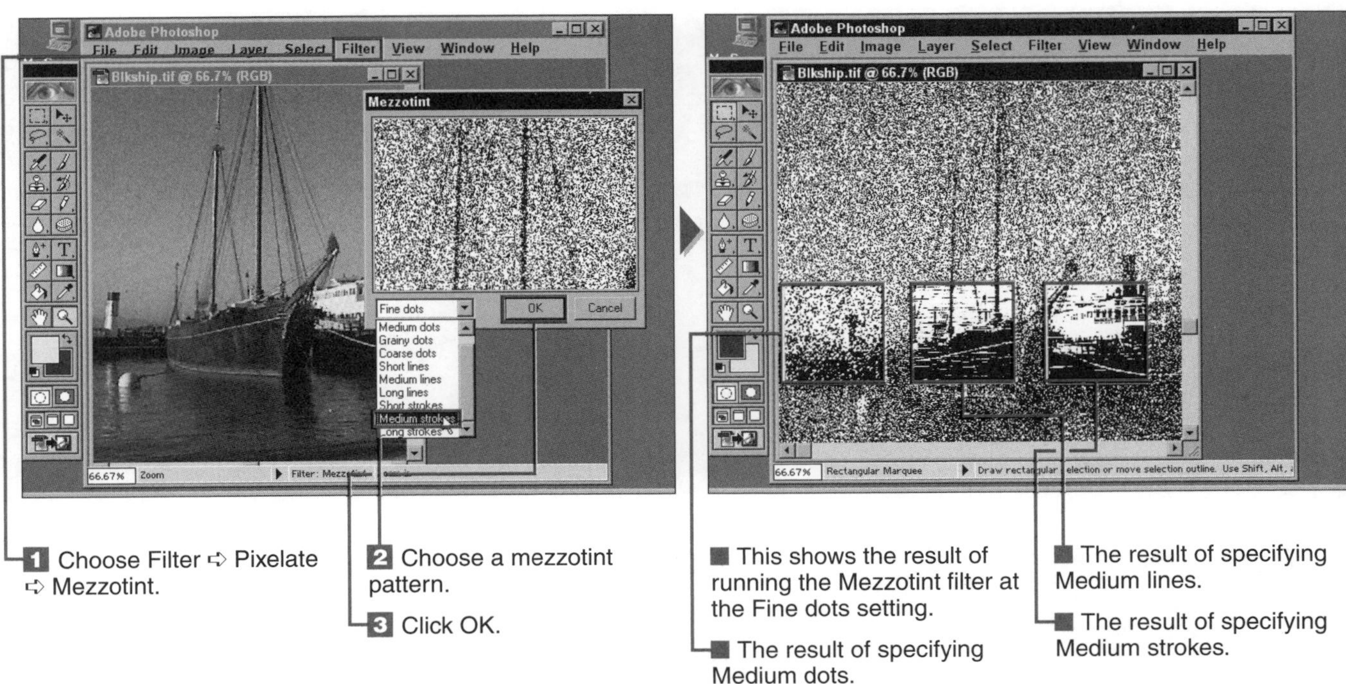

1 Choose Filter ➪ Pixelate ➪ Mezzotint.

2 Choose a mezzotint pattern.

3 Click OK.

■ This shows the result of running the Mezzotint filter at the Fine dots setting.

■ The result of specifying Medium dots.

■ The result of specifying Medium lines.

■ The result of specifying Medium strokes.

CREATE A TEXTURE WITH THE MEZZOTINT FILTER

The Mezzotint filter makes any image grainy — even one that is a solid color. This makes it ideal for use as a texture pattern maker. You can further modify the grain patterns with Photoshop's built-in blur and distortion filters, and then make multiple copies of layers and blend them to get a final texture.

The steps to create a texture with the Mezzotint filter are shown in this exercise, but you can repeat any of these steps in any combination to make an infinite number of texture patterns. I find these patterns especially useful as a relatively easy way to create natural-looking textures that mimic such things as hand-made papers, concrete, newsprint, and watercolor paper.

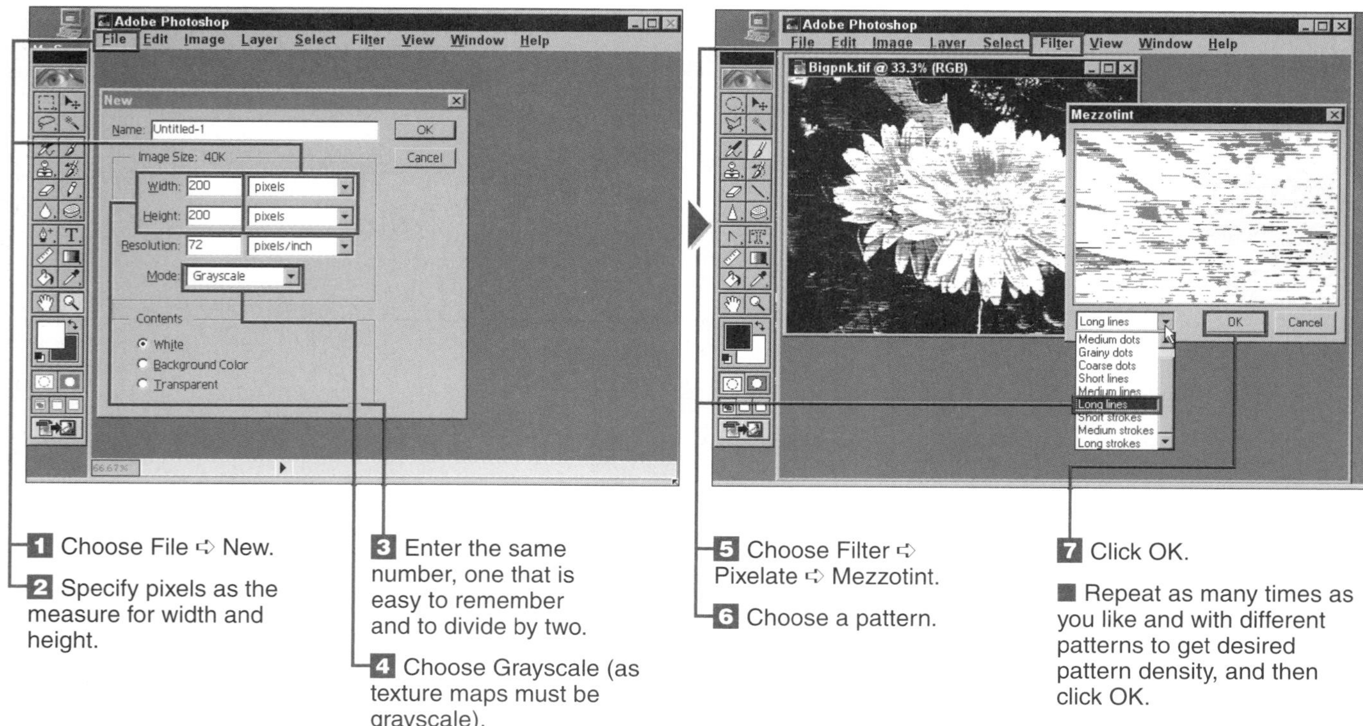

1 Choose File ⇨ New.

2 Specify pixels as the measure for width and height.

3 Enter the same number, one that is easy to remember and to divide by two.

4 Choose Grayscale (as texture maps must be grayscale).

5 Choose Filter ⇨ Pixelate ⇨ Mezzotint.

6 Choose a pattern.

7 Click OK.

■ Repeat as many times as you like and with different patterns to get desired pattern density, and then click OK.

TIPS

Are any particular distortion filters more likely to be useful for making textures?

The Diffuse Glow filter is excellent for softening the edges of the mezzotint patterns so you can get more natural-looking paper and marble textures, for instance. Also, the Glass filter can be good for adding random streaks that look like paper fibers.

Is there any way to make a texture that uses more than one of the mezzotint effects?

Duplicate the unfiltered background layer once for each effect you want to create. Apply a different effect to each layer. Use the transparency slider in the layer's palette to adjust the transparency for each layer. Apply distortion effects to each layer or wait until you've flattened the entire file. After flattening, you may want to use the Threshold filter to boost contrast. Finally, make a seamless tile of the texture (or make the texture big enough to cover an entire image or selection).

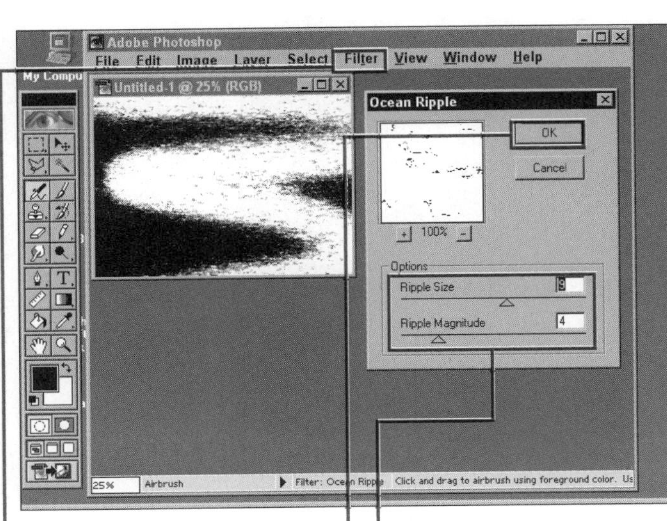

USE A DISTORT FILTER TO MAKE THE PATTERN LESS UNIFORM

1 Choose Filter ⇨ Distort ⇨ Ocean Ripple (or whichever Distort filter you wish to use).

2 Adjust controls.

3 Click OK.

USE A BLUR FILTER TO INCREASE CONTOURS IN DEEPEST PART OF PATTERNS

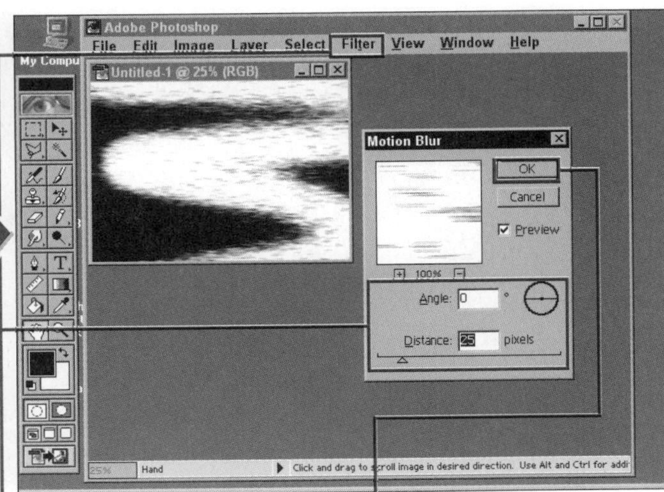

1 Choose Filter ⇨ Blur ⇨ Motion Blur.

2 Adjust controls to stretch and angle the pattern.

3 Click OK.

■ Follow the steps needed to make a seamless tile of this pattern.

Note: For some effects, you may want to repeat this step on duplicated layers.

APPLY THE POINTILLIZE FILTER

The Pointillize filter actually does a fairly credible job of turning your image into a pointillist painting. You can do this more effectively by running the filter so that the dots, or points of paint, vary in size from one area of the image to another. Also, the space between the dots will be in the current background color. You may want one space color for some areas of the image and another for other areas of the image.

The Pointillize filter dialog box has a single control for the size of the dot. It does not contain a Preview check box.

Try duplicating the layer on which you want to use the Pointillize filter. Run the same filter on the new layer, using white as the background color. Use the Underpainting filter on the underlying layer. Next, make the background color transparent by selecting white with the Select ➪ Choose Color Range command and pressing Backspace/Delete. The Underpainted layer will now show through.

1 Choose Filter ➪ Pixelate ➪ Pointillize.

2 Drag to set the size of a color dot.

3 Click OK.

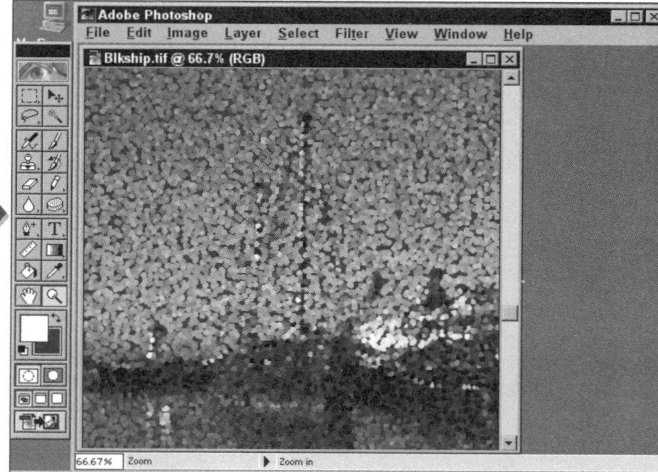

■ Here's the result of running the Pointillize filter at Cell Size set to 10.

APPLY THE DIFFUSE FILTER

The Diffuse filter makes an image look as though it was sprayed with paint from an aerosol can. It produces a sort of diffused grainy effect.

The Diffuse filter dialog box does not contain slider controls for modifying the size of the effect in relationship to the resolution of the image. Instead, three radio buttons enable you to choose between three variations of the effect: Normal, Darken only, and Lighten only.

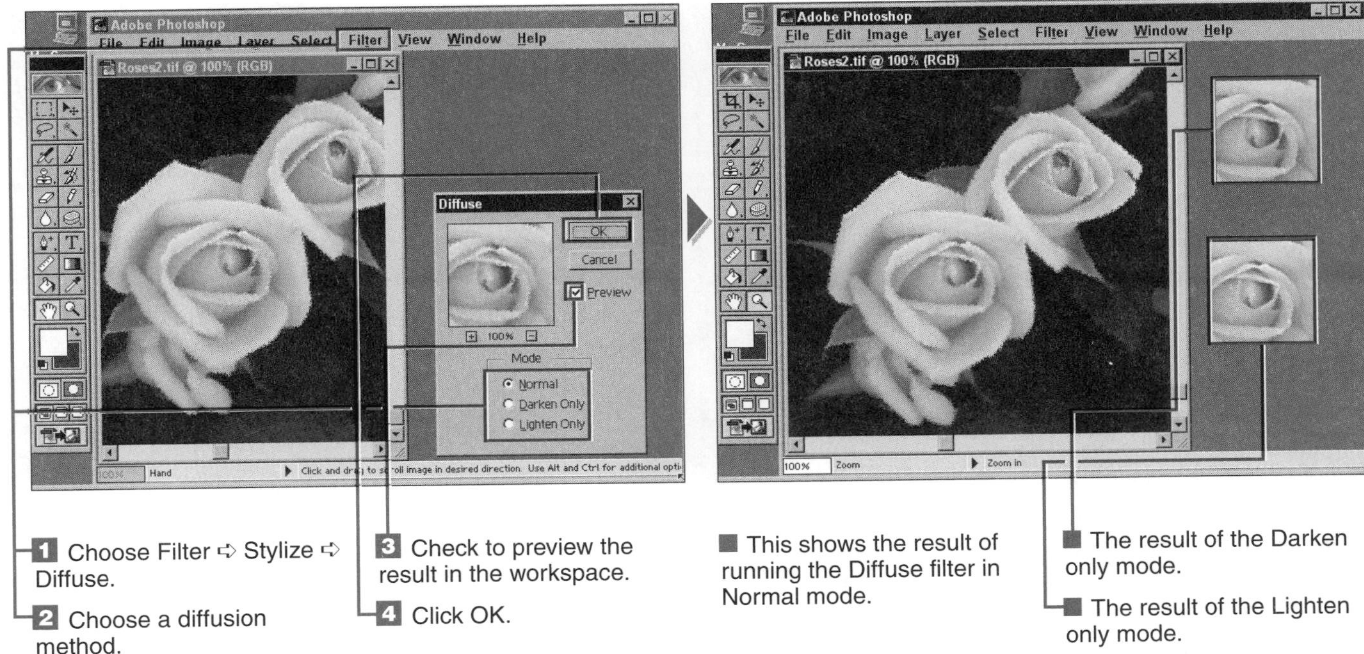

1 Choose Filter ⇨ Stylize ⇨ Diffuse.

2 Choose a diffusion method.

3 Check to preview the result in the workspace.

4 Click OK.

■ This shows the result of running the Diffuse filter in Normal mode.

■ The result of the Darken only mode.

■ The result of the Lighten only mode.

APPLY THE EMBOSS FILTER

The Emboss filter creates a monochrome image that looks as if the elements in the image are stamped into paper — similar to embossed stationery. You will see some color in the image if you move the settings to their upper limits and if you have a very colorful subject.

The Emboss filter dialog box has a Preview check box and three settings: Angle, Height, and Amount. Angle refers to the apparent lighting angle. Height controls the depth of the most prominent edges in the image. Amount refers to the amount of detail that will be seen between the most contrasting edges.

Emboss is an excellent filter to use as a texture map. It's already grayscale, so just choose Image ⇨ Mode ⇨ Grayscale and then save the result in Photoshop (PSD) format. You could also duplicate the layer, use the Emboss filter on the underlying layer, and then use a Blend mode for a different kind of 3D effect.

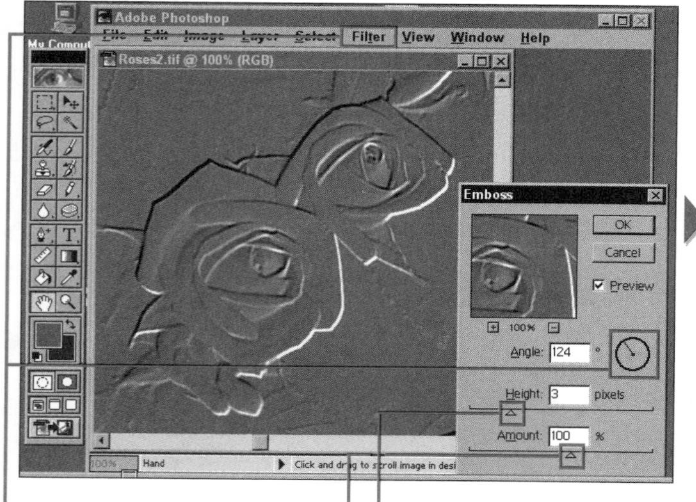

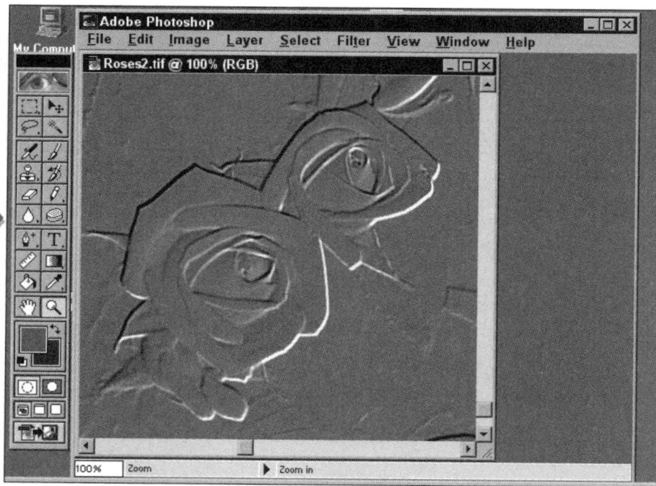

1 Choose Filter ⇨ Stylize ⇨ Emboss.

2 Drag to set the angle of lighting.

3 Drag to make major edges cast deeper shadows.

4 Drag to increase amount of detail.

■ Here's the result of running the Emboss filter.

APPLY THE EXTRUDE FILTER

The Extrude filter makes the image look like it has been glued to raised blocks. You can also use it to convert the image to solid-color 3D blocks or pyramids.

The Extrude filter dialog box has no sliders, but it contains two entry fields, four radio buttons, and two check boxes. The Type control features a pair of radio buttons with which you can choose between square blocks or four-sided pyramids. You can enter the size of a block or pyramid as a number of pixels. You can also specify the depth, but then the depth of individual squares can be either based on color level or randomly assigned, depending on which radio button you choose. Checking Solid Front Faces makes the face of each block a solid color (kind of like using the Mosaic filter at a large size). Checking Mask Incomplete Blocks drops any blocks that can't be completed because of their proximity to the edge.

1 Choose Filter ⇨ Stylize ⇨ Extrude.

2 Choose Blocks or Pyramids.

3 Enter pixel size of blocks/pyramids. Size will be uniform.

■ The image shows the result at the pictured settings.

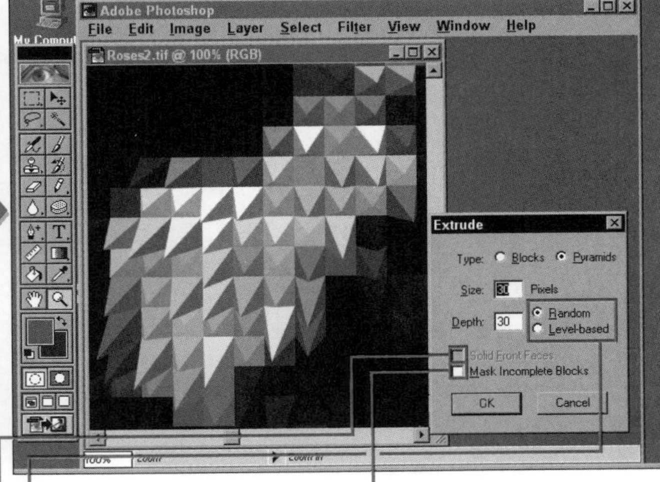

4 Choose Random or Level-based depth of extrusions.

5 Check for solid color blocks (this will be grayed for pyramids, which are always solid).

6 Check to drop blocks too close to the edge to be completed.

■ The image shows the result at the pictured settings.

APPLY THE FIND EDGES FILTER

The Find Edges filter accentuates the edges of the pixels in an image. It traces contrasting edges with a dark line and converts all the other shades in the image to a highlighted pastel of whatever was the image's former color. It causes low-contrast areas of an image to appear white, medium-contrast areas to appear gray, and high-contrast areas to appear black.

The Find Edges filter does not have settings controls and is fully automatic.

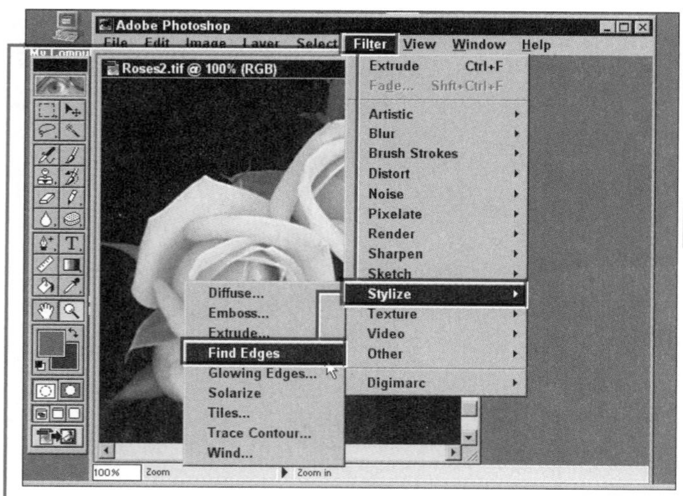

1 Choose Filter ⇨ Stylize ⇨ Find Edges.

■ After a few moments, you should see something similar to the result shown here.

APPLY THE GLOWING EDGES FILTER

The Glowing Edges filter traces contrasting edges with a bright line and converts all the other shades in the image to a charcoal color.

The Glowing Edges filter dialog box has three controls: Edge Width, Edge Brightness, and Smoothness. Edge Width does the expected, setting the span of the edges between strongly contrasting colors. Edge Brightness is less obvious because the brighter the edge, the wider. Smoothness controls how sharp or blurred the line forming the edge will be.

If you want more control over the effects of the Find Edges filter (discussed in the previous exercise), use Glowing Edges. Next, press ⌘/Ctrl+I to invert the image. Also, try duplicating the layer, running Glowing Edges on both, and then inverting the top layer. Afterwards, use the Hard Light Blend mode on the top layer.

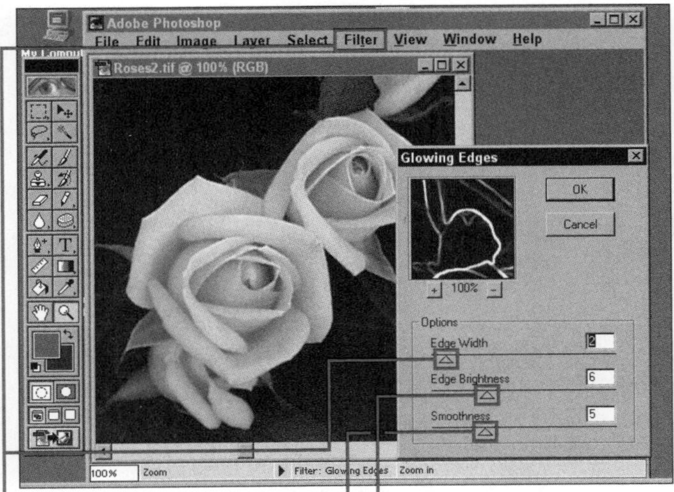

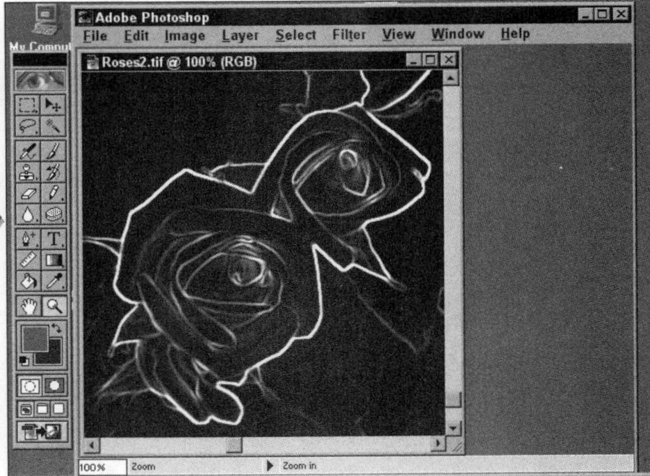

1 Choose Filter ⇨ Stylize ⇨ Glowing Edges.

2 Drag to determine broadness of edges.

3 Drag to determine brightness of edges. (The brighter, the broader.)

4 Drag to soften edges of edges.

■ This shows the result of running the Glowing Edges filter.

APPLY THE SOLARIZE FILTER

If you're familiar with traditional chemical darkroom techniques, solarization results when an image is exposed to light during the developing process. This causes the undeveloped portion of the image to invert so the image is half normal, half negative. The Solarize filter produces an effect similar to this process. It is an automatic filter, meaning it does not have a dialog box for specifying settings.

You can get a much more dramatic effect by choosing Image ➪ Adjust ➪ Auto Levels immediately after running the Solarize filter. Solarization can also be interesting when used to texturize the original image.

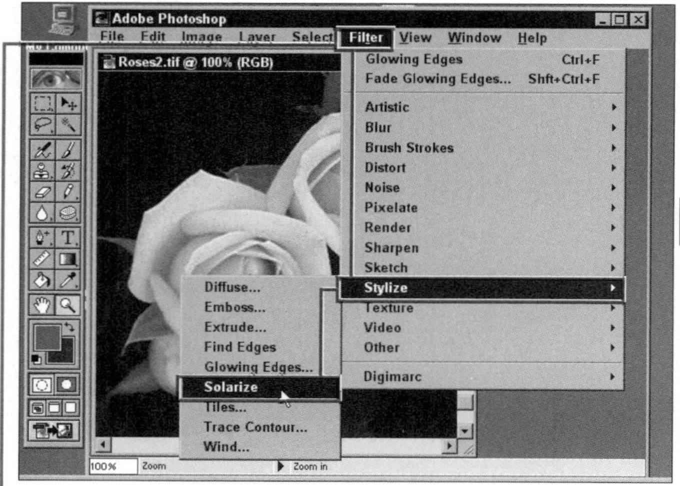

1 Choose Filter ➪ Stylize ➪ Solarize.

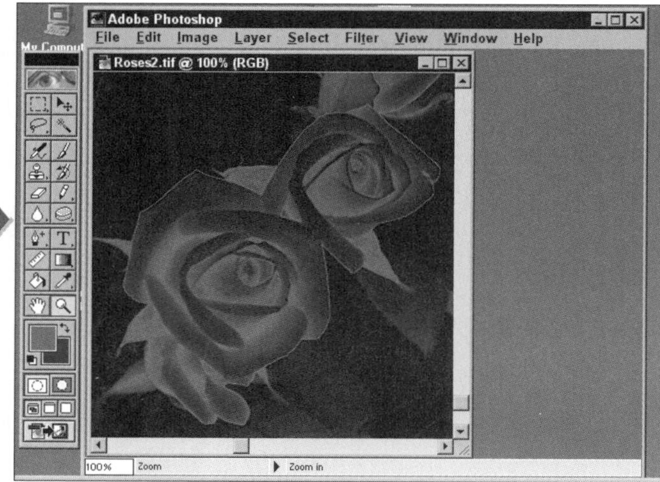

■ Here is the result of running the Solarize filter.

APPLY THE TILES FILTER

The Tiles filter produces an effect that looks similiar to a mosaic, dividing the image up into somewhat irregular square tiles. The "grout" (space between the tiles) can be in the foreground or background, or can take its color from the image or the inverse of the image.

The Tiles filter dialog box has three controls. Two entry fields let you specify the number of tiles across and the percentage of maximum offset between the tiles. The third control is a set of four radio buttons that enable you to choose how the space between tiles will be filled: Background Color, Foreground Color, Inverse Image, or Unaltered Image.

You can try making a real mosaic, with solid-color tiles, by first running the Mosaic filter and then the Tiles filter. The trick is in figuring out how to make the tiles in each filter the same size. (Hint: Choose Window ➪ Show Info and drag a rectangular marquee around a tile.)

1 Choose Filter ➪ Stylize ➪ Tiles.

2 Enter the desired number of tiles across the image.

3 Enter a percentage of image width for maximum distance between tiles.

4 Click to choose what will fill the space between tiles.

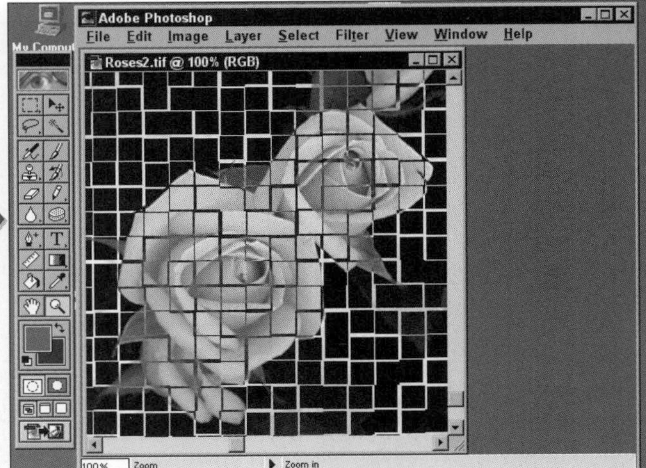

■ This shows the result of running the Tiles filter.

APPLY THE TRACE CONTOUR FILTER

The Trace Contour filter draws a single-pixel line to trace edges and then drops out all the other colors in the image.

The Trace Contour filter dialog box has a couple of controls. One is a Level slider that sets the threshold for finding an edge. Dragging this slider changes the amount of detail and influences the number of colors you see in the tracing. The pair of radio buttons determine whether the edge is chosen from pixels just above or just below the threshold line.

You can make several duplicates of the target layer and run Trace Contours at different threshold settings on each. Next, use the Multiply Blend mode to combine all the traced edges into a more complex result.

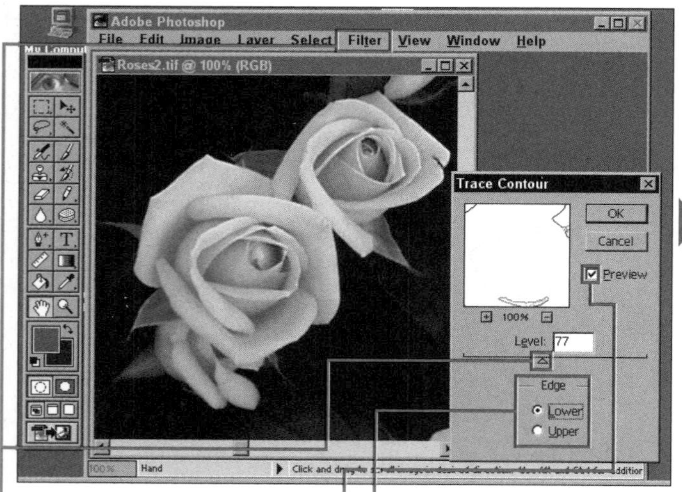

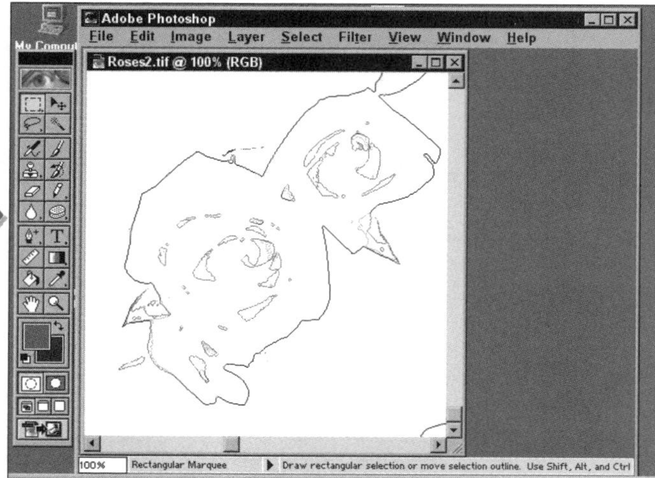

1 Choose Filter ⇨ Stylize ⇨ Trace Contour.

2 Drag to set edge contrast threshold level.

3 Click to choose whether edge is determined by pixels just above or below the threshold.

4 Check to preview changes in the workspace.

■ Here's the result of running the Trace Contours filter.

APPLY THE WIND FILTER

The Wind filter is closely related to the Motion Blur filter. (Why it isn't found on the Blur Filters menu is a mystery that may haunt us for versions of Photoshop to come.) Anyway, this is more of a comic-strip motion blur, with streaked edges — at least, that's the default look. Several variations are available.

The Wind filter dialog box has two sets of radio buttons that determine the specific effect you get. The Method buttons are Wind, Blast, and Stagger. The Direction buttons dictate whether the smears move to the left or to the right from the edge.

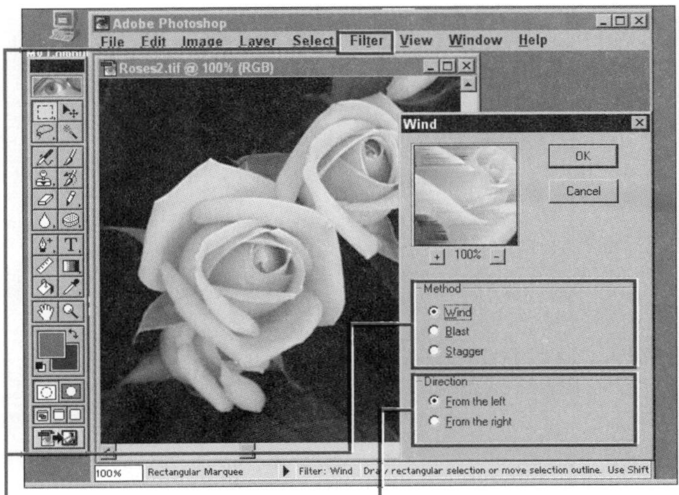

1 Choose Filter ➪ Stylize ➪ Wind.

2 Choose a method (see second paragraph, above).

3 Choose a direction for the smear.

■ Notice the result of running the Wind filter at the pictured settings.

Note: Brighter edges streak farther than darker ones.

CREATE YOUR OWN FILTER EFFECTS: THE CUSTOM FILTER

If you don't like any of the filters Photoshop provides, you can make your own. Even if you don't have the time and patience to make your own filter, the Custom command (Filter ➪ Other ➪ Custom) provides you with a way to load any of the hundreds of custom-made filters that others have posted for free on their Web sites.

This is not to say that the Custom filter enables you to make every kind of filter there is, or that this is a particularly easy-to-use feature of Photoshop. The interface for this filter is fairly obscure. Try to understand the guidelines laid out here, and then experiment.

The Custom filter creates filters that work by mixing pixels within a 5-pixel radius according to the numbers you input into a 5×5 matrix and into two additional fields, Scale and Offset. The types of effects for which the Custom filter is best suited are sharpening, blurring, edge detection, and embossing. Because creating custom filters is so experimental, be sure the Preview box is checked so that you can see the result of your entries almost immediately.

■ This is the image of a bunch of roses, before any customization is applied.

START THE CUSTOM FILTER

1 Choose Filter ➪ Other ➪ Custom.

■ The Custom dialog box appears.

■ Notice the default settings for the Custom filter.

Note: All the numbers add up to 1.

Note: Scale should always be equal to the sum of the numbers (to maintain overall color balance).

2 Check to preview results in the workspace before rendering.

Why do I have to do the math to balance the sum of the Scale value and the matrix numbers? Can't I achieve the same end by changing the Offset value?

Not quite. Balancing the sum of the numbers in the matrix and the Scale value fully maintains the color balance of the original image. Changing the Offset value just adjusts the midtone.

Why can you enter a value up to 9,999 in the Offset field if 255 is absolute white?

Because it's entirely possible to enter numbers in the matrix that will (mathematically, at least) produce results that are much whiter than white or blacker than black. So by entering a high or low enough offset, you bring these pixels back into the visible spectrum.

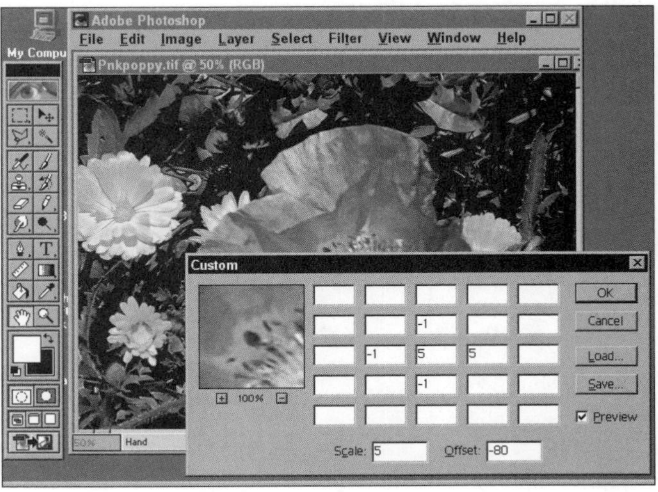

BALANCE COLOR AND CONTRAST WHEN SUM OF MATRIX VALUES ≠ 1

1 Enter a value in the Offset field between —255 and 255 (solid white).

Note: Think of the Offset field as a threshold control, except you have to enter a value instead of dragging a slider. Try several values to help you judge the effect.

Note: Always enter numbers in opposite fields in the matrix. (This isn't a hard and fast rule, by any means — just a good place to start.) If you enter numbers at random, you'll quickly lose track of which settings bring about which effects.

SAVE AND LOAD CUSTOM FILTERS

The moment you create something that looks interesting with the Custom filter, save it using a descriptive name. Next, create a before and after picture, write a small blurb about how others might find it useful or interesting, and put both on your Web site for everyone to share. Then let users click to download the file. You'll find instructions on how to do all this in Chapter 21.

Meantime, you want to be able to save any of your experiments that work so you can use them again yourself. You'll also want to know how to load a custom filter when you need it. It's easy to save and load custom filters, and this exercise shows you all you need to know.

Note: You have to save filters the moment you've made the settings and before you render them by clicking OK in the Custom dialog box.

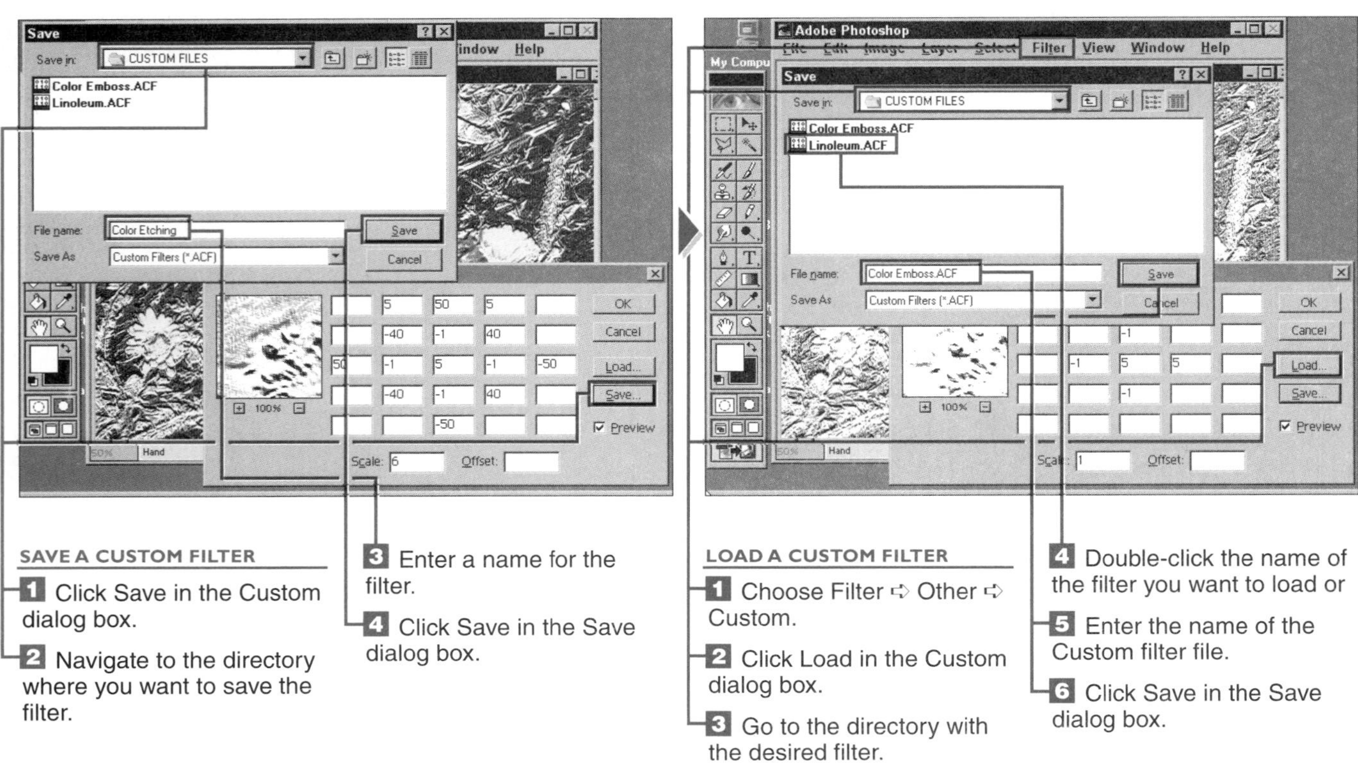

SAVE A CUSTOM FILTER

1 Click Save in the Custom dialog box.

2 Navigate to the directory where you want to save the filter.

3 Enter a name for the filter.

4 Click Save in the Save dialog box.

LOAD A CUSTOM FILTER

1 Choose Filter ➪ Other ➪ Custom.

2 Click Load in the Custom dialog box.

3 Go to the directory with the desired filter.

4 Double-click the name of the filter you want to load or

5 Enter the name of the Custom filter file.

6 Click Save in the Save dialog box.

SHARPEN WITH THE CUSTOM FILTER

The Custom filter is capable of taking Photoshop's Unsharp Masking capabilities to different levels and creating extreme effects.

Sharpening is accomplished by entering a large number in the center value field of the Custom filter dialog box and surrounding it with small numbers that add up to the center value (or come within 20 percent of it). If you want to take sharpening to a more exaggerated state, enter the value in the outside row and increase the center value while leaving the Scale value at 1 (or very low).

Examples of mild and extreme sharpening are shown in the figures below. Experiment by using different numbers in the same positions for different sharpening effects.

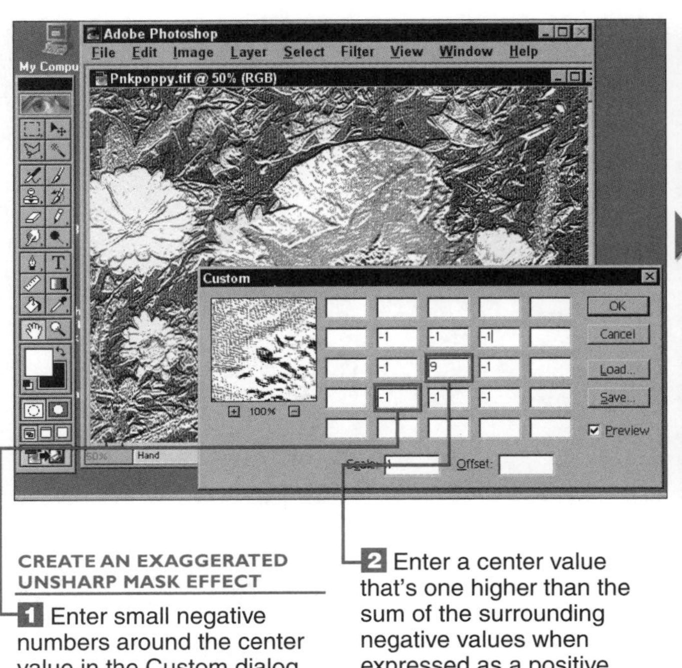

CREATE AN EXAGGERATED UNSHARP MASK EFFECT

1 Enter small negative numbers around the center value in the Custom dialog box.

2 Enter a center value that's one higher than the sum of the surrounding negative values when expressed as a positive number.

3 Save the effect if you like it.

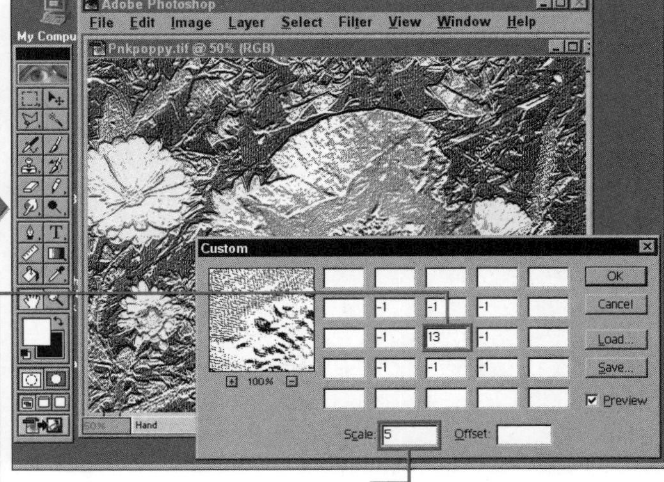

MAKE THE SHARPENING EFFECT MORE SUBTLE

1 Increase the center value in the Custom dialog box.

2 Enter a number that equals the difference between the sum, expressed as a positive, of the matrix numbers and the center value.

CREATE DIRECTIONAL BLURS WITH THE CUSTOM FILTER

If you enter all your values in the Custom filter dialog box in a row rather than surrounding the center value, you end up with a directional blurring effect. To create a blur, make the center value 1, set the other values higher, and make the Scale higher than the total of all the values. To sharpen, use a higher center value, negative matrix values, and a Scale value of 1.

The two examples below show blurring in a horizontal direction and blurring in a diagonal direction.

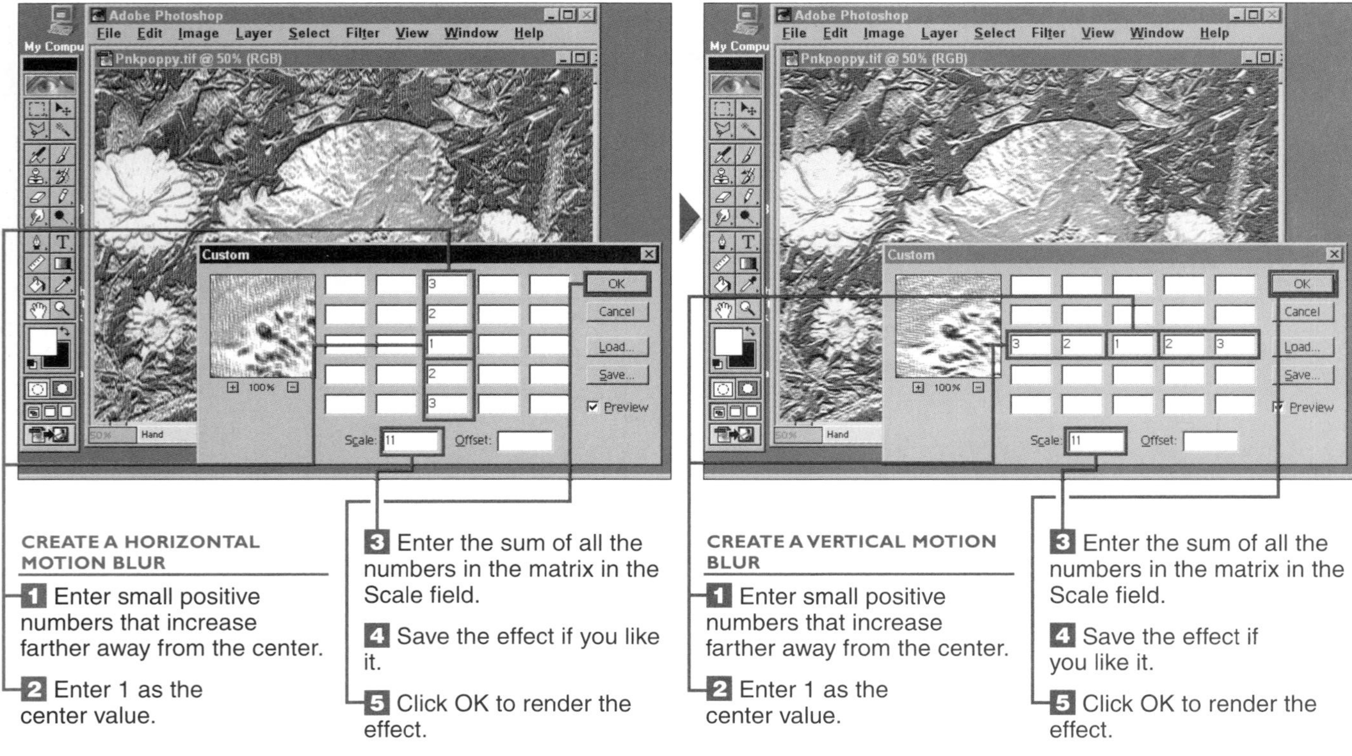

CREATE A HORIZONTAL MOTION BLUR

1 Enter small positive numbers that increase farther away from the center.

2 Enter 1 as the center value.

3 Enter the sum of all the numbers in the matrix in the Scale field.

4 Save the effect if you like it.

5 Click OK to render the effect.

CREATE A VERTICAL MOTION BLUR

1 Enter small positive numbers that increase farther away from the center.

2 Enter 1 as the center value.

3 Enter the sum of all the numbers in the matrix in the Scale field.

4 Save the effect if you like it.

5 Click OK to render the effect.

EMBOSS WITH THE CUSTOM FILTER

Embossing effects are easily created by entering asymmetrical numbers into the Custom filter dialog box matrix. For example, enter positive numbers on one side of the center value and negatives of the same numbers on the other side. You can go berserk with this effect by experimenting with wildly random numbers, so long as the opposite numbers are on the other side of the matrix. To put it another way: Be sure to put positive numbers on one side of the center value, negative numbers on the other.

This can be a confusing concept to grasp, but playing with variations in the exercises below should clear things up. Start by keeping the Scale value set at 1 and leaving the Offset field blank.

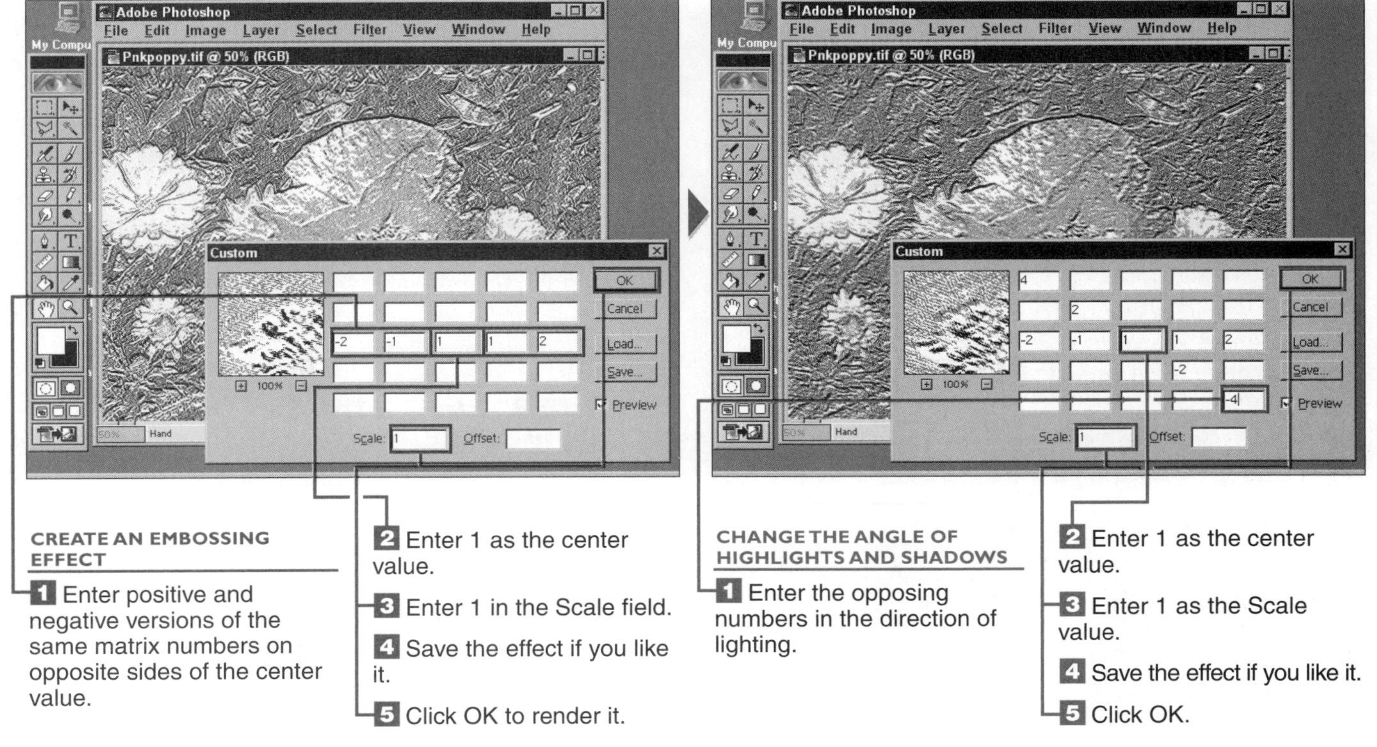

CREATE AN EMBOSSING EFFECT

1 Enter positive and negative versions of the same matrix numbers on opposite sides of the center value.

2 Enter 1 as the center value.

3 Enter 1 in the Scale field.

4 Save the effect if you like it.

5 Click OK to render it.

CHANGE THE ANGLE OF HIGHLIGHTS AND SHADOWS

1 Enter the opposing numbers in the direction of lighting.

2 Enter 1 as the center value.

3 Enter 1 as the Scale value.

4 Save the effect if you like it.

5 Click OK.

SECTION V

18 USING LAYERS TO COMBINE EFFECTS

Using Other Features Expressively 462
Combine Filter Effects Using Layers 464
Define and Save Patterns 466
Paint with Fills 468
Make Nonlinear Gradient Fills 470
Make and Edit Gradient Styles 472
Choose Colors 474
Make Custom Swatch Palettes 476

19 AUTOMATING PHOTOSHOP WITH ACTIONS

Simplify Life with Actions 478
Create a New Action 482
Save and Load a Set of Actions 484
Edit an Action 486
Play Actions 488
Play Actions in Batches 490
Insert the Unrecordable 492

20 PREPARING IMAGES FOR A COMPOSITE

Organization Is the Key to Success 494
Collect and Prep Images 496
Integrate Images in a Collage 498
Clean Up the Edges 500
Rearrange Items on a Layer 502
Cast Shadows 504

ADVANCED TECHNIQUES

18 Using Other Features Expressively

This chapter is a grab bag of tips and techniques on how to create expressive, creative effects with the components of Photoshop I've discussed so far in this book. If you've read the book up to this point, you have already seen all the features discussed in this chapter; however, they are put to different use here.

Before I delve into the exercises, I provide a brief overview of the Color Picker dialog box and the Custom Colors dialog box, as you will use them often when experimenting with Photoshop.

The Color Picker

The Color Picker is an extremely flexible tool, as illustrated by the following figure. Within it, you can choose colors in several ways. You can drag the Color slider and then click in the color spectrum, or you can enter numeric values. You can also enter numbers for RGB, HSB (Hue, Saturation, and Brightness), Lab, and CMYK (Cyan, Magenta, Yellow, and blacK) color models or pick colors from the swatch books of all the most widely used color systems (ANPA, Pantone, DIC, Toyo, and Trumatch) in the Custom Colors dialog box.

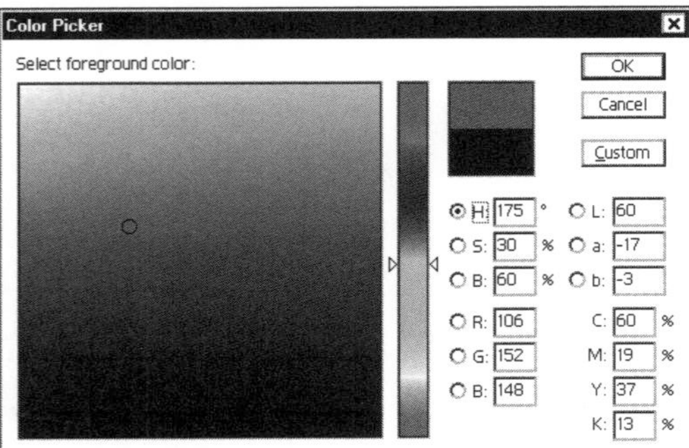

Color Picker Dialog Box Contents

Component	Function
Color field	This window shows you the range of colors you can choose according to the selected Color Mode buttons.
Color marker	Indicates the position of the currently chosen replacement color. You can choose a different replacement color simply by clicking a different point in the Color field.
Previous color	The color you last chose.
New color	The currently chosen color.
Color slider	Indicates the values of colors available to the currently chosen Color Mode component radio button. If you click inside the Color slider, the arrows automatically move to that position.
Color slider arrows	Drag the arrows up and down the Color slider to change the value of the colors shown in the Color field.

Component	Function
Color Mode component radio buttons and fields	Choose a button to change the color schemes shown in the Color field and Color slider.
Custom color button	Switches to the Custom Colors dialog box.

Custom Color

When you click the Custom button in the Color Picker, the Custom Colors dialog box appears, shown here. In this dialog box you are able to select from a set of predefined colors. These colors are from brand-name color libraries.

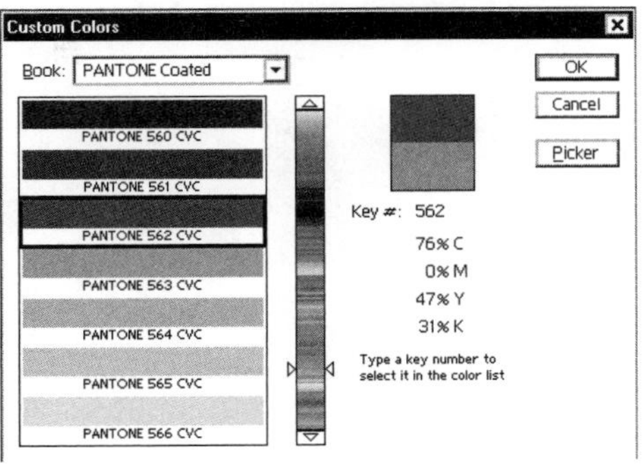

Custom Colors Dialog Box Contents

Component	Function
Book pull-down menu	Chooses a proprietary spot color book.
Color swatch panel	Shows exact colors available within the range indicated by the Color slider.
Color slider	Displays all the colors available in the currently chosen book. Click a color to change the colors in the Color swatch panel.
Color slider scroll buttons	Click the buttons to scroll colors upwards or downwards.
Color slider arrows	Drag to change the colors in the Color swatch panel.
Previous color	The color you last chose.
New color	The currently chosen color.
Color Key number	The code number assigned by the Color swatch book manufacturer to the currently chosen color.
CMYK color value	The percentages of cyan, magenta, yellow, and black contained in the currently chosen color.
Picker button	Switches to the Color Picker.

COMBINE FILTER EFFECTS USING LAYERS

The variety and versatility of Photoshop's filter effects is enriched considerably by the capability to easily duplicate layers and place a different effect on each duplicate. You can then combine these layers in a number of ways. You can erase or partially erase parts of various layers so that other parts show through; you can vary the Transparency setting for layers; and you can use one of the seventeen layer Blend modes.

COMBINING EFFECTS BY ERASING PARTS OF LAYERS

This is a simple idea that can be used to produce some very complex effects. Although only four layers are used in the following exercise, there is no end to the number of layers you can employ in this way. The advantage of erasing parts of layers, rather than creating the effect in a selection, is that the process is interactive, making it easier to visualize the end result.

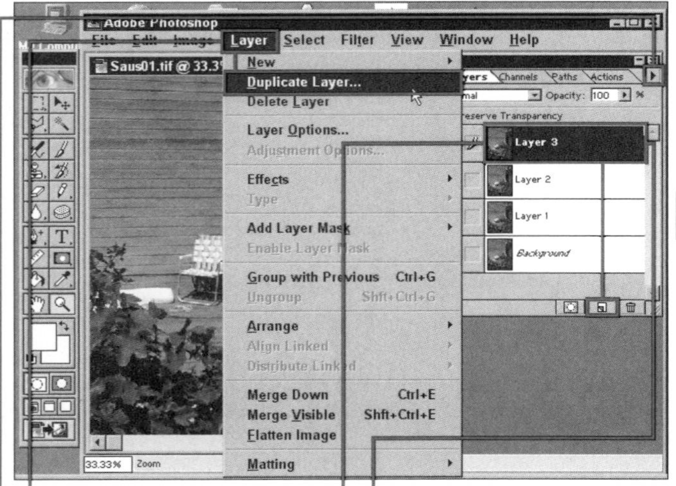

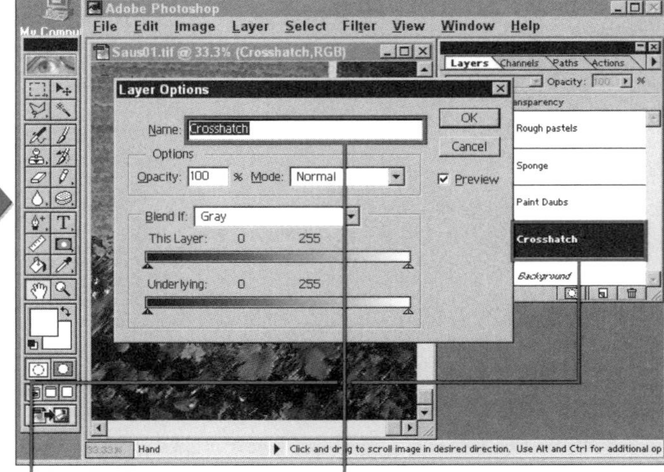

1 Choose Layer ⇨ Duplicate Layer. A dialog box appears in which you can name the layer.

2 Or, choose Duplicate Layer from the Layers palette menu.

3 Or, drag the target layer onto the New Layer icon.

4 Double-click the new layer to bring up the Layer Options dialog box.

5 Select each layer in turn and run a different filter (or the same filter with different option settings) on each.

6 Double-click the layer name.

■ The Layer Options dialog box for that layer appears.

7 Enter the name of the filter used on that layer.

TIPS

Why not use Layer Masks to erase parts of layers?

In fact, that's an even more powerful way to do the job. Layer masks make it easy to gradually erase parts of the image and to control the feathering of the edges of erasures. See Chapter 8 for more information on masking.

Note: This figure shows you the effects of four different filters, side by side. The Layer thumbnails reveal how each filter was erased on each layer to reveal the layer beneath.

■ Sponge filter

■ Rough Pastels filter

■ Paint Daubs filter

■ Crosshatch filter

8 Activate each layer in turn.

9 Select the near objects in the image, invert, and press Delete/Backspace.

10 In the next layer, select the background objects, invert, and press Delete/Backspace.

11 Make the cross-hatching erasing with a large brush set at 50 % transparency.

DEFINE AND SAVE PATTERNS

Photoshop enables you to do all sorts of things with patterns. A *pattern*, as defined by Photoshop, is all or part of any raster image that will fit inside a rectangular selection marquee. All you have to do to define a pattern in Photoshop is to open the file that contains it, make a rectangular selection within that file (this includes the use of the Select All command), and then choose Edit ⇨ Define Pattern.

If you think you may want to reuse that specific pattern, the very next thing you should do is press ⌘/Ctrl+C (to copy the contents of the selection to the Clipboard), choose File ⇨ New, and click OK. The new file will automatically be the same size as the Clipboard. Press ⌘/Ctrl+V to paste the Clipboard contents into the new file and then save it under a new name (preferably inside a folder named Patterns). Now, any time you want to reuse the pattern, open the file, press ⌘/Ctrl+A to Select All, and then choose Edit ⇨ Define Pattern. You need to do this each time you change patterns.

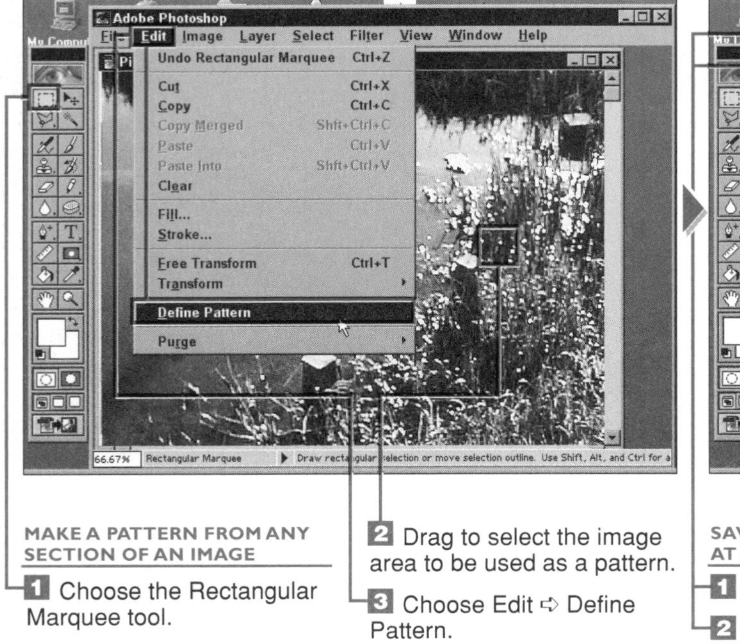

MAKE A PATTERN FROM ANY SECTION OF AN IMAGE

1 Choose the Rectangular Marquee tool.

2 Drag to select the image area to be used as a pattern.

3 Choose Edit ⇨ Define Pattern.

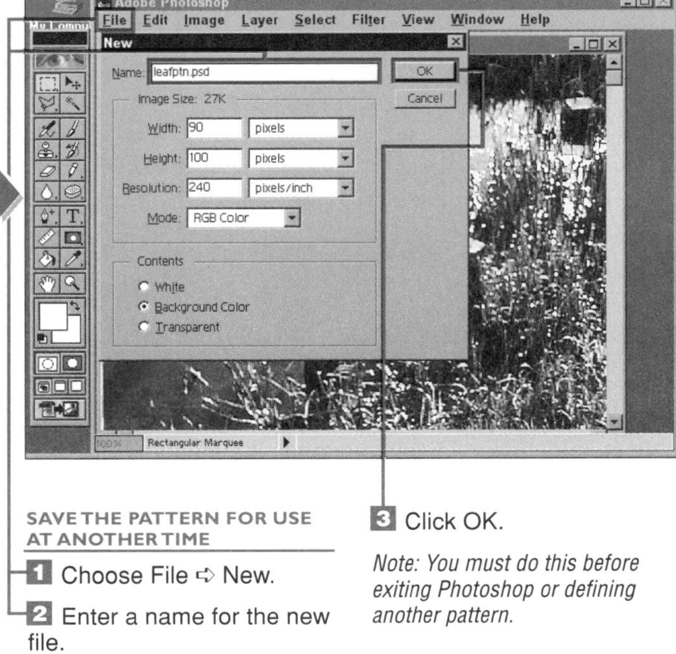

SAVE THE PATTERN FOR USE AT ANOTHER TIME

1 Choose File ⇨ New.

2 Enter a name for the new file.

3 Click OK.

Note: You must do this before exiting Photoshop or defining another pattern.

TIPS

Do I have to make all my own patterns?

No. Several Web sites distribute free seamless tile patterns. Some of these are given away to attract people to a particular site, and others are sold commercially (usually at very reasonable prices).

What can I do with patterns?

You can fill any layer or selection with them. You can use the Paint Bucket to fill colors with them. You can paint with them by choosing Use Pattern as an option for the Rubber Stamp tool. You can also convert a pattern file to grayscale and then use it as a texture file.

How do I make the edges of patterns blend together so there's no obvious break from tile to tile?

See "Create Seamless Pattern and Texture Tiles" in Chapter 14.

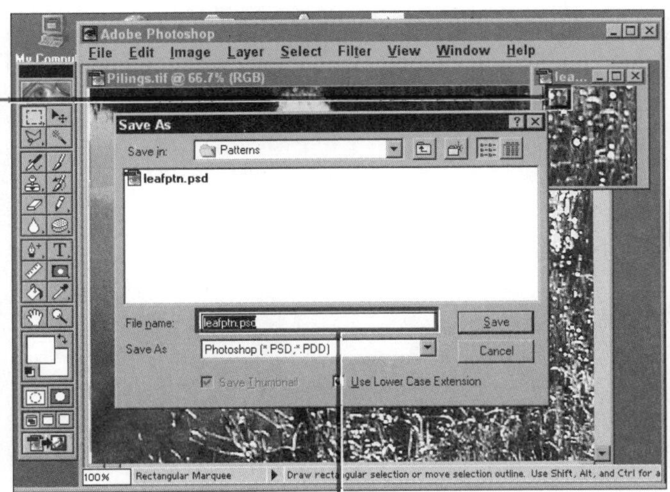

Note: An empty window opens for the new file. Make sure this is the active window.

4 Choose Edit ➪ Paste.

■ The contents of the clipboard are pasted into the new file as a new layer.

5 Choose File ➪ Save As.

6 Enter an appropriate file name.

Note: It is a good idea to create a folder called Patterns and to store all pattern files in that folder.

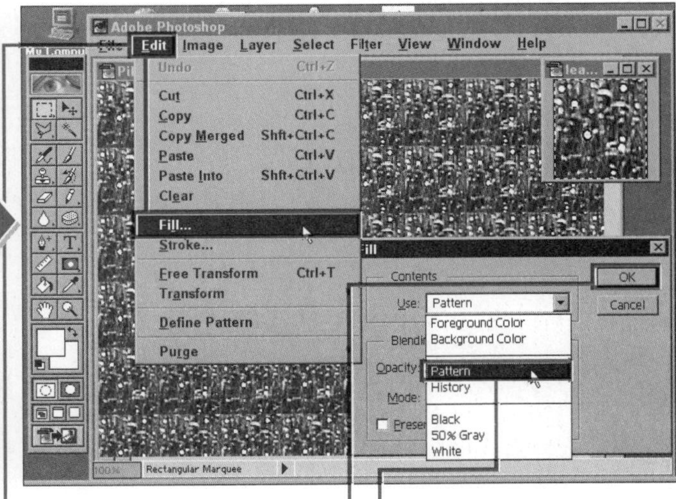

FILL AN IMAGE WITH THE PATTERN

1 Choose Edit ➪ Fill.

2 Choose Pattern from the Use pull-down menu.

3 Click OK.

PAINT WITH FILLS

You can paint sizable areas of an image instantly simply by making use of one of the several methods Photoshop provides for automatically filling images, layers, channels, and selections. You can also fill areas of color without having to first make a selection.

Photoshop also lets you fill with solid colors, gradients, or patterns, or with the contents of any snapshot in the History palette. Filling with the current foreground, background, and pattern can be done with either the Paint Bucket tool or the Edit ➪ Fill command. Filling with a snapshot from the History palette can only be done with the Edit ➪ Fill command. Filling with gradients can only be done with the Gradient Fill tool.

Fills can also be applied by using Blend modes. To use these, you must specify the Blend mode in either the Tools Options palette for the Paint Bucket tool or Gradient tool or in the Fill dialog box for the Edit ➪ Fill command before the fill is applied.

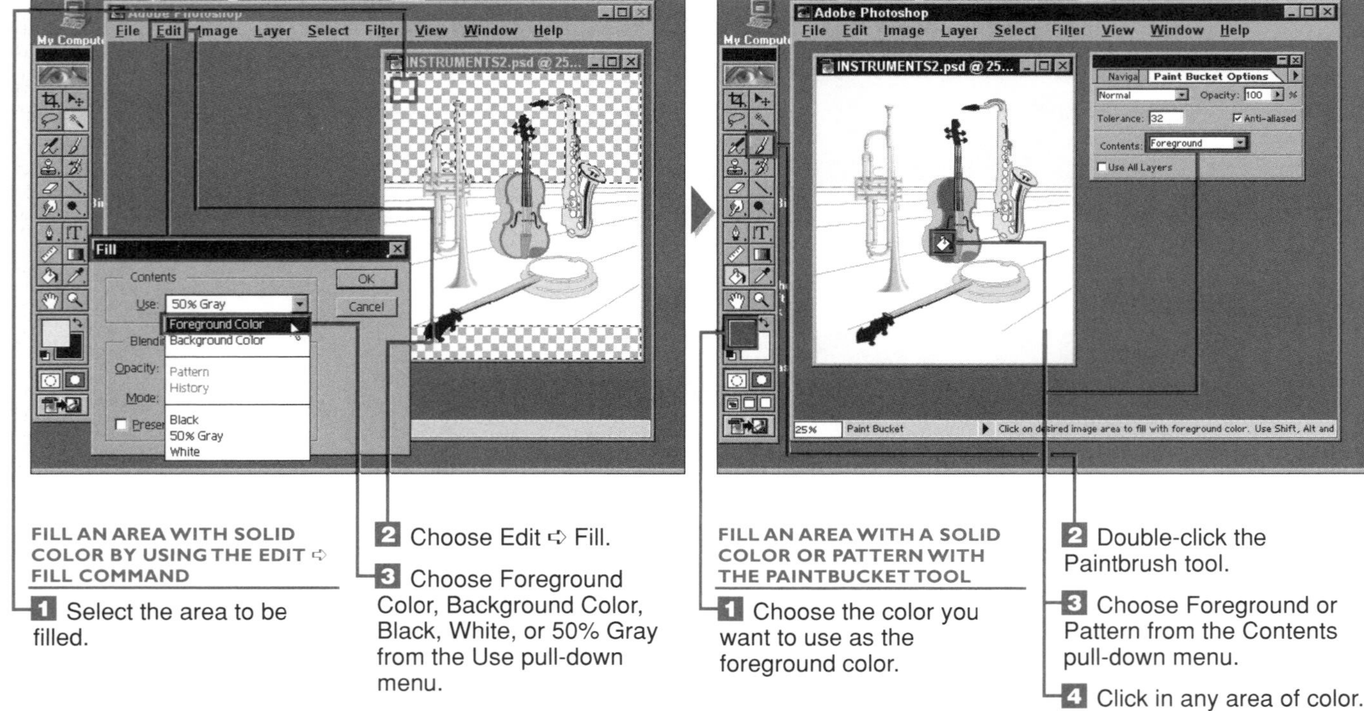

FILL AN AREA WITH SOLID COLOR BY USING THE EDIT ➪ FILL COMMAND

1 Select the area to be filled.

2 Choose Edit ➪ Fill.

3 Choose Foreground Color, Background Color, Black, White, or 50% Gray from the Use pull-down menu.

FILL AN AREA WITH A SOLID COLOR OR PATTERN WITH THE PAINTBUCKET TOOL

1 Choose the color you want to use as the foreground color.

2 Double-click the Paintbrush tool.

3 Choose Foreground or Pattern from the Contents pull-down menu.

4 Click in any area of color.

TIPS

Is a Linear Gradient the only type of Gradient fill?

No. It was used in this example because it's used so frequently. Linear gradients are an excellent way to shade masks, simulate the shading in a blue sky, or simulate the change in tonalities from dark to light as a cue to the depth in an image (use the gradient with one of the Blend modes). See the other layouts on using gradients.

When I fill selections, how can I make them blend along the borders of contiguous selected areas?

Make the selections slightly larger and feather the edges. Continue to do this each time you make a new selection. This way the selected areas that bump into one another cross-fade, and edges that don't run into any others blend more smoothly with their surroundings.

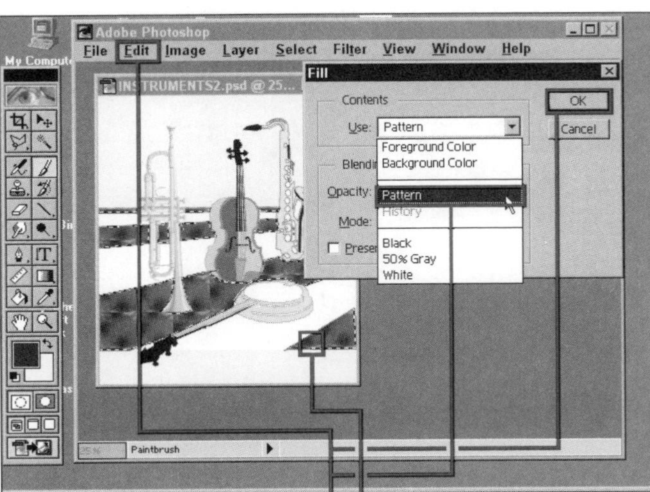

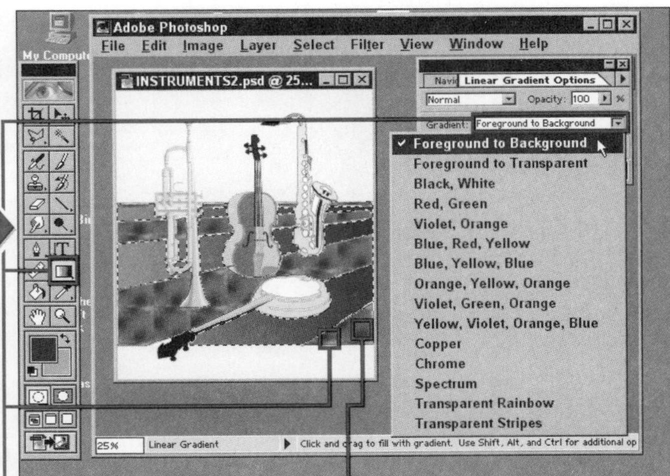

FILL AN AREA WITH A PATTERN USING THE EDIT ⇨ FILL COMMAND

Note: To do this, you must have a pattern defined and stored. See "Define and Save Patterns" earlier in this chapter.

1 Select the area you want to fill.

2 Choose Edit ⇨ Fill.

3 Choose Pattern.

4 Click OK.

FILL A SELECTED AREA WITH A GRADIENT

1 Select the area to fill.

2 Double-click the Gradient tool.

3 Select the gradient color scheme.

4 Drag to indicate the start point, direction, and stop point for the gradient.

5 Release mouse button to fill.

MAKE NONLINEAR GRADIENT FILLS

Photoshop has not one, but five Gradient tools. Each tool creates gradients in a different shape or manner. The names of the tools are Linear Gradient, Radial Gradient, Angular Gradient, Reflected Gradient, and Diamond Gradient. *Linear Gradient* shades in a straight line, perpendicular to the drag line, in even steps from the foreground color to the background color. *Radial Gradient* shades in a circular pattern, with the center at the start point and the diameter at the end point. *Angular Gradient* shades in a counter-clockwise direction from the start point (as though you're looking down on a shaded cone). *Reflected Gradient* mirrors the same linear gradient on either side of the start point. *Diamond Gradient* shades from the starting point outward in a square pattern, with one corner of the square attached to the drag line.

Each Gradient tool has three check boxes in its Gradient Options palette: Transparency, Dither, and Reverse. Check Transparency to enable the transparency mask that is stored with each gradient style. Check Dither to eliminate banding between shades. Check Reverse to make the gradient go from background to foreground color.

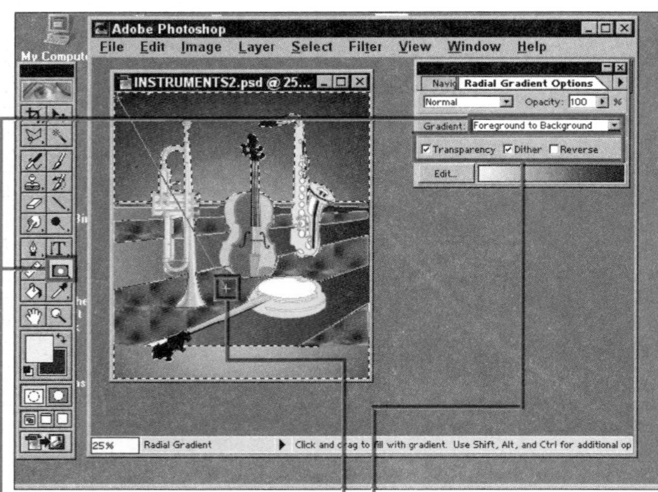

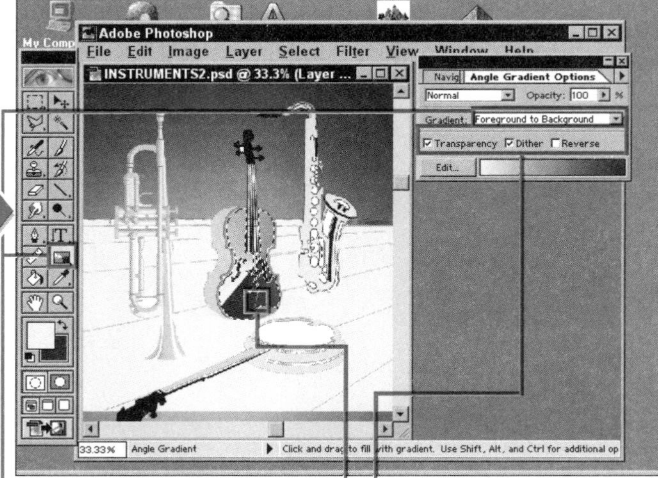

MAKE A RADIAL GRADIENT FILL

1 Double-click the Radial Gradient tool.

2 Choose the gradient style.

3 Check any option you want to employ.

4 Drag to indicate the center of the circle and the distance to the end of the circle.

MAKE AN ANGLE GRADIENT FILL

1 Double-click the Angle Gradient tool.

2 Choose the gradient style.

3 Check any option you want to employ.

4 Drag to indicate the start of the gradient, the angle, and the distance to the end of the gradient.

TIPS

How can I put a gradient into a mask?

Choose Window ⇨ Show Channels. When the Channels palette appears, click the channel name of the alpha channel mask you want to graduate. The image of the mask then fills the workspace. Select the area you want to fill with a gradient, and then proceed as shown in this layout.

Can I use gradients in Quick Mask mode?

Yes. Black masks 100 percent and white is completely transparent (you can choose the reverse as an option), even though you see these as shades of orange in Quick Mask mode. You can also fill a selection in Quick Mask mode, as well as using any of the other Paint tools.

Can I use gradients to affect a Blend mode between layers?

Yes. Make a layer mask for the layer to which you want to apply the Blend mode, and then edit the layer mask from the Channels palette.

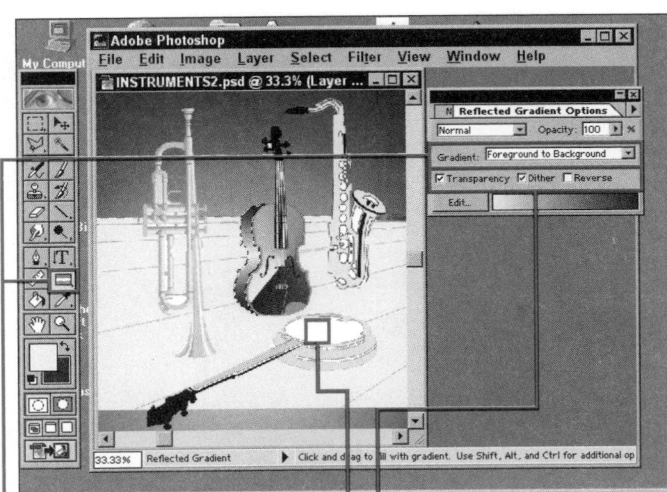

MAKE A REFLECTED GRADIENT FILL

1 Double-click the Reflected Gradient tool.

2 Choose the gradient style.

3 Check any option you want to employ.

4 Drag to indicate the start of the gradient, the direction of reflection, and the distance to the end of the gradient.

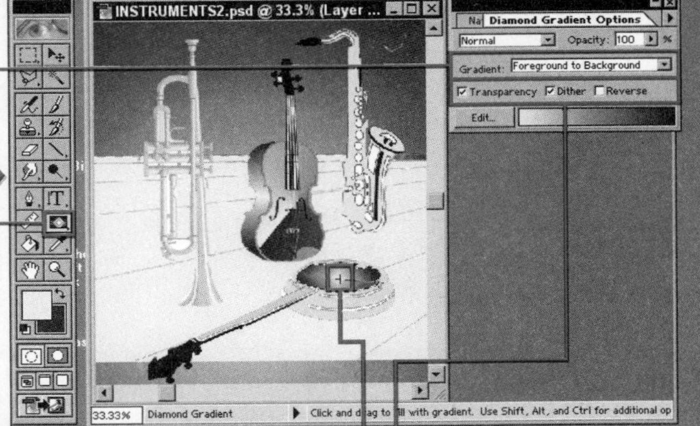

MAKE A DIAMOND GRADIENT FILL

1 Double-click the Diamond Gradient tool.

2 Choose the gradient style.

3 Check any option you want to employ.

4 Drag to indicate the start of the gradient, the direction of reflection, and the distance to the end of the gradient.

MAKE AND EDIT GRADIENT STYLES

Photoshop 5 makes it possible to create gradients that blend from any color to any other color with any number of gradients in between. You can even have part or parts of the gradient fade into transparency so that the gradient "fades in" to the underlying image.

The following 15 premade gradient styles come with the program: Foreground to Background, Foreground to Transparent, Black-White, Red-Green, Violet-Orange, Blue-Red-Yellow, Blue-Yellow-Blue, Orange-Yellow-Orange, Violet-Green-Orange, Yellow-Violet-Orange-Blue, Copper, Spectrum, Chrome, Transparent Rainbow, and Transparent Stripes. (All of these are shown in the color section of this book.)

You can make new styles by starting with any of the premade styles and editing them. Double-click the Gradient tool button to show the Gradient palette. Next, pick a style from the Gradient pull-down menu and click the Edit button.

Note: You can also create new gradients by first clicking the New or Duplicate buttons on the right side of the Gradient Editor dialog box. This protects the default gradients from change. Thereafter, the editing procedure is the same as in the procedure outlined in the following exercise.

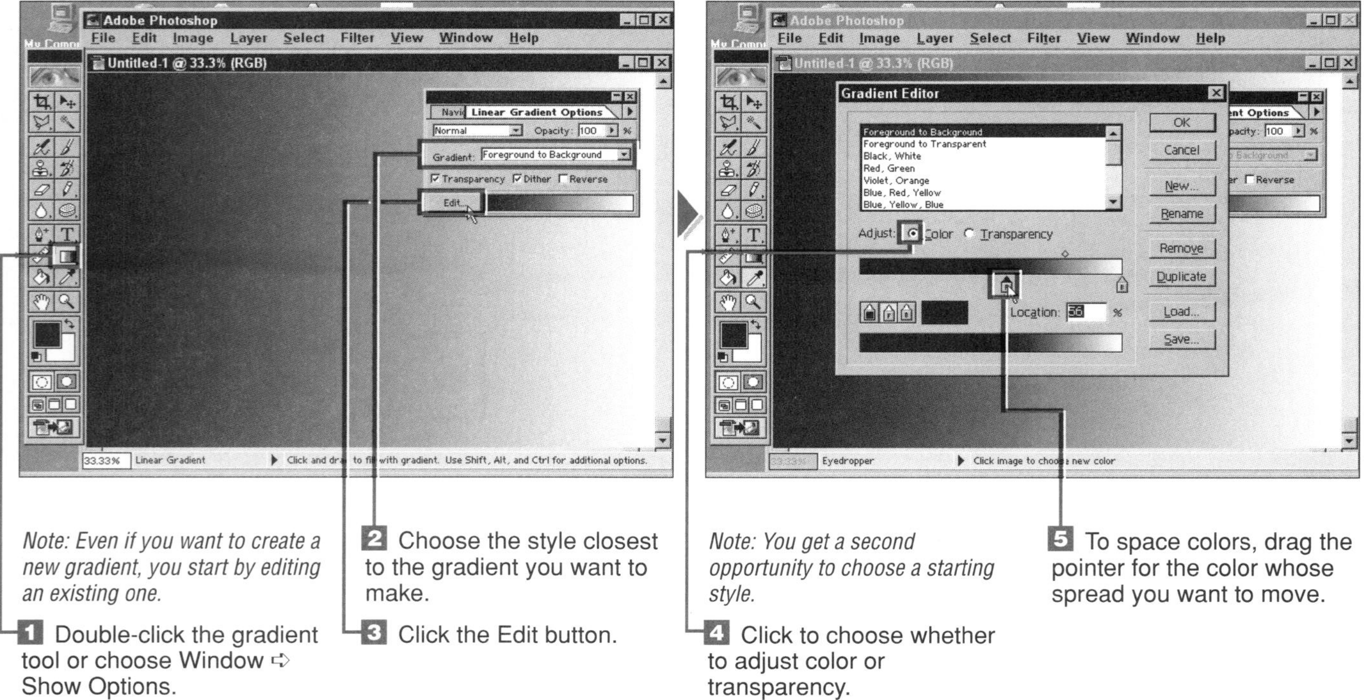

Note: Even if you want to create a new gradient, you start by editing an existing one.

1 Double-click the gradient tool or choose Window ➪ Show Options.

2 Choose the style closest to the gradient you want to make.

3 Click the Edit button.

Note: You get a second opportunity to choose a starting style.

4 Click to choose whether to adjust color or transparency.

5 To space colors, drag the pointer for the color whose spread you want to move.

TIPS

What happens when I click the New button?

You get a Gradient Name dialog box, in which you can name the new gradient. Next, a completely black Gradient bar with a blank New Color pointer at each end appears. Simply follow the steps outlined here to create an entirely new gradient.

Can you explain the use of the New Color, F, and B pointers a bit more?

You can switch any of these pointer types to any other by first selecting the pointer on the Gradient bar and then clicking the desired Pointer Type icon. F is always the current foreground color, and B is always the current background color. A New Color pointer always retains the same color, which you pick from the standard Color Picker.

How do I place and remove pointers?

Click just below the Gradient bar at the place where you want a new pointer to appear. To dump a pointer, click to select it (the tip turns black), and then drag it to the Pointer Icon box.

How do I change the median blending point between two colors?

Drag the diamond-shaped pointer that's just above the Blending bar, or select the pointer and specify a percentage in the Location field.

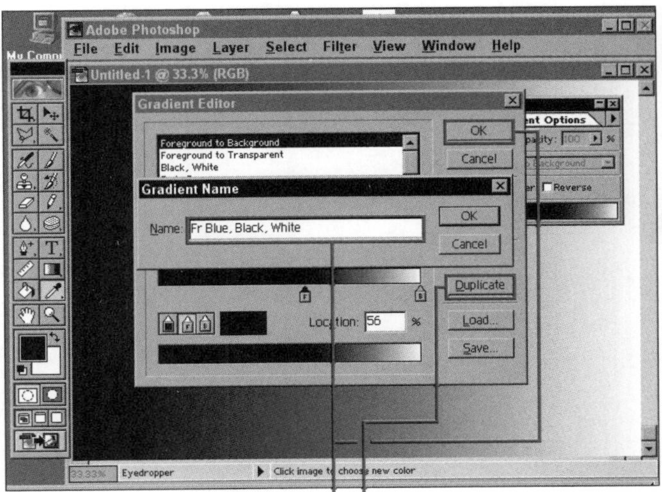

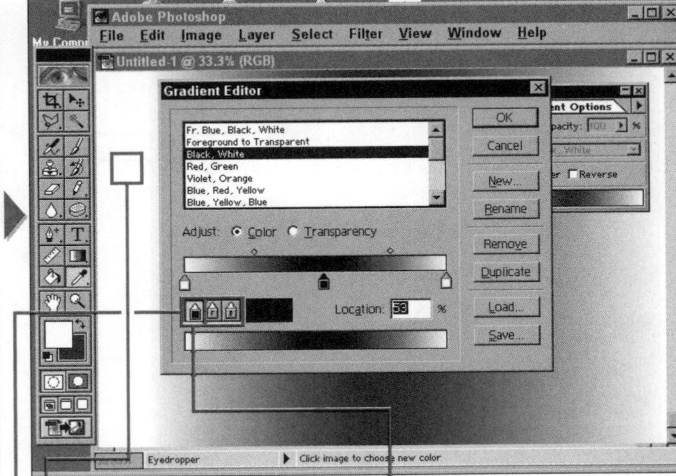

6 To add and change a color, duplicate the current scheme.

7 Click duplicate.

8 Enter a new name for the duplicate.

9 Click OK.

10 Click at the point where you want to add a color.

11 Click to choose one of the pointers.

12 Click to bring up Color Picker and pick a color. You can also double-click on the Color pointer.

13 Drag to adjust the position of any of the sliders.

14 Click OK.

CHOOSE COLORS

Photoshop gives you several ways to choose the colors you want to paint with: You can use the Eyedropper tool, select from the Color Picker, select from the Colors palette, or choose from the Swatches palette.

The Eyedropper is a tool found not only in the Toolbox but also in many Photoshop commands, such as Select ➪ Color Range and Image ➪ Adjust ➪ Levels/Curves. It is always used to designate a color by clicking on that color in the active layer of the working image. This is the tool to use when you need an exact match for an existing color.

The Color Picker lets you choose any of the 16.8 million colors available to a 24-bit color operation. You can also choose swatch book colors from the Color Picker or choose any color from the Colors palette.

The Swatches palette can contain any number of predefined colors. It's best used for painting and text fills when you need to quickly choose from one of several frequently used colors.

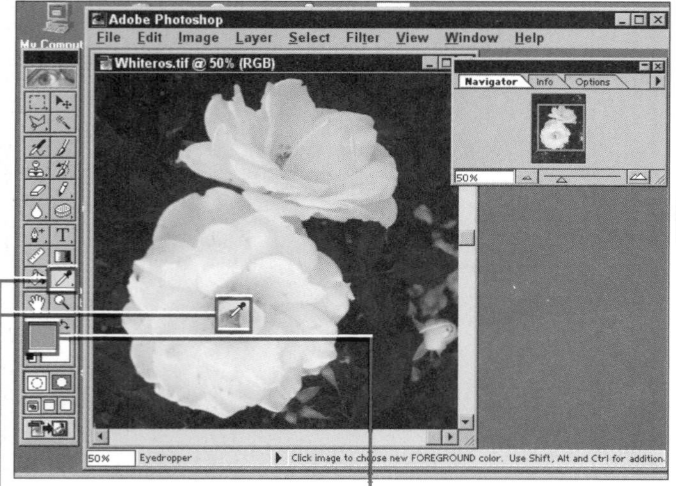

CHOOSE A COLOR WITH THE EYEDROPPER

1 Choose the Eyedropper tool.

2 Click the pixel that is the color you want to use.

■ The color appears as the foreground color.

Note: To choose a background color, use Opt/Alt+click. If you want to exchange the foreground and background colors, click or press X.

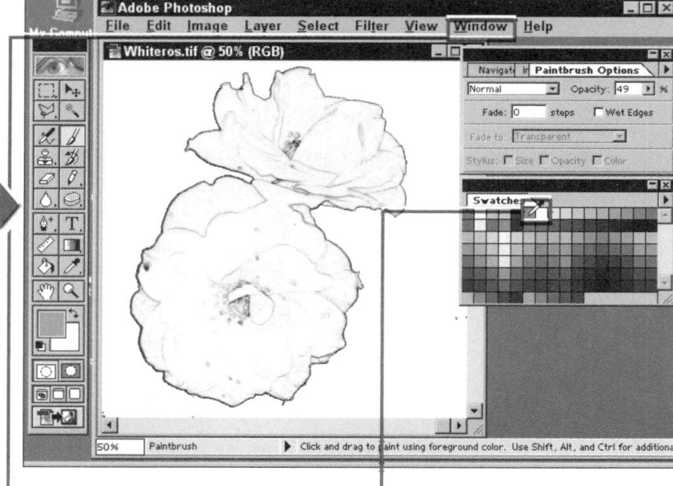

CHOOSE A COLOR FROM THE SWATCHES PALETTE

1 Choose Window ➪ Show Swatches (or click the Swatches tab if it s visible under another palette).

2 Click to choose your foreground color.

Note: See "Make Custom Swatch Palettes," later in this chapter.

TIPS

Is there any way to choose colors that have been mixed, as one would on a traditional palette?

Yes. Create a new, small file. Place your basic colors in this new file. Choose the Smudge tool and a fairly large brush, and mix the colors together. Next, use the Eyedropper to pick colors from the mixture. The chosen colors remain the same when you switch windows.

What if I want subtle changes in color when I make a stroke?

You have to use a pressure-sensitive digitizing tablet, such as the Wacom. In the Options palette for the brush you're using, check the Color box. When you stroke and scrub, the color alternates subtly between the foreground and background colors.

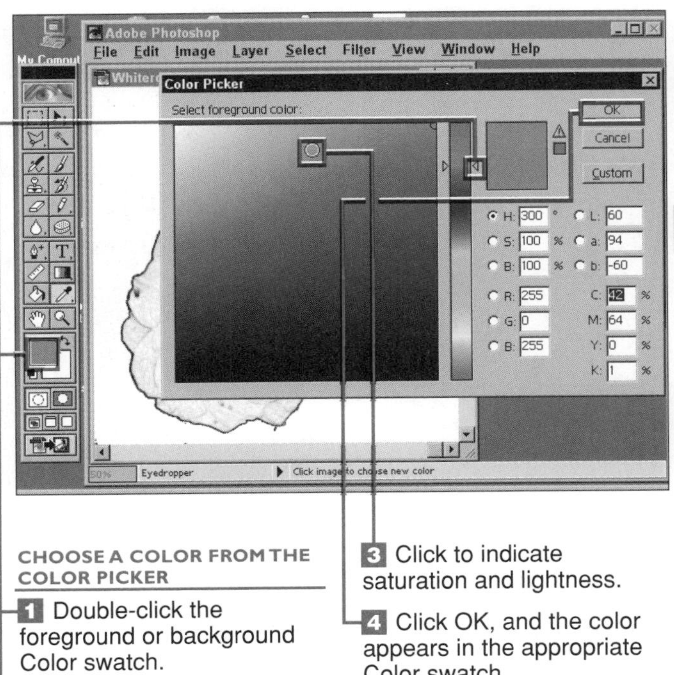

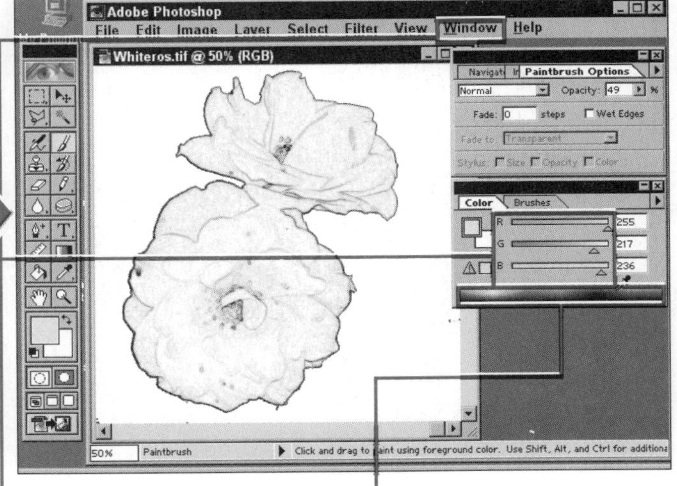

CHOOSE A COLOR FROM THE COLOR PICKER

1 Double-click the foreground or background Color swatch.

2 Drag to pick the base color.

3 Click to indicate saturation and lightness.

4 Click OK, and the color appears in the appropriate Color swatch.

CHOOSE A COLOR BY USING THE COLORS PALETTE

1 Choose Window ⇨ Show Colors.

2 Drag sliders to adjust the color.

3 Or, click in the Spectrum bar to choose a color.

Note: This icon appears if you have chosen a color that is beyond printable range (out of gamut).

MAKE CUSTOM SWATCH PALETTES

If you're creating an original image, as opposed to touching up an existing one, you'll no doubt want to create a custom swatch palette that enables you to quickly choose the colors you need most often. This is easy to do. To change the color in an existing swatch, press Shift (the pointer turns into the Paint Bucket icon) and click the swatch. The color changes to that of the existing foreground color.

You can also insert a new swatch between two existing swatches. Press Shift+Opt/Alt and click a swatch. To add a new swatch without altering any existing swatches, just click the empty area below the swatches. A new swatch in the foreground color is automatically added.

So how do you choose what color will appear in the new swatch? Before you make the new swatch, use any of the methods shown in the previous exercise, "Choose Colors."

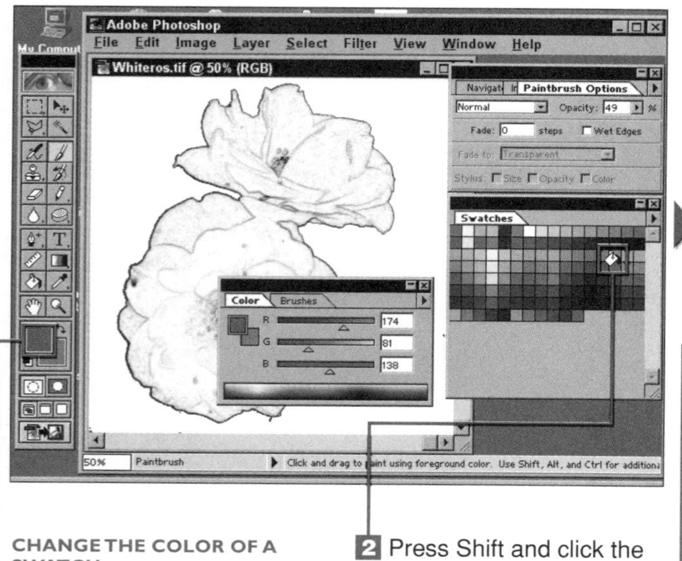

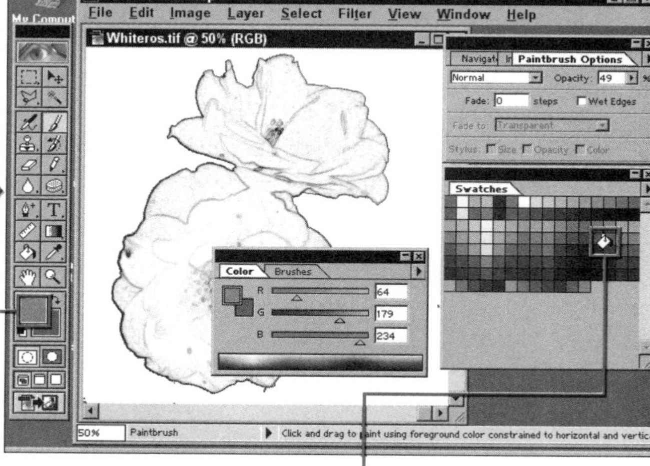

CHANGE THE COLOR OF A SWATCH

1 Choose the color you want to add (use the Color Picker, Eyedropper, or Colors palette).

2 Press Shift and click the target color s swatch.

Note: The cursor changes to the Paint Bucket icon when it is about to change or add colors.

ADD A SWATCH

1 Choose the color you want to use as the foreground color.

2 Press Shift+Opt/Alt and click the swatch in front of which you want to insert the new swatch.

Note: The cursor changes to the Paint Bucket icon, and the swatches move to make room for the new swatch.

TIPS

Is there a quick way to choose colors when I want to create a new palette?

The fastest way to choose colors for a custom palette is to drag the Colors palette alongside the Swatches palette.

What if I want to create a new palette without using any of the current colors?

Press ⌘/Ctrl and click all the colors in the palette. Now you can add colors by simply choosing new foreground colors and clicking in the Swatches palette for each change.

How do I save the new palette?

From the Swatches palette pull-down menu, choose Save Swatches. If you've made a new palette, give it a new name so you won't erase the default palette. When you want to reuse the palette, choose either Load Swatches or Replace Swatches from the pull-down menu. Load Swatches adds the colors to the existing palette.

What if I make a mess of the Swatches palette?

From the Swatches palette pull-down menu, choose Reset Swatches.

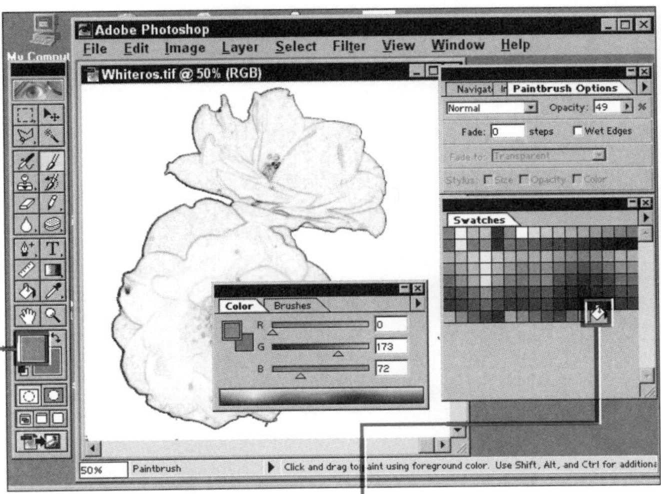

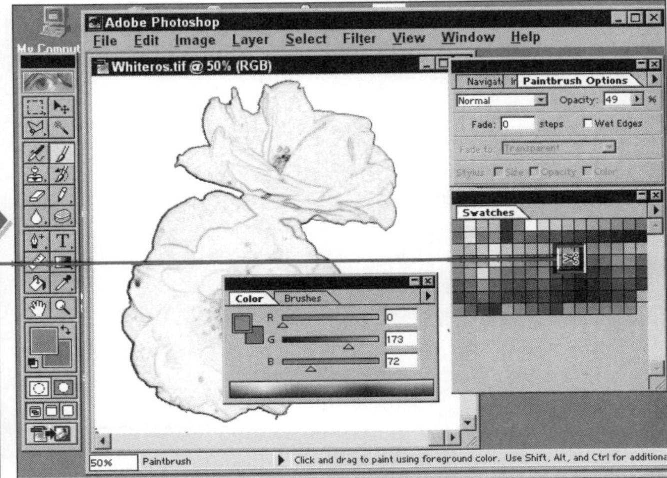

ADD A SWATCH

1 Choose the color you want to add.

2 Click the white space at the bottom of the Swatches palette.

■ A new swatch is added.

DELETE A SWATCH

1 Press ⌘/Ctrl and click the swatch you want to delete.

■ The cursor changes to a scissors icon and the swatch is deleted.

19 SIMPLIFY LIFE WITH ACTIONS

Actions are lists of Photoshop commands that can be performed and tools that can be used with a single keystroke or mouse click. In Photoshop 5 and 5.5, you can now use almost every command and tool in the program through Actions.

Actions can be applied to either the current file or to all the files in a given folder, making it possible to batch-process a whole series of files. You could, for instance, resize a whole folder of images so they fit within the confines of a Web page. The same command could reduce the colors in all those files to a given level and then convert them all to GIF file format.

The Actions Palette

To record an Action, you must first display the Actions palette, shown in the following figure.

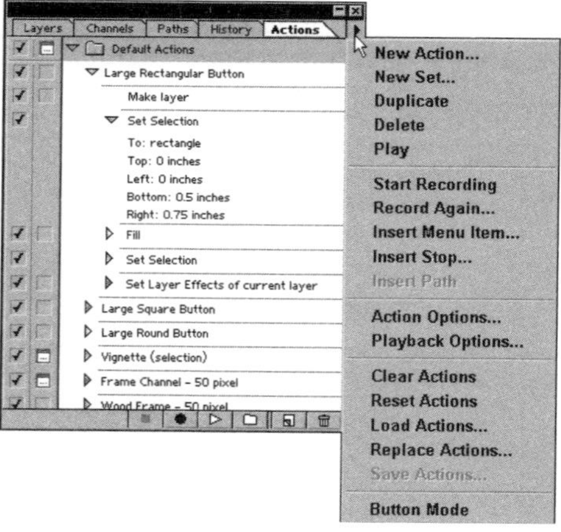

Actions Palette Contents

Component	Function
On/Off check box	Click to toggle command or Action on/off (checked is on).
Modal icon	Click to toggle modal control on/off (appearance of icon indicates on). Modal control enables the command to stop for input during its execution. Essential for operations where settings or filenames vary from one execution of an Action to another.

Component	Function
Set name bar	Actions can be placed in sets so that you can execute a whole series of Actions by choosing the set name bar, and then clicking the Play button. Sets can be saved and retrieved from disk.
Action name bar	This displays the name of the Action (you enter this before recording). You can execute an Action by selecting it and clicking the Play button or by choosing the Play command from the Actions palette menu.
Recorded Command name bar	This displays the command names (entered automatically as recorded), making it easy to see what an Action does and to edit it later.
Stop button	Click to stop playing or recording.
Record button	Click to record or resume recording (you can add commands to the highlighted Action).

Component	Function
Play button	Plays the highlighted Action. You can also play part of an Action by highlighting a Command name bar and clicking the Play button to play the rest of the commands in the Action.
New Set button	Brings up the New Set dialog box through which you can create a new set of Actions.
New Action button	Opens the New Action dialog box.
Trash icon	Deletes the selected command or Action. You can also delete a command or Action by dragging its name bar to the Trash icon.
Actions Palette menu button	Click to drop down the Actions Palette menu.
Actions Palette menu	Drag to select a menu item.

CONTINUED

SIMPLIFY LIFE WITH ACTIONS CONTINUED

Actions Palette Menu Contents

Command	Function
New Action	Brings up the Actions dialog box. Choose this command before starting a new Action.
New Set	Brings up the New Set dialog box. Choose this command if you want to create a new set of Actions.
Duplicate	Makes a copy of the selected Action.
Delete	Eradicates the selected Action.
Play	Executes the selected Action.
Start Recording	Starts recording a new Action or inserts commands after the selected command in an Action.
Record Again	Rerecords an existing Action so you can enter a different sequence of commands.
Insert Menu Item	Inserts a command that can't be recorded, so that you can execute it at the proper time during playback.
Insert Stop	Inserts a stop so you can perform a nonrecordable task while the Action is paused.
Insert Path	Inserts any previously selected path so that the path is recreated when the Action is played on any subsequent file.
Action Options	Opens the Action Options dialog box.
Playback Options	Opens the Playback Options dialog box.
Clear Actions	Removes all the Actions from the Actions palette.
Reset Actions	Restores the default list of Actions and dumps all others.
Load Actions	Adds a set of Actions to the current list by loading them from disk.
Replace Actions	Dumps all the Actions in the current list and loads another from disk.
Save Actions	Saves the currently selected (highlighted) Actions to disk.
Button Mode	Toggles Button mode on/off.

Rules and Guidelines for Actions

The following are things to remember about working with Actions in Photoshop 5:

Actions can include functions of the following tools: Gradient, Marquee, Crop, Polygon Lasso, Lasso, Move, Magic Wand, Paint Bucket, and Type. Palettes whose functions can be recorded include the Paths, Channels, Layers, and History palettes.

Modal commands and tools all provide the user an option to interact with an Action if the Modal icon is turned on. What commands can make use of modal control? Any command that normally requires pressing Return/Enter and the function of any tool that depends on position (Gradient, Magic Wand, Lasso, Marquee, Path, and Type).

Remember that the effect of some commands may depend on such things as the current choice of foreground/background color, image size, current Color mode, currently active layer, and overall image size (horizontal and vertical pixel measurements).

Although not every single Photoshop command can be recorded, you can use the Insert command to add nonrecordable commands to the Action after the fact.

Recordable commands you might normally think could not be recorded include Play on the Actions palette menu, which lets an Action start another Action; and File ➪ Automate ➪ Batch, which would start a batch operation partway through the execution of a command. All the Automate commands can be recorded in an Action, too.

All recorded Actions are automatically saved in the default Actions file: Actions Palette.psp (no three-letter extension is added to the Mac filename).

CREATE A NEW ACTION

Actions can save you time in Photoshop because by using Actions, you do not have to spend extra time looking for and loading each command in a particular series. The right commands are ready for you to use if you've created an Action for them. More important, Actions can also save the tension that comes with having to perform repetitive tasks one command at a time. And even more important, Actions help eliminate mistakes in complicated procedures because they never forget the necessary sequence of commands and never exclude a needed command.

This exercise shows you how to create and record a new Action on your own. Virtually any task you perform in Photoshop more than a couple of times should be turned into an Action.

Because I work a lot with digital cameras that save their files in highly compressed and lossy JPEG format, I want to make sure the files are converted to lossless, cross-platform, cross-application TIFF format before archiving them to a lossless CD-ROM. (*Lossy* refers to *lossless compression*, which is the process of compressing a file such that some data is lost when the file is decompressed. *Lossless compression*, on the other hand, is a compression scheme that conserves space but does not sacrifice image data.) You might find this routine equally useful, so I've made it the example for this exercise.

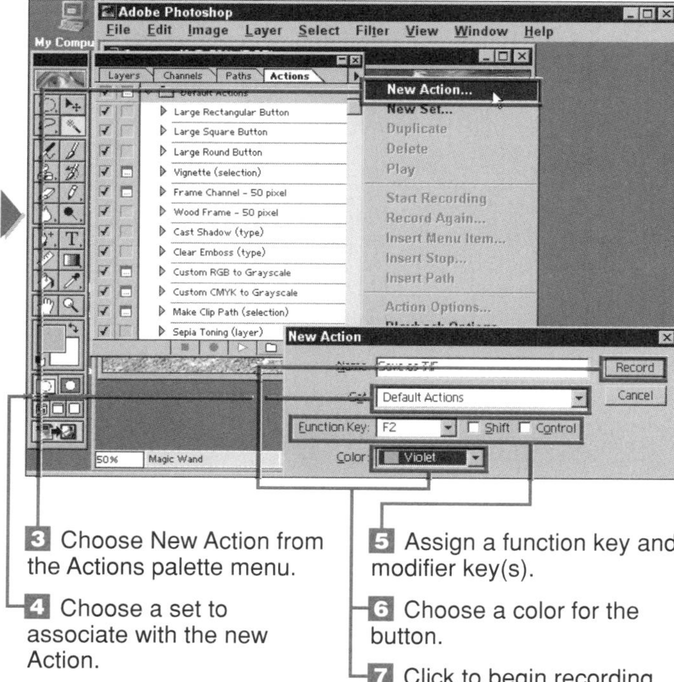

1 Open a file that is a typical target for the Action you want to create.

2 Choose Window ⇨ Show Actions.

■ The Actions palette appears.

Note: The Actions palette must be visible before you can create, edit, and maintain Actions.

3 Choose New Action from the Actions palette menu.

4 Choose a set to associate with the new Action.

5 Assign a function key and modifier key(s).

6 Choose a color for the button.

7 Click to begin recording the new Action.

What if I need to create an Action that uses a painting, focusing, or toning tool?

You can't record the functions of these tools, but you can insert a stop in your Action. This way the Action pauses to let you manually use the tool. You can even write a message instructing what tool to use at what setting and for what purpose. You can also tell the Action to continue once you've finished using the tool.

What if I forget to save my Actions?

They will be automatically saved in the default palette. At any later time, you can create a new set, drag the Action into that set, and then save the new set. This removes it from the default set.

What commands can't be recorded?

Those involving painting tools (Airbrush, Paintbrush, Rubber Stamp, Pencil, Eraser), focus tools (Blur, Sharpen, Smudge), and toning tools (Dodge, Burn, Sponge), as well as Tool options, View commands, and Preferences.

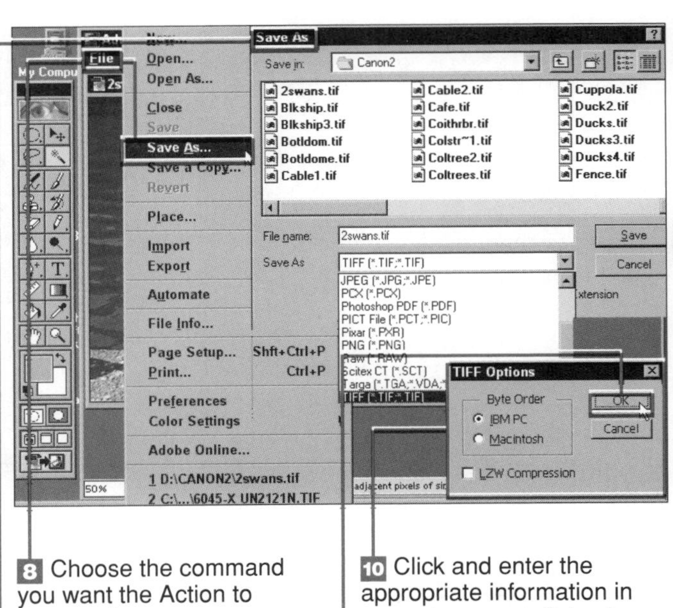

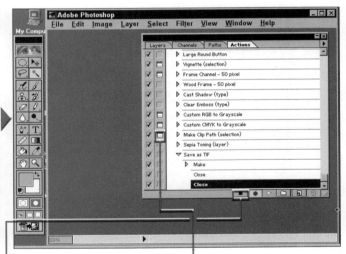

8 Choose the command you want the Action to execute first.

9 If the command has an associated dialog box, make the choices you want to repeat.

10 Click and enter the appropriate information in any subsequent dialog box.

11 Click OK.

12 Repeat Steps 8-10 for as many commands as you want to include.

■ A command to close the file was entered after the Save As command in this example.

13 When you've finished adding commands, click the Stop Recording icon.

14 Click to turn on modal control if you want to change information in a dialog box.

SAVE AND LOAD A SET OF ACTIONS

Actions are automatically saved in a set called Actions Palette.psp (the Mac uses the same filename but doesn't add the .psp extension). However, at times you may want to move an Action to a different set.

You can't save or load individual Actions, only sets of Actions. Of course, you could create a new set and record only one Action (or move only one Action into it). If you saved that set, you'd be saving only that Action. This could be useful if you have one Action you want to place into several sets. If you move an Action out of a set but don't subsequently save it, you'll still have that Action in the original set the next time you load it.

Two commands enable you to load Actions: Load Actions and Replace Actions. Load Actions adds the chosen set to the current set. Replace Actions deletes the current set from the Actions palette and adds the newly chosen palette.

ADD A SET OF ACTIONS TO THE CURRENT SET

1 Choose Load Actions from the Actions palette menu.

2 Navigate to the folder containing the Action (Windows extension = .atn).

3 Double-click the filename of the Action you want to load (or click to enter it in the File name field) and then click Load.

EXCHANGE A SET OF ACTIONS FOR ANOTHER SET

1 Choose Replace Actions from the Actions palette menu.

2 Navigate to the folder containing the Action (Windows extension = .atn).

3 Double-click the filename of the Action you want to exchange (or click to enter it in the File name field) and then click Load.

TIPS

Can I assign the same function key to different Actions in different sets?

You can as long as both sets are not loaded into the same palette.

How do I copy an Action to several other sets without removing it from the original set?

Drag the Action to the New Action icon at the bottom of the Actions palette. A new Action appears, with "copy" appended to the original name. Drag the copy to another set, double-click its name bar, and then rename it in the Options dialog box. Now save the set to which you moved the copy. Repeat for as many different sets as you like.

How do I rename a set?

The same way you rename any Photoshop palette item: Double-click the item's name bar in the palette. The Set Options dialog box appears. Enter a new name.

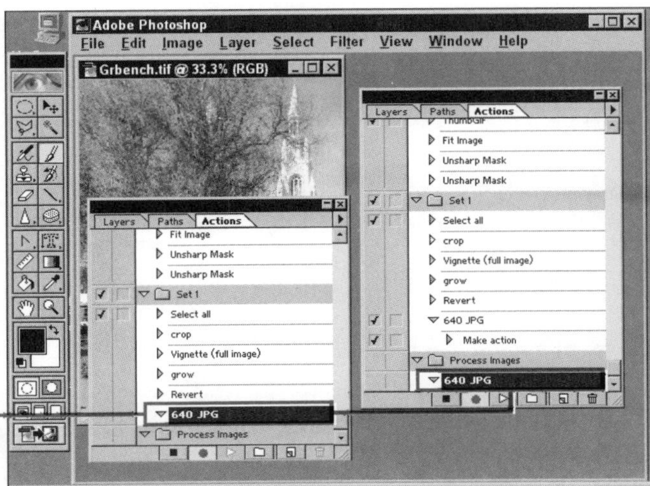

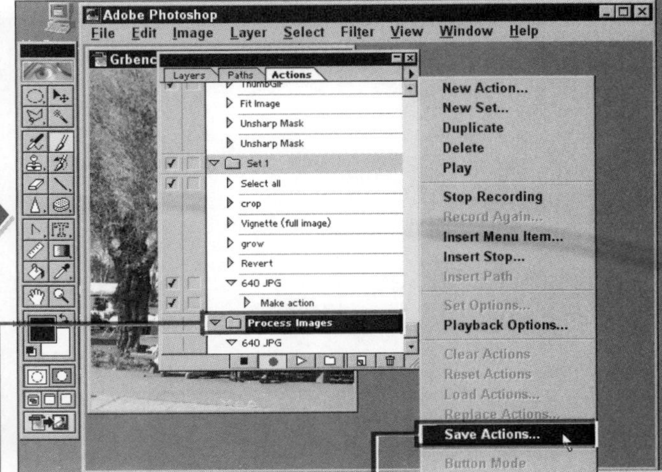

MOVE AN ACTION FROM ONE SET TO ANOTHER

1 Make sure both sets are loaded.

2 Drag the Action from any location in the current set to any location in another set.

Note: To make the new location permanent for both sets, select each set and save it.

Note: You can also change the position of an Action within a set by simply dragging it without moving it to a new set.

SAVE AN ACTIONS SET

1 Click to highlight the target set.

2 Choose Save Actions.

3 Navigate to the desired folder and click Save.

EDIT AN ACTION

Once you've recorded an Action, you can do several things to modify it. You can add new commands at any point in the Action. You can change the values for any commands associated with dialog boxes. You can change the Action Options (Action Name, Button Color, Shortcut Key and modifiers). Finally, you can remove commands from the Action.

The procedures for editing Actions aren't as obvious as those for creating them, but you can learn them in a matter of minutes.

The preceding exercise in this chapter demonstrates how to move a command from one Action set to another. You use the same drag-and-drop technique to move commands within the same Action, except you just drag them to a new location in that Action's stack. Commands are always executed in top-to-bottom order.

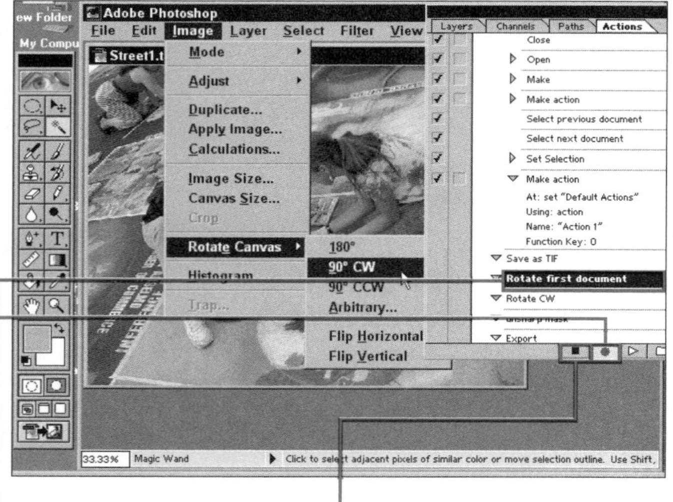

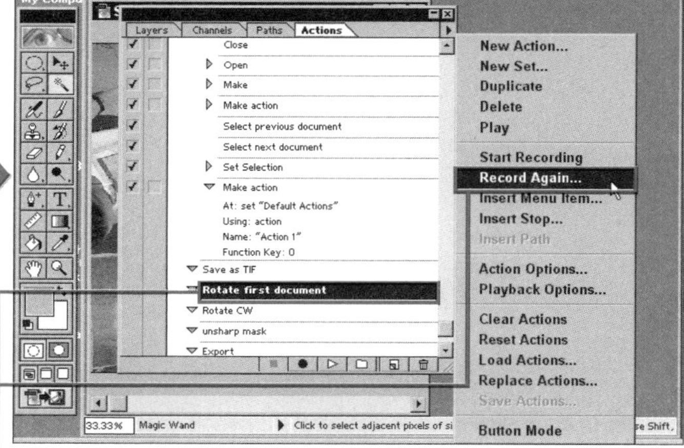

INSERT A NEW COMMAND IN AN EXISTING ACTION

1 Select the command after which you want to insert any new command(s).

2 Click the Begin Recording icon.

3 Execute as many new commands as you d like to add.

4 Click the Stop Recording icon when you want to stop adding commands at this location.

CHANGE THE ORIGINAL CHOICES MADE FOR AN EXISTING COMMAND (OR AN ENTIRE ACTION)

1 Select the command whose parameters you want to change.

2 Choose Record Again.

Note: No need to reissue the command. Any associated tool or dialog box immediately appears.

3 Change any parameter.

4 Click OK. Recording stops automatically.

TIPS

How many ways are there to duplicate an item on the Actions palette list?

Three: 1) Drag the item to the New Action icon at the bottom of the Actions palette. 2) Opt/Alt+drag the item to a new location in the Actions palette. 3) Select as many commands as you like (Shift+click for contiguous items; Ctrl/Opt+click for discontinuous items) and choose Duplicate from the Actions palette menu.

What if I want to delete all the Actions in the palette?

Choose Clear Actions from the Actions palette. Presto! A clean slate. (Don't worry, they're all still in the disk file unless you saved this empty set to the same name.)

What do I do when I find the default set of Actions crowded with stuff?

Move all the Actions you want to keep into other sets. Next, choose Reset from the Actions Palette menu.

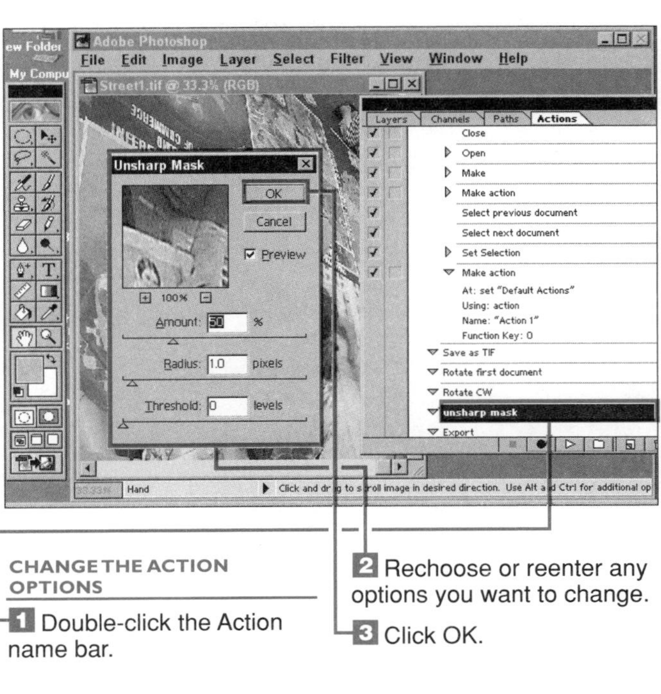

CHANGE THE ACTION OPTIONS

1 Double-click the Action name bar.

2 Rechoose or reenter any options you want to change.

3 Click OK.

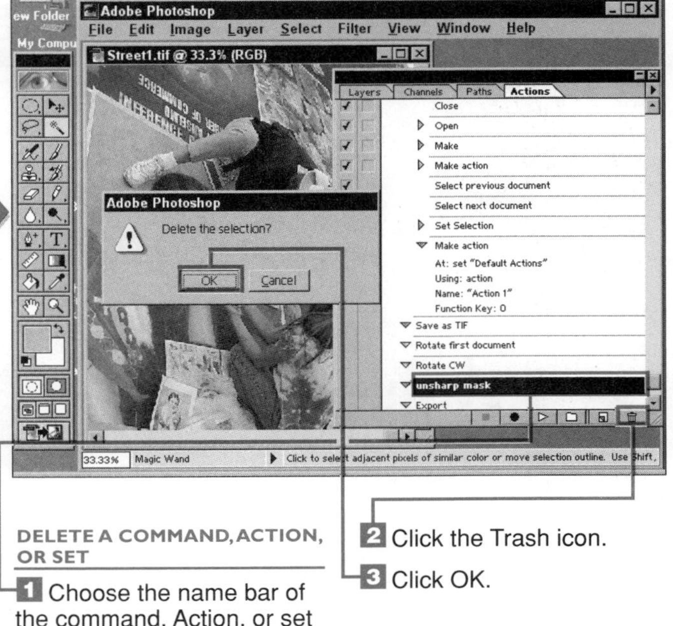

DELETE A COMMAND, ACTION, OR SET

1 Choose the name bar of the command, Action, or set you want to delete.

2 Click the Trash icon.

3 Click OK.

PLAY ACTIONS

On the surface of it, playing Actions is as simple as pressing a function key or clicking an Action's Button mode button. In fact, there are several ways to start the playing of Actions and several ways to make the Actions behave once they start playing.

First, you can start with any of the commands in the Action's list. You can process a single file or, by playing the Action in Batch mode, process a whole folder of files. You can tell Photoshop to play an Action at the fastest speed possible, to slow it down so you can study what's going on, and even to pause it so you can use a tool that can't be recorded.

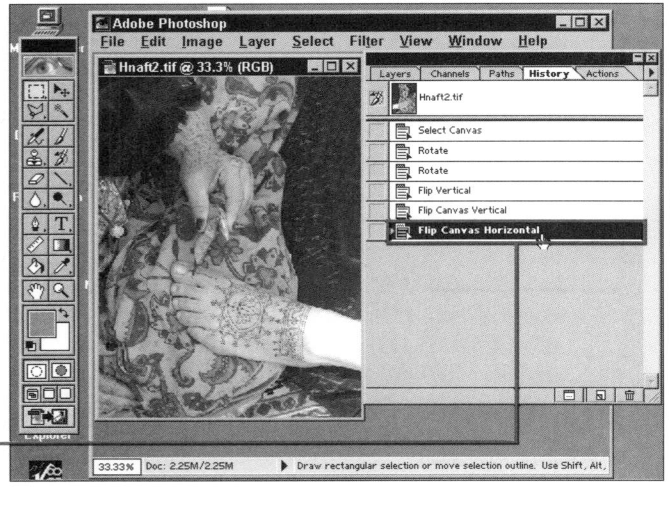

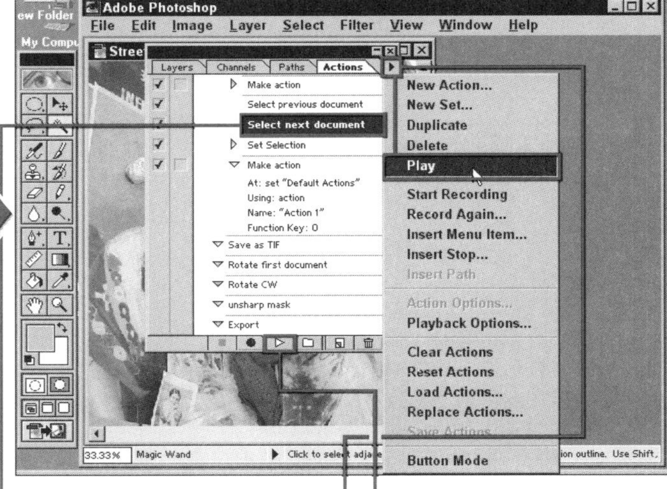

PLAY AN ACTION AT NORMAL SPEED ON A SINGLE FILE (OR THE ENTIRE SET)

1 Select the window containing the file you want to affect. (If there s more than one layer, make sure they are also selected.)

2 Or, choose Button mode from the Actions palette menu.

3 Click the button of the Action you want to play.

4 Or, press a function key.

PLAY A SINGLE COMMAND IN AN ACTION

1 Make sure you re not in Button mode.

2 Select the command you want to play.

3 Click the Play icon.

4 Or, choose Play from the Actions palette menu.

Can I play a whole set of Actions on a single file?

Yes. Just select the name of the set instead of an individual Action, and then proceed according to the instructions under the first screen.

What if I want to undo an Action?

Playing an Action doesn't record all the subsequently executed commands to the History palette. Give yourself a margin of safety by recording a snapshot of the state of the file before you play the Action. This way you can return to the snapshot later. To record a snapshot, choose Window ⇨ Show History and then choose New Snapshot from the History palette menu.

Why would I want to slow down playback of an Action?

Two reasons: 1) To demonstrate to someone else how you did something (such as creating a composite photo). 2) To see what's causing a problem when the Action doesn't behave as you expected.

EXCLUDE COMMANDS OR ACTIONS FROM PLAYBACK

1 Click to turn off command.

Note: You can uncheck as many commands or Actions as you want to turn off. To turn them back on, simply click the same box again.

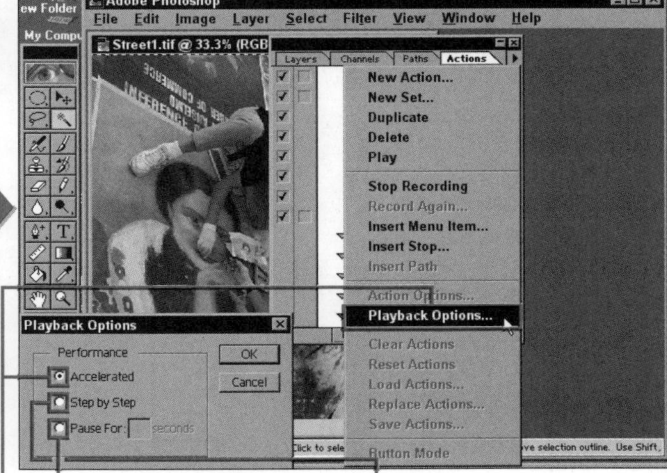

SPECIFY THE SPEED OF PLAYBACK

1 Choose Playback Options.

2 Choose to play without slowing or interruption.

3 Choose to show each change in the image as it occurs.

4 Choose to make each step pause for the number of seconds you enter.

PLAY ACTIONS IN BATCHES

You can apply almost any Action to a batch of figures in just a few steps. If you have captured dozens of frames from a video camera or digital camera, batching your conversion process will save you time. You can convert all the files to a lossless format, make a set of thumbnails or contact sheets from them, run AutoLevels on all of them, and store them all in the folder of your choice while you go take a shower in preparation for your next appointment.

Before starting a batch conversion, it is best to organize your target folders. Place all the files that you want to be converted on the same level of folders. If you want to store the results of the batch conversion to a different folder, make sure that the target folder exists before you start the Action.

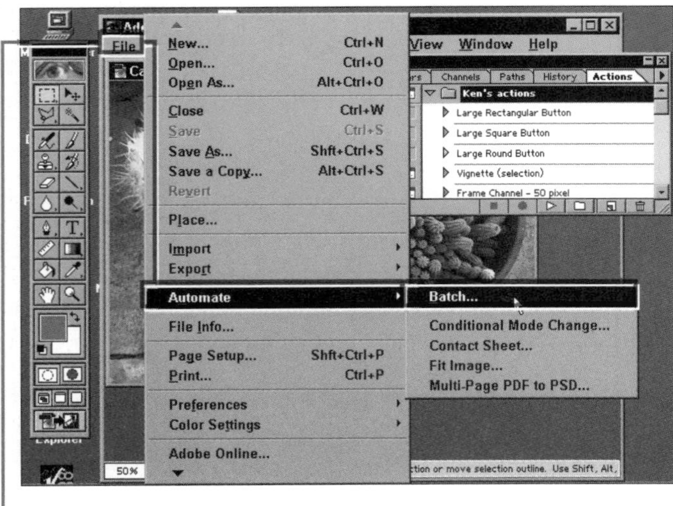

1 Choose File ➪ Automate ➪ Batch.

■ The Batch dialog box appears.

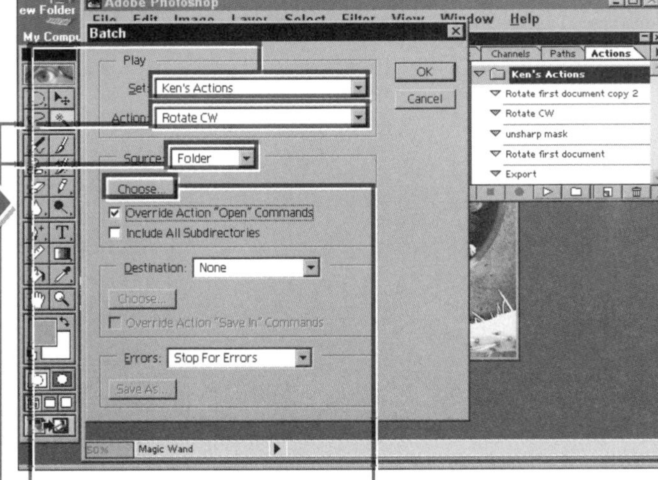

2 Choose Set from the pull-down menu.

3 Choose Action from the pull-down menu.

4 Choose Folder (existing) or Import (to get images from a digital camera).

5 If Folder is the choice, click Choose.

6 Navigate to the folder that contains the files you want processed.

TIPS

What if I want to apply just one command to a batch of files?

If it's a command that's one of only a few in an Action, simply turn off all the others by unchecking their On/Off boxes. Or, you could record a single command as an Action.

Is there any way to apply a complete set to a batch?

Nope. Well, actually, you could drag all the commands in that set into a single Action. (Remember, cheating often works.)

What if I want to process the file but don't want it to overwrite the original?

Make sure you choose Folder from the Destination pull-down menu in the Batch dialog box. It's also mandatory that you either uncheck any Save or Save As commands included in the Action or check the Override Action "Save-In" Commands box — unless you want the files saved in two different places.

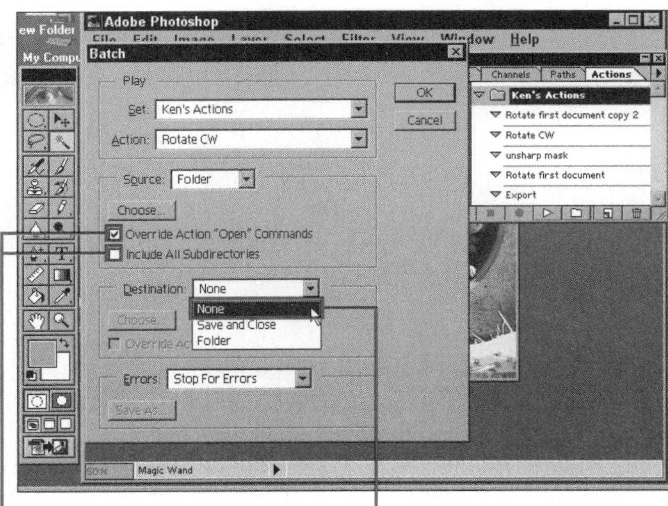

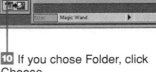

7 Check to ensure files are opened only from the specified folder.

8 Check if you want to include subdirectories of the source folder.

9 Choose a destination.

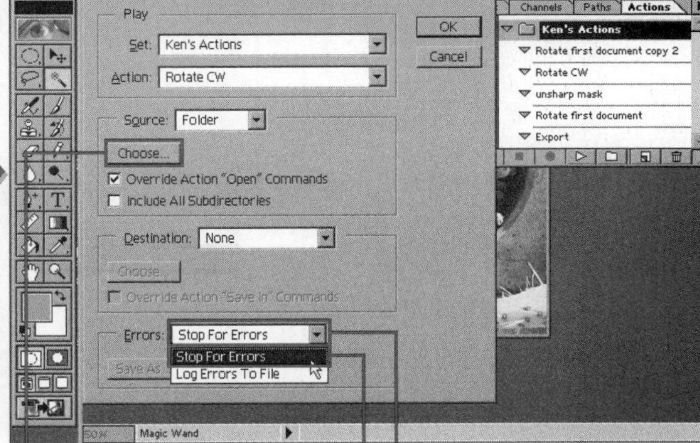

10 If you chose Folder, click Choose.

11 Navigate to the folder you created earlier.

12 Choose Stop for Errors to suspend the batch until you respond to the error.

13 Choose Log Errors to File to continue uninterrupted.

14 Click OK.

INSERT THE UNRECORDABLE

Some tools and commands can't be recorded in Actions. That doesn't mean you can't accommodate them, though. You can insert a Bezier curve path, certain menu items and tools that can't be recorded (Tool options, View commands, and Preferences), and even have the Action wait while you do something unrecordable by hand (such as using painting and toning tools). This exercise shows you how to do this.

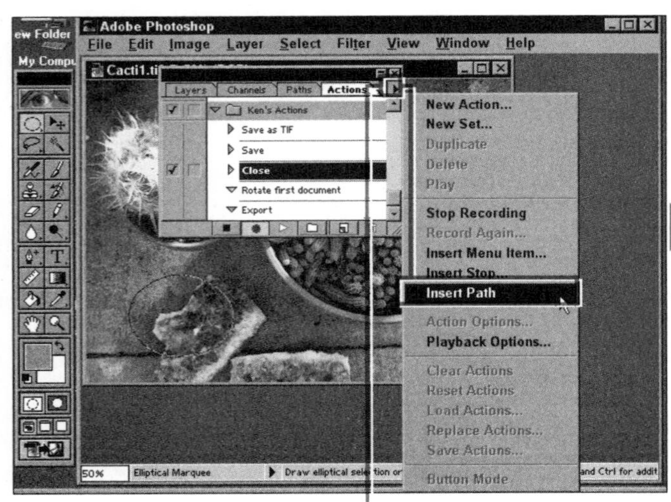

RECORD A PATH

Note: Make sure you have a path drawn on the currently active layer.

1 Select the path.

2 Choose Insert Path.

Note: From now on, regardless of which file is being processed by an Action, the inserted path will be drawn on that file's active layer.

INSERT A NONRECORDABLE MENU ITEM

1 Finish recording the Action.

2 Select the recorded command to succeed the inserted command.

3 Choose Insert Menu Item.

4 Choose any menu item or tool that has an Options dialog box.

5 Or, enter the name of the command here.

TIPS

Why are some inserted commands unavailable when I try to play back the Action?

Because of the stage of processing you're in or because of the nature of the image at the time the Action is played. Because Photoshop doesn't know what the state of a given image will be when a given Action is played, it simply makes it possible to insert all commands. Photoshop always gives you the choice of continuing if you can't access a command.

Can I enter just any command when I insert a command?

If the command has an associated dialog box, the dialog box appears without having to choose the Modal icon in the Actions palette. If there's no associated dialog box (most notably for the Undo, Cut, Copy, Paste, and Clear commands), the command simply executes.

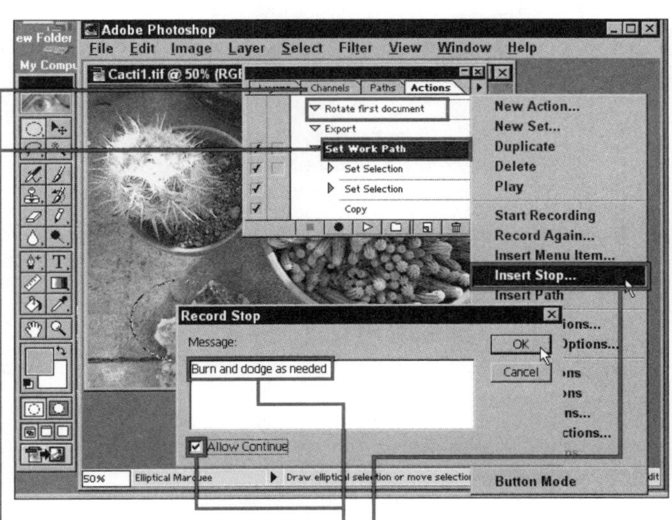

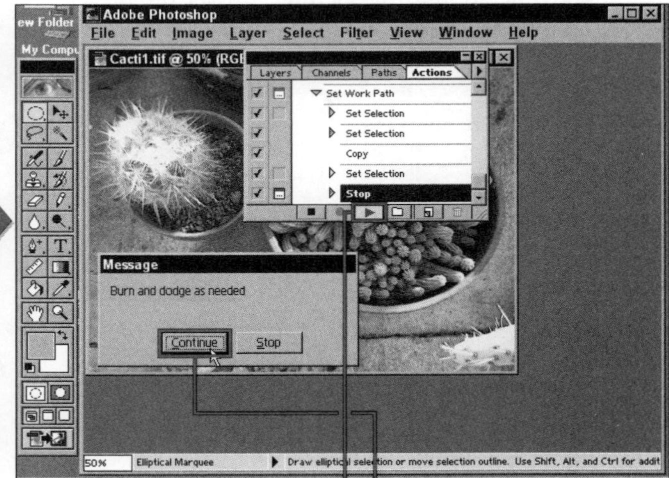

INSERT A PAUSE

1 Select the recorded command that will precede the inserted stop.

2 Or, select the name of the Action to stop at the end of that action.

3 Choose Insert Stop.

4 Enter a reminder of what to do during the pause.

5 Check Allow Continue if you want the Action to resume after the pause.

Note: When you play back an Action with a stop inserted, the Action stops and a message appears; or if you've checked Allow Continue, the Action stops but you'll also be able to continue the Action.

6 If you don't need to do as the message says, click Continue.

7 Click the Play icon to resume the Action.

ORGANIZATION IS THE KEY TO SUCCESS

Just as the three rules for the successful establishment of a retail site are location, location, location, the three rules for the successful production of images made from other images are organization, organization, organization. This chapter deals with those Photoshop 5 tools and features that help you to organize your collection of photos, create a montage, and perfect collage projects.

Almost all the tools, commands, and dialog boxes you use in the following exercises are illustrated in previous chapters of this book. The one that hasn't yet been introduced is the dialog box associated with the File ➪ Automate ➪ Contact Sheet command, which is used to make contact sheets. Turn to the first exercise in this chapter to learn how to create a contact sheet of your own.

Contact Sheets

The File ➪ Automate ➪ Contact Sheet command brings up the Contact Sheet dialog box (see the following figure). The dialog box contains options for opening a folder full of images and assembling them on a single page.

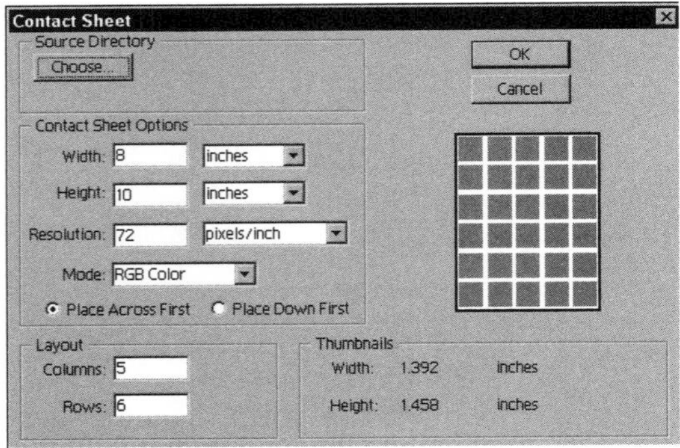

Contact Sheet Dialog Box Contents

Component	Function
Source Directory pull-down menu	Click to open a file browsing window. Navigate to find the folder you want to make contacts from and click. *Note: Subdirectory contents will not be included on the contact sheet.*
Width and Height fields	Enter the width and height of the area into which you want all the thumbnails placed. The most typical size is 8×0 because that is the size used by most photographers and because it fits on the most commonly used size of paper, letter size.
Width and Height units pull-down menus	Choose from inches, centimeters, or pixels.

Component	Function
Resolution field	This should be the resolution of the thumbnail images. Make this as high as your printer is capable of printing, divided by the number of primary colors in the current color (3 for RGB, 4 for CMYK, and so on).
Resolution units pull-down menu	Choose from pixels per inch or pixels per centimeter.
Mode pull-down menu	Choose from RGB, CMYK, or Lab color modes for printing.
Placement order radio buttons	Click one or the other to determine whether images will be placed in left-to-right horizontal order or in top-to-bottom vertical order.
Layout preview window	Shows you the aspect ratio of the thumbnails and the number of rows and columns that will result from the specifications you've chosen.

Component	Function
Columns field	Enter the number of columns across you want. It is best to enter a number of rows and columns that will result in a square thumbnail preview. Otherwise, some images may be smaller than others because verticals or horizontals may need to be shrunk to fit one of the dimensions.
Rows field	Enter the number of rows across you want. If the number of rows and columns you enter results in fewer thumbnails per page than there are images in the chosen folder, Photoshop simply creates multiple contact sheets.
Thumbnails width and height	The figures shown in this area of the dialog box result from the numbers entered in the Rows and Columns fields.

COLLECT AND PREP IMAGES

Collecting and prepping the images you're going to use in a collage or montage, as described here, isn't mandatory, but it can save you time. Furthermore, if you need to move the project to another computer, the job will be far easier. And if you decide to back up your project to CD-ROM, it will be much easier to keep track of your work.

The most important part of this task is to make a special folder for the project and then copy to it all the files you're going to use in the composite. Notice I said *copy*. If you resize, crop, or modify the copied files, you won't have destroyed your originals. The second most important part is to make all the components roughly the size they will be in the composite. This means resizing and trimming them. When you resize, be sure not to make the file any smaller than you could possibly want it to be. If you do, and you have to enlarge it later, you'll lose definition (of course, you could always copy the original back in).

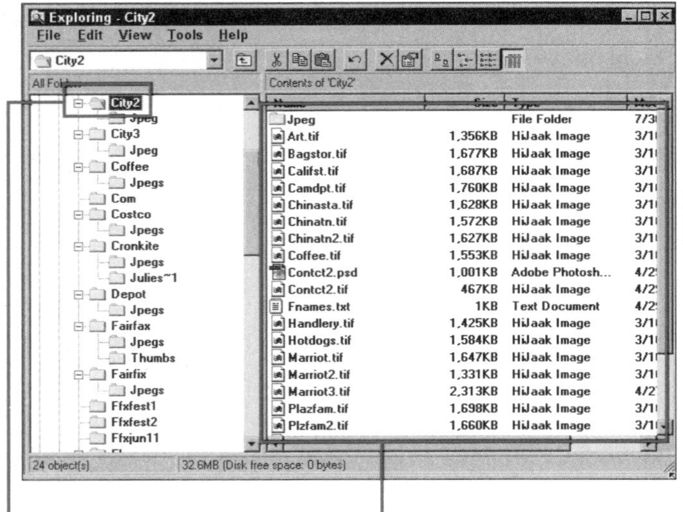

Note: Use your contact sheets to find the images you want in your composite.

1 Create a folder and name it after your project.

2 Copy all the needed files into this folder (remember, don't cut and paste or move them).

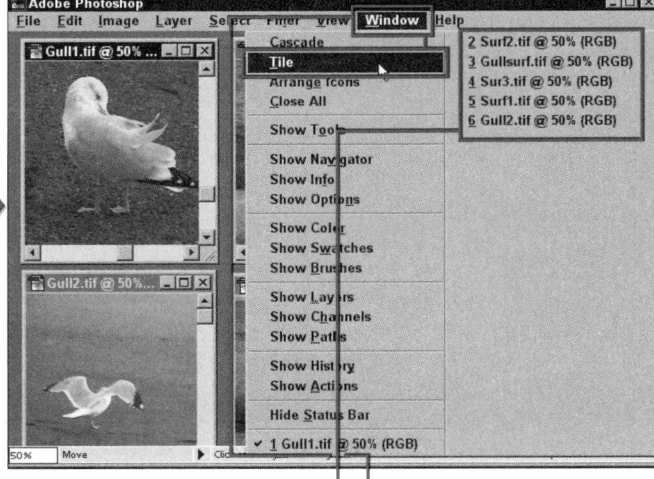

3 Open the folder in Photoshop.

Note: Open the folder and then drag all the files onto the Photoshop icon.

4 Choose Window ➪ Tile.

5 In turn, click to activate each image.

6 Press ⌘/Ctrl+(-) to zoom out until the entire image can be seen in the window.

TIPS

Why is it important to know whether I want to make a collage or a montage?

A *collage* combines multiple images so that each is distinct but contributes to an overall message and composition. A *montage* combines images to create the illusion of a scene that never happened. Which you intend as your final result will determine how you select and blend the individual layers.

Duplicating all these files uses a lot of hard disk space. How can I keep it to a minimum?

Crop each of the originals to the portion used in the target image. This will keep the size of your project folder as small as possible.

What is the best tool for making the initial quick cuts?

I zoom all the way out. If I just want to lop off a portion of a layer, I use the Marquee. Otherwise, I just make a quick freehand selection with the Lasso. Press Delete/Backspace, and you're ready to perform refined edge cutouts and blending.

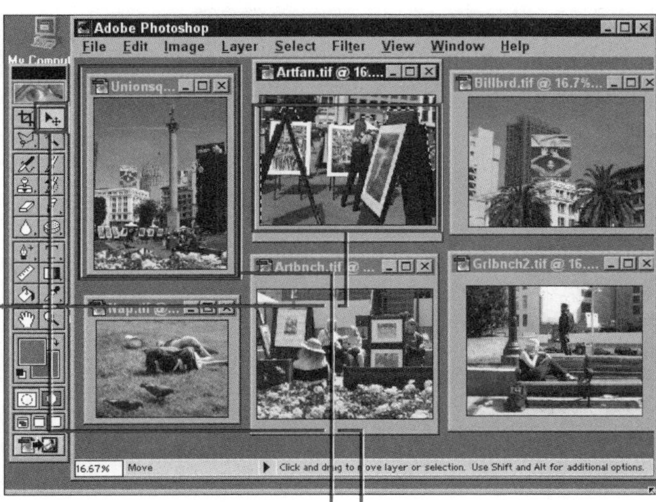

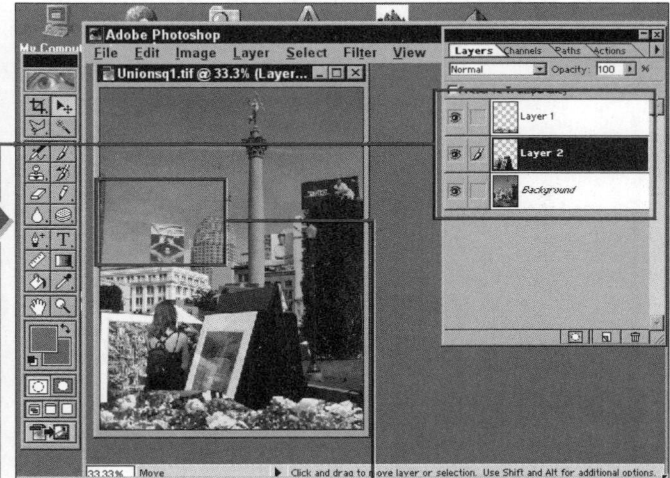

■ Decide which image is going to be the main image or background. You want to place all images inside this one, the target image.

7 In turn, select the portion of each image you want to use.

8 Select the Move tool.

9 Drag the selected portion onto the target image.

■ Each of the dragged-in selections automatically becomes a new layer in the target image.

10 Choose Window ⇨ Show Layers.

11 Drag the layers into their required stacking order.

12 Drag the transparency to see which portions overlap.

13 Make a rough selection of the portion of each layer that won't be needed and press Delete/Backspace to cut.

■ Now you are organized for the considerable fine-tuning that follows.

20

INTEGRATE IMAGES IN A COLLAGE

The difference between a *montage* and a *collage* is that a collage doesn't require you to make the images look as though they are part of the same photo. In fact, it's often effective, as in traditional collage, to simply rough-cut images and then scale and place them to make your composition.

The collages you see in many of today's digitally created ads, illustrations, and fine art tend to look more integrated than their traditional counterparts. Part of the reason is the capability to control exposure, transparency, and Blend mode, but the biggest difference is that images can be made to fade into one another.

The three techniques for doing such edge blending, shown in the exercise here, are quite simple: 1) You can erase the edges with a highly feathered paint brush. 2) You can make a highly feathered selection, invert it, and delete. 3) You can make a layer mask and then place a gradient in it.

■ All the images in this collage fade into one another.

Note: It is important for each of these images to reside on its own layer. You collect these images in the same way as you would collect them for a montage.

FADE AN IMAGE EVENLY

1 Make a selection that surrounds image.

2 Choose Select ➪ Feather and enter a high number of pixels in the dialog box.

3 Invert the selection (press ⌘/Ctrl+I or choose Select ➪ Inverse).

4 Press Delete/Backspace.

TIPS

Are there other techniques for integrating images in a collage?

Scribble with the Eraser, both with and without checking the Use History box in the Eraser Options. This places "sketches" of the underlying layers within the active layer (and vice versa).

Can I fade an image on both sides by using the Gradient tool?

Sure. The width of your gradient is determined by how far you drag. The gradient is made from the foreground color to the background color in the direction you drag; to make a two-sided fade, just make a gradient on both edges of the mask.

Can't Blend modes and filters also affect the effectiveness of a collage?

There is no end to the creative ways you can use Photoshop to enhance (or mess up) your collages and montages. Using various filters and Blend modes can certainly enrich texture and mood and do more to bring an original touch to the work.

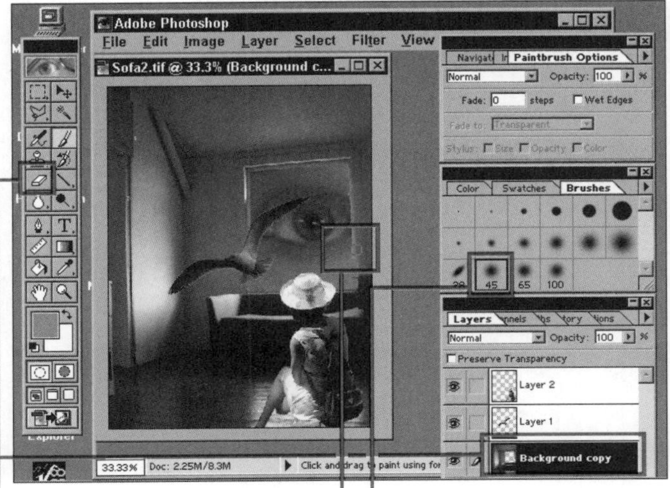

BLEND EDGES WITH THE ERASER

1 Click to activate the layer to be erased.

2 Choose the Eraser tool.

3 Choose the Paintbrush mode from the Options palette and use a highly feathered brush.

4 Erase wherever you want to see an underlying image show through.

MAKE A FADING LAYER MASK

1 Activate the layer you want to fade.

2 Click the Make Layer Mask icon.

3 Switch to the Channels palette, activate the layer mask channel, and make all channels visible.

4 Choose the Gradient tool, and drag to make a gradient that fades from black to white.

CLEAN UP THE EDGES

If you are making a collage and you have already collected and prepped the needed images, the next step is to cut out the components that will be blended together.

The routine goes like this: Select the obviously easy-to-delete portions you know you aren't going to need. If your selection makes a clean edge, fine, but don't waste time on this until you've gotten rid of the bulk of the stuff to be discarded. You'll then have a much easier time positioning items so that they blend into one another as smoothly as possible.

Next, position and scale the individual layers. When everything is in position, use the Eraser and brush tools to retouch any edges as needed.

1 In each layer, cut out material that won t appear in the composite.

2 Make a loose lasso selection around the material to be kept.

3 Press ⌘/Ctrl+ Shift+I to invert the selection.

4 Press Delete/Backspace to delete the unwanted material.

5 Choose Select ➪ Color Range.

6 Click OK.

7 Press Delete/Backspace to clear the selected area.

8 Choose Layer ➪ Matting ➪ Defringe.

9 Enter 1 or 2 in the Width field.

10 Click OK.

TIPS

How do I know how much width to specify in the Defringe dialog box?

If in doubt, enter 1 pixel. If that doesn't do the job, repeat the command until the fringe is all gone. Don't overdo it, or parts of your image will start to disappear. Remember, you can retouch with the Eraser tool.

Why shouldn't I make my selections before I put the image into the composite file?

You'll end up having to tweak it with the Eraser tool anyway. May as well save time by doing it all in one step.

Why do you use the eraser to fine-tune edges instead of just making a selection and inverting it?

Lots of people use selection and inversion, and it's often a good technique. Unfortunately, what works in theory sometimes doesn't work in practice. A correctly selected edge may look too sharp in some places and too soft in others. By using the Eraser, you can control the edges visually. It's like painting the object into place.

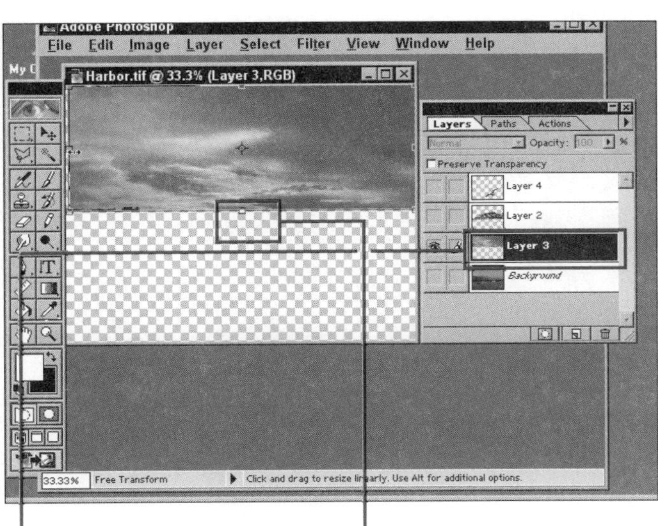

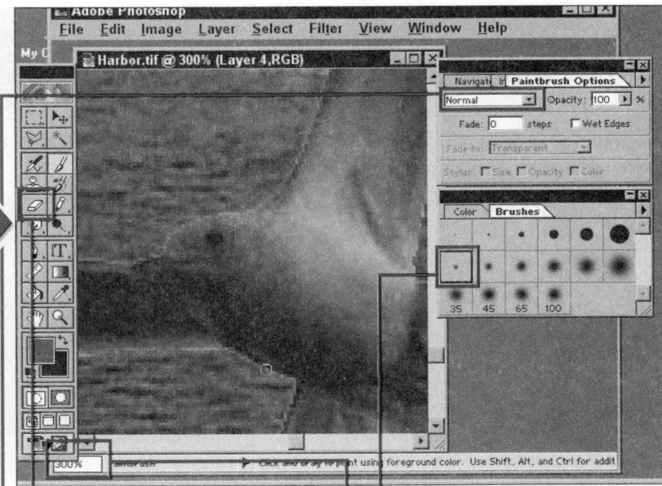

11 After you ve made rough trims for all the layers, use the Layers palette to stack the layers in the order in which you want them to appear.

12 Scale layers to the size they will be in the final composite.

13 Choose Edit ➪ Free Transform, and rescale the layer.

14 Choose the Eraser tool and double-click it to show Eraser options.

15 Choose the Paintbrush mode from the pull-down menu.

16 Choose a fairly small brush with a slightly feathered edge.

17 Zoom in to about 200 percent and stroke the image to erase the exact edge you want.

REARRANGE ITEMS ON A LAYER

Sometimes you need to move something on one of the layers in a composite so that it isn't covered by something on another layer. You may also want to move an item into a more visually prominent place or to improve the composition.

The problem is if you simply select the item and drag it, you'll leave a hole in the spot that it came from. This is easy to work around: Select the item as you've been shown in the preceding exercises in this chapter. Press ⌘/Ctrl+J to lift the contents of the selection to a new layer. Next, turn off everything but the originating layer and clone the original items. Now you can move and transform the new layer any way you like.

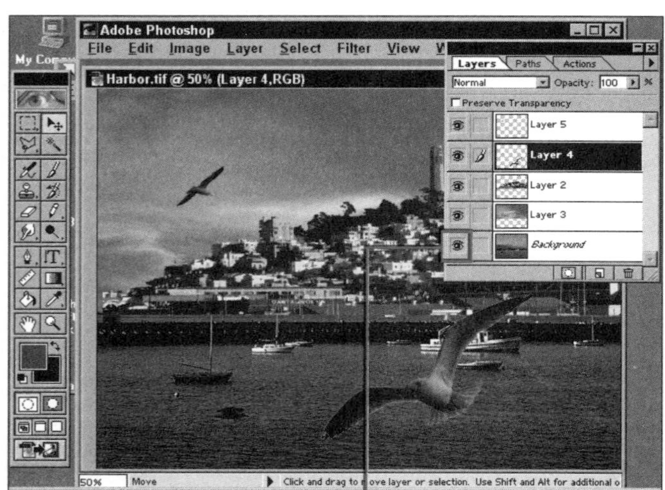

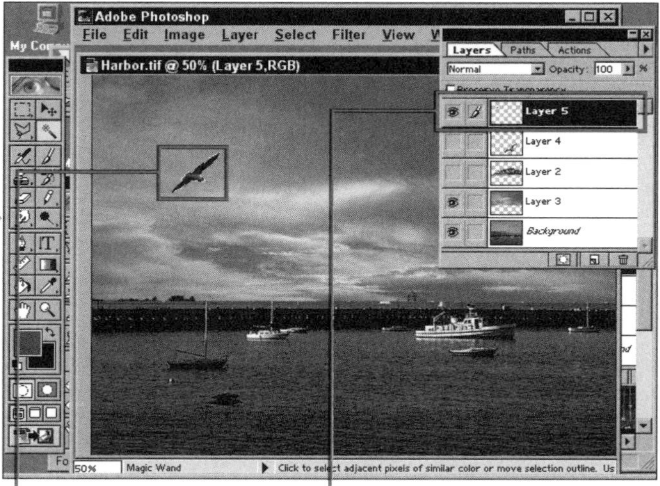

■ The people in the water are hidden by the willow tree.

1 Click the Eye icons to turn off the layers above the target layer.

2 Make a rough selection around the subject you want to move.

Note: Reflections and water tracks must be included, otherwise the subjects won't look natural in their relocated surroundings.

3 If the subject is on a background that will blend with the background in its new location, press ⌘/Ctrl+Opt/Alt+D.

4 Press ⌘/Ctrl+J to lift the selection to a new layer.

TIPS

What is the best way to keep the results of the cloning from being obvious?

Use a feathered brush so you don't get sharp borders. Paint into the same general area from several points of origin; otherwise, you're likely to get repeating patterns, or you'll push lighter areas into darker areas, which results in the appearance of an obvious border.

How much should I feather the selection?

That depends on the overall size of the image and even more on the size of the object you're moving. Generally, anything less than a 5-pixel feather is going to make a visible break.

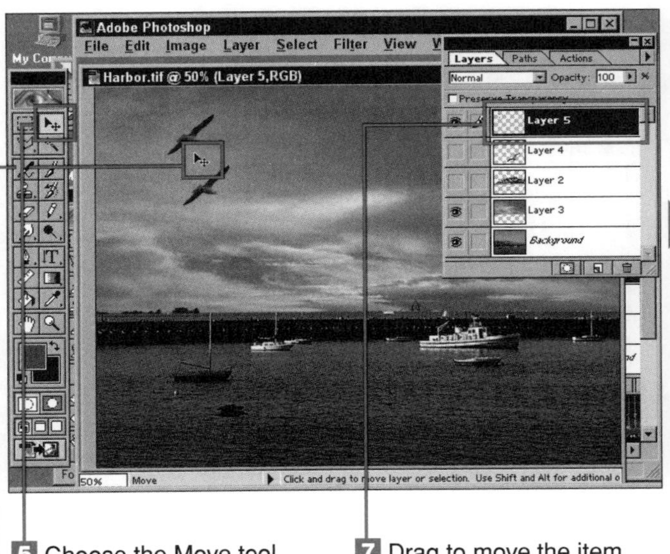

5 Choose the Move tool.

6 Click to activate the new layer.

7 Drag to move the item.

Note: In this case, the item blends perfectly with the water, but this is seldom the case. If you have to blend edges, see the previous exercise.

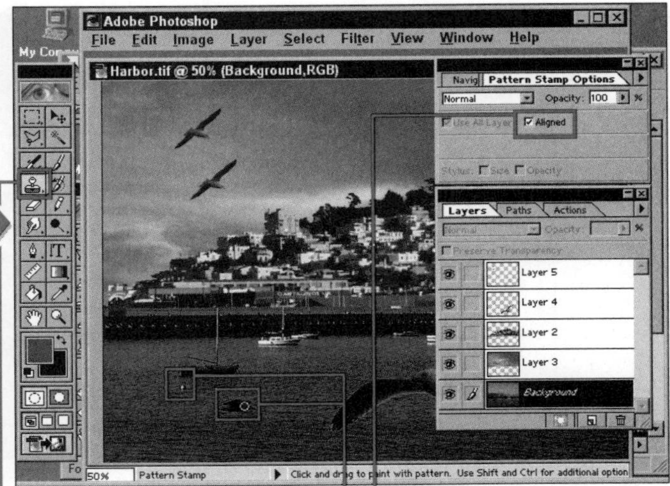

8 To make the original subject disappear, turn off the layer(s) above it.

9 Choose the Rubber Stamp tool (or press S).

10 Check the Aligned check box.

11 Press Opt/Alt+click to set the origin point.

12 Paint out the original subject.

20

CAST SHADOWS

In photomontages, the components should look as if they were taken by one camera in the same instant of time.

The first giveaway in many montages that the image is indeed a montage is inconsistent lighting. Professionals who make montages generally have well equipped studios, so for them, this inconsistency is easy to avoid. They adjust the lighting in their studios to match the background shot and then shoot the components. If you're shooting outdoors, try to shoot all the components at the same time of day. If you can't do that, shoot in the shade or on an overcast day. This way you'll have a fairly evenly lit subject, and you can add your own shadows. Better yet, shoot your background scene(s) on an overcast day (or at least while the sun's behind a cloud).

If you've shot on an overcast day and the lighting is fairly even (the more so, the better), you'll be able to fake some shadows and highlights in Photoshop.

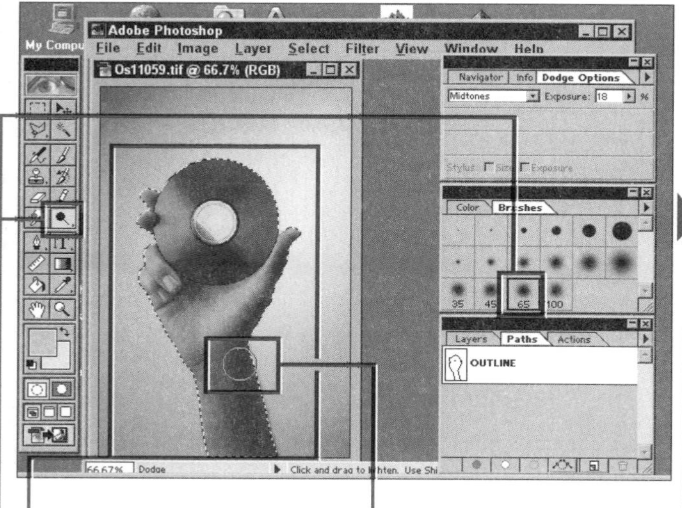

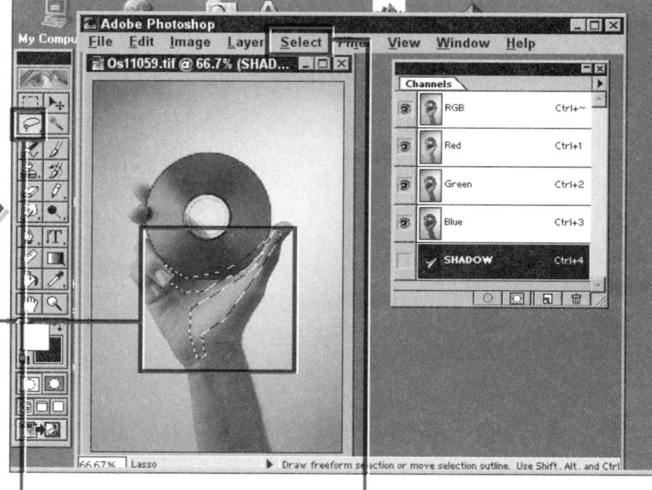

1 Select the item for which you want to change the lighting direction.

2 Choose the Dodge tool.

3 Choose a fairly large, highly feathered brush.

4 Scrub the shadow areas until they come close to matching the highlights.

Note: Subjects with very strong contrast between highlight and shadow are poor candidates.

5 Choose the Lasso tool.

6 Select the area where you want a new shadow to be cast.

7 Choose Select ⇨ Save Selection.

■ This creates a new alpha channel, which you will need for blending the edges of the selection.

TIPS

How do I control the feathering of the edge of the shadow mask?

Of course, you can feather the selection, but this rarely looks natural because the edges of shadows are sharper near the object that casts them and softer at a distance. Soften the edges by painting on the mask with highly feathered brushes of different sizes. Press [and] to change brush sizes. Press D to choose the default colors. Press X to switch the foreground and background colors. Remember, black makes the mask more opaque; white makes it more transparent.

Should I save all of my selections?

Always save your selections. You may be able to use all or part of them again.

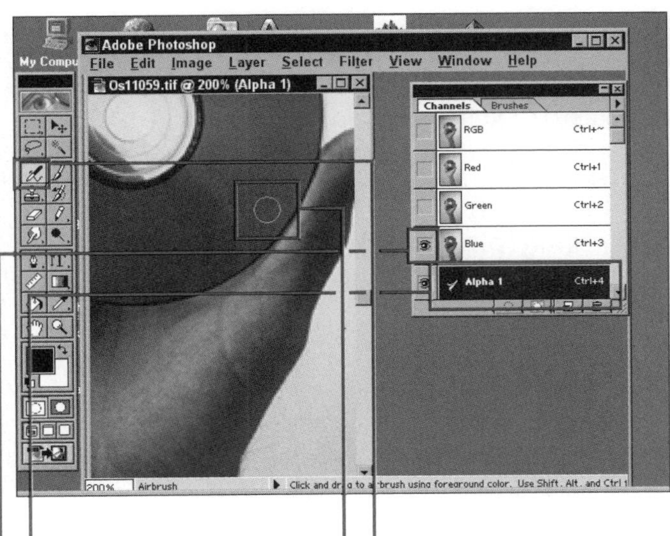

8 Click to activate the alpha channel (the mask appears in the workspace).

9 Click to make one of the color channels visible.

■ Make sure none of the other channels are active.

10 Choose the Airbrush or Paintbrush tool and a large, feathered brush.

11 Paint to soften the edges as needed.

12 Drag the mask channel to the Make Selection icon.

13 Activate the RGB channel

14 Press ⌘/Ctrl+H to hide the selection marquee so you can see how well your effect blends.

15 Choose Image ➪ Adjust ➪ Brightness and Contrast and darken as necessary.

SECTION VI

21 PREPARING WEB IMAGES WITH IMAGEREADY

Getting to Know ImageReady 508
Optimize PNG-8 in ImageReady 513
Optimize GIF Files in Photoshop 5.5 514
Optimize JPEG Files in Image Ready 516

22 DESIGNING INTERACTIVE GRAPHICS

Image Slicing 518
Slice It Up 522
Modify Slices 524
Specify Slices 528
Assign Rollovers to Slices 530
Animate a Rollover State 532

23 MAKING ANIMATIONS FROM PHOTOGRAPHS

Create Motion Tweens 534
Tween a Cross Fade 536
Animate a Series of Photos 538
Create a Slide Show 540
Color Management 542
What's on the CD-ROM 554

PREPARING IMAGES FOR THE WEB

Getting to Know ImageReady

ImageReady used to be a stand-alone Adobe program made strictly for the purpose of optimizing Web graphics. With the introduction of Photoshop 5.5, ImageReady is now an integral part of Photoshop. The new version (2.0) can slice images for faster image loading and create mouse rollover events.

ImageReady optimizes the three most popular Web file formats for bitmap graphics: GIF, JPEG, and PNG. It deals with both types of PNG formats: PNG-8 and PNG-24. ImageReady will convert to a Web format virtually any bitmapped image you can create in Photoshop or bring in from scanner or digitize from film or digital camera.

Photoshop/ImageReady gives you a myriad of settings for optimizing an image and, best of all, lets you preview multiple settings at the same time.

In addition to having terrific facilities for optimizing the performance of still Web images, ImageReady features a complete GIF animation program (which has its own tricks for super-optimization) and lets you slice images and create image maps.

Slices can be linked to URLs or to JavaScript. ImageReady writes its own JavaScript routines for creating mouse roll-over events. You can also modify the image for each event so that when the event occurs, the slice will change its appearance. You can also specify that changes occur in other slices. (For example, on mouse down, an instruction or navigational graphic could appear in another slice.) You can even have an animation appear in another slice.

ImageReady acts as a stand-alone, feature-rich program. However, many of its functions duplicate Photoshop 5.5 functions. Whenever that is the case, those functions will be covered in the previous sections of this book. The few exceptions will occur whenever a shared function has a particularly useful capability for preparing Web images.

Adobe provides three learning tools to help in learning ImageReady: the user guide, the online Help system, and Web service at Adobe's home page, `http://www.Adobe.com`.

The Image Ready Interface

The ImageReady interface is so similar to Photoshop's that it may at first fool you into thinking that you're still working in Photoshop. This was done intentionally to help keep the learning curve between programs at a minimum.

What Is Optimization and Why Is It so Important?

Optimization is the term that has come into general acceptance among Web designers for all of the "tricks" that can be used to make a graphics file as small as possible without losing too much quality.

How much loss of quality is tolerable will vary considerably from image to image, author to author, client to client, and intended purpose to intended purpose. Traditionally, graphics have been optimized by performing several separate operations (image resizing, color reduction, dithering, and compression) independently. These are usually performed on several copies of each image, each using different settings. The results are compared and the smallest image that looks good enough is the one that ends up being used on the Web.

ImageReady saves us gobs of time by letting us apply up to four different sets of compression settings, each including all the categories named previously, at the same time. You can see them all side-by-side. Furthermore, you see the results of all the settings nearly instantly. That makes it easy to change a setting or two and look at the results again. As soon as you're sure that one of the four is the best you can do for that image, you select that view of the image. Only then need you save the file.

Which File Format?

If you are new to preparing graphics for Web publication, it helps to understand which of the four graphics formats supported by ImageReady is most appropriate for optimizing a given image.

Four different file formats (actually three, one of which has two distinctive "flavors") have come into wide acceptance on the Web. In order of popularity, these include GIF (Graphics Interchange Format), JPEG (Joint Photographic Experts Group), PNG-8, and PNG-24. PNG stands for Portable Network Graphics. GIF and PNG-8 are used for 8-bit (256-colors or less) images.

- **GIF**: Use this format for graphic text (logos and such), graphic elements, technical drawings, and most hand-executed art (unless there are lots of soft edges and smooth gradations of color).
- **JPEG**: Use for almost all photos and any other artwork with lots of colors, soft edges, and smooth transitions. This is a 24-bit format, so all colors are legal. Since most computers in use today have true-color display systems, you won't need to worry about Web-safe colors for this type of art work.
- **PNG-8**: Lossless compression makes this a good format for highly detailed, flat-color artwork. Also, multi-level background transparency ensures smooth blending of transparent image edges with the background. (However, GIF files have much more universal browser support.)
- **PNG-24**: This format is capable of lossless compression and can store alpha channels. Use for technically-critical photographs when you're audience is willing to wait for the file to load in order to be able to judge the quality of your portfolio or to study a technical or scientific photo. Also invaluable when you need to display partial or graduated transparency. (Note: this format is supported only in the very latest generations of Web browsers.)

The PNG format is supported directly in the browser only by Internet Explorer 4.0 and later. Versions 2.0 and later of both Netscape and Microsoft browsers can use PNG plug-ins. PNG Live is a popular plug-in that works with both browsers.

LiveViews

ImageReady LiveViews are what you see as a result of choosing one of the tabs in the active document window that show an optimized version of the image. These are four tabs: Original, Optimized, 2-up, and 4-up.

The optimization ImageReady does to an image can be previewed in one of these Live Views. You can see information about the performance of the optimization settings for a given view at the bottom of that window. LiveViews are so called because any time you change an optimization setting, the selected LiveView shows the resulting changes in the image.

CONTINUED

GETTING TO KNOW IMAGEREADY CONTINUED

The layout of 2-up and 4-up LiveViews is automatically determined by ImageReady as a result of the width:height ratio of the image, the aspect ratio of the window, and whether annotations or rules are shown.

The Optimize Palette

All of the settings that are reflected in the currently selected LiveView are made in the Optimize palette.

The contents of the Optimize palette are different for each of the four types of optimized files. (Refer to the following tables for explanations of each of the settings.) The contents of the Optimize palette menu, accessed by clicking the arrowhead in the upper-right corner of the Optimized tab, are the same for all four versions.

The Optimize Palette (8-bit Color)

Item	What It Does
Droplet arrow	Creates a droplet (batch processing icon) that will apply the current settings to any folder you drop on the icon.
File type pull-down menu	Lets you choose the file format (GIF, JPEG, PNG-8, or PNG-24) for optimization.
Color Reduction Algorithm pull-down menu	Choose from Perceptual, Selective, Adaptive, Web, Custom, MacOS, or Windows.
Dither Algorithm pull-down menu	Determines how to simulate colors not in the table. Choose from No Dither, Pattern (uses a halftone pattern), or Diffusion (dither effects randomly diffused).
Transparency checkbox	Indicates a transparent color will be assigned to the file.
Interlaced checkbox	Check to indicate that an interlaced (low resolution) preview image should be created.
Lossy slider (GIF only)	If applied, allows loss of some image data in exchange for smaller file size.
Maximum Colors menu and field	Enter any number between 1 and 256.
Dither Percentage slider and field	Drag to indicate the amount of dithering to be applied.
Matte Color swatch and pull-down menu	Displays a swatches palette that enables you to choose a background color to use to match edge halo pixels to browser background color.
Web Snap Tolerance field and slider	Determines how close a color must come to a color in the Web-safe palette before it will be converted to that color.

The Optimize Palette (True Color)

Item	What It Does
Settings pull-down menu	Enables you to choose from any previously saved settings. (Adobe includes quite of few of the most commonly used.)
Compression Quality pull-down menu (JPEG only)	Enables you to quickly pick between four compression levels: Low, medium, high, maximum.
Progressive/Interlaced checkbox	Check to indicate that an interlaced (low resolution) preview image should be created.
ICC Profile checkbox (JPEG only)	Preserves any pre-existing ICC profile to be saved with the image. May increase file size.
Quality slider (JPEG only)	Drag the slider or enter a number between 1 and 100 to determine the exact amount of loss to be tolerated.
Blur slider and field (JPEG only)	Applies Gaussian blur to reduce critical detail and permit greater compression.
Matte Color swatch and pull-down menu	Displays a swatches palette that enables you to choose a background color to use to match edge halo pixels to browser background color.

Optimize Palette Menu

Item	What It Does
Hide Options	Expands the palette to show additional controls.
Create Droplet	Enables you to save the current settings as a Droplet (an application file that will automatically batch process all the files in any folder you drop on it according to the current optimization settings).
Save Settings	Saves the current settings.
Delete Settings	Deletes saved settings.
Optimize to File Size	Optimizes to a specific file size in one step. Option for sticking with the current file type or enabling ImageReady to choose between GIF and JPEG.
Repopulate View	4-up view only: Regenerates optimization alternatives for all but the original and selected views.
Auto Regenerate	Toggles. Automatically regenerates any selected window according to any changes in the settings.
Regenerate	Forces regeneration of the selected (or Optimized) view if Auto Regenrate is toggled off. Use when you want to edit the image without waiting for regeneration after each stroke.

GETTING TO KNOW IMAGEREADY CONTINUED

Understanding Color Palettes

If you are compressing your files in true-color (JPEG or PNG-24), you needn't worry about palettes.

GIF and PNG-8, on the other hand, are limited to the production of 8-bit, 256 (or fewer) indexed palette colors. Because the number of colors is limited, very specific colors must be assigned to the limited number of locations available in a palette.

The color of a given pixel in the image is actually assigned to a specific location in the palette matrix.

When you optimize a file in Photoshop 5.5 or ImageReady, you are given a choice of seven different palette types (which Adobe also calls Color Reduction Algorithms): Perceptual, Selective, Adaptive, Web, Custom, Mac OS, and Windows. How each of these influences the outcome of your optimization is described here.

Perceptual

Creates a color table based on the colors in the image, but weighted for colors that are most critically perceived by the human eye.

Selective

Default. The choice that is usually most faithful to an original photo. Also creates a color table based on colors in the original image, but favors the preservation of Web colors and those colors that occupy large areas of the image.

Adaptive

Basis selection of colors entirely on the frequency of their appearance in the original image. Very useful for images with one or two highly predominant colors, such as a field of grass.

Web

Uses the Web-safe palette for the color table. All colors in the original are snapped to the closest Web-safe color. Ensures that the target browser will not dither colors. Can result in larger file sizes. Best used for logos and graphic elements with limited colors.

Custom

You have to choose Preceptual, Selective, or Adaptive first. Creates a table from the original image that is maintained regardless of any subsequent changes you make.

Mac OS

The color table is based on the Macintosh Operating System's uniform sampling of 256 RGB colors.

Windows

The color table is based on the Windows operating system's uniform sampling of 256 RGB colors.

OPTIMIZE PNG-8 IN IMAGEREADY

Optimizing to PNG-8 is essentially the same operation as optimizing in GIF. The operation is also essentially the same whether it's done in either Photoshop or ImageReady.

This exercise assumes you have your image opened in Photoshop and that the image contains a transparent background. (If the image you're using doesn't have a transparent background, be sure you don't check the transparent box.)

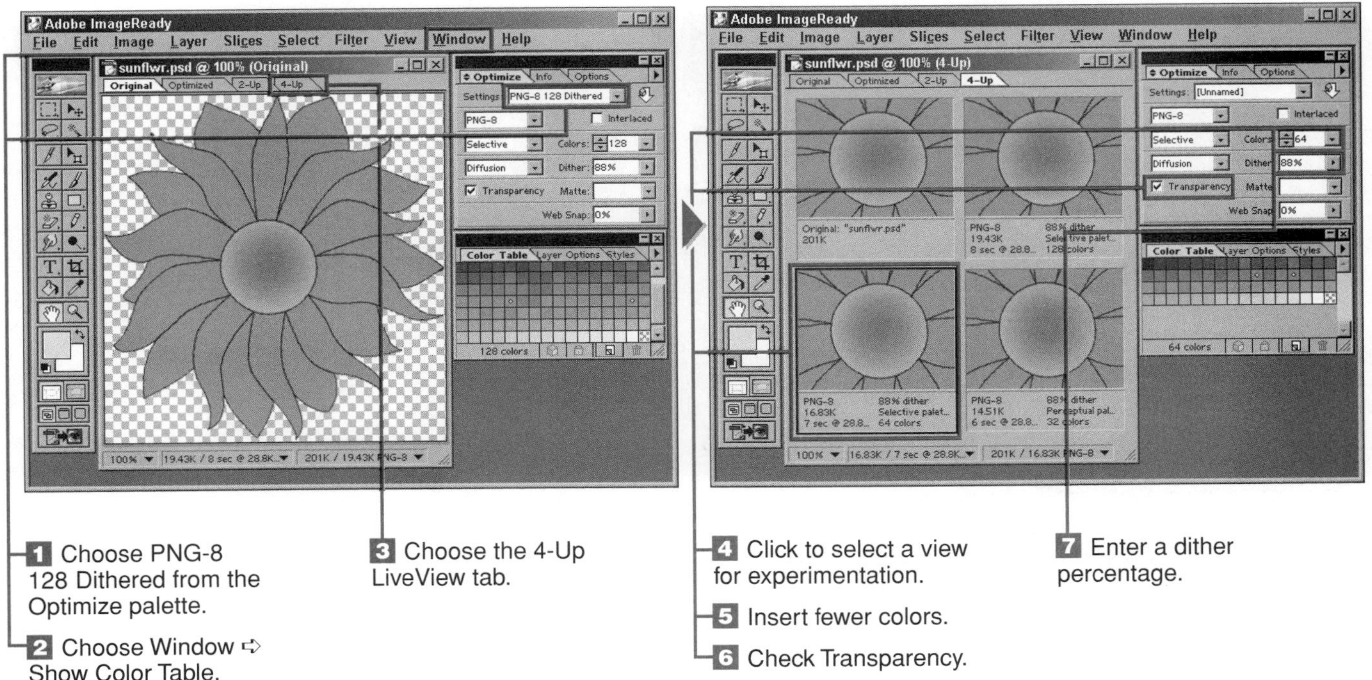

1 Choose PNG-8 128 Dithered from the Optimize palette.

2 Choose Window ⇨ Show Color Table.

3 Choose the 4-Up LiveView tab.

4 Click to select a view for experimentation.

5 Insert fewer colors.

6 Check Transparency.

7 Enter a dither percentage.

OPTIMIZE GIF FILES IN PHOTOSHOP 5.5

You can now optimize GIF files in either Photoshop 5.5 or Image Ready with nearly identical results. Which route you take will depend mostly on which environment you are working in when you decide to optimize the file.

GIF (Graphics Interchange Format) was the first universally adopted standard for network graphics, due to the pioneering efforts of Compuserve. It is still the most widely used graphics format on the Internet because its lossless compression maintains the sharp edges and solid colors needed for effective depiction of graphical text and of interactive elements such as buttons and banners.

GIF graphics are limited to 256 colors or less, which must be stored in a color pallet that is indexed to the location of each pixel. This makes choosing the palette an important decision.

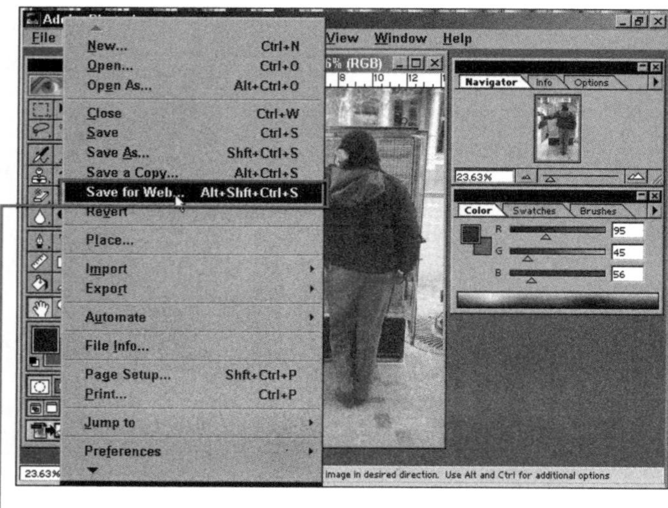

1 Choose File ⇨ Save for Web.

■ The Save for Web dialog box appears.

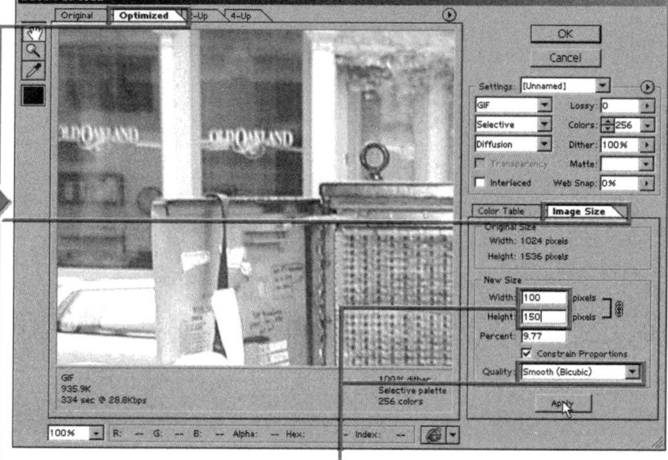

2 Choose the Optimized tab.

3 Choose the Image Size tab.

4 Enter maximum height or width for the Web image.

5 Choose bicubic and click Apply.

TIPS

My normal-size photos of 5–40MB take forever to resize this way. Is there a better way?

Especially if you have a slower computer and less that 96MB of RAM, this will be true. You can save time by resizing the image before choosing File ⇨ Save for Web. Just be sure not to save the resized original unless you save it under another name.

Why did you choose to resize the photo so small?

Because we're saving a full-color photo to a GIF file with a limited range of colors. The loss of colors is much less likely to show in a file with fewer pixels.

How can I tell how much I've improved loading time when I change settings?

Take a look at the information displayed under the image. If you don't see the file size and loading time at a given modem rate, choose View ⇨ Show Optimization Info.

Why haven't you used more of the settings here?

It's seldom necessary, but you can experiment and see your results instantly. If you see a performance gain from one of the other settings and you still find the image quality acceptable, use it.

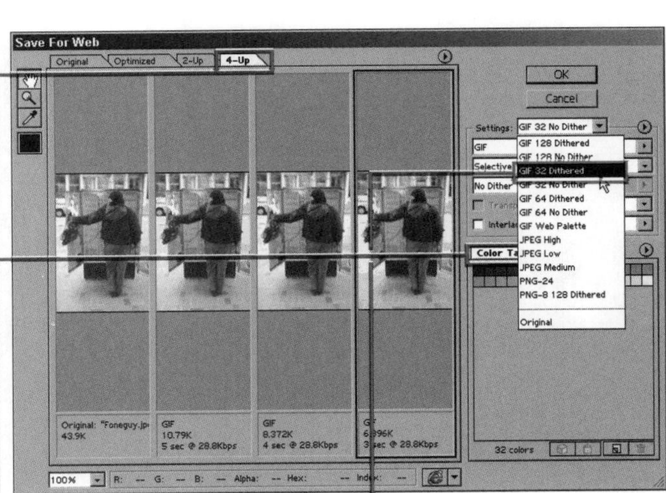

6 Choose the 4-up LiveView tab.

7 Select the Color Table tab so that you can see the effect of further changes on the color table.

8 Select each window in turn and choose dithered scheme with fewer colors for each.

9 Choose Repopulate Views from the Optimize menu.

10 Click to select Fastest File.

11 Click OK.

12 A standard file-save dialog box appears. Name and save the optimized file to the location of your choice.

OPTIMIZE JPEG FILES IN IMAGE READY

The file being optimized in this exercise is a painting. Because it has some continuous gradations of color and some solid-color, hard-edge areas, it's anybody's call whether to choose JPEG or GIF for optimization.

JPEG has been chosen in this instance because it's likely that it will produce a smaller file and, therefore, download much faster.

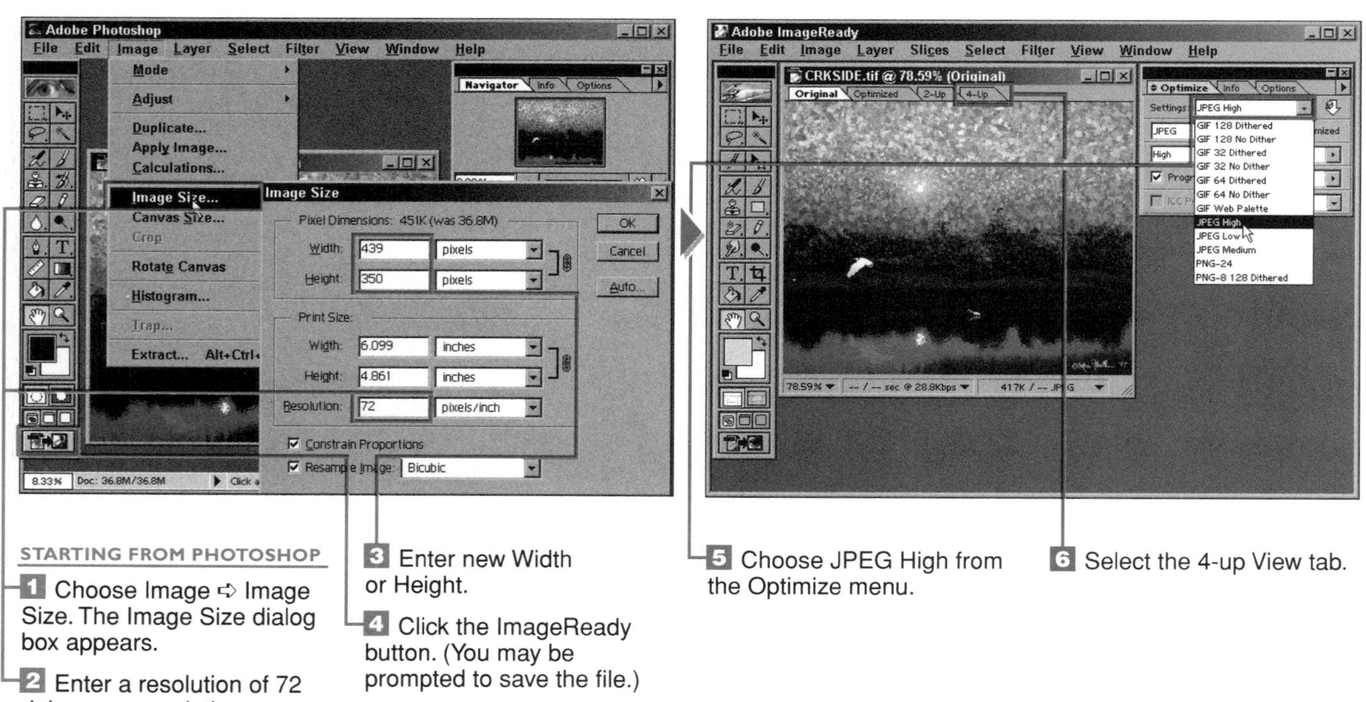

STARTING FROM PHOTOSHOP

1 Choose Image ➪ Image Size. The Image Size dialog box appears.

2 Enter a resolution of 72 dpi screen resolution.

3 Enter new Width or Height.

4 Click the ImageReady button. (You may be prompted to save the file.)

5 Choose JPEG High from the Optimize menu.

6 Select the 4-up View tab.

TIPS

Why isn't the Color Table open?

If it were, you wouldn't see a color table because there's no need to index colors in a true-color file.

Is there a fast way to get to an even smaller, faster file?

Choose Optimize to File Size from the Optimize palette menu. Because you get to preview the result before you save it, you'll know if you've picked too small a file size.

Should you always try blurring the file?

No. Blurring blurs. You'll probably know if your image can tolerate that. If you can, reduce the size of the file. You've been asked to do it here so that you can see the effect.

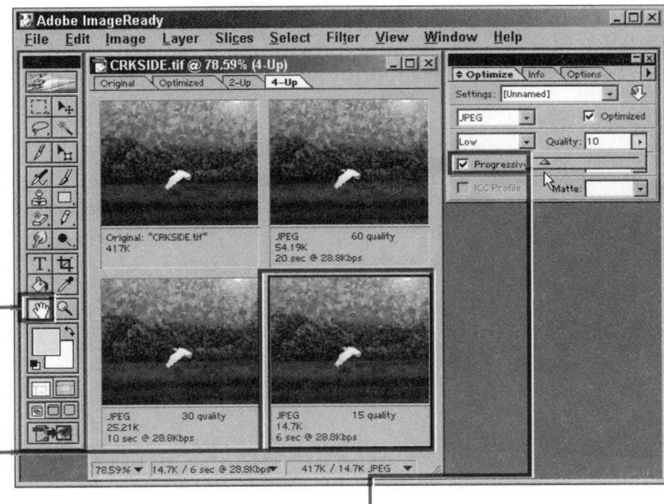

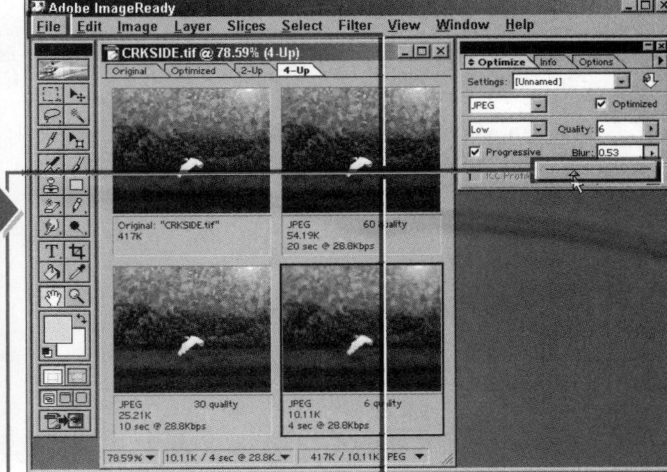

7 Choose the Hand tool and drag in any window to center the image.

8 Select the lowest quality acceptable image and try an even lower Quality set.

9 Check Progressive.

10 Try the Blur slider. If you can get away with a blurred image, you will get a smaller file.

11 Choose File ⇨ Save Optimized.

22 Image Slicing

ImageReady 2.0 included with Photoshop 5.5 makes it possible to divide an image that is destined for the Web into several images. These parts can be loaded onto a Web page so that no seam is visible. This process is known as *image slicing*.

Image slicing provides you with both performance advantages and interface design advantages. Performance may be enhanced for either or both of three reasons:

- Each slice can be individually optimized.
- Slices can be made to contain no image. (You can still make the slice match the HTML page's background color and you can enter HTML text and links into non-image slices.)
- Several smaller images may load into most browsers faster than one large image.

The Interface design advantage is that you can assign JavaScript programming routines, called *rollovers*, to any individual slice. The purpose of rollovers is to make the interface come alive when you mouse over to a menu choice.

Technically, an ImageReady-created slice is any rectangular area of an image that the program turns into a cell in HTML code. That HTML code is part of the code ImageReady writes for each image saved for the Web. Anytime you create new slices in the same image, ImageReady re-writes the code to reflect the creation of the new slice or slices.

User Slices and Auto Slices

Any time you create a slice, Image Ready creates extra slices so that the whole image will fit back together. The slice you created is called a *user* slice. User slices are flexible in that they can have more properties assigned to them. The slices the program creates automatically care called *auto* slices. At any time, you can select an auto slice and promote it to a user slice. You can also create a new slice and the program will automatically reassign the slices and renumber them.

Image Slice Options Defined

The Slice palette, especially when expanded by choosing Show Options from the Slice palette menu, offers you the opportunity to choose from many settings. Their purpose and the directions for use follow.

Name and Appearance

ImageReady names slices automatically according to the preferences you set in the File ➪ Preferences ➪ Slices dialog box.

You can change the naming default of DOC.NAME_## by choosing from any of the slice naming menus. You can also simply enter your own specifications in the fields, but remember that you'll want SLICE NO somewhere in the name if you want to be able to tell where the slice belongs in the image and in what order it was created.

You can also choose to show the lines without symbols and can choose the color of the lines. You can also choose whether the numbers and symbols will appear in the upper-right corner of the slice, as well as their opacity and their size.

Finally, you can choose the relative brightness of user slices and auto slices.

Background Color

When you choose from the Background Color menu, the color doesn't appear in your image. You won't see it until you preview the image in a browser.

The background color is the color you see in a browser before the other contents of a page have loaded. You can choose to use a different background color for a given slice than that of your Web page. Also, if you have a partly transparent image in your slice, it is this background color that shows through.

To choose a background color, use the menu in the Slices palette and drag to pick one of the choices shown.

- The colors in the swatches palette of the Background Color menu are all Web-safe colors.
- If you choose None, the background color of the target Web page will be used.
- If you choose Matte, you will get the Matte color specified in the Optimize palette.
- Foreground Color and Background Color refer to the colors currently chosen in the Toolbox Swatches.

URL

You can assign URLs (Uniform Resource Locators) to link the slice to another file. If you've already created URLs for other objects in the current file, they will be listed on the drop-down menu. You can choose one of those or you can type in a new link.

Target

This option is grayed unless there are frames in the image's HTML document. Frames are HTML instructions that divide a Web page into windows, each containing different content.

If you enter a frame name, it must match that of an actual frame in the HTML document. Otherwise, you can choose one of the following:

- **_blank**: Shows the linked file in a new browser window without closing the current window.
- **_self**: Places the linked file in the same frame as the original link.
- **_parent**: Puts the linked file into the frameset of the original parent. Of course, the document must contain parent/child frames.
- **_top**: Removes all the current frames and replaces the current browser window's contents.

CONTINUED

IMAGE SLICING CONTINUED

Message

By default, when an image begins to load in a given location in an HTML page, the browser displays the name of the file that's loading. If you enter anything else in the message field, that will appear instead.

Alt

Lets you enter text that will appear in place of the slice in non-graphical browsers and in place of the image while the image is loading in graphical browsers.

Text

This field is available for non-image slices. Enter text that you would like to have appear as HTML text in the table cell occupied by the non-image slice.

If you understand how to code HTML, you can also enter code here. If you don't, but have a Web authoring program such as Adobe GoLive or Dreamweaver, you could create the content you want, then cut and paste the code into this field.

Linking Slices

If you don't want to optimize every single slice separately, there's salvation. You can link them, then apply the optimization settings to all. Linked slices also share the same color palette and dither pattern — so they will match in appearance.

Auto slices are automatically linked when they are created. If you manually link an auto slice to a user slice, the auto slice will be automatically promoted to a user slice.

To link slices, select them with the Slice Select tool. Shift+Click to select multiple slices or drag a marquee to surround several. Next, choose Slices ➪ Link Slices. Unlinking slices is just a matter of selecting the slices to be unlinked and choosing Slices ➪ Unlink Slices. If you want to Unlink a set or sets of slices (those that were linked at the same time), you can simply choose one slice in the set and choose Slices ➪ Unlink Set(s). To make sure that no slices are linked, choose Slices ➪ Unlink All.

Changing the Appearance of Slices

ImageReady employs several visual devices to help you to identify and manage slices, including colored slice lines, contrast and brightness, and name and type symbols.

To turn off all characteristics except the slice lines, choose File ➪ Preferences ➪ Slices and check Show Lines Only. To Change the color of lines, choose File ➪ Preferences ➪ Slices and choose a color from the Line Color pull-down menu. To change the contrast and brightness of user and autoslices, choose File ➪ Preferences ➪ Slices and pick a percentage from the appropriate Color Adjustments pull-down menu. To show/hide slices, select the Show Slices or Hide Slices buttons in the Toolbox.

SLICE IT UP

Slicing an image means cutting an image up into smaller files that display edge-to-edge so together they look like one big image. There are two reasons to slice an image: speed and interactivity. You can optimize each slice separately so the total file loads faster. You can also assign mouse events to the slices.

There are two types of slices: Those you draw (called user slices) and those Photoshop auto-creates to fill in empty spaces (called auto slices). All auto slices are linked to one another and are optimized in the same way. User slices can be categorized as Image or No Image. No Image slices can contain a solid color or HTML text.

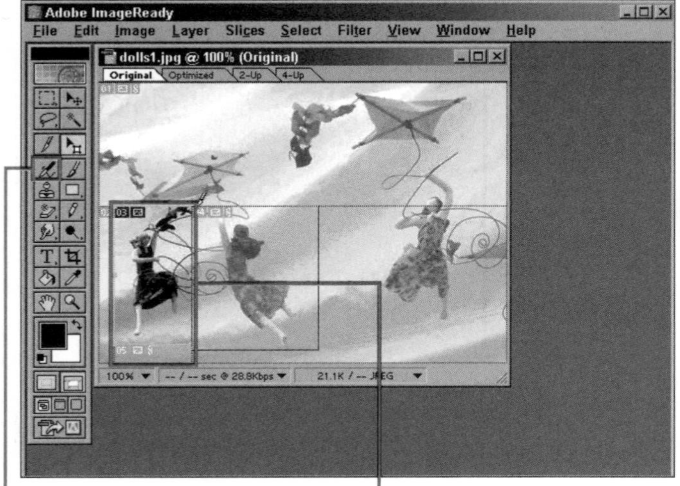

1 Open and size the file you want to slice.

2 Choose the Slice tool.

3 Press ⌘/Ctrl + and drag to indicate slice size.

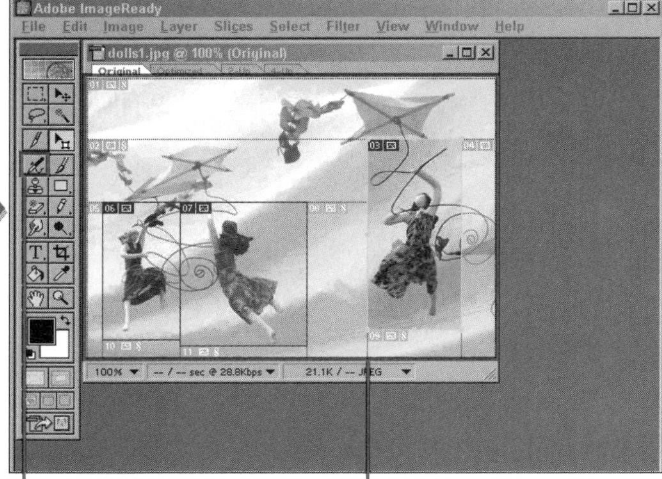

4 Repeat to indicate other major user slices.

5 ImageReady automatically divides the rest of the image into autoslices.

TIPS

Can you create slices from guides you drag in from the rulers?

Sure. Except for how the Guides are placed, it's the same process. You just choose Slices ➪ Create Slices from Guides.

Is there any other way to create slices?

You can also create them from rectangular selections. Choose the Marquee and drag diagonally to indicate the area you want to include in the main slice. Then choose Slice ➪ Create Slice from Selection. You can do this as many times as you like.

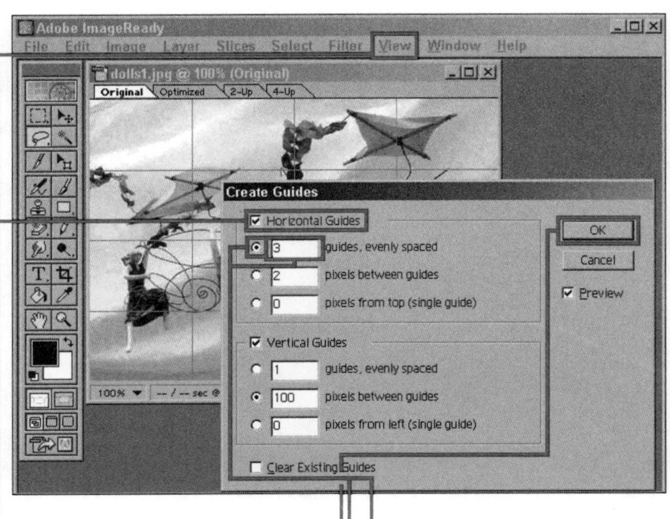

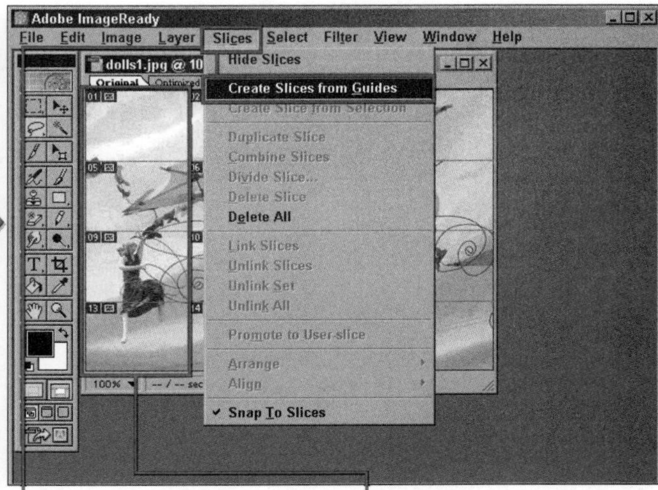

CREATE SLICES FROM GUIDES

1 Choose View ➪ Create Guides.

2 Check to indicate Vertical, Horizontal, or both.

3 Click a radio button to indicate type of division.

4 Enter distance or number of guides.

5 Click OK.

6 Choose Slices ➪ Create Slices from Guides.

7 The slices will be drawn as shown.

MODIFY SLICES

ImageReady provides a bevy of ways to specify and manage slices. Before you can do anything to a slice, you have to select it with the slide selection tool.

Slices can be duplicated, moved, resized, divided, restacked, deleted, snapped to one another (or not), and aligned. You can also promote auto slices to user slices.

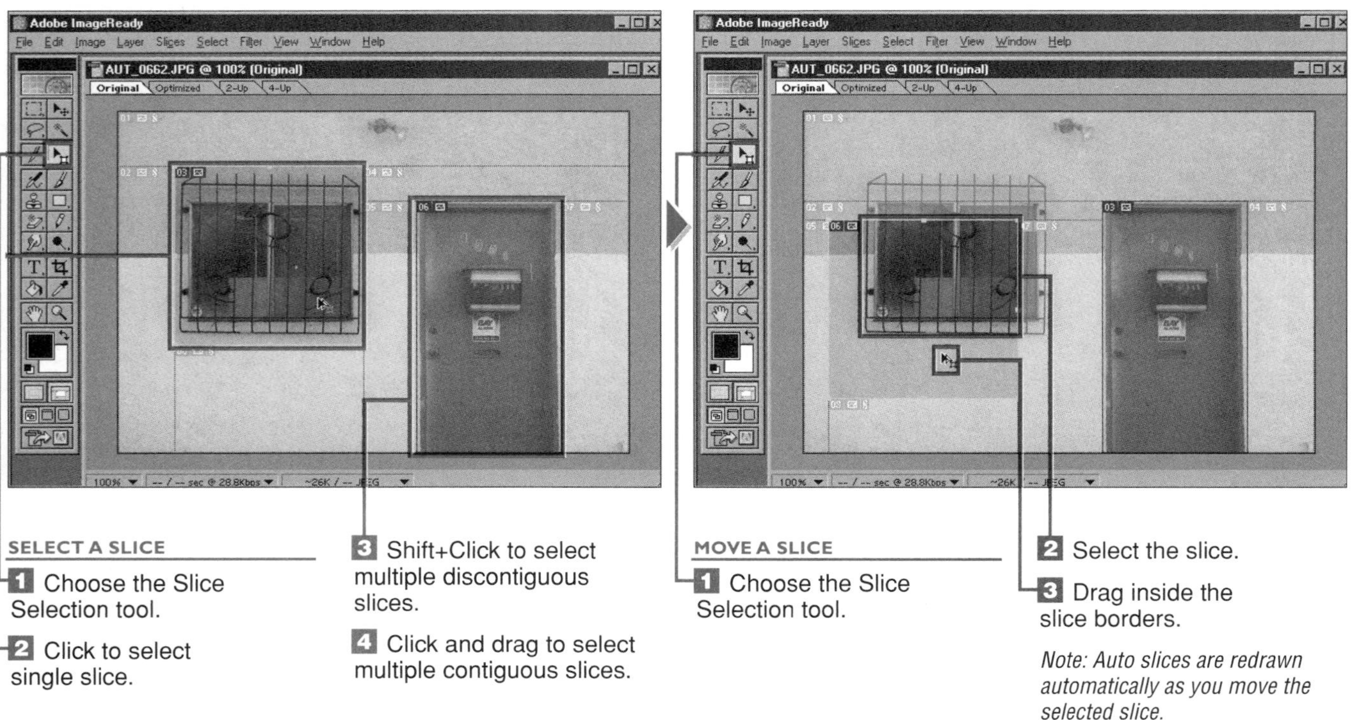

SELECT A SLICE

1 Choose the Slice Selection tool.

2 Click to select single slice.

3 Shift+Click to select multiple discontiguous slices.

4 Click and drag to select multiple contiguous slices.

MOVE A SLICE

1 Choose the Slice Selection tool.

2 Select the slice.

3 Drag inside the slice borders.

Note: Auto slices are redrawn automatically as you move the selected slice.

TIPS

Can I duplicate a slice?

Sure. Choose Slices ⇨ Duplicate Slice. The duplicate will appear over the original, offset 10 pixels down and right. You can also duplicate by pressing Opt/Alt and dragging the Slice Selection tool from inside the slice.

What if I want to select an underlying (sub) slice?

You can click on any visible part of the underlying slice and it will be selected in its entirety.

What if I want to move a slice, but keep it in horizontal alignment with the original location?

Press Shift while dragging. This restricts movement to horizontal, vertical, or 45-degree diagonal from the original location.

If I move a slice, can I make it snap to the edges of other slices?

Choose Slices ⇨ Snap to Slices. If the command is checked when you open the menu, it is already turned on.

How do I promote an auto slice to a user slice?

Choose Slices ⇨ Promote to User-slice(s). If you select multiple auto slices, you can promote them all at the same time.

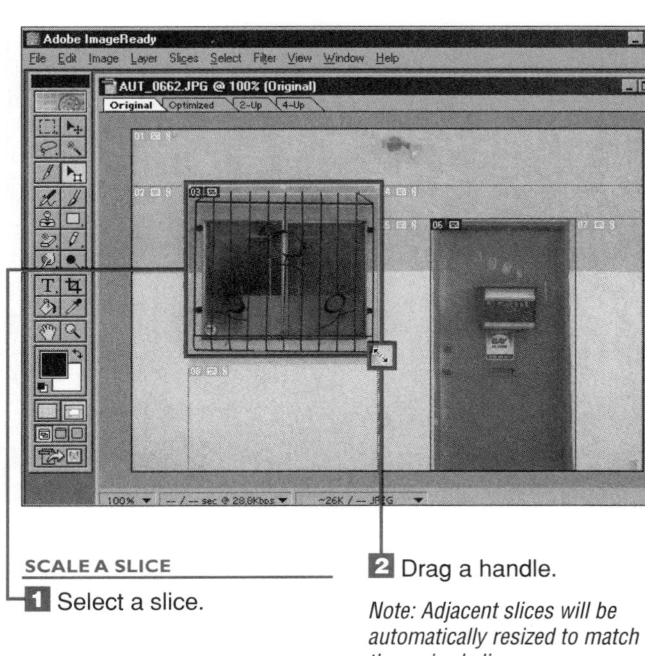

SCALE A SLICE

1 Select a slice.

2 Drag a handle.

Note: Adjacent slices will be automatically resized to match the resized slice.

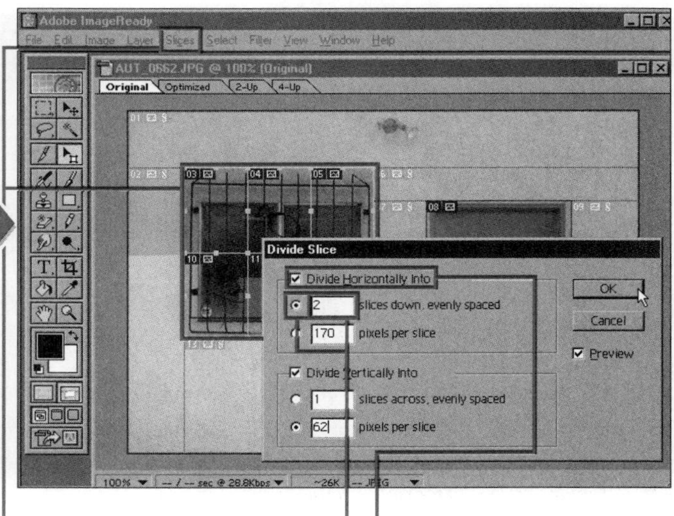

DIVIDE A SLICE

1 Select the slice.

2 Choose Slices ⇨ Divide Slice.

3 Check the dimensions you want to divide.

4 Select a method for making the division.

5 Enter numbers and dimensions and click OK.

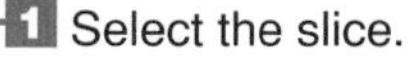
CONTINUED

MODIFY SLICES CONTINUED

Any changes you make to slices causes ImageReady to automatically regenerate the HTML code for that image so that it reflects the changes and redrawing all autoslices.

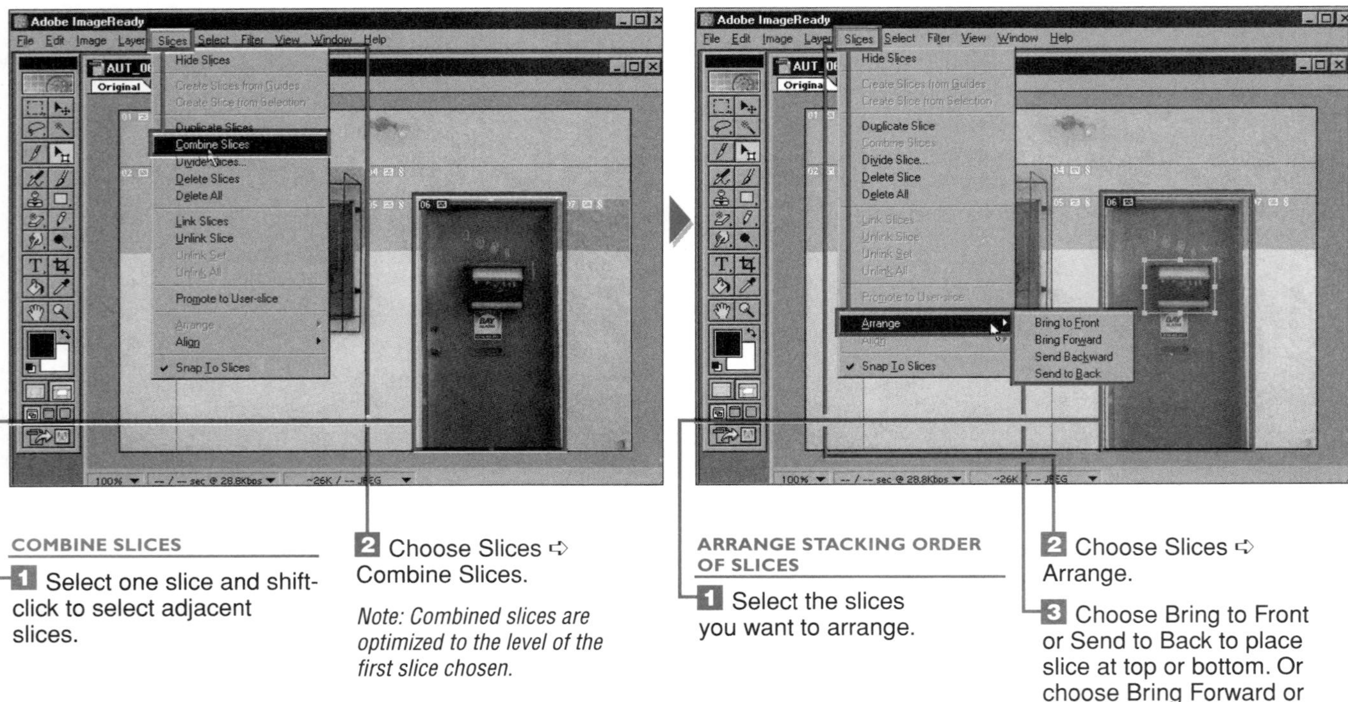

COMBINE SLICES

1 Select one slice and shift-click to select adjacent slices.

2 Choose Slices ➪ Combine Slices.

Note: Combined slices are optimized to the level of the first slice chosen.

ARRANGE STACKING ORDER OF SLICES

1 Select the slices you want to arrange.

2 Choose Slices ➪ Arrange.

3 Choose Bring to Front or Send to Back to place slice at top or bottom. Or choose Bring Forward or Send Backward to move slice one level.

TIPS

How do I delete a slice or slices?

Choose Slices ➪ Delete Slice(s). If you want to delete all slices and don't want to take any changes that you haven't preselected one, just choose Slices ➪ Delete All slices.

What happens if you change the stacking order of overlapping slices?

ImageReady rewrites the HTML to reflect which slices have been subdivided.

How can I tell what the stacking order is?

The last slice created is always the one on top. To put it another way, slices are piled atop one another as they are created.

Is there a way to select all the slices at once?

Choose the Slice Selection tool and drag a rectangle that covers the entire image. You can select any number of slices in this way — just drag to enclose those you want to select.

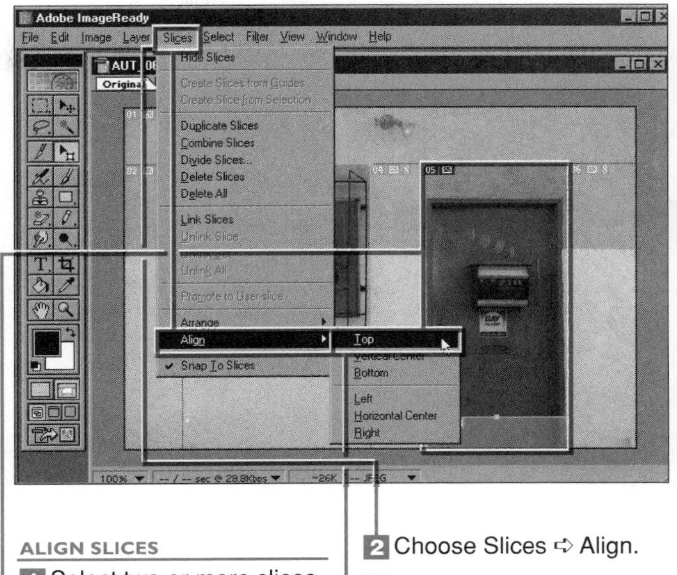

ALIGN SLICES

1. Select two or more slices.
2. Choose Slices ➪ Align.
3. Choose an option.

Note: Aligning slices can eliminate small, unneeded slices to produce a smaller file.

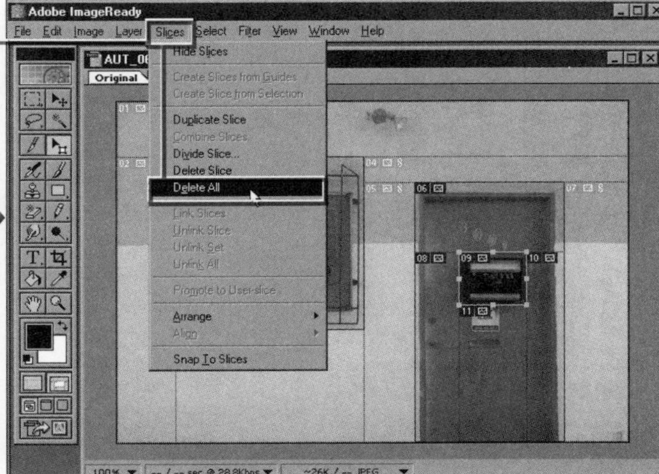

DELETE ALL SLICES

1. Choose Slices ➪ Delete All.

SPECIFY SLICES

ImageReady makes slices to fit within an HTML table that it generates automatically when you create the slices. Because you create the slice from an image, the content from each slice is part of that image. You can change that by specifying a given slice as "No Image."

You can also change the slice type, which is a good thing because only user images can be No Image slices.

Finally, you can change the slice content. For example, you could change a slice to a solid color and enter text in it. Or, you could change it to match the background color of the page, thus saving on upload time.

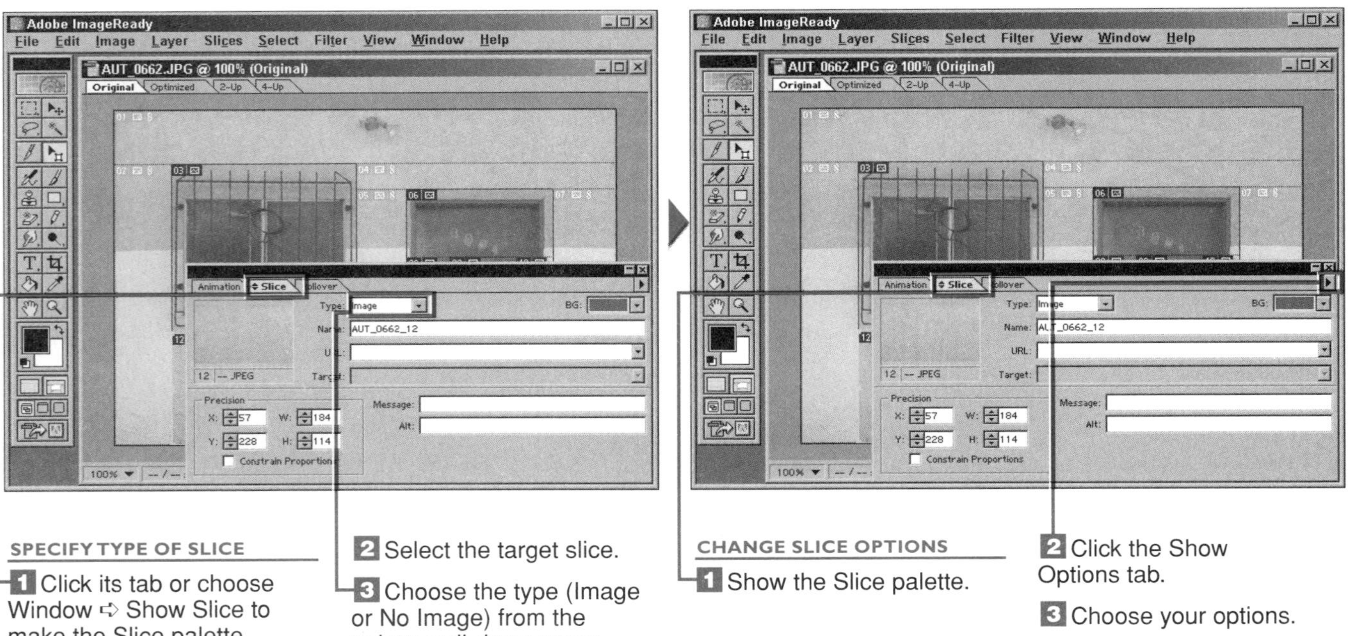

SPECIFY TYPE OF SLICE

1 Click its tab or choose Window ➪ Show Slice to make the Slice palette visible.

2 Select the target slice.

3 Choose the type (Image or No Image) from the palette pull-down menu.

CHANGE SLICE OPTIONS

1 Show the Slice palette.

2 Click the Show Options tab.

3 Choose your options.

TIPS

Can you describe the option choices in more detail?

Choices include Name (enter a name you can use as a target), Background Color (choose from a menu or Web palette), URL (enter one if you want to link the slice), Target (assigns the image to appear in a given frame in the HTML document), Message (this appears in the browser while waiting for the file to load), Alt (lets you assign an alternative image to appear in place of this slice), and Precision (lets you specify a precise X-Y coordinate for the slice within the browser window).

Can you assign a URL to a slice?

Yes, to either user or auto slices. Linked auto slices are automatically converted to user slices.

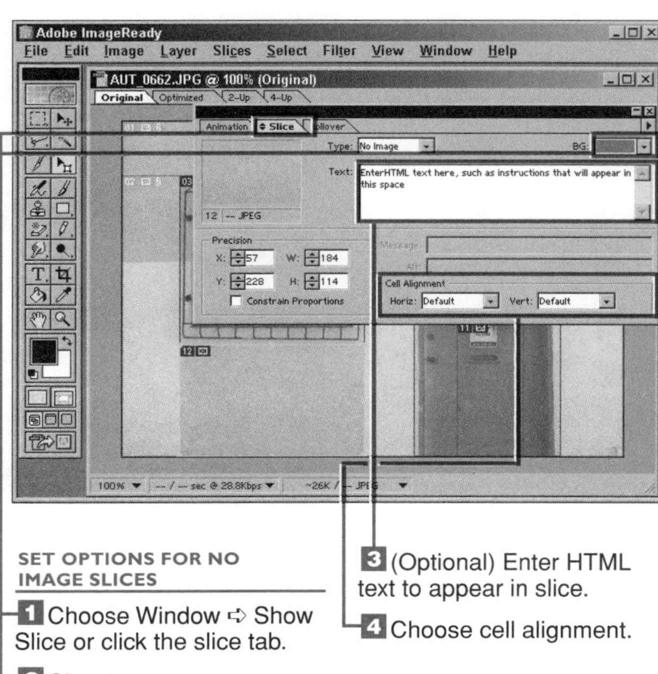

SET OPTIONS FOR NO IMAGE SLICES

1 Choose Window ➪ Show Slice or click the slice tab.

2 Choose a background color.

3 (Optional) Enter HTML text to appear in slice.

4 Choose cell alignment.

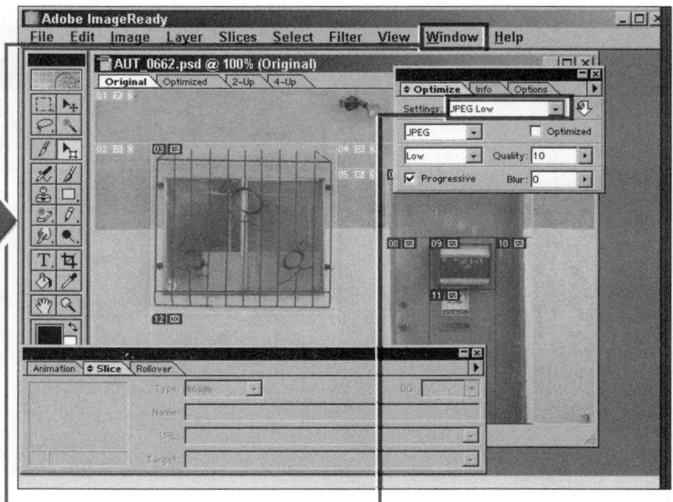

OPTIMIZE SLICES

1 Select one or more slices.

2 Choose Window ➪ Show Optimize.

3 Choose an Optimization Scheme from the Settings menu.

Note: The advantage of optimizing slices individually is that less important areas can tolerate greater image reduction.

ASSIGN ROLLOVERS TO SLICES

Rollovers are effects that can be made to happen when you use the mouse to move over a specific slice of the image. You can create many different effects for rollovers and you can create them for different mouse *states* or *events*.

There are seven mouse states: Normal, Over, Down, Click, Out, None, and Custom. Rollovers can cause several the image in the specified slice to change in some aspect.

To create a rollover, you simply copy the image in that slice to a new layer, change the copied layer in any way you wish, then assign that layer to whatever mouse event you'd like by simply creating an activating that even in the Rollover palette. The exercise here will even make an image appear elsewhere (called a *secondary rollover*) and turn a button into an animation.

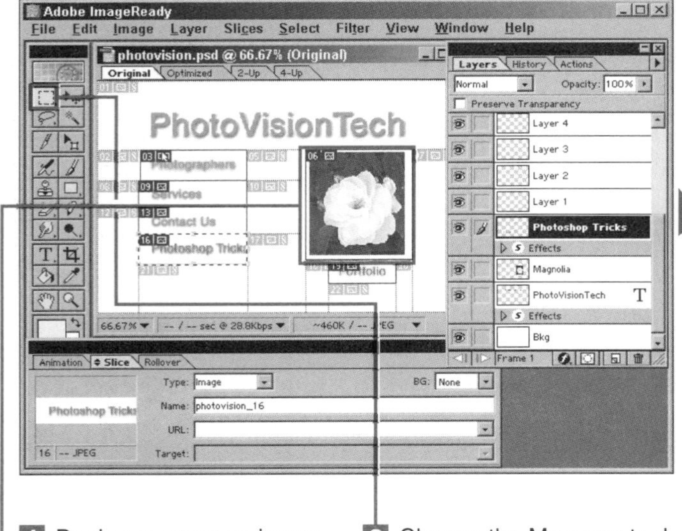

1 Design or open an image that you'd like to place into a Web page.

2 Divide the image into slices.

3 Choose the Marquee tool and drag to select an area of a slice.

4 Press ⌘/Ctrl+C, then ⌘/Ctrl+V to copy the area to as many new layers as you will have mouse events.

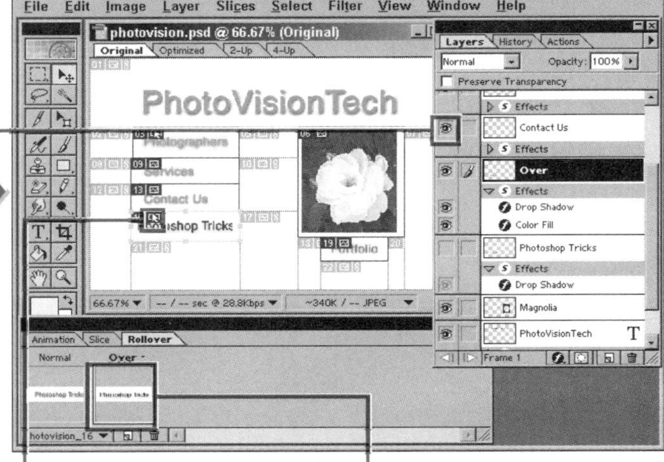

5 Click the New State button to create a new event.

6 Click the eye icons to Turn off all but the layer for the rollover state you want to create.

7 Choose the type of event from the Rollover State menu.

8 Change the selected layer as you want it to appear in the new state.

TIPS

Should I size and optimize images I'm going to import before I import them?

It is best to plan ahead if you're going to import an image onto a layer you're assigning to an event. You can, however, size and optimize it in ImageReady after the fact.

Could an event bring up another menu?

Sure. Just hide everything in the slices where the menu items will appear. Then put the menu on the layer that responds to the Up mouse event. Make the menu an image map and assign a different URL to each menu choice.

Can you suggest some things I might do to change a layer for an event?

Some easy changes include rescaling, distorting, running a filter over the image, breaking the image apart as though it had exploded, and so on.

Do I have to create a new layer for each event?

Depends on what you want to do. Yes, to add new art; no, if you change the layer by executing a layer command, such as a blend mode or changing opacity. Whenever you create a new layer for an event, it's a good idea to rename the layer for the event.

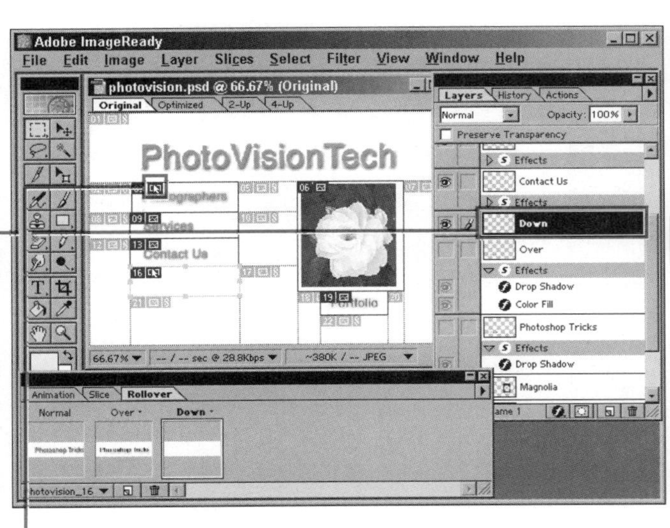

9 Click the New State button to create another state.

10 Select another layer and turn off all the others as before.

11 Delete the image on that layer.

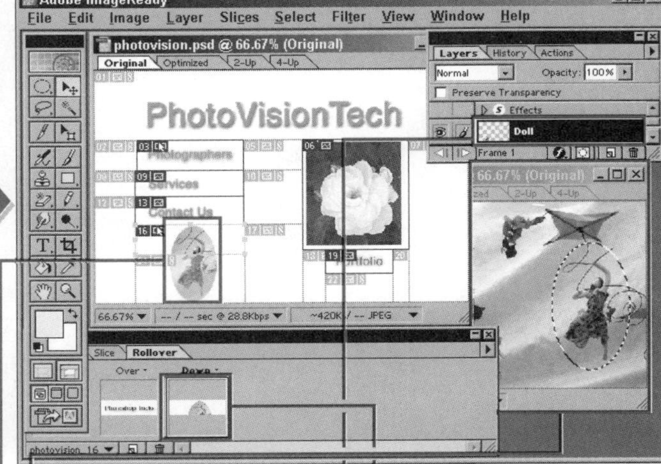

12 One option is to have another image appear in another location: Open another image.

13 Drag it onto the target image in the position where you'd like it to appear.

14 Select the new state.

15 Select and name the layer created when the image was dragged in.

ANIMATE A ROLLOVER STATE

Animating a rollover state involves little more than creating an animation in the Animations palette (or importing one), then substituting the animation for the layer in the rollover state. Of course, it probably won't be clear just how you go about that until you look over the steps below.

You can get very elaborate with this procedure, but remember that the more complex your efforts, the bigger your files are likely to grow.

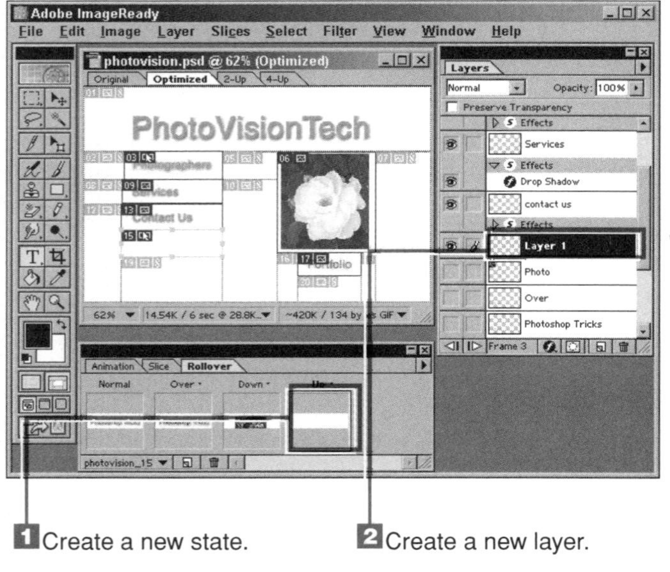

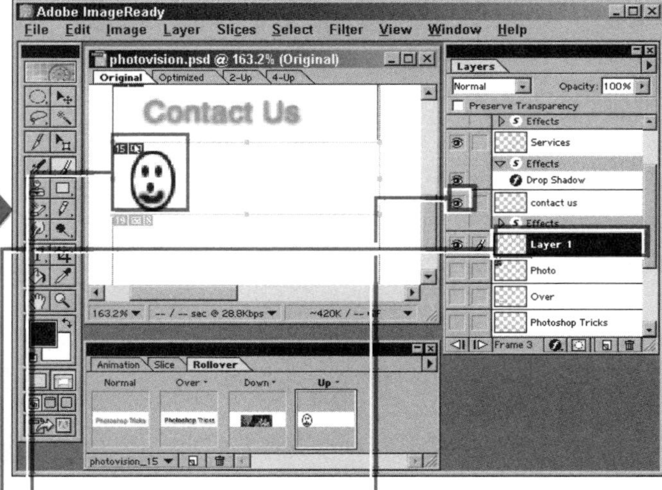

1 Create a new state.

2 Create a new layer.

3 Place content in the layer. Draw, type text, or import a selection from another file.

4 Make sure that the layer stays selected.

5 Turn off layers created for other states that won t be visible in this state.

Note: Be sure you do not turn off layers that contain information that will display in other slices.

How do I prevent something that was moved outside the frame in an animated layer from showing up during the preview?

Create a mask for that layer before saving the file. The layer mask should reveal only the contents of the slice.

Can I import an animation?

You can create your animation in another file using multiple layers. When finished, choose Select All Frames from the Animation Palette menu. Switch to the file you want to place the animation and choose.

Can I include multiple layers in the animation?

Yes. Just as you do with rollover states, but in the Animation palette. Select a frame. Turn off (click the eye icon) the layer that was shown in the previous frame. Turn on a different frame. If you create multiple frames for the animation in a state, make sure only the layer that should be showing in a particular frame is chosen.

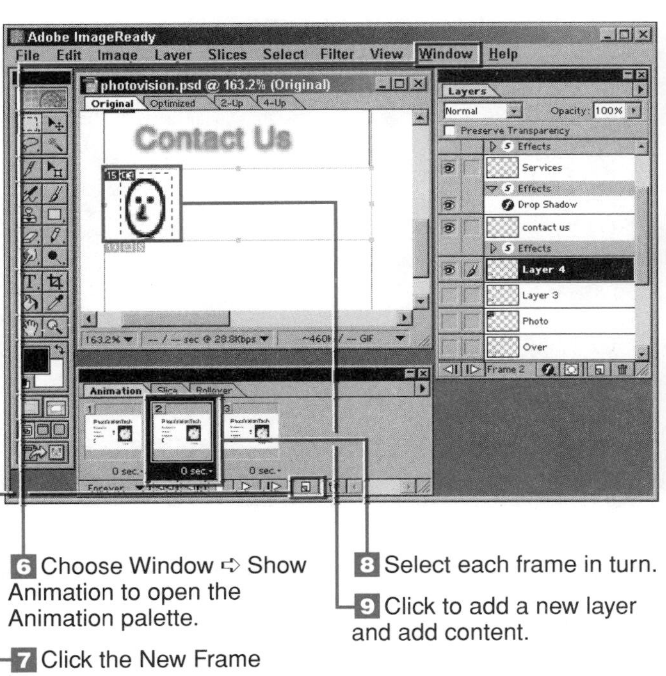

6 Choose Window ⇨ Show Animation to open the Animation palette.

7 Click the New Frame button to create new frame(s).

8 Select each frame in turn.

9 Click to add a new layer and add content.

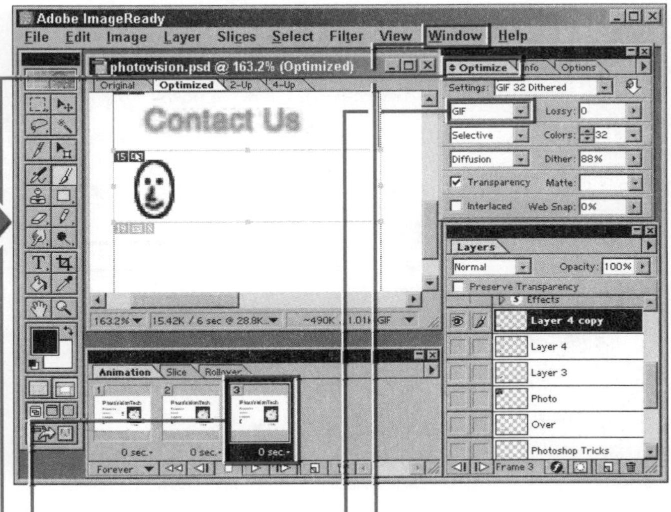

10 Make sure the slice you are animating, the layer, and the rollover state are selected.

11 Click the Optimized tab.

12 Choose Window ⇨ Show Optimized.

13 Choose a GIF optimization format.

CREATE MOTION TWEENS

One of the easiest ways to produce an effective animation is by creating a motion tween. *Tweening* is an animation industry term that refers to the drawing of frames in-between the start and the peak of a movement.

With ImageReady, you draw or photograph the start and stop frames and ImageReady automatically draws the *tweens*. ImageReady is only capable of drawing tweens for two types of changes between *keyframes* (the start and peak frames): motion and opacity.

This exercise will show you how to tween motion. The principle is simple: You create two frames for a layer, move the content of that layer to a different position in each frame, and then have the program draw frames that move the item between the two points.

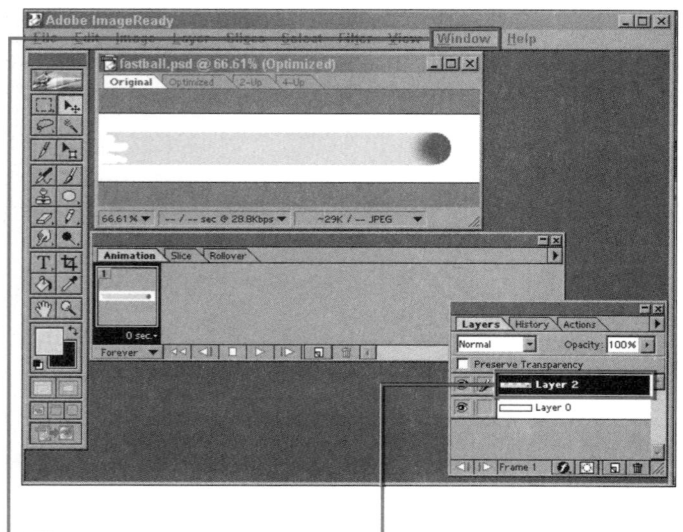

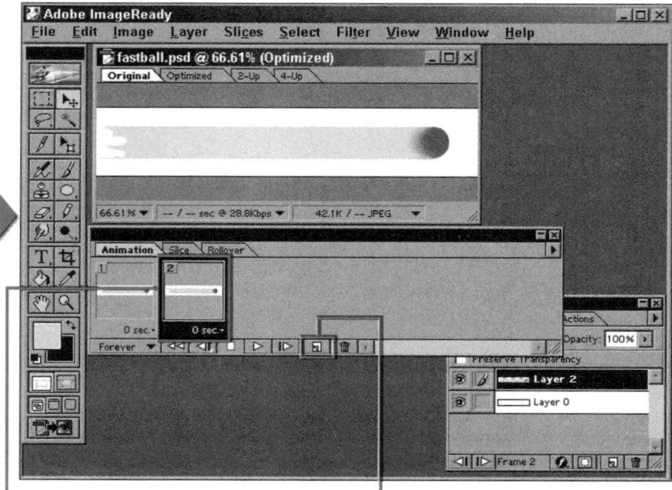

1 Open a GIF image.

2 Choose Window ➪ Show Layers. The Layers Palette appears.

3 Select Layer 2.

4 Choose Window ➪ Show Animation.

5 The Animation Palette appears. The selected layer is shown as one frame in the animation

6 Click the New Frame icon to copy the selected frame.

TIPS

What if I want to do more complex tweens, such as morphs?

There are several third-party animation programs that will do more sophisticated tweening. (Macromedia's Director [bitmap] and Flash programs, are some examples.) You could create the tweens in those programs and then export their animations frame-by-frame, then place the sequence on layers in Photoshop and use ImageReady to animate them.

What about morphing?

There are several Photoshop plug-ins that do morphing. Again, you'll need to do the morphing frame-by-frame, then place each stage on a separate layer.

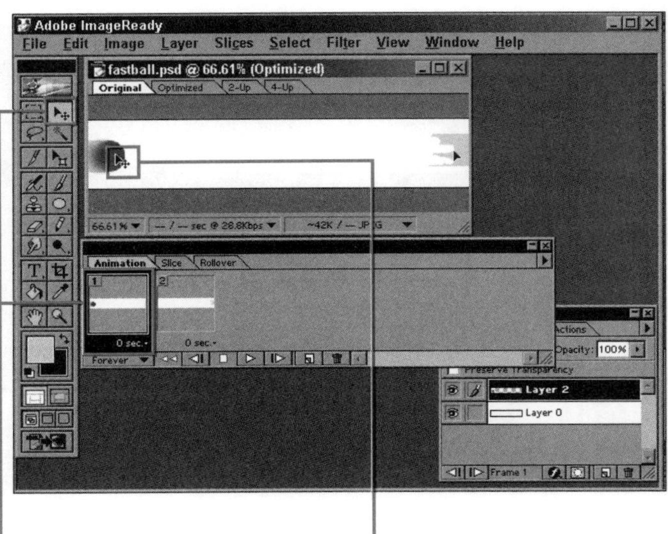

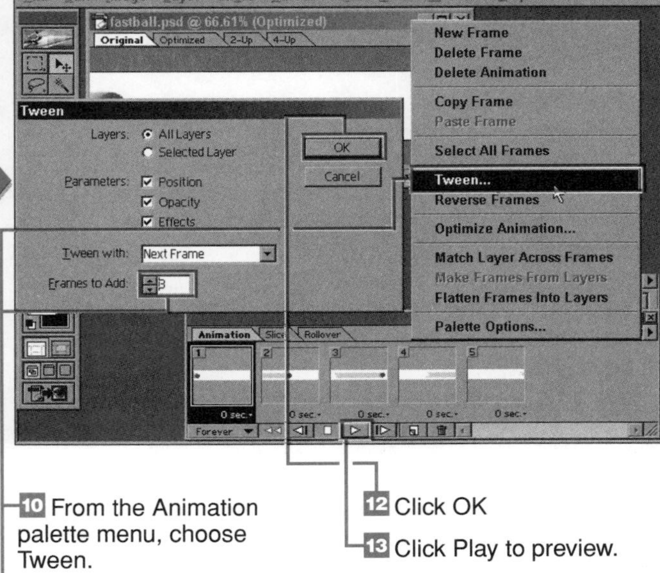

7 Choose the Move tool and drag the layer to its end position.

8 Select the first frame.

9 Choose the Move tool and drag the layer to its start position.

10 From the Animation palette menu, choose Tween.

11 Enter number of in-between frames to create.

12 Click OK

13 Click Play to preview.

TWEEN A CROSS FADE

Because ImageReady's Animation palette can tween opacity, it is very easy to make an image fade to black or fade to white. You just have the tween occur between an image frame and a black or white frame (or any other color frame).

You use almost exactly the same technique to cross-fade from one image to the next. This can give your animation a cinematic look. Be careful, though. You could easily create animations that take several minutes to load. That's a sure way to encourage viewers to leave your Web site. Also, keep the number of frames in the transition between 3 and 5.

If you want to cross-fade between two entirely different scenes, scale two photos to the exact same size and place them in the same folder. Then choose File ➪ Import ➪ Folder as Frames.

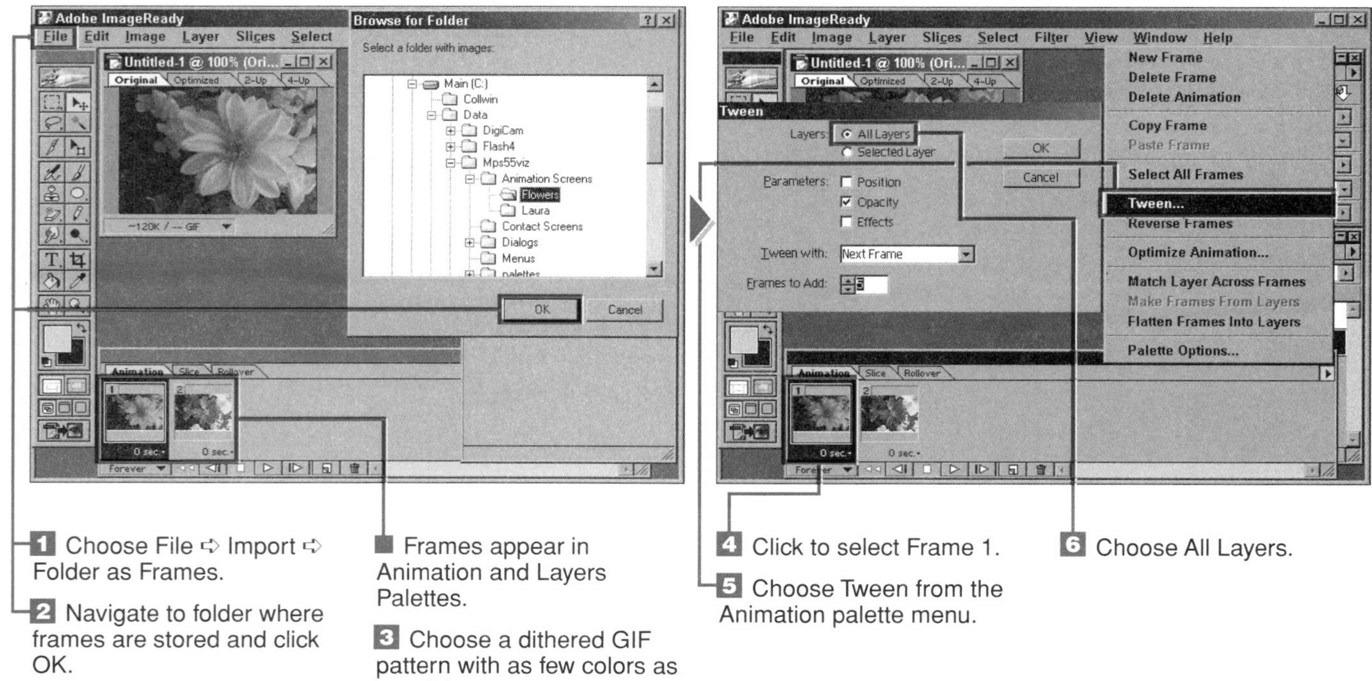

1 Choose File ➪ Import ➪ Folder as Frames.

2 Navigate to folder where frames are stored and click OK.

■ Frames appear in Animation and Layers Palettes.

3 Choose a dithered GIF pattern with as few colors as possible.

4 Click to select Frame 1.

5 Choose Tween from the Animation palette menu.

6 Choose All Layers.

TIPS

Do I need to optimize each frame?

No. If you choose a GIF optimization when you first load the folder into the Animation palette, all of the frames will be optimized to that level. You can also experiment with the other settings in the Optimize palette.

How do I make the first and last frames stay on-screen longer?

Each frame has a delay menu in the lower right corner of its icon. Choose a longer time from that menu.

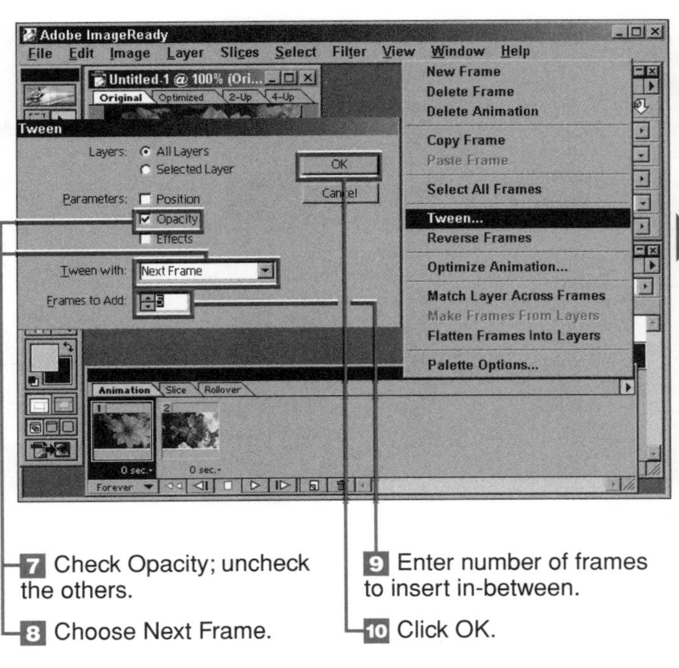

7 Check Opacity; uncheck the others.

8 Choose Next Frame.

9 Enter number of frames to insert in-between.

10 Click OK.

■ The Frames will be inserted and you can see the transition between frames.

11 Click the Play button to preview the animation.

12 Choose File ➪ Preview In ➪ Your Browser to preview the animation in a browser.

23

ANIMATE A SERIES OF PHOTOS

One of the coolest techniques for creating an attention-getting Web animation is to take a series of still photos of a sequence. You could capture a series of stills from videotape frames, shoot with a motorized still camera, use burst mode in a digital camera, or just carefully pose your subject and shoot one frame at a time.

This last technique is especially suitable for time-lapse sequences that show such slow actions as a flower growing or a caterpillar morphing into a butterfly.

Once you have the photos, name the files sequentially (for example, Laura01, Laura02, and so on) and store them in the same folder. It's also a good idea to size them to their final size before storing them.

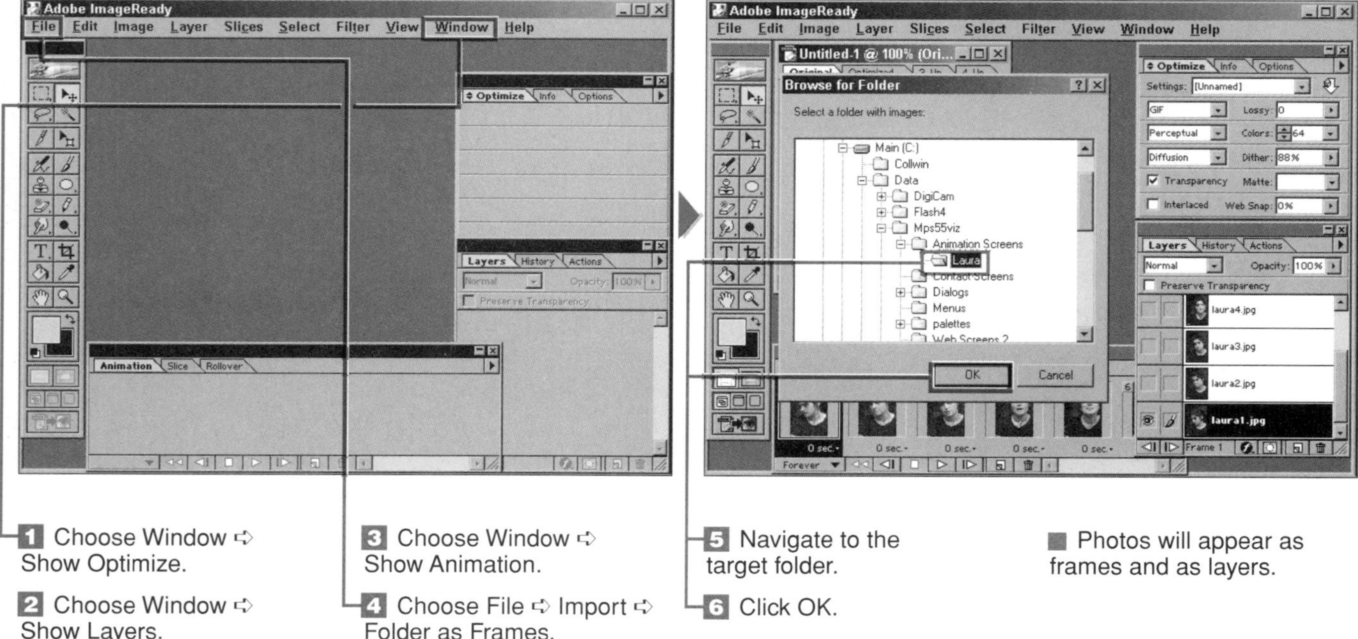

1 Choose Window ➪ Show Optimize.

2 Choose Window ➪ Show Layers.

3 Choose Window ➪ Show Animation.

4 Choose File ➪ Import ➪ Folder as Frames.

5 Navigate to the target folder.

6 Click OK.

■ Photos will appear as frames and as layers.

TIPS

How can I speed up the process of sizing, naming, and storing the files in the same folder?

Choose Window ➪ Show Action and then choose New Action from the Actions palette. Name the Action in the dialog box and then do everything you need to do to resize, sharpen, and save the images. Put a pause in the save command so that you can place the file in the new folder and enter the right name.

What file formats can you import into an animation?

Any file format that Photoshop supports. However, the animations are always animated GIFs, so you must remember to choose a GIF optimization in the Optimize palette before attempting to preview in a browser.

7 Choose a dithered GIF Optimization.

8 Choose Perceptual.

9 Choose Diffusion.

10 Click Play icon to preview the animation.

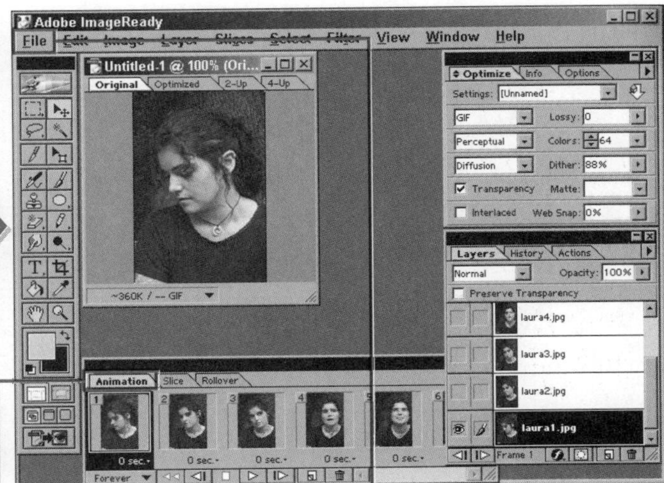

11 Change the sequence of frames by dragging, if needed.

12 Choose Optimize Animation from the Animation palette menu.

13 Choose File ➪ Preview In to preview in your choice of browsers.

14 Choose File ➪ Save As GIF to save the file.

CREATE A SLIDE SHOW

One of the most effective types of animated GIFs is a slide show. A slide show is made in the same way as any other animation, but there's a much longer pause between frames. Also, within a slide show you may want frames to stack on top of one another, or you may want them to appear in different places on your screen.

Slide shows are especially useful if you want to show a series of products or if you need to show larger images in the animation than would be efficient in a full-motion animation.

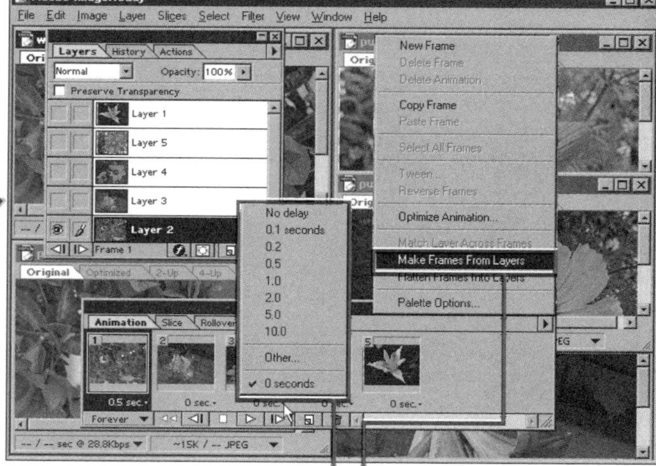

1 Open all the files you want to include in the slide show.

2 Click to select each open window except the first. Press ⌘/Ctrl+A to Select All.

3 Click in the window of the file you want to turn into the animation and press ⌘/Ctrl+V.

■ The copied image is pasted as a new layer in the target window.

4 Repeat until all images are pasted into the same window.

5 Choose Make Frames From Layers from the Animation palette menu.

6 Choose a frame delay for each frame.

TIPS

Why did you enlarge the canvas?

So that there would be room to move the images off-center from one another. The idea is to make the animation look as though the images are randomly dropped on top of one another.

What about saving and optimizing the finished animation?

When you've finished the animation and like the preview, Choose Optimize Animation from the Animation palette menu. Then choose File ⇨ Save Optimized and name and place the file.

7 Choose Image ⇨ Canvas Size.

8 Enter a larger size than the current image.

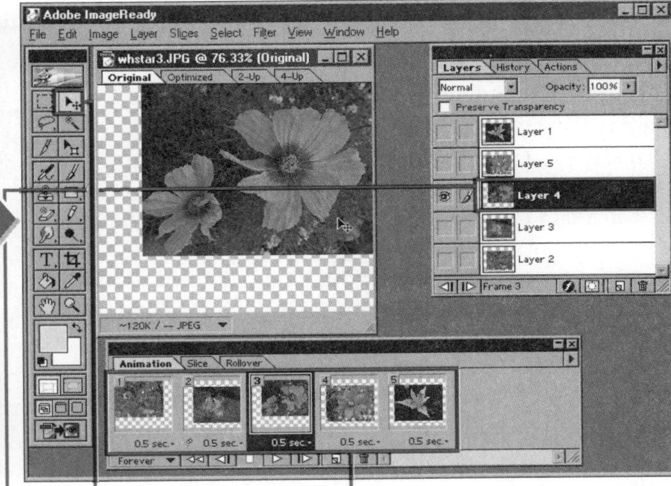

9 Select each frame.

10 Select the corresponding layer.

11 Choose the Move tool and drag each image to a different position.

12 Ctrl/right-click each frame and choose Do not dispose.

APPENDIX A

COLOR MANAGEMENT

Here I discuss the basics of color management and how Photoshop revolutionized the color management process by basing it on a device-independent color model and International Color Consortium (ICC) device profiles. Next, I show you the most direct and frequently needed steps for calibrating your working system: monitor, input devices (such as cameras and scanners), and output devices (such as printers and slide recorders). In the last two sections, I cover considerations and processes for converting legacy files and special-purpose color management workflows.

DEVICE INDEPENDENT COLOR

The exciting news about the changes in Photoshop's color management scheme is that once a system has been calibrated, the files produced by that system can be transported to any other system or device that supports the same open-to-all color management system device profiles.

Until now, most of the processes and devices used to produce color images were device specific. Actually, that's still the case, but now Photoshop and many other applications, devices, and operating systems can reconcile the differences between the way different devices see color through industry-standard color management and standardized device "profiles." The idea is to ensure what you see at one stage of production is consistent with what you see in subsequent stages of production.

This capability has become much more important since the advent of digital imaging, because different stages of production are often accomplished by different people in different places using different hardware — even using different applications and operating systems.

COLOR MANAGEMENT DEFINED

If you're wondering exactly what is meant by the term *color management,* it is a fairly simple concept to grasp. A color management system is simply a means of coordinating (or reconciling) the color properties inherent in the different devices that may be used to create and then reproduce a color digital image. These devices include digital cameras, print and slide scanners, monitors, and printers. Though not obvious choices, possible devices also include the operating system you use, the applications you use, and the plug-ins you use. The purpose of using a color management system is to make the qualities of the final image, such as color balance and contrast, as predictable as possible.

Until recently, virtually every print house had its own, thoroughly tested, internally devised and administered color management system. This was possible because the process of producing the proof and the final print could be localized and tightly controlled.

The color management systems incorporated into Adobe's current products, particularly Photoshop 5 and 5.5, adhere to a single set of standards for managing all the steps in the color production and reproduction process. Adobe has adopted an open set of standards for measuring color called *CIELAB*. The CIELAB standard for measuring color is based on how the human eye perceives color. (The name for this color management system is derived from *Commission Internationale de l'Eclairage,* which translates to International Committee on Illumination.)

Photoshop also uses industry-standard color management models devised and specified by the International Color Consortium. Adobe and several other powerful makers of computerized color systems are members of this group.

The ICC Color Management Model is designed to be a part of the operating system so that all applications will eventually be capable of taking advantage of a common color control system. The ICC Color Management System (CMS) consists of three components:

- The **Reference Color Space**, which is a device-independent color model (also known as a color space).
- **ICC device profiles**, which are sets of data that explain how colors created by their host device are to be interpreted by other devices.
- A **Color Management Module** (CMM) that translates or interprets profiles as they are transferred from one device to another.

The aforementioned CIELAB color model is used by the ICC as its basic color model because its accuracy does not depend on whether the image is seen by transmitted or reflective light. For this reason, it is ideal as a device-independent color model.

In a device-independent CMS, a CMM is used to convert the color gamut of one device (as defined by its ICC profile) so that it can take optimal advantage of the gamut of the target display device. Any given CMS has a default CMM but can also host other predefined CMMs.

How a CMM remaps colors from one device to another depends on rendering intent. *Rendering intent* **is divided into four categories: Perceptual, Saturation, Relative Colorimetric, and Absolute Colorimetric, which are defined as follows:**

- **Perceptual:** Maintains the visual consistency of colors from one device to another. Use this rendering intent when you want to maintain the way the image looks to the human eye. This is the default rendering intent in Photoshop.
- **Saturation:** Maintains the vividness of the original when it's converted to the target color space. Use this rendering intent primarily for business graphics, where photographic realism is less important than the impact of the image on the viewer.
- **Relative Colorimetric:** Maps colors that are out of gamut in the target to the closest possible equivalent. Colors that will stay within gamut when converted to the target device are unmolested. All versions of Photoshop predating Version 5 defaulted to this method of conversion.
- **Absolute Colorimetric:** The overall brightness of the image doesn't change (white and black points are not adjusted). Colors match precisely. It is important to use this rendering intent when pleasing continuous-tone color balance is less important than matching a key color. Matching key colors is especially important when corporate logos or trademarks are part of the image design.

I stated earlier that device-independent color management systems work best at the operating system level. Windows 95 and NT 4.0 do not host a color management system, so you'll have to configure Photoshop (and your other applications) to use either the Kodak KCMS or Agfa's FotoTune.

The MacOS uses Color Sync 2.0 as its CMS, and the Linotyp-Hell CMM is the default Color Management Module. Windows 98 and NT 5 use Microsoft's ICM 2.0, which also uses the Linotype-Hell CMM default.

APPENDIX A

Conventional Color Management Models

Two characteristics of color devices make it difficult to have real device-independent color: 1) The process requires that the color spectrum be constantly compressed along the path that moves from perception to reproduction. 2) Some of the needed devices (film, monitors, projectors) work with transmitted light, whereas any device that reproduces an image on paper must work with reflected light.

The color management models traditionally used for seeing, capturing, and manipulating color images use mixtures of the primary colors for transmitted light — namely red, green, and blue. Thus, the color model most frequently useful for film, cameras, scanners, and monitors is called the RGB model.

Devices that put the RGB images on paper use primary colors that are the polar opposites of red, green, and blue: cyan, magenta, and yellow. These don't produce as many colors as red, green, and blue, and, worse, can't produce a neutral black. So most color models used for printing use the CMYK color model (cyan, magenta, yellow, and black).

Device Profiles

Device profiles, as stated earlier, are needed in any device-independent color management system. Otherwise, there would be no way to automatically manage the way the image recorded by one device (say a camera or scanner) is recorded into another device (for instance, a Photoshop file). Each device in the system needs to have its own device profile. There are three categories of device profiles:

- **Input or Source profiles:** Used by such devices as digital cameras and scanners.
- **Display profiles:** Used by monitors, flat-panel displays, and digital projection systems.
- **Output profiles:** Used by printers, film recorders, and printing plate makers.

A profile can also be embedded into image files. By default, this is done in Photoshop to make files transportable from one application or computer system to another and to ensure the destination system will understand exactly how to interpret that file.

Image file formats that can contain embedded profiles include the following:

- **PSD:** The native Photoshop file format.
- **PDF:** Adobe Acrobat Portable Document Format.
- **TIFF:** Tagged Image File Format. This is the most universally understood file format for true-color, high-resolution image files. However, this format does not support layers.
- **EPS:** Encapsulated PostScript.
- **JPEG:** The most popular format for compressed true-color images and for Web photos.
- **PICT:** A Macintosh format that can contain both vector and bitmapped graphics (technically called a metafile format). Can be read by most modern graphics programs, whether Mac or Windows based, but few Windows programs will save files to this format.

Monitor Calibration

The first and most vital part of establishing a CMS for your own use is to calibrate your monitor. After all, many digital photographers, artists, and designers do all the creative work on their own computer and then send the file elsewhere (for instance, to a publisher, ad agency, or service bureau) for final output. So calibrating your monitor may be the only calibration you need to do.

Calibrating your monitor eliminates color tints and sets a known white point. Monitor calibration is also important because your monitor is the place where you view the image as it is created. If the ICC profile for the device that will output the final image (or proof) is accurate, then what you see on the monitor will also be what you get from that device.

The bad news is that your monitor and display card don't display color consistently. Monitor *phosphors*, the coating on the video tube that lights up when struck by scanning beams, fade over time (as a rule of thumb, plan on buying a new monitor every three to five years). Dust and dirt may coat the face of the tube. Most important, the intensity and quality of the room light at any time of the day influences your perception of on-screen color.

The good news is that it's easy to calibrate your monitor to a degree acceptable to most users. If you're a person who makes color separations for printing or have other critical work to do, you should invest in automatic color calibration systems and monitors from such manufacturers as Barco, Radius, and X-Rite. If your budget doesn't allow that option, consider using third-party software-only calibration. Currently, two such systems can work with either Mac OS or Windows: Pantone Personal Color Calibrator and Sonnetech Colorific. (You will find a trial version of the Pantone Personal Color Calibrator on the CD-ROM that accompanies this book. There's also a short preview of how to use the Personal Color Calibrator later in this chapter.)

Using the Adobe Gamma Control Panel

The Adobe Gamma Control Panel isn't an internal part of Photoshop. However, you can find it on the Photoshop CD-ROM. The following text describes the preparatory steps you should take before actually using Adobe Gamma. After that, two additional step-by-step procedures are presented: one for using the Adobe Gamma Wizard or Assistant, the other a more advanced procedure for making settings in Adobe Gamma.

Getting Ready Turn on your monitor and leave it on for at least a half-hour before beginning the calibration process. You should also make sure your monitor has been on for the same period of time before doing any color-critical Photoshop work.

Clean the screen of your monitor.

Position lights and the face of the monitor so that no glare shows on the screen.

Set the room lighting to as soft and as low a level as possible, consistent with your other work requirements. It's best if the room is nearly dark, but that's not practical for most working situations. You probably want enough room light to read by.

Try to set the room lighting so that it will be nearly the same at all hours of the day. Otherwise, you may have to make different calibrations that adjust for the lighting at different times of the day.

Press the degauss button on your monitor (if it has one).

Set your monitor's color temperature control at either 5000 or 6500. If you ever change the color temperature, recalibrate.

Using the Adobe Gamma Wizard (Windows) or Assistant (Mac OS) Open the Adobe Gamma Control Panel. On the Mac, this control panel is located in the Systems folder under Control Panels. In Windows, from the Start menu choose Settings ⇨ Control Panel. The Control Panel window opens. Double-click the Adobe Gamma icon. Click the Wizard button (the Assistant button on the Mac).

The Adobe Gamma Wizard/Assistant dialog box opens. If you have created more than one monitor profile, you can use the Load button to locate a file that is appropriate for your current monitor (some folks use more than one) or lighting conditions. First-time calibrators should click the Next button.

The Adobe Gamma Wizard dialog box appears. Crank your contrast control to its highest setting.

Turn your brightness control down until the inside box is nearly black but the border remains pure white. If the frame goes slightly gray, you've turned brightness down a bit too much. When you're satisfied that you've got this right, click Next.

Choose the correct settings for your monitor from the Phosphors pull-down menu. (You need to check your monitor's documentation for its phosphor type code.) If you don't see your monitor's code on the list (or can't find one), choose Custom, and then click Next.

You now have a choice of setting midtone gamma by a single-tone grayscale setting or for each individual primary color. The simplest method is to leave the View Single Gamma Only option checked. Squint to blur the horizontal lines in the box, and drag the slider until the shade of the center box matches the shade of the lines. Or, uncheck the View Single Gamma box. You now see three boxes, one for each primary color. Squint and drag the slider for each box until you can't distinguished between the box in the center and its ruled frame. When all three boxes are adjusted properly, click Next.

You are next asked to input the white point of your monitor. You can choose from one of several preset Kelvin temperatures (5000, 5500, 6500, 7500, or 9300 degrees) or enter a Custom temperature (as provided by the manufacturer of your monitor or a monitor testing organization). Better yet, use a colorimeter or spectrophotometer. Or, click the Measure button.

The next screen instructs you to eliminate all ambient light. In other words, make sure it's dark outside, turn off all the room lights, and then click OK.

The screen blanks, and a row of three gray squares appears. Click to choose the most neutral of the three. If you choose either of the outside squares, it becomes the center square. Keep this up until the color of the center square is absolutely neutral, and then click the center square or press Return/Enter to confirm your final choice. You are be returned to the previous screen. Click Next.

Enter a name for your monitor settings in the File Name box or accept the default of Adobe Monitor Settings_copy.icm. Click Finish.

That's all there is to it. You should repeat this process every few months so that you compensate for changes in your monitor's phosphors. You should also repeat this process for each significantly different set of lighting circumstances. For instance, if you work both days and evenings, you may have a great deal of daylight during the day and dimmer light at night. So you should calibrate your monitor for both, and save the settings to different filenames. You can then quickly recalibrate for each set of conditions by opening the Adobe Gamma Control Panel, running the Wizard/Assistant, and loading the appropriate ICC monitor profile.

If you need a more accurate calibration of your monitor, but still aren't ready to invest in an automatic hardware calibration system, you can try two other more accurate software-only methods: Use Adobe Gamma to manually custom calibrate your monitor, or use a third-party software calibrator such as the Pantone Personal Color Calibrator or Sonnetech Colorific. (As the Pantone product was licensed from the Sonnetech product, you won't find a big difference in the two.)

Using Adobe Gamma sans Wizard If you choose the manual route for using Adobe Gamma, you won't gain anything in accuracy, but you may save time if you have a set of custom phosphor settings you want to enter directly or simply want to adjust the gamma for different lighting conditions.

Manual adjustments made through the Adobe Gamma Control Panel are exactly the same as those you make using the Wizard/Assistant, except that you access the controls directly by clicking the appropriate item in the control panel.

To adjust brightness and contrast, use the hardware adjustment on your monitor to turn contrast up to the brightest level. The dark strip at the top of the Brightness and Contrast box displays alternating black and gray squares.

Adjust the monitor's brightness control until you see as little difference as possible between the shade of the alternating squares without dimming the brightness of the white strip below.

Next, choose the appropriate Phosphors setting. If you know that your phosphors conform to one of the standards on the list (because the monitor documentation indicates this is so or because the monitor has a Trinitron tube), choose the name from the pull-down menu. Or, enter a custom phosphor specification provided by a colorimeter or spectrophotometer after choosing Custom from the Phosphors pull-down menu.

To make a quick, overall gamma adjustment, leave the View Single Gamma box checked. Squint until the horizontal lines in the border of the gamma square blend. While still squinting, drag the slider until the center square's tone matches the border's tone.

To set the monitor's white point, choose Custom from the White Point pull-down menu, and then enter the *x* and *y* values specified by your measuring instrument or from the manufacturer's specifications. Or, to choose a predefined white point, pull down the White Point menu and make your choice. To choose a white point from your monitor settings, click the Measure button. Click the squares on the ends of the row that appears until the square in the center is a neutral gray, and then click the center square.

When you click the center square, you are returned to the Control Panel window. Simply close the control panel. Your settings have been recorded.

Using Pantone or Colorific Software-Only Calibration

Sonnetech of San Francisco, California, makes a software-only color calibration system that works on computers that use either the Mac OS or Windows (3.1 and over).

They have licensed this software to many hardware and software manufacturers, so you may already have a copy. Check the software that came with your scanner or digital camera. One of the software manufacturers to whom Sonnetech has licensed their calibration software is Pantone. Pantone sells the product as the Pantone Personal Color Calibrator (P^2C^2) in separate versions for Windows and Macintosh. Sonnetech sells their software as Colorific on a CD-ROM that contains versions for both MacOS and Windows 95/98/NT. If you are still using Windows 3.1 (a bad idea for Photoshop users), you will need to special order the Windows 3.1 version. Both the Pantone and Sonnetech versions of this product retail for less than $60 at the time of this writing.

These systems do a much more accurate job of calibrating your printer/monitor than the Adobe Gamma Control Panel does, as you may gather from the steps that follow.

The interface screens for P^2C^2 and Colorific differ slightly, as do the interfaces for Mac and Windows. Furthermore, this book isn't intended as a substitute for the manual for any third-party products. The example shown in the following text demonstrates the Windows 95 version of the interface and leaves out some of the optional steps for the sake of brevity. In other words, this serves only as a preview of options that are available to you outside Photoshop. In instances where significant differences exist between the operating systems, I point them out to you. Otherwise, the steps are so similar that you will be able to easily sort out the difference from the cues you are given on screen. (You can find demo versions of both products on the CD-ROM that accompanies this book, if you want to explore further.)

Calibrating with Colorific To begin the calibration process, place the Colorific CD-ROM in your CD-ROM drive. If you are running Windows, the CD-ROM begins playing automatically, and you are interactively led through the installation process. If you're on the Mac, run the installation program according to the instructions in the operating manual.

Once the program is properly installed, open the Colorific Control Panel: Do this in Windows by opening the Colorific program group folder and clicking the Colorific Control Panel icon. Mac users need to open the Colorific folder and then click the Colorific icon.

The Colorific Control Panel opens. Click the Recalibrate button to open the monitor/printer setup screen.

From the pull-down menu, choose the make and model of your monitor. Your monitor may be too old or too new to be included on this list, in which case you should contact the manufacturer for exact color temperature specifications. If you have a new monitor, you may find its specifications on the Colorific site at `www.colorific.com` under Tech Support. Once you have chosen a monitor, the brightness adjustment screen appears.

Turn the contrast control on your monitor to its highest (brightest) setting, and then adjust brightness so that the blacks are as black as possible without dimming the whites. When finished, click Continue.

The first in a series of monitor gamma measurement screens appears next. This screen works in much the same way as the Adobe Gamma control, except that it's easier to pick the right measurement. Instead of making adjustments, click the square that comes closest to matching its surroundings. Colorific makes you repeat this process several times for each primary color so that you end up with the best possible adjustment. In between each gamma adjustment, you make black point adjustments when the black point adjustment screen appears.

To make a black point adjustment, choose the first square that shows enough color to separate it from the background. You will be asked to do this several times (twice for each color), alternating with the gamma adjustment screens. When you are done, the light source type screen appears.

You start to set your monitor's white point by choosing the type of room lighting (for example, incandescent, halogen, or daylight) that you are currently using from the menu. Once you've made the choice, the white point measurement screen appears.

You are prompted to raise the level of room lighting to as bright as possible. In other words, turn on all the lights.

Place the plastic Color Reference card on your monitor. This isn't really a card but a piece of soft vinyl with small squares cut out of it. Static electricity will hold it in place on the face of the monitor tube. Turn down the contrast control until the color of the card is the same color as the surrounding background. Be sure to leave the card on the tube when you click OK.

Click to choose the square that most closely matches the color of both the card and the background. Be sure you match color, not brightness. Colorific then automatically creates a profile for your monitor and printer. If your default printer doesn't have an ICC profile set for it, you are asked to set one. You may need to refer to your system documentation to be able to do so correctly.

To accept the settings, Windows users need to restart their systems at this point. Mac users only need to click OK.

Input Device Calibration

The next logical step is to calibrate the devices that digitize existing images for subsequent use by Photoshop. (However, this varies depending on the device, as further discussed in the following text.)

Digital Cameras

Much of the software that comes with late-model digital cameras automatically creates an ICC color profile, which is embedded in the image as it is downloaded. If this is not the case for your camera, you can still make adjustments in Photoshop that will print as they look — assuming you've calibrated your monitor.

Scanners

Most scanning is done with a flatbed scanner. You need to check the documentation of your scanner and its bundled software to look for ways to calibrate your scanner. Models of scanners and types of scanner calibration software are too numerous to document effectively here. However, here are some hints that should help you in calibrating your scanner:

- Make sure you have calibrated your monitor for your printer, as described previously.
- Open a file that contains a full range of primary colors, flesh tones, and an intermediate gray, and print it. You can find a file, called Olé No Moiré, that is ideal for this purpose on your Photoshop CD-ROM in the Other Goodies/Calibration folder.
- Print the file on your color printer using high gloss photo paper.
- Place the print on your scanner's flatbed and start the scanner software. Adjust the preview so that it matches the printed image as closely as possible.
- Scan the image. If necessary, open it in Photoshop.
- Convert from Profile to Profile, if possible. To do this, choose Image ➪ Mode ➪ Profile to Profile. From the From pull-down menu, choose the model of your scanner. Choose RGB from the To pull-down menu (unless you have a special reason for wanting to work in another color model). Choose Perceptual from the Intent pull-down menu. (If your scanner isn't on the menu, either try to get an ICC profile from its manufacturer's Web site, or skip this step if an ICC profile isn't available.)
- Open the original file alongside the converted file in another window. If the scan isn't a close match, go back to the scanner software and make further adjustments until you get as close a match as possible. Note the settings in a place where you can find them easily in case you have to temporarily change the settings for a special-case scan. Also, some scanner software resets itself to the default settings each time it is restarted.

Of course, you can use Photoshop to change the appearance of a scanned image if you don't like the original scan. However, if you want to ensure that you get as rich a range of tonal detail as possible in the finished output, you want to capture as much of the image's detail as possible during input.

It's also a good idea to set Photoshop to 16-bit-per-channel mode before scanning. You will then be able to capture all the color depth that your scanner is capable of producing (unless the scanner software reduces the image to 24-bit color automatically on import). Most of today's scanners capture 30- or 36-bit color, rather than the standard 24-bit color. Later, when you are sure that you have adjusted the image to your satisfaction, you can safely reduce it to 24-bit color (to keep file size to a minimum and to have access to all the Photoshop commands).

If you use a slide scanner, a high-end professional flatbed scanner, or a drum scanner, you need to closely follow the instructions that come with that device. Most of the time, you will be able to work with such devices by doing an ICC profile-to-profile conversion (see the sixth step in the preceding bulleted list).

APPENDIX A

Converting Legacy Files to Photoshop

Photoshop has to interpret several types of files when it loads them for the first time. This includes files created in earlier versions of Photoshop (*legacy* files), files from sources that are ignorant of Photoshop's requirements, and files that you have reason to want to convert from one ICC profile to another.

Converting Files from Earlier Versions of Photoshop

Files created in earlier versions of Photoshop do not have embedded ICC profiles. Photoshop, by default, converts such files to your chosen color space and simultaneously embeds the appropriate profile. Photoshop needs to do this only the first time it opens the legacy file. When you save the file, the profile is automatically included so that this conversion need never take place again.

Importing Files Without Affecting Them You can change settings in Photoshop so that it will open files without converting them or embedding a profile. Remember, however, that when you do this you are no longer working with device-independent color. To import a file without affecting the original color space, choose File ➪ Color Settings ➪ RGB Setup. The RGB Setup dialog box appears.

From the RGB pull-down menu, choose Monitor RGB. Uncheck the Display Using Monitor Compensation check box. From the menu bar, choose File ➪ Color Settings ➪ Profile Setup. The Profile Setup dialog box appears.

From the RGB pop-up menu, choose Apple RGB (even if you're working in Windows). The exception here is if the file was created on a Mac using ColorSync in the earlier version of Photoshop. In that case, choose your system profile.

Converting Files from Photoshop–Ignorant Sources

When you open a file from a Photoshop-ignorant source (for example, the file was created and manipulated in an image-editing program made by another manufacturer, or came from external scanner software that creates no ICC profile), you can simply open the file using the default settings and let Photoshop automatically convert it.

Performing Profile-to-Profile Conversions

There many be times when you want to convert files from one profile to another. Photoshop makes this a piece of cake.

From the menu bar, choose Image ➪ Mode ➪ Profile to Profile. The Profile to Profile dialog box appears.

Choose the profile for the current image from the From pull-down menu; the destination profile from the To pull-down menu; and the desired intent from the Intent menu (Perceptual is the intent type used most often). Click OK.

Importing from a Variety of Sources

You can set up Photoshop so that when a file opens, you are asked how you want the file to be converted. You will then be in a position to cover all of the preceding situations as they arise. This is the best course for service bureaus and other businesses that must accept input from an unpredictable variety of sources. To set up Photoshop to ask how to convert files when opening, from the menu bar choose File ➪ Color Settings ➪ Profile Setup. The Profile Setup dialog box opens.

From the RGB pull-down menu in the Assumed Profiles section, choose Ask When Opening. Also choose Ask When Opening from the CMYK and Grayscale pull-down menus. Leave all the other settings at their defaults, and click OK.

WHAT'S ON THE CD-ROM

On the CD-ROM found in the back of this book you will find limited-use or limited-capability demonstration versions of third-party software for Photoshop. These items, along with information about the companies that created them, are listed here.

ADOBE SYSTEMS, INC.

345 Park Avenue
San Jose, CA 95110
Phone: 408-536-6000
Fax: 408-537-6000

Photoshop 5.5

(Macintosh and Windows) Don't yet have a copy of Photoshop 5.5? Try out the demo version on the CD-ROM. Create, retouch, and enhance images with Adobe Photoshop, the de facto standard photo design and production tool for Macintosh and Windows.

ALIEN SKIN

1100 Wake Forest Rd., Suite 101
Raleigh, NC 27604
Toll Free: 888-921-7546
Phone: 919-832-4124
Fax: 919-832-4065

Alien Skin's filters are remarkable for their attractive and easy-to-use interface, which features extra-large previews and game-like design.

Eye Candy 3.0.1

(Macintosh and Windows) The Eye Candy filters are Photoshop 5-compatible and fully scriptable with Photoshop 5 actions. These filters include the following: Antimatter, Carve, Chrome, Cutout, Drop Shadow, Fire, Fur, Glass, Glow, HSB Noise, Inner Bevel, Outer Bevel, Perspective Shadow, Smoke, Squint, Star, Swirl, Water Drops, Weave.

AUTO F/X CORPORATION

Main Street
Alton, NH 03809
Phone: 603-875-4400
Fax: 603-875-4404

Most of the Auto/FX applications (especially those that create edge effects) come in a variety of volumes, with each volume priced separately.

Photo/Graphic Edges 4.0

(Macintosh and Windows) This is the classic Auto F/X filter set, recently echoed by Extensis. The new version has a much larger selection of edge styles and is markedly quicker. Unlike any previous versions or imitators, it also does bevels, glows, shadows, carves, distortions, grains, sepia tones, lighting, matte textures, and colors. Another great feature is that these filters finally come in a box that you can put on the shelves alongside your other software.

Page/Edges 3.0

(Macintosh and Windows) This software works with any application compatible with Photoshop plug-ins to place the selected edge effect around the entire page (rather than the current selection, as in Photo/Graphic Edges). You can control border width, scale, softness, opacity, texture, color, lighting direction, and drop shadows. An unlimited number of effects are compatible with the program.

Photo/Graphic Patterns

(Macintosh and Windows) This plug-in actually creates surface textures that make the image look as though it has been projected onto natural materials such as wood, stressed metal, or concrete. There are over 1,000 textures, both full-sized and seamless tiles. You can also incorporate any textures you create in Photoshop or that come with another program. The interface allows control over a wide range of properties for each surface type: hue, scale, softness, opacity, highlight intensity, shadow intensity, highlight and shadow color, and lighting direction.

Universal Animator

(Macintosh and Windows) This software works inside virtually any popular program, from Adobe Illustrator to Photoshop to Word. Automatically generates an animation frame from the contents of any working application window. Animations are automatically compressing into highly efficient GIFs that can be played directly on the Web or used as templates for vector animations in Macromedia Flash. Built-in palettes include a Web-safe 216 palette, a Web-adaptive palette, and an image-adaptive palette. You can have as many as four global and four local transparency regions. Features anti-alias fringe controls, displays accurate download times and frame statistics, has full interframe delay and looping controls, and features 1:1 and simulated download previews. Universal Animator even enables you to have independent frame sizing and delay (pause as long as you want on any frame).

WebVise Totality

(Macintosh and Windows) WebVise Totality works as either a plug-in or stand-alone application. The package can perform batch processing of images. It includes ultra-high GIF and JPEG compression engines; an animation module for creating animations inside Photoshop; digital watermarking; a Web-safe color converter that enables you to dither any color from any Photoshop palette into a Web-safe color; and a dithering engine that's capable of reproducing any color accurately on the Web.

Ultimate Texture Collection

(Macintosh and Windows) This collection features three volumes of 1,000 textures each: Paper and Fabrics, Stone and Metal, and Art and Organics.

Digital Dominion

1910 Byrd Avenue, Suite 204
Richmond, VA 23230
Phone: 804-282-5868
Fax: 804-282-3768

Cinematte

(Windows) Cinematte is handy for blue or green screen compositing. This excellent plug-in enables you to do highly automatic masking of objects shot or modeled in front of solid blue or green backgrounds. Automatically masks translucent, transparent, or hairy objects. Works with homemade blue and screens made from standard paints or fabrics. Also provides for automatic color spill removal.

Extensis Corporation

1800 SW First Avenue, Suite 500
Portland, OR 97201
E-mail: info@extensis.com
Toll-Free: 800-796-9798
Phone: 503-274-2020
Fax: 503-274-0530

Portfolio 4.0

(Macintosh and Windows) Extensis Portfolio 4.0 enables the individual, workgroups, and corporations to share, repurpose, and distribute digital assets to team members, partners, and customers anywhere.

Mask Pro 2.0

(Macintosh and Windows) Mask Pro 2.0 is a great time-saving tool. Use it to dramatically reduce the time necessary for masking and selecting complex objects in Adobe Photoshop.

Intellihance 4.0

(Macintosh and Windows) Intellihance is a great tool for enhancing images from any source, including digital cameras, flatbed and drum scanners, and original digital artwork. Streamline image enhancement and color correction with this tool.

PhotoTools 3.0

(Macintosh and Windows) Extensis PhotoTools 3.0 is a versatile collection of real-world special effects tools for print, multimedia, and Web design. It also includes 3 components — PhotoTexture, PhotoAnimator, and PhotoGroove — that ease such common Photoshop tasks as creating seamless tile textures, complex GIF animations, and custom bevels.

PhotoFrame 1.0

(Macintosh and Windows) PhotoFrame enables you to create customized edge effects. Go beyond the ordinary with special effects like shadows, glows, textures, and bevels.

Flaming Pear Software

Phone: 510-601-5244

BladePro

(Macintosh and Windows) This software creates a wide variety of beveled edges and textures that are especially useful with clipart and type. Features an incredible number of textures, all of which can be given virtually endless variations. You can also control the radius, height, texture, color, gloss, glare, reflection, glassiness, causticity, iridescence, tarnish, angle, color, and brightness of the light. Finally, you can adjust the shape of the edge bevel. You can even import a PICT file to use as a background texture. The fully working copy found on the CD-ROM is shareware.

GAMUT IMAGING

44 Yorba Linda Boulevard, Suite G-500
Yorba Linda, CA 92887
Toll Free: 888-426-8844
Phone: 714-779-2421

Image Book 2.5

(Macintosh and Windows) Here's a portfolio-type image manager. Catalogs folders with thumbnail images. You can annotate the images with keywords and file information, and then print the whole thing as a contact sheet or even a CD-ROM cover. Software automatically recognizes over 40 bitmap image formats.

IMAGEXPRESS

3545 Cruse Road, Suite 103
Lawrenceville, GA 30044
Phone: 770-564-9924

ScanPrepPro 3.5.2, Alius v.1.0.1, Deep-Bit Filters v.1.0

(Macintosh) ScanPrepPro is a highly professional application for correcting color and tonal values in scans and for applying prepress corrections such as screen frequency and dot gain. Prepress experts can further fine-tune under-color removal, prepare for stochastic screening, and set unsharp masking. Custom adjustments can be saved for retrieval later.

INTENSE SOFTWARE

3495 Cambie Street #310
Vancouver, BC Canada V5Z 4R3
E-mail: intense@pro.net
Toll-Free: 888-251-3586
Phone: 604-244-3501
Fax: 604-267-1125

PowerTone

(Macintosh and Windows) This plug-in generates duotones that can be printed with two inks but look like full-color images. Good trick for saving a lot of money on your next printing job.

SilverTone

(Macintosh) Here's a plug-in for producing metallic-color separations. You can add channels for special spot colors, such as metallic inks.

MICROFRONTIER, INC.

PO Box 71190
Des Moines, IA 50325
Phone: 515-225-9800
Fax: 515-996-9022

Digital Darkroom

(Macintosh and Windows) Digital Darkroom is an introductory image-editing program. With it you can create your own images, improve existing images, apply 3D effects, and generate Web graphics.

RAYFLECT SA

9, rue Duphot 75001
Paris, France

Four Seasons VI

(Macintosh and Windows) Here's a filter plug-in that creates the effects of natural elements and atmospheres. Comes with 150 prebuilt skies. Wonderful for creating interesting skies in photos shot on gray days. Also useful for creating haze, fog, and rainbows.

Site Jazz Corporation

11835 Roe. Suite 140
Leawood, KS 66211
Phone: 913-491-1305
URL: www.sitejazz.com

SmartGIF 1.0.2

(Macintosh) SmartGIF distinguishes itself from other plug-ins that create optimized GIFs in two significant ways: 1) You can cut up an image into separate GIFs that will appear as one. This can make large images appear to load faster, and makes it possible to assign a different link to each section of the image. 2) You don't have to flatten the image before you export it as a GIF.

Vertigo Technology, Inc.

1255 W. Pender Street
Vancouver, B.C., Canada V6E 2V1
Phone: 604-684-2113
Fax: 604-684-2108

Vertigo 3D Dizzy

(Macintosh) This plug-in filter enables you to import surface-mapped 3D objects within Photoshop. Can import any model created in the 3DMF format and comes with over 400 models. You can control lighting, viewing angle, size, surface texture, orientation, and location within the frame.

How to Install the Programs on the CD-ROM

The CD-ROM accompanying this book is a partitioned disc, compatible for both Macintosh and Windows. Macintosh users should have a Power PC processor, System 7.6 or later, 64MB of RAM, and 125MB hard disk space. PC users should have a Pentium processor, Windows 9x/NT, 64MB of RAM, and 125MB hard disk space.

All of the software included on the CD-ROM is contained in separate folders listed by company name. To access the software, insert the CD-ROM into your CD-ROM drive, and then follow the instructions below.

Macintosh

Once the CD-ROM is inserted into your CD-ROM drive, a CD icon named P5.5Vis appears on your desktop. Double-click the CD icon to open the CD-ROM.

To install and run the individual programs, open the folder of your choice, double-click the installer icon, and follow the prompts.

Windows

Once the CD-ROM is inserted into your CD-ROM drive, double-click the My Computer icon on your desktop (or access your CD-ROM drive through Windows Explorer). In the My Computer window, double-click the CD-ROM icon. The CD-ROM window opens on your desktop.

To install and run the individual programs, open the folder of your choice, double-click the installer icon, and follow the prompts.

COLOR PLATES

This section is a visual guide to the effects generated by Photoshop's Apply Modes, Blend Modes, and Filters. Apply and Blend modes are illustrated as one, as the results they produce are the same. The effect is called a *Blend Mode* when it pertains to the way one of the tools applies color to the active layer. The same effect is called an *Apply Mode* when one layer is blended with one or more others.

The Filters chart shows you a single setting for each of Photoshop's built-in filters. Each of these filters' effects can be varied over a wide range of settings. It is less confusing, however, if you see each filter demonstrated at it's most popular setting (usually the default) so that you get a clearer idea of the difference between the filters themselves. Of course, when you use that filter, you should experiment for the optimum settings.

APPLY/BLEND MODES

Blend Modes are available to all of the Photoshop tools that are used to paint, including the Edit ➪ Fill command. To apply a Blend Mode, simply select the mode to be used by a tool from the tool's Options dialog box, or select the mode to be used by the Fill command from the Fill dialog box. To select the mode to be used by a layer you must go to the Layers window. Shown here are samples of the Apply/Blend Modes at their default setting.

Normal

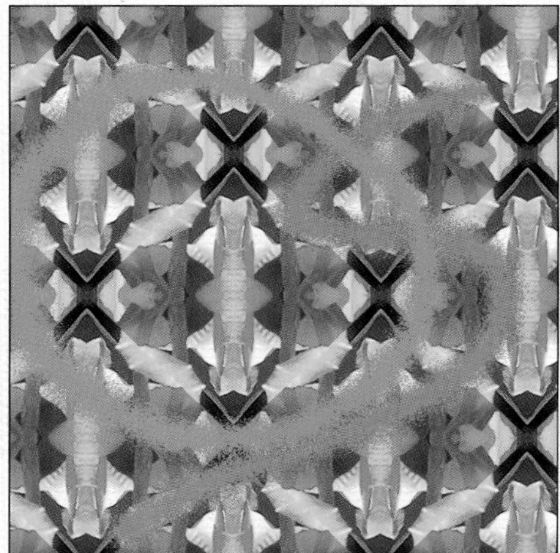
Dissolve

Behind

Multiply

Screen

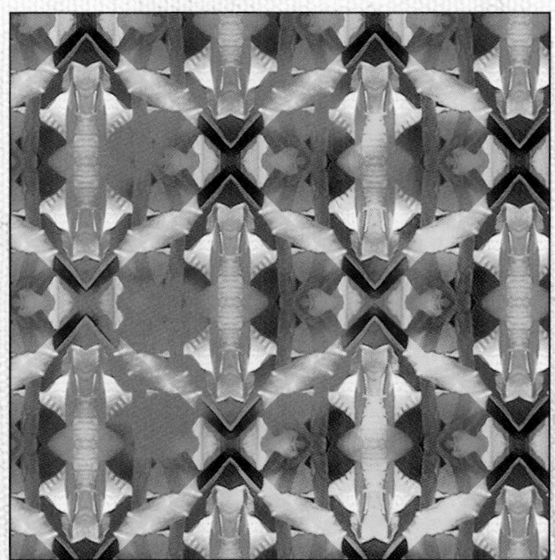

Overlay

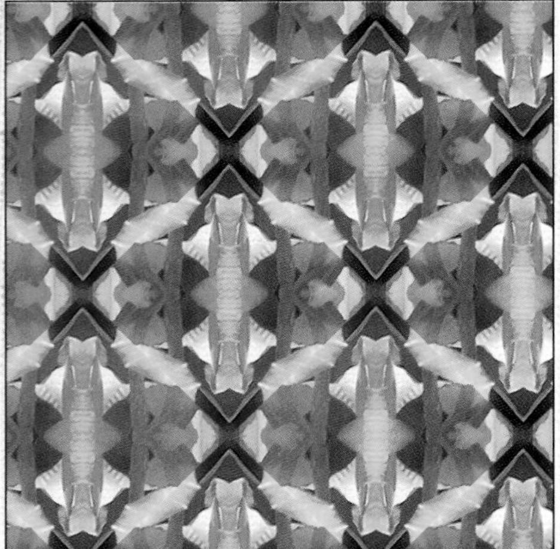
Soft Light

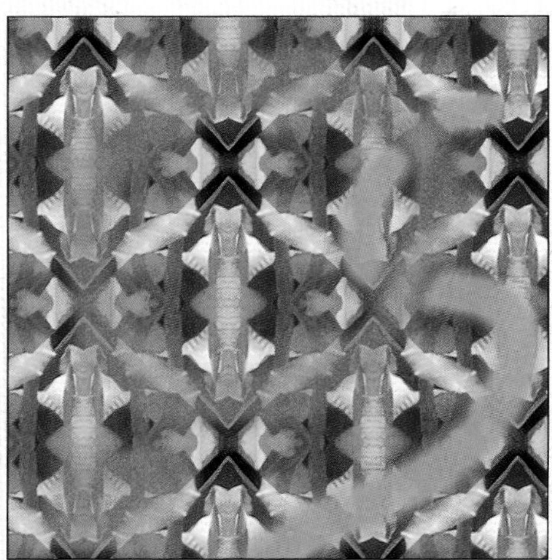
Hard Light

Color Dodge

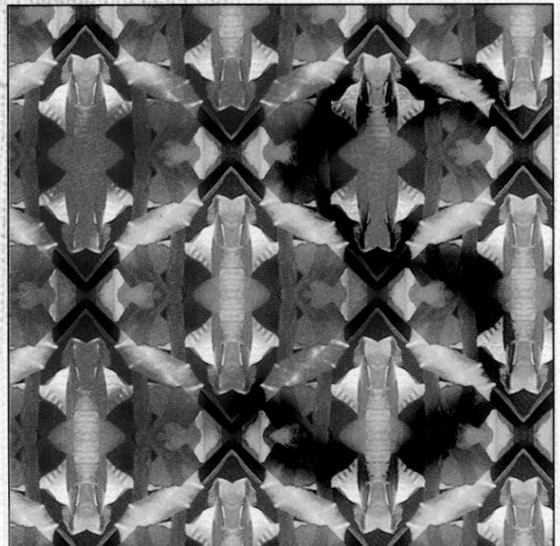
Color Burn

Darken

Lighten

Difference

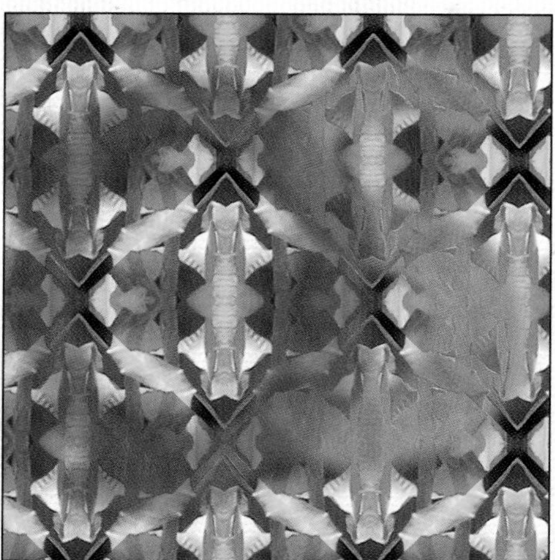
Exclusion

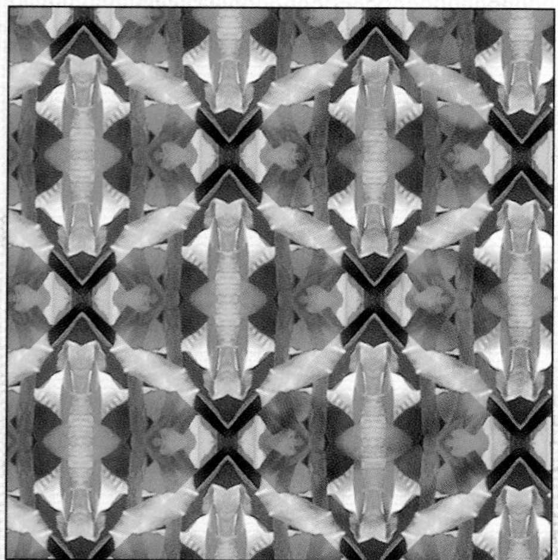
Hue

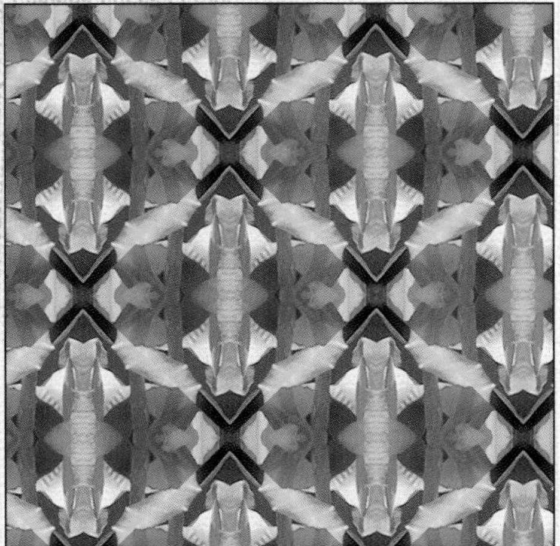

Saturation

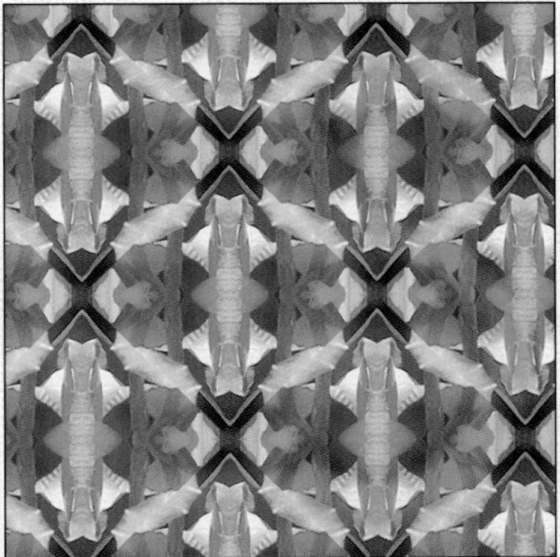

Color

Luminosity

Photoshop Filters

Following is a chart of all of the built-in Photoshop filters, organized by category. Order of appearance follows the order on the Filters menu. If you see a filter effect you think might be appropriate to the image you are working in, you will know exactly where to find it on the menu.

Artistic

Colored Pencil

Cutout

Dry Brush

Film Grain

Fresco

Neon Glow

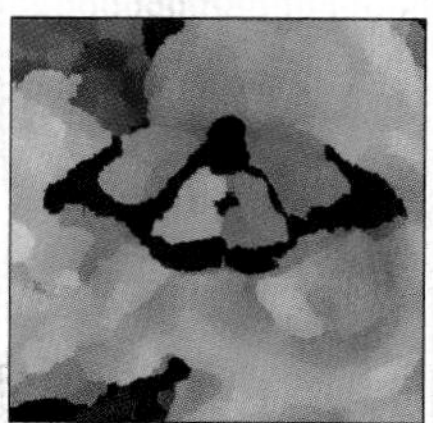

Palette Knife

Plastic Wrap

Poster Edges

Rough Pastels

Smudge Stick

Sponge

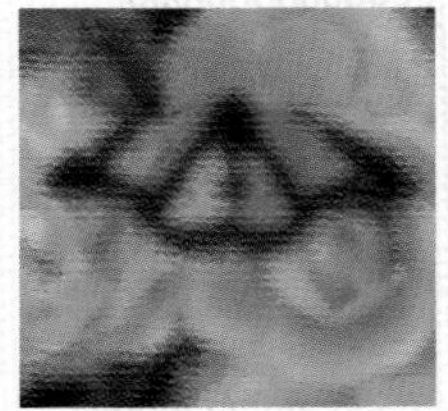
Underpainting

Watercolor

BLUR

Blur

Blur More

Gaussian Blur

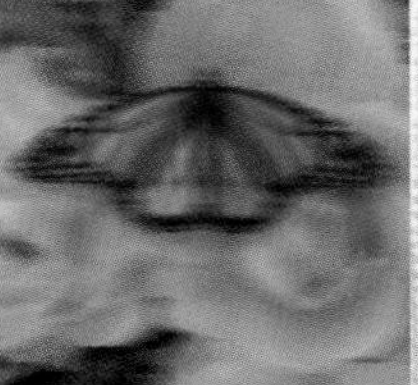
Motion Blur

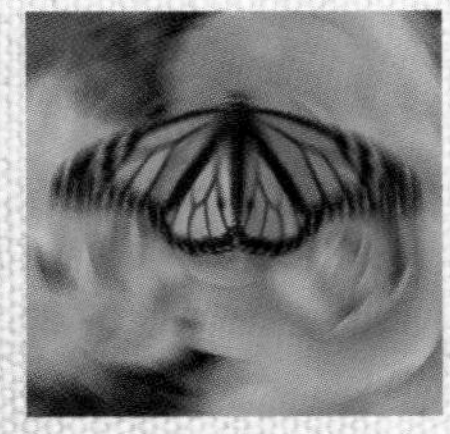
Radial Blur

Smart Blur

Accented Edges

Angled Strokes

Crosshatch

Dark Strokes

Ink Outlines

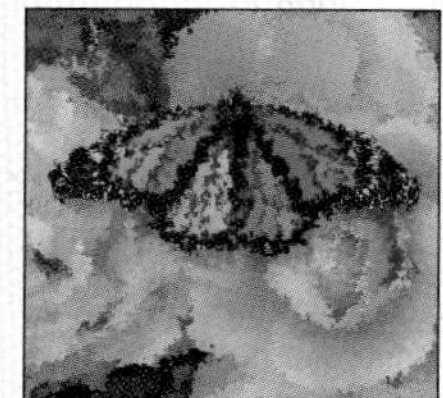
Spatter

Sprayed Strokes

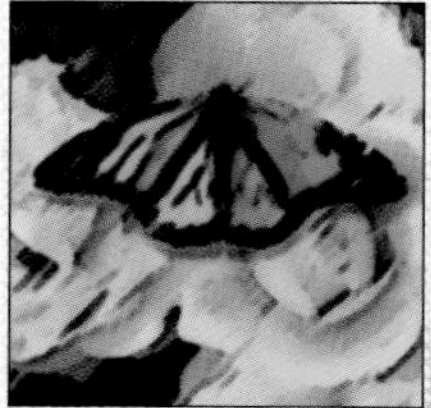
Sumi-e

Diffuse Glow

Displace

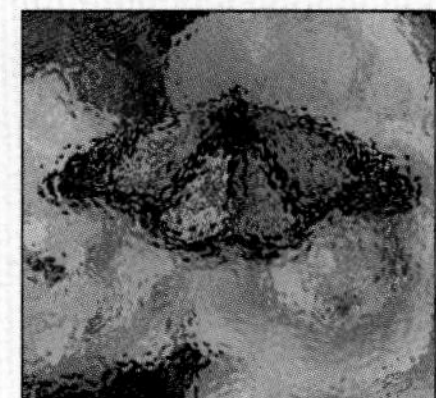
Glass

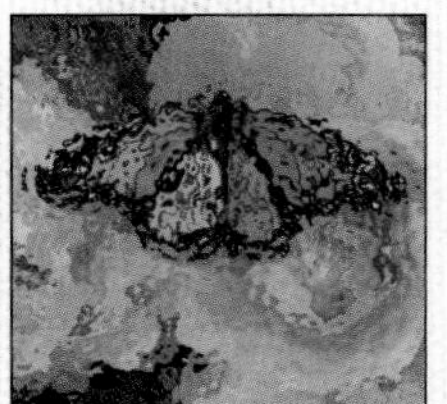
Ocean Ripple

Pinch

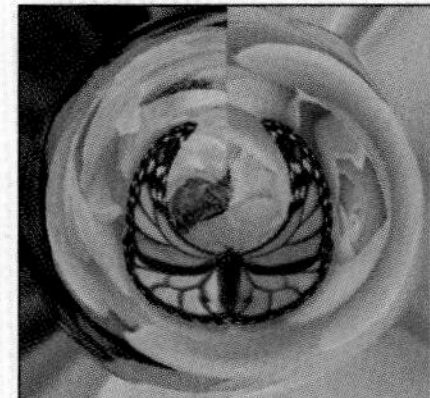
Polar Coordinates

Ripple

Shear

Spherize

Twirl

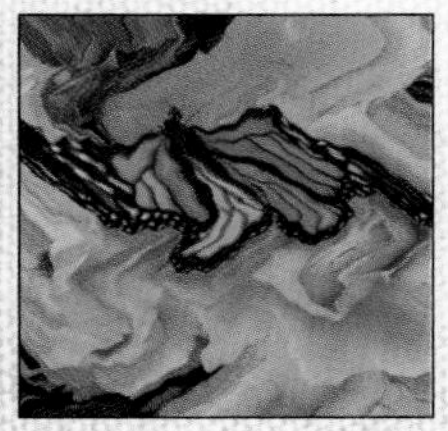
Wave

ZigZag

Noise

Add Noise

Despeckle

Dust & Scratches

Median

Pixelate

Color Halftone

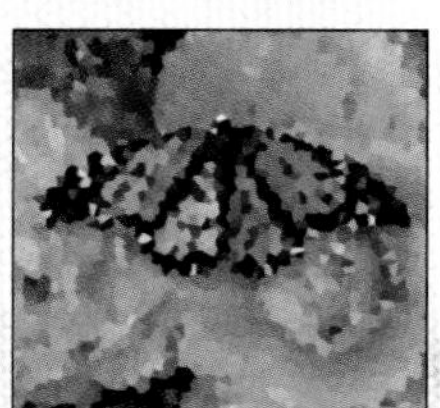
Crystalize

Facet

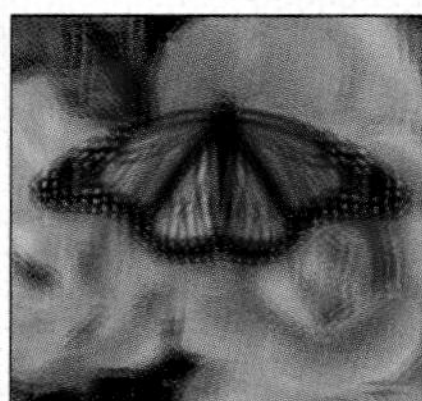
Fragment

Mezzotint

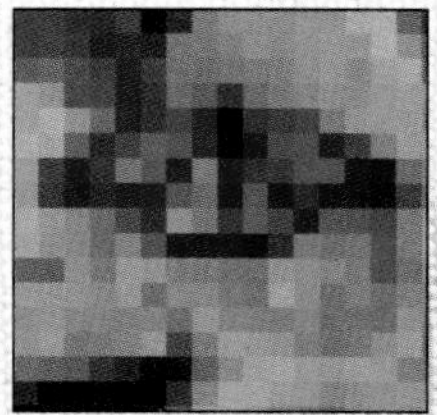
Mosaic

Pointillize

Render

3D Transform

Clouds

Difference Clouds

Lens Flare

Lighting Effects

Texture Fill

Sharpen

Sharpen

Sharpen Edges

Sharpen More

Unsharp Mask

SKETCH

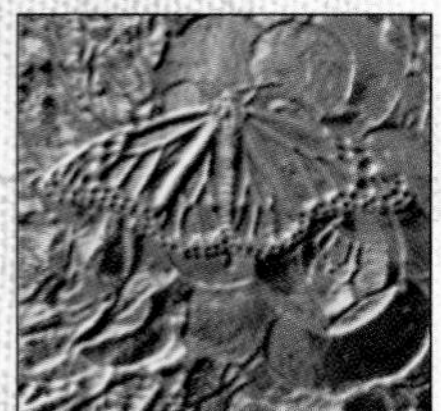
Bas Releif

Chalk & Charcoal

Charcoal

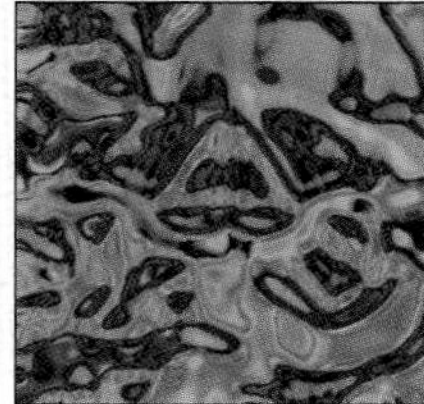
Chrome

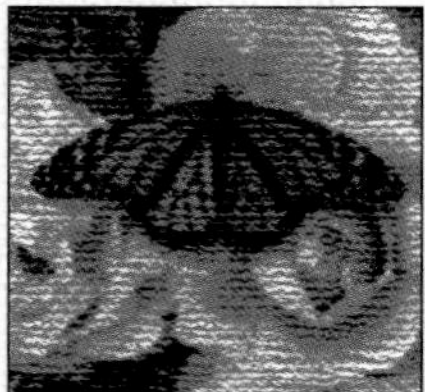
Conte Crayon

Graphic Pen

Halftone Pattern

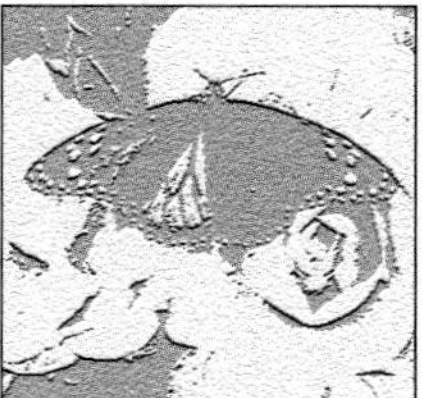
Note Paper

Photocopy

Plasteer

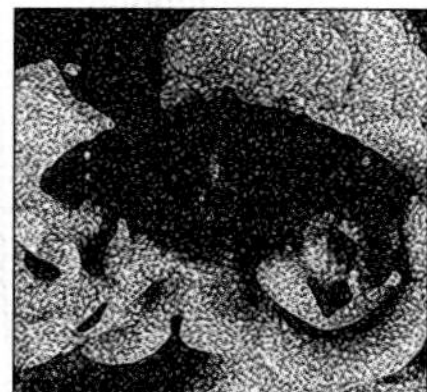
Reticulation

Stamp

Torn Edges

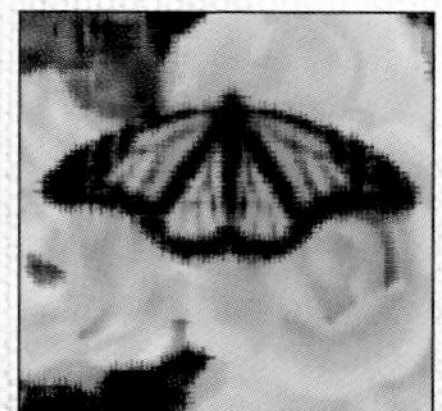
Water Paper

Diffuse

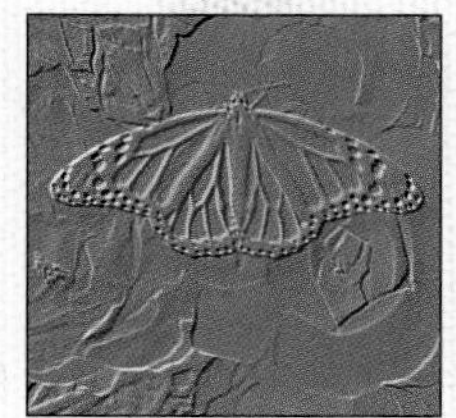
Emboss

Extrude

Find Edges

Glowing Edges

Solarize

Tiles

Trace Contour

Wind

Texture

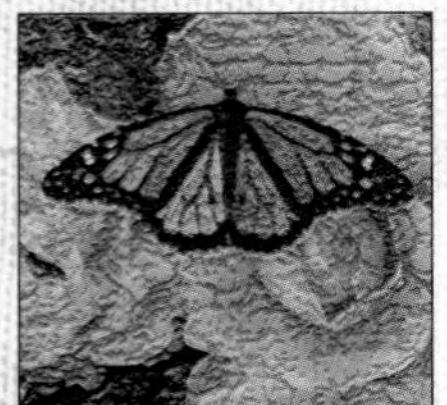
Craquelure

Grain

Mosaic Tiles

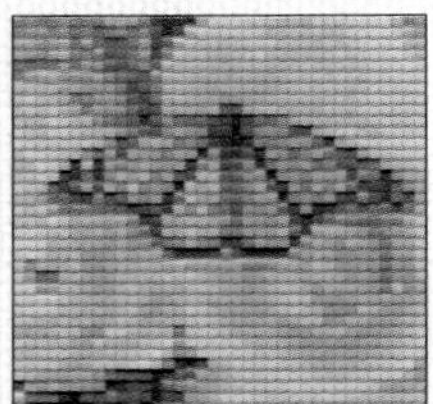
Patchwork

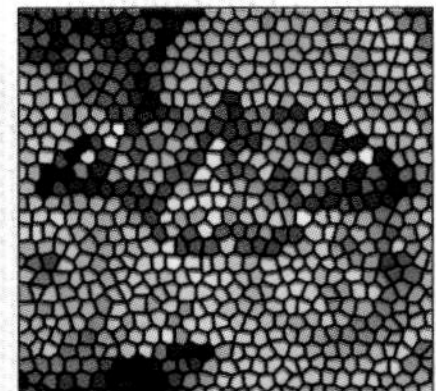
Stained Glass

Texturizer

Other

High Pass

Maximum

Minimum

Offset

INDEX

A

ABR files, 285

Accented Edges filter, 350, 381

acquisitions devices, 50

Actions

- Action Options, 480
- Actions palette, 44
- ActionsPalette.psp, 481
- create, 482–483
- edit, 486–487
- improvements, 7
- overview, 478–480
- play, 488–491
- plug-ins, 11
- rules and guidelines, 481
- save and load, 484–485
- scripts, 10
- unrecordable, 492–493

add color tone, 304–307

Add Noise filter, 325

Add Point tool, 156

Adjustment Layer, 7, 230–231

Adjustment Options command, 203

Adobe Illustrator, 34, 158, 168–169, 259

Adobe ImageReady, 9

Adobe PageMaker, 259

Adobe Web site, 34

Advance Photo System (APS), 56

Airbrush tool, 111, 274, 280

AIS files, 169

Align Linked command, 205

aligned cloning, 118

Alignment commands, 10

alpha channel, 171

Amplitude, 420

Anchor box, 64

Andromeda plug-ins, 422

Angled Strokes filter, 350–351, 382

Angular Gradient tool, 470

anti-aliasing, 132, 148, 150, 170

Apply Image command, 250–251

Apply modes, 220

applying filters, 331

APS. *See* Advance Photo System

arbitrary method, 108

Around Center option, 421

Arrowhead Shape command, 275

Art History Brush, 7, 292–293

artifacts, 53, 322–325

Artistic filters

- Accented Edges filter, 350, 381
- Angled Strokes filter, 350–351, 382
- Bas Relief filter, 353–354, 388
- Chalk & Charcoal filter, 354, 389
- Charcoal filter, 355, 390
- Chrome filter, 355, 391
- Colored Pencil filter, 342, 366
- Conté Crayon filter, 355–356, 392

continued

INDEX

Artistic filters *(continued)*
Crosshatch filter, 351, 383
Cutout filter, 342–343, 367
Dark Strokes filter, 351–352, 384
Dry Brush filter, 343, 368
Film Grain filter, 343–344, 369
Fresco filter, 344, 370
Graphic Pen filter, 356–357, 393
Halftone Pattern filter, 357, 394
Ink Outlines filter, 352, 385
Neon Glow filter, 344–345, 371
Note Paper filter, 357, 395
overview, 342
Paint Daubs filter, 345, 372
paintings, creating, 362–363
Palette Knife filter, 345–346, 373
Photocopy filter, 358, 396
Plaster filter, 358, 397
Plastic Wrap filter, 346, 374
Poster Edges filter, 346–347, 375
Reticulation filter, 359, 398
Rough Pastels filter, 347, 376
Sketch filter, 364–365
Smudge Stick filter, 348, 377
Spatter filter, 353, 386
Sponge filter, 348, 378
Stamp filter, 359, 399
Sumi-e filter, 353, 387
Torn Edges filter, 360, 400
Underpainting filter, 349, 379
Water Paper filter, 361, 401
Watercolor filter, 349–350, 380

Assorted brush palette, 284
asymmetrical curves, 160
Auto Erase check box, 282
Auto Levels command, 83, 300
auto slices, 518, 522–523
automated retouching, 435
automatic spotting, 119–120
automation improvements, 7

B

Background command, 203
Background Eraser, 152–153
Bas Relief filter, 353–354, 388
base unit of measure, 19
baseline shift, 254
Behind blend mode, 221
Bevel and Emboss effect, 234
Bezier curves, 166
bicubic interpolation, 15, 61
Bilinear resampling, 61
bipolar interpolation, 218
bitmap images, 23
black-and-white images, 304
Black-White gradient style, 472
_blank, 519
Blast button, 453
bleed, 389
blemishes, removing, 119

blend

correcting defects, 121

selections, 148–149

text, 264–265

Blend modes, 193, 211, 220–221, 280, 468

block eraser, 197

blotchiness, 189

Blue-Red-Yellow gradient style, 472

Blue-Yellow-Blue gradient style, 472

blur

Blur brush, 184

Blur filter, 182

Blur tool, 113–114

Border command, 142

border effect, 6

boundaries, 309

Brightness/Contrast command

adjust, 87, 230

image quality, 76, 300

brightness curve, 74

brightness percentage, 185

Bring Forward command, 204

Bring to Front command, 204

Brush Detail slider, 343, 368

Brush Size slider, 343, 368

brushes

airbrush options, 280

Airbrush Options palette, 273

Arrowhead Shape command, 275

Art History Brush, 292–293

Brushes palette, 275–277

choosing, 278–279

create from postscript image, 289

create from types, 288

custom shapes, 286–287

eraser options, 283

Line Options palette, 275

load brush palettes, 284–285

New Brush Options command, 277

overview, 272

paint from a snapshot, 290–291

Paintbrush Options palette, 273–274, 281

Pencil Options palette, 274, 282

Brushes palette, 275–277, 285

Burn tool, 154, 294, 298

Button Mode command, 480

C

cache, 22

Calculations command, 252–253

Cancel sign, 5

Canvas Size command, 33, 64

Canvas texture, 412

captions, 40

categories, 40

CD-ROM recorder, 32

Cell Size slider, 428

CGSD, 326

Chalk & Charcoal filter, 354, 389

change size, layers, 218–219

Channel Mixer command, 80, 94–95, 230

Channel name bar, 173

channel operations (CHOPS)
- Apply Image command, 250–251
- Calculations command, 252–253
- Channel Options command, 242
- Channels palette, 238–240
- Channels Palette Options command, 243
- Duplicate Channel command, 241
- merge, 246–249
- Merge Channels command, 243
- New Channel command, 240
- New Spot Channel command, 241–242
- split out, 244
- spot colors, 245

Channel Options command, 174, 242
Channels palette, 173–174, 238–240, 243
Charcoal Area slider, 354
Charcoal filter, 355, 390
checkerboard pattern, 18
choosing brushes, 278–279
CHOPS. *See* channel operations
Chrome filter, 355, 391
Chrome gradient style, 472
Clear Actions command, 480
Clear blend mode, 221
Clear Effects command, 203
Clipboard, 33
clipping group, 229
Clipping Path, 6
Clone tool, 6, 112–113, 214
Clumped effect, 327, 333
CLUT. *See* Color Lookup Table
CMYK colors, 9, 18, 43
collage, 498–499
Color Balance command, 72, 75, 84–85, 106
Color blend mode, 221
Color Burn blend mode, 221
Color channels, 94–95, 173, 194–195
color conversion, 10
color correction aids, 86
Color Dodge blend mode, 221
color family, 89
Color from the Apply Modes pull-down menu, 90
Color Halftone filter, 426, 437
Color Indicates radio buttons, 176
Color Lookup Table (CLUT), 101
Color Management, 8
Color palettes, 100–101, 512
Color Picker command, 307, 462–463
Color Range command, 135
Color Reduction Algorithm, 510
Color Sampler, 6
Color Swatch, 176, 240
Color Table command, 100
Colored Pencil filter, 342, 366
Colorize box, 88
colors, choosing, 474–475
column size, 19
comic strip blur, 313
Composite channel, 94, 173
composite channel, 172
composite images, 84
compound selections, 138–139

compression, 53, 322
Compression Quality pull-down menu, 511
Compuserve, 514
Conditional Mode Change, 44–45
Constrain Proportions, 226
Contact Sheet, 32, 42–43
Contact Sheet command, 32, 43, 494–495
Conté Crayon filter, 355–356, 392
Contiguous checkbox, 150
Contrast command, 72, 142
Contrasty effect, 327, 333
control points, 166
Convert Anchor Point tool, 158
Convert Point tool, 157, 162
Copper gradient style, 472
Copy Effects command, 203
copyrights, 40
CorelDRAW!, 158, 168, 259
counterclockwise rotation, 227
Crack Brightness, 332
Crack Depth, 332
Craquelure Filter, 326–327, 332
create
  Custom filters, 454–455
  layers, 210–211
Create Layer command, 203
Crop tool, 33, 65
Crosshatch filter, 351, 383, 465
Crystallize filter, 426–427, 438
Cursors, 17
Curve Fit, 155, 162
Curve Point button, 74
Curves adjustment, 230
Curves command
  color values, 106–107
  image quality, 74
  special effects color changes, 108–109
  tonal values, 104–105
cusp point, 166
Custom Colors command, 463
Custom filters
  create, 454–455
  directional blurs, 458
  emboss, 459
  save and load, 456
  sharpen, 457
custom mask, 95
custom shapes, brushes, 286–287
custom swatch palettes, 476–477
cut and paste, 118
Cutout filter, 342–343, 367

D

Dark Rough brush type, 372
Dark Strokes filter, 351–352, 384
Darken blend mode, 221
darkroom effects
  add color tone, 304–307
  artifacts, eliminating, 322–325
  Burn tool, 294
  depth of field, 310–311
  Dodge tool, 295

continued

darkroom effects *(continued)*
- hand-color, monotone images, 308–309
- match color, 303
- motion blur, 312–313
- preset sharpening filters, 318–319
- radial blur, 314–315
- Sharpen tool, 296–298
- simple tonal effects, 298–301
- smart blur, 316–317
- Sponge tool, 295–296, 302
- unsharp mask, 320–321

DeBabelizer software, 34
defaults, 21
Define Brush command, 289
Defringe command, 205, 233
Delete Anchor Point tool, 166
Delete Channel command, 174
Delete Channel icon, 173
Delete Layer command, 202, 217
Delete Point tool, 156–157
Density control, 398
depth of field, 310–311
Desaturate command, 83, 90
Despeckle filter, 434
Diamond Gradient tool, 470
DIC, 305
Difference blend mode, 221
Diffuse filter, 428, 445
Diffuse Glow filter, 402, 410
digital cameras, 31, 50, 52–53
Direct Selection tool, 157
Direction Balance slider, 351
Direction buttons, 453
direction points, 166
directional blurs, 458
Disable Layer Mask command, 204
Displace filter, 402–403, 411
Display and Cursors, 17
Dissolve blend mode, 221
Distort command, 218, 222–223
distort filters
- Diffuse Glow filter, 402, 410
- Displace filter, 402–403, 411
- Glass filter, 403–404, 412
- Ocean Ripple filter, 404, 413
- overview, 402
- Pinch filter, 404–405, 414
- Polar Coordinates filter, 405, 415
- Ripple filter, 405–406, 416
- Shear filter, 406, 417
- Spherize filter, 406–407, 418
- third-party surface filter, 422–423
- 3D surface filter, 422–423
- Twirl filter, 407, 419
- Wave filter, 407–408, 420
- ZigZag filter, 409, 421

Distribute Linked command, 205
Dither Algorithm, 470, 510
Dodge tool, 295, 298
DOS file extensions, 16
double-exposure effect, 220
Drop Shadow effect, 64, 234, 284

Droplet arrow, 510
Dry Brush filter, 343, 368
duotone effect, 95
Duplicate Channel command, 174, 241
Duplicate command, 480
Duplicate Layer command, 25, 202, 208
Dust and Scratches command, 119
Dust and Scratches filter, 425, 435

E

Edge Contrast, 132, 155
Edge Fidelity slider, 343, 367
Edge Simplicity slider, 343, 367, 375
Edge Thickness slider, 347, 375
edges, cleaning up, 500–501
edit selections, 140–141
effects layers, 234–237
Elliptical Marquee, 129
Emboss filter, 429, 446, 459
Encapsulated PostScript, 34
Enlarged effect, 327, 333
EPS format, 168
Epson Stylus Color printer, 63
Equalize command, 83, 98–99, 300
Equilibrium Software, 34
Erase to History check box, 283
eraser options, brushes, 283
Exclude Alpha Channels check box, 39
Exclusion blend mode, 221
Expand command, 142
Export command, 169
extraneous colors, eliminating, 12
Extrude filter, 429–430, 447
Eye icon, 213
Eyedropper tool, 64, 116

F

Facet filter, 439
Fade steps field, 110
Fade to mode, 280, 315
Feather Selection command, 176–177, 301
feathering, 129, 148
Fiber Length control, 361, 401
Fidelity, 292
File
  Info, 40–41
  New, 33
  Open, 34–35
  Save, 36
  Save a Copy, 36–37
file extensions, 11
file formats, 9, 509
file size, minimizing, 38
files, flattening, 214
fills
  edit with, 186–187
  nonlinear gradient, 470–471
  paint with, 468–469
Film Grain filter, 343–344, 369
Find Edges filter, 81, 429–430, 448
Finger Painting check box, 115
flash memory cards, 52

Flashpix, 9
flatbed scanners, 54–55
flatness value, 168
Flatten Image command, 39, 202, 340
Flip command, 218
float, 129
Flop command, 218
fluorescent effect, 245
Focoltone, 305
folders, organizing projects with, 31
foreground, 212, 278
Foreground Level slider, 356
Foreground to Background gradient style, 472
Foreground to Transparent gradient style, 472
Fractal Design, 439
Fragment filter, 440
Free command, 219
Free Form mode, 218
Free Transform command, 224–225
Freeform tool, 156
Freehand Pen, 159
Frequency, 155
Fresco filter, 344, 370
Front Image button, 70
Frosted texture, 412
function keys, 87
Fuzziness field, 78, 317

G

gamma, 72
Gaussian Blur filter, 120, 199, 311
General, 15
geometric shapes, 159
GIF files, 34–35514–515
Glass filter, 403–404, 412
Global Angle command, 203
Glow Amount slider, 402
Glow Brightness slider, 345
Glow Color Swatch, 371
Glow size slider, 345
Glowing Edges filter, 430–431, 449
Gradient Fill tool, 468
gradient styles, 472–473
Gradient tool, 7, 468
graffiti, 185
Grain Filter, 327, 333
Grain slider, 343, 402
grainy pictures, 123
Graphic Pen filter, 356–357, 393
grayscale images, 94
Group with Previous Layer check box, 209, 231
Grow command, 144–145
Guides and Grid, 20

H

Halftone Pattern filter, 357, 394
halo, 151
hand-color, monotone images, 308–309
hand-spotting, 122–123
Hand tool, 215
handles, 166
Hard Light blend mode, 221

Hide All Effects command, 203
Hide Selection command, 204
hiding selections, 147
High Color monitor setting, 12, 14
Highlight Area slider, 343
Highlight Eyedropper, 102, 339
histograms, 22
History Brush, 6, 290
History Brush Source box, 283
History List, 26
History palette, 7
Horizontal command, 203
Horizontal effect, 327, 333
Hue blend mode, 221
Hue/Saturation command, 77, 88–89, 230

I

ICC Profile checkbox, 511
Image Balance control, 397
Image Controls, 290
image quality
  Brightness/Contrast command, 76
  Channel Mixer command, 80
  Color Balance command, 75
  Curves command, 74
  Hue/Saturation command, 77
  Levels command, 73
  overview, 72
  Posterize command, 82
  Replace Color command, 78
  Selective Color command, 79
  Threshold command, 81
  Variations command, 82–83
image size
  canvas size, 64–65
  crop, 66–71
  Image Size command, 218
  overview, 60–61
  scanners, 55
image slicing
  auto slices, 518, 522–523
  modify, 524–527
  overview, 518–521
  user slices, 518, 522–523
ImageReady
  Color palettes, 512
  file format, 509
  GIF files, 514–515
  JPEG files, 516–517
  LiveViews, 509–510
  Optimize palette, 510–511
  overview, 508–509
  PNG-8, 513
images
  collecting and prepping, 496–497
  importing, 52–55
  integrating in collages, 498–499
  resizing, 60
Impressionist mode, 118
improvements
  Action scripts, 10
  Actions, 7

continued

improvements *(continued)*
Actions plug-ins, 11
Adjustment layers, 7
Adobe ImageReady, 9
Alignment commands, 10
Art History Brush, 7
Automation, 7
Cancel sign, 5
Clipping Path, 6
Clone tool, 6
CMYK images, 9
color conversion, 10
Color Management, 8
Color Sampler, 6
file extensions, 11
file formats, 9
Flashpix, 9
Freeform Pen, 6
Gradient tool, 7
History Brush, 6
History palette, 7
instant scrolling, 5
instant zooming, 5
Layer Effects, 7
Magnetic Lasso, 6
Magnetic Pen, 6
Measure tool, 6
Pattern Stamp tool, 6
Purge All, 5
Purge History, 5
Reselect Command, 10
save, large files, 11
Save Selection command, 5
16–bit channels, 9
spot color support, 9
status line, 5
3D Transform, 8
Transformations, 8
Type layers, 7
Vertical Type Mask, 6
Vertical Type tool, 6
Indexed Color, 101
infrared effect, 244
Ink Outlines filter, 352, 385
Inner Glow effect, 234
Inner Shadow effect, 234
Input Hues bar, 77
input/output axis, 74
Insert Path command, 480
Insert Stop command, 480
instant scrolling, 5
instant zooming, 5
Intensity slider, 343
International Press Telecommunications Council (IPTC), 40
Interpolation, 15
Invert adjustment, 230
Invert command, 83, 91
IPTC. *See* International Press Telecommunications Council
irregular shapes, drawing, 159

J

jaggies, 63

Job Print, 46–47
JPEG format, 35, 40, 247, 516–517

K

Kai Power Tools, 326
kerning, 254
keyboard shortcuts, overview, 4
keywords, 40
Kodak 50 percent gray card, 109

L

Lab mode, 322–323
Lasso, 129
layers
- Adjustment Layer, 230–231
- blend modes, 220–221
- change size, 218–219
- clipping group, 229
- create, 210–211
- delete, 217
- Distort command, 222–223
- Duplicate Layer command, 208
- effects, 7, 234–237
- erasing parts of, 464–465
- flattening, 38
- Free Transform, 224–225
- Layer Effects, 7
- Layer Options command, 202
- Layer via Copy command, 203
- Layer via Cut command, 203
- Layers menu contents, 203–205
- Layers palette, 200–202
- link, 228
- mask, 232–233
- merge, 214–215
- moving, 212
- New Adjustment Layer command, 208–209
- New Layer command, 207
- Numeric command, 226–227
- overview, 198–200
- Perspective command, 222–223
- rearranging items on, 502–503
- show and hide, 213
- Skew command, 222–223
- stack and reorder, 212
- transparency, 216

leading, 254
Levels adjustment, 230
Levels command, 73, 102–103
levers, 166
Light/Dark Balance slider, 357
Light Position control, 397
Light Rough brush type, 372
Lighten blend mode, 221
Lighting Effects, 373
Line Options palette, 275
Linear Gradient tool, 470
link layers, 228
Linked command, 205
LiveViews, 509–510
Load Actions command, 480, 484
load brush palettes, 284–285

Load Selection command, 178–179
lossless compression, 482
lossy compression, 482
Lossy slider, 510
Luminosity blend mode, 221

M

Macintosh setup, 14
Macromedia Director, 100
Macromedia FreeHand, 158, 168, 259
Magic Eraser, 150–151
Magic Wand, 129, 131, 163, 233
Magnetic Lasso tool, 6, 129, 132–134
Magnetic Pen tool, 6, 155
Make Mask icon, 173, 198
Make Selection icon, 173, 175
Make Work Path dialog box, 163
Marquee tool, 66, 129
masks
  alpha channels, 174–175
  brushes, edit with, 184–185
  Channels palette, 173–174
  color channels, 194–195
  definition, 39
  Feather Selection command, 176–177
  fills, edit with, 186–187
  layer, 198–199
  Load Selection command, 178–179
  overview, 172–173
  Quick Mask mode, 175–176, 188–189
  Save Selection command, 177–178, 180–181
  Spot channels, 174–175
  texture, 190–193
  threshold, 196–197
  thumbnail, 198
match color, 303
matte, 233
Matte Color swatch, 510
Measure tool, 6
measurement, system of, 19
Median filter, 425–426, 436
megapixel resolution, 52
Memory and Image Cache, 22
memory requirements, 214
merge
  channel operations (CHOPS), 246–249
  layers, 214–215
  Merge Channels command, 174, 243
  Merge Layers/Linked command, 202
  Merge Spot Channel command, 174, 239
  Merge Visible command, 202
metallic ink, 245
Mezzotint filter, 427, 441–443
Microsoft Windows setup, 12–13
Midtone Eyedropper, 102
midtones, 301
modify
  image slicing, 524–527
  selections, 142–145
monitor settings, 12
Monochrome check box, 80
monotone effect, 95
montage, 498

morphing. *See* distort filters
Mosaic Tiles Filter, 327–328, 334
motion blur, 312–313
Move tool, 215
Multichannel option, 248
Multiply Blend mode, 220–221, 452

N

NAA. *See* Newspaper Association of America
Navigation palette, 103
Nearest Neighbor resampling, 61
negatives, converting into positives, 91
Neon Glow filter, 344–345, 371
New Action command, 480
New Adjustment Layer command, 202, 208–209
New Brightness Values bar, 74
New Brush Options command, 277
New Channel command, 174, 240
New File command, 33
New Layer command, 202, 207
New Set command, 480
New Spot Channel command, 174, 239, 241–242
Newspaper Association of America (NAA), 40
Nikon, 31
Noise filters
    Add Noise filter, 424–425, 433
    Despeckle filter, 434
    Dust & Scratches filter, 425, 435
    Median filter, 425–426, 436
    overview, 424
nonlinear gradient fills, 470–471
Normal blend mode, 221
Note Paper filter, 357, 395
Number of Levels slider, 343
Numeric command, 226–227
Numeric dialog box, 219

O

object distance, 231
Ocean Ripple filter, 404, 413
offset cloning, 117
Offset Filter, 329–330
Olympus DL500, 52
opacity, changing, 216
Opacity field, 110, 176
Open As command, 35
Open command, 34–35
optical resolution, 54
Optimize palette, 510–511
Orange-Yellow-Orange gradient style, 472
organization, importance of, 494
Out from Center option, 421
out of gamut colors, 18
Outer Glow effect, 234
Output Hues bar, 77
overadjust, 97
overall brightness, 72
overall tonal range, 72
overcompressed JPEG files, 247
Overlay blend mode, 221

P

PageMaker, 168
Paint Bucket tool, 468
Paint Daubs filter, 345, 372
paint from a snapshot, 290–291
Paintbrush Options palette, 273–274, 281
Paintbrush tool, 110–111
painting cursors, 17
paintings, creating, 362–363
Palette Knife filter, 345–346, 373
Palette Options command, 174, 202
Pantone, 305
Paper Brightness effect, 366
_parent, 519
Paste Effects command, 203
Paste Effects to Linked command, 203
Patchwork Filter, 327–328, 335
paths
- clipping, 166–167
- complex, 160–161
- edit, 166–167
- export, 169
- freehand, 162
- learning to draw, 158
- overview, 158–159
- paint, 170–171
- reshape, 166–167
- save, 169
- selections, converting to, 163
- stroking, 170
- trace, 164–165

Pattern mode, 118
Pattern Stamp tool, 6
patterns, define and save, 466–467
PCMCIA. *See* Personal Computer Memory Card Interface Adapter
Pen tool, 154
Pen Width, 155
Pencil Options palette, 274, 282
Pencil tool, 111–112
Personal Computer Memory Card Interface Adapter (PCMCIA), 52
Perspective command, 218, 222–223
PhotoCD, 31
Photocopy filter, 358, 396
photos, create textures from, 338–339
Photoshop format, 40
pica size, 19
Picture Package, 46–47
Pinch filter, 404–405, 414
pixel placement, 17
Pixelate filters
- Color Halftone filter, 426, 437
- Crystallize filter, 426–427, 438
- Facet filter, 439
- Fragment filter, 440
- Mezzotint filter, 427, 441–443
- overview, 424
- Pointillze filter, 427–428, 444

pixels, 19, 60
Plaster filter, 358, 397
Plastic Wrap filter, 346, 374
Play command, 480
Playback Options command, 480

Plug-Ins, 21
Plus and Minus Eyedroppers, 93
PNG-8, 509, 513
PNG-24, 509
point of view, changing, 223
point size, 19
Pointillze filter, 427–428, 444
Polar Coordinates filter, 405, 415
Polygon Lasso tool, 129–130
polygonal crystal, 438
Pond Ripples, 421
Poster Edges filter, 346–347, 375
Posterization slider, 347
Posterize adjustment, 230
Posterize command, 82
postscript image, create brushes from, 289
Precise option, 17
Preferences
  Cursors, 17
  Display and Cursors, 17
  General, 15
  Guides and Grid, 20
  Memory and Image Cache, 22
  Plug-Ins and Scratch Disks, 21
  Saving Files, 16
  Transparency and Gamut, 18
  Units and Rulers, 19
premade gradient styles, 472
Preserve Luminosity check box, 75
Preserve Transparency box, 283
preset sharpening filters, 318–319
Pressure mode, 280
pressure sensitivity, 164
Preview check box, 102
preview icons, 16
printing resolution, 47
Progressive/Interlaced check box, 511
projects, organizing by folder, 31
proportionate cropping, 68
PSD files, 37
Purge All, 5
Purge History, 5
Pyramids radio button, 430

Q

Quark Generic EPS files, 34
QuarkXPress, 168, 259
Quick Edit mode, 28–29
Quick Mask mode
  masks, 175–176, 188–189
  selections, 129, 136–137

R

radial blur, 314–315
Radial Gradient tool, 470
Radius, 119
raindrops, 185
Randomize, 420
raster image, 23
Rasterize Generic EPS dialog box, 289
Real Texture Tools, 326
recolor, 92

Record Again command, 480
Recover from mistakes
 Duplicate Layer, 25
 History List, 26
 Revert, 24
 Snapshots, 27
 Undo, 23
rectangle, rounded corner, 143
Rectangular Marquee, 68–69
Red channel, 244
Red-Green gradient style, 472
Reflected Gradient tool, 470
Relief slider, 349
Remove Black Matte command, 205
Remove White Matte command, 205
Render Layer command, 204
Repeat Edge Pixels radio button, 408
Replace Actions command, 480, 484
Replace Brushes command, 284
Replace Color command, 78, 92–93
Reselect Command, 10
Reset Actions command, 480
resizing images, 60, 167
Reticulation filter, 359, 398
retouching, 121–122
Reveal All command, 203
Reveal Selection command, 203
Revert, 24
RGB colors, 18, 43
Ridges control, 421
Ripple filter, 187, 405–406, 416
Ripple Magnitude, 413
Ripple Size setting, 413
rollovers, 518
Rotate command, 167, 218
Rough Pastels filter, 347, 376
Rubber Band, 154, 161
Rubber Stamp tool, 112–113, 467
rule of thirds, 20

S

Sampling menu, 153
Saturation blend mode, 221
Save a Copy command, 36–37
Save Actions command, 480
save and load, 456
Save As command, 36–37
save files, 11, 16
Save Selection command, 5, 177–178, 180–181
Scale command, 218
Scaling slider, 167, 347
scanners, 50
Scrapbook Page, 48–49
scratch disks, 21
scratches, removing, 119
Screen blend mode, 221
scrubbing, 296
seamless pattern and texture tiles, 340–341
Select All, 146
Select Inverse, 146
Select None, 146

selections
  Background Eraser, 152–153
  blend, 148–149
  Color Range command, 135
  compound, 138–139
  edit, 140–141
  Grow command, 144–145
  hiding, 147
  Magic Eraser, 150–151
  Magic Wand tool, 131
  Magnetic Lasso tool, 132–134
  modify, 142–145
  overview, 128–129
  Polygon Lasso tool, 130
  Quick Mask mode, 136–137
  Similar command, 144–145
  wholesale changes, 146–147
Selective Color command, 79, 230
_self, 519
Send Backward command, 204
sepia tinting, 94
settings, switching quickly, 13
setup
  Macintosh, 14
  Microsoft Windows, 12–13
Shadow Eyedropper, 102
shadows, 504–505
Sharpen Edges filter, 63
sharpen filters, 318–319, 457
Sharpen tool, 296–298
Sharpness slider, 345
Shear filter, 406, 417
show and hide, 213
Show Color command, 86
Show Swatches, 309
shrink to fit, 132
silhouette, 229
Similar command, 144–145
Simple brush type, 372
simple tonal effects, 298–301
Sine Type radio button, 408
single-color toning, 304
Single Column Marquee, 129
Single Row Marquee, 129
16–bits-per-channel mode, 9, 85
Sketch filter, 364–365
Skew command, 167, 218, 222–223
skin blemishes, 123
slide scanners, 50, 56–57
smart blur, 316–317
smart cards, 52
Smooth command, 142
Smoothness slider, 386
Smudge Stick filter, 348, 377
Smudge tool, 114–115
Snapshots, 27
Soft effect, 327, 333
Soft Light blend mode, 221
Solarize filter, 450
solid fill, 187
Sparkle brush type, 372
Spatter filter, 353, 386

specification, 70
Speckle effect, 327, 333
Spectrum gradient style, 472
Spherize filter, 406–407, 418
Spin mode, 315
Split Channel command, 174, 240
split out, 244
Sponge filter, 348, 378
Sponge tool, 295–296, 302
Spot channels, 174–175
spot color support, 9
spot colors, 245
Sprinkles effect, 327, 333
Square brush palette, 284
stack and reorder layers, 212
Stagger button, 453
Stained Glass Filter, 328–329, 336
Stamp filter, 359, 399
Start Recording command, 480
status line, 5
Stippled effect, 327, 333
streaks, avoiding, 299
stretch image, 222–223
Stretch to Fit radio button, 403
stretching, 167
Stroke Length slider, 347
Stroke Subpath dialog box, 279
Stylize filters
  Diffuse filter, 428, 445
  Emboss filter, 429, 446
  Extrude filter, 429–430, 447
  Find Edges filter, 429–430, 448
  Glowing Edges filter, 430–431, 449
  overview, 424
  Solarize filter, 450
  Tiles filter, 431, 451
  Trace filter, 431–432, 452
  Wind filter, 432, 453
Stylus Pressure, 155
Sumi-e filter, 353, 387
symmetrical border, 64

T

Target Mode, 45
Technology Without An Interesting Name (TWAIN), 50–51
Terrazzo, 326
text
  blend, 264–265
  Text Tools Pop-Out Menu, 254
  transparency, 264–265
  Type Layer, 255, 260–261
  Type Selection Tool, 262–263
  Type tool, 255–259
  vertical type, 266–267
Text Tools Pop-Out Menu, 254
textures
  applying filters, 331
  Craquelure Filter, 326–327, 332
  creating from photos, 338–339

examples, 191
Grain Filter, 327, 333
masks, 190–193
Mosaic Tiles Filter, 327–328, 334
Offset Filter, 329–330
overview, 326
Patchwork Filter, 327–328, 335
seamless pattern and texture tiles, 340–341
Stained Glass Filter, 328–329, 336
Texture Explorer, 326
Texture slider, 343
Texturizer Filter, 329, 337
third-party surface filter, 422–423
3D surface filter, 422–423
3D Transform, 8
Threshold command, 81, 119, 196–197, 230
thumbnails, 16, 68
TIFF format, 4–0, 37, 168
Tiles filter, 431, 451
Tiny Lens texture, 412
Tolerance setting, 131, 292
tonal range, finding, 290
tonal values, correct, 102–105
Tone Balance radio buttons, 75
_top, 519
Torn Edges filter, 360, 400
Toyo, 305
Trace filter, 431–432, 452
tracking, 254
transformations, 8, 167
transparency, 216, 264–265
Transparency and Gamut, 18
transparency scanners, 56
transparent background, 18, 65
Transparent Rainbow gradient style, 472
Transparent Stripes gradient style, 472
Trash Can icon, 217
True Color monitor setting, 12, 14
Trumatch, 305
Turpentine brush, 439
TWAIN. *See* Technology Without An Interesting Name
24mm Advanced Photo System (APS), 56
Twirl filter, 407, 419
Type Layer, 7, 255, 260–261
Type Selection Tool, 262–263
Type tool, 255–259
types, create brushes from, 288

U

Umax PowerLook scanner, 54
Underpainting filter, 349, 379
Undo command, 23
Units and Rulers, 19
Unsharp mask, 63, 247, 320–321
Urgency pull-down menu, 41
URLs, 40
Use All Layers checkbox, 150
Use Diffusion Dither, 17
Use Global Angle check box, 234
Use System Palette, 17
user slices, 518, 522–523

V

Variations command

  adjust, 96–97

  image quality, 82–83

varnish, 245

vector programs, 261

Vertical command, 203

Vertical effect, 327, 333

vertical type, 6, 266–267

video cameras, 50

Video LUT animation, 17

Violet-Green-Orange gradient style, 472

Violet-Orange gradient style, 472

virtual memory files, temporary, 21

Visibility icon, 173

visual aids, nonprinting, 20

W

wallpaper, 12–13

warping. *See* distort filters

Water Paper filter, 361, 401

watercolor effect, 286

Watercolor filter, 349–350, 380

Wave filter, 407–408, 420

Wavelength, 420

Web Snap Tolerance, 510

Web thumbnails, 68

Wet Edges option, 110, 278

white balance, 109

White Level control, 398

wholesale changes, 146–147

Wide Blurry brush type, 372

Wide Sharp brush type, 372

Wind button, 453

Wind filter, 432, 453

X

Xaos Tools, 326

Y

Yellow-Violet-Orange-Blue gradient style, 472

Z

ZigZag filter, 409, 421

IDG Books Worldwide, Inc. End-User License Agreement

<u>READ THIS.</u> You should carefully read these terms and conditions before opening the software packet(s) included with this book ("Book"). This is a license agreement ("Agreement") between you and IDG Books Worldwide, Inc. ("IDGB"). By opening the accompanying software packet(s), you acknowledge that you have read and accept the following terms and conditions. If you do not agree and do not want to be bound by such terms and conditions, promptly return the Book and the unopened software packet(s) to the place you obtained them for a full refund.

1. <u>License Grant.</u> IDGB grants to you (either an individual or entity) a nonexclusive license to use one copy of the enclosed software program(s) (collectively, the "Software") solely for your own personal or business purposes on a single computer (whether a standard computer or a workstation component of a multiuser network). The Software is in use on a computer when it is loaded into temporary memory (RAM) or installed into permanent memory (hard disk, CD-ROM, or other storage device). IDGB reserves all rights not expressly granted herein.
2. <u>Ownership.</u> IDGB is the owner of all right, title, and interest, including copyright, in and to the compilation of the Software recorded on the disk(s) or CD-ROM ("Software Media"). Copyright to the individual programs recorded on the Software Media is owned by the author or other authorized copyright owner of each program. Ownership of the Software and all proprietary rights relating thereto remain with IDGB and its licensers.
3. <u>Restrictions On Use and Transfer.</u>

   (a) You may only (i) make one copy of the Software for backup or archival purposes, or (ii) transfer the Software to a single hard disk, provided that you keep the original for backup or archival purposes. You may not (i) rent or lease the Software, (ii) copy or reproduce the Software through a LAN or other network system or through any computer subscriber system or bulletin-board system, or (iii) modify, adapt, or create derivative works based on the Software.

   (b) You may not reverse engineer, decompile, or disassemble the Software. You may transfer the Software and user documentation on a permanent basis, provided that the transferee agrees to accept the terms and conditions of this Agreement and you retain no copies. If the Software is an update or has been updated, any transfer must include the most recent update and all prior versions.

4. **Restrictions on Use of Individual Programs.** You must follow the individual requirements and restrictions detailed for each individual program in Appendix B of this Book. These limitations are also contained in the individual license agreements recorded on the Software Media. These limitations may include a requirement that after using the program for a specified period of time, the user must pay a registration fee or discontinue use. By opening the Software packet(s), you will be agreeing to abide by the licenses and restrictions for these individual programs that are detailed in Appendix B and on the Software Media. None of the material on this Software Media or listed in this Book may ever be redistributed, in original or modified form, for commercial purposes.

5. **Limited Warranty.**

   (a) IDGB warrants that the Software and Software Media are free from defects in materials and workmanship under normal use for a period of sixty (60) days from the date of purchase of this Book. If IDGB receives notification within the warranty period of defects in materials or workmanship, IDGB will replace the defective Software Media.

   (b) IDGB AND THE AUTHOR OF THE BOOK DISCLAIM ALL OTHER WARRANTIES, EXPRESS OR IMPLIED, INCLUDING WITHOUT LIMITATION IMPLIED WARRANTIES OF MERCHANTABILITY AND FITNESS FOR A PARTICULAR PURPOSE, WITH RESPECT TO THE SOFTWARE, THE PROGRAMS, THE SOURCE CODE CONTAINED THEREIN, AND/OR THE TECHNIQUES DESCRIBED IN THIS BOOK. IDGB DOES NOT WARRANT THAT THE FUNCTIONS CONTAINED IN THE SOFTWARE WILL MEET YOUR REQUIREMENTS OR THAT THE OPERATION OF THE SOFTWARE WILL BE ERROR FREE.

   (c) This limited warranty gives you specific legal rights, and you may have other rights that vary from jurisdiction to jurisdiction.

6. **Remedies.**

   (a) IDGB's entire liability and your exclusive remedy for defects in materials and workmanship shall be limited to replacement of the Software Media, which may be returned to IDGB with a copy of your receipt at the following address: Software Media Fulfillment Department, Attn.: *Master Photoshop 5.5 Visually*, IDG Books Worldwide, Inc., 10475 Crosspoint Blvd., Indianapolis, IN 46256, or call 1-800-762-2974. Please allow three to four weeks for delivery. This Limited Warranty is void if failure of the Software Media has resulted from accident, abuse, or misapplication. Any replacement Software Media will be warranted for the remainder of the original warranty period or thirty (30) days, whichever is longer.

(b) In no event shall IDGB or the author be liable for any damages whatsoever (including without limitation damages for loss of business profits, business interruption, loss of business information, or any other pecuniary loss) arising from the use of or inability to use the Book or the Software, even if IDGB has been advised of the possibility of such damages.

(c) Because some jurisdictions do not allow the exclusion or limitation of liability for consequential or incidental damages, the above limitation or exclusion may not apply to you.

7. U.S. Government Restricted Rights. Use, duplication, or disclosure of the Software by the U.S. Government is subject to restrictions stated in paragraph (c)(1)(ii) of the Rights in Technical Data and Computer Software clause of DFARS 252.227-7013, and in subparagraphs (a) through (d) of the Commercial Computer—Restricted Rights clause at FAR 52.227-19, and in similar clauses in the NASA FAR supplement, when applicable.

8. General. This Agreement constitutes the entire understanding of the parties and revokes and supersedes all prior agreements, oral or written, between them and may not be modified or amended except in a writing signed by both parties hereto that specifically refers to this Agreement. This Agreement shall take precedence over any other documents that may be in conflict herewith. If any one or more provisions contained in this Agreement are held by any court or tribunal to be invalid, illegal, or otherwise unenforceable, each and every other provision shall remain in full force and effect.

my2cents.idgbooks.com

Register This Book — And Win!

Visit **http://my2cents.idgbooks.com** to register this book and we'll automatically enter you in our fantastic monthly prize giveaway. It's also your opportunity to give us feedback: let us know what you thought of this book and how you would like to see other topics covered.

Discover IDG Books Online!

The IDG Books Online Web site is your online resource for tackling technology — at home and at the office. Frequently updated, the IDG Books Online Web site features exclusive software, insider information, online books, and live events!

10 Productive & Career-Enhancing Things You Can Do at www.idgbooks.com

- Nab source code for your own programming projects.
- Download software.
- Read Web exclusives: special articles and book excerpts by IDG Books Worldwide authors.
- Take advantage of resources to help you advance your career as a Novell or Microsoft professional.
- Buy IDG Books Worldwide titles or find a convenient bookstore that carries them.
- Register your book and win a prize.
- Chat live online with authors.
- Sign up for regular e-mail updates about our latest books.
- Suggest a book you'd like to read or write.
- Give us your 2¢ about our books and about our Web site.

You say you're not on the Web yet? It's easy to get started with IDG Books' *Discover the Internet,* available at local retailers everywhere.

S A T I S F I E D U S E R S !

from:

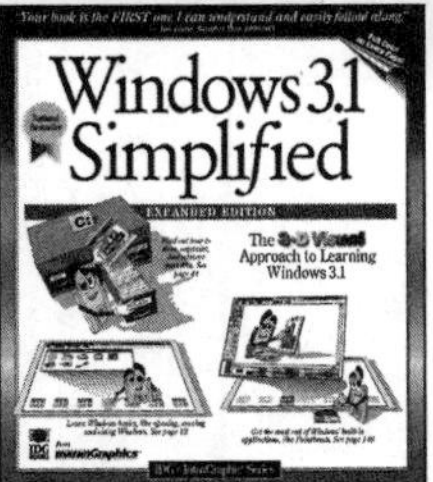

Windows 3.1 Simplified
ISBN 1-56884-654-1
$19.99 USA/£18.99 UK

Word 97 Simplified
ISBN 0-7645-6011-5
$24.99 USA/£23.99 UK

Word For Windows 95 Simplified
ISBN 1-56884-681-9
$19.99 USA/£18.99 UK

Word 6 For Windows Simplified
ISBN 1-56884-660-6
$19.99 USA/£18.99 UK

Excel 97 Simplified
ISBN 0-7645-6022-0
$24.99 USA/£23.99 UK

Excel For Windows 95 Simplified
ISBN 1-56884-682-7
$19.99 USA/£18.99 UK

Computers Simplified, 4th Edition
ISBN 0-7645-6042-5
$24.99 USA/£23.99 UK

America Online Simplified
ISBN 0-7645-6033-6
$24.99 USA/£23.99 UK

PC Upgrade and Repair Simplified
ISBN 0-7645-6049-2
$24.99 USA/£23.99 UK

The 3-D Visual Dictionary of Computing
ISBN 1-56884-678-9
$19.99 USA/£18.99 UK

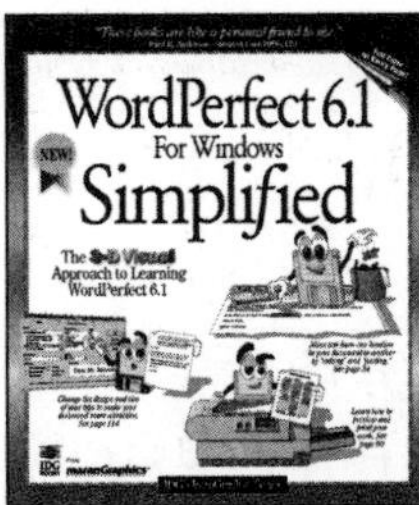

WordPerfect 6.1 For Windows Simplified
ISBN 1-56884-665-7
$19.99 USA/£18.99 UK

Lotus 1-2-3 R5 For Windows Simplified
ISBN 1-56884-670-3
$19.99 USA/£18.99 UK

ALSO AVAILABLE:

Windows 3.1 Visual PocketGuide
ISBN 1-56884-650-9
$14.99 USA/£13.99 UK

Excel 5 For Windows Visual PocketGuide
ISBN 1-56884-667-3
$14.99 USA/£13.99 UK

WordPerfect 6.1 For Windows Visual PocketGuide
ISBN 1-56884-668-1
$14.99 USA/£13.99 UK

Lotus 1-2-3 R5 For Windows Visual PocketGuide
ISBN 1-56884-671-1
$14.99 USA/£13.99 UK

FOR CORPORATE ORDERS, PLEASE CALL: 800-469-6616